terra australis 31

Terra Australis reports the results of archaeological and related research within the south and east of Asia, though mainly Australia, New Guinea and island Melanesia — lands that remained *terra australis incognita* to generations of prehistorians. Its subject is the settlement of the diverse environments in this isolated quarter of the globe by peoples who have maintained their discrete and traditional ways of life into the recent recorded or remembered past and at times into the observable present.

Since the beginning of the series, the basic colour on the spine and cover has distinguished the regional distribution of topics as follows: ochre for Australia, green for New Guinea, red for South-East Asia and blue for the Pacific Islands. From 2001, issues with a gold spine will include conference proceedings, edited papers and monographs which in topic or desired format do not fit easily within the original arrangements. All volumes are numbered within the same series.

List of volumes in Terra Australis

Volume 1: *Burrill Lake and Currarong: Coastal Sites in Southern New South Wales.* R.J. Lampert (1971)
Volume 2: *Ol Tumbuna: Archaeological Excavations in the Eastern Central Highlands, Papua New Guinea.* J.P. White (1972)
Volume 3: *New Guinea Stone Age Trade: The Geography and Ecology of Traffic in the Interior.* I. Hughes (1977)
Volume 4: *Recent Prehistory in Southeast Papua.* B. Egloff (1979)
Volume 5: *The Great Kartan Mystery.* R. Lampert (1981)
Volume 6: *Early Man in North Queensland: Art and Archaeology in the Laura Area.* A. Rosenfeld, D. Horton and J. Winter (1981)
Volume 7: *The Alligator Rivers: Prehistory and Ecology in Western Arnhem Land.* C. Schrire (1982)
Volume 8: *Hunter Hill, Hunter Island: Archaeological Investigations of a Prehistoric Tasmanian Site.* S. Bowdler (1984)
Volume 9: *Coastal South-West Tasmania: The Prehistory of Louisa Bay and Maatsuyker Island.* R. Vanderwal and D. Horton (1984)
Volume 10: *The Emergence of Mailu.* G. Irwin (1985)
Volume 11: *Archaeology in Eastern Timor, 1966–67.* I. Glover (1986)
Volume 12: *Early Tongan Prehistory: The Lapita Period on Tongatapu and its Relationships.* J. Poulsen (1987)
Volume 13: *Coobool Creek.* P. Brown (1989)
Volume 14: *30,000 Years of Aboriginal Occupation: Kimberley, North-West Australia.* S. O'Connor (1999)
Volume 15: *Lapita Interaction.* G. Summerhayes (2000)
Volume 16: *The Prehistory of Buka: A Stepping Stone Island in the Northern Solomons.* S. Wickler (2001)
Volume 17: *The Archaeology of Lapita Dispersal in Oceania.* G.R. Clark, A.J. Anderson and T. Vunidilo (2001)
Volume 18: *An Archaeology of West Polynesian Prehistory.* A. Smith (2002)
Volume 19: *Phytolith and Starch Research in the Australian-Pacific-Asian Regions: The State of the Art.* D. Hart and L. Wallis (2003)
Volume 20: *The Sea People: Late-Holocene Maritime Specialisation in the Whitsunday Islands, Central Queensland.* B. Barker (2004)
Volume 21: *What's Changing: Population Size or Land-Use Patterns? The Archaeology of Upper Mangrove Creek, Sydney Basin.* V. Attenbrow (2004)
Volume 22: *The Archaeology of the Aru Islands, Eastern Indonesia.* S. O'Connor, M. Spriggs and P. Veth (2005)
Volume 23: *Pieces of the Vanuatu Puzzle: Archaeology of the North, South and Centre.* S. Bedford (2006)
Volume 24: *Coastal Themes: An Archaeology of the Southern Curtis Coast, Queensland.* S. Ulm (2006)
Volume 25: *Lithics in the Land of the Lightning Brothers: The Archaeology of Wardaman Country, Northern Territory.* C. Clarkson (2007)
Volume 26: *Oceanic Explorations: Lapita and Western Pacific Settlement.* S. Bedford, C. Sand and S. P. Connaughton (2007)
Volume 27: *Dreamtime Superhighway: Sydney Basin Rock Art and Prehistoric Information Exchange.* J. McDonald (2008)
Volume 28: *New Directions in Archaeological Science.* A. Fairbairn and S. O'Connor (2008)
Volume 29: *Islands of Inquiry: Colonisation, Seafaring and the Archaeology of Maritime Landscapes.* G. Clark, F. Leach and S. O'Connor (2008)
Volume 30: *Archaeological Science Under a Microscope: Studies in Residue and Ancient DNA Analysis in Honour of Thomas H. Loy.* M. Haslam, G. Robertson, A. Crowther, S. Nugent and L. Kirkwood (2009)
Volume 31: *The Early Prehistory of Fiji.* G. Clark and A. Anderson (2009)

terra australis 31

THE EARLY PREHISTORY OF FIJI

Edited by Geoffrey Clark and Atholl Anderson

© 2009 ANU E Press

Published by ANU E Press
The Australian National University
Canberra ACT 0200 Australia
Email: anuepress@anu.edu.au
Web: http://epress.anu.edu.au

National Library of Australia Cataloguing-in-Publication entry

Title: The early prehistory of Fiji [electronic resource] / editor Geoffrey Clark, Atholl Anderson.

ISBN: 9781921666063 (pbk.) 9781921666070 (ebook)

Series: Terra Australis ; 31.

Notes: Bibliography.

Subjects: Antiquities, Prehistoric—Fiji.
            Fiji—Antiquities.

Other Authors/Contributors:
            Clark, Geoffrey R. (Geoffrey Richard), 1966-
            Anderson, Atholl

Dewey Number: 996.11

Copyright of the text remains with the contributors/authors, 2009. This book is copyright in all countries subscribing to the Berne convention. Apart from any fair dealing for the purpose of private study, research, criticism or review, as permitted under the *Copyright Act*, no part may be reproduced by any process without written permission. Inquiries should be made to the publisher.

Series Editor: Sue O'Connor

Typesetting and design: Rachel Lawson

Cover image: Geoffrey Clark. *Kabara Island with worked beach rock in the foreground and view of Vuaqava Island.*

Back cover map: *Hollandia Nova*. Thevenot 1663 by courtesy of the National Library of Australia.
Reprinted with permission of the National Library of Australia.

Terra Australis Editorial Board: Sue O'Connor, Jack Golson, Simon Haberle, Sally Brockwell, Geoffrey Clark

Contents

1 Research on the early prehistory of Fiji
   Atholl Anderson and Geoffrey Clark — 1

2 Palaeofaunal sites and excavations
   Trevor H. Worthy and Atholl Anderson — 19

3 Results of palaeofaunal research
   Trevor H. Worthy and Atholl Anderson — 41

4 Vegetation histories from the Fijian Islands: Alternative records of human impact
   Geoffrey Hope, Janelle Stevenson and Wendy Southern — 63

5 Fieldwork in southern Viti Levu and Beqa Island
   Atholl Anderson and Geoffrey Clark — 87

6 Fieldwork in northern Viti Levu and Mago Island
   Geoffrey Clark and Atholl Anderson — 121

7 Site chronology and a review of radiocarbon dates from Fiji
   Geoffrey Clark and Atholl Anderson — 153

8 Molluscan remains from Fiji
   Katherine Szabó — 183

9 The fish bone remains
   Geoffrey Clark and Katherine Szabó — 213

10 Bird, mammal and reptile remains
   Trevor H. Worthy and Geoffrey Clark — 231

11 Ceramic assemblages from excavations on Viti Levu, Beqa-Ugaga
    and Mago Island
    Geoffrey Clark — 259

12 Post-Lapita ceramic change in Fiji
    Geoffrey Clark — 307

13 Compositional analysis of Fijian ceramics
    Geoffrey Clark and Douglas Kennett — 321

14 Stone artefact manufacture at Natunuku, Votua, Kulu and Ugaga, Fiji
    Chris Clarkson and Lyn Schmidt — 345

15 Characterisation and sourcing of archaeological adzes and flakes from Fiji
    Barry Fankhauser, Geoffrey Clark and Atholl Anderson — 373

16 Colonisation and culture change in the early prehistory of Fiji
    Geoffrey Clark and Atholl Anderson — 407

Contents

1. Research on the early prehistory of Fiji
   Atholl Anderson and Geoffrey Clark — 1

2. Palaeofaunal sites and excavations
   Trevor H. Worthy and Atholl Anderson — 19

3. Results of palaeofaunal research
   Trevor H. Worthy and Atholl Anderson — 41

4. Vegetation histories from the Fijian Islands: Alternative records of human impact
   Geoffrey Hope, Janelle Stevenson and Wendy Southern — 63

5. Fieldwork in southern Viti Levu and Beqa Island
   Atholl Anderson and Geoffrey Clark — 87

6. Fieldwork in northern Viti Levu and Mago Island
   Geoffrey Clark and Atholl Anderson — 121

7. Site chronology and a review of radiocarbon dates from Fiji
   Geoffrey Clark and Atholl Anderson — 153

8. Molluscan remains from Fiji
   Katherine Szabó — 183

9. The fish bone remains
   Geoffrey Clark and Katherine Szabó — 213

10. Bird, mammal and reptile remains
    Trevor H. Worthy and Geoffrey Clark — 231

11 Ceramic assemblages from excavations on Viti Levu, Beqa-Ugaga
    and Mago Island
    Geoffrey Clark — 259

12 Post-Lapita ceramic change in Fiji
    Geoffrey Clark — 307

13 Compositional analysis of Fijian ceramics
    Geoffrey Clark and Douglas Kennett — 321

14 Stone artefact manufacture at Natunuku, Votua, Kulu and Ugaga, Fiji
    Chris Clarkson and Lyn Schmidt — 345

15 Characterisation and sourcing of archaeological adzes and flakes from Fiji
    Barry Fankhauser, Geoffrey Clark and Atholl Anderson — 373

16 Colonisation and culture change in the early prehistory of Fiji
    Geoffrey Clark and Atholl Anderson — 407

1

Research on the early prehistory of Fiji

Atholl Anderson
Department of Archaeology and Natural History, The Australian National University

Geoffrey Clark
Department of Archaeology and Natural History, The Australian National University

Introduction

This volume describes results of a research program on the early phases of prehistory in Fiji. The research began in 1995 as a collaborative project of the ANU and the Fiji Museum entitled 'Prehistoric colonisation and palaeoenvironment of Fiji' (Anderson et al. 1996). The initial emphasis was on the period beginning about 5000 BP and extending up to about 2000 BP, with the objective of studying the pre-human landscape and then the arrival, spread and environmental impact of human colonisation. At the time, human colonisation was thought to begin somewhere between 3000 and 4500 BP, depending on whether archaeological (3200–3700 BP) or paleoenvironmental (4000–4500 BP) data were preferred, and the colonising Lapita phase was regarded as persisting up to about 2000 BP (Frost 1979:64; Gibbons and Clunie 1986; Southern 1986; Davidson et al. 1990:131; Davidson and Leach 1993:102–103).

Our initial fieldwork involved sediment coring for pollen, July–August 1995 in Viti Levu and Vanua Levu, including at sites where previous data had suggested unusually early dates of possible human impact (Hope and Anderson 1995). During the first season of archaeological fieldwork, in 1996, Clark began doctoral research on the early and middle phases of Fijian prehistory with the objective of studying transformations that led from Lapita towards a more distinctly Fijian cultural facies (Clark 2000). Thus, the Fiji project was broadened, and renamed 'The Early Prehistory of Fiji Project' (abbreviated to the EPF). Its objectives were to consider initial colonisation and its effects, and later transformations before the last millennium of Fijian prehistory: approximately equating to the Sigatoka and Navatu phases in the standard sequence (Green 1963a). Papers on themes of the Fiji project have been published already, notably on the chronology and modulation of colonisation (Anderson and Clark 1999; Anderson 2001; Anderson et al. 2001a; Anderson et al. 2006), intra-archipelagic dispersal (Clark and Anderson 2001), and aspects of faunal (Worthy et al. 1999; Anderson et al. 2001b) and vegetation change (Hope et al. 1999), and inland (Anderson et al. 2000) and small-island (Clark et al. 2001) settlement, among others.

Our main intention in the current volume, consistent with the aim of *Terra Australis*, is to present and interpret the basic data of the project. In this chapter, we describe the background to the project as it was seen in 1995.

The Fiji Islands

Fiji lies in an area of 570,000 sq. km of the Central Pacific Ocean, 12–22°S, with the main islands at 16–17°S. At 18,272 sq. km, it is more like Vanuatu (14,760 sq. km) and New Caledonia (19,060 sq. km) than Tonga (748 sq. km) or Samoa (2850 sq. km), its main regional neighbours. It has 300 to 500 islands, depending on how they are counted (a common figure being 330), of which 110 are inhabited. Viti Levu (10,429 sq. km) and Vanua Levu (5556 sq. km) are the largest (Pernetta and Watling 1979). In addition to these geologically complex volcanic and sedimentary islands, there are high volcanic islands and various coral limestone islands, upraised or as atolls. The geological complexity of Fiji arises from its position on the continental side of the Andesite Line (Figure 1), either directly on the Indo-Australian plate, or on an independent micro-plate which is being deformed by the movement of the Indo-Australian and Pacific plates along a subduction zone north and east of Fiji, in fact 1000 km east in the Tonga trench (Nunn 1994a:37). Viti Levu is the oldest island in the archipelago, dating to Late Eocene to Early Oligocene age (Rodda 1994), but it is not known whether it was exposed terrestrially at that time. Land was certainly present during the deposition of the Wainimala Group (Late Oligocene–Middle Miocene), and probably has been continuously present since about 16 million years ago (Chase 1971; Rodda 1994). The land area was about 50% larger than it is now during the last glacial era, when Vanua Levu, Taveuni and Viti Levu formed a single large island (Watling 1982). Subsequently, sea level rose to about 1.5 m to 2 m above present at 4000–3000 BP (Nunn 1999:230) and then receded to complete the modern topography.

Fiji divides into two geographical provinces, the western province, which is dominated by large islands, and the eastern province, east of a line from Taveuni to Kadavu, which is made up entirely of small islands, including the Lau Group, which lies equidistant between the western province and Tonga. The main islands are rugged rather than mountainous, rising generally to 500–800 m, with small areas about 1000 m in altitude. There are two major river catchments, the Rewa and Sigatoka, both on Viti Levu, which, with the Ba, provide good access into the interior. The climate is tropical, with average daily temperatures remaining in the range 22–26°C all year round, but there is considerable variation in precipitation. Rainfall is highest in southeastern, or windward, districts, about 3000–6000 mm per annum, depending on altitude, and up to 13,000 mm per annum in the mountains of Taveuni. Associated with it in the natural state are dense rainforests. Northwestern districts get about half that rainfall and sustain dry forest and savannah. There is a wet season, November to April, during which 10 to 15 cyclones track across Fiji from the northwest each decade, sometimes causing major flooding, windfall and erosion.

If the main impression of the late Holocene environment of Fiji is of its variety, then a similar idea has permeated the common view of its people and culture. Human colonisation began in the late Holocene with Lapita migrations from the west, after which, in ways very poorly understood, there were changes that resulted in the Fijian people and culture encountered by Europeans. Abel Tasman, the first European visitor, sailed through the northeastern islands of Fiji in January 1643, and the Master of the *Resolution* left some presents on a beach at Vatoa in July 1774. The earliest regular contact seems to have been in western Vanua Levu, during the sandalwood rush, 1804–1810, and sustained interaction was associated with the trade in *beche-de-mer*, 1820s–1850s (Howe 1984:258–259). As a result of these encounters, the Fijian people and culture were perceived to be a mixture of Polynesian and Melanesian elements. There was regular contact between eastern Fiji and Tonga, and to a lesser extent with Samoa, so some mixing of populations was expected. William Mariner (Martin 1817 II:194, 199) found that the Tongans got their canoes, and learned much about the manufacture of them, from the Fijians, while the earthenware pots used in Tonga came from Fiji, and subsequent historical research has produced evidence of a thriving exchange network among Samoa, Tonga and Fiji (Kaeppler 1978). However, the idea of racial and cultural mixing went well beyond that.

The philologist Horatio Hale (1846:194) regarded Fijians as primarily Melanesian but derived through Papua, which included some Malaysian elements, and augmented by Malaysian

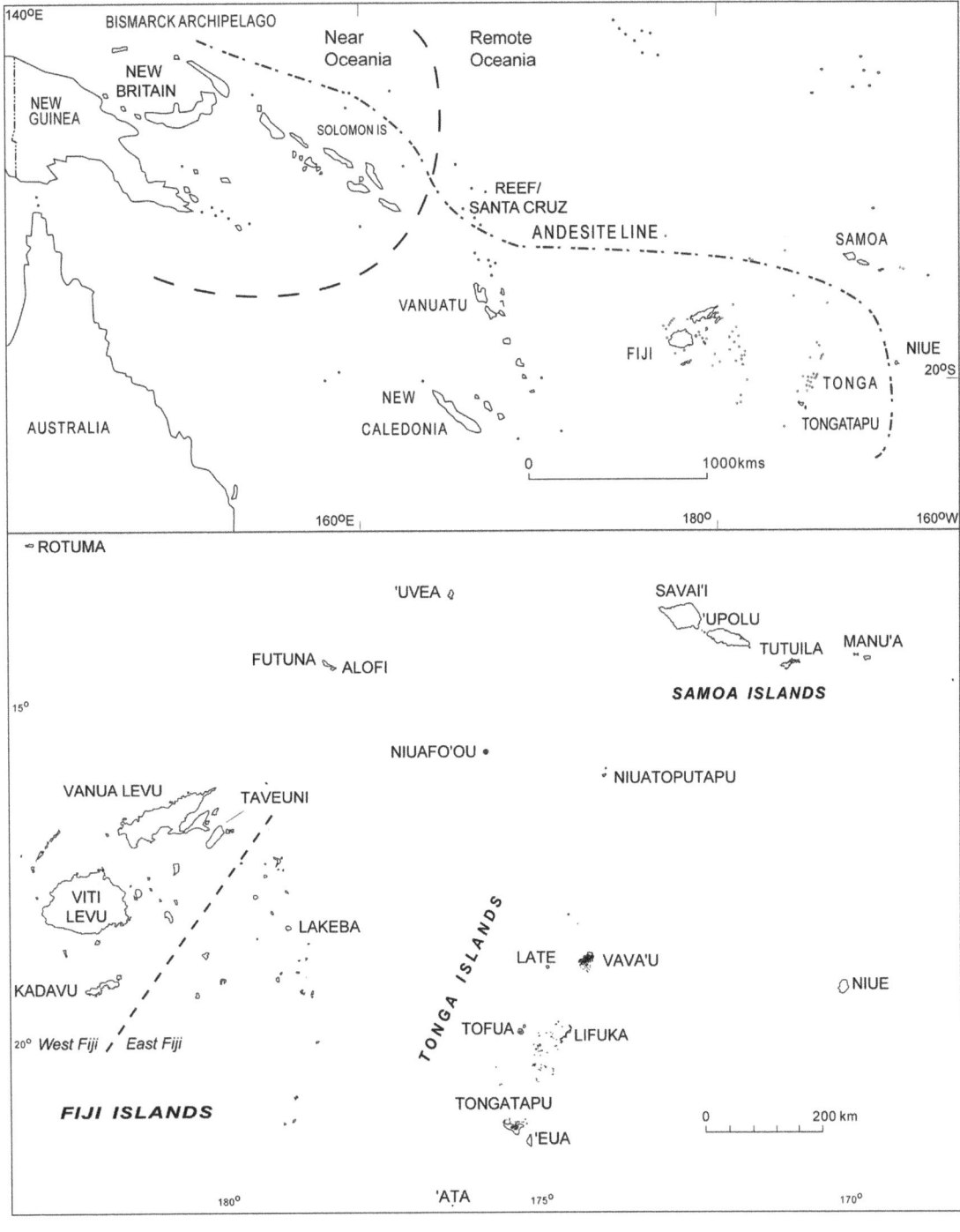

Figure 1. Map of the West and Central Pacific (top) and Fiji–West Polynesia (bottom).

influence through Polynesia. Similarly, Howells (1973:158, 168) placed Fiji in Melanesia but argued that the population: 'should be viewed as Melanesianized Polynesian rather than the reverse'. Linguists, however, placed Fijian in the Central Pacific subgroup of Oceanic languages. In this assemblage, otherwise entirely of conventional Polynesian languages, Proto-Central Pacific was located in Fiji and developed into a dialect chain that split into Rotuman, Fijian and West Polynesian languages (Pawley and Ross 1995:53–54). On that ground, Fiji was placed in Polynesia. Archaeological opinion, founded on the assumption that Lapita culture was spread by people of predominantly 'southern Mongoloid' origin (Bellwood 1996), proposed that Melanesian connections generally came later, and relatively weakly, to Fiji compared with Vanuatu and New Caledonia, the relative influence of these extracting Fiji from the remainder of historical 'Island Melanesia' (notably in Spriggs 1997).

The matters bound up in these views are far more complex than outlined here, but the point about Fiji being in a marginal or transitional position (e.g. Frost 1979) between Melanesia and Polynesia (leaving aside here the history and validity of those concepts; see Clark 2003) was basic to archaeological interest in the archipelago when our project began. The issues centred on the Navatu phase – in Green's (1963a) Fijian sequence dating 100 BC–AD 1100, and situated between the Sigatoka phase, which was seen as ancestral Polynesian, and the Vuda and Ra phases, regarded as exhibiting Melanesian culture. Both the ways in which the transition was conceptualised and its empirical nature remained very much open to debate (Hunt 1986).

Field research on Fiji's early prehistory, human and environmental, also had comparative value for the wider Central Pacific (Fiji–West Polynesia, also the eastern Lapita region). There had been frequent archaeological research on Lapita in Tonga since 1957 (Golson 1961; Groube 1971; Poulsen 1987; Kirch 1988), and a substantial project, based at Simon Fraser University, was underway in the early 1990s (Dickinson et al. 1994; Shutler et al. 1994). Only one Lapita site was known in Samoa, and it was underwater (Jennings 1974; Green and Richards 1975), but new efforts were being made to refine its chronology. Lapita-related fieldwork was in a quiet phase in Fiji by the early 1990s, but accelerated erosion at Sigatoka prompted renewed attention (Hudson 1994; Petchey 1995; Burley 1997; Wood et al. 1998). Some progress had been made in respect of faunal extinctions around the period of human advent in Tonga (Pregill and Dye 1989; Pregill 1993; Steadman 1993; Koopman and Steadman 1995), and there were sparse records from Lakeba (Best 1984), creating a potential basis for comparison. Investigation of vegetation changes in the prehistoric human era, however, had hardly begun (Hope et al. 1999). There were no records from Samoa, only a small project on mangrove pollen directed at sea-level issues in Tonga (Ellison 1989), and preliminary work in Fiji (Latham 1983; Southern 1986; and a project underway on Totoya Island by Clark et al. 1999).

The prehistory of Fiji in the post-colonisation period was also enigmatic, with potential stylistic influences from Southeast Asia and several Melanesian Islands (New Guinea, Solomon Islands, Vanuatu, New Caledonia) seen in Fijian ceramics (Gifford 1951:224, 236–237; Solheim 1952a, b; Frost 1970:252; Garanger 1971; Vanderwal 1973:209; Golson 1974:568, 573). Large-scale investigations on Lakeba Island by Best (1984:216, 493) suggested a ceramic record that had received inputs from New Caledonia and Vanuatu, and a broader pan-Melanesian ceramic style was suggested by Wahome (1997, 1998:189), who proposed that '. . . contacts between the various regions of Island Melanesia continued through the Lapita, post-Lapita, late prehistoric times and after'. Navatu phase sites containing ceramics and material-culture items were studied to examine unresolved issues relating to the cause and sequence of prehistoric culture change in Fiji.

Within Fiji, therefore, the main archaeological research focus at the beginning of the EPF was, first, the timing, nature, spread and impact of Lapita colonisation and, second, the definition, timing and causes of change through the Navatu phase. There was clearly a need to resolve questions about the chronology of Lapita and Navatu sites, and their distribution on islands of different sizes and types and coastally versus inland. In such a large and diverse archipelago, we also hoped to gain some insight into the dispersal of initial colonists through the Fiji Islands. The existence of substantial areas of limestone held out the promise of locating remains of extinct faunas, with the terrestrial ecological diversity of prehistoric fauna used to investigate the directions and rate of human impact on the botanical landscape. Thus the Fiji project was divided into three areas of research: faunal change, landscape change and early archaeology. The background, objectives and fieldwork of each are described briefly here.

Faunal change

The modern vertebrate fauna of Fiji is characterised by a lack of terrestrial mammals, as in other Pacific Islands, but it has six species of bats (Flannery 1995). Fruit bats are mainly of *Pteropus* spp., but also include *Pteralopex acrodonta*, which otherwise occurs only in the Solomons. Historically, the Fijian archipelago had 69 indigenous breeding land birds, 47 on Viti Levu. About 56% of the land birds are endemic, yet few are as distinctive as might be expected in an avifauna from relatively old oceanic islands ('oceanic' meaning islands beyond a continental shelf). Even more unusual for an oceanic island is the fact that few species are known to have become extinct historically. Prominent larger taxa (Ryan 2000) include the reef heron *(Egretta sacra)*, the collared lory *(Phigys solitaries)*, two species of musk parrots *(Prosopeia* spp.), several fruit doves *(Ptilinopus* spp.) and their common predator the peregrine falcon *(Faico peregrinus)*, the banded rail *(Gallirallus philippensis)* and the swamp hen *(Porphyrio porphyrio)*. The avifauna of Fiji is most similar to that of Tonga and Samoa, with overlap of many species in the Lau Group (Watling 1982).

There is a diverse herpetofauna of frogs *(Platymantis,* 2 spp.), iguanas *(Brachylophus,* 3 spp.), geckos (9 spp.), skinks (9 spp.) and snakes (2 spp.). This fauna contains several endemic species that have no equivalents on truly oceanic islands, including two *Platymantis* frogs which are terrestrial, salt-intolerant taxa for which over-water dispersal seems unlikely. Their nearest relatives are in the Solomon Islands archipelago (Gorham 1965; Gibbons 1985). Of the iguanas *(Brachylophus* spp.*),* one is shared with Tonga, but otherwise no close relatives occur elsewhere. One snake, *Ogmodon vitianus*, is an endemic monotypic genus, while the boid *Candoia bibronii* is more widespread (Gibbons 1985). Interestingly, the Fijian invertebrate fauna retains a number of very large taxa, including giant stick insects *(Hermarchus* spp.), coconut beetles *(Olethrius tyrranus)* and longhorn beetles *(Xixuthrus* spp.), which seem to have survived predation by introduced rats (Ryan 2000).

The low incidence of historical extinctions and the scarcity of prehistoric extinctions (exceptions were remains of two megapodes and a pigeon) of relatively large-bodied terrestrial fauna compared with evidence from Tonga and several other Pacific islands (Balouet and Olson 1987; Steadman 1994, 1995; Steadman et al. 2000) begged the question about the faunal history of Fiji. Was a substantial sector of the terrestrial fauna (including land birds) missing from the historical and archaeological record? If the fauna existed, had it gone extinct before the arrival of people, possibly as a result of biogeographical changes resulting from post-Pleistocene sea-level rise? Alternatively, were faunal extinctions culturally coincident? These matters were set down for investigation, primarily by Worthy, in fieldwork involving survey and excavation of sediments preserved in cave sites (Worthy and Anderson 1999; Worthy 2000), mostly in the limestones of Viti Levu (Gilbert 1984).

Fieldwork

In June 1997, there was a preliminary survey of caves in the lower and middle Sigatoka Valley and in September–October 1997, there was a survey of caves in the upper Sigatoka, and on Navo Island. In March–April 1998, Volivoli, Tuvu, Tau and Joskes Thumb were investigated and, in September–October 1998, research shifted mainly to the Wainibuku area near Suva. In November 1999, sites inland from Nadi were visited, along with caves in the Wainibuku Valley, and at Delaniqara at Wailotua. Research also occurred on Vatulele Island.

Landscape change

Fiji has strong floristic links to the west, with 90% of its genera occurring in New Guinea (Ash 1992). Dense tropical rainforest was the main prehistoric vegetation cover in windward districts of Fiji. It included stands of gymnosperms, notably *Agathis macrophylla* (*A. vitiensis*, dakua makadre), *Dacrydium nidulum* (yaka) and the cycad *Cycas rumphii* (logologo), as well as *Cyathea* tree-ferns, several hundred species of ground ferns such as the edible sovanigata *(Asplenium australasicum)* and some palms such as *Veitchia joannis* and *Pritchardia pacifica*. West and north coasts have a dry season and annual rainfall of 1500–2000 mm. Late Holocene rainfall was sufficient to support dry forest, dominated by *Casuarina* spp. and *Pandanus* spp. in the driest areas, while on the limestone islands there is often high forest in which the vesi *(Instia bijuga)* is a prominent tree and the main source of timber for carving (Ash 1992; Ryan 2000).

It was expected that entry of people into the forested landscapes of Fiji, and the changes that occurred during human history, would be disclosed by sedimentary coring and palynological analysis. The evidence of such palaeoenvironmental investigations was regarded as vital to the overall objectives because it offered insight into two basic issues of island colonisation. The first was its potential value as an independent measure of colonisation chronology through radiocarbon-dating evidence of sedimentary and vegetational disturbance that was potentially of synanthropic origin. There was some disagreement in the mid-1990s about the interpretation of sedimentary and pollen sequences in the Pacific, notably about how to explain the considerable gap between palynological and archaeological chronologies of human colonisation in east Polynesia (e.g. Kirch and Ellison 1994; Anderson 1995) In Fiji, this was also a looming issue. Southern (1986) had a radiocarbon date of 4000 BP from the basal level of Bonatoa Bog, in the Rewa delta, where it was associated with a substantial level of fine charcoal under a decline in sago (*Sagu vitiensis*) pollen. Uncertainty was compounded by evidence, in pollen sequences from southern Viti Levu, of enigmatic perturbations that could be interpreted as cultural interference dating to as early as 4500 BP (Southern 1986; Shepherd 1990). The waters were muddied still further by arguments that the history of sea-level change was such that it was premature for prehistorians to rule out human colonisation during the last glacial era, when the Central Pacific archipelagos were several times larger and closer together than they are now (Gibbons 1985; Nunn 1994a, b).

More research on the specific issue of age and on the general pattern of anthropogenic disturbance was clearly needed. There were diverse opinions about the later vegetation history as well. Conventional wisdom had assigned the major role in formation of the modern lowland grasslands of New Caledonia and Fiji to anthropogenic burning (e.g. Cumberland 1963:196; Hughes et al. 1979; Ash 1992), but Latham (1983), Southern (1986) and Nunn (1994b) did not discount a largely natural origin for the extensive *talasiga* grasslands of the leeward districts of Viti Levu and on other islands.

Investigating the age and extent of deforestation in Holocene sequences was also important in other ways. Establishing the pattern of forest retreat could suggest whether it was 'front-loaded' into a general early clearance indicative of widespread exploration and use, or progressively cleared coastal to inland as might reflect population growth and agricultural expansion. Searching for pollen of introduced plants would help to estimate the timing and character of agricultural development.

Fieldwork

In July–August 1995, Hope and Anderson (1995; Hope et al. 2000) cored eight swamp localities in Viti Levu and Vanua Levu to obtain palynological sequences from which a more comprehensive picture of coastal vegetation change during the pre- and post-human Holocene could be constructed. The cores were also intended as a test of the Southern (1986) hypothesis of pre-Lapita intervention in coastal vegetation. In July 1996, Hope cored the Volivoli swamp at Sigatoka and a mangrove location near the Natunuku site at the mouth of the Ba River to investigate the effects of Lapita occupation on the local environment. In November 2000, Hope took a core from the flood plain near the Navatu 17A site to investigate the effects of post-Lapita human settlement, and undertook additional work in the Sigatoka Valley. In November–December 2000, Hope took cores from Vanuabalavu and Yacata in northern Lau.

Human colonisation and cultural transformation

When the Fiji project began, only a handful of Lapita sites had been examined archaeologically in any detail: Natunuku (Mead et al. 1973; Davidson et al. 1990), Sigatoka (Birks 1973), Yanuca (Birks and Birks 1978; Hunt 1980), Lakeba (Best 1984) and Naigani (Best 1981), although some additional sites had been recorded. The Sigatoka ceramic sequence had been used to define a Fijian culture history (Green 1963a, b; Green and Palmer 1964) comprising Lapita and plain-ware assemblages in the Sigatoka phase (1200–100 BC), paddle-impressed wares in the Navatu phase (100 BC–AD 1100), incised and shell-impressed assemblages in the Vuda phase (AD 1100–1800), and ornate modern wares in the Ra phase (about AD 1800–1900). Excavations by Birks (1973) put more precise dates to the two early phases, at least at Sigatoka: Level 1 (Sigatoka phase) radiocarbon dating to 789–405 BC (GaK-946, 2460±90 BP) and Level 2 (Navatu phase) dating to about 300 AD. He estimated Level 3 (Vuda phase) as about 1300 AD.

Radiocarbon dating of other Lapita sites suggested colonisation had begun earlier than 1000 BC. Among the Fijian Lapita dates listed by Kirch and Hunt (1988:Table 2.3) was an early age (GaK-1218, 3240±100 BP), calibrated as 1684–1416 BC from the basal cultural layer 6 at Natunuku (recalculated by Davidson et al. (1990:131) as 1736–1266 BC), and another of 1377–1052 BC (GaK-1226, 2980±90 BP) from Yanuca, both on charcoal samples. Layer 6 at Natunuku produced a ceramic assemblage of early eastern Lapita type, with some connections to western Lapita, which was possibly older than other Fijian assemblages known at the time (Davidson et al. 1990). New dates on marine-shell samples from Layer 5 at Natunuku provided a much younger age, about 350 BC (Davidson and Leach 1993), which simply highlighted the fact that in these sites and generally '. . . the Fijian sequence cannot yet be said to be well-dated' (Davidson and Leach 1993:102). Clearly one fundamental issue in understanding the early prehistory of Fiji had to be whether it was possible to obtain a more precise chronology of colonisation using various chronometric techniques in conjunction with evidence from site stratigraphy and material culture. As the Fiji archipelago is extensive, a related issue was whether there was evidence of delay in the initial colonisation of west versus east, or of small versus large islands.

Related to those matters was a cluster of questions about Lapita settlement patterns in general. Were they as exclusively coastal as they appeared, and was this more or less so in Remote Oceania where an absence of pre-existing inland occupation could be assumed? Was Lapita occupation largely associated with small islands? What did the answers to these questions imply about the nature of subsistence and about social patterns? Birks (1973) had used the Sigatoka dunes sequence to propose a dynamic model of Fijian prehistory, which argued that relatively slow dune formation in early prehistory followed by late rapid change indicated an increased rate of erosion in the Sigatoka catchment due to forest firing, which, in turn, reflected relatively late population growth and settlement penetration into the island interior (Figure 2). To put it another way, Lapita settlement was very much coastally tethered.

Yet it was difficult to avoid pondering the significance of the location of Natunuku and Sigatoka Lapita sites at the mouths of two of the largest rivers on Viti Levu (Sigatoka and Ba), where reef resources must have been comparatively poor even at the beginning of occupation, but where there was unparalleled watercraft access far into the interior. Looking at Lapita sites in general, Lepofsky (1988) had found that all were coastal and had ready access to the open sea, but there was no particularly evident proximity to reefal and lagoonal resources, arable land was generally close by, and a locational emphasis on small islands was less apparent than was generally believed. Other syntheses of Lapita site characteristics (Butler 1988; Nagaoka 1988) showed that faunal remains were relatively sparse overall and lent no strong support to either of the competing hypotheses: that Lapita expansion was fuelled largely by littoral and marine foraging – the so-called 'strandlooper hypothesis' (Groube 1971); or that it was mainly an agricultural expansion (Green 1979; Kirch and Green 1987), as documented by remains of introduced animals. As Kirch pointed out (1988:160), the evidence for horticulture, which was the core strategy at issue, remained indirect. As for social interaction, the coastal location of Lapita sites was clearly conducive to mobility by sea (Lepofsky 1988), but whether lithics and ceramics had been moved about within the Fijian archipelago (Hunt 1980; Best 1984) or from further afield, or were mainly of local procurement or manufacture, was a question that needed to be addressed.

Figure 2. View of the landscape inland from the Sigatoka Sand Dunes.

Fieldwork – Lapita sites

Archaeological fieldwork began in July 1996 with investigations at the two Lapita sites best known from previous research, Natunuku and Sigatoka, with the objective of defining more precisely the nature of the early Lapita phase in Fiji (or, indeed, of any earlier phase of settlement) in terms of both chronology and content. At Sigatoka (Figure 3), on the windward coast of Viti Levu, early archaeological remains are stratified in the lower levels of a coastal dune system and appear to represent periods of relative stability. Since dune-building began earlier than the lowest archaeological deposits, it was essential to determine whether there were phases of similar stability lower in the sequence than the archaeological remains and therefore whether there were prior periods when the locality could have been settled had there been people available to do so. The main objectives in this work were to obtain sediment profiles and samples and to date the changes. To do this we took samples for the (then quite new) method of optically stimulated luminescence dating, the only practical means of getting a detailed chronology of the dune system. Concurrently with work at Sigatoka were test excavations in the vicinity, at Malaqereqere rock shelter (Figure 4) along the coast to the west, and at two rock shelters in the Volivoli limestone massif behind Sigatoka (Volivoli I and Volivoli II). The purpose of these was to determine whether Lapita occupation could be picked up away from the main site along the coast or immediately inland in the lower Sigatoka Valley.

Figure 3. Sigatoka Sand Dune in south Viti Levu, west view along dunes.

Figure 4. Malaqereqere rock shelter prior to excavation.

At Natunuku, on the leeward coast, were the eroding remains of a once-larger site (Mead et al. 1973), possibly the oldest in Fiji. Our objective was to locate and excavate additional areas of Layer 6 which had produced the very early radiocarbon date and to test sediments beneath for any earlier signs of occupation. We also wanted to date the sedimentary history of the site and beneath it using OSL dating. On a small coastal plain immediately behind the Lapita site another extensive site (approximately 1.0 ha) was observed in 1995. There was no evidence that this was a Lapita site, but as it extended to within 20 m of Lapita Location C (Davidson et al. 1990), it could have concealed early cultural layers at depth and on that ground it needed to be investigated.

Fieldwork on the Navatu phase began in August 1996. The Navatu 17A site (Figure 5) containing paddle-impressed pottery was relocated and excavated by Clark and a small team from the Fiji Museum and villagers from Narewa and Vitawa.

In November–December 1997, the Votua Lapita site on Mago Island (Figure 6) was discovered and excavated during an expedition to the Lau Group organised by Professor Patrick

Figure 5. Uluinavatu volcanic plug in north Viti Levu. The Navatu 17A site is on the lower flanks of the plug just in from the edge of the sugar cane field.

Nunn (USP). Deposits from the Sovanibeka rock shelter were collected by Clark and Hope. The Votua site was revisited in December 2000 and excavated by Clark, Hope and L. Schmidt (ANU). In May 1997, attention turned to Beqa Island (Figure 7), offshore from the south coast of Viti Levu. Lapita pottery had been reported from several localities by Crosby (1988). Two of these were especially interesting. One site in Kulu Bay was located in a damp area behind the coastal sand plain. This was targeted for an exploratory excavation to determine whether it was, or contained, a wet site of Lapita province.

Another site with early paddle-impressed wares was on the small lagoonal island of Ugaga (Figure 8). At this site, the transition from late Lapita to the middle phase of Fijian prehistory could be investigated.

Figure 6. The Vutuna headland (west view) on Mago Island. The Votua Lapita site lies behind the beach berm beside the Tokelau Stream.

Figure 7. Beqa Island viewed from Ugaga Island.

Figure 8. Ugaga Island in the Beqa Lagoon.

Oceanic context

Although a distinct project, the Fiji research was also part of the Indo-Pacific Colonisation Program (IPCP) devised by Anderson to pursue an interest in the late-Holocene migration of people, mostly presumed speakers of Austronesian languages, across the remote regions of the Indian and Pacific oceans, their colonisation of oceanic islands and the reciprocal relations that developed between settlement and environmental change. The IPCP originated in response to two concerns. The more important methodologically was that while oceanic archaeology structured as longitudinal culture–historical research by island or archipelago is fundamental to understanding regional prehistory, and it is certainly reflected in the Fiji project, it may not be the most useful way to investigate specific issues of extensive distribution, such as those of migration and colonisation, which are often, by their nature, relatively brief but wide-ranging. A project that focused on the scale of the oceanic landscape as a whole seemed a more useful and efficient approach. The Fiji research is interesting in its own right, but it will become, as well, part of the larger study of the prehistoric human colonisation of the oceans.

A more immediate and pragmatic concern was a crisis of research funding in 1995 that loomed in the Institute of Advanced Studies (ANU) because the institute had no direct access to the research funding through the Australian Research Council that was available to the ANU Faculties and all other Australian universities. Research survival demanded alternative resourcing strategies, a point driven home in 1996 by the reduction of the Division of Archaeology and Natural History to the status of a small department. The IPCP involved focused investigation of the colonising phases of numerous islands of various sizes, types and environmental zones, a strategy that required multiple, focused projects with shared resources in collaboration with colleagues with research interests across the island world.

Existing projects on Niue Island (Walter and Anderson 2002) and Norfolk Island (Anderson and White 2001) were taken into the IPCP and new projects were undertaken in Fiji, Christmas Island, Kiritimati Island (Anderson et al. 2002), Lord Howe Island, French Polynesia (Maupiti, Huahine, Mangareva, Rapa), the Pindai caves in New Caledonia, subantarctic New Zealand, Batanes Islands (Philippines), Yaeyama Islands (Japan), and the Juan Fernandez and Galapagos Islands of the far-eastern Pacific (Anderson 2004). The IPCP continues in the Indian Ocean. In due course, the Fiji project and all the others will be considered within a broad synthesis of the evidence and its implications for the human colonisation of the oceans.

Acknowledgments

'The Early Prehistory of Fiji' project, directed by Atholl Anderson (Department of Archaeology and Natural History, ANU), received research funding from the Australian Research Council (with P. White), the Royal Society of New Zealand, the Wenner-Gren organisation and the National Geographic Society, for which we are most grateful. Staff at the Fiji Museum were instrumental in facilitating project fieldwork. In particular, we thank K. Vusoniwailala (Director), T. Sorovi-Vunidilo (Director, archaeologist), C. Burke (archaeologist), S. Matararaba (Mata) (Field Officer, archaeologist), J. Naucabalavu (Field Officer, archaeologist), W. Copeland and K. Nanda (Education Officer). We are very appreciative of the generous support of Professor P. Nunn (University of the South Pacific) who supported investigations at several locations and arranged site permissions and logistics, as well as providing study materials and student assistants. Significant assistance and advice was also provided by D. Watling, P. Geraghty, G. Udy, D. Burley, C. Ollier, P. Ryan, P. Rodda, W. Dickinson, R. Green, J. Clark, G. Irwin, C. Sand, A. Parke, S. Best, D. Argue, A. de Biran and F. Valentin, who gave generously of their time and knowledge. We are especially thankful to L. Schmidt and D. O'Dea in the Department of Archaeology and Natural History for assisting in the processing of archaeological and palaeoenvironmental materials.

We also thank the Roko Tui Nadroga/Navosa, Mr I. Kedralevu and the Provincial Officers, U. Kunaturaga, S. Moceacagi and M. Nagata, for helping with access to the Sigatoka sites. We are grateful for the aid of the Assistant Roko Tui Vuda/Vitoga, Mr S. Vaturu, for facilitating access to Nawaqadamu village, and thank, from Nawaqadamu village, Mr J. Nanauwalu (Turangi-ni-koro), the Ratu M. Bitu, and the guides A. Raakuma and A. Kuruisaqila for access to caves in their care, particularly Vatumu Cave. Thanks are due to the following landowners who gave access to their lands and caves. Volivoli – Mrs L. Tubou (owner), Mr N. Tubou and Mr S. Batimala (Turanga-ni-koro); Wainibuku Area – Mr D. Singh, K. Vukeiono; Wailotua – Ratu A. Roseru and E. Cavu. We are grateful to H. Crawford and M. Livingston for hosting the team at Vatulele Resort while we conducted fieldwork. We thank the Ratu A. Racara-Tui of Ekubu village for permission to visit caves in the area, and for help in locating the caves we acknowledge P. Niutoga, A. Yabaki and A. Venuki.

The University of the South Pacific is thanked for funding the Northern Lau expedition headed by Professor P. Nunn, and the Tokyu Corporation of Japan is acknowledged for allowing research on Mago Island. The people of Mago, Yacata and Kaibu gave generously of their time, knowledge and hospitality during project investigations. The village of Naceva generously hosted the excavation crew during fieldwork on Beqa-Ugaga. Special thanks go to the Roko Tui Rewa, J. Cagi, V. Qaranivalu (village headman), P. Vakaolo, M. Tubanavau (Rukua village), J. Ledua Cagi, Professor M. Davis (Sociology, USP), J. Clark, N. Lawson, F. Ericsson, J. Naucabalavu, S. Mataraba, K. Lawson, Dr R. McGovern-Wilson (DoC, New Zealand). Excavations at Navatu were organised and carried out with the assistance of the Fiji Museum and thanks go to the people of Narewa village, particularly the late I. Donu who looked after the field crew of G. Clark, H. Kiguchi (JOCV-Fiji Museum), S. Matararaba, J. Nancabalaru, C. Tuitubou, V. Sadrugu, J. Tikoibau (Narewa) and V. Vakabua (Vitawa).

The palaeofaunal investigations were advanced by the assistance of curators and collections managers in the following institutions: Australian National University (ANU) – C. Campbell; Auckland Institute and Museum (AIM) – B. Gill; American Museum of Natural History (AMNH) – P. Sweet, A. Andors, C. Blake; Australian National Wildlife Collection, Canberra (ANWC) – J. Wombley; Natural History Museum, London (BMNH) – J. Cooper for measurements and X-Rays of specimens; Canterbury Museum, Christchurch, NZ (CM) – G. Tunnicliffe; Museum of New Zealand Te Papa Tongarewa, Wellington, NZ (MNZ) – A. Tennyson, S. Bartle; Queensland Museum, Brisbane, Australia (QM) – S. van Dyke; Smithsonian Institution (USNM) – S. Olson, P. Angle, R. Crombie; South Australian Museum, SA, Australia (SAM) – B. McHenry; Burke Museum, University of Washington, Seattle, USA (UWBM) – R. Faucett and C. Filardi.

We also thank S. Best for loans of casts of Naigani faunal material, G. Irwin for access to the Naigani collections, E.S. Gaffney for turtle identifications (American Museum of Natural History) and D. de Gusta (Stanford University) who examined and identified the human bone from Navatu. Chert samples were kindly provided by S. Best, J. Clark and C. Sand. The Fiji Museum is gratefully acknowledged for allowing us to examine chert artefacts from Sigatoka. Chert samples were prepared by W. Ambrose (ANU) with thanks to G. Summerhayes (University of Otago) for providing access to the Lucas Heights accelerator and to P. White (Sydney University) for undertaking the PIXIE/PIGME analysis. The Statistical Consulting Unit at the ANU and P. Sheppard (Auckland University) provided helpful advice on the chert data for which we are grateful. Analyses of various materials was made by W. Ambrose, J. Chappell, D. Kennett, G. Robertson, R. Roberts and L. Wallis whom we thank. Land-snail identifications for Volivoli II were made with access to the shell collections held at the Netherlands National Museum of Natural History, and we thank E. Gittenberger, W. Maasson and J. de Vos for their support and also S. Walker for discussion of coenobitid hermit crab behaviour. The late R. Green (University of Auckland) kindly located and copied the excavation documents for Karobo, and the Fiji Museum gave permission for the Karobo collection to be studied at the ANU.

We are grateful for assistance in the collection of pollen cores from F. Areki, J. Ash, A. de Biran, C. Burke, the late L. Cavu, C. Corby, R. Kumar, P. Nunn, S. Matararaba, N. Ram, L. Schmidt, E. Tawake, N. van Dijk and B. Weatherstone. We owe a particular debt of gratitude to the University of South Pacific, which supported Southern and Hope's work, and the Fiji Museum. Financial support for pollen dating was provided by AINSIE and the late John Head of the ANU.

References

Anderson, A.J. 1995. Current approaches in East Polynesian colonization research. *Journal of the Polynesian Society* 104: 110–132.

Anderson, A.J. 2001. Mobility models of Lapita migration. In: Clark, G.R., Anderson, A.J. and Vunidilo, T. (eds), *The archaeology of Lapita dispersal in Oceania: Papers from the Fourth Lapita Conference*. Terra Australis 17: 15–23.

Anderson, A.J. 2004. It's about time: The Indo-Pacific colonization project. In: Murray, T. (ed), *Archaeology from Australia*, pp. 3–17. La Trobe University, Melbourne.

Anderson, A.J., Ayliffe, L., Questiaux, D., Sorovi-Vunidilo, T., Spooner, N. and Worthy, T. 2001b. The terminal age of the Fijian megafauna. In: Anderson, A.J., Lilley, I. and O'Connor, S. (eds), *Histories of old ages: Essays in honour of Rhys Jones*, pp. 251–264. Pandanus Books, Canberra.

Anderson, A., Bedford, S., Clark, G., Lilley, I., Sand, C., Summerhayes, G. and Torrence, R. 2001. A list of Lapita sites containing dentate-stamped pottery. 2001a. In: Clark, G.R., Anderson, A.J. and Vunidilo, T. (eds). *The archaeology of Lapita dispersal in Oceania*, pp. 1–13. Terra Australis 17, Pandanus Press, Canberra.

Anderson, A.J., Burke, C. and Clark, G.R. 1996. Prehistoric colonisation and settlement of Fiji: An initial report to the Fiji Museum. Unpublished report to the Fiji Museum, Suva.

Anderson, A.J. and Clark, G.R. 1999. The age of Lapita settlement in Fiji. *Archaeology in Oceania* 34: 31–39.

Anderson, A.J., Clark, G.R. and Worthy, T.H. 2000. An inland Lapita site in Fiji. *Journal of the Polynesian Society* 109: 311–316.

Anderson, A.J., Martinsson-Wallin, H. and Wallin, P. 2002. *The prehistory of Kiritimati (Christmas) Island, Republic of Kiribati: Excavations and analyses.* Occasional Papers of The Kon-Tiki Museum, Volume 6.

Anderson, A., Roberts, R., Dickinson, W., Clark, G., Burley, D., de Biran, A., Hope G. and Nunn, P. 2006. Times of sand: Sedimentary history and archaeology at the Sigatoka dunes, Fiji. *Geoarchaeology* 21: 131–154.

Anderson, A.J. and White, J.P. (eds) 2001. *The prehistoric archaeology of Norfolk Island, Southwest Pacific.* Supplement 27, Records of the Australian Museum.

Ash, J. 1992. Vegetation ecology of Fiji: Past, present and future perspectives. *Pacific Science* 46: 111–127.

Balouet, J.C. and Olson, S.L. 1987. An extinct species of giant pigeon (Columbidae: Ducula) from archaeological deposits on Wallis (Uvea) Island, South Pacific. *Proceedings of the Biological Society of Washington* 100: 769–775.

Bellwood, P. 1996. Early agriculture and the dispersal of the southern Mongoloids. In: Akazawa, T. and Szathmáry, E. (eds), *Prehistoric Mongoloid dispersals*, pp. 287–302. Oxford University Press, Oxford.

Best, S. 1981. Excavations at Site VL 21/5 Naigani Island, Fiji, a preliminary report. Department of Anthropology, University of Auckland.

Best, S. 1984. Lakeba: The prehistory of a Fijian Island. Unpublished PhD thesis, Department of Anthropology, University of Auckland.

Birks, L. 1973. Archaeological excavations at Sigatoka dune site, Fiji. *Bulletin of the Fiji Museum* No.1.

Birks, L. and Birks, H. 1978. Archaeological excavations at site VL 16/81, Yanuca Island, Fiji. *Oceanic Prehistory Records* No. 6. University of Auckland.

Burley, D.V. 1997. Archaeological research, Sigatoka Sand Dune National Park. Unpublished report to the Fiji Museum, Suva.

Butler, V.L. 1988. Lapita fishing strategies: The faunal evidence. In: Kirch, P.V. and Hunt, T.L. (eds), *Archaeology of the Lapita cultural complex: A critical review*, pp. 99–115. Thomas Burke Memorial Washington State Museum Research Report No. 5. Burke Museum, Seattle.

Chase, C.G. 1971. Tectonic history of the Fiji Plateau. *Geological Society of America Bulletin* 82: 3087–3110.

Clark, G.R. 2000. Post-Lapita Fiji: Cultural transformation in the mid-sequence. Unpublished PhD thesis, Australian National University.

Clark, G. 2003. Shards of meaning: Archaeology and the Melanesia-Polynesia distinction. *Journal of Pacific History* 38(2): 197–213.

Clark, G.R. and Anderson, A.J. 2001 The pattern of Lapita settlement in Fiji. *Archaeology in Oceania* 36: 77–88.

Clark, G.R., Anderson., A.J. and Matararaba, S. 2001. The Lapita site at Votua, northern Lau Islands, Fiji. *Archaeology in Oceania* 36: 134–143

Clark, J.T., Cole, A.O. and Nunn, P.D. 1999. Environmental change and human prehistory on Totoya Island, Fiji. In: Lilley, I. and Galipaud, J-C. (eds), *Le pacifique de 5000 à 2000 avant le présent. Suppléments à l'histoire d'une colonisation*, pp. 227–240. Editions de l'ORSTOM, Paris.

Crosby, A. 1988. Beqa: Archaeology, structure and history in Fiji. Unpublished MA thesis, Department of Anthropology, University of Auckland.

Cumberland, K.B. 1963. Man's role in modifying island environments in the southwest Pacific: With special reference to New Zealand, pp. 187–206. In Fosberg, F.R. (ed), *Man's place in the island ecosystem*, pp. 187–206. Bishop Museum, Honolulu.

Davidson, J., Hinds, E., Holdaway, S. and Leach, F. 1990. The Lapita site of Natunuku, Fiji. *New Zealand Journal of Archaeology* 12: 121–155.

Davidson, J. and Leach, F. 1993. The chronology of the Natunuku site, Fiji. *New Zealand Journal of Archaeology* 15: 99–105.

Dickinson, W.R., Burley, D.V. and Shutler, R. Jr. 1994. Impact of hydro-isostatic Holocene sea-level change on the geologic context of archaeological sites. *Geoarchaeology* 9: 85–111.

Ellison, J.C. 1989. Pollen analysis of mangrove sediments as a sea level indicator: Assessment from Tongatapu, Tonga. *Palaeogeography, Palaeoclimatology, Palaeoecology* 74(3–4): 327–341.

Flannery, T.F. 1995. *Mammals of the South-west Pacific and Moluccan Islands*. Reed Books in association with the Australian Museum, Sydney.

Frost, E.L. 1970. Archaeological excavations of fortified sites on Taveuni, Fiji. Unpublished PhD thesis, University of Oregon.

Frost, E.L. 1979. Fiji. In: Jennings, J.D. (ed), *The prehistory of Polynesia*, pp. 61–81. Australian National University Press, Canberra.

Garanger, J. 1971. Incised and applied-relief pottery, its chronology and development in southeastern Melanesia, and extra areal comparisons. In: Green, R.C. and Kelly, M. (eds), *Studies in oceanic culture history*, Volume 2, pp. 53–99. Pacific Anthropological Records No. 12.

Gibbons, J.R.H. 1985. A brief environmental history of Fiji. *Domodomo* III(3): 110–123.

Gibbons, J.R. and Clunie, F.G. 1986. Sea level changes and Pacific prehistory, new insight into early human settlement of Oceania. *The Journal of Pacific History* XXI (2): 58–82.

Gifford, E.W. 1951. Archaeological excavations in Fiji. *University of California Anthropological Records* 13: 189–288.

Gilbert, T. 1984. Limestone and volcanic caves of the Fiji Islands. *Transactions of the British Cave Research Association* 11(2): 105–118.

Golson, J. 1961. Report on New Zealand, western Polynesia, New Caledonia and Fiji. *Asian Perspectives* 5: 166–180.

Golson, J. 1974. Both sides of the Wallace Line: New Guinea, Australia, Island Melanesia and Asian prehistory. In: Barnard, N. (ed), *Early Chinese art and its possible influence in the Pacific Basin*, pp. 533–595. Proceedings of a symposium arranged by the Department of Art History and Archaeology, Columbia University, New York City and Taiwan.

Gorham, S.W. 1965. Fiji frogs, life history data from field work. *Zoologische Beitrage* 14: 427–446.

Green, R.C. 1963a. A suggested revision of the Fiji sequence. *Journal of the Polynesian Society* 72: 235–253.

Green, R.C. 1963b. Two collections of pottery from Sigatoka, Fiji. *Journal of the Polynesian Society* 72: 261–264.

Green, R.C. 1979. Lapita. In: Jennings, J.D. (ed), *The prehistory of Polynesia*. pp. 27–60. Australian National University Press, Canberra.

Green, R.C. and Palmer, J.B. 1964. Fiji sequence: Corrections and additional notes for Sigatoka. *Journal of the Polynesian Society* 73: 328–333.

Green, R.C. and Richards, H.G. 1975. Lapita pottery and lower sea level in western Samoa. *Pacific Science* 29: 309–315.

Groube, L.M. 1971. Tonga, Lapita pottery, and Polynesian origins. *Journal of the Polynesian Society* 80: 278–316.

Hale, H. 1846. *United States exploring expedition: Ethnology and philology*. Lea and Blanchard, Philadelphia.

Hope, G. and Anderson, A. 1995. A reconnaissance survey of Holocene deposits on Viti Levu and Vanua Levu, Fiji. Unpublished report, Australian National University.

Hope, G., Anderson, A., Stevenson, J. and O'Dea, D. 2000. Vegetation histories from Fiji: Alternative records of human impact. Unpublished ANH working paper.

Hope, G., O'Dea, D. and Southern, W. 1999. Holocene vegetation histories in the Western Pacific: Alternative records of human impact. In: Lilley, I. and Galipaud, J-C. (eds), *The Pacific from 5000 to 2000 BP: Colonisation and transformations*, pp. 387–404. IRD Editions, Paris.

Howe, K.R. 1984. *Where the waves fall*. Allen and Unwin, Sydney.

Howells, W. 1973. *The Pacific Islanders*. Weidenfeld and Nicolson, London.

Hudson, E. 1994. Sigatoka Sand Dune Site archaeological rescue project 1993. Unpublished report, Auckland Uniservices Limited, Auckland.

Hughes, P.J., Hope, G.S., Latham M. and Brookfield, M. 1979. Prehistoric man-induced degradation of the Lakeba landscape: Evidence from two inland swamps. In: Brookfield, H.G. (ed), *Lakeba: Environmental change, population and resource use*, pp. 93–111. UNESCO/UNFPA Island Reports 5.

Hunt, T.L. 1980. Toward Fiji's past: archaeological research on southwestern Viti Levu. Unpublished MA thesis, University of Auckland.

Hunt, T.L. 1986. Conceptual and substantive issues in Fijian prehistory. In: Kirch, P.V. (ed), *Island societies: Archaeological approaches to evolution and transformation*, pp. 20–32. Cambridge University Press, Cambridge.

Jennings, J.D. 1974. The Ferry Berth site, Mulifanua district, Upolu. In: Green, R.C. and Davidson, J.M. (eds), Archaeology in Western Samoa, Volume 2. *Auckland Institute and Museum Bulletin* 7: 176–178.

Kaeppler, A. 1978. Exchange patterns in goods and services: Fiji, Tonga and Samoa. *Mankind* 11: 246–252.

Kirch, P.V. 1988. *Niuatoputapu: The prehistory of a Polynesian chiefdom*. Thomas Burke Memorial Washington State Museum Monograph No. 5. The Burke Museum, Seattle.

Kirch, P.V. and Ellison, J. 1994. Palaeoenvironmental evidence for human colonization of remote Oceanic islands. *Antiquity* 68: 310–321.

Kirch, P.V. and Green, R.C. 1987. History, phylogeny and evolution in Polynesia. *Current Anthropology* 28: 431–456.

Kirch, P.V. and Hunt, T.L. 1988. The spatial and temporal boundaries of Lapita. In: Kirch, P.V. and Hunt, T.L. (eds), *Archaeology of the Lapita cultural complex: A critical review*, pp. 9–31. Thomas Burke Memorial Washington State Museum Research Report No. 5. Burke Museum, Seattle.

Koopman, K.F. and Steadman, D.W. 1995. Extinction and biogeography of bats on 'Eua, Kingdom of Tonga. *American Museum Novitates* 3125: 1–13.

Latham, M. 1983. Origin of the *talasiqa* formation. In: Latham, M. and Brookfield, H.C. (eds), *The eastern islands of Fiji*, pp. 129–142. UNESCO/UNFPA, Paris.

Lepofsky, D. 1988. The environmental context of Lapita settlement location. In: Kirch, P.V. and Hunt, T.L. (eds), *Archaeology of the Lapita cultural complex: A critical review*, pp. 33–47. Thomas Burke Memorial Washington State Museum Research Report No. 5. Burke Museum, Seattle.

Martin, J. 1817 *An account of the natives of the Tongan Islands, compiled and arranged from the communications of Mr William Mariner*, 2 vols. London.

Mead, S., Birks, L., Birks, H. and Shaw, E. 1973. The Lapita pottery style of Fiji and its associations. *Journal of the Polynesian Society Memoir* 38: 1–98.

Nagaoka, L. 1988. Lapita subsistence: The evidence of non-fish archaeofaunal remains. In: Kirch, P.V. and Hunt, T.L. (eds), *Archaeology of the Lapita cultural complex: A critical review*, pp. 117–153. Thomas Burke Memorial Washington State Museum Research Report No. 5. Burke Museum, Seattle.

Nunn, P.D. 1994a. *Oceanic islands*. Blackwell, Oxford.

Nunn, P.D. 1994b. Beyond the naive lands: Human history and environmental change in the Pacific Basin. In: Waddell, E. and Nunn, P.D. (eds), *The margin fades: Geographical itineraries in a world of islands*, pp. 5–27. Institute of Pacific Studies, USP, Suva.

Nunn, P.D. 1999. *Environmental change in the Pacific Basin*. John Wiley, Chichester.

Pawley, A. and Ross, M. 1995. The prehistory of the Oceanic languages: A current view. In: Bellwood,

P., Fox J.J. and Pawley, A. (eds), *The Austronesians: Historical and comparartive perspectives*, pp. 39–74. Anthropology, RSPAS, ANU, Canberra.

Pernetta, J.C. and Watling, D. 1979. The introduced and native terrestrial vertebrates of Fiji. *Pacific Science* 32: 223–244.

Petchey, F. 1995. Archaeology of Kudon: Archaeological analysis of Lapita ceramics from Mulifanua, Samoa and Sigatoka, Fiji. Unpublished MA thesis, University of Auckland, New Zealand.

Poulsen, J. 1987. *Early Tongan prehistory*. (2 volumes). Terra Australis 12. Department of Prehistory, Research School of Pacific Studies, Australian National University.

Pregill, G.K. 1993. Fossil lizards from the late Quaternary of 'Eua, Tonga. *Pacific Science* 47: 101–114.

Pregill, G.K. and Dye, T. 1989. Prehistoric extinction of giant iguanas in Tonga. *Copeia* 1989: 505–508.

Rodda, P. 1994. Geology of Fiji. In: Stevenson, A.J., Herzer, R.H. and Ballance, P.F. (eds), Geology and submarine resources of the Tonga–Lau–Fiji Region. *SOPAC Technical Bulletin* 8: 131–151.

Ryan, P. 2000. *Fiji's natural heritage*. Southwestern, Auckland.

Shepherd, M.J. 1990. The evolution of a moderate energy coast in Holocene time; Pacific Harbour, Viti Levu, Fiji. *New Zealand Journal of Geology and Geophysics* 33: 547–556.

Shutler, R. Jr., Burley, D.V., Dickinson, W.R., Nelson, E. and Carlson, A.K. 1994. Early Lapita sites, the colonisation of Tonga and recent data from northern Ha'apai. *Archaeology in Oceania* 29: 53–68.

Solheim, W.G. II. 1952a. Oceanian pottery manufacture. *Journal of East Asiatic Studies*. 1(2): 1–39.

Solheim, W.G. II. 1952b. Paddle decoration of pottery. *Journal of East Asiatic Studies*. 2(1): 35–45.

Southern, W. 1986. The late Quaternary environmental history of Fiji. Unpublished doctoral dissertation, Australian National University.

Spriggs, M. 1997. *The Island Melanesians*. Blackwell, Oxford.

Steadman, D.W. 1993. Biogeography of Tongan birds before and after human impact. *Proceedings of the National Academy of Sciences, USA* 90: 818–822.

Steadman, D.W. 1994. Bird bones from the To'aga site, Ofu, American Samoa: Prehistoric loss of seabirds and megapodes. *University of California Archaeological Research Facility, Contributions* 51: 217–228.

Steadman, D.W. 1995: Prehistoric extinctions of Pacific island birds: Biodiversity meets zooarchaeology. *Science* 267: 1123–1131.

Steadman, D.W., Worthy, T.H., Anderson, A.J. and Walter, R. 2000. New species and records of birds from prehistoric sites on Niue, Southwest Pacific. *Wilson Bulletin* 112: 165–186.

Vanderwal, R.L. 1973. Prehistoric studies in central coastal Papua. Unpublished PhD thesis, Australian National University.

Wahome, E.W. 1997. Continuity and change in Lapita and post-Lapita ceramics: A review of evidence from the Admiralty Islands and New Ireland, Papua New Guinea. *Archaeology in Oceania* 32(1): 118–123.

Wahome, E.W. 1998. Ceramic and prehistoric exchange in the Admiralty Islands, Papua New Guinea. Unpublished PhD thesis, Australian National University.

Walter, R. and Anderson, A. 2002. *The archaeology of Niue Island West Polynesia*. Bishop Museum Bulletin in Anthropology 10. Bishop Museum Press, Honolulu.

Watling, D. 1982. *Birds of Fiji, Tonga and Samoa*, Millwood Press, Wellington.

Wood, S., Marshall, Y. and Crosby, A. 1998. Mapping Sigatoka Site VL 16/1: The 1992 field season and its implications. Unpublished report, Fiji Museum, Suva.

Worthy, T.H. 2000. Fossil faunas from Vatulele Island, Fiji. Unpublished report, Fiji Museum, Suva,.

Worthy, T.H. and Anderson, A.J. 1999. Research on the caves of Viti Levu, Fiji, June 1997–October 1998, and their significance for palaeontology and archaeology. Unpublished Report, Fiji Museum, Suva.

Worthy, T.H., Anderson, A.J. and Molnar, R.E. 1999. Megafaunal expression in a land without mammals: The first fossil faunas from terrestrial deposits in Fiji (Vertebrata: amphipibia, reptilia, aves). *Senckenbergiana biologica* 79: 237–242.

2

Palaeofaunal sites and excavations

Trevor H. Worthy
School of Biological, Earth and Environmental Sciences, The University of New South Wales

Atholl Anderson
Department of Archaeology and Natural History, The Australian National University

Introduction

Fieldwork investigating fossil sites occurred in Fiji between June 1997 and November 1999. We concentrated on the limestone areas of Viti Levu, but also investigated the upraised coral island of Vatulele. Access and permission to the various sites was facilitated by the Fiji Museum, in particular by Sepeti Matararaba (Fiji Museum Field Officer). All research on fossil sites was directed by Worthy, as follows:

1. In June 1997, assisted by Matararaba and Gavin Udy (New Zealand caver), we made a preliminary survey of caves in the Sigatoka Valley. Limestone areas around Volivoli, Raiwaqa, Toga, Tuvu and Saweni were examined (Figure 9). Most caves had no or few fossils. In a few sites, small collections of recent bones were made from cave entrances, where *Tyto alba* (lulu, or barn owl) had been nesting.

2. In March–April 1998, assisted by Anderson, Matararaba and Tarisi Sorovi-Vunidilo (Fiji Museum), work continued in the Volivoli and Tuvu areas. The previously unrecorded caves at Tau (Nakidro Land Division) were also examined and the former falcon colony at Joskes Thumb was visited.

3. In October 1998, assisted by Matararaba and Udy, a brief visit to the Volivoli caves was made with Fiji Museum staff and students from the University of the South Pacific. Most of the time, however, was spent examining caves in the Wainibuku area near Suva. These were Wainibuku Cave, Udit Cave and Dharam Singh Cave, *sensu* Gilbert (1984). A visit to Wailotua was also made and two caves were prospected for fossils – the main Wailotua Cave and Delaniqara.

4. In November 1999, assisted by Matararaba, Jone Naucabalavu (Fiji Museum) and Udy, limestone outcrops in the hills about 14 km inland of Nadi near Nawaqadamu village were investigated. Caves were again visited in the Wainibuku Valley, and a visit was made

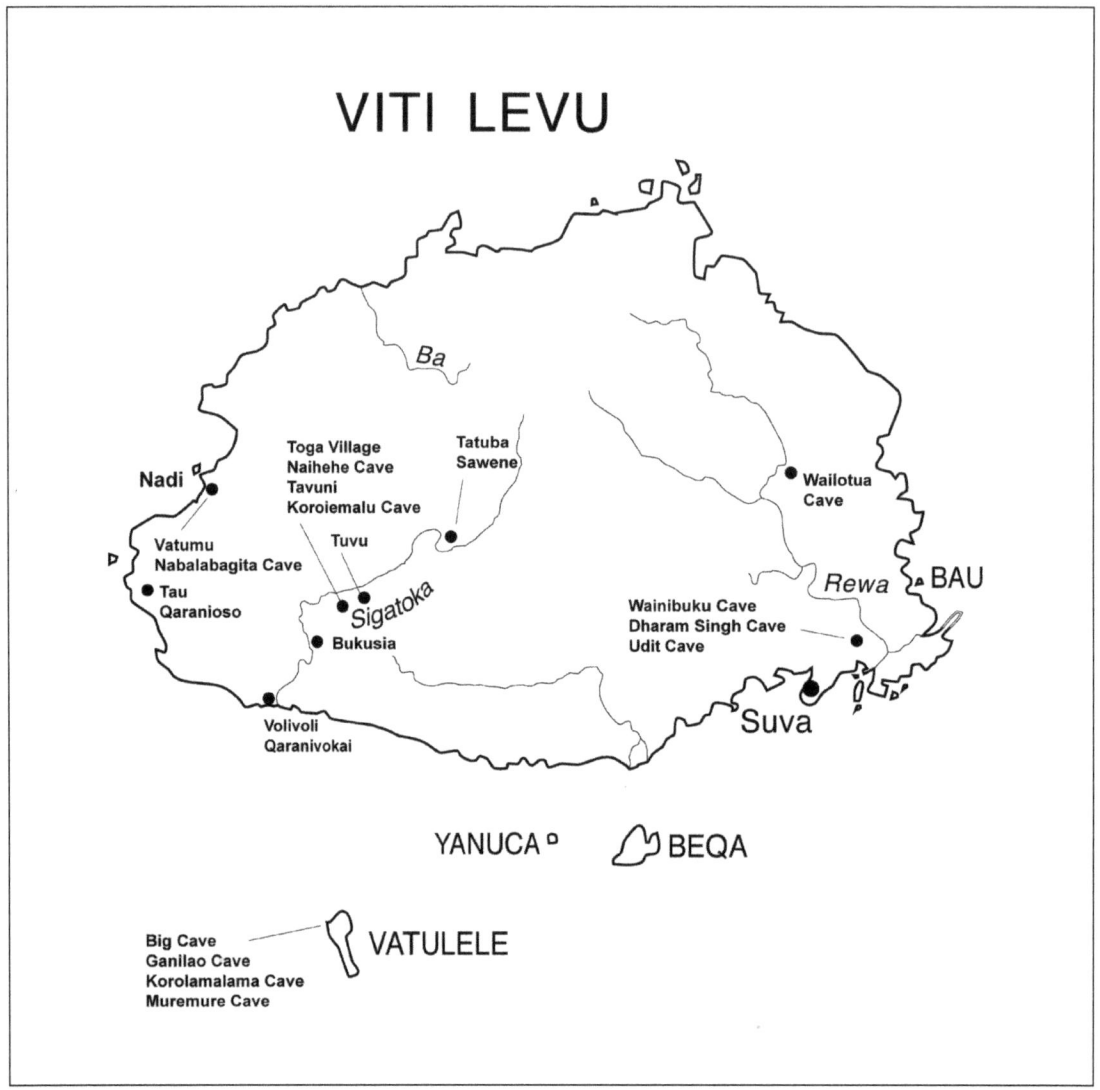

Figure 9. Viti Levu, showing locations where fossil sites were searched for.

to Naivucini, near Vunidawa, to look at cliffs that peregrine falcons were reported still to inhabit. Ledges high on the cliff may warrant investigation for fossil deposits, but were inaccessible with the equipment at hand. The team also revisited Delaniqara at Wailotua for a more detailed examination of the cave. A cave nearby, with a 20 m entrance pitch into a regularly flooded chamber with a large stream and a large bat colony in the roof, was explored but no fossil deposits were found. The work on Vatulele Island also occurred during this period of fieldwork.

In the descriptions which follow, grid references to sites are on the 1:50,000 Series 31 topographical maps. Latitude and longitude were obtained using a Garmin 38 GPS instrument. Fossils were either collected from cave floors or excavated from sediment by trowel. Unconsolidated sediments were sieved with 6 mm, 4 mm or 2 mm sieves, using the smallest mesh that was possible in each circumstance, and the sediment retained on the finer mesh was sorted under laboratory conditions. Subsequent bone conservation treatment, restoration and identification was accomplished by Worthy. All fossils are catalogued in the fossil bird collection of the Museum of New Zealand Te Papa Tongarewa, Wellington, New Zealand, and the results are listed in the following chapter.

Fossil sites in the Sigatoka Valley: Volivoli Cave system

Location: L29 659713; edition 1, 1992; 18° 09' 39"S, 177° 28' 53"E. Visits: Investigations were conducted in this cave (Figure 10) on several occasions: 4, 14 and 16 June 1997; 25–28 March, 1 April and 30 September 1998.

Volivoli submergence

Archaeological structures (walls) and midden deposits are in primary position in the main submergence entrance, but the latter have been eroded by intermittent stream flows and spread along the stream bed of the cave for about 150 m. Examination of the debris in the stream bed revealed many undecorated pottery sherds and shells, but no bones of food species. Several fragments of adzes were collected from the stream bed by Matararaba and placed in the Fiji Museum. Remains of three human burials were noted in the cave: one at the entrance, one in an alcove opposite and immediately downstream of the fossil site, and one at the end of the side passage downstream of and on the same side as the fossil site. The cave is generally about 8 m wide for the first 60 m and the stream has eroded sediments down to clean rock along its bed throughout this area. Beside the stream, banks of red, lateritic, silty clay remain in places. The floors of all sediment surfaces and the sections in the sediment banks were examined for fossils. About 50 m from the entrance, the Volivoli fossil site 1 (VV1) was discovered on the true left (Figure 10).

Volivoli fossil site 1

Volivoli 1 is the first fossil site containing Quaternary terrestrial animal remains to be located in Viti Levu. It is a steep, 5 m high bank of mainly clay sediment with some boulders that appear to be coming into the cave from a now-blocked entrance. A few metres further into the cave, a hole in the roof leads into a steeply ascending passage, which appears to come from the same old entrance. It was too difficult to follow this passage up slope, but midden debris (*Trochus* shells and some bivalves) were on the floor of this passage, presumably having been washed into the cave during wet periods. Overlying this site on the surface is a doline, which has a rock shelter (Volivoli III) in it from which a shaft drops into the roof at VV1. The deposit in which the fossils occur is a consolidated, red lateritic silty-clay matrix, which forms part of a once more extensive cave infill. The bones are very sparse and also generally very fragmented, making their recovery difficult. The consolidated silty-clay nature of the sediment precluded wet-sieving methods to extract fossils, nor was this desirable as it would have destroyed the association of the bone fragments. The fossils were kept associated in sediment, and dried, after which the clay was able to be rinsed off under a gentle flow of water. The bones were then redried and reconstructed.

The taphonomy of VV1 is difficult to interpret but the fragmented nature of the material, which comprises mainly terrestrial species, suggests it may have been scavenged or predated, probably by the crocodilian (below). Fossils were buried in massive unstructured sediment with limestone rocks, so fluvial deposition can be ruled out. Subsequent diagenesis has resulted in sediment compaction and crushing of many fossils. The presence of slickensides in the clay sediments indicates that it has been alternatively wet and dried to some extent and the associated expansion and contraction probably contributed to the bone fragmentation.

The undisturbed sediment contained no charcoal inclusions (although fine charcoal fragments derived from coconut torches are common on surfaces), was unstratified, and was not capped by any speleothem deposits, thus dating by methods employing these elements was not possible. Samples of crocodile and other bone were submitted to Beta Analytic for AMS radiocarbon dating. However, they were found to contain no collagen, so direct radiocarbon

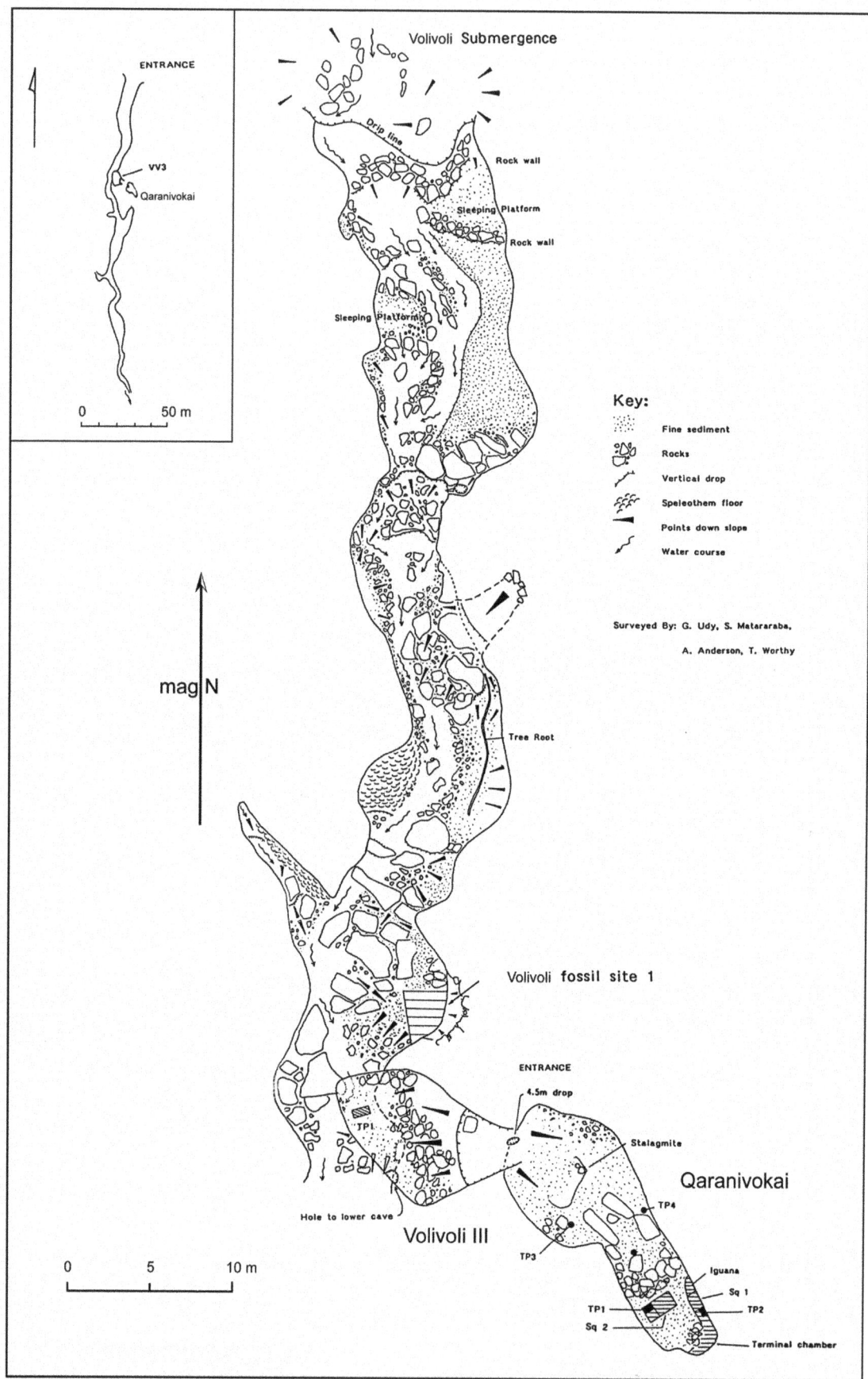

Figure 10. Volivoli Cave system, showing the location of Volivoli III, the newly discovered cave Qaranivokai and the test pits excavated in it, and Volivoli fossil site 1.

dating of the bones was not possible. Preliminary optically stimulated luminescent dates from Volivoli Cave indicate an age of 10,000–20,000 years ago for the fossiliferous clay (Anderson et al. 2001).

Species recovered from the site include notably a crocodilian, a tortoise, a giant iguana (*Lapitiguana*), a boid snake, three species of frog (*Platymantis* spp.) and several birds, including a previously unknown giant megapode (*Megavitiornis*) and giant pigeon (*Natunaornis*).

Qaranivokai

On the entrance slope leading into Volivoli III, a small slot leads down a vertical drop of about 5 m into a 15 m long and 4 m wide chamber (Figure 10). We first entered this site on 26 March 1998 and were the first people in it. Remains of a giant iguana skeleton were found on the surface near the end, and on its account, we named the cave Qaranivokai (cave of the iguana).

The deposits in Qaranivokai differ greatly from those in VV1 in the cave below. The sediment has washed into the cave via the entrance slot where a talus cone has built up. Test pits at several spots in the passage (Figure 10) showed a similar stratigraphy of a surface layer 20–30 cm thick that contains bones. This layer comprises fine brown unconsolidated silt that readily passes dry through a sieve. In the terminal chamber, the fossiliferous loam is deeper, extending to 46 cm, but below this, as shown in a test pit excavated to 1.5 m depth (Figure 11), are several layers of dark material assumed to be derived from swiftlet guano. The age of the Qaranivokai fossil deposit was estimated to be mid-Holocene, as the absence of pottery and charcoal shows that it antedates the arrival of people in the area, and hence it must be older than about 3000 years BP. U-series ages of overlying speleothems in the terminal chamber clearly indicate that deposition had ceased there by about 4500 BP (Anderson et al. 2001). Two fossil bones, one a shaft of a femur from the iguana skeleton found on the surface, and the other a piece of iguana humerus collected from the surface of the terminal chamber, both approximately 5 g in weight, did not yield separable collagen and so could not be directly radiocarbon dated. However, radiocarbon dates on sediment presumed to derive from guano and fine charcoal fragments from the sediments enclosing the fossils suggest a Conventional Radiocarbon Age of 20,020±660 BP (ANU-11010) to 25,540±630 BP (ANU-11011) (Anderson et al. 2001).

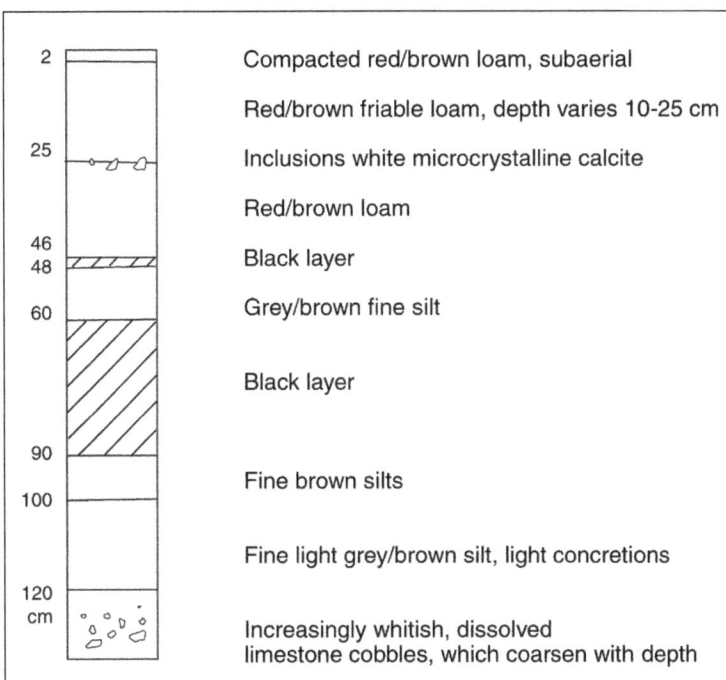

Figure 11. Stratigraphy of Test Pit 1, Qaranivokai.

We excavated areas of the final chamber as shown in Figure 10. Sediment was dry-sieved through a 6 mm mesh. Slight dampness of the silt made it impossible to put it through a 2 mm mesh and no water was available in the area. However, the presence of few stones and no shell made recovery of bone relatively easy and many small pieces were obtained. The fauna includes 15 species of bird, including the giant pigeon, three frogs, giant iguana and banded iguana, two types of bat, two species of gecko and a skink.

Volivoli Swamp owl site

On 3 April 1998, we surveyed the bluffs along the eastern escarpment of the Volivoli limestone block and found no further cave features. However, at the foot of the slope, beside the swamp which separates the escarpment from Volivoli village, an owl midden was found in an alcove on a boulder just above winter water level. A small sample from this revealed an interesting fauna, including fish bones indicating the owl responsible foraged over the wetland.

Bukusia, Raiwaqa village

Location: L28 c. 776846; edition 1, 1992. Visit: 5 June 1997.

The cave system is in a small, forested limestone hill. The grid reference given above is for the resurgence cave at the foot of imposing overhanging bluffs, and is about 100 m up a side stream of the river in the valley. However, the resurgence cave is only passable for about 30 m before it ends in a room with a skylight more than 30 m overhead. The stream emerges from an impenetrable passage. A colony of swiftlets (*Collocalia spodiopygia*) has deposited much guano in the final chamber, but beneath the skylight are some wall-like man-made structures, and a huge mound of midden material.

Exploration overland northwards from the resurgence revealed a shelter high up the hillside at the head of a steep rocky gully. From this shelter, a small crawl-way led off into a series of chambers with about 200–300 m of passages, some up to 20 m wide. These intersected several large skylights from the 'plateau' above and so had large quantities of freshwater mussel-shell midden with broken pottery in them. Charcoal figures were drawn on the walls in one place. One chamber allowed access to the plateau above and a very well-preserved hill fort – the single point of access from above ground, at one end still had a more or less complete wall across it. This hill fort is presumed to date from the Kai Colo uprising of 1875–76, having been built by Kunatui and his people after they were evicted from Tavuni.

Archaeological deposits were abundant all around the plateau and under all skylights within the cave. In places, heaps of midden were metres thick, but no bones were visible in them. All pottery sherds inspected were undecorated. Although no sediments containing fossils were found, two bones of the giant iguana were found on the surface at the small, eastern crawl-way entrance. Under the cliffs south of the resurgence were abundant bones beneath a barn-owl roost. This bone deposit was no more than 10 cm deep and overlaid up to 50 cm of cultural sediments, as indicated by charcoal, midden shells and pottery sherds.

Sites near Toga village: Naihehe Cave

Location: M28 812906; edition 1, 1993. Visit: 7 June 1997.

Naihehe Cave is at the eastern end of the impressive limestone cliffs backing Toga. It is a resurgence cave well known to the village, and is used as a tourist cave. A low roof at the entrance opens into large caverns that extend about 150 m from the entrance. At this point the stream emerges from a flooded passage. Along the true left side of the passage, ledges are present that slope upwards and appear to have been formed by solution upwards along the limestone bedding planes, suggesting a phreatic origin for the cave. We climbed up to most of the higher ledges seen along the cave.

The only fossils found were bat bones in a series of old rimstone pools. Many bones of the fruit bat *Notopteris macdonaldi* were present. In the Sigatoka Valley, the only known colony of this bat is in Tatuba Cave near Saweni. A few bones of the small sheath-tailed bat (*Emballonura semicaudata*) were also found.

Tavuni owl site

Location: L28 776905; edition 1, 1992 (17° 59' 17"S, 177° 35' 326"E). Visit: 7 June 1997.

At the western end of the limestone bluffs and west of Vunaivilela Creek under an almost vertical cliff some 200 m high, known as Naqalimare, is a small resurgence used as the water supply for Toga village. Barn owls nest in the cave above the water supply and a large downy chick was present on our visit. About 20 m along the cliff from the resurgence cave, a slot leads into a round room of about 3 m diameter, which is essentially the base of a shaft rising up into the cliff. Owl midden debris was on the floor.

A test excavation 60 cm² to a depth of 125 cm was made on the side of the round room nearest to the spring. Its stratigraphy was as follows: Layer 1, 0–2 cm – unconsolidated dust with owl midden bones; Layer 2, 2–7 cm – fluvial silts; Layer 3, 7–90 cm – black loam (paddle-impressed pottery at 60–70 cm, layer of limestone rocks at 40–60 cm; Layer 4, 90–100 cm – grey-black loam, many fragments limestone; Layer 5, 100–125 cm – patches of red earth in grey soil, no bones.

Sediment samples were taken at 30, 45, 60 and 90 cm (now at ANU). Most bones were rats, which were common to 35 cm, sparse between 35 and 45 cm, and absent below 45 cm. On the surface, bones of *Rattus rattus* were present, but most on the surface and all those to 35 cm were *R. exulans*. Some of the deepest specimens were *R. praetor*. The owl midden was only a surface feature, no more than 10 cm deep.

Vunaivilelu Creek, Naqalimare – Mt Koroiemalu

Location: South of the road between the Tavuni site and Toga village. Detailed locations given below. Visits: 9–10 June and 28–29 September 1997.

The dry bed of Vunaivilelu Creek was searched for caves along the flanks of the huge limestone bluffs of Naqalimare. No fossil deposits were found. However, in the area to the south of Mt Koroiemalu, at the head of Valivali Creek, we found cavernous limestone and a few caves.

Koroiemalu Cave

Location: 17° 59' 31"S, 177° 36' 36"E.

The major cave, which we named Koroiemalu Cave, has three entrances in grassland near the base of a small valley leading towards the back of the forested Mt Koroiemalu. One of the entrances is a 15 m shaft, and the other two may be climbed into. We explored about 200 m of passages but were stopped by a 6 m deep shaft needing tackle. Although our 'guides' did not know of the cave, charcoal symbols on the walls were evidence of previous visitors. No fossiliferous deposits were found and the clean-washed nature of the passage attests to seasonal flushing of the cave. A nearby cave led from the end of a valley in tall bamboo, down an impressive 35 m deep shaft, but there it ended. Across the top of the pitch, 10 m of guano-rich passage also had no fossils.

Tatuba Cave – Saweni and environs

Location: The resurgence entrance is at M28 992004; edition 1, 1993; the hill above the cave is at: 17º 54' 02"S, 177º 47' 56"E. Visits: 12–13 June and 29 September 1997.

Tatuba Cave is one of the best-known caves in the Sigatoka Valley (Gilbert 1984) and has an impressive wall across its lower entrance. Large numbers of swiftlets inside the cave have built up huge piles of sediment. At one point is a roost of the fruit bat *Notopteris macdonaldi*. Sediments below the present bat roost are highly acidic and so bones are rapidly dissolved – even those few on the surface were essentially destroyed. We searched all surfaces in the cave and only a very few bat and swiftlet bones were found. It is improbable that any fossiliferous sediment is present in these upper levels of the cave as a result of the leaching caused by the guano. At the upstream end of the cave are three further entrances, beneath which lie abundant undecorated pottery sherds and other archaeological debris. No bone deposits were found. In the surrounding large depression, seven other cave entrances were located (Figure 12). These are:

No. 1. This appeared to be an excellent pitfall trap. A 2 m drop to a ledge was followed by a further 4 m pitch to a floor. A test pit revealed clay containing worked stone and pottery to 50 cm depth, where apparent bedrock was encountered. Therefore, all sediment is of post-human age.

No. 2. A deep 30 m doline had an impenetrable water sink on one side, but on the other, a partly walled-up small hole led to 15 m shaft. At its base, parts of at least five human skeletons were partly buried by washed-in clay. The bones were completely decalcified. While the floor looked suitable for fossils, none were seen, and all sediments are probably very recent.

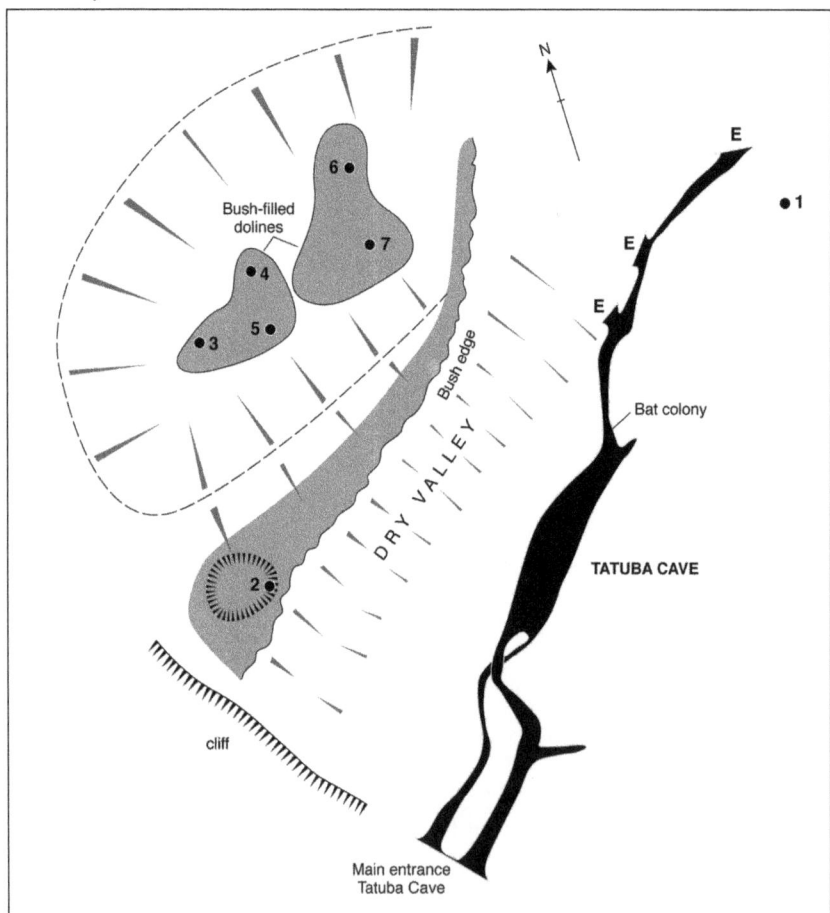

Figure 12. The Tatuba Cave system and the location of other cave features (1–7) described in the text. Cave map is after Gilbert (1984).

No. 3. A shaft with 3 m, 4 m, and 7 m steps led to a terminal room with clay deposits all over the walls, which obviously floods seasonally, and had no fossils.

No. 4. At the upper end of the doline containing sites 3 and 5, a slot opens to drops of 5 m then 6 m followed by a narrow rift, then another 8 m pitch to a narrow passage; no fossils.

No. 5. A 5 m diameter shaft about 4 m deep. On the upper side, a cave led in about 6 m and contained one burial. Sparse remains of owl midden were present. Downslope, a crawl led into a well-washed cave about 15 m long, with no fossils.

No. 6. A small 6 m deep shaft with much flowstone on its walls, but no fossils.

No. 7. A small water sink, with an unexamined shaft.

Our general impression was that run-off from surrounding land has mobilised lots of sediment, filling these caves with sediment in the past 1000–2000 years. As the run-off is from non-limestone substrates, it is acidic and would soon dissolve any bones that might have been there. As a result, there appears to be little potential here for fossils.

Tuvu

Location: The chief's house on the old village site at the north end of the limestone hill affords the most direct access. It is at: 17° 55' 52"S, 177° 42' 18"E; grid reference M28 892969; edition 1, 1993. Visits: 17 June 1997 and 31 March 1998.

The limestone hill at Tuvu is about 1 km long and a little narrower. The road passes along the eastern boundary of the hill, enabling ready access to it. Apart from the well-known burial cave on the eastern flanks of the hill (Gilbert 1984), several other features were found (Figure 13). Near the top of the hill (about M28 890966), a large collapsed canyon feature can be followed roughly northwest. In it, many crevices lead deep underground, but the rocks were very unstable. Despite examination of several rooms and chambers well out of daylight, no fossil

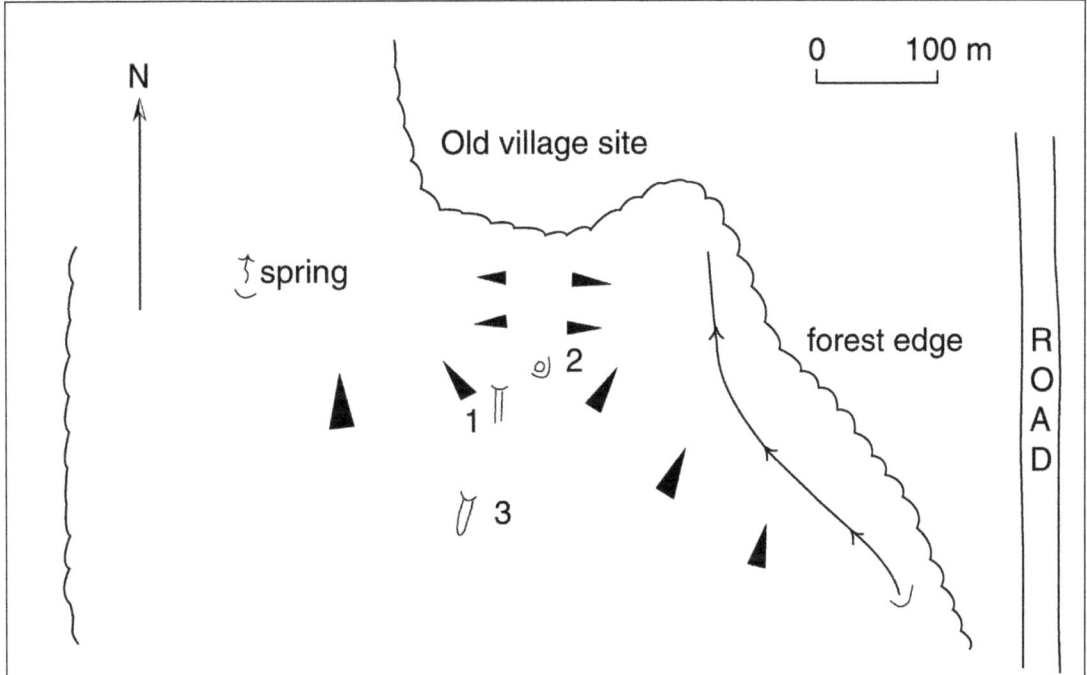

Figure 13. The location of caves (1–3) investigated at Tuvu.

bones were found. We think the instability of the caves and fissures means that all 'floors' are of very recent age. On the north side of the outcrop, immediately south of the old village site, are three caves:

No. 1. About 30 m in from the forest edge and just on the west side of a low ridge running off the limestone towards the village site is a small horizontal cave. This had many human bones in it, and was not explored.

No. 2. A few metres from No. 1, a shaft drops about 7–8 m down into a small cave. A few human bones were on the floor at the base of the shaft, but despite the cave's promising location, no fossil deposits were found. Much of the floor floods seasonally.

No. 3. About 70 m up the hill above the two caves described above is a solution cave about 5 m high, 2–6 m wide and 15 m long.

In No. 3, there was a low entrance to a back chamber of the cave, probably a burial chamber. It was partially walled in and was not investigated. A small colony of swiftlets inhabited the cave on our visit. In the front chamber, a test pit 0.8 x 0.5 m was excavated in 10 cm spits. The stratigraphy disclosed was as follows: Layer 1 Spit 1, a soft grey silt containing pottery sherds. Spit 2 was largely occupied by a soft, lensed white ash or calcite. Layer 2 Spits 3–5, a grey-brown silt containing a few shells, pottery sherds and some charcoal, with weakly defined lenses, but no layering. Layer 3, excavated to 105 cm depth, consisted of soft, orange-brown silt, probably originating in guano. It contained no cultural material and continued beyond spade depth at approximately 150 cm. Lack of an entrapment mechanism makes this an unpromising site for fossils.

Fossil sites in Tau district

Location: L28 455917; edition 1, 1992; near 17º 58' 29"S, 177º 17' 18"E. Visit: 30 March 1998.

This, the westernmost cave site examined, is about 3 km from the coast. A small area of limestone outcrops on the hill above Tau village and near the top of a forested gully on the outcrop at about 200 m above sea level contains a large cave called Qaranioso #1. Gilbert (1984) did not record this cave. It opens from an entrance about 4 m wide and 6 m high into a large chamber some 15 m wide and 30+ m high (Figure 14). Skylights in the roof allow light into this chamber, but a voluminous 60 m long cavern extends from here to the north, and is completely in the dark. On our visit, there was a large colony of swiftlets. The villagers informed us that many years before, people had mined the guano from the cave, and that at one stage a fire had burned within it for many days. About 25 m from the mouth of the cave, downhill to the northwest, is a large rock shelter, or remnant cave chamber entering the side of the hill, which we termed Qaranioso #2.

At the mouth of Qaranioso #1 are remnants of flowstone deposits and calcified infill breccias that are likely to be some of the oldest cave deposits found in Fiji. On the sloping floor, just inside the entrance, are remnant archaeological deposits that in an exposed section appear to be up to 0.5 m deep. Some 30 m into the cave, on the level floor at the start of the big cavern, there are extensive surface scatters of midden and pottery sherds. At the break of slope into the cave a section was cut to record the stratigraphy (below). Sediments from fallen debris, originating from the skylights, slope down to the base of the first chamber, and no fossils were evident. The floor of the final chamber is covered in guano in piles up to 10 m high.

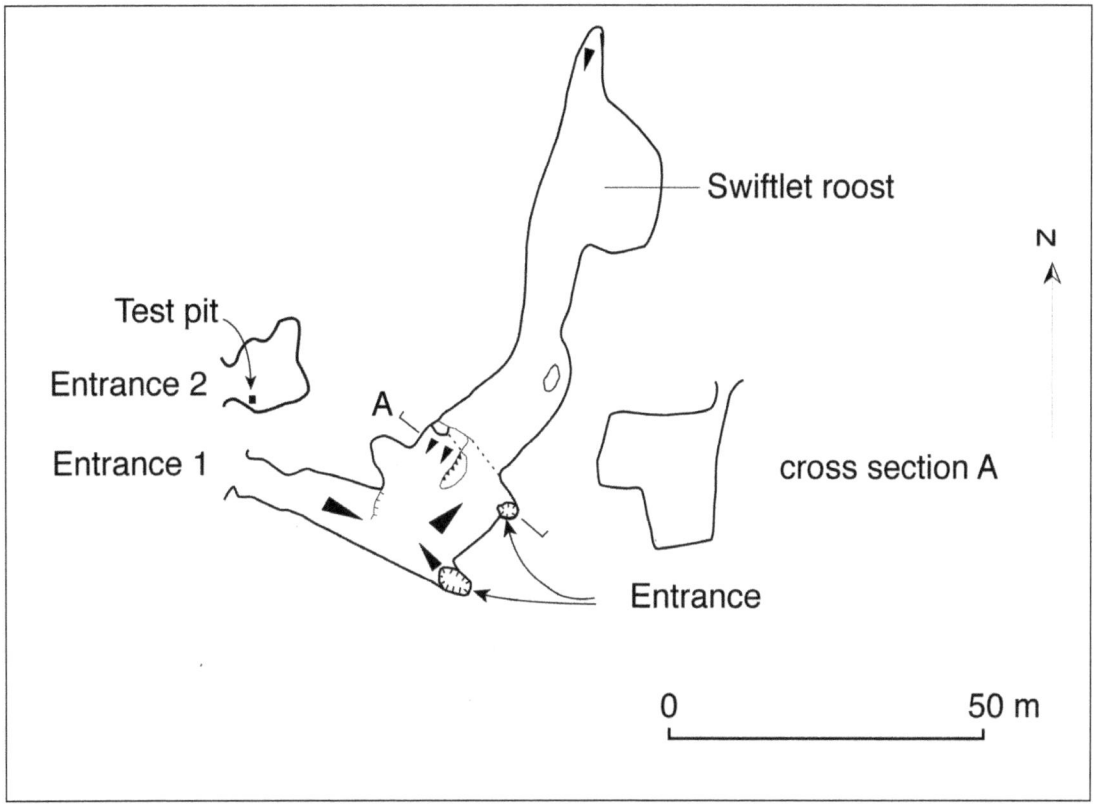

Figure 14. Plan of the cave Qaranioso, Tau, showing the location of the test pit.

Qaranioso #2 is a largely flat-floored chamber that is dry, and throughout which light penetrates. Much of the floor was covered in owl-midden debris, but towards the entrance, archaeological midden was evident. A test pit was excavated (see Chapter 3).

Sites inland of Nadi: Nabalabalagita Cave

Location: Near Nawaqadamu village (17° 55' 44.3"S, 177° 25' 45.6"E; L28 601969). Visit: 16 November 1999.

This is a small rock shelter 4 m wide at the entrance by 6.5 m long. A test pit (50 x 50 cm) was excavated to basement limestone at 62 cm depth. Layer 1 (0–2 cm) was loose brown sediment, rich in bones from an owl midden. Layer 2 (2–8 cm) was ash and charcoal, with some midden shell. Layer 3 (8–23 cm) was brown sediment with charcoal, midden shell, abundant pottery and abundant bones of *R. exulans*. Layer 4 (23–38 cm) was red, compacted lateritic clay sediments containing a lens of ash in the top 5 cm of the layer. Rat bones (*R. exulans*) were present. Layer 5 (38–62 cm, base) was a friable organic soil. Only the top 5 cm of this layer, which was more organic and compacted, had rat bones in it. The lower part of the layer was less dark, more friable and lacked rats entirely. However, pottery sherds, some decorated, midden shell and some unidentified large bird bone fragments were in the lower layer. The paddle-impressed pottery sherds were at 55 cm depth.

The sequence suggests the site was under forest and contained organic rich (forest-derived) soils when people first used the cave, and notably indicates that people arrived before owls if it is assumed the onset of rat-bone deposition marked owl arrival. The marked change in sedimentation indicated by the onset of deposition of red sediment suggests forest clearance and presumed gardening activities on the slopes above the cave at that time. Then after an unknown period, sedimentation in the cave changed to conditions more like those at present, except that people camped regularly in it. The surface of the site was covered in an owl midden from which a sample yielded fauna.

Outcrop of limestone at L28 609984

The hard crystalline limestone of this outcrop was explored for caves and fossil deposits on 17 November 1999. The limestone is very fractured with well-developed karren on the surface. Some of the fractures contained lithified fissure-fill sediments (breccias) of red earth and basalt gravels with *Placostylus* and other land snails incorporated in them. A cave, formed by fracturing of the outcrop, was explored to about 40 m below the entrances in the top of the outcrop. Swiftlets lived in it. Extensive examination of this cave failed to find any fossiliferous sediments, but in an exposure of the hard (probably Pleistocene) breccias, a single bone of the extinct frog *Platymantis megabotoniviti* was found.

Vatumu

Location: About 7 km north of the hill site described above at 17° 52' 56.9"S, 177° 28' 29.0"E; L28 647020. Visit: 18 November 1999.

The limestone outcrop is small and had a fort constructed on it at one time. There are at least two cave features, but the most obvious is a large entrance in the west side of the outcrop that immediately opens to a 10 m pitch to the floor of a chamber 5 m wide by about 15 m long. A test pit showed the floor of the chamber has been filled in by rocks for at least 1 m depth: they overlay fine silts derived from swiftlet guano.

The cave has unconsolidated sediment infill in several places with archaeological materials incorporated in them, e.g. midden shells and pottery sherds, and one side passage has a human burial in it. A single fossil site was located in an alcove below the entrance pitch. Bones were incorporated in consolidated clays, which lacked charcoal and pottery sherds and so are assumed to be of prehuman age. The fragmented nature of the bones and species present in the fauna suggests they may derive from falcon prey. The fauna included the extinct frog *Platymantis megabotoniviti*, an extinct *Ducula*, an extinct snipe (*Coenocorypha miratropica*), a duck and two petrel species.

Sites in eastern Viti Levu: Wainibuku area

There are a number of described caves in the southeastern region of Viti Levu (Gilbert 1984). The descriptions of geologically young, small caves, with active streamways at, for example, Quaia, Kalabo and Lami, give little hope that fossiliferous sediments would be present in them. In contrast, the more extensive karst area centred on the Wainibuku Valley has several more extensive caves with some passages now abandoned by the streams that made them. This fact and the fact that all had more than one entrance made them potential fossiliferous sites. Here, caves are referred to by the names given by Gilbert (1984), who described and mapped them. Figure 15 is adapted from Gilbert (1984:Figure 8) and shows the relationships between the various caves.

Wainibuku Cave

Location: O28 722827; edition 1, 1990; resurgence at 18° 03' 36.7"S, 178° 29' 11.4"E. Visits: 1, 2, 6 and 7 October 1998; 23 November 1999.

This is the cave referred to as Bureivulu Caves by J. Koroikata. The cave is owned by Mr Dharam Singh. The entrance to the main cave is a resurgence which debouches into a deep round pool of water in a small forested valley beside the vehicle track (Figure 15). Two other cave entrances are also found here. About 30 m from the pool, the access track passes an entrance to a smaller cave that is about 4 m high and 1.5 m wide. About 20 m inside the cave, the passage forks. Straight on leads, after about 20 m, to a rockfall that terminates progress. Bones of the bat *Notopteris* were present on the floor and in sediment between the rocks here. The other passage branch leads after about 40 m to another rockfall that also blocks the cave. Again, a few bat bones were present on the floor. The second cave is about 4 m to the true right of the main cave entrance, and is accessed by a traverse above the pool. This leads to about 40 m of passage that gets progressively narrower. Some sediment is present on the floor, but no bones were noticed.

The main cave is initially 10 m high and 4 m wide. The stream is present in a narrower canyon incised in the floor and progress is along ledges above it. The cave is notable for the large numbers of swiftlets living/nesting in it. The cave is about 200 m in length and comes from an upstream submergence entrance. We did not investigate the upstream third of the passage, which has deep water. About 120 m upstream of the resurgence there is a side passage on the true right that extends about 30 m. Roosting in the roof of this passage were thousands of individuals of the fruit bat *Notopteris macdonaldi*.

On the floor of this side passage, in the last 15 m, are pot-hole type erosion features formed by a former stream that are filled with alluvial sediments. The floor is covered in sloppy guano and non-flowing water sits in the pot holes. Upstream, the passage is terminated by a speleothem blockage, but it is assumed that the stream that formed the passage and deposited the sediment came from beyond this blockage. Fossils were located in the sediment in these pot holes. On the surface were numerous bones of *Notopteris*, but a few bones of the large frog *P. megabotoniviti* encouraged us to search more thoroughly. There were five pools and a few

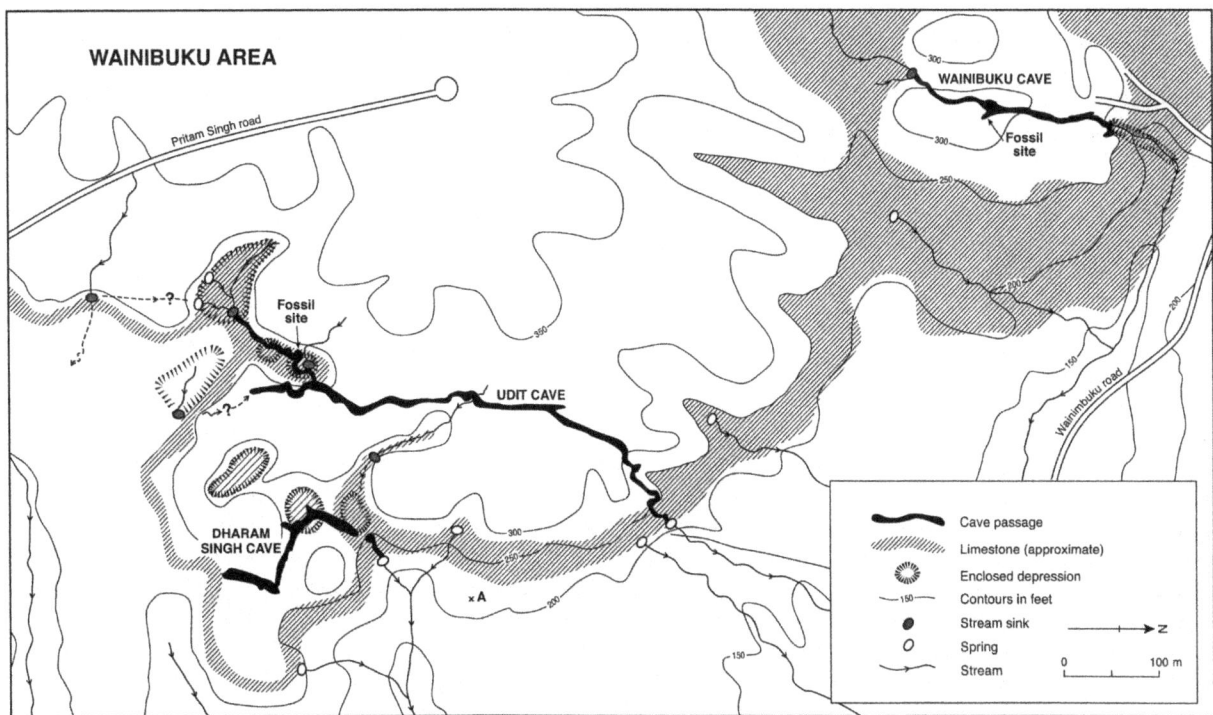

Figure 15. A plan of the caves in the Wainibuku area, after Gilbert (1984), showing local contours and stream drainages.

metres of interconnecting trench. The fossiliferous sediment was wet-sieved in the nearby stream through a 5 mm mesh and the concentrate was sorted in laboratory conditions later.

Starting at the flowstone blockage, the deposit is as follows. A narrow (ca. 20–40 cm wide) and shallow (<20 cm) deposit of silts extends for about 4 m to the first pool. No bones were found in the sediment extending from the flowstone blockage. The first pool is about 80 cm wide and about 40 cm deep. Under a surface layer of silts about 20 cm thick is clay. Two fossils were found in the silts and none in the clay. From this point downstream the deposits are covered in wet, fresh guano a few centimetres deep. About 2 m 'downstream' over bare rock is a second pool of similar size which contained several fossils at the clay-silt interface. Another metre or so 'downstream' is a third pool about 1 m in diameter with few fossils, and then, after another 1 m, is an elongated pool about 0.5 m wide and 2 m long. This feature is deeper, the silt layer is up to 30 cm thick and the clay extends to about 60 cm depth. Fossils were found in the silt and in the upper part of the clay layer.

The last deposit is a 1.5 m wide, shallow, circular pool just above a slope leading down to the present stream. Under the guano deposit, which is deepest at this point, is a layer 10 cm thick of sand, containing sticks and abundant bat bones (L1). About 5 cm of consolidated clay (L2) separates the next silt and sand layer (L3), which is also 5–10 cm deep. This layer contains many bones, all stained black, including boa vertebrae and crocodilian bones. A 15–20 cm layer of fine clay (L4) devoid of bones underlies this fossil layer. Then a layer (L5) about 10 cm thick, comprised of sloppy clay with a gritty texture and mudstone inclusions (equates to Layer 2 in the upper pools), contains fossils. Unlike the black bones encountered above, these are stained light brown and have dark brown concretions growing on them. Fine clay without fossils extends to the deepest point of the pool at a further 40 cm depth.

The black bones from the lowest pool show little evidence of stream transport and the crocodilian bones are from two individuals. However, many crocodilian teeth are from substantially larger animals than those represented by the bones. The bones in the lower, more clayey layer from all pools have the same preservation and were relatively stream worn by the time of their burial, indicating considerable lateral transport.

Dharam Singh Cave

Location: The most easily located entrance to Dharam Singh Cave is found on the slopes of an enclosed doline, about 40 m up to the true right of the short cave leading from it (Figure 15). The small cave is about 30 m long and carries a stream to a resurgence at a house at 18° 03' 54"S, 178° 29' 30"E, which is at the end of a vehicle track; shown as point A in Figure 15. Visit: 2 October 1998.

This cave is known as Tokorokolulu to the present (1998) leasee, Kemueli Vukeiono. It was not owned in 1998, and nor has it been owned by Mr Dharam Singh to our knowledge, so it is not known why Gilbert (1984) used this name for the cave.

A steep scramble down a slope leads into passages of impressive dimensions. To the north (left), the passage is 30–40 m wide and high, and extends nearly 100 m to a rockfall collapse. Southwards, the passage is smaller but still usually several metres wide. A large rockfall slopes upwards more than 50 m on the right close to the entrance. A narrow section where rockfall nearly blocks the passage leads to the final chamber that is 55 m long and 9 m wide and opens to the second, larger entrance. The northern limb of the cave has a floor with rockfall on it and the only fossils found were some *Notopteris* bones in a small deposit of consolidated sediment on one wall. Several bones of a chicken (*Gallus gallus*) were found at one point. The southern branch of the cave has flat, clay-covered floors over which water seasonally flows, and no fossils were found.

Udit Cave

Location: Udit Cave is the longest known cave in the Wainibuku area, with 790 m of passage (Gilbert 1984). It extends from depressions beside Pratam Singh Road to the resurgence in the Wainibuku Valley (Figure 15). Visits: 2, 3, 6 and 7 October 1998; 20 November 1999.

The upstream submergence is a low cave entrance (<0.5 m high) beneath overhanging vegetation, into which a stream flows and into which much domestic rubbish unfortunately has been tipped. Inside the cave, the passage is 2–3 m wide and 1–2 m high, with abundant stalactites descending from the roof. Rubbish is wrapped around most rocks and stalactites where it has been left by floodwaters. We did not follow this passage to its end, but believe it to be blocked by rubbish about 100 m downstream.

The cave can be accessed via a doline about 150 m to the northeast. Here, a steep climb down one side of the doline allows eventual access to the stream. Upstream and downstream it is blocked by rubbish, so making impossible the traverse to the cave in either of the directions surveyed by Gilbert (1984). A dry cave entrance opens into the side of the doline and this was investigated. It is only about 4 m long and boulders rise up to the back of the cave. However a gap between the boulders leads to a small cavity at floor level where a fossil deposit was found, which we called the Udit Cave Pitfall site.

In the valley running northeast of the Udit Cave Pitfall site are two shafts. One is narrow and about 8 m deep and ends at the water level. The other is about 5 m deep and goes to a flat floor, 2 m wide by 5 m long. No fossil deposits were found in them. The resurgence of Udit Cave has a weir built across the stream and the inhabitants of the local houses use the water. We entered the cave here and climbed the 6 m waterfall blocking access and explored upstream 500–600 m through the rest of the cave. Gravel deposits are present in several parts of the upper reaches of the cave but none of these were found to contain any fossil bones. The rubbish-choked connection to the doline with the Udit Cave Pitfall site in it was located.

Udit Cave Pitfall site

Location: O28; edition 1, 1990; 18° 04' 02.6"S, 178° 29' 21.0"E.

The deposit in this site is very small and initially was probably 1 m long by 0.5 m wide and 30 cm deep. The site is confined, with walls about 0.5 m apart and the working space about 1 m long. The deposit is visible initially as bones loose on the floor and a cross-section of cobbles capped with flowstone about 30 cm above the floor. The visible deposit on the floor is thus a lag derived from erosion of the primary deposit by dripping water. The sediment was excavated by trowel and passed outside for processing. The primary deposit was found to be *in situ* on the inner side of the 'chamber' and some articulated elements were recovered. The sediment is wet clay. Once the floor was excavated to about 25 cm, a low passage was found extending upstream, in which perennial water flow was apparent. The fossil material seems to have had its source somewhere upstream and to have been washed downstream to the site where it accumulated in sediment against the rockfall. A speleothem sample was obtained, but the crystal structure is too contaminated by silt for uranium series dating. Bone samples from the deposit lack preserved collagen, so are unsuitable for radiocarbon dating.

Wailotua Cave

Location: West (main) entrance O27 638157; edition 1, 1993; east entrance O27 644157; edition 1, 1993. Visits: 5 October 1998 and 24 November 1999.

This is the longest cave in Viti Levu, with about 1500 m of passage mapped by Gilbert (1984). Entry is usually via the fossil resurgence or western entrance beside Wailotua village, and the large passages are easily traversed. The eastern end is preceded by a huge cavern with myriads of swiftlets and bats in it, notably *Notopteris macdonaldi*, but possibly also including *Emballonura*. The floor of this cavern has seen extensive guano mining and the floor of the cave from here to the western entrance has been modified to allow a small railway to transport the material. Sediments throughout most of the cave are cobbles and sands deposited by the precursor of the present large stream that enters the eastern entrance and disappears down passages to the northwest. The high energy of this stream and the modifications caused by the mining make it unlikely that any fossiliferous sediment is present and none was found. In the main chamber, on what is labelled the Terrace, the sediments forming this feature appear to be of colluvial nature and lack bedding and lack the rounded nature of stream-transported sediments. Despite several extensive cross-sections of these sediments being available for examination, not a single fossil was found.

Delaniqara

This cave is on the top of the hill above Wailotua Cave and is unmapped. It was not completely explored by us. Access is via a 4–5 m diameter pitfall entrance down a steep climb into a large cavern, which leads down between giant blocks of rock to successively lower levels. The upper regions are characterised by extensive deposits of flowstone covering all floor surfaces, and in most places such floors are composed of boulders. Large colonies of swiftlets and bats (*Notopteris macdonaldi*) were present in 1998 and in 1999.

Substantial areas of the cave were explored, but apart from numerous bat bones, we only located two fossil specimens – a part skeleton of the giant megapode *Megavitiornis altirostris* in October 1998 and a rail (*Nesoclopeus poicilopterus*) in November 1999. Numerous bat and swift bones litter the floors of many chambers. The extensive flowstone deposits make detection of an old surface on or in which fossils might be found difficult.

Fossil sites on Vatulele Island

Vatulele is a small island about 30 km south of Viti Levu, some 12.9 km long north to south, and with a maximum width of 4.9 km in the north (Figure 16). It has greatest elevations above sea level along the western coast, with a maximum of 38 m in the northwest, but is generally much lower. Thin soils formed on limestone, or limestone rock, cover most of the ground surface on the western plateaus and slopes above a few metres altitude. Along the eastern coast, narrow sand dunes enclose a low-lying, marshy area, with deep latosolic soils. Inland of these are well-drained inland flats with thin soils (Nunn 1988). Most of the marshy areas are modified by gardening or by coconut plantations.

Near the coast in the more elevated northern and western parts of the island, the limestone is extensively eroded into a *makatea* landform – a sharply eroded karst typical of tropical coastal limestone and usually of reefal limestone. Caves are numerous but large features are few. None are mapped, but my observations suggest that the larger ones (Muremure, Big Cave) developed at the water table where freshwater was concentrated in a route that drained the central and eastern parts of the island towards the coast. This is likely to have occurred when sea levels were as much as 120 m lower during the last glacial period of the Pleistocene when the present eastern lowlands and lagoons with their sandy basements might have been wetlands. Big Cave, at least,

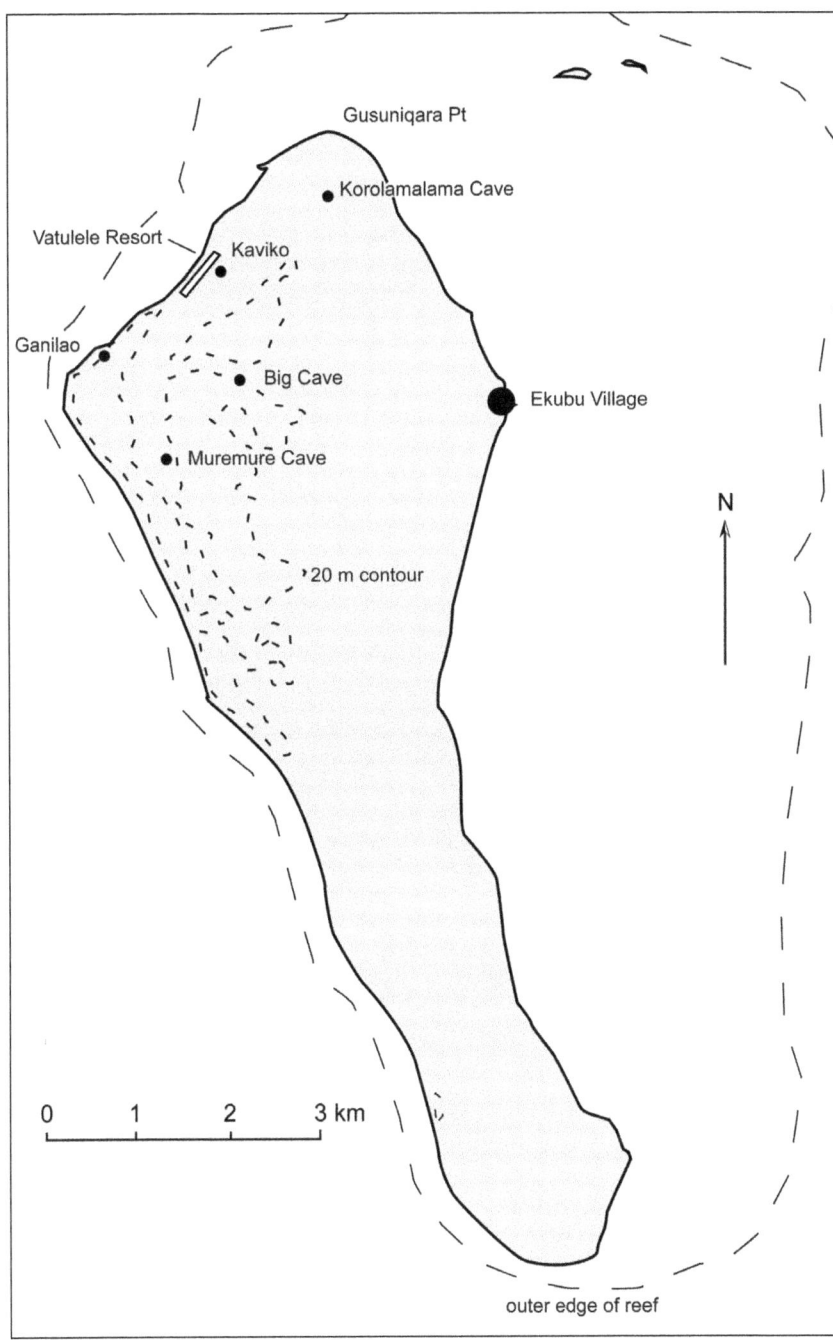

Figure 16. The island of Vatulele showing outer reef limit, 20 m contour, and the location of the major caves in relation to Ekubu village and Vatulele Resort.

is developed along a major southwest–northeast joint system parallel to the Naura cliff. Muremure does not exhibit marked geological structural control, but rather is typical of phreatic development in unstructured limestone down a shallow drainage gradient, as seen, for example, in Anahulu Cave on Tongatapu (Worthy et al. 1991). Both caves are extensively modified by subsequent drainage, collapse and secondary speleothem development. Most caves on Vatulele have been briefly described by Gansser (1994) and his names for the features are followed here.

The age and geomorphological history of an island are significant factors in predicting features of its fauna, therefore a summary of the geomorphological development of Vatulele is taken from Nunn (1988). Briefly, it began when limestone began accumulating in deep water about 14 million years ago (Ma). Regional uplift resulted in its emergence above sea level towards the end of the Miocene, possibly as early as six Ma. Volcanic activity about 4.72 Ma resulted in lava intruding through the limestone to emerge on the surface, where it is now preserved as small exposures at Nabale and Nasarava, near Ekubu village. With the cessation of volcanic activity in the late Pliocene, Vatulele began to gradually subside. However, irregular uplift due to earthquakes, as evidenced by the presence of notches incised in the coastal cliffs, has offset the subsidence. These are best preserved at Gusuniqara Point, where a series of four notches is preserved at 2.2 m, 4.0 m, 6.2 m and 7.8 m above mean sea level. The best preserved notch (2.2 m), extending along much of the west coast, contains remnants of a lithified infill that has had a *Tridacna* shell dated from it at 37–38 kyr BP. Nunn (1988) considered that this date and another at 44.7 kyr for the 4.0 m notch markedly underestimated the true ages, and he interpreted the 2.2 m notch as representing the high stand of the last interglacial shoreline (ca. 125 kyr BP). Then, relative sea level was assumed to be about 6 m above present level, and so Nunn suggested there had been 3.8 m subsidence of the island in the past 125 kyr.

Palaeosea-level curves indicate that relative sea level has been 70–120 m lower than present from ca.110 to eight kyr BP (Shackleton 1987), so it is inconceivable that the 2.2 m notch could have been eroded about 40 kyr BP. Moreover, since the notch was incised, beach deposits were laid up against the cliff between Vetau and Naura beaches, infilling the 2.2 m notch, and then became lithified with the inclusion of land snails (pers. obs.). The lithification of these sediments would have taken a considerable period of time and thus their presence supports the suggestion that they were deposited at the end of the last interglacial period, about 100 kyr BP. Since sea level attained near its present height in the past 6000 years, these lithified sediments have largely been eroded from the notch, but exposures up to 1 m thick still remain on the primary wave-cut platform of the beach.

More recently, Nunn (1998) has doubted this sequence of events, and has suggested that all notches were formed within the Holocene. We doubt this for several reasons. Worthy's experience with fossil sites in solution notches in relatively pure Oligocene limestone in New Zealand indicates that cliffs can exhibit little or no headward erosion in 20–30 kyr. The limestone at Vatulele is sufficiently hard and homogenous in its cliff exposures to withstand tens if not hundreds of thousands of years' weathering. Moreover, to infer the sequence of notch excision, formation of beach deposits of coral rubble on the wave platform and infilling the notch, sea level fall, beach sediment consolidation, sea level rise, some erosion of the infill beach deposits, and lastly, the deposition of stalagmitic deposits up to 0.5 m diameter in the notches, all within the last few thousand years of the Holocene, seems very improbable. Furthermore, the incision of the higher notches under this Holocene scenario requires relative sea level fall (or island rise) which must have been accompanied by downcutting of the present beach platforms, which are incised in limestone, at this same rapid rate of island rise. While problems are well known to exist in dating shell near the limit of radiocarbon dating and gross underestimations of true age are likely, overestimating age is unlikely. However, dating of the speleothem deposits that are seen in several places to also infill these notches would test Nunn's premise. Furthermore, the development of the cave systems has necessarily occurred in concert with the above-ground geomorphology and the notches, and caves the size of Muremure and Big Cave, would require much longer than some 7000 years to form. It is likely they have had their present form for tens if not hundreds of thousands of years: people have certainly occupied the present floors for the past 2000 years.

Thus, we have two contrasting hypotheses of island age. One suggests it may be as old as six Ma, and the other that its subaerial history may be measured at most in hundreds of thousands of years. However, the mere presence of a subaerial landmass does not mean it could sustain much of a terrestrial vertebrate fauna. It would need to have been of a certain minimum size and to have supported a well-developed vegetation community to maintain a diverse avifauna. The age of the higher sea level notch, at about 8 m, is probably critical in this respect, as then, the hill at Korolamalama was a protruding rock with marine caves in it and very little of the rest of the island is higher than 20 m, not much of it was outside the impact zone of storm events. In this respect, tsunamis generated from volcanic events in the Tonga or Kermadec Trench regions are likely to have had severe impacts on such a low-lying island.

The fauna of Vatulele has some potential for corroborating either the young or the old hypothesis of island development. If the island has had a long period of subaerial exposure and has been isolated from the mainland, then endemic forms could evolve. No endemic extant taxa are documented, but island endemics are likely to be terrestrial and flightless and the faunal component most prone to human-induced extinction. This is demonstrated to have been the case on Viti Levu (Worthy et al. 1999) and in many other places in the Pacific (e.g. Steadman 1989, 1995). The fossil record of Vatulele can therefore contribute to this debate by determining the former presence or absence of such endemic species.

Big Cave system

Location: 18° 30' 44.7"S, 177° 36' 38.2"E. Visits: 8–9 November 1999.

The cave is in walking distance of Vatulele Resort and the main entrance is a recreational destination for visitors to the resort (Figure 16). The main cave, called Big Cave, has a large walk-in type entrance with slopes down to deep pools of water on the left (Figure 17). The chamber is about 30 m wide and trends northeast but collapsed rocks bar progress beyond about 30 m in that direction. A few bones were found among the rocks of this chamber, and on the slope in the middle of the chamber just inside the drip-line of the entrance, a deposit of bones from an owl roost was present. On the southwest side of the same entrance feature, another chamber headed southwest contains a large colony of swiftlets. No fossils were found in this section. Off the southeast side of the same entrance feature is another chamber within which no fossil deposits were found.

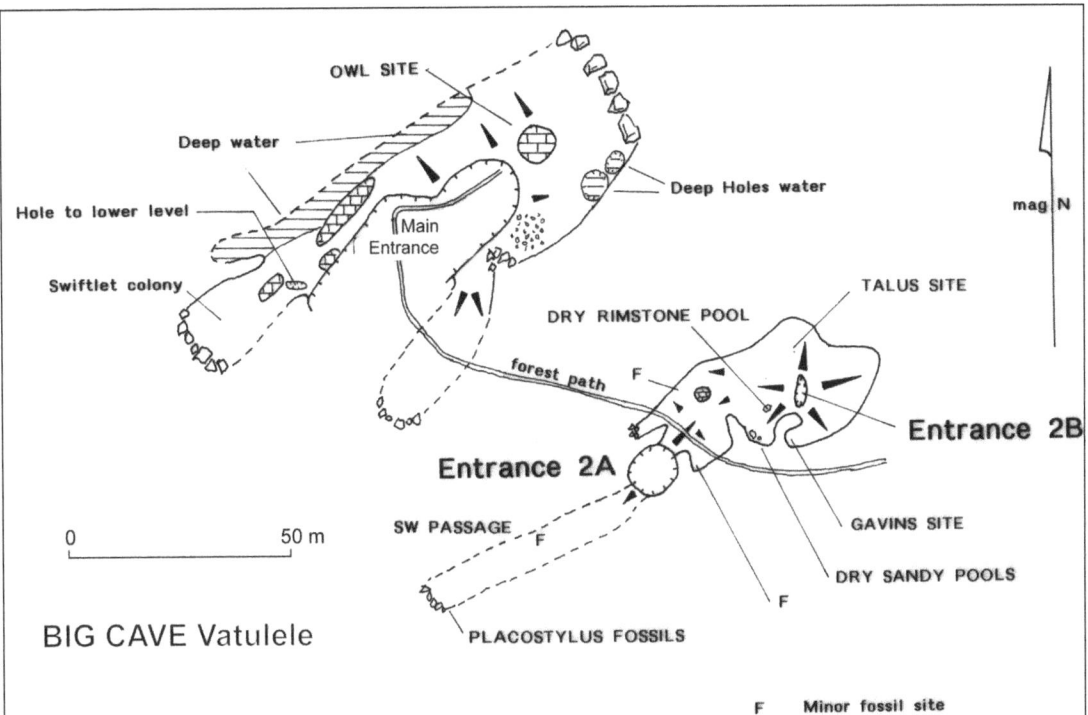

Figure 17. Map of Big Cave, Vatulele Island, showing the location of the major fossil sites. The cave was surveyed with a tape (0.1 m) and compass (1°). Unsurveyed passages are defined by dashed lines.

About 70 m before the main Big Cave entrance, the access path passes two vertical entrances dropping into caves below. The most obvious is an entrance about 10 m diameter on the southwest side of the path, here called Entrance 2A (Figure 17). About 30 m distant and on the other side of the path is Entrance 2B, which is smaller but with more difficult access. The two entrances are connected by a cave passage, and other passages extend either side of them. Many fossils were found in surface deposits in the chamber below Entrance 2B. This is partly because it is an excellent pitfall trap, and partly because its more difficult access meant barn owls could live undisturbed in it. Large deposits of bones accumulated by them are present, but all are post-human-arrival in age, as indicated by the presence of rats.

Ganilao Cave

The site Ganilao is in a large solution notch in the cliff about 200 m from the Prawn Grotto, with its base about 7 m above the ground level (Figure 16). This cave is reputed to have been the home of a legendary giant predatory bird. The site is surrounded by natural forest. The feature is about 5 m wide and 10 m long with a high roof, but the bone deposit lies within a hollow about 3 m wide by 6 m long.

The deposit is dry and dusty and is mainly an accumulation by barn owls, though nesting white-tailed tropicbirds *Phaethon lepturus* probably have added some fish bones to it. The surface bone deposit is about 5 cm deep and overlies consolidated sediments. We sieved the material from an area 3 m x 2.5 m of the surface deposit through a 6 mm and a 2 mm sieve. Material on the 6 mm sieve was sorted *in situ* and the concentrate remaining on the 2 mm sieve was sorted under laboratory conditions. A test pit 20 cm x 20 cm was excavated in three 5 cm spits, after which basement rock was encountered, to assess the faunal composition of the subsurface deposits. Bones were found throughout the subsurface sediments, and charcoal and pottery fragments were present in the first 10 cm, but not in the last 5 cm above the base. The bones on the surface therefore post-date people inhabiting the island and the cave, but nevertheless provide a rich record of barn-owl prey from a relatively undisturbed forest environment. The site contains a damp ledge at its rear with sediment in it from which a separate sample was collected and analysed. A white-tailed tropicbird with a downy chick occupied an alcove in the site at the time of our visit on 10 November 1999.

Korolamalama Cave

Korolamalama Cave is in the top of a small hill about 1 km inland from Gusuniqara Point (Figure 16). The hill is now forested but coconut plantations are close by. Neither bats nor swiftlets were living in the cave at the time of our visit. The hill is basically hollow, as around its summit several entrances lead down into a central, daylight-lit chamber. On the south side of the hill, a distinct, very smoke-blackened passage leads into the hill towards the northeast. There are deep archaeological deposits throughout all cave features and fortification terraces line the hillside. Fossil deposits, if any, are thus deeply buried by archaeological deposits, and their location is impossible to predict. The sample of bones is an accumulation made by barn owls since people last lived in the cave. It comes from the floor of the central chamber in the cave, and was in daylight.

Muremure Cave

Muremure Cave (Figure 18) is a complex linear system formed by drainage from the centre of the island towards the west coast. We took a GPS reading (18° 31' 15.2"S, 177° 36' 26.5"E) in a small garden clearing on the path traversing the island from the west coast, which is where the path to the cave diverges from it. The cave is about 500 m from this point at an estimated map reference of 798E 313N. Passages appear to have been formed on one level at or below the water table, as shown by pocket solution features over the walls and roof, but are now entirely drained. In some chambers, speleothem deposition is abundant. In the chambers towards the bat colony from the crawl (Figure 18) and west of the vertical pitfall entrance, all floors are covered in rockfall debris. Between the three entrances, the floors are flat and mainly covered in silt.

The cave is unmapped, but we visited about 1 km of passage with three entrances on 11 November 1999. Between Entrances 1 and 2, which are horizontal 'walk-in' type features, the floors are much modified by prehistoric human activities, with many stone walls and terraces and infilled hollows. Human burials and pottery fragments are scattered through the cave. The cave depicted by Gansser (1994:Fig. 25) is presumed to be passages seen extending eastward out of the doline, containing what we have called the 'Main Entrance', which we did not visit.

Most fossils were found near the westernmost entrance, which is a vertical 'pitfall' feature, and so trapped ground birds. All were surface deposits. A single barn-owl deposit was seen on the floor in the daylight zone in the middle or second entrance. No potential fossil deposits within sediment sequences were noted. This is the only cave where small bats, presumed to be the sheath-tailed bat *Emballonura semicaudata*, were seen alive. Swiftlets were not present.

Caves around the resort

On 10 November 1999 we visited caves close to the resort. Kaviko Cave is a small, drowned feature with no accessible deposits. Another small cave, partially developed for the resort, was also too close to the water table and no deposits of interest were noted. Lastly, Bua Cave, on the path leading towards Ekubu village, is about 5 m wide and 10 m long. Again, it is close to the water table, and has no entrapment mechanism to accumulate fossils.

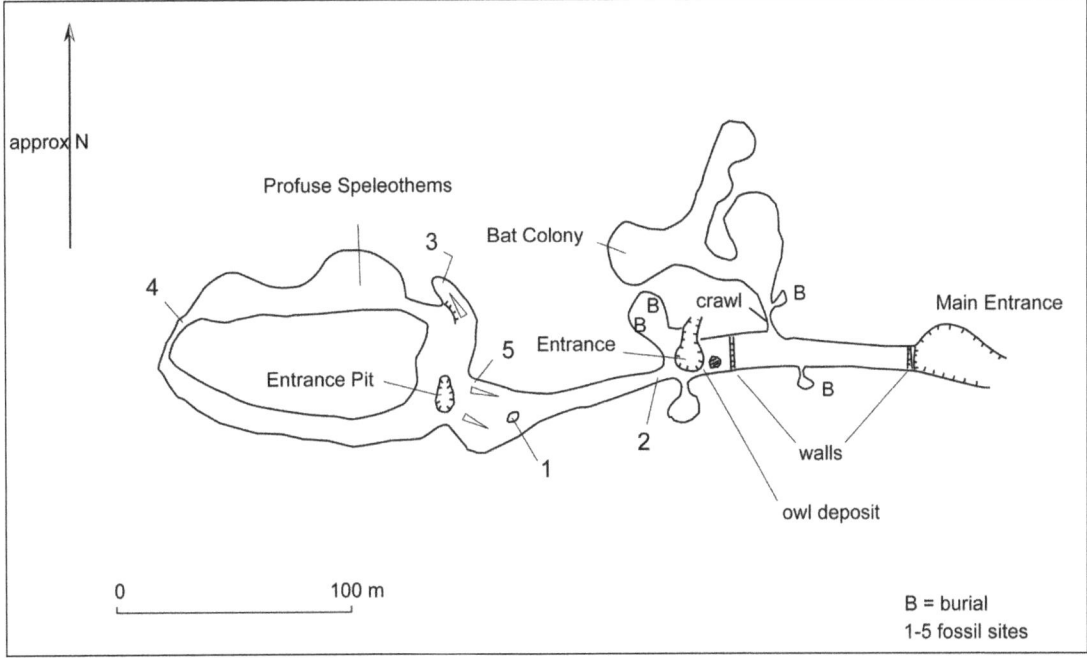

Figure 18. Sketch map of Muremure Cave, Vatulele Island.

References

Anderson, A.J., Ayliffe, L., Questiaux, D., Sorovi-Vunidilo, T., Spooner, N. and Worthy, T. 2001. The terminal age of the Fijian megafauna. In: Anderson, A.J., Lilley, I. and O'Connor, S. (eds), *Histories of Old ages: Essays in honour of Rhys Jones*, pp. 251–264. Pandanus Books, ANU, Canberra.

Baumel, J.J. and Witmer, L.M. 1993. Osteologia. In: Baumel, J.J., King, A.S., Breazile, J.E., Evans, H.E and Vanden Berge, J.C. (eds), *Handbook of avian anatomy: Nomina Anatomica Avium*, Second Edition. Publications of the Nuttall Ornithological Club 23: 45–132. Cambridge, Massachusetts, USA.

Gansser, A. 1994. *Enigmas of Vatulele Island*. La Buona Stampa, Switzerland.

Gilbert, T. 1984. Limestone and volcanic caves of the Fiji Islands. *Transactions of the British Cave Research Association* 11(2): 105–118.

Nunn, P.D. 1988. Vatulele, a study in the geomorphological development of a Fiji island. *Mineral Resources Department Memoir* 2, Fiji.

Nunn, P.D. 1998. Uplift of islands along the Vatulele–Beqa ridge. In: *Pacific Island Landscapes*, pp. 43–60. Institute of Pacific Studies, The University of the South Pacific, Suva.

Shackleton, N.J. 1987. Oxygen isotopes, ice volume and sea-level. *Quaternary Science Review* 6: 183–190.

Steadman, D.W. 1989. Extinction of birds in Eastern Polynesia: A review of the record, and comparisons with other Pacific Island groups. *Journal of Archaeological Science* 16: 177–205.

Steadman, D.W. 1995. Prehistoric extinctions of Pacific island birds: Biodiversity meets zooarchaeology. *Science* 267: 1123–1131.

Worthy, T.H. and Anderson, A. 1999. *Research on the caves of Viti Levu, Fiji, June 1997 – October 1998, and their significance for palaeontology and archaeology*. Report to the Fiji Museum, ANH, RSPAS, ANU, Canberra.

Worthy, T.H., Wilde, K. and Williams, D. 1991. Anahulu Cave, Tongatapu. *New Zealand Speleological Bulletin* 8: 525–528.

Worthy, T.H., Anderson, A.J. and Molnar, R.E. 1999. Megafaunal expression in a land without mammals – the first fossil faunas from terrestrial deposits in Fiji (Vertebrata: Amphibia, Reptilia, Aves). *Senckenbergiana biologica* 79(2): 237–242.

3

Results of palaeofaunal research

Trevor H. Worthy
School of Biological, Earth and Environmental Sciences, The University of New South Wales

Atholl Anderson
Department of Archaeology and Natural History, The Australian National University

Introduction

In this chapter, we describe the results of identifications of the faunal remains described in Chapter 2. We restrict the results to data from the fossil sites rather than the archaeological sites, which are described in Chapter 10. Analyses were carried out by Worthy using the reference collections noted in Chapter 10, which include relatively modern material in order to examine changes in the Fiji fauna.

The following abbreviations have been used for both single and plural reference to the elements: cmc, carpometacarpi; cor, coracoids; fem, femora; fib, fibulae; hum, humeri; pt, part; quad, quadrates; rad, radii; scap, scapulae; stern, sterna; tmt, tarsometatarsi; and tib, tibiotarsi. When listing material, bones are sometimes identified as left (L) or right (R) elements. L or R prefixed by 'p', 's' or 'd' indicates 'proximal', 'shaft' or 'distal' part of the element respectively, e.g. pR fem means the proximal part of a right femur. Anatomical nomenclature for specific bone landmarks follows Baumel and Witmer (1993), but terms are Anglicised after first mention. Some common terms are abbreviated as follows: *proc.* for *processus*; *artic.* for *articularis*.

Owl middens – insights into modern faunas

In many of the sites described in the preceding chapter, middens accumulated by the barn owl (*Tyto alba*) were present (Table 1). In several cases, the bone deposits were relatively thin (<10 cm) and generally they overlay archaeological deposits, indicating initiation of deposition after human use of the site. At Nabalabalagita Cave, the test pit indicated abundant bones of *Rattus exulans* to 45 cm depth. They are probably derived from owl midden, but human use of the cave is indicated by archaeological material to 62 cm depth. At the Tavuni site near Toga, the sediment containing owl-derived fauna and *Tyto* bone extended to 45 cm depth, and there, also, human influence in the site extended to about 60 cm depth. While still dominated by *Rattus exulans*, bones of *R. praetor*, *Gallicolumba stairii* and *Porphyrio porphyrio* are probably several hundred years old. In no case was there evidence of owl-midden deposits in sediments older than the period of human colonisation.

Table 1. Faunas from barn owl (*Tyto alba*) sites showing NISP.

Species	Common name	VVS	Buk	Tav	Q2	Nab
*Rattus exulans	Pacific rat	100s	100s	100s	100s	100s
*Mus musculus	Mouse		21	73	88	6
*Rattus rattus/norvegicus	Rat	64		17		5
*Rattus ?praetor	Rat			4		
Emballonura semicaudata	Microbat		54	2	4	
Tyto alba	Barn owl	5	4	4	8	1
Egretta sacra	Reef heron		24	100		
Halcyon chloris	White-collared kingfisher				1	3
Collocalia spodiopygia	White-rumped swiftlet		127	9	158	
Gallicolumba stairii	Friendly ground dove			1		
Ptilinopus perousii	Many-coloured fruit dove dove		2			
Ptilinopus luteovirens	Golden dove					?1
Poliolimnas cinereus	White-browed crake	8				
Porzana tabuensis	Spotless crake	5				
Porphyrio porphyrio	Purple swamphen			1		
Foulehaio carunculatus	Wattled honeyeater					2
*Acridotheres fuscus	Indian myna			13		4
*Pycnonotus cafer	Bulbul		58		1	45
Aplonis tabuensis	Fiji starling	1				
Turdus poliocephalus	Island thrush		2			
Zosterops ?lateralis	Fiji white-eye	5	25			30
Erythrura cyanovirens	Parrot bill finch					1
Undetermined passerines			7	6		Y
Gehyra oceanica	Gecko	2	5	7		18
Nactus pelagicus	Gecko	1		2		
Gecko sp. indet	Gecko	17			2	
Skink sp. indet	Skink	6				
Brachylophus ?vitiensis	Banded iguana				1	

VVS – Volivoli Swamp site, Buk – Bukusia, Tav – Tavuni at Toga, Q2 – Qaranioso #2 at Tau, Nab – Nabalabalagita Cave. 'Y' indicates the taxon was present.
* means taxon is introduced. While rats appear to dominate these assemblages there is a consistent high diversity of birds and other vertebrates present.

The owl middens are observed as large surface deposits of rat bones. While most bones appeared to be whole, bulk samples show many are fragmented. Most are of the Pacific rat (*Rattus exulans*), but large numbers of geckos and a lesser number of birds are always present. Samples from such sites were collected to compare to the older fossil sites and provide indications of modern deposition in caves. It was hoped these could be compared to prehistoric owl-accumulated faunas, but none of those were found.

In all sites, rodents dominated the faunas (Table 1), with *Rattus exulans* most common. However, larger rats were also present, with *Rattus praetor* at deeper levels in one site, and *Rattus rattus/norvegicus* in surface deposits with *Mus musculus*. The small bat *Emballonura semicaudata* was common in some sites, where suitable roosting caves were present nearby. At least 17 species of birds plus other undetermined passerines were recorded from these owl middens. Two geckos and the banded iguana complete the fauna.

The fauna in each site appear to have been highly influenced by the local environment and the availability of prey species. For example, the small bat *Emballonura* and the swiftlets *Collocalia* were only present when there were caves near the sites, and then their bones were common, indicating they were favoured owl prey. The Volivoli Swamp site was the only one near a wetland and it was also the only one that had wetland birds such as white-browed crake *Poliolimnas cinereus* and spotless crake *Porzana tabuensis*. Fish bones were also present and, together with the crake bones, indicate the owl foraged over the wetland. The modern deposits often contained historically introduced birds, such as Indian myna *Acridotheres fusca* and bulbul *Pycnonotus cafer*, which, together with white-eyes *Zosterops lateralis*, were often the most common birds in the site. These taxa indicate that the owls were hunting in open grassland–shrubland habitats rather than in closed forest. One species notable by its absence among these faunas was the long-tailed cuckoo *Eudynamis taitensis*. Its bones were common in owl middens on Vatulele Island (see below), and this observation bears out the observations of local ornithologists (D. Watling, pers. comm., Environment Consultants, Fiji) that the long-tailed cuckoo is rare or absent on Viti Levu, yet common on smaller islands.

The most important conclusion from these data is that humans were already present in Viti Levu, and had been for some time, before barn owls *Tyto alba* arrived. The presence of suitable rodent prey introduced by people presumably at or near colonisation about 3000 years ago (Anderson and Clark, 1999; White et al. 2000) was probably the prerequisite that allowed barn owls, which are specialist predators of small mammals and specifically rodents, to self-colonise, presumably from the Solomon Islands.

The fossil faunas

Fossil vertebrate faunas were obtained from five main sites: Volivoli #1, Qaranivokai, Wainibuku Cave, Udit Tomo and Vatumu. Isolated finds were made at Delaniqara at Wailotua, Bukusia and Qaranioso. The fossil faunas available from these sites reveal a minimum of 11 herpetofaunal species, 24 birds plus at least four undetermined passerines, and four bats (Table 2) (Worthy and Anderson 1999; Worthy et al. 1999; Molnar et al. 2002; Pregill and Worthy 2003; Worthy 2000a, 2001a, b, 2003, 2004). Of great significance, this fossil fauna revealed the presence of some extinct taxa, of which several are sufficiently large to be termed megafauna. Foremost among these were herpetofaunal species: a terrestrial crocodilian, a giant iguana, a giant frog and a tortoise. Among the birds were a giant flightless megapode and an equally large flightless pigeon, rivalling the dodo in size. Other extinct species include another megapode, a large fruit pigeon, and another large rail, in addition to the historically extinct barred-wing rail *Gallirallus* (=*Nesoclopeus*) *poicilopterus*, a snipe and a duck.

Herpetofauna

Three species of frog are represented. Bones of the two extant species, *Platymantis vitiensis* and *P. vitianus*, are present, with those of a newly discovered extinct species named *Platymantis megabotoniviti* (Worthy 2001a). Growing to about 150 mm snout–vent length, the latter was a very much larger and more robust ground frog than *P. vitianus*. *Platymantis megabotoniviti* was found in most fossil sites in Viti Levu (Figure 19).

Iguana fossils include some attributable to one of the extant species, but many are of a new, extinct giant iguana up to 1.5 m long (Worthy et al. 1999), recently named *Lapitiguana impensa* (Pregill and Worthy 2003). This iguana has been found in four sites (Volivoli #1, Qaranivokai,

Table 2. A list of taxa and NISP recorded from the main fossil sites in Viti Levu.

Species	Common Name	Volivoli I	Qaranivokai	Wainibuku Cave	Udit Pitfall Cave	Vatumu	Wailotua	Joskes Thumb
†*Platymantis megabotoniviti*	Giant ground frog	36	795	53	6	11	1	
Platymantis vitiensis	Fiji tree frog		15			2		
Platymantis vitianus	Fiji ground frog	4	375			3		
Gehyra aff. *G. vorax*	Large gecko		9			1		
Gecko sp.			13					1
Skink large sp.			2					
†*Lapitiguana impensa*	Giant iguana	35	134					
Brachylophus ?vitiensis	Modern iguana	1	3					
Candoia sp.	Boa	1		157				
†*Volia athollandersoni*.	Land crocodilian	13		112				
†*Tortoise* nsp	Tortoise	1						
?†*Tortoise* nsp fragments	?Tortoise	13						
Pseudobulweria rostrata	Tahiti petrel					6		
Pterodroma ?brevipes	Collared petrel					2		180
Pterodroma leucoptera	New Caledonian petrel							1
Pterodroma externa or *Pt. cervicalis*	Juan Fernandez petrel							5
Nesofregetta albigularis	White-throated storm petrel							4
Puffinus lherminieri	Audubon's shearwater							20
Sterna fuscata	Sooty tern							4
†*Vitirallus watlingi*	Viti Levu rail	7	544		1			
Gallirallus philippensis	Banded rail		5					
†*Nesoclopeus poicilopterus*	Barred-wing rail			2	2		18	
†Rail indet sp. 1	?Gallinule			1	2			
†*Megavitiornis altirostris*	Giant megapode	7	6	17	200		5	
†*Megapodius amissus*	Viti Levu scrubfowl	2	2		89			
†*Anas* sp. indet.	Fiji teal					1		
Natunaornis gigoura	Giant pigeon	10	16	13	29			
Columba vitiensis	White-throated pigeon		2					
Ducula latrans	Peale's pigeon		3			3		53
†*Ducula* sp. cf *D. lakeba*	Large fruit pigeon	1		1	1	2		
Gallicolumba stairii	Friendly ground dove					24		
Ptilinopus ?lutiovitrens	Golden dove		1					
Ptilinopus perousii or *P. luteovirens*	Many-coloured or golden dove					7		
Ptilinopus sp. indet	Indet dove sp.							3
Prosopeia personata	Musk parrot		31			2		6
Vini solitarius	Collared lory					1		8
†*Coenocorypha miratropica*	Fiji snipe					17		
Accipiter rufitorques	Fiji goshawk							39
Halcyon chloris	White-collared kingfisher							1
Aplonis tabuensis	Polynesian starling	1	3					2
Rhipidura cf *spilodera*	Spotted fantail		1					
Zosterops sp.	White-eye		1					
Foulehaio carunculata	Wattled honeyeater		1					
Gymnomyza viridis	Giant forest honeyeater							5
Collocalia spodiopygia	Swiftlet					1		
Turdus poliocephalus	Island thrush	1	7		?1			
Passerine sp.	Small perching birds		10			7 (4 sp)		
Pteropus tonganus	Large fruit bat	2			?1	?1		204
Notopteris macdonaldi	Small fruit bat		10	647		34	209	
Emballonura semicaudata	Small bat	3	98	2		14		
Chaerephon bregullae	Fijian mastiff bat			6				

† Species globally extinct. Joskes Thumb is attributed to falcon predation, and is after Worthy (2000b) with addition of new material collected.

Bukusia, Qaranioso), all in western Viti Levu (Worthy and Anderson 1999). Its large size is unrivalled in the Pacific, and also indicates that it was a terrestrial species (Figure 20). It has not been found in the wetter rainforest regions of the east despite the presence there of suitable fossil sites, indicating it favoured drier habitats. Banded iguanas in Fiji have recently been shown to comprise three distinct species, with *Brachylophus bulabula* erected for populations formerly known as *B. fasciatus* in the wet forests of Viti Levu, Vanua Levu and Kadavu (Keogh et al. 2008). Populations in the dry vegetation zones of the northwestern side of Viti Levu and offshore islands are *B. vitensis*, and *B. fasciatus* is now restricted to populations in the Lau Group. We follow this nomenclature here, but note that the referral of iguana bones from Vatulele or Sigatoka to either *B. vitensis* of *B. bulabula* is problematic, as extant populations, if present, have not been identified (Keogh et al. 2008).

The new species (and genus) of extinct terrestrial crocodilian *Volia athollandersoni* and the tortoise were both found in Volivoli #1 on the first investigation (Worthy et al. 1999). Remains of the tortoise have not been identified with certainty from any other site. The only identifiable bone, although there are several fragments with internal turtle osteological morphology, is an ungual, which is similar to that of the meiolaniids, or terrestrial horned turtles, known from, for example, New Caledonia and Lord Howe Island.

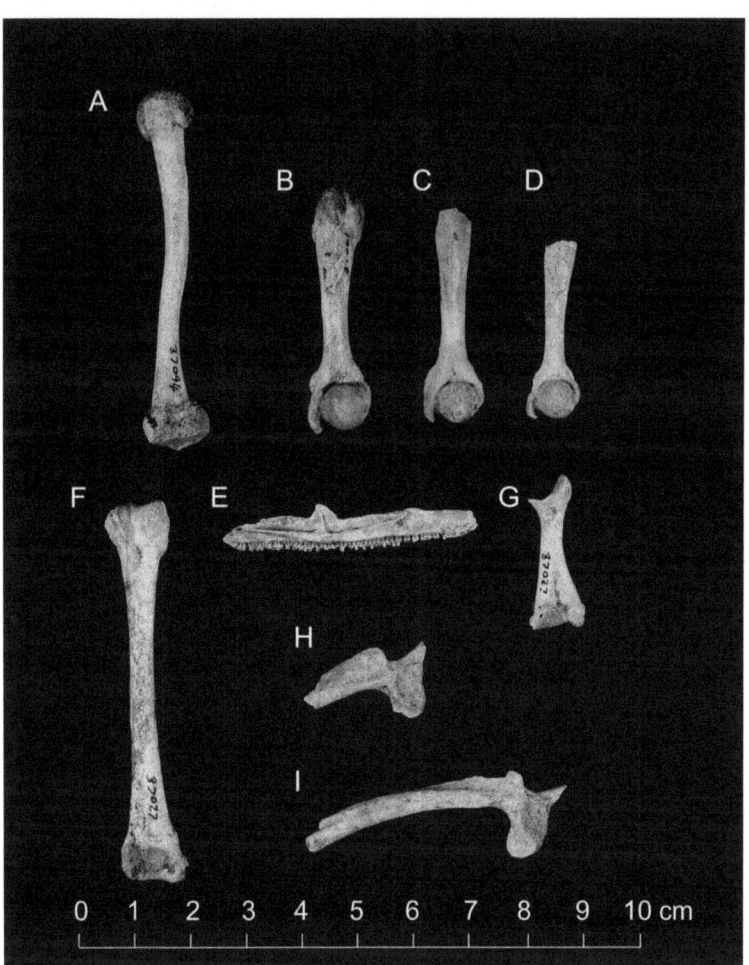

Figure 19. Selected bones of *Platymantis megabotoniviti*. A, femur MNZ S37094. B–D, adult left humeri in ventral view: S37027, S37068 and S37065. E, right maxilla S37061 in lingual view. F, left tibiofibula S37027 in anterior view. G, right radioulna S37027 in lateral view. H–I, left ilia S37057C and S37057A in lateral view. Reproduced from Worthy (2001a) with the permission of *Palaeontology*.

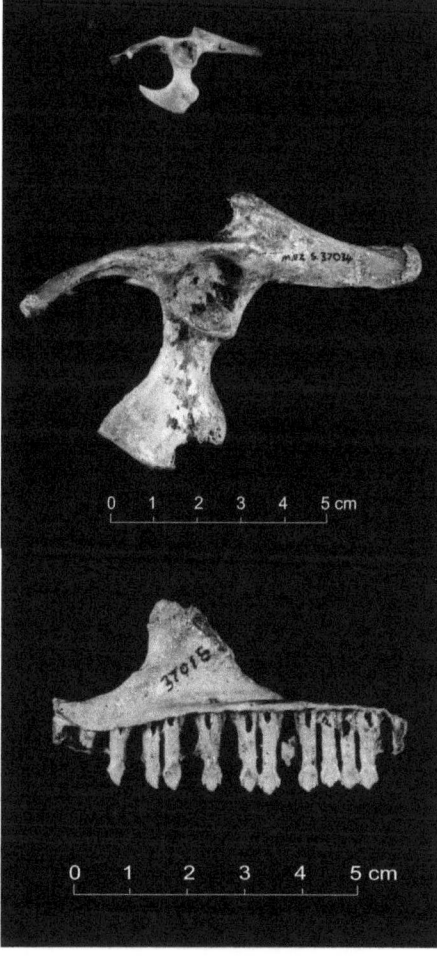

Figure 20. Giant iguana (*Lapitiguana impensa*) remains. Bottom, right maxilla (MNZ S37015) lingual view. Middle and top, pelves (left side) of modern *B. vitensis* and *Lapitiguana impensa* (MNZ S37034).

The crocodilian *Volia athollandersoni* is represented by material from Volivoli #1 and Wainibuku Cave in the west and east of Viti Levu respectively (Figure 21). The better-preserved remains found in Wainibuku Cave have enabled the species to be described (Molnar et al. 2002). It is a terrestrial species most similar to *Mekosuchus inexpectatus* (Balouet and Buffetaut 1987) from New Caledonia and *M. kalpokasi* from Vanuatu (Mead et al. 2002), as well as fossil mekosuchine taxa from Australia (Molnar et al. 2002). *Volia athollandersoni* grew to at least 3 m in length.

The remaining fossil herpetofauna includes remains of a boid snake, presumably the extant *Candoia bibronii*, and undetermined skinks and geckos, including large (ca. 20–30 cm long) species of each.

Avifauna

The 24 taxa of birds so far known from these fossil faunas, even when augmented by at least four undetermined passerines, is a considerably smaller total than the 47 known historically from Viti Levu (Watling 1982). However, eight of the fossil taxa are newly discovered, extinct taxa. Most of the fossil species are ground-dwelling species, with canopy-dwelling forest species under-represented, and wetland taxa virtually absent.

Megapodes are one of the most characteristic ground birds of the South Pacific, with either extant or extinct species spread from Indonesia across the Pacific to Western Samoa (Jones et al. 1995; Steadman 1999, 2006a). The largest and most unusual species is *Sylviornis*

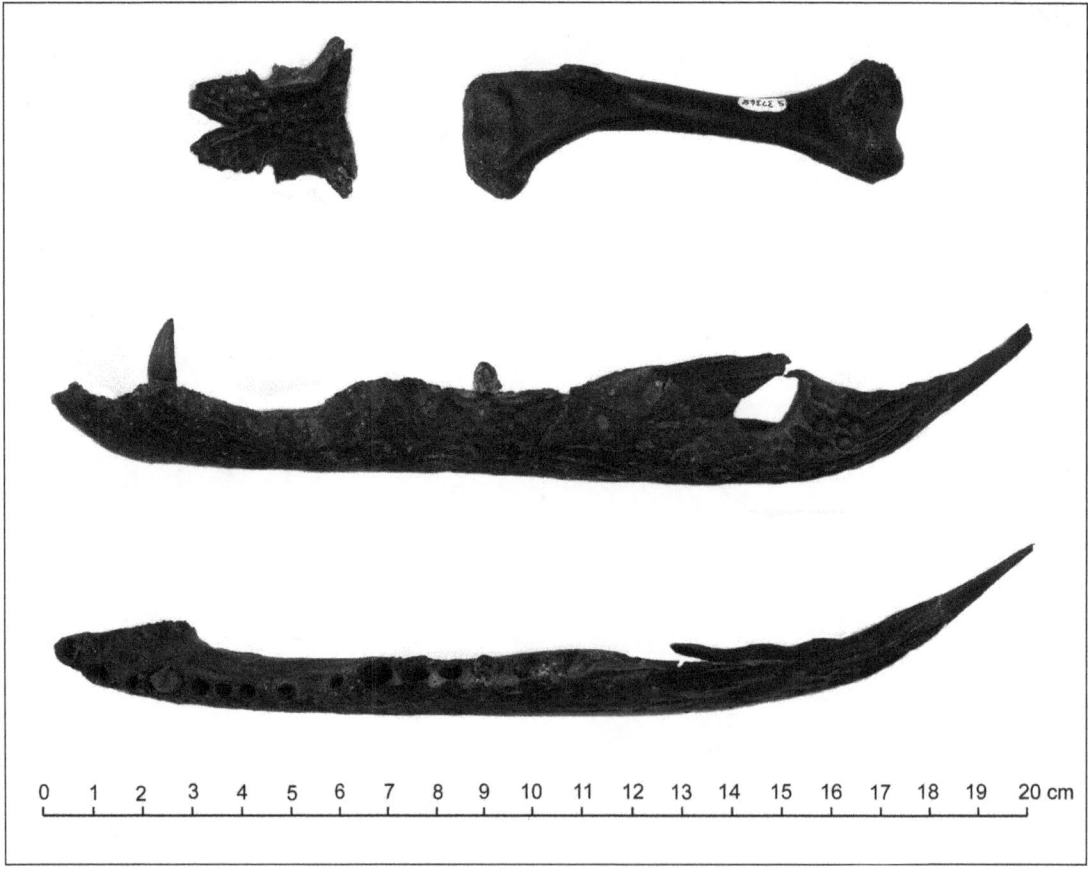

Figure 21. Terrestrial crocodilian (*Volia athollandersoni*) remains. Top left, coalesced parietals (MNZ S37342) dorsal view. Top right, humerus (right) (MNZ S37348). Middle, mandible (MNZ S37332) lateral view. Bottom, mandible (MNZ S37332) dorsal view.

neocaledoniae from New Caledonia (Poplin and Mourer-Chauviré 1985; Balouet 1991), but the fossils discovered in Viti Levu reveal a smaller, but still very large species. Recently described as *Megavitiornis altirostris* (Worthy 2000a), this flightless species was perhaps up to 15 kg in weight and stood near 1 m tall. Its bones were found in Volivoli #1, Qaranivokai, Udit Cave and Delaniqara at Wailotua, so the species lived in both wet and dry habitats (Figures 22–

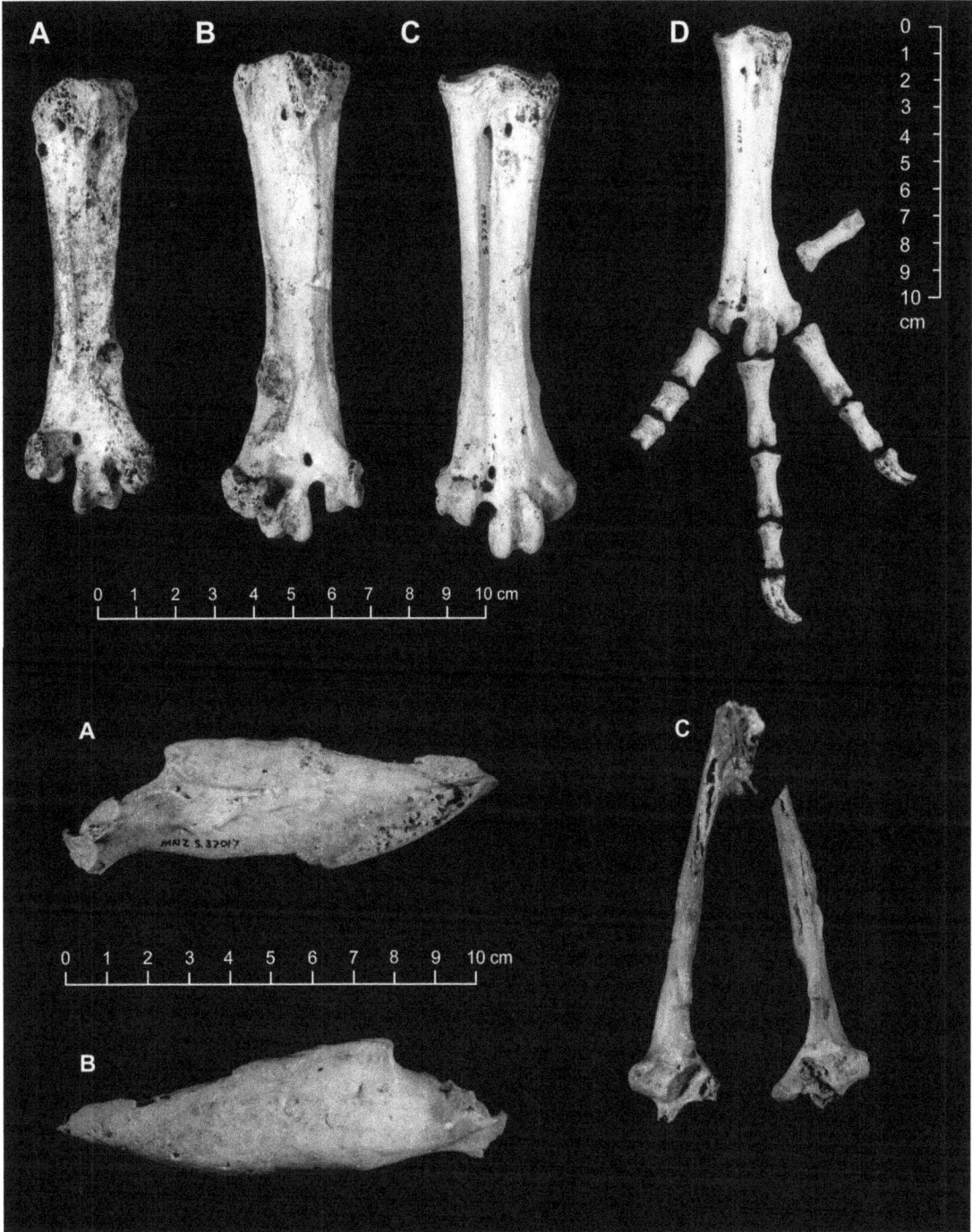

Figure 22. Top, Tarsometatarsi and phalanges of the giant megapode *Megavitiornis altirostris* from Viti Levu. A, paratype MNZ S37369; B–D, holotype MNZ S37362. Reproduced from Worthy (2000a) with the permission of the Royal Society of New Zealand. Bottom, the incredibly stout mandible of *Megavitiornis altirostris*, MNZ S37017 in A, medial, B, lateral, and C, dorsal, aspects. Reproduced from Worthy (2000a) with the permission of the Royal Society of New Zealand.

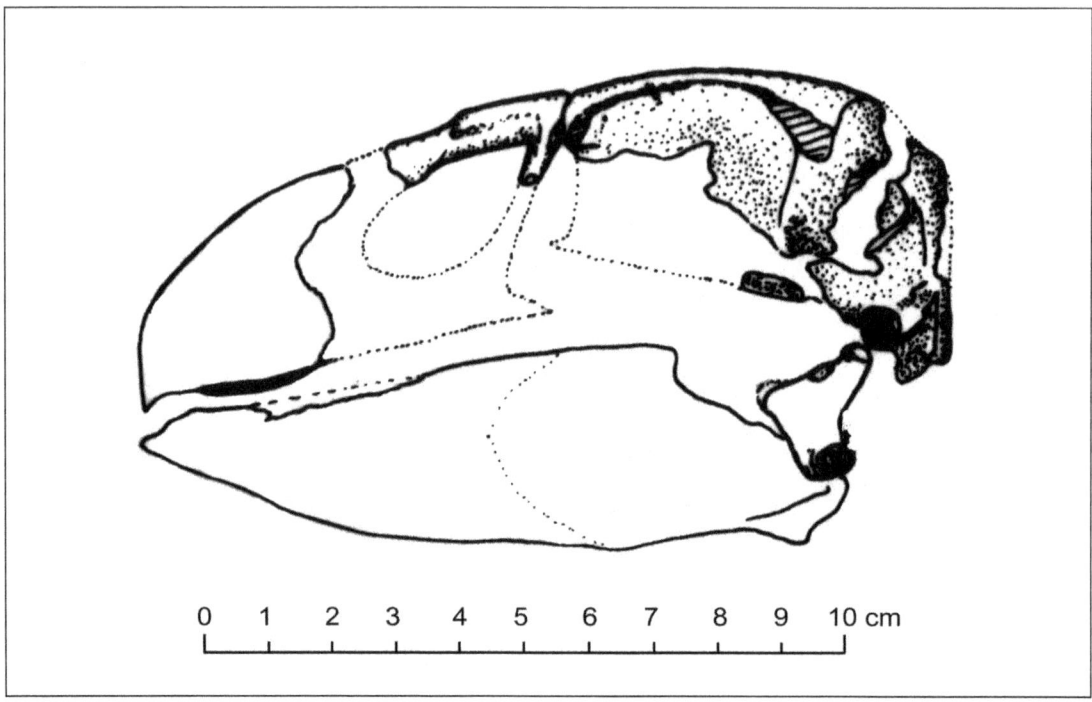

Figure 23. Reconstruction of the skull of *Megavitiornis altirostris* based on MNZ S37455 and MNZ S37017. Reproduced from Worthy (2000a) with the permission of the Royal Society of New Zealand.

23). A smaller extinct megapode was also found in Volivoli #1, Qaranivokai and Udit Cave, a flightless or weakly volant form of the widespread genus *Megapodius* (Jones et al. 1995) named *Megapodius amissus* (Worthy 2000a). It was larger than all its congeners except *M. reinwardt* in Australia and *M. molistructor* (Balouet and Olson 1989) extinct of New Caledonia.

The second giant flightless species of bird was a pigeon. Large flightless pigeons are rare in insular faunas (Goodwin 1967): they are otherwise unknown in the Pacific and represented in the Indian Ocean by the dodo *Raphus cucullatus* and solitaire *Pezophaps solitaria*. The giant extinct species from Fiji was nearly the same size as the dodo and has been recently described as the new genus and species *Natunaornis gigoura* (Worthy 2001b), allied to the crowned pigeons *Goura* of Papua New Guinea. Its genus name honours Kiniviliame Natuna, the senior chief of Volivoli in Nadroga, while its specific name reflects its likeness to a gigantic *Goura* species. A few bones indicate the presence of a large fruit pigeon, which may be *Ducula lakeba*, described recently by Worthy (2001b) from Lakeba Island. This species is a larger pigeon than the extinct *Ducula david* of Wallis Island (Balouet and Olson 1987) and *Ducula harrisoni* of Henderson Island (Wragg and Worthy 2006), but Viti Levu bones are of either undiagnostic parts or elements not shared with the Lakeba assemblage, precluding a certain referral. However, both the Viti Levu species and *Ducula lakeba* are larger than any other *Ducula* so far described.

As might be expected from their remarkable radiation elsewhere in the Pacific (Steadman 1987, 1995, 2006a; Steadman et al. 2000), there are several rails in the Viti Levu fauna, of which three are extinct, and only one was historically known. One is a very distinctive form, recently described as *Vitirallus watlingi* (Worthy 2004), the long bill of which approaches the proportions of that in *Aphanapteryx* in the Mascarene Islands, but the bird was the size of the weka *Gallirallus australis* of New Zealand. Three bones attest to the probable presence of a gallinule, which would not be unexpected given the presence of *Gallinula pacifica*, historically known from Samoa, and *Gallinula silvestris*, from the Solomon Islands, both listed in the genus *Pareudiastes* by Steadman (2006a). Last and rarest of the extinct taxa within the fossil record is the historically extinct *Gallirallus* (=*Nesoclopeus*) *poicilopterus*, of which few bones have been found. Four extant rails are also present in the fossil fauna: the banded rail *Gallirallus philippensis*, the spotless crake *Porzana tabuensis*, the purple swamphen *Porphyrio porphyrio*, and the white-browed crake *Poliolimnas cinereus*.

An unexpected discovery was that of a new species of extinct snipe *Coenocorypha miratropica*, found at Vatumu, near Nadi (Worthy 2003). This genus is otherwise not known from Fiji, but has been recorded in New Caledonia (Balouet and Olson 1989) outside its stronghold in the New Zealand archipelago (Holdaway et al. 2001; Worthy and Holdaway 2002).

Also at Vatumu, a single bone of a small duck *Anas* sp. was recovered. This is the only anatid fossil so far recovered from Fiji. It is not referable to *Dendrocygna arcuata*, which is a small, highly vagile species, reported historically from Fiji (Watling 1982). The single scapula is not differentiable from the New Zealand brown teal *Anas chlorotis*, and so it is possible Fiji had a member of the Australasian radiation to which this species belongs. A teal that is very like *Anas gracilis* has been recorded from New Caledonia (Balouet and Olson 1989; Worthy unpubl. data).

Fossil sea birds are so far known only from the one fossil site at Vatuma near Nadi. Two petrels, *Pterodroma brevipes* and *Pseudobulweria rostrata*, are present in this fauna, which was probably accumulated by a predator, assumed to be the peregrine falcon *Falco peregrinus*. Clunie (1972) and Worthy (2000b) studied a recent fauna, accumulated by peregrine falcons, found at Joskes Thumb a few kilometres west of Suva. It was dominated by numerous species of birds, including canopy dwellers like *Ducula*, *Vini* and *Foulehaio*, and sea birds such as *P. brevipes* and *Sterna fuscata*, and fruit bats, and so was similar to the fauna found at Vatumu. The modern prey faunas of peregrines from Joskes Thumb (Clunie 1972) and downtown Suva (Clunie 1976) clearly show that the peregrine captures prey both over the ocean, outside the reef, and within forests.

Only the sites of Qaranivokai and Vatumu provide data on the volant and canopy species component of the prehuman avifauna. Theses sites have fossils of three fruit pigeons, a ground dove, one or two fruit-doves, the musk parrot, the collared lory and several passerines (Table 2). Only one of these, the largest fruit pigeon, is extinct.

Mammals

Four species of bats are represented in the fossil faunas (Table 2). These include the large fruit bat *Pteropus tonganus*, the endemic smaller fruit bat *Notopteris macdonaldi*, and the small sheath-tailed bat *Emballonura semicaudata*. A surprise was the discovery of the Fijian mastiff bat *Chaerephon bregullae* in the Wainibuku site, as this species is now known in the Fiji archipelago only from Vanua Levu and Taveuni (Flannery 1995; Palmeirim et al. 2007), but it is also known from Vanuatu, and a congener *Chaerephon solomonis* is known from the Solomon Islands (Flannery 1995:406).

No rodents were found in the fossil deposits, but in the archaeological site of Qaranioso #2 and in the barn owl site at Tavuni (Worthy and Anderson 1999), *Rattus praetor* was found with *R. exulans*. *Rattus praetor* is a Western Pacific species, occurring nearest in Vanuatu, and recorded recently from Mago Island in the Lau Group, Fiji, to which it was presumably taken by human colonisers about 2800 years ago (White et al. 2000). It is now extinct and has been replaced in upper layers of owl sites by *Rattus rattus*.

Significance of the faunas

The fossil record of birds throughout the Pacific has revealed many extinct species, and range reductions of others (Steadman 2006a, and references therein). In the New Zealand geographic region, 66, or 26.9%, of the original 245 breeding species are now globally extinct (Holdaway et al. 2001; Worthy and Holdaway 2002: where New Zealand was defined as North, South and Stewart Island and associated islets; Chatham Islands; the subantarctic Snares, Bounty, Antipodes, Auckland, Campbell and Macquarie Islands; and the tropical Norfolk Island and Kermadec Islands). At least 41% of the endemic species from the New Zealand region are extinct. On main islands, losses are even higher, e.g. the North Island lost 51% of its original fauna (Holdaway et al. 2001; Worthy and Holdaway 2002), and total losses have only been reduced because of the presence of small refuge islands adjacent to larger ones (Holdaway 1999). Gigantism and flightlessness have been significant evolutionary trends on mammalian predator-free islands, as shown in New Zealand by the 10 species of moa (Dinornithiformes, Tennyson and Martinson 2006), large rail-like birds (Aptornithidae), *Aptornis* (two species) and waterfowl (Anatidae), *Cnemiornis* (two species) (Olson and James 1991; Quammen 1996). The Hawaiian archipelago lost more than half its bird diversity (James and Olson 1991; Olson and James 1991), including at least four species of large, flightless, browsing anatids, called moa-nalos. Elsewhere in the Pacific, often up to half the fossil species were found to be extinct (Steadman 2006a), as in the Marquesas (Steadman 1989a; Steadman and Rolett 1996), Easter Island (Steadman 1995), Henderson Island (Wragg and Weisler 1994; Wragg and Worthy 2006; Worthy and Wragg 2003, 2008), Society Islands (Steadman 1989a), Samoa (Steadman 1994), and on the Tongan and Cook Island groups (Steadman 1989a, 1993, 1995). Among the extinct taxa are many species of rails, megapodes, columbids and parrots (Balouet and Olson 1987; Kirchman and Steadman 2005, 2006a, 2006b, 2007; Steadman 1987, 1989b, 1992, 2006a, 2006b, 2006c; Steadman and Zarriello 1987; Wragg and Worthy 2006; Worthy and Wragg 2003, 2008). A similar history of extinction has also been found in New Caledonia (Balouet and Olson 1989) and there are indications of them in Micronesia (Steadman and Intoh 1994; Steadman 2006a). Throughout the Pacific, most of the documented species diversity that has been lost is among the birds, but bats (Koopman and Steadman 1995), lizards (Pregill 1993) and iguanas (Pregill and Dye 1989; Pregill and Steadman 2004) all suffered losses prehistorically.

The recent palaeontological investigations have contributed substantially to knowledge of the prehuman terrestrial fauna of Viti Levu in the Fiji group. A remarkable fauna of large herpetofaunal species (crocodilian, tortoise, iguana and frog) has been revealed (Worthy et al. 1999). The tortoise and the crocodilian (Molnar et al. 2002) have their parallels in *Mekosuchus* and *Meiolania* on New Caledonia, Vanuatu and Lord Howe Island. The iguana *Lapitiguana impensa* (Pregill and Worthy 2003) and the extinct frog *Platymantis megabotoniviti* (Worthy 2001a) are both substantially larger than the extant taxa in each group, and together consolidate the notion of a long evolutionary history in Fiji for each of these groups. They also typify the phenomenon of island taxa having a tendency to evolve large terrestrial forms that are more at risk of extinction when new animals enter their habitats (Quammen 1996).

To the 47 historically known land birds (Watling 1982), eight more extinct species can be added. These include two of the most remarkable species known from the Central Pacific. Of these, the giant megapode *Megavitiornis altirostris* was exceeded in size only by *Sylviornis* of New Caledonia (Poplin and Mourer-Chauviré 1985). The giant, flightless pigeon *Natunaornis gigoura* represents a unique evolutionary course in the Pacific, but has its parallel in the Mascarene Islands with the solitaire and dodo. While considerably derived, this giant pigeon has several resemblances to *Goura* from Papua New Guinea (Worthy 2001b). The other extinct species, such as the smaller megapode *Megapodius amissus*, the large fruit pigeon *Ducula* cf. *lakeba*, the duck *Anas* sp., the three rails, and the snipe *Coenocorypha miratropica*, all have parallels elsewhere in the Pacific and were to be expected, in view of palaeontological research on other islands (Steadman 1995, 2006a).

Before these discoveries, Fiji was unique among larger Pacific islands in seemingly having lost only two taxa historically, with none known to be lost prehistorically. The new palaeontological data show the all-too-familiar pattern seen in insular faunas, that after humans and their commensals colonise an island for the first time there are numerous changes in the fauna, commonly with the large flightless birds and other ground-dwelling taxa becoming extinct (e.g. Olson and James 1991; Quammen 1996; Steadman 1995, 1999, 2006a; Worthy and Holdaway 2002). The large extinct taxa doubtless fell victim to over-hunting by the first humans (Anderson 1996; Quammen 1996). The evidence for this in Viti Levu is still largely lacking, but there is no other plausible reason why large taxa should persist for millennia through many climatic cycles then drop from the record about the time of human arrival. To date, no significant archaeological bone middens of extinct fauna have been recovered from Viti Levu. But *Lapitiguana* was present in the basal layers of a test pit in the archaeological deposit in Qaranioso near Tau, which is the only inland archaeological site dating to the first contact period of humans with the fauna. A test pit in Volivoli II has revealed one of the extinct rails and small petrels. The archaeological site VL 21/5 on Naigani (Best 1981) contained remains of a giant megapode, as first reported by van Tets (1985) and later by Jones et al. (1995). These bones were identified as *Megavitiornis altirostris* by Worthy (2000a). There are also bones of the giant iguana *Lapitiguana* and the crocodilian *Volia* present in this fauna (Irwin and Worthy in prep). The archaeological record would be immensely enhanced by the discovery of first-contact faunas from sites on Viti Levu. The very small faunas available from these few early sites do attest, however, to the use of some of the extinct taxa by humans, suggesting they had a significant hand in that process.

On Viti Levu, extinction is not just a prehistorical or a historical phenomenon. Viti Levu has the usual range of rodents (*Rattus exulans*, *R. rattus*, *R. norvegicus*, *Mus musculus*) found on many islands. These are disastrous enough on their own, but in addition to cats and dogs, Viti Levu has a mustelid, the mongoose, which is a highly efficient predator. The mongoose *Herpestes auropunctatus* was introduced in 1883 (Pernetta and Watling 1979), and the barred-wing rail *Gallirallus* (=*Nesoclopeus*) *poecilopterus* was probably extinct soon after: the only specimens were collected in the mid-19th century. Since then, the purple swamp hen *Porphyrio porphyrio* has become extinct on Viti Levu and other islands with mongoose. Moreover, no colonies of petrels are known to survive on Viti Levu, yet *Pterodroma brevipes*, *Pseudobulweria rostrata*, *Nesofregetta albigularis*, *Puffinus pacificus* and *P. lherminieri*, at least, are likely to have had breeding populations in the past. The large ground frog *Platymantis vitianus* is very rare and seemingly headed for extinction on Viti Levu, while remaining common on mongoose-free parts of its former range. Similarly, banded iguanas (*Brachylophus* spp.) are rare now on Viti Levu, yet can be abundant on predator-free islands. In New Zealand, birds like kaka *Nestor meridionalis*, kokako *Callaeas cinerea*, parakeets *Cyanoramphus* sp. and yellowheads *Mohoua ochrocephala* are unable to maintain populations in the presence of the stoat *Mustela ermina* without management of stoat numbers. It is probable that the same is true of several species in Viti Levu, and that the true predatory effects of the mongoose may not yet have been realised. Several birds, notably the pink-billed parrot-finch *Erythrura kleinschmidti*, the greater forest warbler *Trichocichla rufa* and the friendly ground dove *Gallicolumba stairii* are very rare and are likely headed for extinction.

Even bats are not immune from extinction. The fauna from Wainibuku revealed that the Fiji mastiff bat *Chaerephon bregullae* was formerly on Viti Levu, though presently it is only known from Vanua Levu and Taveuni in Fiji (Palmeirim et al. 2007). While fossils indicate the sheath-tailed bat was widespread in Viti Levu even recently, we only saw one individual in Volivoli cave, and since then the species has not been found at all and is now considered extinct on Viti Levu (Palmeirim et al. 2007). Thus, extinction is an ongoing phenomenon on Viti Levu.

These new discoveries shed some light on the origin of the Fiji fauna, and that of Viti Levu in particular. As noted above, the affinities of the Fijian avifauna are generally held to be with Samoa and Tonga (Watling 1982; Steadman and Franklin 2000; Steadman 2006a). However, the former presence of the crocodilian, tortoise and three frogs, along with the megapodes and the giant pigeon, all indicate a western relationship for the older, endemic component of the fauna of Viti Levu, as centres of abundance of these taxa and/or their nearest relatives lie to the west. The duck and the snipe probably have an Australasian derivation.

The fossil fauna of Vatulele

Most of the fossil faunas located in caves on Vatulele arise from predation by the barn owl *Tyto alba* so most species are its preferred prey. Reptiles were very common in these prey assemblages, with hundreds of geckos present, represented mainly by *Gehyra oceanicus* and some *Nactus pelagicus*. Also present were some skinks large enough to be the green tree skink *Emoia concolor*, rare banded iguanas *Brachylophus ?bulabula*, and rarely, small boas *Candoia bibroni*. However, the most obvious component of the owl faunas were rats. Three species were present, with the Pacific rat *Rattus exulans* most common. The larger, European species *R. norvegicus* and *R. rattus* were always present, clearly indicating that these owl deposits mainly post-dated European arrival. Even the subsurface deposits at Ganilao had large rat bones attributed to *R. rattus* or *R. norvegicus*, and therefore were post-European in age. However, in the small sample from the subsurface deposits, we found a single lower mandible, referred to the Fijian mastiff bat *Chaerephon bregullae*, now known only from Taveuni.

Only in sites associated with Big Cave entrances 2A and 2B and at Muremure were deposits found that could conceivably pre-date human occupation on the island. In all cases, these were small deposits attributed to single individuals on cave floors.

A total of at least 25 species of birds were recorded as fossil bones from the caves of Vatulele (Table 3). Most of these were in the owl sites. The main birds hunted by the owls were the swiftlet *Collocalia spodiopygia*, small *Ptilinopus* doves, Polynesian starling *Aplonis tabuensis* and wattled honeyeater *Foulehaio carunculata*. Other regular prey species were kingfishers *Halcyon chloris* and long-tailed cuckoos *Eudynamys taitensis*. The common presence of the latter species is interesting, as bones from the species have been not been found on mainland Viti Levu, despite several owl sites having been investigated. Moreover, it is seen only rarely on the main islands of Fiji (D. Watling, pers. comm.). Perhaps it avoids the main islands when it migrates to Fiji. The doves could be either *Ptilinopus porphyraceus* or *P. perousii*, both of which are extant on the island. They are of similar size, and the size range of the fossil bones, illustrated by humerus length in Figure 24, has an apparently normal distribution, with a few small individuals. The available reference specimens of *P. perousii* and *P. porphyraceus* fall within the size range of the fossils, which thus could be either. Other than these taxa, the owl preyed on a range of smaller passerines (undetermined) and some coastal species.

Big Cave entrances 2A and 2B and Muremure Cave provided pitfall faunas, which were dominated by bones of the purple swamp hen *Porphyrio porphyrio*, typical of the small, slender Pacific races *P. p. vitiensis* and *P. p. samoensis*, with the banded rail *Gallirallus philippensis* also common. No bones of megapodes or those of any other flightless bird were found. No bones of the frog *Platymantis* spp. were found.

Extinctions on Vatulele

Few species have demonstrably gone extinct on Vatulele. It seems likely the Fijian mastiff bat lived on the island in the past, and it is presumed extinct there. Of the birds, the swamp hen has gone extinct on Vatulele in living memory, as on Viti Levu. On Vatulele, the mongoose is absent, but the marshy areas are now cultivated, and the swamp hen population may have relied on the mainland population to offset declines in bad seasons. Now that the Viti Levu

Table 3. A list of the birds, reptiles and mammals from Vatulele Island at present and recorded here as fossils. Data for extant birds is from Dick Watling.

	Taxon	Common Name	Extant Status	Fossil
Reptiles	*Brachylophus ?bulabula*	Banded iguana	B	Y
	Skink, cf. *Emoia concolor*	Green tree skink	B	Y
	Gehyra oceanicus	Oceanic gecko	B	Y
	Nactus pelagicus	Pacific slender-toed gecko	B	Y
	Candoia bibroni	Pacific boa	B	Y
Birds	*Puffinus ?lherminieri*	Shearwater sp.	V	Y
	Puffinus pacificus	Wedge-tailed shearwater	V	Y
	Pterodroma ?brevipes	Gadfly petrel ?Collared	V	Y
	Phaethon lepturus	White-tailed tropic bird	B	Y
	Sula dactylatra	Masked booby	B	
	Sula leucogaster	Brown booby	V	
	Sula sula	Red-footed booby	B	
	Fregata ariel	Lesser frigate bird	V	
	Ardea novaehollandiae	White-faced heron	?B, V	
	Egretta sacra	Reef heron	B	
	Anas superciliosa	Pacific black duck	B	
	Circus approximans	Swamp harrier	B	
	Gallus gallus	Jungle fowl	B	Y
	Gallirallus philippensis	Banded rail	B	Y
	Porphyrio porphyrio	Purple swamphen	Locally extinct	Y
	Porzana tabuensis	Sooty crake	?	Y
	Poliolimnas cinereus	White-browed crake	?	Y
	Pluvialis fulva	Pacific golden plover	V	Y
	Tringa incana	Wandering tattler	V, common	Y
	Tringa brevipes	Siberian tattler	V, rare	
	Arenaria interpres	Ruddy turnstone	V	
	Limosa lapponica	Bar-tailed godwit	V	
	Sterna bergii	Crested tern	V	
	Sterna sumatrana	Black-naped tern	B	
	Sterna anaethetus	Bridled tern	V	
	Anous minutus	Black noddy	?B	Y
	Anous stolidus	Common noddy	B	Y
	Gygis alba	White tern	B	
	Columba vitiensis	White-throated pigeon	B	
	Ducula pacifica	Pacific pigeon	B	Y
	Ptilinopus porphyraceus	Crimson-crowned fruit-dove	B	Y
	Ptilinopus perousii	Many-coloured fruit dove	B	
	Gallicolumba stairii	Friendly ground dove	?locally extinct	Y
	Streptopelia chinensis	Spotted turtle dove	I	
	Vini solitarius	Collared lory	B	
	Cacomantis pyrrophanus	Fan-tailed cuckoo	?	Y

Continued on next page

Table 3 *continued*

	Taxon	Common Name	Extant Status	Fossil
Birds	*Eudynamys taitensis*	Long-tailed cuckoo	?	Y
	Tyto alba	Barn owl	B	Y
	Collocalia spodiopygia	White-rumped swiftlet	B	Y
	Hirundapus caudacutus	Spine-tailed swift/White-throated needletail	V	
	Halcyon chloris	Kingfisher	B	Y
	Mayrornis lessoni	Slaty monarch	B	
	Clytorhynchus vitiensis	Lesser shrikebill	B	?Y
	Myiagra vanikorensis	Vanikoro broadbill	B	
	?Zosterops lateralis	Grey-backed white-eye	B	Y
	Aplonis tabuensis	Polynesian starling	B	Y
	Foulehaio carunculata	Wattled honeyeater	B	Y
	Passerine sp. indet.			Y
	Acridotheres tristis	Common mynah	I	
	Acridotheres fuscus	Jungle mynah	I	
Mammals	*?Chaerephon bregullae*	?Fijian mastiff bat	Locally extinct	Y
	Emballonura semicaudata	Sheath-tailed bat	B, rare	Y
	Pteropus cf. *tonganus*	Fruit bat	B	Y
	Rattus exulans	Pacific rat	B	Y
	Rattus rattus	Black rat	B	Y
	Rattus norvegicus	Norway rat	B	Y

B, breeding; V, visitor; I, introduced species.

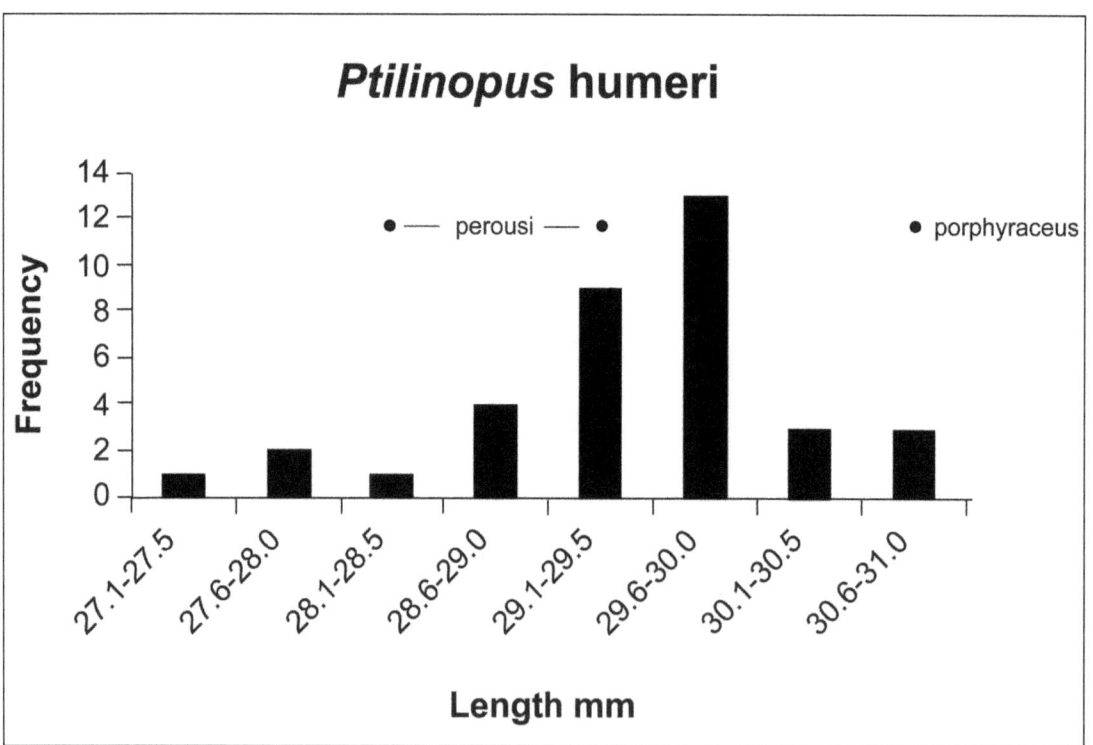

Figure 24. A frequency distribution of humerus length for *Ptilinopus* humeri from Ganilao plotted with measurements for modern specimens of two *P. perousii* and one *P. porphyraceus*.

population has gone, so has that on Vatulele. The sooty crake probably still lives on the island, though no record exists for it. At least two small rails are seen in the forest near the resort (M. Livingston, pers. comm.), and these are likely to be the banded rail and sooty crake.

The only other possibly extinct bird is the friendly ground dove. This is a shy bird of the forest and it may still be extant in the western forests of the island: Dick Watling's observations of extant fauna were mainly around the resort in the north (D. Watling, pers. comm.). However, the presence of abundant mammalian predators (cats, black rats and Norway rats) militates against this possibility, as this dove has been found to be susceptible to these predators in many other places.

The absence of fossils suggest megapodes were absent from Vatulele, as these ground-frequenting birds surely would have been in the deposits if they were present on the island. Two species of megapodes have been found on Viti Levu, and a further species was present on islands in the Lau Group (Worthy et al. 1999; Worthy 2000a).

Differences from the Viti Levu fauna

The fossil faunas from Viti Levu include a number of distinctive extinct endemic species. These include a crocodilian, a giant iguana, a new giant frog to add to the two species already known (Worthy 2001a; Worthy et al. 1999), a giant megapode, and another weakly flightless one (Worthy 2000a), a giant flightless pigeon and a new large *Ducula* species (Worthy 2001b), a new flightless rail *Vitirallus watlingi* (Worthy 2004), a small duck, and a snipe *Coenocorypha miratropica* (Worthy 2003). The terrestrial giants and the frogs appear to be or have been restricted to Viti Levu and nearshore islands that were connected to it during low sea levels of the Pleistocene. None of these taxa were recorded from Vatulele, which is about 30 km distant. The deep intervening water (>250 m) would have ensured Vatulele was an island throughout the Pleistocene glacial–interglacial cycles.

The species that constitute the fauna on Vatulele are all good dispersers. The arboreal iguana, boa, skinks and geckos, for example, could easily have arrived on trees washed down the Sigatoka River during cyclones. Large trees remained on the Vatulele reef in November 1999 from the last cyclone, and Worthy was told they arrived only two days after the storm. The birds are all highly volant taxa, and characteristic of the many small atoll islands in Fiji and elsewhere in the South Pacific (Steadman 2006a). However, the terrestrial species from Viti Levu have not populated Vatulele, so presumably 30 km of water was an effective barrier.

The lack of any distinct species on Vatulele suggests this island has not been isolated for any great length of time in a form capable of supporting a fauna. In comparison, Henderson Island in the southeast Pacific first emerged only 380 kyr ago (Blake 1995), yet three endemic pigeons and a sandpiper have evolved in that period (Wragg 1995; Wragg and Worthy 2006; Worthy and Wragg 2003, 2008). The lack of any distinct species, particularly of flightless forms, on Vatulele suggests that its subaerial history may be quite short indeed. This provides some support for the relatively recent history of rising land suggested by (Nunn 1998). However, if the true age of Vatulele lies somewhere between the contrasting scenarios outlined above, it is possible that during the last interglacial high stand of sea level, the island was mostly, if not entirely, inundated. Only a small area of the present Naura cliff may have been emergent, an area insufficient to support a diverse terrestrial fauna. Moreover, such a small and low island could have had its fauna periodically removed by storm events. Thus, the present fauna may have a history no older than 70–80 kyr BP. Investigations to better date the antiquity of Vatulele, such as dating the speleothems in the wave-cut notches or in caves, are needed to test this suggestion.

Appendix: Vatulele fauna from Big Cave, Ganilao, Korolamalama and Muremure

Trevor H. Worthy

School of Biological, Earth and Environmental Sciences, The University of New South Wales

Appendix: Table 4. Faunas from the fossil sites on Vatulele. Big Cave System. This cave system comprises two discrete sections of cave now separated by collapsed rockfalls. Fossils were found mainly associated with entrances 2A and 2B. The faunas are listed by the sites they were collected from. All fossils were on the surface. Values are NISP/MNI.

Taxon	Name	Entrance 2A area	SW passage off 2A	2B, Gavin's Site	2B, Talus slope	2B, Isolated sites	2B, Dry rim-stone pool	2B, Dry sandy pool	Big Cave main Ent.
Brachylophus fasciatus	Banded iguana			9/1					
Candoia bibroni	Boa			2/1				6 vert	
Skink, cf *Emoia concolor*	Green skink			1 bone					
Gecko sp. indet	Gecko								Y
Puffinus pacificus	Wedge-tailed shearwater	17/1							
Porphyrio porphyrio	Purple swamp hen		1/1, 30/1	90/4	45/2	1/1	3/1	62/1, x/1	
Gallirallus philippensis	Banded rail		6/1, 16/1, 2/1	75/5	29/3		45/2	34/2, x/1	
Porzana tabuensis	Sooty crake			5/1					
Gallus gallus	Chicken				7/1				
Tyto alba	Barn owl				2/1				
Ptilinopus porphyraceus	Crimson-crowned fruit-dove				3/2				
Gallicolumba stairii	Friendly ground-dove	1/1	2/1	2/1		7/1, 1/1			
Eudynamys taitensis	Long-tailed cuckoo								21/1
Aplonis tabuensis	Polynesian starling		4/1						1/1
Foulehaio carunculata	Wattled honeyeater								1/1
Passerine sp. indet.				Yes	Yes				Yes
Pteropus tonganus	Fruit bat	1 dentary							
Emballonura semicaudata	Sheath-tailed bat			7 bones				20 bones	28 bones
Rattus exulans	Pacific rat		Y	74 bones	196 bones		53 bones		Skeleton
Rattus rattus	Black rat		Y						
Rattus rattus /norvegicus	Norway rat		Y	12 bones	30 bones		5 bones		

Appendix: Table 4 *continued*. List of species from the Ganilao barn owl midden. Faunas are listed here from the five separate samples. Values are NISP/MNI.

Taxon	Common name	Surface	Test pit 0–5 cm	Test pit 5–10 cm	Test pit 10–15 cm	Damp alcove
Brachylophus fasciatus	Banded iguana	28/1				9 bones
Skink, cf *Emoia concolor*	Green tree skink	34 bones			1 bone	1 bone
Gehyra oceanicus	Oceanic gecko	100s/94	30 bones	10 bones	8 bones	68/6
Nactus pelagicus	Pacific slender-toed gecko	X/26				3 bones
Gecko species						X/2
Puffinus sp. ?lherminieri	?Audubon's shearwater					1/1
Pterodroma ?brevipes	White-winged petrel	5/2			4/1	
Phaethon lepturus	White-tailed tropic bird	7/2				
Pluvialis fulva	Lesser golden plover	4/1				
Anous minutus	Black noddy	5/1		2/1	1/1	1/1
Anous stolidus	Common noddy	8/4			2/1	14/4
Tringa incana.	Wandering tattler	2/1		1/1		
Gallirallus philippensis	Banded rail	25/6				7/2
Porzana tabuensis	Sooty crake					2/1
Poliolimnas cinereus	White-browed crake	4/1				
Tyto alba	Barn owl	2/1				
Ducula pacifica	Pacific pigeon	9/2	1/1			
Ptilinopus porphyraceus	Crimson-crowned fruit-dove	447/33	11/2	1/1		46/5
Gallicolumba stairii	Friendly ground dove	54/6				12/3
Cacomantis pyrrophanus	Fan-tailed cuckoo		3/2			
Eudynamys taitensis	Long-tailed cuckoo	66/7	4/1			13/3
Halcyon chloris	Kingfisher	31/5	1/1		2/1	9/2
Collocalia spodiopygia	Swiftlet	451 bones	20 bones	9 bones	8 bones	81 bones
Aplonis tabuensis	Polynesian starling	158/15	3/1	2/1	2/1	13/3
Foulehaio carunculata	Wattled honeyeater	87/8				3/1
?Zosterops lateralis	Grey-backed white-eye	4/1				6/2
?Clytorhynchus vitiensis	Lesser shrikebill					1/1
Passerine sp.		2 spp.	Yes			Yes
?Chaerephon bregullae	?Fijian mastiff bat			R dentary		
Emballonura semicaudata	Sheath-tailed bat	120 bones	7 bones	1 bone	4 bones	11 bones
Rattus exulans	Pacific rat	X/100s	100s/20	100s/5	X/1	100s
Rattus rattus	Black rat	X/23				X/1
Rattus norvegicus	Norway rat	X/10				X/3
Rattus rattus /norvegicus	Black or Norway rat		30 bones	6 bones		

Appendix: Table 4 *continued*. List of specimens from Korolamalama Cave owl midden. Values are NISP/MNI.

Taxon	Common name	Specimens
Gehyra oceanicus	Oceanic gecko	100+
Nactus pelagicus	Pacific slender-toed gecko	1
Gallirallus philippensis	Banded rail	2/1
Gallus gallus	Chicken	9/1
Tyto alba	Barn owl	8/1 juv
Ptilinopus porphyraceus	Crimson-crowned fruit-dove	90/11
?Cacomantis pyrrophanus	?Fan-tailed cuckoo	4/1
Aplonis tabuensis	Polynesian starling	75/7
Foulehaio carunculata	Wattled honeyeater	51/6
Passerine sp.		Yes
Emballonura semicaudata	Sheath-tailed bat	30 bones
Rattus exulans	Pacific rat	100s
Rattus rattus	Black rat	X/16
Rattus norvegicus	Norway rat	Nil

Appendix: Table 4 *continued*. List of faunas from Muremure Cave. Fossils are listed under each discrete site they were found in. Values are NISP/MNI.

Taxon	Common name	Site 1	Site 2	Site 3	Site 4	Site 5	Owl site
Brachylophus fasciatus	Banded iguana		1/1				
Porphyrio porphyrio	Purple swamp hen	27/2		30/1	3/1, 1/1	22/1	
Gallirallus philippensis	Banded rail	7/2				4/1	
Porzana tabuensis	Sooty crake			3/1			
Tyto alba	Barn owl						12/2
Ptilinopus porphyraceus	Crimson-crowned fruit-dove						9/2
Gallicolumba stairii	Friendly ground dove			5/1			
Eudynamys taitensis	Long-tailed cuckoo						3/1
Aplonis tabuensis	Polynesian starling						4/1
Foulehaio carunculata	Wattled honeyeater						3/2
Rattus exulans	Pacific rat						40 bones
Rattus rattus /norvegicus	Black or Norway rat						23 bones

References

Anderson, A.J. 1996. Te whenua hou: Prehistoric Polynesian colonisation of New Zealand and its impact on the environment. In: Hunt, T.H. and Kirch, P.V. (eds), *Historical ecology in the Pacific Islands*, pp. 271–283. Yale University Press, Yale.

Anderson A.J. and Clark, G.R. 1999. The age of Lapita settlement in Fiji. *Archaeology in Oceania* 34: 31–39.

Anderson, A.J., Clark, G. and Worthy, T.H. 2000. An inland Lapita site in Fiji. *Journal of the Polynesian Society* 109: 311–316.

Balouet, J.C. 1991. The fossil vertebrate record of New Caledonia. In: Rich, P.V., Monaghan, J.M., Baird, R.F., Rich, T.H., Thompson, E.M. and Williams, C. (eds), *Vertebrate palaeontology of Australasia*, pp. 1383–1409. Pioneer Design Studio, Melbourne.

Balouet, J.C. and Buffetaut, E. 1987. *Mekosuchus inexpectatus* n. g., n. sp., Crocodilien nouveau de l'Holocene de Nouvelle Caledonie. *Comptes Rendus de l'Academie des Sciences, Paris* 304: 853–857.

Balouet, J.C. and Olson, S.L. 1987. An extinct species of giant pigeon (Columbidae: Ducula) from archaeological deposits on Wallis (Uvea) Island, South Pacific. *Proceedings of the Biological Society of Washington* 100(4): 769–775.

Balouet J.C. and Olson, S.L. 1989. Fossil birds from late Quaternary deposits in New Caledonia. *Smithsonian Contributions to Zoology* 469: 1–38.

Baumel, J.J. and Witmer, L.M. 1993. Osteologia. In: Baumel, J.J., King, A.S., Breazile, J.E., Evans, H.E and Vanden Berge, J.C. (eds), *Handbook of avian anatomy: Nomina Anatomica Avium*, pp. 45–132, Second Edition. Publications of the Nuttall Ornithological Club 23. Cambridge, Massachusetts.

Best, S. 1981. Excavations at site VL 21/5, Naigani Island, Fiji. A preliminary report. Department of Anthropology, University of Auckland.

Blake, S.G. 1995. Late Quaternary history of Henderson Island, Pitcairn Group. *Biological Journal of the Linnean Society* 56: 43–62. [Reprinted as: *The Pitcairn Islands: Biogeography, ecology and prehistory*. Edited by Benton, T.G. and Spencer, T., Academic Press, 1995]

Clunie, F. 1972. A contribution to the natural history of the Fiji peregrine. *Notornis* 19: 302–322.

Clunie, F. 1976. A Fiji peregrine (*Falco peregrinus*) in an urban-marine environment. *Notornis* 23: 8–28.

Flannery, T.F. 1995. *Mammals of the South-west Pacific and Moluccan Islands*. Reed Books in association with the Australian Museum.

Goodwin, D. 1967. *Pigeons and doves of the world*. Trustees of the British Museum (Natural History), London.

Holdaway, R.N. 1999. Introduced predators and avian extinction in New Zealand. In: MacPhee, R.D.E. (ed), *Extinctions in near time: Causes, contexts, and consequence*, pp. 189–238. Advances in Paleobiology. Plenum Press, New York.

Holdaway, R.N., Worthy, T.H. and Tennyson, A.J.T. 2001. A working list of breeding bird species of the New Zealand region at first human contact. *New Zealand Journal of Zoology* 28(2): 119–187.

James, H.F. and Olson, S.L. 1991. Descriptions of thirty-two new species of birds from the Hawaiian Islands: Part 2. Passeriformes. *Ornithological Monographs* 46: 1–88.

Jones, D.N., Dekker, R.W.R.J. and Roselaar, C.S. 1995. *The megapodes, Megapodiidae*. Bird families of the World, Oxford University Press.

Keogh, J.S., Edwards, D.L., Fisher, R.N. and Harlow, P.S. 2008. Molecular and morphological analysis of the critically endangered Fijian iguanas reveals cryptic diversity and a complex biogeographic history. *Philosophical Transactions of the Royal Society of London B* 363: 3413–3426.

Kirchman, J.J. and Steadman, D.W. 2005. Rails (Aves: Rallidae: *Gallirallus*) from prehistoric sites in the Kingdom of Tonga, including a description of a new species. *Proceedings of the Biological Society of Washington* 118: 465–477.

Kirchman, J.J. and Steadman, D.W. 2006a. New species of rails (Aves: Rallidae) from an archaeological site on Huahine, Society Islands. *Pacific Science* 60: 281–297.

Kirchman, J.J. and Steadman, D.W. 2006b. Rails (Rallidae: *Gallirallus*) from prehistoric archaeological sites in Western Oceania. *Zootaxa* 1316: 1–31.

Kirchman, J.J. and Steadman, D.W. 2007. New species of extinct rails (Aves: Rallidae) from archaeological sites in the Marquesas Islands, French Polynesia. *Pacific Science* 61: 145–163.

Koopman, K.F. and Steadman, D.W. 1995. Extinction and biogeography of bats on 'Eua, Kingdom of Tonga. *American Museum Novitates* 3125: 1–13.

Livezey, B.C. 1993. An ecomorphological review of the dodo (*Raphus cucullatus*) and solitaire (*Pezophaps solitaria*), flightless Columbiformes of the Mascarene Islands. *Journal of Zoology London* 230: 247–292.

Mead, J.I., Steadman, D.W., Bedford, S.H., Bell, C.J. and Spriggs, M. 2002. New extinct mekosuchine crocodile from Vanuatu, South Pacific. *Copeia* 2002(3): 632–641.

Molnar, R.E., Worthy, T.H. and Willis, P.M.A. 2002. An extinct Pleistocene endemic Mekosuchine crocodylian from Fiji. *Journal of Vertebrate Paleontology* 22(3): 612–628.

Nunn, P.D. 1998. Uplift of islands along the Vatulele-Beqa ridge. In: *Pacific Island landscapes*. Institute of Pacific Studies, The University of the South Pacific, Suva, Fiji.

Olson, S.L. and James, H.F. 1991. Descriptions of thirty-two new species of birds from the Hawaiian Islands: Part 1. Non-Passeriformes. *Ornithological Monographs* 45: 1–88.

Palmeirim, J.M., Champion, A., Naikatini, A., Niukula, J., Tuiwawa, M., Fisher, M., Yabaki-Gounder, M., Thorsteinsdóttir, S., Qalovaki, S. and Dunn, T. 2007. Distribution, status and conservation of the bats of the Fiji Islands. *Oryx* 41(4): 509–519.

Pernetta, J.C. and Watling, D. 1979. The introduced and native terrestrial vertebrates of Fiji. *Pacific Science* 32: 223–244.

Poplin, F. and Mourer-Chauviré, C. 1985. Sylviornis neocaledoniae (Aves, Galliformes, Megapodiidae), Oiseau géant éteint de L'ile des Pins (Nouvelle-Caledonie). *Geobios* 18: 73–97.

Pregill, G.K. 1993. Fossil lizards from the late Quaternary of 'Eua, Tonga. *Pacific Science* 47: 101–114.

Pregill, G.K. and Dye, T. 1989. Prehistoric extinction of giant iguanas in Tonga. *Copeia* 1989: 505–508.

Pregill, G.K. and Steadman, D.W. 2004. Human-altered diversity and biogeography of South Pacific iguanas. *Journal of Herpetology* 38: 15–21.

Pregill, G.K. and Worthy, T.H. 2003. A new iguanid lizard (Squamata, Iguanidae) from the late Quaternary of Fiji, Southwest Pacific. *Herpetologica* 59: 57–67.

Quammen, D. 1996. *The song of the dodo. Island biogeography in an age of extinction*. Hutchinson, London.

Steadman, D.W. 1987. Two new species of rails (Aves: Rallidae) from Mangaia, Southern Cook Islands. *Pacific Science* 40: 27–43.

Steadman, D.W. 1989a. Extinction of birds in Eastern Polynesia: A review of the record, and comparisons with other Pacific Island groups. *Journal of Archaeological Science* 16: 177–205.

Steadman, D.W. 1989b. New species and records of birds (Aves: Megapodiidae, Columbidae) from an archaeological site on Lifuka, Tonga. *Proceedings of the Biological Society of Washington* 102(3): 537–552.

Steadman, D.W. 1992. New species of *Gallicolumba* and *Macropygia* (Aves: Columbidae). *Los Angeles County Museum of Natural History, Science Series* 36: 329–348.

Steadman, D.W. 1993. Biogeography of Tongan birds before and after human impact. *Proceedings of the National Academy of Sciences U.S.A.* 90: 818–822.

Steadman, D.W. 1994. Bird bones from the To'aga site, Ofu, American Samoa: Prehistoric loss of seabirds and megapodes. *University of California Archaeological Research Facility, Contributions* 51: 217–228.

Steadman, D.W. 1995. Prehistoric extinctions of Pacific island birds: Biodiversity meets zooarchaeology. *Science* 267: 1123–1131.

Steadman, D.W. 1999. The biogeography and extinction of megapodes in Oceania. In: Dekker, R.W.R.J., Jones, D.N. and Benshemesh, J. (eds), Proceedings of the Third International Megapode symposium. *Zoologische Verhandelingen Leiden* 327: 7–21.

Steadman, D.W. 2006a. *Extinction and biogeography of tropical Pacific birds*. The University of Chicago Press, Chicago and London.

Steadman, D.W. 2006b. A new species of extinct parrot (Psittacidae: *Eclectus*) from Tonga and Vanuatu, South Pacific. *Pacific Science* 60: 137–145.

Steadman, D.W. 2006c. An extinct species of tooth-billed pigeon (*Didunculus*) from the Kingdom of Tonga, and the concept of endemism in insular landbirds. *Journal of Zoology* 268: 233–241.

Steadman, D.W. and Franklin, J. 2000. A preliminary survey of landbirds on Lakeba, Lau Group, Fiji. *Emu* 100: 227–235.

Steadman, D.W. and Intoh, M. 1994. Biogeography and prehistoric exploitation of birds from Fais Island, Yap State, Federated States of Micronesia. *Pacific Science* 48: 116–135.

Steadman, D.W. and Rolett, B. 1996. A chronostratigraphic analysis of landbird extinction on Tahuata, Marquesas Islands. *Journal of Archaeological Science* 23: 81–94.

Steadman, D.W., Worthy, T.H., Anderson, A.J. and Walter, R. 2000. New species and records of birds from prehistoric sites on Niue, Southwest Pacific. *Wilson Bulletin* 112(2): 165–186.

Steadman, D.W. and Zarriello, M.C. 1987. Two new species of parrots (Aves: Psittacidae) from archaeological sites in the Marquesas Islands. *Proceedings of the Biological Society of Washington* 100: 518–528.

Tennyson, A. and Martinson, P. 2006. *Extinct birds of New Zealand*. Te Papa Press, Wellington.

Van Tets, G.F. 1985. *Progura gallinacea* The giant Australian megapode. In: Rich, P.V., Van Tets, G.F. and Knight F. (eds), *Kadimakara extinct vertebrates of Australia*, pp. 195–199. Pioneer Design Studio, Victoria.

Watling, D. 1982. *Birds of Fiji, Tonga and Samoa*. Millwood Press, Wellington.

White, J.P., Clark, G. and Bedford, S. 2000. Distribution, present and past, of *Rattus praetor* in the Pacific and its implications. *Pacific Science* 54(2): 105–117.

Worthy, T.H. 2000a. The fossil megapodes (Aves: Megapodiidae) of Fiji with descriptions of a new genus and two new species. *Journal of the Royal Society of New Zealand* 30: 337–364.

Worthy, T.H. 2000b. The prey of peregrine falcons *Falco peregrinus* as determined by skeletal remains from Joske's Thumb, Viti Levu. *Domodomo* 12(2)[1999]: 44–48.

Worthy, T.H. 2001a. A new species of *Platymantis* (Anura: Ranidae) from Quaternary deposits on Viti Levu, Fiji. *Paleontology* 44(4): 665–680.

Worthy, T.H. 2001b. A giant flightless pigeon gen. et sp. nov. and a new species of *Ducula* (Aves: Columbidae), from Quaternary deposits in Fiji. *Journal of the Royal Society of New Zealand* 31: 763–794.

Worthy, T.H. 2003. A new extinct species of snipe *Coenocorypha* from Viti Levu, Fiji. *Bulletin of the British Ornithologists' Club* 123(2): 90–103.

Worthy, T.H. 2004. The fossil rails (Aves: Rallidae) of Fiji with descriptions of a new genus and species. *Journal of the Royal Society of New Zealand* 34(3): 295–314.

Worthy, T.H. and Anderson, A. 1999. *Research on the caves of Viti Levu, Fiji, June 1997 – October 1998, and their significance for palaeontology and archaeology*. Report to the Fiji Museum, ANH, RSPAS, ANU, Canberra, ACT 0200, Australia.

Worthy, T.H., Anderson, A.J. and Molnar, R.E. 1999. Megafaunal expression in a land without mammals – the first fossil faunas from terrestrial deposits in Fiji (Vertebrata: Amphibia, Reptilia, Aves). *Senckenbergiana biologica* 79(2): 237–242.

Worthy, T.H. and Holdaway R.N. 2002. *The lost world of the moa: Prehistoric life of New Zealand*. Indiana University Press, Indiana.

Worthy, T.H., Walter, R. and Anderson, A.J. 1998. Fossil and archaeological avifauna of Niue. *Notornis* 45: 177–190.

Worthy, T.H., Wilde, K. and Williams, D. 1991. Anahulu Cave, Tongatapu. *New Zealand Speleological Bulletin* 8: 525–528.

Worthy, T.H. and Wragg, G.M. 2003. A new species of *Gallicolumba*: Columbidae from Henderson Island, Pitcairn Group. *Journal of the Royal Society of New Zealand* 33: 769–793.

Worthy, T.H. and Wragg, G.M. 2008. A new genus and species of pigeon (Aves: Columbidae) from Henderson Island, Pitcairn Group. In: Clark, G.R., Leach, F. and O'Connor, S. (eds), *Islands* of inquiry: Colonisation, seafaring and the archaeology of maritime landscapes*, pp. 499–510. Terra Australis 29. ANU EPress, Canberra.

Wragg, G.M. 1995. The fossil birds of Henderson Island, Pitcairn Group: Natural turnover and human impact. *Biological Journal of the Linnean Society* 56: 405–414. [Reprinted as: *The Pitcairn Islands: Biogeography, ecology and prehistory.* Edited T. G. Benton and T. Spencer. Academic Press, 1995.]

Wragg, G.M. and Weisler, M.I. 1994. Extinctions and new records of birds from Henderson Island, Pitcairn Group, South Pacific Ocean. *Notornis* 41: 61–70.

Wragg, G.M. and Worthy, T.H. 2006. A new species of extinct imperial pigeon (*Ducula*: Columbidae) from Henderson Island, Pitcairn Group. *Historical Biology* 18(2): 127–140.

4

Vegetation histories from the Fijian Islands: Alternative records of human impact

Geoffrey Hope
Department of Archaeology and Natural History, The Australian National University

Janelle Stevenson
Department of Archaeology and Natural History, The Australian National University

Wendy Southern
Department of Prime Minister and Cabinet, Australian Government

Introduction

The Melanesian high islands of Tertiary and Quaternary volcanic origin provide a natural laboratory for assessing the impact of human settlement on bounded habitats. In Fiji, the three largest islands, Viti Levu, Vanua Levu and Tavieuni, formed a single landmass at glacial times in the Pleistocene, while other high islands occur with a range of isolation from nearest land. Human settlement is known from about 3000 years ago from locations throughout the archipelago. The islands lie at about 16–23°S latitude in the tropical southeast trade-wind belt, and exhibit a marked zonation of climate. The eastern and southern windward coast and slopes are humid to hyperhumid and relatively aseasonal, compared with the northwest lee slopes which have a pronounced dry season (though not as extreme as that of Hawaii). Annual rainfall varies from 13,300 mm at 800 m on the crestal ridge of Tavieuni, to 880 mm on the coast of northeastern Vanua Levu.

The vegetation at the time of European arrival reflected that climate, with *Sporobolus indicus* grasslands or shrublands of disturbance plants (*talasiga*), as well as woodlands of *Casuarina* and *Santalum* widespread on the drier areas of the large islands (Mueller-Dombois and Fosberg

1998). In many places the *talasiga* occurs on slopes where the original topsoil layer has been lost through erosion. Dry tropical forests of *Fagraea gracilepes*, Myrtaceae, legumes and Euphorbiaceae are present today only as remnants. Disturbance is more limited on the southern and eastern (windward) coasts, where forests dominated by Myristicaceae, *Calophyllum* and Myrtaceae prevail. It is likely that the grasslands and most of the scrubs of Fiji are anthropogenic, since rainfall is sufficient to support at least a dry rainforest throughout the region (Ash 1992). This presumption can be tested by studying sedimentary sequences in swamps and alluvial fills using palaeoenvironmental techniques, as it is possible to compare Holocene pre-human sequences with the post-settlement effects, given that humans arrived relatively late to the Central Pacific (Spriggs 1997).

Swamps often build up deposits over thousands of years and sediment cores from these can be analysed for pollen, phytoliths, charcoal, algae and the various inorganic components such as inwashed soil or carbonates. Samples are taken at close intervals for analysis, allowing a picture of change in the swamp and surrounding landscape over time. Changes in cores can be radiocarbon dated using peat, wood, charcoal or shell samples. These analytical techniques have proven powerful in establishing the impact of phenomena such as cyclones, fires or volcanic ash falls on the stability of the natural vegetation. But they can also discern the effects and timing of human disturbance on the surrounding environment at the same time as establishing the nature of local resources available to human settlements. In addition, the evidence from sedimentary and palynological sequences can be used to examine proposals such as the 'AD 1300 event' argued to have been caused by significant climate shifts (Nunn 2007).

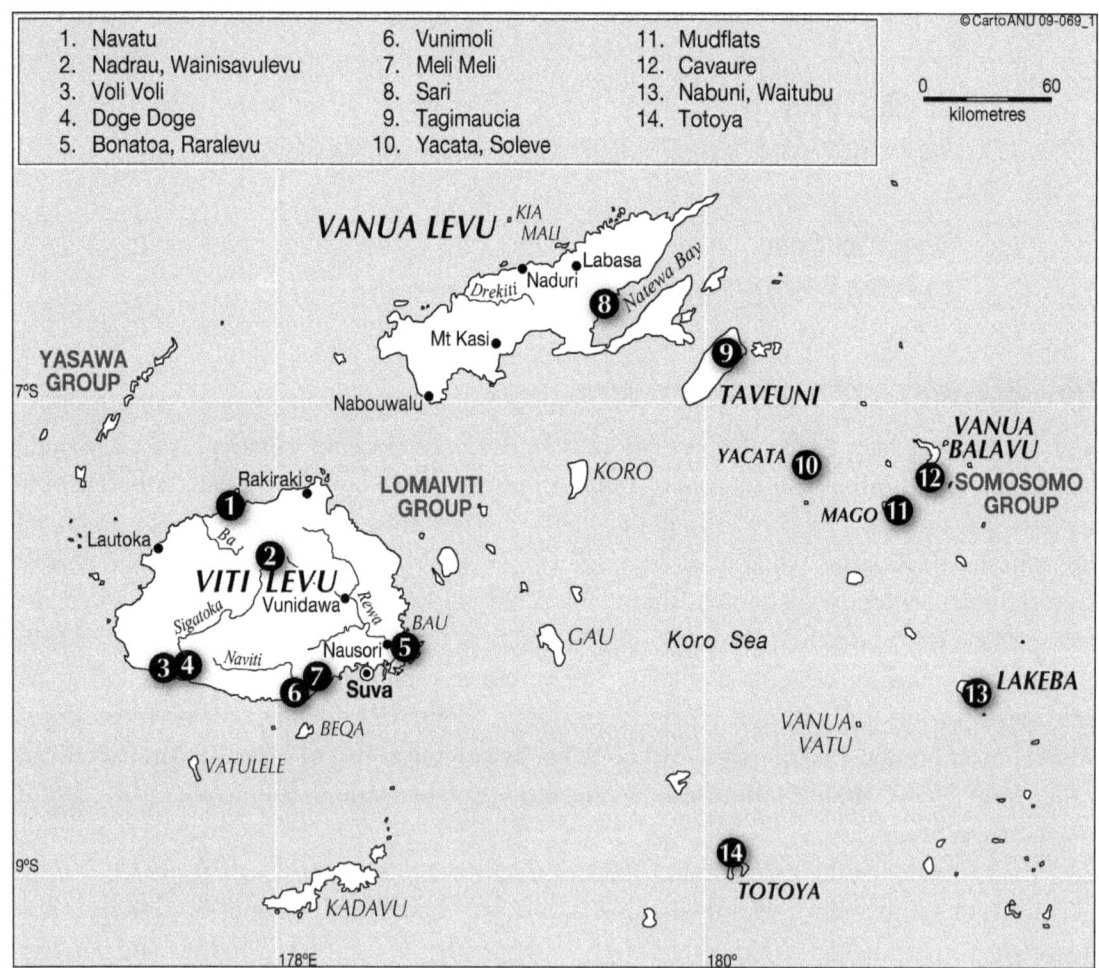

Figure 25. Location of dated mire sequences in Fiji as well as other sites mentioned in the text.

Six pollen records from Viti Levu and one from Tavieuni were prepared by Wendy Southern in her unpublished PhD (Southern 1986) and some of her results have been summarised by Geoff Hope (1996) and Hope et al. (1998). Additional sites on Viti Levu and Vanua Levu were collected by Hope and Atholl Anderson in 1996, and in Lau cores were collected by Muriel Brookfield in 1980 (Latham et al. 1983) and by Hope, Patrick Nunn and Geoffrey Clark in 1997 and 2000 (Clark and Hope 2001). Anthony Cole studied six short estuarine cores covering the past 2000 years from the southern island of Totoya for his PhD at Massey University (Cole 1996; Clark and Cole 1997; Clark et al. 1999).

This chapter outlines progress in the interpretation of the palaeoecological record from Fiji. Southern's pioneering work allowed us to develop pollen recognition of important elements in the Fijian flora more quickly than otherwise would have been possible, but a continuing effort by Janelle Stevenson, aided by Mike Macphail (ANU), has been necessary to improve our taxonomic recognition of the complex flora. In all, 23 sites have been sampled and dated, although analyses of some cores are not complete (Table 5, Figure 25). Some critical levels in Southern's sites have been redated using material from her original cores.

In the following discussion, calibrated ages before present (cal. BP) will be used. The records can be divided into three groups, based on the type of sedimentary record and its location.

1. Humid montane mires and lakes with long records.
2. Infilled coastal swamps and alluvial fills.
3. Non-estuarine mires with short records.

Table 5. Sites with dated and pollen analysed sequences from Fiji. Waitubu and Nabuni on Lakeba Island are charcoal records only as the pollen recovered was sparse. The analysis of Cavaure has not been completed.

Site name	Altitude	Location	Site type	Setting	Cal. age range (ka)	Analyst
Lake Tagamaucia	680	Tavieuni	1	Fault lake	0–17	W. Southern
Wainisavulevu	720	Nadrau Plateau, Viti Levu	1	Buried peat	24–29	W. Southern
Bonatoa Swamp	4	Rewa delta, Viti Levu	2a	Infilled estuary	0–5.8	W. Southern
Meli Meli	1	Navua delta, Viti Levu	2a	Infilled estuary	0–5	W. Southern
Raralevu	1	Rewa delta, Viti Levu	2a	Infilled estuary	0–2.2	W. Southern
Vunimoli	1	Navua delta, Viti Levu	2a	Infilled estuary	0–3	W. Southern
Sari	1	Natewa Bay, Vanua Levu	2b	Infilled estuary	0–6.5	J. Stevenson
Navatu	4	Raki Raki, Viti Levu	2b	Infilled estuary	0–4.5	J. Stevenson
Volivoli	2	Sigatoka delta, Viti Levu	2b	Sand plain lagoon	0–5.8	D. O'Dea
Yacata	2	Yacata Is, Cakadrove	2c	Infilled karst	0–6.5	D. O'Dea
Soleve	2	Kaibu Is, Cakadrove	2c	Infilled karst	0–7.9	D. O'Dea
Mudflat	2	Mago Is, Lau	2c	Infilled karst	5–7	D. O'Dea
Cavaure	0	Namalata, Vanua Balavu, Lau	2c	Mangrove karst	0–6	G. Hope
Mangrove sites (six)	1	Totoya Is	3b	Infilled estuaries	0–2.2	A. Cole
Nadrau Swamp	680	Nadrau Plateau, Viti Levu	3a	Sedge swamp	0–2.2	W. Southern
Doge Doge	8	Sigatoka valley, Viti Levu	3a	Sedge swamp	0–2.2	D. O'Dea
Nabuni	23	Lakeba Is, Lau	3c	Valley fill	0.8–2	G. Hope
Waitubu	43	Lakeba Is, Lau	3c	Valley fill	0.5–2	G. Hope

1. Humid montane mires and lakes

Lake Tagamaucia (Southern 1986; Hope 1996) is a shallow lake on the windward slope of Tavieuni Island at an altitude of 680 m and with a modern annual precipitation of about 11,000 mm. Southern obtained a 1340 cm core of algal muds from the lake and analysed it at 20 cm intervals. The pollen diagram extends from the late Pleistocene at 17,000 cal. BP through the Holocene to the present. She also analysed the oldest peat in Fiji, a buried deposit at Wainisavulevu, at 720 m altitude near Nadrau in the centre of Viti Levu. The 2 m bed of peat and organic-rich clay was exposed about 5 m below the surface during the construction of a dam. The top of the peat was dated to 27,000 cal. BP and the site seems to have been a swamp forest before the last glacial maximum. Twelve levels were counted from this deposit and these can be considered as extending the Tagamaucia record back beyond the Last Glacial Maximum (LGM) as the deposits occur at similar altitudes, although the Nadrau Plateau has somewhat lower precipitation than Tagamaucia. The combined record (Figure 26) provides the longest record of vegetation change from Fiji. Dating of the lacustrine sediments at Tagamaucia suggests steady accumulation until the development of floating sedgelands in the past 1000 years.

Before 15,000 BP the forests are rich in *Ascarina* and gymnosperms such as *Podocarpus*, suggesting a mist forest grew at Nadrau and around the lake, but that conditions were slightly drier than present. There are no indications of fire or other evidence for human intervention. In the Holocene Myrtaceae become dominant and *Balanops* and palms are important in the mid-Holocene. There is an increase in secondary tree taxa such as *Macaranga* in the past 1400 years, which may possibly reflect the widespread disturbance of forest at lower altitudes. This remote cloud-bound lake has remained very wet throughout its history and has not attracted any local settlement or disturbance. The humid conditions make the montane forests insensitive to minor changes in rainfall or temperature.

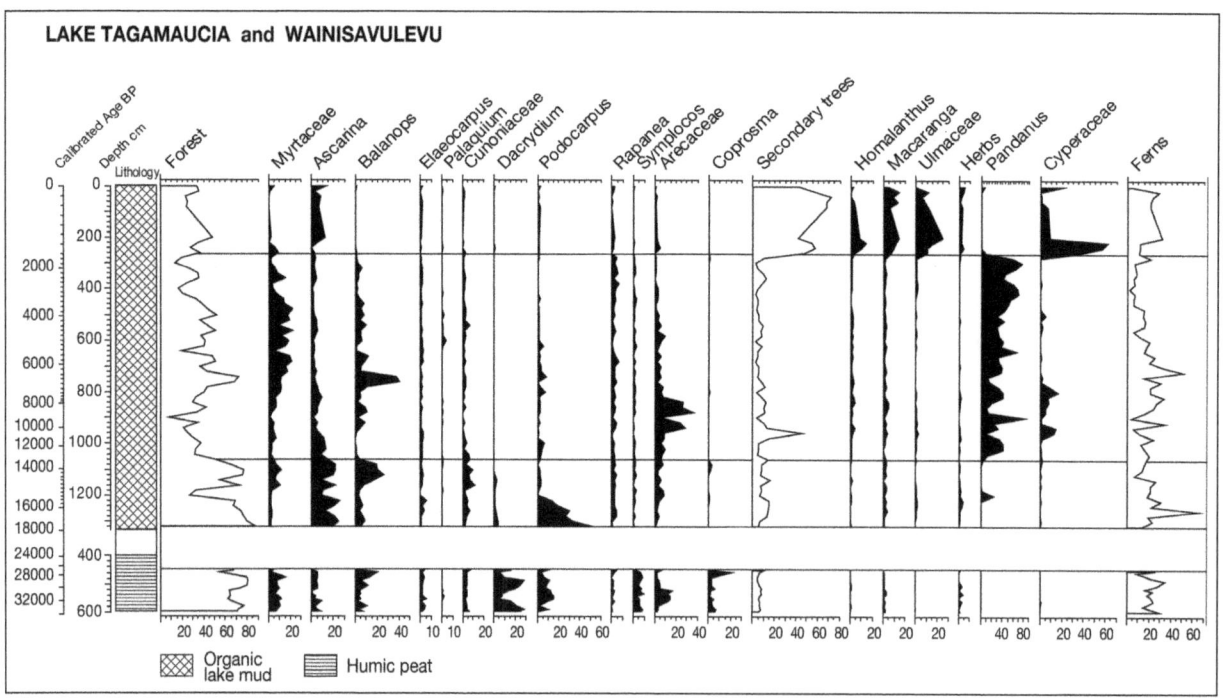

Figure 26. Summary pollen diagram combining Wainisavulevu and Tagamaucia records of Southern (1986). Hollow curves are summarising individual components. The pollen sum is dryland trees, shrubs and herbs.

2. Infilled coastal swamps and alluvial fills

The rise of sea level from 17,000 years ago culminated in a higher-than-present sea-level stand about 6500 cal. BP in the Central Pacific (Dickinson 2001). This process flooded valleys that had cut down to a base level 100 m below present and formed extensive estuaries. This rise also drowned former coral reefs, providing a phase of high-energy coasts with beach formation. Infilling of embayments, expansion of mangroves and the gradual reappearance of reefs resulted in sedimentation and lake formation along the coastline. In addition, raised base level meant flooding of low-lying areas such as solution hollows in limestones formed by raised former reefs. It is now reasonably well established that sea level has been falling since the mid-Holocene (Dickinson 2001; Nunn and Peltier 2001). This has hastened the transition from estuarine sands and muds to freshwater swamp sediments. Several of these former estuaries and flooded sinkholes have been analysed for records as they span the period of human arrival and subsequent erosion of sediment into the valleys from farmed slopes. The transition is palynologically visible because of the distinctive zonation of mangroves, saline tolerant swamp forest and freshwater species. Fiji has a limited mangrove flora, with species of *Rhizophora* and *Brugieria* (Rhizophoraceae) and *Lumnitzera* (Combretaceae) indicating frequent saline inundation. Saline or brackish flats support *Excoecaria agallocha* (Euphorbiaceae), which produces a pollen type that is dominant in some pollen diagrams. This could reflect brackish or fresh habitat and interpretation is complicated by the fact that a regrowth forest tree, *Homolanthus*, has similar pollen. Freshwater swamp woodland is reflected by the Fijian sago palm, *Metroxylon vitiense*, some *Barringtonia* species and some *Pandanus* species. Sedges (Cyperaceae) and waterlilies (*Nymphaea*) suggest more waterlogged or open pond conditions.

Here we look at the sites in three groups – the high rainfall windward coastal swamps, the seasonally dry southern and northern valley fills, and the infills and swamps in solution hollows in raised reef limestones.

The windward coast of Viti Levu and Vanua Levu

Southern studied *Bonatoa*, *Raralevu*, *Meli Meli* and *Vunimoli* swamps in southeastern Viti Levu, claiming evidence for relatively early (>3500 BP) settlement from Bonatoa Bog near the mouth of the Rewa River.

Bonatoa

Bonatoa is a peat bog today, highly disturbed and near ring forts. The basal sediments at 400–300 cm are sandy clays representing aggradation of the Rewa delta and these grade through brown clay to humic peat above 270 cm as the delta extends seawards. The peat becomes more fibrous above 170 cm, with a 2 cm band of clay at 160 cm.

The basal zone indicates a well-developed dryland forest of Myrtaceae, *Calophyllum*, palms, *Podocarpus* and *Palaquium*, while sago palm (*Metroxylon vitiensis*) dominated the swamp (Figure 27). Moderate levels of fine charcoal are present below 290 cm. Above 270 cm there is a marked decline of sago and surrounding forest elements, coincident with an increase in grasses and sedges and decreasing charcoal. These changes are most likely associated with the growth of a sedge-grass peat swamp at the site. While this may represent a natural decline in the growth of sago, it is noted that human exploitation also prevents sago from flowering and could be a cause of the plant's decline. Charcoal increases again after 200 cm, which Southern (1986) regarded as most likely having an anthropogenic origin. However, she noted that on these grounds the earlier forest decline might also reflect human clearance. She reported a modern age for a bulk sediment section at 275–300 cm, and a date of 2265 cal. BP at 240 cm (Table 6). The chronology

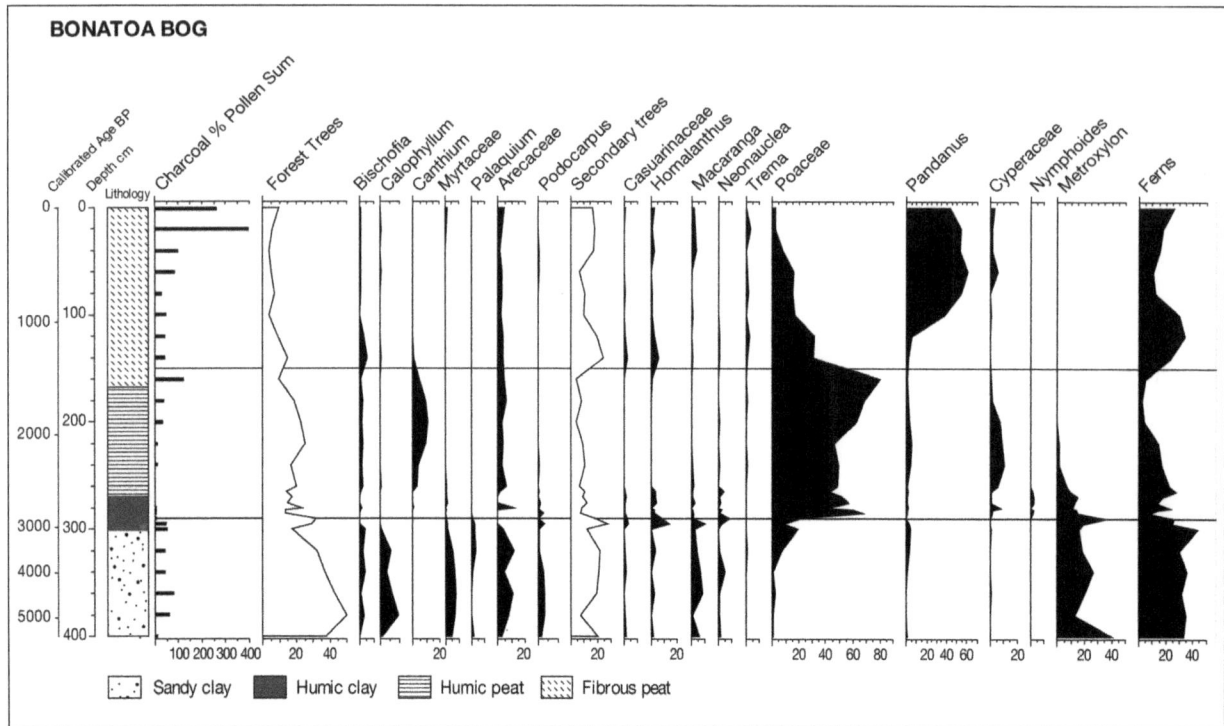

Figure 27. Summary diagram of Bonatoa Bog. Charcoal particles are calculated as a percentage of total pollen. Hollow curves are summaries incorporating individual elements.

Table 6. Radiocarbon dates from Bonotoa.

Sample	Depth (cm)	Date	Cal. age	Cal. age BP	Material Dated	Lab No
FV-BON-1	140–150	1470 ± 100	1365	1435–1290	Bulk peat	ANU 3814
FV-BON-2	230–250	2290 ± 75	2265	2365–2165	Bulk peat	ANU 3813
FV-BON-4	290	2710 ± 40	2805	2840–2770	ABA fines in silts	OZE-471
FV-BON-5	380–390	4360 ± 180	5055	5295–4810	Bulk organic clay	ANU 3816

made it difficult to guess the real age at 290 cm, where the sediment changes from clay to peat. Pretreated organic material from the original core at 290 cm has now been redated by AMS to 2800 cal. BP, showing that the considerable environmental change at this level coincides in time with the probable appearance of human settlement. Active burning of the swamp only becomes marked around 2100 BP. Within the past 800 years, bracken and *Pandanus* increase, along with charcoal and secondary trees such as *Celtis* and Euphorbiaceae. These changes may reflect increasing human use of the wetlands.

Three other swamps on the Rewa and Navua coastal plains were also investigated by Southern (1986).

Raralevu

Raralevu lies east of the Rewa river in formerly ditched and gardened swampland. The sample section was taken from a buried ditch and consists of 80 cm of peat overlying grey-brown silty clay. A date of 2030 cal. BP (2070±90, ANU 4559) was obtained from a piece of wood at 80–100 cm depth at the base of the peats.

The early ditch system seems to have been abandoned about 2000 years ago when peat starts to accumulate in the hollow. The record covers 2100 years and is interpreted as showing some forest disturbance with low burning until about 1000 years ago, when more complete clearance and local burning occurs. The site may thus record two phases of occupation for wetland agriculture.

Meli Meli

Meli Meli is an isolated *Pandanus*-fern swamp 2 km east of the Navua delta. A 5 m sequence provides a complete record of the past 5000 years (Table 7). Southern (1986) considered that the basal sands and shell hash (380–500 cm) started to accumulate in an open estuary around 5000 cal. BP. The sands gradually incorporate increasing organic material and grade to humified peat at 300 cm depth. There is a further transition after 1600 cal. BP to fibrous peat.

The record shows a sago palm forest occupied the site in its early stages as at Bonatoa, but it declined and finally disappeared around 1500 cal. BP. *Bruguiera* and other mangroves maintain a presence throughout the record, but the swamp seems to have been an open fernland, with *Pandanus* and possibly grass, set in a forested catchment. There is insufficient resolution to be certain, but no changes attributable to human disturbance are seen in the record.

Table 7. Radiocarbon dates from Meli Meli.

Sample	Depth (cm)	Date	Cal. age	Cal. age BP	Material
FV-MEL-1	190–195	1630 ± 250	1560	1302–1820	Bulk peat
FV-MEL-2	415–425	4940 ± 90	5670	5591–5754	Coral
FV-MEL-3	485–500	4400 ± 90	4960	4861–5063	Shell hash

Vunimoli Bog

Vunimoli Bog is a tall grassy sedgeland inland of Pacific Harbour, an infilled inlet of the Qaraniqio River, 7 km west of the Navua River delta that has been developed as a residential and resort area. Four beach ridges underlie the swamp (Shepherd 1990) and lie roughly parallel to the present coastline. They are below present sea level and are buried beneath a peat bog which is about 1 m deep on the east and up to 4 m deep on the west. A fifth sand ridge is higher than the others, standing about 2.5 m above MHWS and overlying buried fibrous peat that formed from before 4500 cal. BP until after 3400 cal. BP. Shepherd interpreted the front of the ridge as having been eroded by waves, and its formation above the peat argues for a construction event which moved sand shorewards. It may be the result of a storm surge or tsunami after 3000 cal. BP.

Southern worked on a shallow section on the northwest edge of Vunimoli swamp. Here, 130 cm of peat overlies a 20 cm organic palaeosol with *in situ* tree stumps built on estuarine sands at around 2820 cal. BP (2710±80, ANU 3808). Like the Rewa sites, *Metroxylon* is an important element in the early stages of swamp accumulation as part of a hardwood forest that grew on the site. Increasingly peaty conditions eventually forced *Metroxylon* to decline. The peat section has changes in surrounding forest composition from sub-coastal rainforest to a forest with more secondary species such as *Celtis* and *Trema*. This change is associated with an increase in charcoal at 60 cm, with an inferred age of 1700 cal. BP. The swamp loses *Metroxylon* and becomes dominated by sedges and ferns, along with *Pandanus*. Hence, the Navua sites appear to have had less impact from human disturbance than Bonatoa, and the changes date to 1500–1700 cal. BP.

Eastern Vanua Levu

Sari Swamp

Sari Swamp is a sedge-*Pandanus* swamp located on eastern Vanua Levu near Natewa Bay, a high rainfall location equivalent to the southeastern sites of Viti Levu. The swamp is extensive, infilling a small catchment with an area of 90 ha. A sedgeland lies inland of a complex swamp forest of *Pandanus*, which is separated from the bay by a zone of mangroves and *Excoecaria agallocha* woodland. The core site is located within the sedgeland near the southern margin of the swamp. The catchment vegetation is a mosaic of grassland, *talasiga* and dry rainforest. Dating and pollen analysis shows that the section covers the period since post-glacial sea level rise (Table 8, Figure 28).

The dating results reveal a gradual reduction in sediment accumulation rate as the site moves from a rapidly accumulating estuarine system to a coastal swamp with a small catchment. The sediment core records the transition from estuarine peaty clays before 4000 cal. BP through peaty muds that supported mangrove and sago swamp forest to fibrous peats supporting a freshwater fern swamp with evidence for catchment disturbance in the upper 57 cm (Figure 28). Charcoal appears consistently after 2700 cal. BP, followed by some evidence for forest clearance about 2350 cal. BP, at a time when mangrove pollen is also rapidly declining. Charcoal rises dramatically in association with the disappearance of most primary forest taxa after 1700 BP. The transition from estuarine to freshwater swamp after 2300 cal. BP may reflect sea-level fall or coastal progradation, but the swamp was apparently affected by fire as this change occurred and it became dominated by ferns. The period of clear human impact is contained in the upper 60 cm of the core, but it may be incomplete.

Table 8. Radiocarbon dates from Sari.

Sample	Depth (cm)	Date	Cal. age	Cal. age BP	Material	Lab No
FL-AAS-5	70	2290 ± 35	2246	2175–2355	Organic fines	Wk 20993
FL-AAS-1	125–135	2770 ± 140	2885	2500–3270	Organic fines	ANU 10112
FL-AAS-2	260–275	3800 ± 80	4200	3980–4420	Organic fines	ANU 10101
FL-AAS-3	400–418	4870 ± 140	5615	5320–5910	Organic fines	ANU 10102
FL-AAS-4	588–604	5620 ± 450	6500	5570–7430	Organic fines	ANU 10110

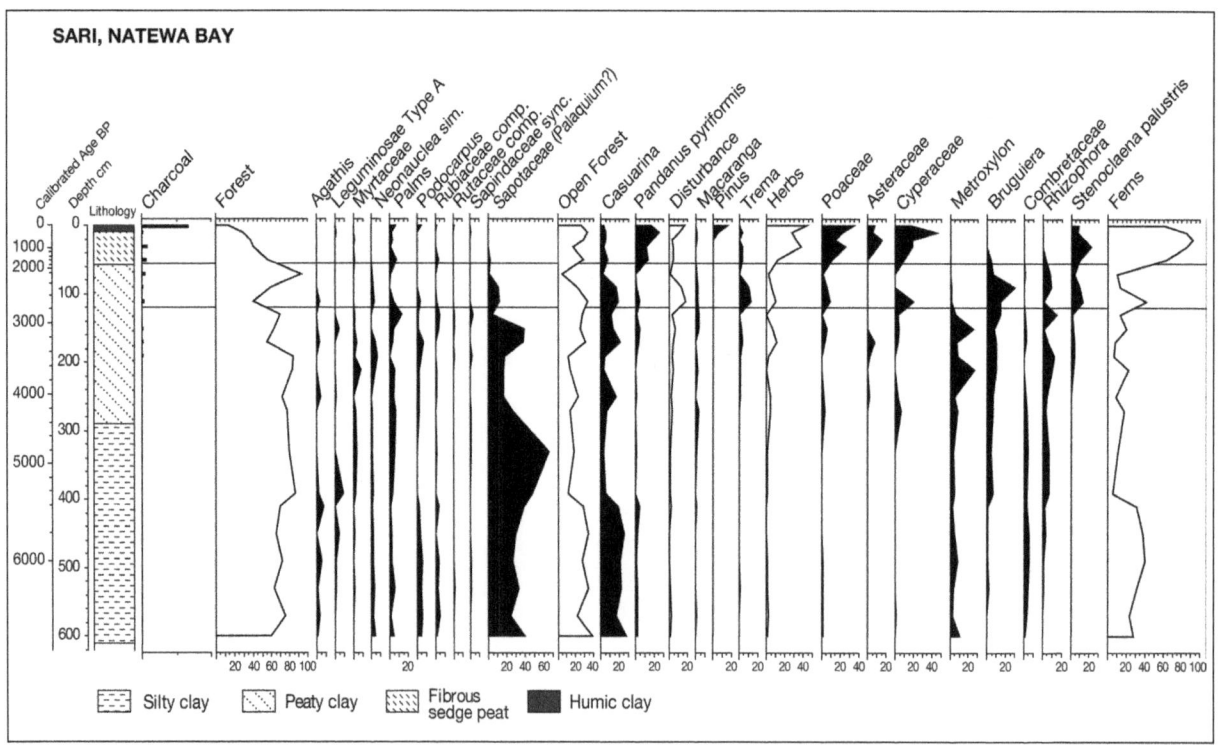

Figure 28. Summary pollen diagram from Sari Swamp, Vanua Levu.

Totoya Island estuarine cores

Anthony Cole cored six coastal mangrove swamps around Totoya Island, a crescentic high island south of Viti Levu (Cole 1996; Clark et al. 1998). The cores from Dravawal, Jigo Jigo, Keitera, Lawakile, Udu and Yaro are high-resolution cores 140–295 cm in depth that extend into estuarine muds and record the decline of already disturbed coastal forests of *Maniltoa, Aleurites,* Apocynaceae, *Calophyllum, Diospyros* and *Ficus* and increasing grass and fernland over the past 1700–2000 years. At some sites the forest is effectively lost by ca. 750 cal. BP when there are peaks in charcoal. Charcoal is present throughout all six cores and varying inputs of terrestrial sediment demonstrate continuing disturbance of the catchments.

Estuarine mires on seasonal coasts

Navatu Swamp

Navatu Swamp is on the northern coast of Viti Levu 15 km west of Rakiraki about 200 m from the sea. A swampy valley floor of red silty clay has built up behind a limestone barrier that may be an old raised reef in which a karst valley developed at a time of lower sea level. Narewa Creek, which drains the steep grassy slopes of the Kroqela Range, spreads across the valley floor. The swamp is at the base of a steep hill that has boulder rock shelters, including the Navatu 17A rock shelter, that have been investigated archaeologically by Gifford (1951) and Clark (2000), with the settlement history extending back at least 2000 years. A 450 cm section was collected from the floor of the valley about 80 m from the rock shelter 17A site. The section was composed of black organic sediments buried by 180 cm of red-brown silts and clays that are a mix of slope wash and alluvium. Samples from the upper 150 cm were collected by auger, below which D-section cores were recovered (Table 9).

The dates indicate an inversion presumably caused by the incorporation of old charcoal or wood in the slope wash. Movement of a modern humic component or young roots down profile is also demonstrated. The dates on the more organic underlying sediment are presumably more reliable. The site appears to be an infilled estuary that was buried by mixed slope-wash materials sometime after 1200 cal. BP to form a sedge swamp (Figure 29). During the estuarine phase, the vegetation is dominated by *Excoecaria*, and after about 3000 cal. BP there are only very low levels of primary rainforest or the dry forest indicator, *Casuarina*. There is a dramatic change around 160 cm when mangroves and associated taxa cease and secondary (disturbance) trees, herbs and ferns increase. This follows the change in sedimentation to inorganic clay above 187 cm. Charcoal analysis shows some charcoal over the history of the deposit, but the highest values are all above 160 cm, and suggest the sustained presence of fire within the immediate landscape. The diagram therefore seems to record a disturbed catchment with fire from possible pre-human times but with increased forest loss around 3000 years ago. Local impact on slope vegetation and a possible increased sediment load in Narewa Creek seems to have infilled the peaty swamp after 1100 cal. BP. The upper 30 cm of silts record an increase in herbs and charcoal, probably representing clearance during colonial times. However, increased resolution and dating of individual pieces of charcoal will be required to establish a more reliable chronology.

Volivoli Lagoon

Volivoli Lagoon is an intermittently flooded area of about 20 ha on the northern side of the beach ridge plain that has infilled the Sigatoka River delta where it meets a steep limestone slope. The sand plain gradually infilled a flooded former valley around 4000–5000 years ago (Anderson et al. 2006). Lapita and later settlement has been recorded from the sand plain (Dickinson et al. 1998), while a cave in the Tertiary limestone to the west above Volivoli has

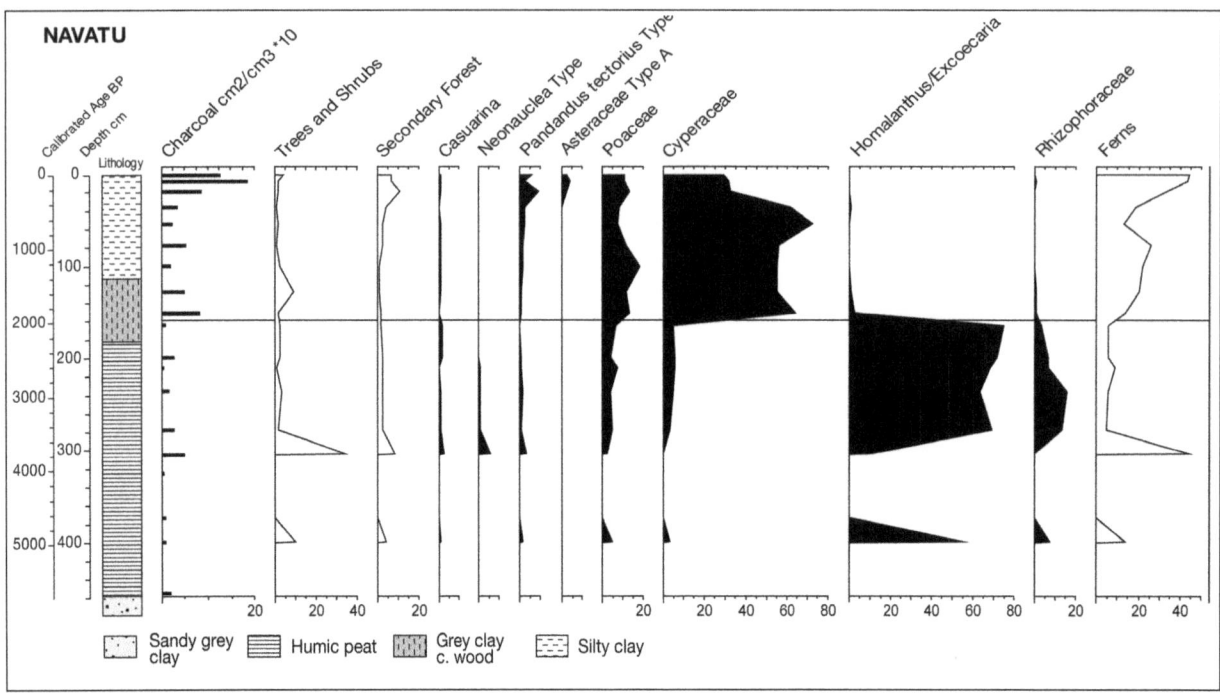

Figure 29. Summary pollen diagram from Navatu.

Table 9. Radiocarbon dates from Navatu.

Sample	Depth (cm)	Date	Cal. age	Cal. age BP	Material	Lab No
FV NAV-1	160	2630 ± 170	2770	2340–3200	Peaty clay fines NaOH insoluble from bucket auger	ANU 10762B
FV NAV-1	160	120.1 ± 5.2 Modern	0	20–270	Organic clay NaOH insoluble fraction	ANU 10762
FV NAV-2	192–204	1190 ± 80	1120	960–1280	Peaty clay fines NaOH insoluble	ANU 10761A
FV NAV-3	290–297	3370 ± 70	3640	3450–3830	Organic clay fines NaOH insoluble	ANU 10760

provided an extinct fauna including birds and reptiles (see Chapter 3). The outlet from Volivoli Lagoon is blocked by sand ridges and by the Sigatoka sandhills, a dune system derived from transported non-calcareous sands that have built up within the past 3000 years. The lagoon is shown on maps as a permanent lake, but is often dry during the dry season. The flooded area is floored by humic black clay over brown clays which overlie humic peat with wood and deltaic sands. The deepest sections occur close to the steep limestone slope on the east and may occupy former karstic depressions. Samples were taken from a pit wall in 1996, and a D-section core was obtained from 80–205 cm in 1999 to provide a more detailed sediment record (Table 10).

The dating is internally consistent and based on acid-alkali pretreated fine organics, as well as one marine and one freshwater shell date. The age at ca. 50 cm, based on freshwater molluscs hand-picked from the sediment, is older than the extrapolated age–depth curve based on the organic series. At this level, there is a strong clay disturbance signal, raising the possibility that the date is too old due to the presence of 'old' carbon in the lagoon. However, the organic dates indicate that sedimentary and charcoal changes above 140 cm pre-date known human settlement and clearance. A large correction of 1700 years would have to be applied to the terrestrial peat and shell dates to cause the age depth curve to agree with the likely settlement date, well established on the delta and beach ridges as ca. 2850 cal. BP (Dickinson et al. 1998; Burley and Dickinson 2004). If the freshwater shell date from 50 cm is rejected, then extrapolating the sedimentation rate from surface to the marine shell date at 28 cm provides an estimate for the base of the clay at 87 cm of 2400 cal. BP. The date of 4610 cal. BP at 90 cm may be incorporating older organics, and the underlying sample ages suggest there may be a significant gap in the sediment record around 90 cm. The age model used in Figure 30 assumes an extrapolated age at 90 cm of 2200 cal. BP and continuous slow sedimentation to the 113.5 cm dated level below. This is admittedly speculative, as the highly inorganic layers between 50 cm and 80 cm may have infilled more quickly than the long-term infill rate suggests.

The pollen and sediments indicate an early estuarine lake that was colonised by a backswamp forest of *Excoecaria agallocha* (but not obligate saline mangroves except possible Combretaceae) near the forested limestone cliffs. The dry forest indicators *Casuarina* and *Neonauclea* are present, suggesting a mosaic of drier and wetter forest in the catchment. The *Excoecaria* forest is replaced above 140 cm by a freshwater lagoon flora of *Nymphoides*, with *Metroxylon* and sedges possibly

Table 10. Radiocarbon dates from Volivoli Lagoon.

Sample	Depth (cm)	Date	Cal. age	Cal. age BP	Material	Lab No
FV-VOL-1	28	1010 ± 70	590*	490–690	Turbo shell	ANU 9925
FV-VOL-2	48–52	3610 ± 110	3530	3260–3800	Fine shells	ANU 9927H
FVOL99-5	89.5	4040 ± 50	4610	4420–4800	Organics	OZF531
FVOL99-6	113.5	4250 ± 50	4775	4590–4960	Organics	OZF532
FV-VOL-3	115–122	4640 ± 80	5350	5260–5585	Wood	ANU 9926
FVOL99-7	140.5	4720 ± 50	5455	5320–5590	Organics	OZF533
FVOL99-8	201	5120 ± 60	5790	5720–5860	Organics	OZF534

Notes: Organic fraction between 10 and 125µm, with Acid-Base-Acid pre-treatment. Southern hemisphere marine correction of -300yr applied prior to calibration.

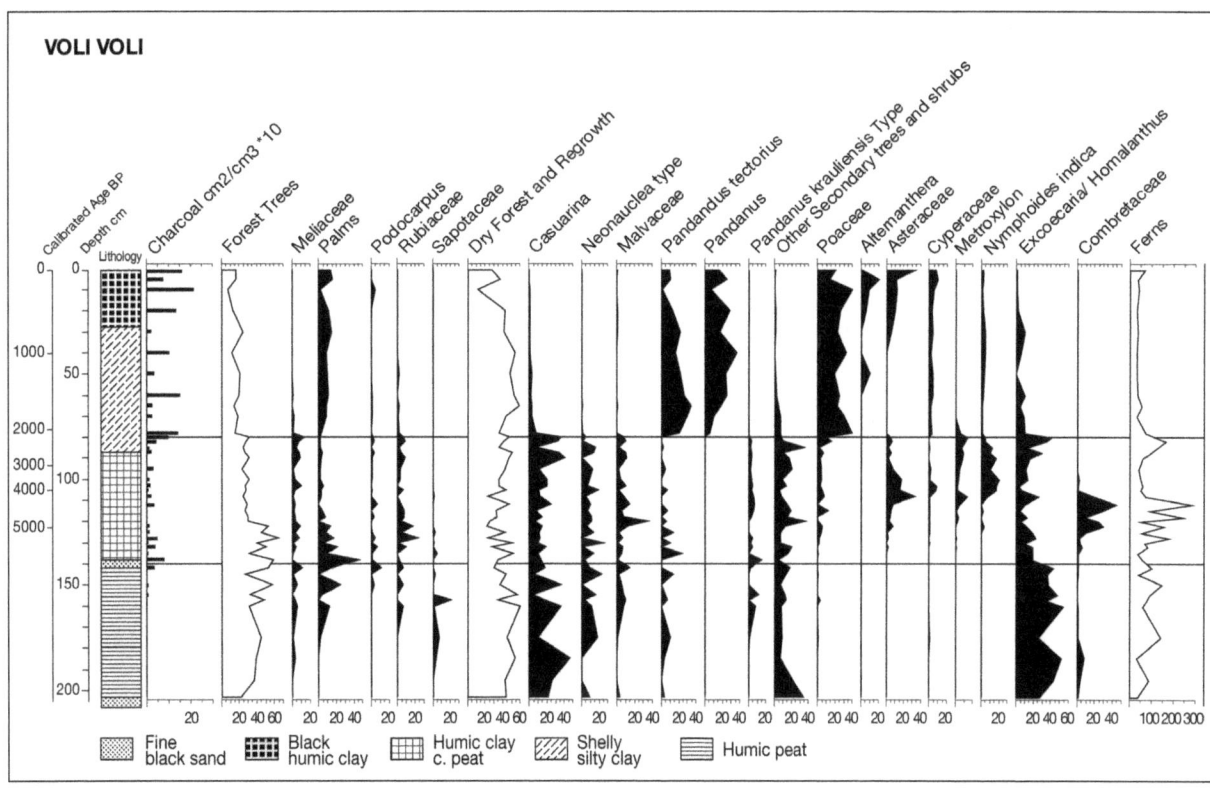

Figure 30. Summary diagram from Volivoli showing increasing charcoal and a transition to inorganic sedimentation.

reflecting blockage of the drainage by dune development. Consistent burning starts at 145 cm (5200 cal. BP) and, above this, lenses of clay alternate with peaty clays until 92 cm when peat formation ceases and the swamp is buried by 60 cm of clays. Grass and disturbance herbs such as daisies are present in significant quantities once burning begins. The lagoon then becomes more ephemeral and *Metroxylon* disappears by 80 cm, while *Pandanus*, sedges, weeds and grass increase. The clay input was derived from slope erosion in the local catchment, and possibly reflects increasing catchment fires. Above 80 cm, grass and *Pandanus* become dominant and primary forest stabilises at moderate levels. The sediment is more organic above 30 cm but has oxidised layers, suggesting a return to a fluctuating lagoonal phase but relative landscape stability. The continuing low level of primary forest and high charcoal influx indicates that the forest on the steep slope above the site was being disturbed.

Infilled karstic ponds

Pleistocene raised reefs are common in Fiji and the limestone is subject to solution that produces a karst landscape called *makatea* that has jagged ridges, dolines and closed valleys. Where the limestone is close to present sea level the dolines have often developed at times of low sea level to below the present base level. These are now infilled by lagoons, lakes and swamps or are buried by alluvium. Sites investigated at Yacata, Kaimbu, Namalata and Mago islands in eastern Cakadrove and northeastern Lau preserve several metres of organic-rich sediments below 1–3 m of terrigenous mud. The sites all have similar features in that they occupy karst depressions in raised limestone reefs just one or two metres above present sea level and usually have red or grey silty clay at the surface.

Yacata Pond

Yacata Island has a central core of volcanic soils with a fringing raised limestone *makatea* to the north and east. A Holocene beach ridge plain has extended the island by 1 km to the east where the only village is situated. The Yacata community depends for a permanent water supply on four ponds on the margins of the *makatea* and volcanics. This line of ponds appears to be a former stream valley of karstic hollows now fed by groundwater and separated by coastal sands from the sea at the southern end. Stratigraphic work was carried out on the northernmost pond at an altitude of around 3.5 m (Clark and Hope 2001). The basin sediments proved to be variable in depth, although generally deeper close to the volcanic slopes on the west. The basin is now infilled by clays derived from the volcanic interior and supports a sedge swamp which is growing in about 60 cm of standing freshwater. A core was collected from a point 80 m from the eastern margin and the clays were found to overlie several metres of organic ooze with small gastropod shells and leaves. The dating resulted in a series of internally consistent ages (Table 11).

The pollen data (Figure 31) show that the site was a deep pond from before 6500 years ago. It is uncertain whether the water was initially saline but Combretaceae pollen is present from the base. The muds on the edge of the pond were probably dominated by *Excoecaria agallocha* which is saline tolerant. The site has a very long history as a pond with a surrounding coastal forest dominated by Myrtaceae, *Macaranga* and *Casuarina*. Low levels of charcoal before 2700 cal. BP suggest that occasional fires occurred on the island in the mid-Holocene. The organic pond sediments are buried by silty clays containing greater quantities of charcoal and a significant increase in grass pollen after 2700 cal. BP. *Excoecaria* (or *Homolanthus*) remains important until 130 cm (ca. 1600 cal. BP) when the site becomes a sedge swamp. The initiation of slope erosion and a regime of burning and swamp vegetation development starts around 2700 cal. BP and the sedge swamp on silty clays is in place by 2050 cal. BP. It seems likely that this transition

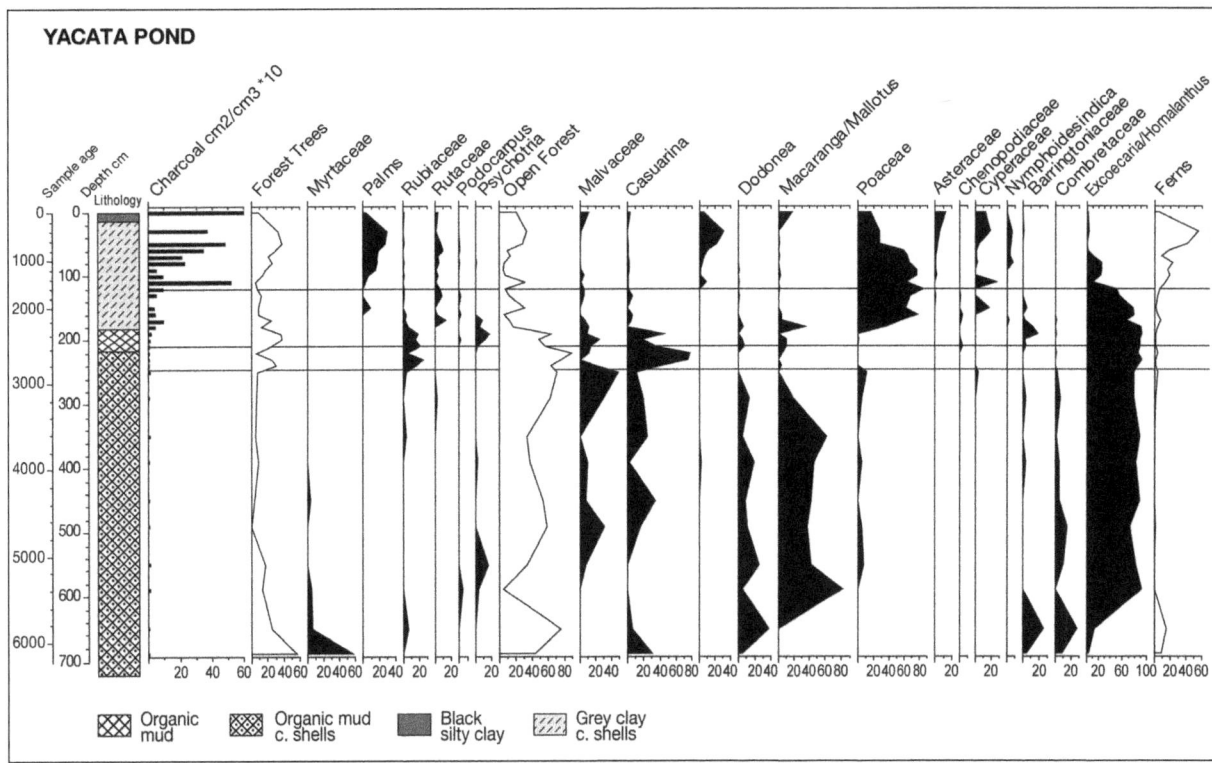

Figure 31. Summary pollen diagram from Yacata Island.

Table 11. Radiocarbon dates from Yacata Swamp.

Sample	Depth (cm)	Date	Cal. age	Cal. age BP	Material	Lab No
FL-YAK-1	140–158	2000 ± 70	1980	1810–2150	Acid insoluble shelly peat	ANU-10812
FL-YAK-7	220	2618 ± 34	2650	2735–2765	Organic fines	Wk-20994
FL-YAK-2	235–248	3370 ± 60	3635	3450–3820	Organic fines	ANU-10813
FL-YAK-6	731–745	5670 ± 470	6485	5470–7500	Organic fines	ANU-10821

is anthropogenic as it overlaps with the established archaeological record and the lake may have been an attractive resource for the first colonists. The post-settlement vegetation alternated between grass and fern dominance, and weed pollen (Asteraceae, Caryophyllaceae) is prominent throughout but increases to the present. Pollen from Ivi (Tahitian chestnut, *Inocarpus fagiferus*) is rarely preserved but this nut tree is prominent around the margins of the swamp today.

Soleve 2

Three swampy karst hollows (Sol 1–3) on Kaibu Island, a few kilometres east of Yacata, hold water after rain, one forming a permanent lagoon (Sol 3). These sites lie near the western coast at around 4 m altitude at the transition of the *makatea* to the volcanic soils and are accessible from garden areas. The swamp area may have been the main freshwater source in the past, and wells are present in two of the three basins. The basins are surrounded by a pure stand of Ivi trees about 1.2 ha in extent, growing in moist dark brown mud. The least disturbed hollow, Soleve 2, was cored, giving a similar stratigraphy to Yacata of clay overlying organic muds and clayey muds.

The pollen results show that disturbance and burning is associated with the appearance of clays above 350 cm (Clark and Hope 2001). Unfortunately, the chronology contains a significant inversion and the cause of the young age at 387 cm is unknown (Table 12). The initial clay input increases gradually above this level, representing the infill of a shallow lake which was finally buried by terrestrial sediment from the local catchment. If related to human settlement, this seems to represent less intensive use of the swamp catchment over a longer time than in the case of Yacata Swamp.

Table 12. Radiocarbon dates from Soleve 2.

Sample	Depth (cm)	Date	Cal. age	Cal. age BP	Material	Lab No
FL- KMB-2	218–230	2690 ± 240	2775	2160–3390	Fine organics in clay	ANU 10819
FL- KMB-4	380–395	1240 ± 340	1230	620–1840	Organic muds, fine fraction	ANU 10814
FL- KMB-10	771–779	7040 ± 70	7840	7700–7980	Organic muds, fine fraction	ANU 10820

Mudflat, Mago Island

The volcanic central part of Mago Island is drained eastwards by a small stream (Waitambo River) to the Butoni mudflat where the stream sinks into a doline in the marginal *makatea*. Coring at four locations on the plain established that the red clays overlie 150 cm to 320 cm of sticky grey clays with fragments of charcoal. These slope-wash sediments bury up to 5 m of peats and shelly organic lake muds with abundant wood. The main sampled site, MMF-1, lies 25 m southwest of the road bridge over the stream, at the lower end of the catchment. Similar sequences were found both closer to the exit doline and 1 km upstream, confirming the widespread nature of the deposit. Pollen and charcoal analyses were made on this sequence.

The swamp-lake phase from ca. 7500 to 5000 years ago is dominated by swamp forest that includes Araliaceae, Myrtaceae, Sapotaceae and Rubiaceae. Ferns are abundant but sedges are intermittent and no mangroves or *Excoecaria* are present. Low levels of charcoal are scattered through the section. Clay increases above 410 cm, associated with increased disturbance taxa such as *Macaranga*. Inorganic clays above 240 cm contain increased charcoal, together with grass, monolete ferns and Asteraceae, while forest elements decline abruptly. The major change in sedimentation processes at the site is possibly the result of changes to the vegetation cover of the island from forest to *talasiga*, which released clays that buried a forested peat swamp into which only minor sediment inputs from the surrounding catchment had occurred over previous centuries. The probable cause is human clearance for gardens throughout the catchment, an event that must post-date the Lapita settlement known from the island (Clark et al. 2001). However, the bulk date of 5580 cal. BP from 280 cm is much older than the likely date of human colonisation and may result from the incorporation of older organics in the clay (Table 13). If so, there may have been loss of the upper parts of the swamp sediments due to erosion. The appearance of red mottling around 185 cm depth suggests a minor soil formation event which indicates that the catchment erosion has had at least two phases. The most recent was possibly caused by the establishment of plantations and the growth of cotton and sugarcane on the riverine plain in the 19th century (Ward 2002).

The raised reef karst hollow sites so far investigated are all on the small islands of northeast Fiji but suitable sites occur elsewhere, such as saline lakes containing anoxic muds on Vanua Levu and Lakeba Island. These sites have been reported as important sources of fish as the muds are periodically disturbed, causing all the fish to surface due to anoxia. Additional karst hollows have been tested on Vanuabalavu and on nearby Namalata Island, where a 700 cm core from Cavaure sinkhole has been shown to preserve a 6500 year record of saline muds that contain marine diatoms.

Table 13. Radiocarbon dates from Mudflat-1.

Sample	Depth (cm)	Date	Cal. age	Cal. age BP	Material	Lab No
FL-MMF1-1	272–288	4920 ± 130	5580	5320–5930	Organics	ANU 11032
FL-MMF1-2	350–365	5380 ± 200	6145	5720–6570	Organics	ANU 11033
FL-MMF1-3	740–755	6810 ± 150	7685	7430–7940	Organics	ANU 11034

3. Non-estuarine mires with short records

Nadrau Swamp

Southern (1986) carried out extensive coring across a 150 ha sedge swamp at ca. 680 m on the Nadrau Plateau of Viti Levu. The site lies on the main divide of the island close to the margin of humid forest and the anthropogenic grasslands of the dry side of the island. The swamp, dominated by grasses and sedges, has colonised a side valley that was impounded behind a stream levee. It contains 2–5 m of fibrous sedge peat over 2 m of brown silty clay. A few remnant trees from former rainforest cling to the slopes around the swamp.

The basal date (Table 14) marks the start of the development of peat on an inorganic alluvium. The pollen diagram shows a rapid decline in a montane forest of *Dacrydium*, Cunoniaceae in the basal alluvium and after ca. 2200 cal. BP there is little change to the surrounding cleared area (Hope et al. 1998). Charcoal is abundant throughout and supports the pollen evidence for clearance and burning that was already occurring at the base of the section, which has an estimated age of 2200 cal. BP. People may have played a role in forming the peatland by causing slope erosion that blocked the valley and by increasing the run-off to the swamp by clearing land in the swamp catchment. Around 750 cal. BP the swamp has increased sedges and ferns and there is a slight increase in forest cover, suggesting wetter conditions or reduced impact.

Table 14. Radiocarbon dates from Nadrau Swamp.

Sample	Depth (cm)	Date	Cal. age	Cal. age BP	Material	Lab No
FV NDR-1	182	850 ± 47	745	685–800	Pollen sample	Wk 21522
FV NDR-2	472.5–482.5	2090 ± 110	2045	1924–2168	Bulk peaty clay	ANU 3810

Doge Doge Swamp

About 12 km from the mouth of the Sigatoka River in southwestern Viti Levu, Parry (1987) described a peat swamp in a tributary valley south of the Nasuto ridge and 400 m west of Nadrala village. Two sedgelands occur on separate small tributaries of Nadrala Creek, both evidently fed by springs at the base of the northern ridge. A swamp forest occupies part of the eastern swamp. The western swamp is about 5 ha in extent and dominated by a cutting sedge (*Cyperus*) with a general water depth of about 45 cm. The sedge *Elaeocharis* sp., a shrub *Melastoma* and small pools supporting waterlilies also occur. A 320 cm core was recovered from the northeastern end of the swamp, with a radiocarbon date returning an age of 2000 cal. BP at 215 cm (Table 15).

The pollen diagram (Figure 32) shows that forest had already declined at the base of the deposit, during a time of rapid local sedimentation, while grass and charcoal is increasing, suggesting continuous human disturbance of the surrounding vegetation. *Casuarina*, palms and secondary trees such as *Trema* increased after 2100 cal. BP as the immediate slopes stabilised. The swamp first supported *Metroxylon*, but later may have become a pond, evidenced by the replacement of sago palm by a woodland of *Excoecaria* which persists until very recent times,

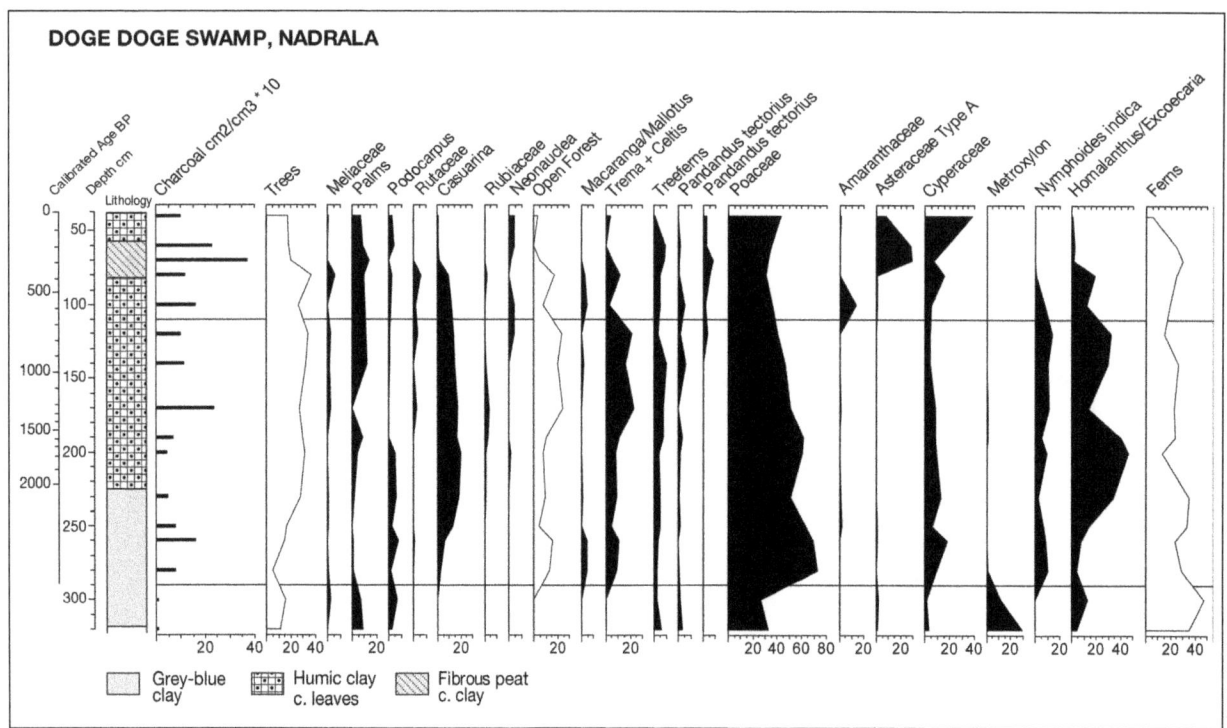

Figure 32. Summary pollen diagram from Doge Doge Swamp, Nadrala.

Table 15. Radiocarbon dates from Doge Doge Swamp.

Sample	Depth (cm)	Date	Cal. age	Cal. age BP	Material	Lab No
FV NAD1	165–178	1330 ± 130	1240	960–1520	Organic fines	ANU 10104
FV NAD2	205–225	2090 ± 160	2050	1630–2470	Organic fines	ANU 10103

when the swamp became a sedgeland. There is a marked decline in forest after 700 cal. BP. Doge Doge is a swamp confined by stream levee building that may have resulted from deforestation in the surrounding hills, which seem to have been entirely cleared by around 2000 BP. This site is effectively anthropogenic, and Nadrala Creek itself is graded to the large flood plain of the Sigatoka, suggesting that the latter might have been constructed during a period of great sediment supply.

Nabuni and Waitubu

Muriel Brookfield cored several swamps on Lakeba Island in the Lau Group in 1978 and two were selected for charcoal analysis in addition to carbon dating. Nabuni and Waitubu are swampy areas at 23 m and 43 m altitude respectively in valleys on the eastern side of Lakeba. In both, about 1 m of slightly peaty brown clays rich in charcoal overlie 5–6 m of red clays with scattered charcoal that infill valley lines. Monolete fern spores and grass pollen were found throughout but in low numbers below the upper horizon (Latham et al. 1983). Table 16 gives the radiocarbon dates, which largely reflect the age of charcoal fragments and hence may slightly overstate the age of the fires.

These records are evidence for a massive deforestation event around 2000 cal. BP in which several metres of sediment were deposited. The dating inversions probably indicate secondary remobilisation of sediment, with older sediments burying younger. The pollen data indicates that only regrowth vegetation was present and the charcoal demonstrates that fire was the cause of the instability.

Table 16. Dating the Waitubu (WTB1) and Nabuni (NMB1) valley fills on Lakeba Island.

Sample	Depth (cm)	Date	Cal. age	Cal. age BP	Material	Lab No
WTB1-1	82–100	945 ± 170	896	738–1054	Charcoal, peat	GX 5616
WTB1-2	225–240	1505 ± 165	1440	1280–1603	Charcoal	GX 5617
WTB1-3	315–335	1910 ± 210	1870	1622–2121	Charcoal	GX 4851
WTB1-4	460–490	1820 ± 150	1755	1582–1925	Charcoal	GX 5618
WTB1-5	618–638	1805 ± 140	1735	1576–1892	Charcoal	GX 4852
NMB1-1	90–105	1645 ± 105	1560	1435–1685	Charcoal	GX 5619
NMB1-2	125–150	1005 ± 145	940	790–1090	Charcoal	GX 5620

Discussion

Prehuman landscapes and vegetation

The large islands of Fiji were cooler but possibly slightly drier during glacial times. Lower sea levels tripled the land area of the largest island and probably resulted in enhanced differentiation between the windward and dry sides. While Pleistocene records from Fiji are restricted to the orographic high rainfall areas, vegetation histories from southern New Caledonia (Hope and Pask 1998; Stevenson et al. 2001; Stevenson and Hope 2005) point to natural fire and the periodic expansion of disturbance scrubs (*maquis*) on several occasions before this, suggesting climate shifts towards greater seasonality and possibly lower rainfall. Latham (1986) infers from terrace building and the formation of soil calcretes that rainfall on the dry side of New Caledonia was 30% lower than present at 25,000 cal. BP, and Hope and Pask (1998) interpret their New Caledonia records as indicating that cyclones were rare in the Pleistocene compared with the Holocene. However, Fiji is somewhat more tropical than New Caledonia and the changes there may have been less distinct.

The rapid rise of sea level from around 16,000 to 7000 cal. BP changed Fiji by drowning reefs, separating islands and flooding into river valleys (Dickinson 2009). The stratigraphies of all dated pollen sites in Fiji are shown in Figure 33, which demonstrates that many of them develop from estuaries to peat swamp under sedge or tree cover. Some sites record burial by slope wash after 2200 cal. BP. With the stabilisation of sea level around 7000 cal. BP, Fiji had a phase of beach-ridge development and estuarine infilling because the absence of mature coral reefs led to a generally higher energy coastline. As reefs developed and interfered with wave patterns, sandy coasts became lagoonal and mangroves colonised the calmer strandlines. This process took variable time to complete, but by 2000 cal. BP, reefs had reached an equilibrium, with sea level and coasts largely protected. Coastal stabilisation was accelerated by small falls in sea level around 4500 and 2200 years ago, which offset any slight isostatic sea level rises due to shelf loading by the sea. Dickinson (2009) suggests that the fall improved the liveability of some islands, particularly atolls.

At the time of first colonisation around 3000 cal. BP there were more sandy beaches and slightly less extensive but rapidly growing productive reefs. The estuaries led further inland to dense mangrove stands and swamps with abundant sago palms. Wild coconuts were most likely present along strands and sand plains. If the core chronologies are correct, the pre-3000 cal. BP records from two seasonal sites, Volivoli and Navatu, show a distinct increase in charcoal after 4500 years ago. More significantly, forest cover was evidently not continuous around either site, as herbs, grass and secondary taxa are present. This raises the possibility that the dry side of Viti

Levu was partly open with a mosaic of forest and savannah patches in the mid-Holocene. Better sites with reliable dating will be needed to check this, but based on current experience, fire would have been caused by lightning and could have spread most easily during drought periods associated with El Niño phases. Fire certainly occurred before human arrival, as shown by the site at Keiyasi on the middle reaches of the Sigatoka River (Nunn et al. 2001). Here, bands of charcoal occur near the base of a 6 m terrace and are dated to around 5400 cal. BP (4630±60, NZA-12539). Nunn considers that the substantial sediment mobilisation may indicate a widespread dry phase at that time. Even wet coastal sites such as Bonatoa contain mid-Holocene charcoal, but some sites, such as Tagamaucia, were evidently too humid to support fire.

Early human impact

Most records show distinct changes in vegetation around 2700–3100 years ago, usually associated with a sustained increase in charcoal. Yacata Pond provides the best record for human impact and slope instability so far and provides a model for accelerated slope erosion that infilled the depositional basin after 2700 cal. BP (Figure 33). Bonatoa and Sari also have distinctive changes, but were undergoing successional changes at the time that may obscure the level of human impact. Other regional pollen studies that provide persuasive evidence for significant human impact accompanying human arrival are from Avai' o'vuna in Tonga (Fall 2005), Mangaia Island in the Cook Islands (Ellison 1994; Kirch and Ellison 1994), St Louis Lac, Plum and Koumac in New Caledonia (Stevenson and Dodson 1995; Stevenson 1998; Hope et al. 1998) and Aneityum in Vanuatu (Hope and Spriggs 1982). At all these sites the arrival of humans radically changed the catchment forest vegetation to shrublands, *talasiga* or grasslands, which was accompanied by the influx of inorganic sediment into lakes or swamps.

An increase and sustained signal of fire in these landscapes is the best indicator of prehistoric human presence. Figure 34 summarises the charcoal (fire) histories of representative palaeoecological sites from Fiji, New Caledonia, Vanuatu and Tonga based on our best estimate of their chronologies. In general, fire becomes a constant at most sites after 2700 cal. BP, but the records are quite variable and often show moderate or low charcoal until 800–1600 cal. BP, followed by an order-of-magnitude increase in charcoal influx. In sites such as Volivoli, Yacata, Nabuni and possibly Keitera on Totoya Island, the major increase in charcoal is associated with slope losses. Once sites stabilise, the inorganic sediment and charcoal influx may fall. This may reflect increased surface cover by grass and ferns that reduces charcoal transport from burned slopes into basins. It would be premature to tie the records directly to the amount of burning, and hence human activity, in the catchments or in the swamps.

While all near-coastal sites in Fiji record abrupt changes in sedimentation associated with a decline in primary forest, increases in secondary and disturbance taxa and increased grass, ferns and charcoal, the dating in several cases is problematic. Several sites seem to have convincing evidence for fire-caused vegetation change, but the onset of this disturbance is much older than the established archaeological record for Fiji. The Volivoli Lagoon record shows distinct changes in vegetation and sedimentation associated with increased fire, which commenced around 5100 cal. BP. The transition from peat to clay at Mudflat on Mago Island around 5000 cal. BP may indicate a hiatus in deposition after 5000 cal. BP until burial by slopewash at an unknown date. However the alluvial muds that bury this swamp are the result of burning that could be ascribed to human-caused disturbance. AMS dating of individual burned particles will be necessary to obtain more precise dating for the peat-to-clay transition event.

Both Soleve, on Kaibu Island, and Navatu, on Viti Levu, record young dates for the onset of post-settlement disturbance, at around 1200 cal. BP, from the top of organic sediments buried

Vegetation histories from the Fijian Islands: Alternative records of human impact 81

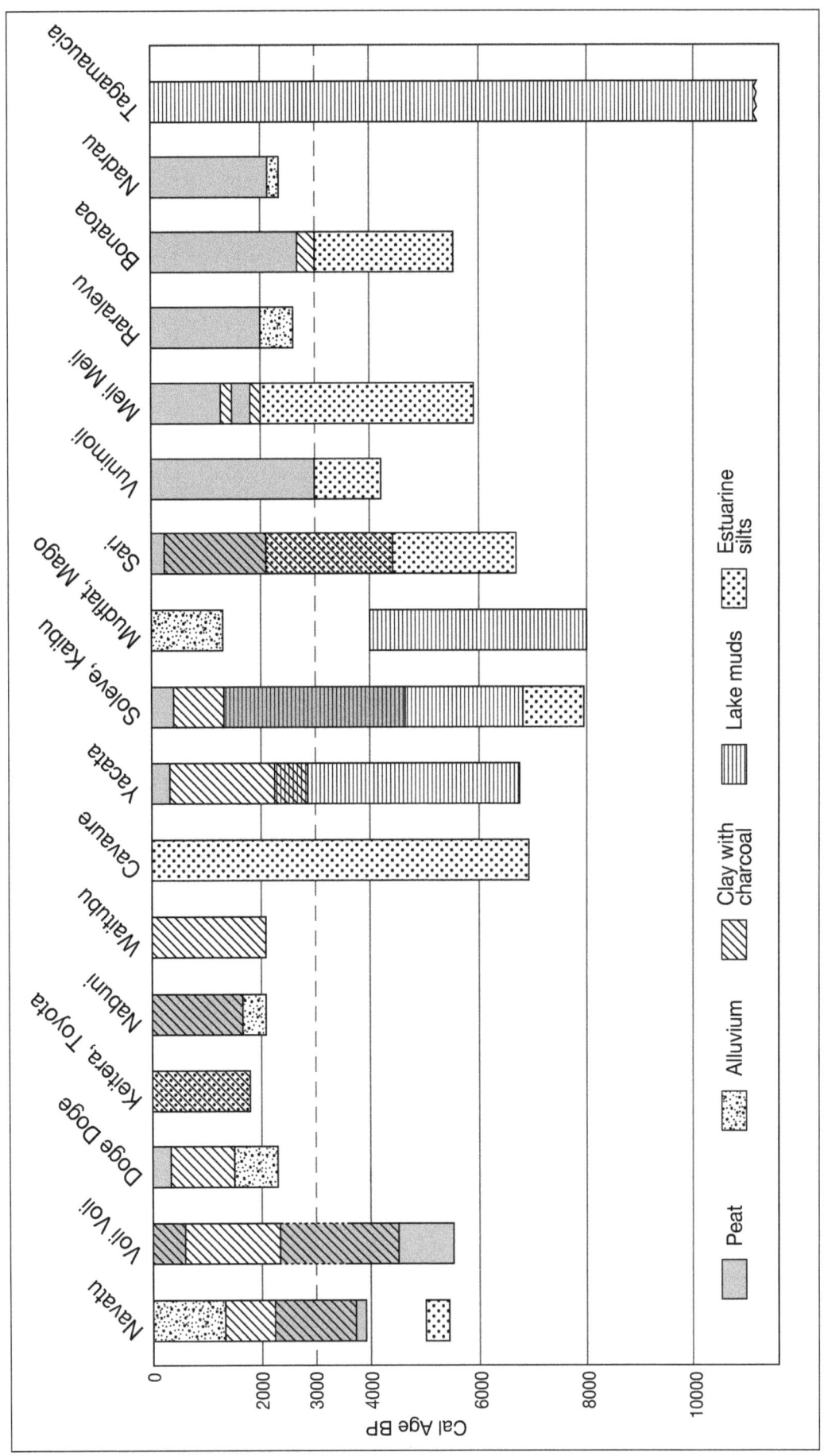

Figure 33. Available dated sedimentary records from Fiji arranged from driest to wettest site.

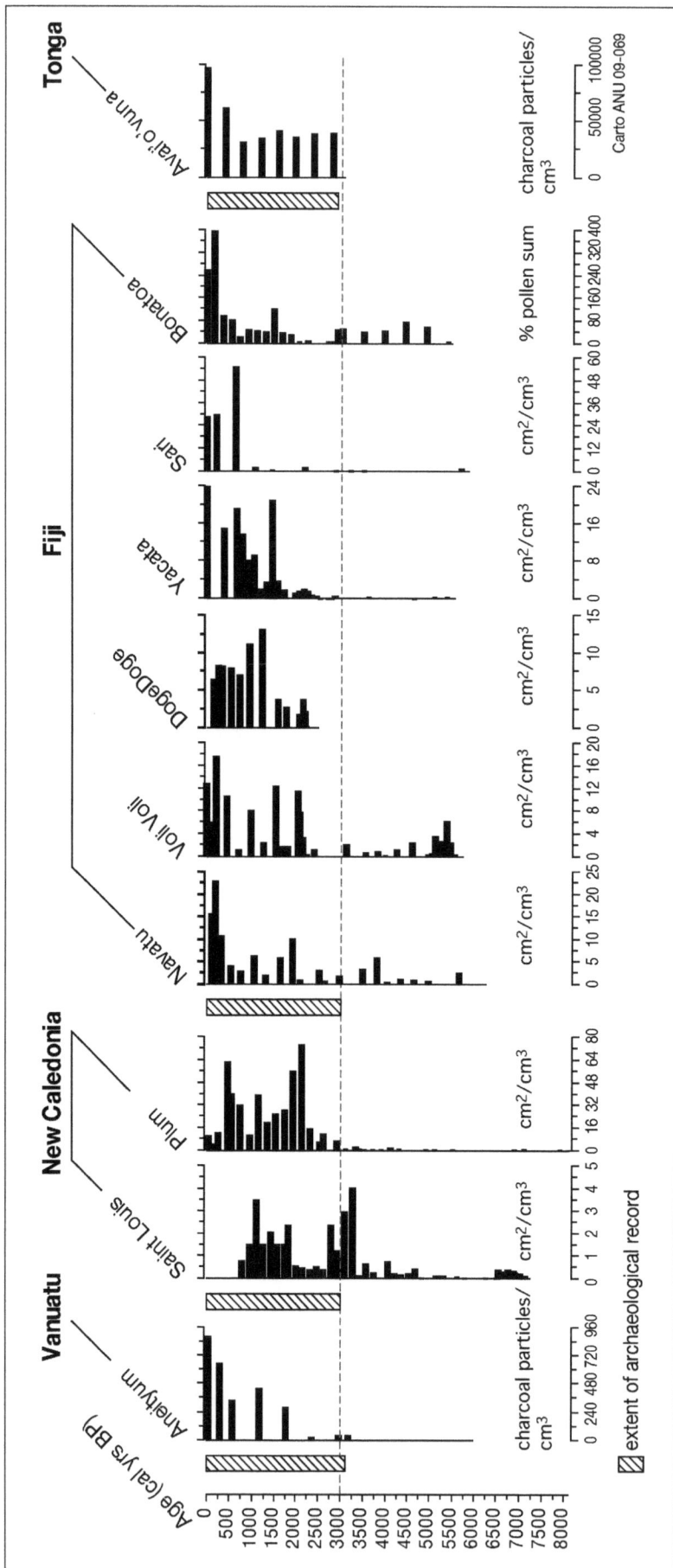

Figure 34. Charcoal as a disturbance index for selected sites in the southwest Pacific (age estimates cal. BP).

by alluvial infills. At both sites, however, the overlying alluvial clays return older dates because they have probably incorporated older organic material from their catchments. Anderson (1994, 1995) has noted that human settlement is often associated with surface erosion, which can result in anomalously old dates for human colonisation.

Hence, problems with dating the pollen sections remain. Anelcahat Swamp, Aneityum, Vanuatu, has a clear association of increased fire, vegetation change and burial of a peatland by terrigenous red clays. Dating of the organic components in the base of the clay resembles the Mudflat site on Mago, with an age of 6000 cal. BP (5220±80, ANU 9787). However, extrapolation of peat accumulation rates from the base of the core suggests an age of 2750 cal. BP for the same level. This is in agreement with a date from the base of the clay from a pit on the side of the swamp of 3000±80 BP (Hope and Spriggs 1982). The Anelcahat site may resemble St Louis Lac or Yacata, and a new section is currently being processed for macrofossils that can be directly dated.

Landscape response 2200–1200 cal. BP

While some sites, such as Yacata, indicate abrupt and lasting impacts soon after 2700 cal. BP, other sites, such as Bonatoa, record relatively low impact from initial settlement, followed by more widespread clearance and increased burning after 2200–1800 cal. BP. This age range also dates the probable clearance event at the source of the Sigatoka River that initiated swamp development at Nadrau around 2200 cal. BP. It may also coincide with the major slope collapse on Lakeba Island, which is estimated to have taken place about 200–300 years after slope erosion attributable to fire and clearance along the lower Sigatoka appears to have initiated Doge Doge Swamp by stream blockage. These dates support the hypothesis that parts of Fiji had started to be altered soon after human arrival, but that many of the major transformations took place 500–1100 years after colonisation.

Building on his work at Aneityum, Spriggs (1997) postulated that the erosion of slopes due to fire and forest clearance in the Pacific led to the construction of lowland silt plains that were highly suitable for cropping. He speculates that some of the destruction may in fact have been intentional, resulting in greater net agricultural productivity despite forest loss and the spread of *talasiga* on slopes. Fiji possessed widespread lowland alluvial plains before settlement, but the subsequent erosion (and possible sea-level fall) did convert numerous estuarine swamps into alluvial valley floors that were used for agriculture. There is a wide range of dates for the major alluviation phase in Fiji, but it is true that it seems to be a phase with definite limits. For example, Volivoli appears to stabilise, with lower inputs of slope materials in the past 1000 years, and similar observations apply to Yacata. While this may be tied to changes in human impact, it is also possible that better-organised gardening and exhaustion of erodible sediment contributed to stabilisation.

In some cases, the result of deforestation was to convert valley floors to swampland. Doge Doge is a relatively early peatland that was created as a result of levee building, possibly by sediments released by vegetation clearance. Removal of the forest can increase water yields and this may contribute to the initiation of swamp conditions. Other examples include Nadrau and the Lakeba Island sites, where very rapid sediment accumulation was followed by rapid peat build up or slower accumulation of organic-rich clay. Lakutu and Mela are near coastal swamps on Guadacanal Island, Solomons, which experienced an initial clay influx with charcoal around 3000 years ago with the loss of forest cover (Haberle 1996). The sites then developed into peat bogs. Similarly, sites on Erromango and Aneityum Islands, Vanuatu, developed organic deposits after clearance around 1800–2000 years ago (Hope et al. 1998). It is possible that the Korowaiwai peatlands at 130 m altitude in central Vanua Levu are of this type.

Marine and climatic influences

The transition from estuary to swamp, and the variable influxes of sediment associated with late-Holocene burning, tend to conceal possible impacts of climate and minor changes in sea level on the vegetation reconstructed from pollen diagrams. The only undisturbed site, Tagamaucia, is buffered climatically by extremely high rainfall and the record is disturbed by the development of floating sedge islands in the last millennium, so minor changes in forest taxa cannot be attributed to climate changes on the scale of minor temperature and rainfall fluctuations. The most sensitive sites to aridity and natural fires are Volivoli and Navatu. If our tentative discovery of a changed fire regime around 5000 cal. BP is correct, it may reflect increased variability in climate and more extreme El Niño fluctuations after that time, as postulated by Gagan et al. (2004).

The falls in local sea level which are suggested between 4500 and 2000 cal. BP by Dickinson (2001) and Nunn (2007) seem to have accelerated vegetation successions and possibly curtailed swamp accumulation in some coastal sites. It is a moot point whether, as Nunn (2007) claims, this allowed human occupation of valley floors, as these locations were often buried by an influx of slope alluvium, which also raised the sites above sea level, and storm waves were impeded by more emergent offshore barriers.

The resolution is low for the pollen data from Fiji, but there appears to be no indication of any widespread and abrupt changes around 700 years ago that might support the well-publicised 'AD 1300 event' proposed by Nunn (2007) and Kumar et al. (2006). Clark and Cole (1997) note that the Totoya sequences cover both the Little Ice Age and a possible warm period with no obvious changes. While we acknowledge the warnings of Nunn (1991, 1994) against assigning environmental changes to human agency, we suggest that minor sea level and climate events are unlikely to be the cause of the vegetation and sediment sequences and charcoal records we have found in many parts of Fiji.

Conclusion

Virtually all of the research on vegetation history in Fiji has been undertaken to compare prehuman vegetation and landscape processes with those after human settlement. Although more than 20 pollen diagrams and charcoal records exist, relatively few sites provide unproblematic sequences recording human settlement and change to the vegetation. Some sites are in areas where humans have had little impact, while others have sedimentary breaks or dating problems. Despite this, the present study shows that there is great potential for high-resolution palaeoecology using well-dated multi-proxy work. The results demonstrate that the landscape history is complex, with individual responses at each site examined.

Most sedimentary basins are created as a response to sea-level stabilisation around 6000–7000 cal. BP. Fire, apparently linked to increases in catchment erosion, is seen in some sites after 5000 cal. BP. In broad terms, smaller islands and the dry sides of the large islands respond to increased fire at the time of human arrival soon after 3000 cal. BP. After 2200 cal. BP, clearance and conversion to scrub and *talasiga* is widespread. More humid sites, while recording increased burning, maintain forest cover, although secondary species become more common, particularly after 1700–2000 cal. BP. Some swamps are caused by levee damming and possibly increased run-off within the past 2400 years, while others are buried by alluvium. The palaeoenvironmental records assembled here illustrate the potential sedimentary basins have to provide independent evidence of human impact, but they also illustrate the complexity inherent in this approach, particularly that human impact is not necessarily a straightforward and homogeneous historical process. Evidence for a marked environmental change associated with the Little Ice Age was not noted, and, in fact, several sites record reduced inorganic inputs after 800 years ago.

References

Anderson, A.J. 1994. Palaeoenvironmental evidence of island colonization: A response. *Antiquity* 68: 845–847.

Anderson, A.J. 1995 Current approaches in East Polynesian colonisation research. *Journal of the Polynesian Society* 104: 110–132.

Anderson, A., Burley, D., Clark, G., de Biran, A., Dickinson, W., Hope, G. and Roberts R. 2006. The times of sand: Sedimentary history and archaeology at the Sigatoka Sand Dunes, Fiji. *Geoarchaeology* 21: 131–154.

Ash, J. 1992. Vegetation ecology of Fiji: Past, present, and future perspectives. *Pacific Science* 46: 111–127.

Burley, D.V. and Dickinson, W.R. 2004. Late Lapita occupation and its ceramic assemblage at the Sigatoka Sand Dune Site, Fiji and their place in oceanic prehistory. *Archaeology in Oceania* 39: 12–25.

Clark, G. 2000. Post-Lapita Fiji: Cultural transformation in the mid-sequence. Unpublished PhD thesis, Australian National University.

Clark, G., Anderson, A. and Matararaba, S. 2001. The Lapita site at Votua, northern Lau Islands, Fiji. *Archaeology in Oceania* 36: 134–145.

Clark, J.T. and Cole, A.O. 1997. Environmental change and human prehistory in the Central Pacific: Archaeological and palynological investigations on Totoya Island, Fiji. Report to the Fiji Museum, Suva.

Clark, J.T., Cole, A.O. and Nunn, P.D. 1999. Environmental change and human prehistory on Totoya Island, Fiji. In: Lilley, I. and Galipaud, J-C. (eds), *Le pacifique de 5000 à 2000 avant le présent. Suppléments à l'histoire d'une colonisation. The Pacific from 5000 to 2000 BP. Colonisation and transformations,* pp 227–240. Actes du colloque Vanuatu, 31 Juillet – 6 Aout 1996. Editions de l'ORSTOM. Collection Colloques et séminaires, Paris.

Clark, G. and Hope, G. 2001. Archaeological and palaeoenvironmental investigations on Yacata Island, northern Lau, Fiji. *Domodomo* 13(2): 29–47.

Cole, A.O. 1996. A dynamical systems framework for modelling plant community organisation. Unpublished PhD thesis, Massey University.

Dickinson, W.R. 2001. Paleoshoreline record of relative Holocene sea levels on Pacific Islands. *Earth Science Reviews* 5: 191–234.

Dickinson, W.R. 2009. Pacific atoll living: How long already and until when? *GSA Today* 19(3): 4–10. doi: 10.1130/GSATG35A.1.

Dickinson, W.R., Burley, D.V., Nunn, P.D., Anderson, A., Hope, G., de Biran, A., Burke C. and Matararaba, S. 1998. Geomorphic and archaeological landscapes of the Sigatoka Dunes Site, Viti Levu, Fiji: Interdisciplinary investigations. *Asian Perspectives* 37: 1–31.

Ellison, J.C. 1994. Palaeo-lake and swamp stratigraphic records of Holocene vegetation and sea level changes, Mangaia, Cook Islands. *Pacific Science* 48: 1–15.

Fall, P.L. 2005. Vegetation change in the coastal-lowland rainforest at Avai'o'vuna Swamp, Vava'u, Kingdom of Tonga. *Quaternary Research* 64: 451–459.

Gagan, M.K., Hendy, E.J., Haberle, S.G. and Hantoro, W. 2004. Post-glacial evolution of the Indo-Pacific Warm Pool and El Niño–Southern Oscillation. *Quaternary International* 118–119: 127–143.

Gifford, E.W. 1951. Archaeological excavations in Fiji. *University of California Anthropological Records* 13: 189–288.

Haberle, S. 1996. Explanations for palaeoecological changes on the northern plains of Guadalcanal, Solomon Islands: The last 3200 years. *Holocene* 6(3): 333–338.

Hope, G.S. 1996. Quaternary change and historical biogeography of Pacific Islands. In: Keast, A. and Miller, S.E. (eds), *The origin and evolution of Pacific Island biotas, New Guinea to Eastern Polynesia: Patterns and process,* pp. 165–190. SPB Publishing, Amsterdam.

Hope G.S., O'Dea, D. and Southern, W. 1998. Holocene vegetation histories in the Western Pacific – alternative records of human impact. In: Lilley, I. and Galipaud, J-C. (eds), *Le pacifique de 5000 à 2000 avant le présent. Suppléments à l'histoire d'une colonisation. The Pacific from 5000 to 2000 BP.*

Colonisation and transformations. Actes du colloque Vanuatu, 31 Juillet – 6 Aout 1996. Editions de l'ORSTOM. Collection Colloques et séminaires, Paris.

Hope, G.S. and Pask, J. 1998. Tropical vegetational change in the late Pleistocene of New Caledonia. *Palaeogeography, Palaeoclimatology, Palaeoecology* 142: 1–21.

Hope, G.S. and Spriggs, M.J.T. 1982. A preliminary pollen sequence from Aneityum Island, Southern Vanuatu. *Bulletin of the Indopacific Prehistory Association* 3: 88–94.

Hughes, P.J., Hope, G.S., Latham M. and Brookfield, M. 1979. Prehistoric man-induced degradation of the Lakeba landscape: evidence from two inland swamps. In: Brookfield, H.G. (ed), *Lakeba: Environmental change, population and resource use*, pp. 93–111. UNESCO/UNFPA Island Reports 5.

Kirch, P.V. and Ellison, J.C. 1994. Palaeoenvironmental evidence for human colonisation of remote oceanic islands. *Antiquity* 68: 310–321.

Kumar, R., Field, J.S., de Biran, A. 2006. Human responses to climate change around AD 1300: A case study of the Sigatoka Valley, Viti Levu Island, Fiji. *Quaternary International* 151: 133–143.

Latham, M. 1986. *Alteration et pédogenése sur roches ultrabasiques en Nouvelle-Calédonie*. ORSTOM, Paris.

Latham, M., Hughes, P.J., Hope, G. and Brookfield, M. 1983. Sedimentation in the swamps of Lakeba and its implications for erosion and human occupation of the island. In: Latham, M. and Brookfield, H.C. (eds), *The eastern islands of Fiji – a study of the natural environment, its use and man's influence on its evolution*, pp. 103–120. Travaux et Documents de l'ORSTOM, Paris. 162.

Mueller-Dombois, D. and Fosberg, F.R. 1998. *Vegetation of the tropical Pacific Islands*. Springer Press, New York.

Nunn, P.D. 1991. *Human and non-human impacts on Pacific island environments*. Environment and Policy Institute East West Center Occasional. Paper 13.

Nunn, P.D. 1994. Beyond the naive lands: Human history and environmental change in the Pacific Basin. In: Wadell, E. and Nunn, P.D. (eds), *The margin fades: Geographical itineraries in a world of islands*, pp. 5–27. Institute of Pacific Studies, USP, Suva.

Nunn, P.D. 2007. *Climate, environment and society in the Pacific during the last millennium*. Elsevier, Amsterdam.

Nunn, P.D. and Peltier, W.R. 2001. Far-field test of the ICE-4G (VM2) model of global isostatic response to deglaciation: Empirical and theoretical Holocene sea level reconstructions for the Fiji Islands, Southwest Pacific. *Quaternary Research* 55: 203–214.

Nunn, P.D., Thaman, R.R., Duffy, L., Finikaso, S., Ram, N. and Swamy, M. 2001. Age of a charcoal band in fluvial sediments, Keiyasi, Sigatoka Valley, Fiji: Possible indicator of a severe drought throughout the Southwest Pacific 4500–5000 years ago. *South Pacific Journal of Natural Science* 19: 5–10.

Parry, J.T. 1987. The Sigatoka Valley – pathway into prehistory. *Bulletin of the Fiji Museum* 9.

Shepherd, M.J. 1990. The evolution of a moderate energy coast in Holocene time; Pacific Harbour, Viti Levu, Fiji. *New Zealand Journal of Geology and Geophysics* 33: 547–556.

Southern, W. 1986. The Late Quaternary environmental history of Fiji. Unpublished PhD thesis, Australian National University.

Spriggs, M.J.T. 1997. *The island Melanesians*. Blackwell, Oxford.

Stevenson J. 1998. Human impact from the palaeoenvironmental record of New Caledonia. In: Lilley, I. and Galipaud, J-C. (eds), *Le pacifique de 5000 à 2000 avant le présent. Suppléments à l'histoire d'une colonisation. The Pacific from 5000 to 2000 BP. Colonisation and transformations*, pp. 251–259. Actes du colloque Vanuatu, 31 Juillet – 6 Aout 1996. Editions de l'ORSTOM. Collection Colloques et séminaires, Paris.

Stevenson, J. and Dodson, J.R. 1995. Palaeoenvironmental evidence for human settlement of New Caledonia. *Archaeology in Oceania* 30: 36–41.

Stevenson, J. and Hope, G.S. 2005. A comparison of late Quaternary forest changes in New Caledonia and northeastern Australia. *Quaternary Research* 64: 372–383.

Stevenson, J., Dodson, J.R. and Prosser, I.P. 2001. A late Quaternary record of environmental change and human impact from New Caledonia. *Palaeogeography, Palaeoclimatology, Palaeoecology* 168: 97–123.

Ward R.G. 2002. Land use on Mago, Fiji: 1865–1882. *The Journal of Pacific History* 37(1): 103–108.

5

Fieldwork in southern Viti Levu and Beqa Island

Atholl Anderson
Archaeology and Natural History, The Australian National University

Geoffrey Clark
Archaeology and Natural History, The Australian National University

Introduction

This chapter is concerned with research in southern Viti Levu and on Beqa Island, which lies off the south coast of Viti Levu. The investigations can be divided into four parts, based on site geography (Figure 35). Much of the early fieldwork effort concentrated on the lower and middle Sigatoka Valley and nearby areas of the south coast of Viti Levu. The Sigatoka, at 137 km long, is the second largest river in Fiji, after the Rewa. Its lower and middle reaches run through the relatively dry leeward zone of Viti Levu and annual rainfall in the valley is around 2000 mm. Originally forested, the Sigatoka Valley is noted for its soil fertility and had become intensively cultivated and densely populated by the 19th century; Parry (1987:53) estimates a protohistorical population of 18,000–22,000. His aerial-photo survey of archaeological sites counted 212 settlements, the majority, not unexpectedly, exhibiting earthworks. The fortification tradition, according to Parry (1987:119), was particularly well developed in the Sigatoka and has origins which can be traced as far back as the second millennium AD (Field 2004). If the significance of the Sigatoka through the last millennium suggests it was regarded as attractive for settlement, then perhaps this was so from the earliest period of human habitation in Fiji. Investigations were focused, therefore, at the Sigatoka Sand Dunes where Lapita ceramics had been recorded along a beach-front section by Birks (1973).

From about the Sigatoka Valley to the west, there are substantial areas of Pliocene sedimentary rocks, in the Sigatoka series and the Viti Limestones (Geological Map of Fiji, 1961). A second project investigated these potentially habitable caves, which in general would have been more accessible in this district of Viti Levu, where precipitation is lower than elsewhere and where natural vegetation was relatively light forest. As rock shelters often contain archaeological remains in sequence, a number of shelters were test-excavated to attempt to establish how early people had begun to use the coastal hinterland and interior.

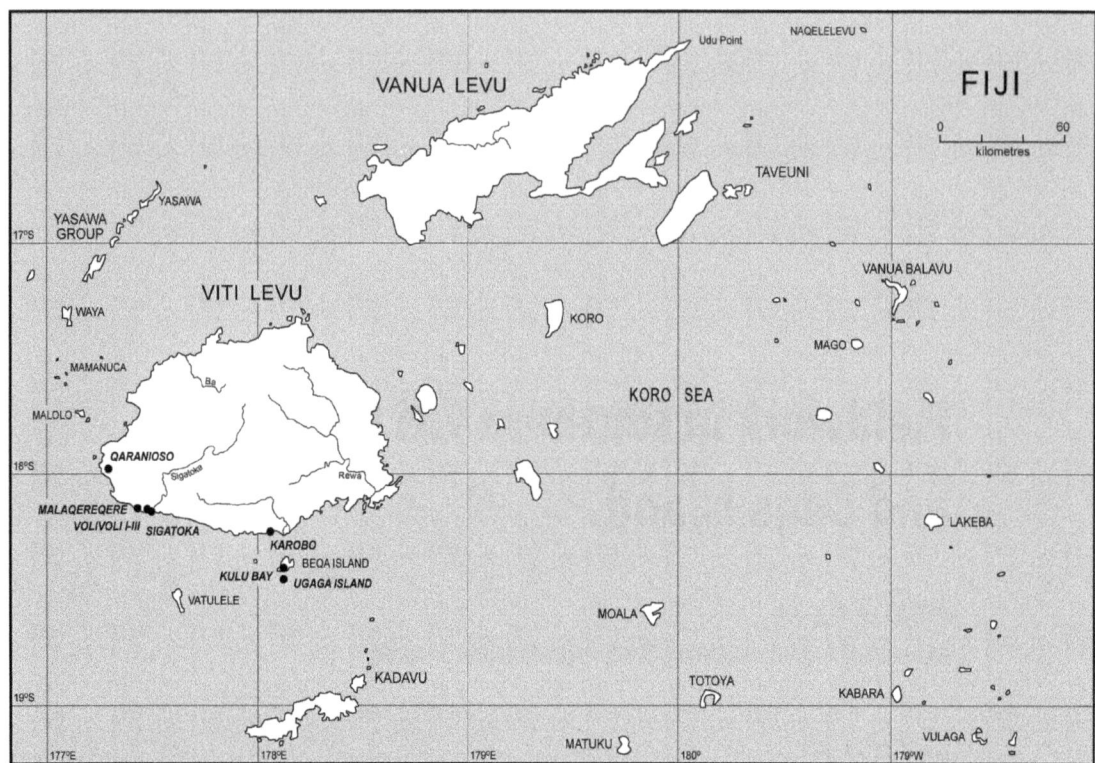

Figure 35. Map of Fiji showing research locations.

A third project was to analyse remains from the Karobo (VL 18/1) site held by the Fiji Museum. Karobo was excavated by Jack Golson, Bruce Palmer and others in the 1960s, and was an important site (Karobo was substantially destroyed by tourism development in 2002) as it yielded materials from the middle of the Fiji sequence. Fieldwork documents from the Karobo excavations were copied from the originals held at the Auckland Museum by Roger Green, and were used to determine site stratigraphy.

Beqa Island is the remnant of an eroded stratovolcano and lies 7.5 km south of the Navua Delta. The island has a maximum height of 480 metres above sea level and is conspicuous from the south coast of Viti Levu. In the 1980s, survey and excavation by Andrew Crosby (1988) recorded dentate-stamped sherds from four locations on Beqa, including Kulu Bay (BQ175A), and impressed sherds on Ugaga Island. A fourth project in 1997 aimed to recover larger samples of cultural material from these two sites than had been obtained from excavations in southern Viti Levu.

Fieldwork in southern Viti Levu

Sigatoka Dunes, VL 16/1

At the Sigatoka River mouth there is an extensive archaeological site (Sigatoka dunes site, VL 16/1), which has a sequence encompassing all the main phases of Fijian culture history. It has been the primary focus of research in Fijian archaeology, in fieldwork and in sequence analysis (Gifford 1951; Green 1963; Green and Palmer 1964; Dickinson 1968; Palmer et al. 1968; Birks 1973; Frost 1979; Southern 1986; Hunt 1986, 1987; Parry 1987; Best 1987a, 1989; Visser 1988, 1994; Crosby 1991, 1992; Hudson 1994; Petchey 1995; Burley 1997, 2003; Dickinson et al. 1998; Wood et al. 1998; Burley and Shortland 1999; Marshall et al. 2000; Burley and Dickinson 2004).

As a prime settlement locality, the Sigatoka dunes site offered a chance to test the possibility raised by Southern (1986) and Gibbons (1985) that evidence of human activity might be earlier than predicted by the conventional archaeological sequence of Green (1963). It was hoped that archaeological deposits in limestone shelter and cave sites at nearby Volivoli, and in the middle reaches of the valley, might also contain sequences which would assist our understanding of early settlement patterns and, in particular, produce faunal and other organic remains which would help to fill out the archaeological evidence at the dunes, where these materials are very scarce. The main Sigatoka Valley and its lower tributaries also presented an ideal opportunity to investigate aspects of the early sedimentary and vegetational history of the district. We were interested in looking at the nature and timing of anthropogenic change in relation to the geomorphology of the dunes, including whether changes occurred in the hinterland early or later in relation to the cultural sequence, and whether substantial change was 'front-loaded' in the sequence, had occurred cumulatively or had increased over time. Investigation of another aspect of palaeoenvironmental change, the impact of people on indigenous vertebrates, was also favoured by the availability of limestone cave sites suited to palaeontological deposition. Abutting the inland edge of the Sigatoka dunes is the Volivoli limestone massif, and other formations equally riddled with caves exist upstream, notably the spectacular outcrops at Toga.

Our basic aim was to set the early archaeological sequence of the district, essentially the first millennium of habitation, into its local context of environmental change. Our methods included coring for sedimentary and palynological records and palaeontological investigations, which are reported in Chapters 2–4, and archaeological research, described here.

After frequent archaeological excavations at the Sigatoka dunes site over the past 50 years, a new phase was beginning in 1996 with a project by Simon Fraser University and the Fiji Museum (Burley 1997, 2003, 2005). Our research was restricted, therefore, to the most pertinent issues of our overall project, those concerning the colonising status of Lapita remains at the site. Did Level 1 (Birks 1973) represent the first human habitation at the site, or was it only the earliest archaeological horizon to survive in a volatile sedimentary sequence? This is an important question from several points of view concerning colonisation. One is whether landscape preferences in the early Lapita era had included the large river valleys, route ways into the interior and obvious sources of many kinds of resources, yet not at all conspicuous among known Lapita site locations. None are recorded from the Rewa Valley; Natunuku, a site of early Lapita facies, stands fairly close to the mouth of the Ba River but not directly at it, while the Sigatoka Lapita site is at the river mouth but has ceramics and radiocarbon dates largely indicative of fairly late Lapita occupation. The question also bears importantly on the relationship of human habitation to the development of the dunes, and especially on whether the dune formation is substantially anthropogenic through the impact of people, by deforestation, on the sedimentary regime.

The main issue was devolved into several operational questions about the lower levels of the stratigraphy at the Sigatoka dunes. Was it possible to determine whether any remains of earlier human activity underlay the Level 1 palaeosol? Was the Lapita occupation contemporaneous with the stable (Level 1 palaeosol) phase or did it begin only after a significant period of soil formation, i.e. later than there existed a suitable locality for settlement? We sought to recover archaeological materials suitable for establishing the age of Lapita occupation at the site by radiocarbon dating, and to compare those results with others obtained on samples of sand by OSL dating (Anderson et al. 2006). The sand samples would provide a sedimentary chronology that began before and spanned the phases of soil formation. Those had been described by Birks (1973) according to a basic stratigraphic profile encompassing three periods of occupation,

Levels 1–3, marked by the association of cultural remains with phases of soil development. The simplicity of that model has been challenged by Marshall et al. (2000), but it remains the most useful description of the greater part of site VL 16/1, certainly for comparative purposes with earlier research results, irrespective of the validity of Marshall et al.'s (2000) views on the age and origin of dune building.

In 1996, we sought a representative stratigraphic sequence and decided to concentrate on an area which began at about the 1200 foot point in the Birks' excavation, which is approximately at the 500 m datum in the 1992 site survey plan (Marshall et al. 2000:Fig. 5.1), and which extended east to the western boundary of the main burial areas investigated by Best (1987a, b, 1989). These lie immediately east of the Marshall et al. (2000) datum point at 200 m. Our choice of this area was strongly influenced by the results of an archaeological salvage project two years earlier, after severe damage to the seaward dunes in this area by cyclone Kina. Hudson's (1994) report suggested both that Levels 1 and 2 ran through this area, though they were difficult to separate, and that the ceramics from the lower horizon included early Lapita types (Petchey 1994) not previously reported from Sigatoka.

Located in very mobile sand dunes which extend for several kilometres along a high-energy beach front, the Sigatoka dunes site is constantly changing and few of its archaeological features remain visible from year to year. So by 1996, the exposures investigated by Hudson (1994) were well covered by recent sand deposition and none of the surface features she recorded remained recognisable. The difficulty of re-locating her excavations was compounded by survey problems in the available site plans. These consisted of an early version of the 1992 survey plan of the Sigatoka site, which was both extensive and detailed (later versions were made available as Wood et al. 1998 and Marshall et al. 2000), and Hudson's localised plans based on it. The latter indicated that the centre of the 1993 excavations, as represented by profile 2, lay about 60 m east of the 500 m datum of the 1992 plan (Hudson 1994:Figure iii). This put the 1993 salvage excavations seaward of a prominent remaining area of Level 2 palaeosol which could be recognised on the ground and in the 1992 survey map. Coring soon showed that the assumed Hudson excavation area had been washed out and refilled by recent sands and that no clearly recognisable Level 1 horizon could be found below the adjacent Level 2 exposure. However, we were not confident about this result because Hudson (1994:Figure ii) shows the centre of the 1993 excavations about 150 m east of the 500 m datum, not 60 m, as in Figure 36. We cored transects in this area as well, with similar results, on the assumption that the datum shown in Hudson (1994) ought to be 400 m not 500 m.

These difficulties should have been resolvable by reference to the 1992 survey map, but that also contained an error. It was apparent as soon as we sought to match the map to the distribution of recognisable features on the ground, initially by tape measurement and later by total station survey, that the distances were substantially different (see also Burley and Dickinson 2004:note 2). Despite considerable effort using aerial photos, we could not resolve this problem in the field. The 1992 survey map was not keyed to an adequately described site datum feature, the site datum lay 60 m or so outside the boundary of the printed map, and the 100 m datum marker poles had been washed away (these deficiencies remain in Marshall et al. 2000). Consequently, it was not possible in 1996 to fix the 1992 survey precisely on the ground. From the later versions of the map (Wood et al. 1998; Marshall et al. 2000), it is now apparent that the version available to us in 1996 had been produced, in error, about 25% larger than its scale.

In the light of these difficulties, the essential features in the area of interest were re-mapped by total station survey (Figures 36–37) and tied to the fixed location of the Club Masa buildings. A sand corer with a diameter of 100 mm was then used to attempt to locate a suitable area for

Fieldwork in southern Viti Levu and Beqa Island 91

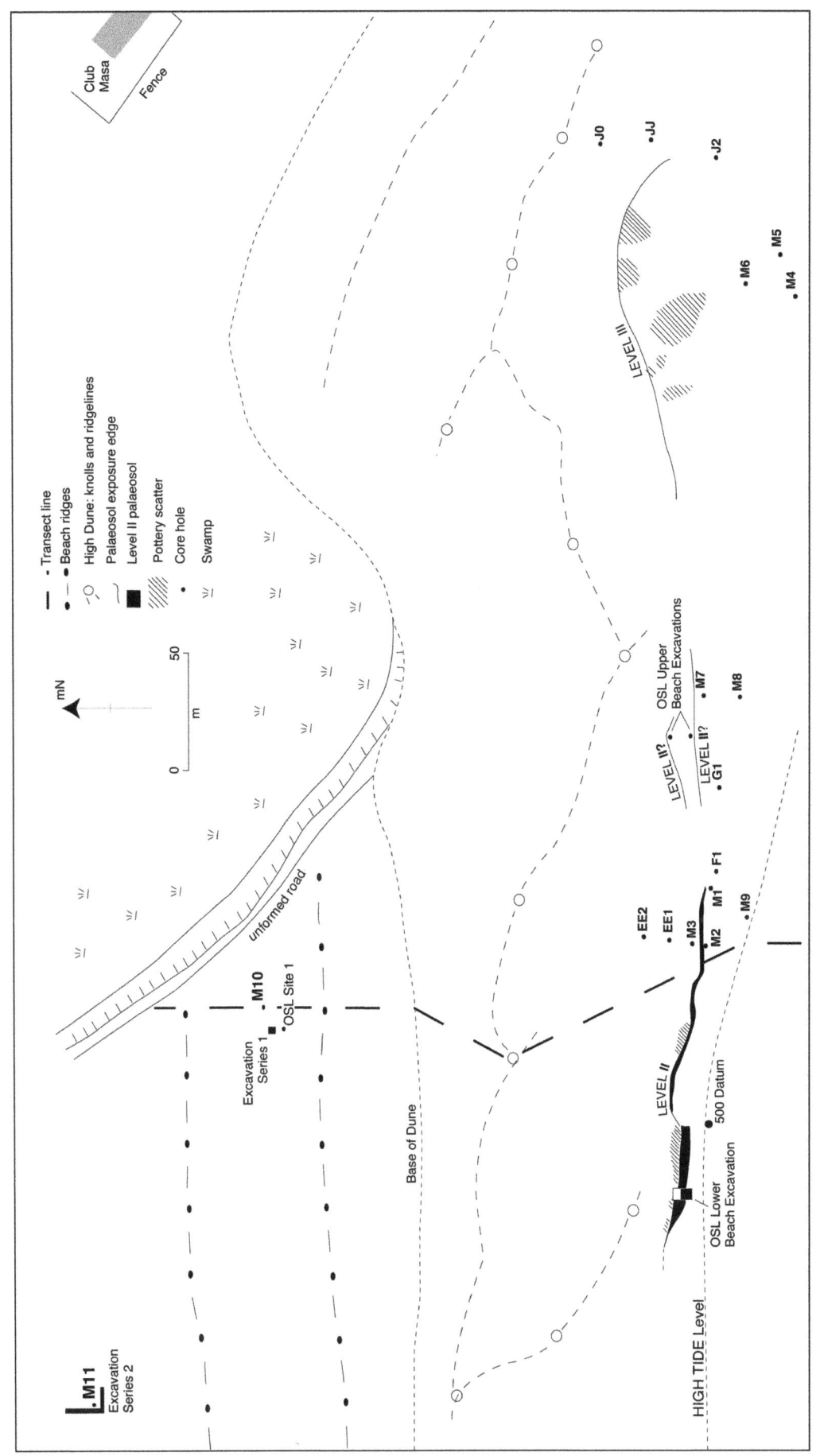

Figure 36. Sigatoka Sand Dunes, plan view of investigations.

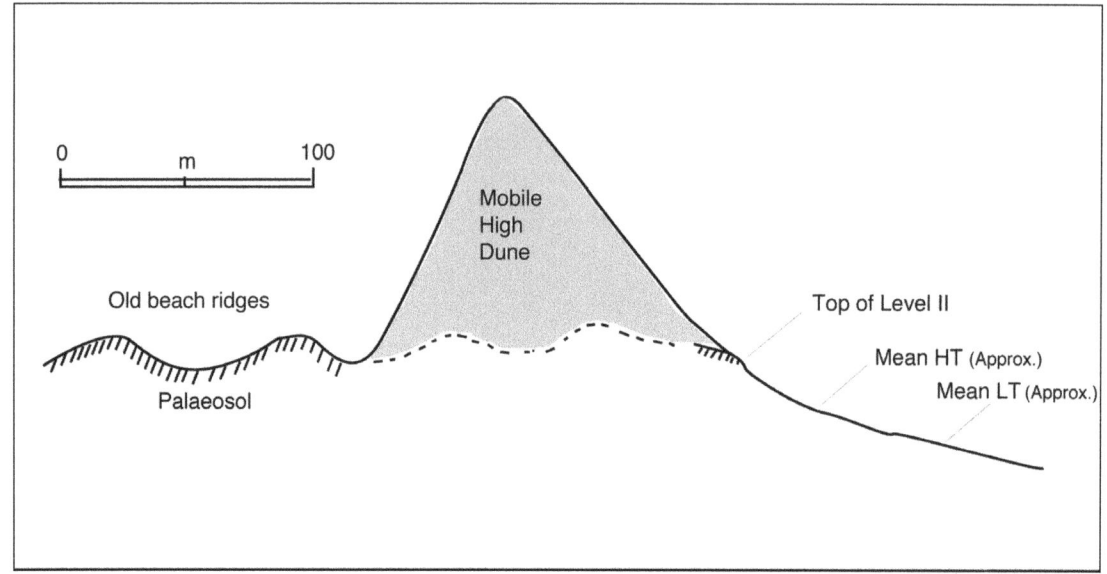

Figure 37. Sigatoka Sand Dunes, cross-section of dune system. Note vertical scale is exaggerated.

detailed investigation and sample collection. Eighteen cores were drilled, recorded and mapped (Figure 36), most going down to about 5 m or to the water table, where sediments could no longer be recovered satisfactorily. The most informative results are from cores which were started in compact, brown sands or weakly developed soils containing in their upper levels, or deposited immediately on them, ceramics of Navatu phase types, notably pieces of leaf-impressed trays and paddle-impressed pot sherds (Figure 38). The pedogenic horizon is assumed to be Level 2 of Birks (1973) where it is exposed in the seafront dunes and to represent it, perhaps more complexly and less exclusively, in the sand plain behind it.

The cores show a broadly uniform stratigraphy but differences in colour between the various sand units at Sigatoka are difficult to interpret and some may have no significance beyond exposure time. Marshall et al. (2000:21) note that even moist green-brown sands, found at depth, dry to yellow-brown and then yellow. Some differences in colour also reflect the degree of iron sand admixture which is variable and unpredictable. It was really only weathering and organic enrichment at periods of stability and pedogenesis which provided horizons that can be readily traced stratigraphically and geographically.

Below the Level 2 palaeosol, there is a layer of relatively uncompacted sand, finely laminated, which varies from yellow-brown or buff near the top to yellow-grey below. This overlies dark-brown to khaki-coloured or green-brown sand which is weakly compacted and which, on various grounds, we eventually concluded was the Level 1 horizon. It lay at about the right elevation relative to approximate high tide for Level 1. In the top 30 cm or so it contained slight evidence of organic enrichment (cf. Burley and Shortland (1999:35) who also noted the weak soil development in Level 1). Quantities of small yellow-to-orange pebbles of pumice occurred mainly near the surface of the layer and these had been associated with Level 1 by Hudson (1994), and Matararaba (pers. comm., Fiji Museum). The Level 1 attribution also seems very probable in light of the conclusion by Marshall et al. (2000:21) that '. . . the green-brown moist sand proved a universal base beneath Level 1 and occasionally beneath Level 2. It was never found between Levels 1 and 2.' Since our cores went through Level 2 at the surface, the green-brown sand in them must signify Level 1, on that basis. However, we recovered no diagnostic ceramics by coring and were doubtful at the time whether cultural remains of Level 1 still existed in the area we investigated, following the devastation wrought by cyclone Kina (Anderson et

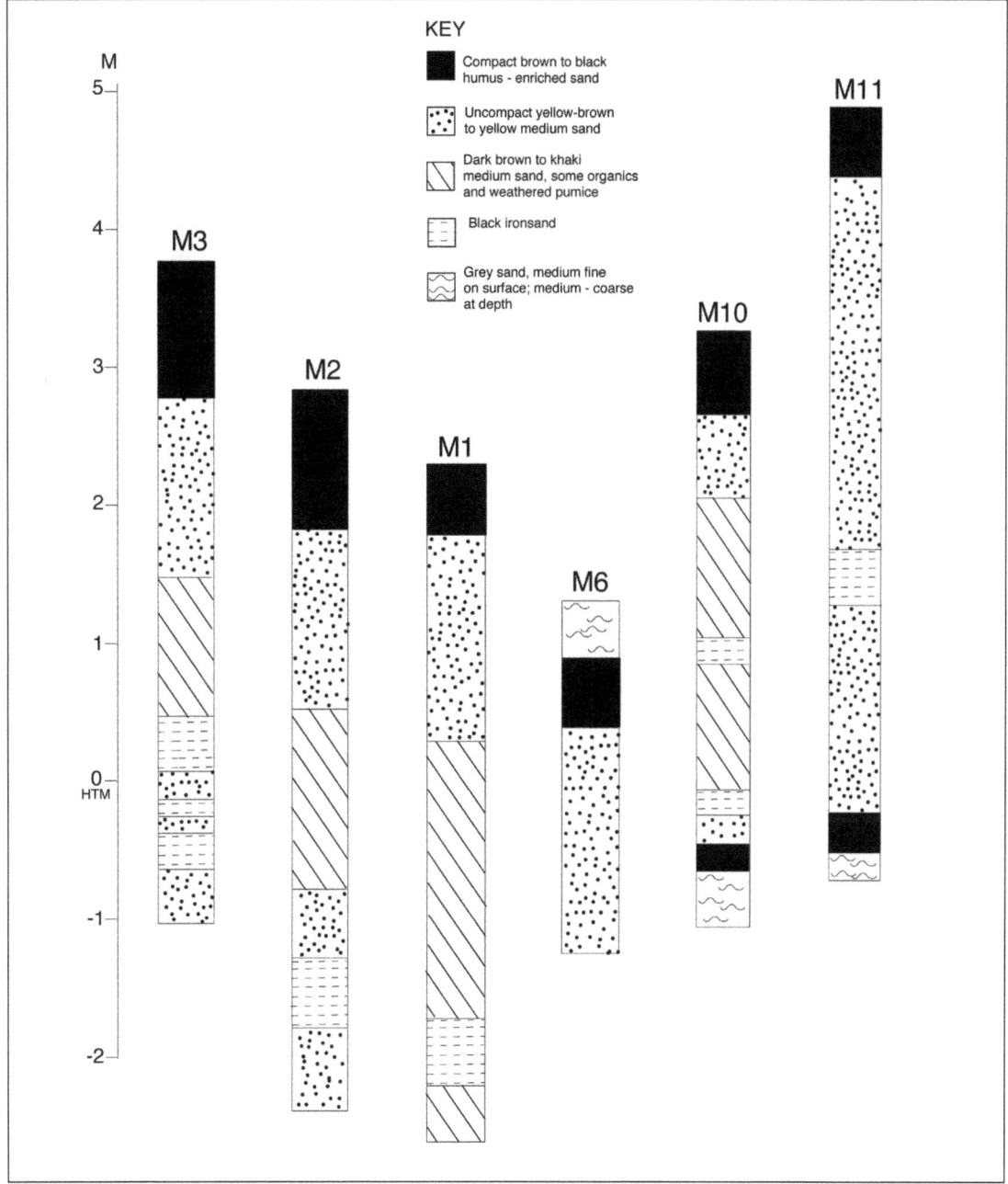

Figure 38. Sigatoka Sand Dunes, core results.

al. 1996). It seems, additionally, that Level 1 has always been less extensively evident in the area of our investigations. According to Marshall et al. (2000:24), it was generally absent as an outcropping horizon containing cultural material from about 300 to 640 m on their map, and was conflated with Level 2 at 400 to 500 m. Nevertheless, while cultural material was sparse or missing in the area, there seems little doubt that we recorded and sampled a sequence which included Level 1 and Level 2.

Below the assumed Level 1 unit were bands of yellow-grey to yellow-brown sands interspersed with bands and lenses of black iron sand. No Level 1 unit was encountered in the area of low ground cored by M4 to M6 (Figure 36), and in the sand-plain cores (M10, M11) there were some slight variations, including organic enrichment of a thin layer, perhaps an old incipient soil horizon, but of unknown age or situation in the Sigatoka sequence, at about 5 m depth (Figure 38).

De Biran's (2001) recent analysis of the geomorphology of the Sigatoka dunes and sand plain has proposed a sequence of formation similar to that outlined by Dickinson et al. (1998). According to de Biran, the present sand plain (or, more precisely, 'strandplain', de Biran 2001:41) in the Sigatoka delta was built as a series of sand ridges accreting seaward, a process beginning about the mid-Holocene. Level 1 represents a period of stability and soil formation, beginning approximately 900 BC, on the back-beach of the prograding delta. It was buried by a new episode of sand deposition, possibly early in the first millennium AD, on which, about AD 350, there began to develop the deep and extensive Level 2 soil. This covers the entire sand plain and outcrops at the seafront of the dunes. After about the 7th century AD, it was covered near the coast by the beginnings of the high dune development, in which, at intervals rather than as a single phase, there was patchy development of the Level 3 soil, beginning about the 14th century AD.

As well as this interpretation, there are some minor (Dickinson et al. 1998) or major (Marshall et al. 2000) variations in earlier works. Marshall et al. (2000) suggest that the settlement sequence at Sigatoka was more complex and continuous than is allowed in the conventional model – although they continue to find that necessary to their exposition; and that dune building had begun very early in the sequence, probably before initial human occupation. This is potentially an important argument, from several points of view which they canvass, but the evidence on which it is based, especially the uncertain identification and provenance of early ceramics at relatively high points in the dunes west of the main archaeological site areas, is open to question. We agree with Hudson (1994:12) and Marshall et al. (2000) in regarding at least Level 2 as having developed on a fairly strongly undulating surface. Our cores show variation of 3–4 m height in the lower boundary of Level 2 at the dunes' front (Figure 38), and there is at least 2 m of height variation in the upper surface of the sand ridges behind the dunes. Nevertheless, this is still comparatively low relief and hardly indicative of the kind of dune-building evident in the modern parabolic forms. The geomorphological model of Dickinson et al. (1998), substantially confirmed by de Biran (2001), has proven the most plausible in interpreting the archaeological and chronological evidence (Burley 2003; Burley and Dickinson 2004; Anderson et al. 2006).

Test excavations in rock shelters

Volivoli shelters

Approximately 1.5 km inland from the coast and the same distance west of the Vatueta distributary of the Sigatoka River is Volivoli village. Running immediately behind it along the western edge of the delta plain is an ancient channel of the Sigatoka River, and above that loom the Volivoli bluffs. They are on the edge of a 250 m high spur of fossiliferous Tertiary limestones and sandstones which dip seaward at 15–20^0 (Sawyer and Andrews 1901:92; see also Gilbert 1984:114). The southern margin of the spur abuts the inland edge of the Sigatoka dunes, forming a saddle through which pass the railroad and the Queen's Highway. Around the periphery of the spur and in dolines on its upper surface are numerous caves and shelters. Some of these have been investigated in pursuit of subfossil faunal remains (Chapters 2–3). Archaeological investigations consisted of test excavations in three sites (Figure 39), with the primary purpose of establishing occupation sequences.

Volivoli I

A small shelter is formed by a cluster of large boulders at the base of the bluffs adjacent to the Volivoli swamp. A test excavation of a 0.5 m x 1.0 m test pit disclosed a shallow deposit of a

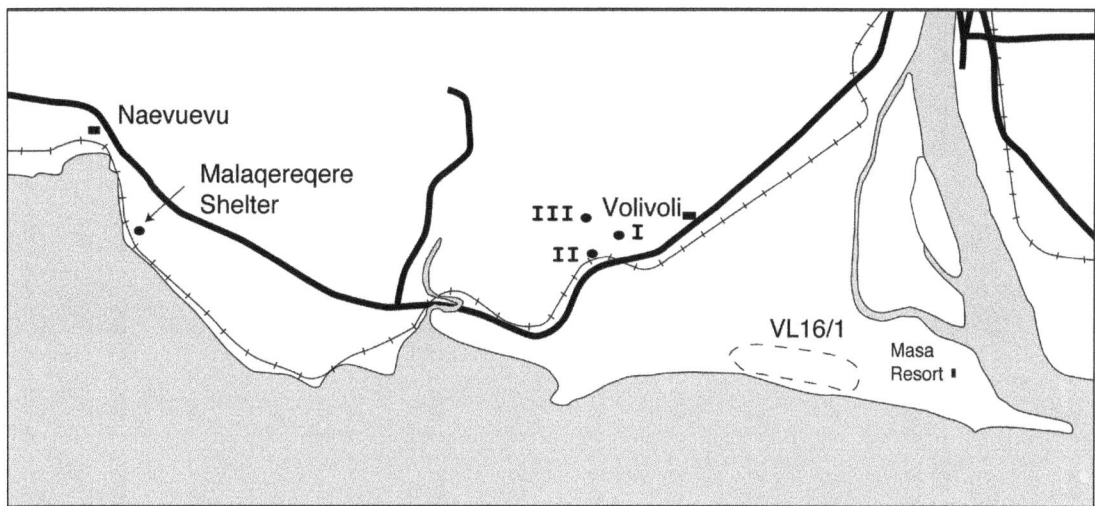

Figure 39. Location of Volivoli and Malaqereqere shelters.

damp, sticky, dark-brown to black loam (Layers 1 and 2) overlying weathered carbonate grit (Layer 3) (Figure 40). The shelter surface is only 0.5 m above the ground surface of the swamp. Small quantities of shell, bone and pottery were recovered by wet-sieving through 3 mm mesh.

Volivoli II

On the southern edge of the Volivoli bluffs, a rock shelter, formed by very large boulders, lies 14 m north of the railroad, at 106 m from the northern buttress of the rail bridge over the Queen's Highway. The rock shelter is 15 m long and about 2 m wide for most of its length. An excavation of a 1.0 x 1.5 m unit was made at the middle of the shelter (Figure 41). The excavation was by 10 cm spits within natural layers and all material was sieved. For Layer 1 it was possible to use a 3 mm sieve, but for Layers 3, 5 and 6 the stiff, dense clay resisted anything but the 6 mm sieve. Stratigraphy in this was as follows:

Layer 1: Fine, dusty, mid-brown loam containing pottery, some roof-fall and candlenut fragments, 0–12 cm.

Layer 2: A grey-white calcite layer extending discontinuously at 12–17 cm.

Layer 3: Mid-brown clay loam, stiff and slightly damp. Contained scattered charcoal, pottery, shell and small limestone clasts.

Layer 4: A grey-white discontinuous calcite band, 2 cm thick, which sloped from 44 cm to 63 cm across the west baulk.

Layer 5: Below the calcite, a stiff, orange-to-red clay loam packed with roof-fall and boulders up to 50 cm maximum length. This extended to 110 cm, but pottery and other cultural material disappeared at 80 cm.

Layer 6: From 110 cm to 130 cm, at which point the base of the deposit was reached in weathered, yellow limestone. A red-brown clay loam and gravel with relatively few larger limestone clasts. Several sherds were recovered at 110–115 cm.

Variation in the stratigraphy, including in the nature of the material and its colour, and in the existence of two calcite layers, suggested that Volivoli II represented a relatively long and varied occupational sequence, broken at intervals by periods of abandonment.

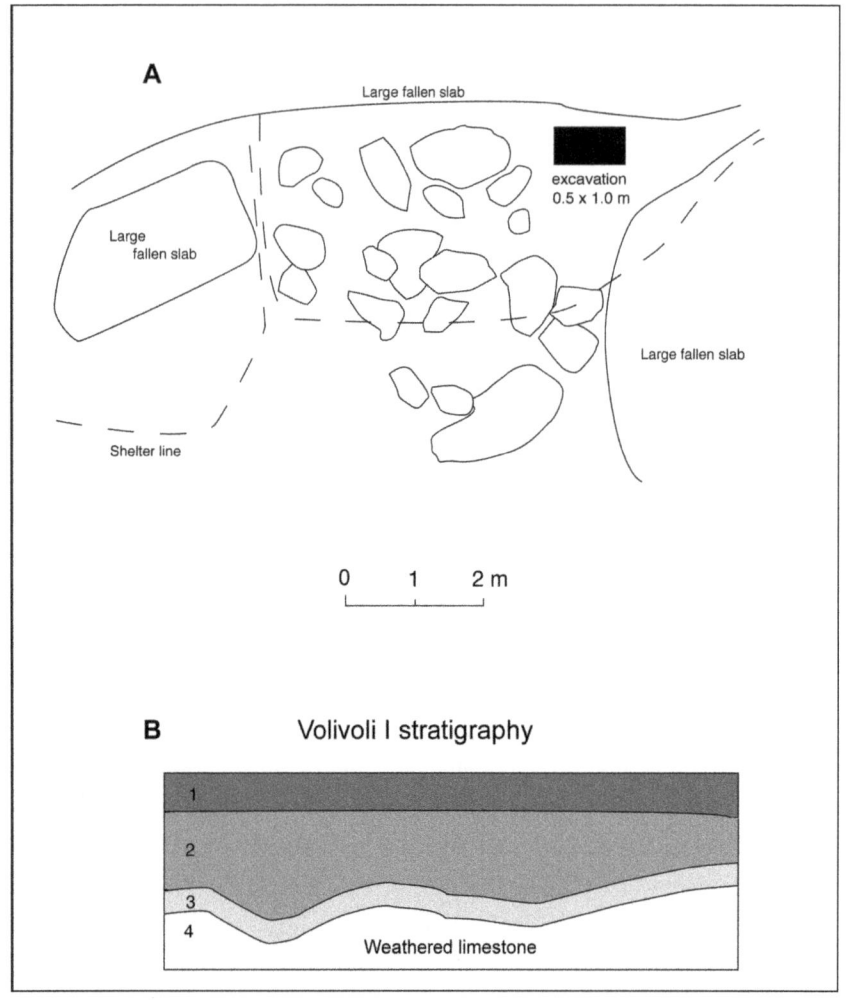

Figure 40. Volivoli I, plan of shelter (A) and excavation section (B).

Volivoli III

Directly above the Volivoli fossil site 2, named Qaranivokai, there is a small rock shelter formed in a doline. A 1.0 m x 1.0 m test pit was excavated in the floor of this shelter (Figure 42). Excavation was by 10 cm spits in natural layers. Material to 30 cm was sieved to 3 mm, but below that level to 6 mm. Below 30 cm depth, the excavation area was reduced by half. The stratigraphy was as follows:

Layer 1: Dark-brown, friable to blocky clay loam, with abundant fire-cracked stone, shell and pottery and small amounts of bone. At 10–12 cm were several calcite lenses. The soil became more blocky and clay-rich with depth. A 3–5 cm thick white ash at 35–40 cm. Adhering to its base were numerous pieces of charcoal.

Layer 2: Medium-brown fine sediment with abundant fragments of limestone from 45 cm to 80 cm depth. Cultural material sparse and diminishing with depth.

Layer 3: From 80 cm to 110 cm an orange-brown blocky clay with abundant limestone clasts and boulders. Some shell and pottery but scarcely any bone or charcoal was found down to 80 cm, where several calcite lenses were encountered. Below the calcite lenses was a tough, yellow-orange clay containing numerous pieces of limestone and no cultural material. It ran out on a flowstone or limestone floor which could not be penetrated.

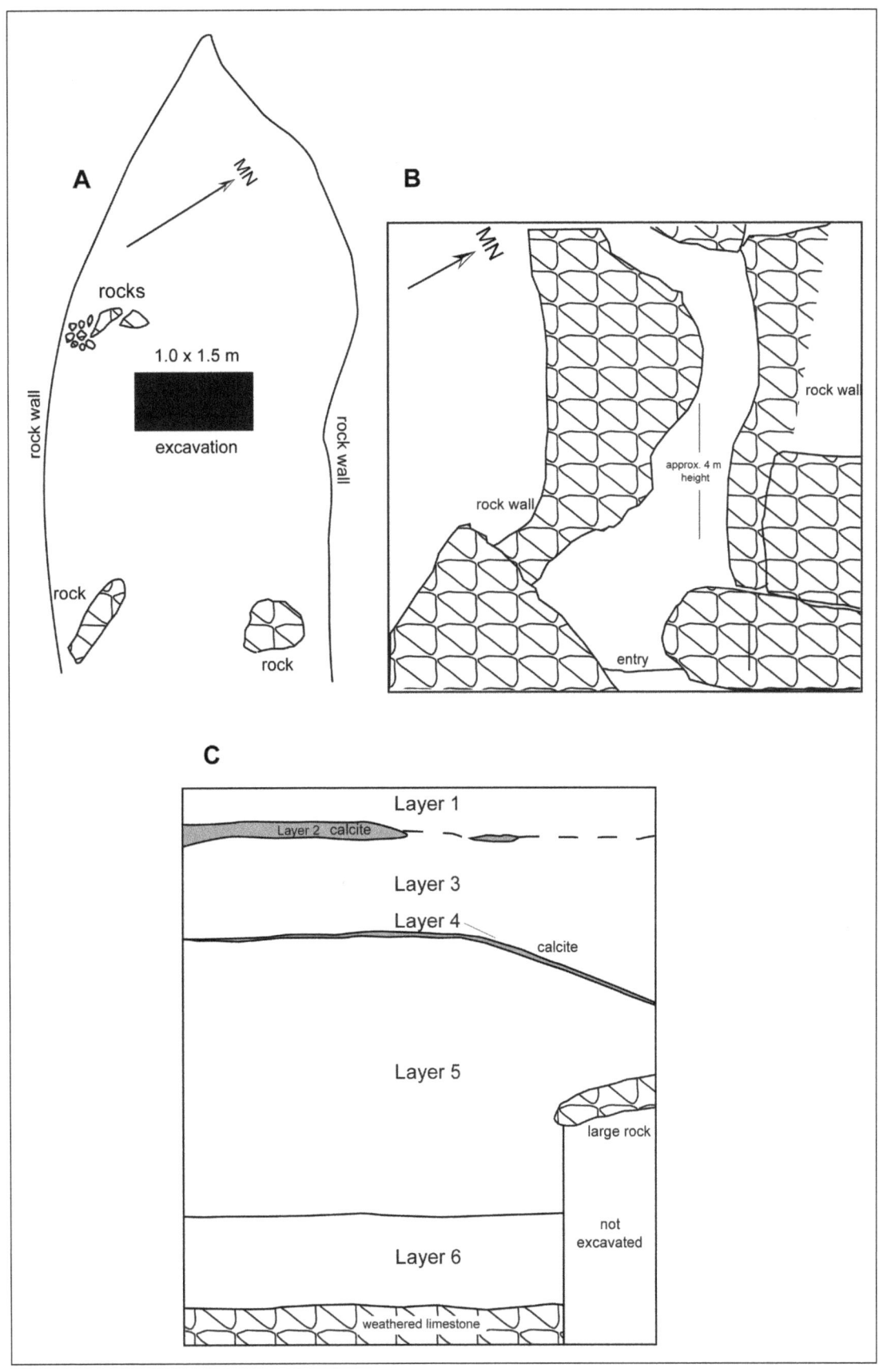

Figure 41. Volivoli II, plan of shelter (A), front entrance (B) and excavation section (C).

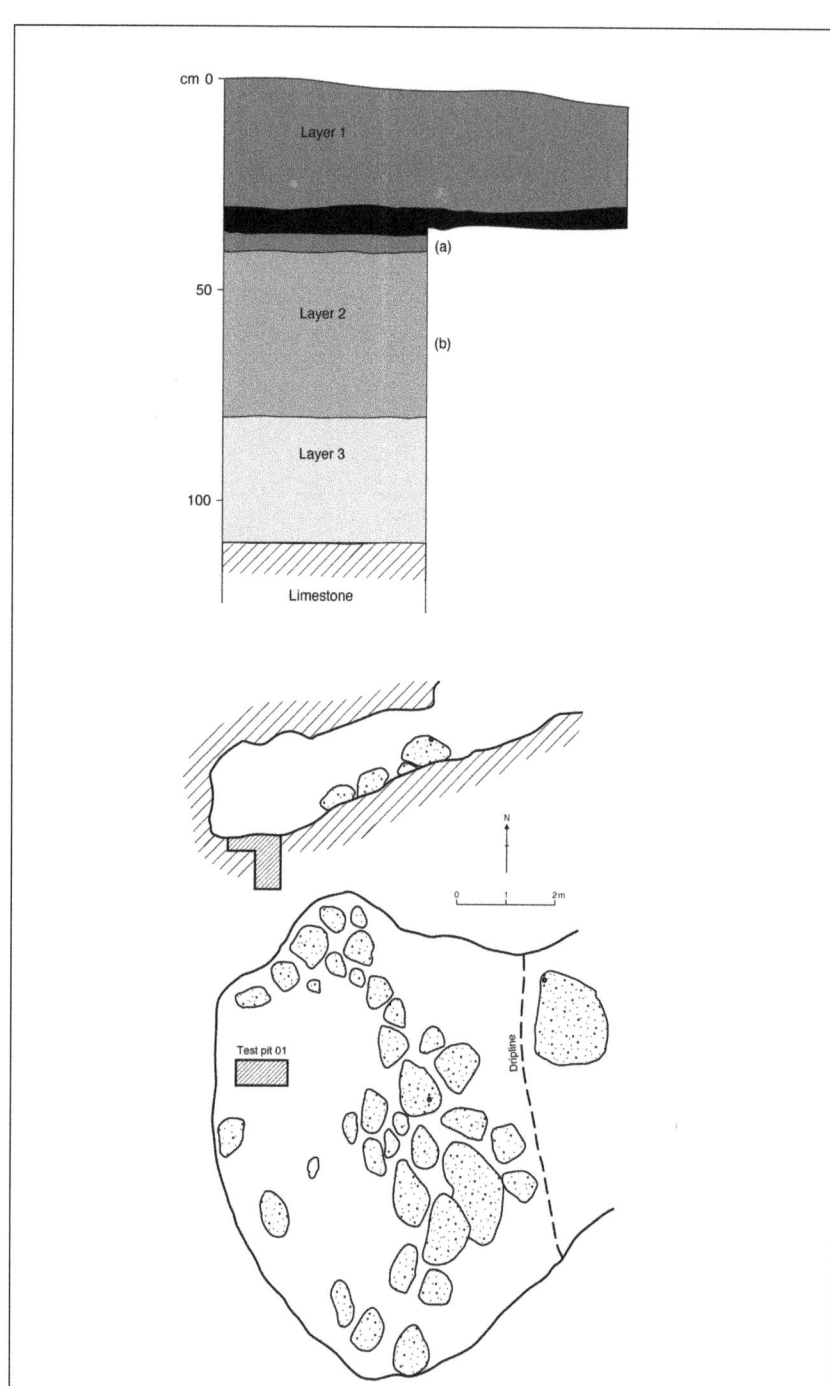

Figure 42. Volivoli III, plan (bottom) and profile of shelter (middle) and excavation section (top).

Malaqereqere shelter

This is a south-facing rock shelter located 1 km east of Naeuvevu village along the railway line (Figure 43). The shelter entrance is 12 m above the lagoon and 21 m north of the railroad cutting. At the entrance of the shelter is a 2 m wide flat, separated from an inner chamber, 10 m x 6 m, by a low wall of placed stones. A 1 m x 2 m excavation was laid out behind the rock wall (Figure 44). Excavation was by 10 cm spits, but followed the main layer changes, and material was sieved to 3 mm.

The stratigraphy was too finely complex in detail (Figure 44) to follow by stratigraphical excavation in plan. It consisted mainly of alternating thin layers and lenses, 0.5–5 cm thick, often disturbed by crab holes, of a soft, friable, brown to black loam and compact white to

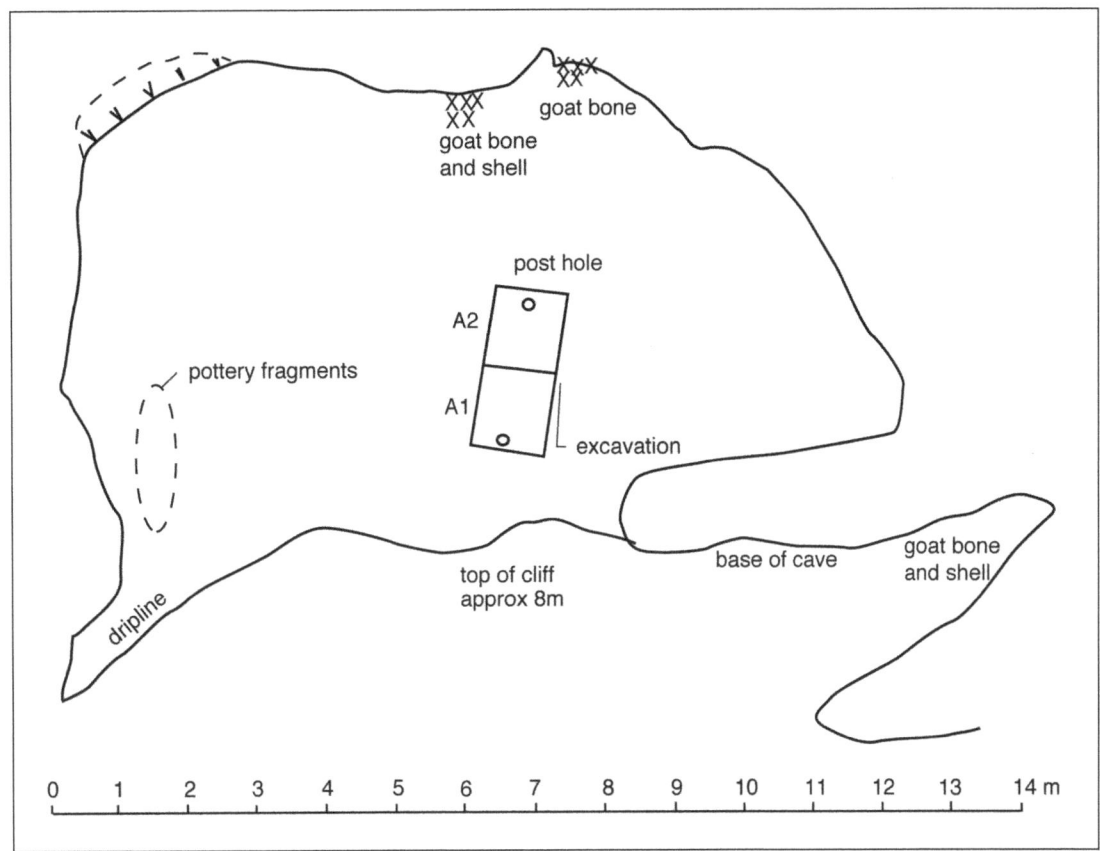

Figure 43. Malaqereqere, plan of shelter.

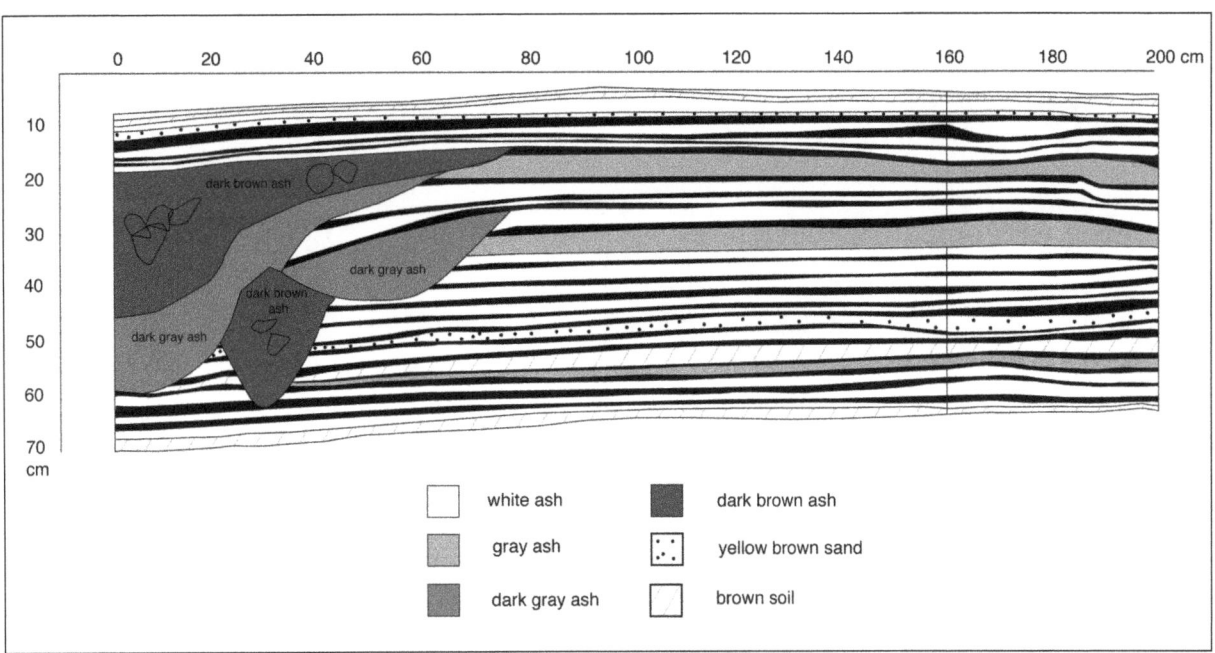

Figure 44. Malaqereqere, excavation section.

grey ash. At 40–50 cm, and again at 50–60 cm, the loam units were separated by yellow-brown sand. The base of the excavation, which reached to 68 cm, was formed by a flat, impenetrable, limestone floor. In Square A1, there was extensive disturbance resulting from the construction of a series of inter-cutting ovens. That aside, the main stratigraphy was as follows:

Layer 1: 5–15 cm (site datum was 5 cm above the surface). Consists of thin brown and white foliations of ash and loam, the ash containing much calcined shell which fell into dust at contact.

Layer 2: 15–25 cm. Similar to Layer 1 but separated from it by a spread of continuous white ash, approximately 3 cm thick, containing charcoal and fine black foliations.

Layer 3: 25–50 cm. Similar appearance but separated from Layer 2 by a continuous spread of black ash and charcoal, 2 cm thick. Layer 3 also contained remnants of a small oven in Square A1, marked by ash, charcoal and burnt coral. At the base of this layer is a continuous thin spread of yellow-brown sand.

Layer 4: 50–55 cm. Mostly yellow-brown sand lenses separating thin foliations of brown loam and grey ash, with one 2–3 cm loam layer extending the length of the excavation and separating this unit from Layer 5.

Layer 5: 55–68 cm. Similar material to Layer 4. At the base of the site there is a thicker (5 cm) lens of brown loam containing charcoal, ash and bone.

There were faunal remains throughout the layers, but in the ash, especially, were calcined and finely fragmented molluscan and crab shell and echinoderm spines. Fish bone occurred sparsely. Pottery was scattered throughout the deposit, mostly in the brown loam, and it was mostly thick-walled material from deep bowls and straight-sided vessels.

Qaranioso shelters

Large caves and shelters lie high up in a 300 m high limestone massif in the Tau district (Figure 35). Some of the caves have been mined for guano. Two small test excavations were undertaken.

Qaranioso I

This is very large cave, still inhabited by substantial colonies of swiftlets. Immediately inside the entrance is a steeply sloping sedimentary face going down approximately 5 m to the main cave floor, the latter covered in deep guano. The face was formed by guano mining. A re-faced section disclosed the following stratigraphy (Figure 45):

Layer 1: 0–80 cm of stiff, red-brown clay containing sparse shell (*Anadara*, *Turbo*), some fish spines and charcoal. A few plain body sherds were recovered. At 30 cm depth was a small hearth, which was sampled for charcoal.

Layer 2: 80–140 cm of loose brown guano. This contained no cultural material and a probe showed that it continued down for at least another 70 cm.

Qaranioso II

About 20 m below Qaranioso I is another, but much smaller cave. It is bell-shaped and open at the top but has substantial shelter around the sides and near the entrance (Figure 45). A 0.5 m x 1.0 m test pit was excavated in the entrance shelter, by 10 cm spits, with sieving to 4 mm for all material, but to 2 mm for that which contained small bone. The stratigraphy was as follows (see also Anderson et al. 2000):

Layer 1: 0–13 cm of powdery silt containing abundant pottery and shell. The layer terminates in a thin calcite or ash.

Layer 2: 13–49 cm. An orange-brown friable silty-loam, containing large pieces of limestone, marine shell, bird and reptile bones and abundant pottery.

Layer 3: 49–53 cm at west end of the trench, 50–65 cm at east end. Soft chalky calcite containing many limestone concretions and pebbles, plus large ?land snail shells and some reptile, rat and bat bone.

Layer 4: Extends down to at least 90 cm. Loose, brown guano.

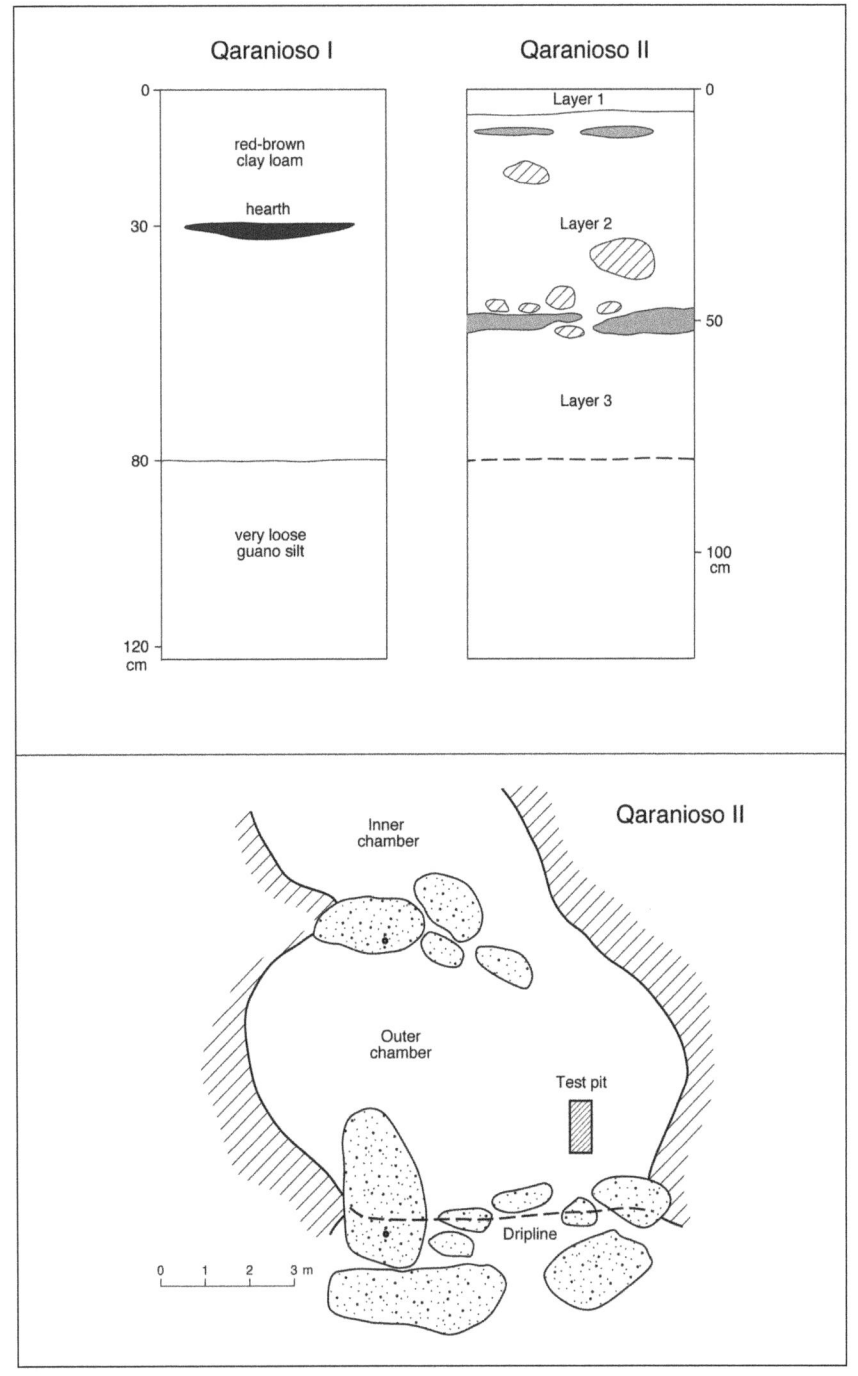

Figure 45. Qaranioso I and II, stratigraphy (I and II) and plan of shelter (II).

Paddle-relief pottery extended down to Layer 2 and one tooth-impressed sherd, possibly of Lapita age, was recovered from Layer 3. Further excavations were planned for this site in 2000, but were cancelled on account of the political emergency.

Tuvu shelter

In the middle reaches of the Sigatoka River is Tuvu village and nearby is a shelter, one of several recorded initially by Gifford (1951). The shelter is 14 m x 6 m, with a low rock pile at the entrance, from which it is a step down on to a dry floor scattered with sherds of plain pottery. At the back of the shelter is a low entrance to a second chamber (Figure 46). Several metres inside that a rock wall seals the rest of the cave. It is believed to be a burial chamber. A test pit of 0.8 m x 0.5 m, was excavated in 10 cm spits and by natural layers, in the centre of the shelter, 1 m behind the entrance rock pile. This disclosed the following stratigraphy:

Layer 1: 0–10 cm of grey silt or guano with sherds.

Layer 2: 10–18 cm depth. Soft, foliated calcite.

Layer 3: 18–52 cm. This is a brown-grey slightly compacted silt and guano layer, with some faint lenses of charcoal and scarce shell and pottery.

Layer 4: From 52 cm to at least 130 cm is a soft, orange-brown guano containing no cultural material.

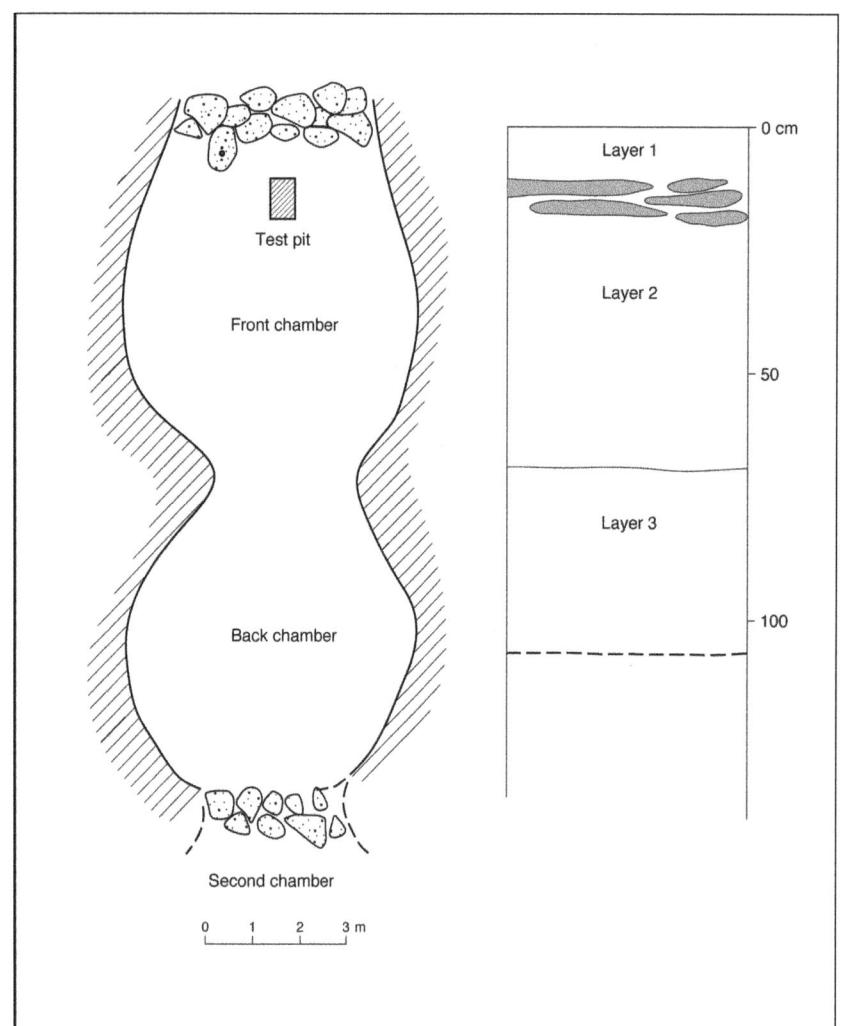

Figure 46. Tuvu, plan of shelter and excavation section.

Research on data from Karobo VL 18/1

The site of Karobo was discovered and excavated in the 1960s by the Director of the Fiji Museum, Bruce Palmer. Despite Palmer (1965) making some introductory remarks about the Karobo site, he never subjected the ceramic material to detailed examination nor had the site dated. The VL 18/1 assemblage was, however, frequently mentioned as an important site for understanding the ceramic dimensions of the Navatu phase, as the site was well stratified and contained an intact decorated pottery 'horizon' (Palmer 1965; Golson 1974; Frost 1979). Permission was given in 1997 to re-examine the Karobo material held by the Fiji Museum. The unpublished field notes and illustrations relating to the Karobo excavations were traced to the Auckland Institute and Museum by Professor Roger Green (Department of Anthropology, Auckland University), who copied the material. The following site descriptions derive primarily from those documents.

Location and environs

The site was located at the eastern end of Karobo beach (Shepherd 1990) on a narrow sand spit/ dune ridge to the east of a small unnamed stream. The site lies 6.5 km east of the mouth of the Navua River and 1.2 km west of the Taunovo River (Figure 47). A mangrove swamp lay behind the sand ridge and on its seaward side was a narrow white-sand beach. Small water-cut channels ran through the swamp and bordered the base of the dune. At its highest point the dune ridge was 80 cm higher than the beach surface and was between 6 m and 10 m wide (Figure 48).

Karobo was discovered by Fergus Clunie in late 1963 or early 1964. Clunie collected sherds from a stream-cut channel below the sand ridge and recognised their similarity to leaf and paddle-relief sherds from Sigatoka. Karobo was visited by Bruce Palmer (Fiji Museum), Clunie, Roger Green and others who examined the site and made a collection of the surface ceramics. The site was then surveyed by Les Thompson, Clunie and Palmer. The first excavation, conducted by Palmer, a Fiji Museum worker and local assistants, took place from June 18 to 20, 1964. Palmer and others then excavated from July 1 to 3, and July 15 to 18. Jack Golson, of the Australian National University, excavated from August 26 to 28 and Thompson surveyed two cross-sections of the site on August 30. Further excavations were conducted from January 28 to

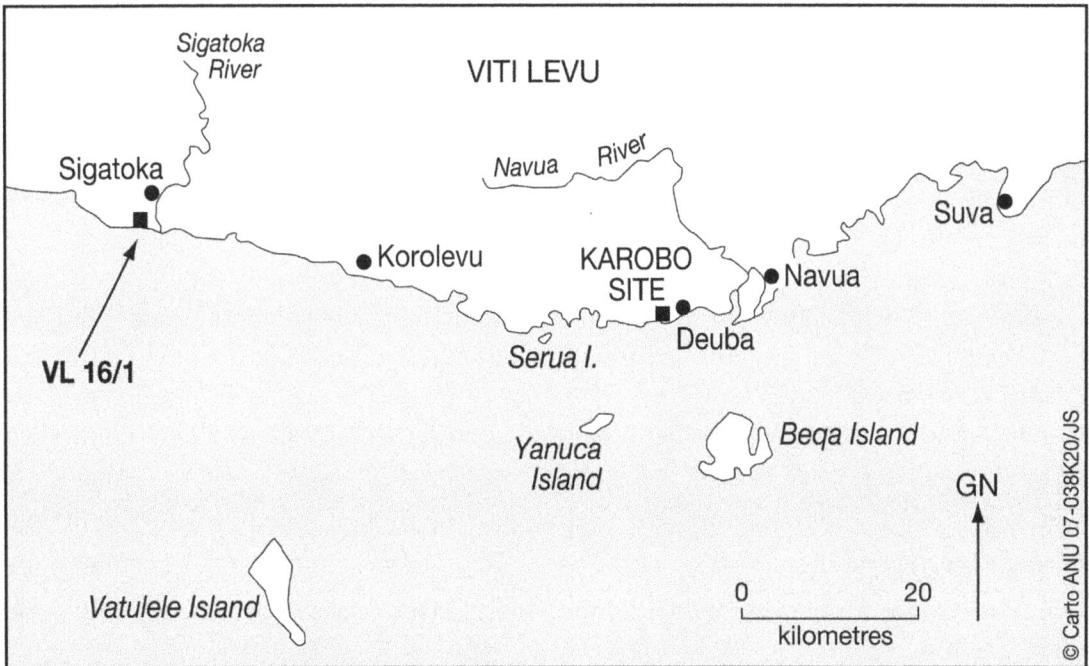

Figure 47. Location of Karobo (VL 18/1) (after Palmer 1965).

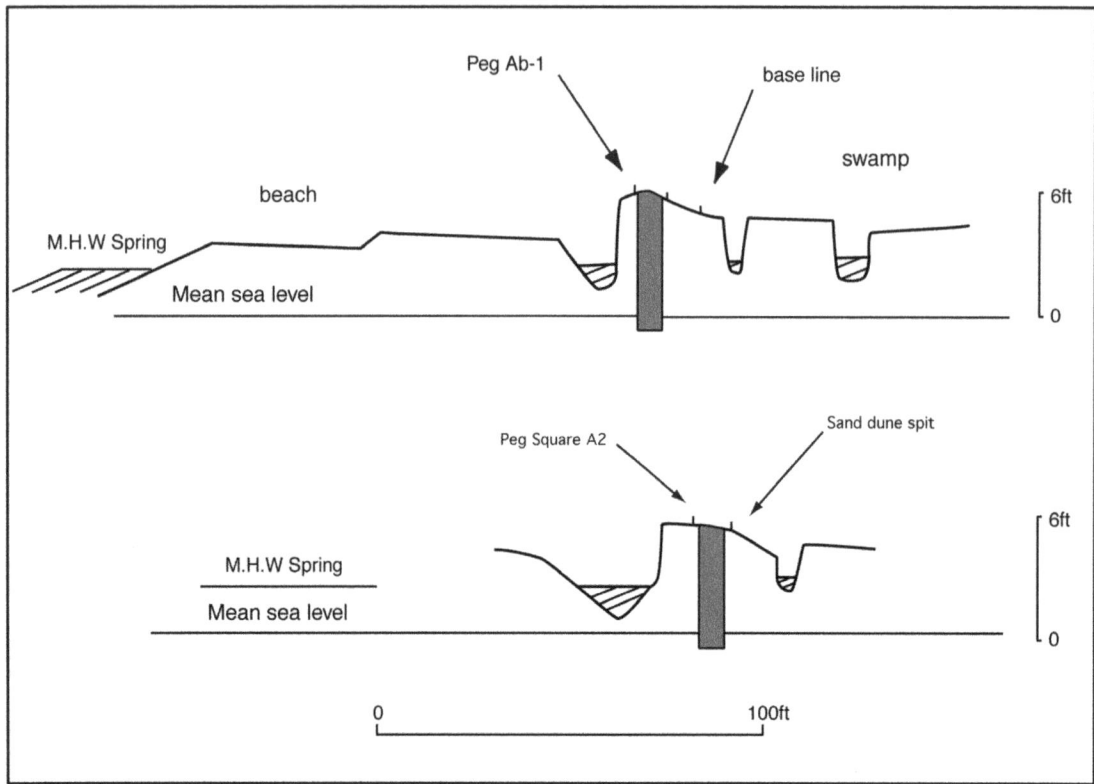

Figure 48. Karobo excavation cross-sections. Redrawn from Thompson 30/08/1964.

31, and February 1 to 8, 1965, with the final excavation taking place from May 16 to 20, 1966. Thus, at least 28 days of excavation are represented by the seven periods of work at Karobo.

A 140 ft baseline running east–west was placed along the landward side of the sand ridge. Squares 10 ft x 10 ft were marked along the grid from east to west using the southeast corner of each square as a reference point. Squares were labelled alphabetically in the north–south plane and numerically in the east–west line. The square with the eastern datum peg was A1, that to its left A2 and the square immediately north of A1 was B1. Squares behind the baseline were identified by lower-case letters. Square Aa-1 was directly south of Square A1 and Square Ab-1 was south of Aa-1. A plan of the site reconstructed from Palmer's description is given in Figure 49. The baseline-square identification system does not appear to have been used in the excavation of Squares X and Y, because if it had they would be located between 73 m and 76 m north of the sand ridge. These squares do not appear to have been excavated by Palmer and a report on Square Y makes it clear that these squares were placed on the seaward side of the sand spit, but at an unknown distance east or west of the baseline datum point.

The sand ridge was heavily vegetated and the presence of trees and stumps meant that square excavation was by quadrant, with the southeast quadrant called Quadrant 1 and remaining quadrants numbered clockwise. There was variation in quadrant size. Six-inch baulks were left within each square and each quadrant, leaving a 1 ft baulk between adjoining quadrants. This approach was followed by Palmer and Golson but may not have been adhered to by other excavators.

Methods and stratigraphy

Excavation was by natural layer using a trowel when cultural remains were dense and by spade when 'non-productive' zones were encountered. Material was sieved (mesh size unknown), or the spoil was examined if the density of archaeological material was low. When the water table was

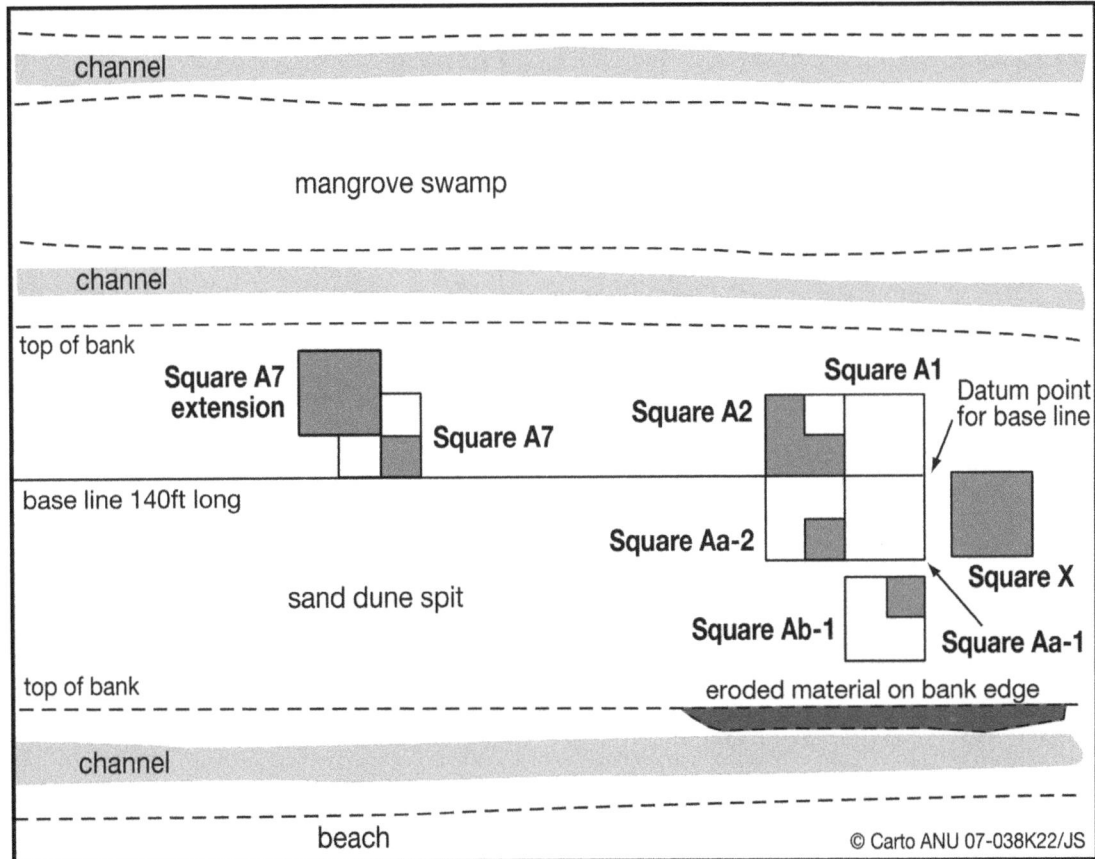

Figure 49. Karobo, plan view of excavated squares (shaded) and environs.

reached, spoil was mounded to form a dam and the matrix removed to the surface for sorting.

The stratigraphy at Karobo consisted of alternating layers of different-coloured sand interspersed in the lower levels by lenses of charcoal and pottery. The stratigraphy of the primary squares is summarised below to provide an overall picture of the deposits across the site. Depth measurements are given in metric units.

Square A2, Quadrants 1 to 3 (Figure 50)

Layer 1: Thin grey-sand humus layer 5–15 cm deep.

Layer 2: Discontinuous white sand 5–10 cm in depth. The layer contained small quantities of eroded ceramics, pumice and oven stones.

Layer 3: Compacted brown sand around 60 cm deep. One *Trochus niloticus* shell, with small flecks of charcoal, a few pot sherds and pumice.

Layer 4: Yellow-brown damp and compacted sand with rotted pumice, between 10 cm and 25 cm thick. This layer lensed out in Quadrant 3 and was thicker in the south of the square.

Layer 5: Grey-brown sand very damp and in its upper 20 cm mottled with orange-yellow patches. Beneath the mottled material was a clean, grey, very damp sand. Cultural material was abundant at 1.30 m depth and included fragments of cut wood, seeds, leaves, pottery and charcoal.

Square A7 (Figure 50)

Layer 1: Thin humus layer with grey sand approximately 5–15 cm deep.

Layer 2: Clean white sand up to 20 cm in depth.

Layer 3: Brown sand with abundant humus and many roots. Some pumice but no ceramics or other cultural material. Depth 30–40 cm.

Layer 4: Yellow sand with small flecks of charcoal, pumice and a few ceramic sherds, approximately 30–40 cm deep.

Layer 5a and b: Grey sand which was lighter in the upper margins (5a) and darker below (5b). Few ceramics or other cultural remains were excavated from this square. Below this were layers described as thin and highly stratified natural deposits.

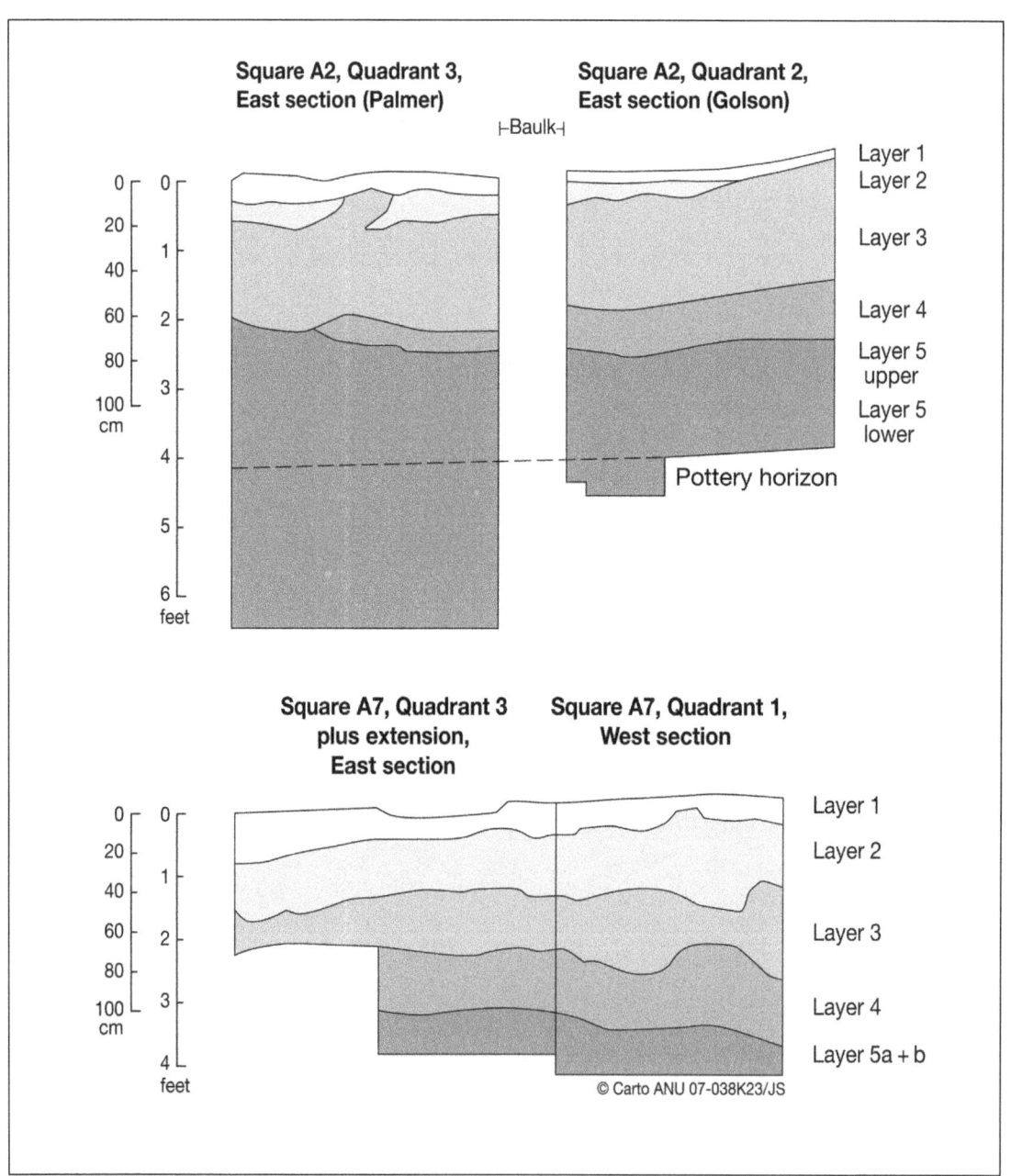

Figure 50. Karobo sections, Squares A2 and A7.

Squares Aa-2 and Ab-1 (Figure 51)

Layers 1 and 2: As above, but Layer 1 was thinner and Layer 2 thinner and more patchy than comparable layers from Square A2.

Layer 3: Dark-black sand layer with abundant charcoal and roots. Around 20 cm in depth. The layer contained small quantities of pot sherds, heat-cracked oven stones and pumice.

Layer 4: Dense layer of charcoal which lensed out toward the north of Square Aa-2. Layer thickness was 5–20 cm. No cultural material was recorded from this layer.

Layer 5: Grey-brown stained sand found in patches in Square Ab-1. Not continuous through the squares. In Square Aa-2 patches of Layer 5 intruded into Layer 6 (Figure 51), but in Square Ab-1 the layer was more regular, around 10–20 cm thick.

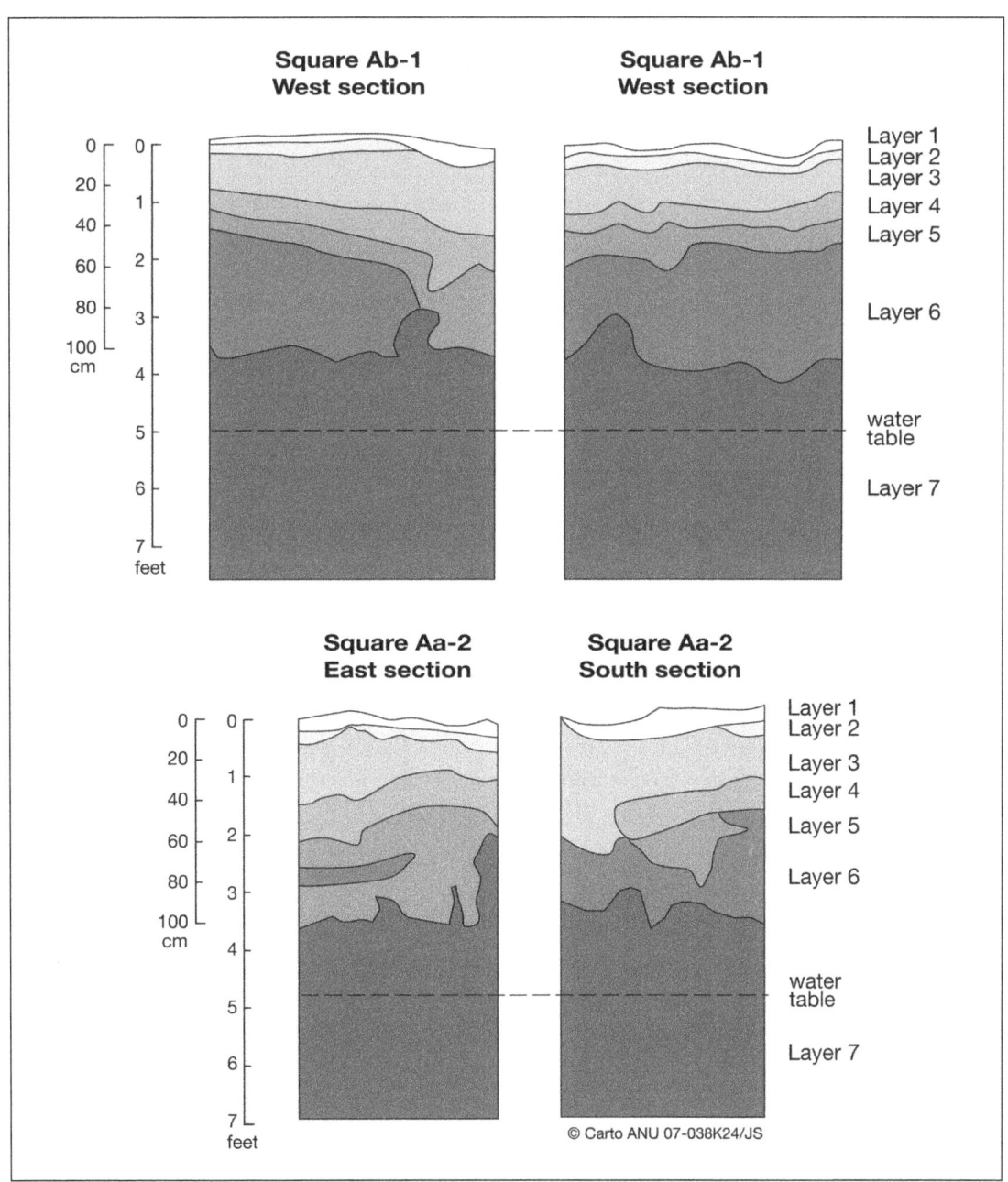

Figure 51. Karobo sections, Squares Ab-1 and Aa-2.

Layer 6: Yellow-brown sand with pumice, occasional oven stones and ceramic sherds. Towards the bottom of the layer the sand became cleaner and more yellow in colour. This layer was variable in depth, ranging from 10 cm to 45 cm.

Layer 7: Dark-grey sand mottled in its upper margins with small patches of yellow-brown sand. Below the mottled zone was the wet grey sand in which ceramics, charcoal, seeds and wood were abundant. This layer continued below the water table and was more than 1 m thick.

Squares X and Y

The stratigraphy of Square X was similar to that of Square A2 where bands of white and yellow sand gave way to a lower layer of grey sand (Layer 5b) at 75 cm depth. This layer was excavated to 1.7 m and at the base was the 'pottery horizon' identified by Palmer and Golson in Square A2. Square Y contained four layers; humus layer followed by a clean white beach sand and then a blackish compacted soil with abundant charcoal, oven stones and a few ceramic sherds. Below this was Layer 4 which consisted of a yellow sand with flecks of charcoal and pieces of pumice. Most of the ceramics were found in the upper 15 cm of Layer 4 and the excavation finished at a depth of 60 cm.

Excavation features

Features were recorded from Square A2, Quadrants 2 and 3, and Square Y. In Square A2 (Quadrant 3) groups of large sherds belonging to flat-based platters were found at 1.3 m depth (Layer 5). Under the platter sherds were concentrations of charcoal, ash and large numbers of oven stones. In Quadrant 2 a large log projected from the south wall at the level of the pottery horizon (1.3–1.5 m depth). Remains of oven building and rake out were identified in Square Y in Layer 3 at 25–35 cm depth.

Site formation and use

As there is little detailed information available on the Karobo environs and sediments, the following description of site formation is preliminary and requiring further investigation. The earliest *in situ* occupation level at Karobo appears to be 1.4 m below the current sand spit/ridge surface, represented by the hearth in Square A2, Quadrant 3. That is, near the top of Layer 5 in Square A2 and the top of Layer 7 in Squares Ab-1 and Aa-2. At this time, the site appears to have been a low beach ridge. Proximity of the cultural deposits to the water table probably results from sediment compaction rather than a post-1600 BP rise in sea level (W. Dickinson, pers. comm., University of Arizona). The geomorphology of Domona Beach just east of Karobo suggests that the past 2000 years witnessed substantial progradation of beach ridges when sediments from the developing Navua/Deuba Delta were transported westwards by the prevailing southwesterly waves. Shepherd (1990:553) dated a log in the Holocene beach ridge deposits of Domona Beach at 1600±50 BP (NZ-7554). It seems probable that the prograding coastline at Karobo had, therefore, reached its present position by ca.1600 BP and the Karobo occupation took place on the beach berm. Introduction of fluvial-borne sediments behind the berm led to the development of swamp conditions and expansion of mangrove communities.

No bone and little marine shell was recovered from the Karobo excavations. However, Palmer recorded that a variety of nuts, including *Canarium* and *Pandanus*, was present. Most of the botanical remains were found in the lower water-logged layers and Palmer suggested that a cultural origin was probable for the remains, although acknowledging that crabs and water transport of seeds and leaves could introduce some of the smaller fragments. Use of the nuts to manufacture coconut oil using the flat-based platters was suggested as a primary activity at Karobo (Palmer 1965). At Sigatoka it has been suggested that similar vessels were used to recover salt through evaporation. However, Golson was far more hesitant about attributing purposeful prehistoric human activity to the nut specimens, noting that in the sump hole excavated into Layer 5 of Quadrant 2, Square A2, shell fragments from two nuts occurred in a crab hole. The low height of the dune spit could also argue against Palmer's suggestion, as both wave action seaward, and flooding and channel cutting landward, could be responsible for the deposition of the wood, nuts and leaves. Nuts are commonly deposited on beaches in Fiji (Smith 1990) and, as Matthews and Gosden (1997) note, care needs to be taken when interpreting botanical remains from archaeological sites. Overall, the prehistoric activities at the Karobo site are not well understood, although cooking, the manufacture of flat-based platters and the preparation of domestic products such as salt or coconut oil are possibilities.

Beqa Island and Ugaga Island

Beqa Island has an area of 36 sq. km and it formed from a subaerial stratovolcano about 5 million years ago, while Ugaga Island is a small volcanic island about 0.25 km^2 located 3.5 km southwest of Beqa within the 390 sq. km Beqa lagoon (Figure 52). Beqa is high enough to create a marked orographic effect with more rainfall (about 300 cm annually) on the windward or southeastern side than the leeward side (Rajotte and Bigay 1981). Kulu Bay is situated on the southwest coast of Beqa Island and faces southwest towards Ugaga Island, 3.5 km distant. Dentate-stamped sherds were among a small surface collection of 141 sherds collected by Crosby (1988) and the location was given the code BQ175A.

Kulu Bay 1

Sherds, including some of Lapita type, are scattered on the surface approximately 65 m directly inland from the HTM in the middle of the bay (Figure 52). They lie in a shallow swale between two low ridges which lie more or less parallel to the beach front. The seaward ridge is of sand, but the inland ridge is of unsorted boulders and soil. It is an irregular feature sloping gently back into the forest floor inland and is probably an old stream bank. In any event, it is apparent that water moves periodically down the swale. A 3.0 sq. m excavation was set out in the swale in an area where some dentate-stamped sherds were recovered. The stratigraphy was as follows:

Layer 1: 0–25 cm of stiff, blocky, chocolate-brown clay loam, containing sherds and scarce shell. It was probably a garden soil.

Layer 2: From 25 cm to 110–130 cm in square C11. The matrix is of stiff, exceptionally sticky, dark-brown clay and shell hash, with some shell midden. The layer is increasingly wet with depth. Below 50–60 cm there is an increase in the quantity of bone, especially of fish bone. Chert, quartz and basalt flakes occur throughout and pottery is common. The latter is mostly plainware but it includes dentate and paddle-impressed wares, mixed together.

Layer 3: From 110 cm to 130–160 cm in square C11. The matrix is the same stiff, exceptionally sticky, dark-brown clay. It has no shell hash, but a few thin lenses of yellow carbonate sand near the bottom. Large shells of *Turbo* and other taxa are more conspicuous. Bone is both relatively more abundant than above and in greater diversity, including bird bone. The same pottery and lithics as above occurred in conjunction with candlenut and other woody fragments.

Layer 4: This is a beach deposit at 160 cm+ (excavated to 170 cm and probed to at least 0.5 m below that) of blue-grey coarse sand and shell grit, with broken shell and coral pieces in clasts up to 10 cm long.

Throughout the stratigraphy there is abundant evidence of crab-hole disturbance, which might account for the mixing of pottery types. The water table occurs at about 1.1 m and is probably responsible for acidic conditions in which the shell hash of Layer 2 has disappeared in Layer 3, leaving only the larger shells. The absence of any features, the relative scarcity of charcoal, and an impression of a broad homogeneity in the material from top to bottom suggests this is a transported site. It has either (or both) been washed down the swale from further inland – although there was no surface indication of that upstream in the swale; or deposited by storm surge. The mixing of substantial quantities of shell hash with clay might indicate the latter mechanism.

The first square excavated was C10, which was taken out in 0.2 m spits down to 0.6 m. When the nature of the material was apparent, and despite the difficulties of doing so, the remainder of the excavation was in 10 cm spits. Material was bucketed down to the beach and washed in sea water. The stiff, exceptionally sticky clay would not wash through any sieve, even with considerable effort. It had a toffee-like consistency and for the most part it was pulled into small pieces over the sieves, to extract the larger pieces of pottery and midden, the residue then being rubbed through 4 mm, and in bone-rich areas, 2 mm, sieves. Inevitably, this led to some

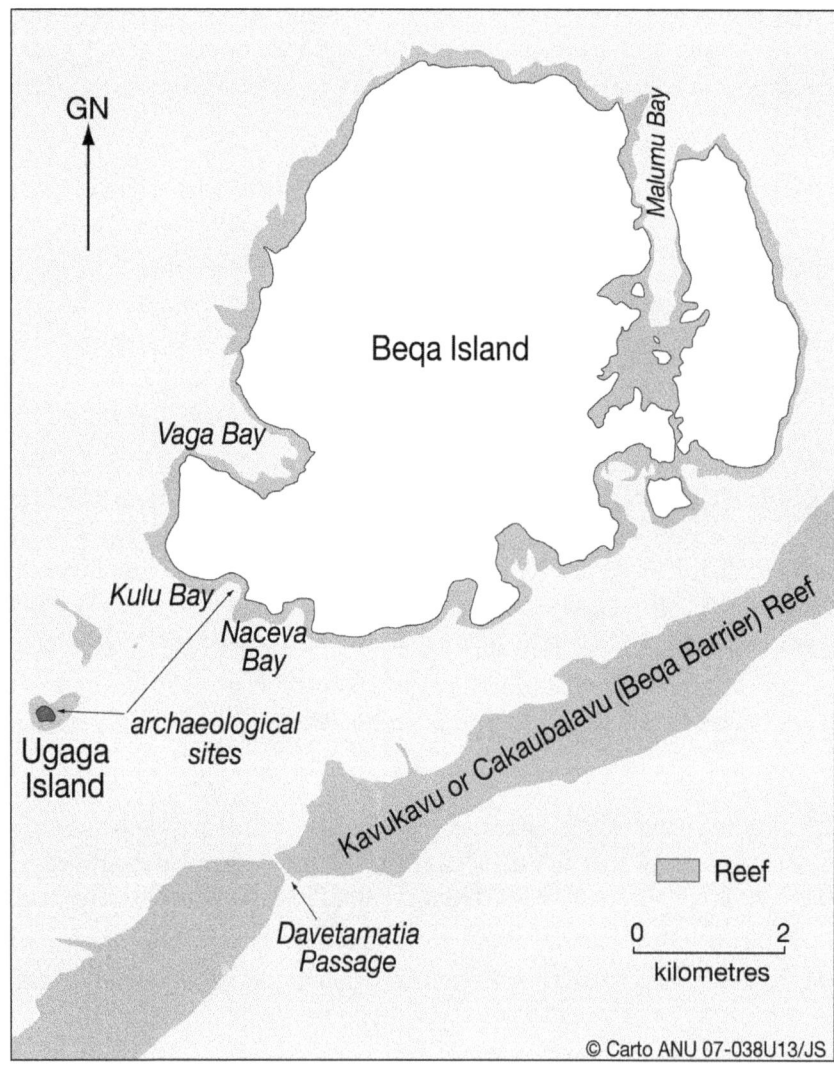

Figure 52. Location of Ugaga Island and Kulu Bay.

damage to the material, and while the site is quite rich it was decided not to excavate below 1 m in C9 and C10, nor to open any additional squares until some means of dealing with the stickiness of the matrix could be found. Subsequent enquiries were not encouraging, since the usual de-flocculating chemicals cannot be used safely, in environmental terms, at the industrial levels required.

Kulu Bay 2

Halfway between site 1 and the beach is Kulu 2. It was located not because of any surface evidence but to test the seaward extent of the Kulu 1 stratigraphy. In fact, excavation encountered two bundle burials, of one larger and one smaller adult individual, only 20 cm below the surface. There was some paddle-impressed sherds in the vicinity, but not obviously associated with the burials. The latter were exposed and photographed, then reburied in the same place. Our workers from Naceva village, in the next bay, conducted a brief service and set a margin of stones and a headstone at the grave. The stratigraphy of Kulu 2 shows that yellow beach sand extends for at least a metre below a 20 cm topsoil of sandy brown loam.

Ugaga Island

Ugaga Island is located 3.5 km southwest of Naceva Bay on Beqa Island (Figure 52). The island is about 150–200 m in diameter and surrounded by a fringing reef. It has small beaches on the southern, northern and western sides, but only the northern beach, which is sheltered from the prevailing southeast trade winds, is of any extent. The island is composed of augite-olivine basalt breccia of early Pliocene age (Band 1968; Whelan et al. 1985). The main ridge of this material runs east–west and reaches an elevation of 20 m above sea level. There is no permanent freshwater source on the island. A small sand plain below the volcanic ridge, with an area approximately 30 m x 35 m contains archaeological deposits. To its north, the sand plain has been eroded by wave action and forms a terrace edge which is 1.5–2.0 m above the high-tide water level. Outlier coconut palms 2–4 m from the terrace edge indicate recent storm erosion. The beach zone is 20–28 m wide at low tide. Behind the beach terrace, the sand plain is bordered by soil and rock-covered slopes (Figure 53). Vegetation consists of numerous economic introductions, including coconut, pandanus, banana, breadfruit and lemon trees and grasses (e.g. *Panim* and *Pennisteum*). No root crops were observed on the island in 1997.

Ugaga Island was given to the Vunivalu of Serua, as payment for defending Naceva village against attack from Rukua around 1830. Food crops planted on the island by the people of Naceva were said to have been taken to Serua. In 1997, links with Serua were still strong but there was some uncertainty over the ownership of Ugaga Island, with the Vunivalu of Serua, Naceva village and the Lawaki Mataqali all having some claim. In practice, permission to visit the island is sought through Naceva village. Fishing rights around Ugaga Island are jointly held by villagers from Sawau, Rukua, Naceva and Yanuca Island. The prehistoric site on Ugaga Island was first recorded by Andrew Crosby, then a student at Auckland University, in the mid-1980s (Crosby 1988). Two sites on the northern beach edge were identified (UG 1 and UG 2) and estimated as covering 1500 sq. m. Pottery sherds were obtained from a thin charcoal-stained surface layer 150 mm in depth. Between 46% and 52% of the recovered sherds were decorated. Heavy impressed 'ribs', parallel ribs, chevron ribs and cross-hatch-impressed sherds were abundant. Rims were mostly expanded but some sharply everted rims were found. Crosby (1988:115) concluded from the ceramic collection that Ugaga was likely to be a single-phase site that recorded the transition from the Sigatoka to the Navatu phase (2200–1800 BP). Further, there was the possibility that Ugaga was undisturbed and therefore provided an '... opportunity to gain a full areal record of site layout from this poorly understood period of Fiji's prehistory' (Crosby 1988:223).

112 Atholl Anderson and Geoffrey Clark

An initial walk-over survey of the island suggested the main archaeological deposits were located on the sand plain behind the northern beach edge. Ceramics and shell fragments were eroding along the terrace edge from the eastern edge of the beach to a distance 35 m west of that position. The first excavation was a 1 m x 1 m square called Test Pit 1, located to test the area immediately behind the daily camp site and north of a water tank built in 1992 (Figure 53). Although a post hole and a large *Tridacna maxima* shell were found in Test Pit 1, the ceramics were few, fragmentary and eroded.

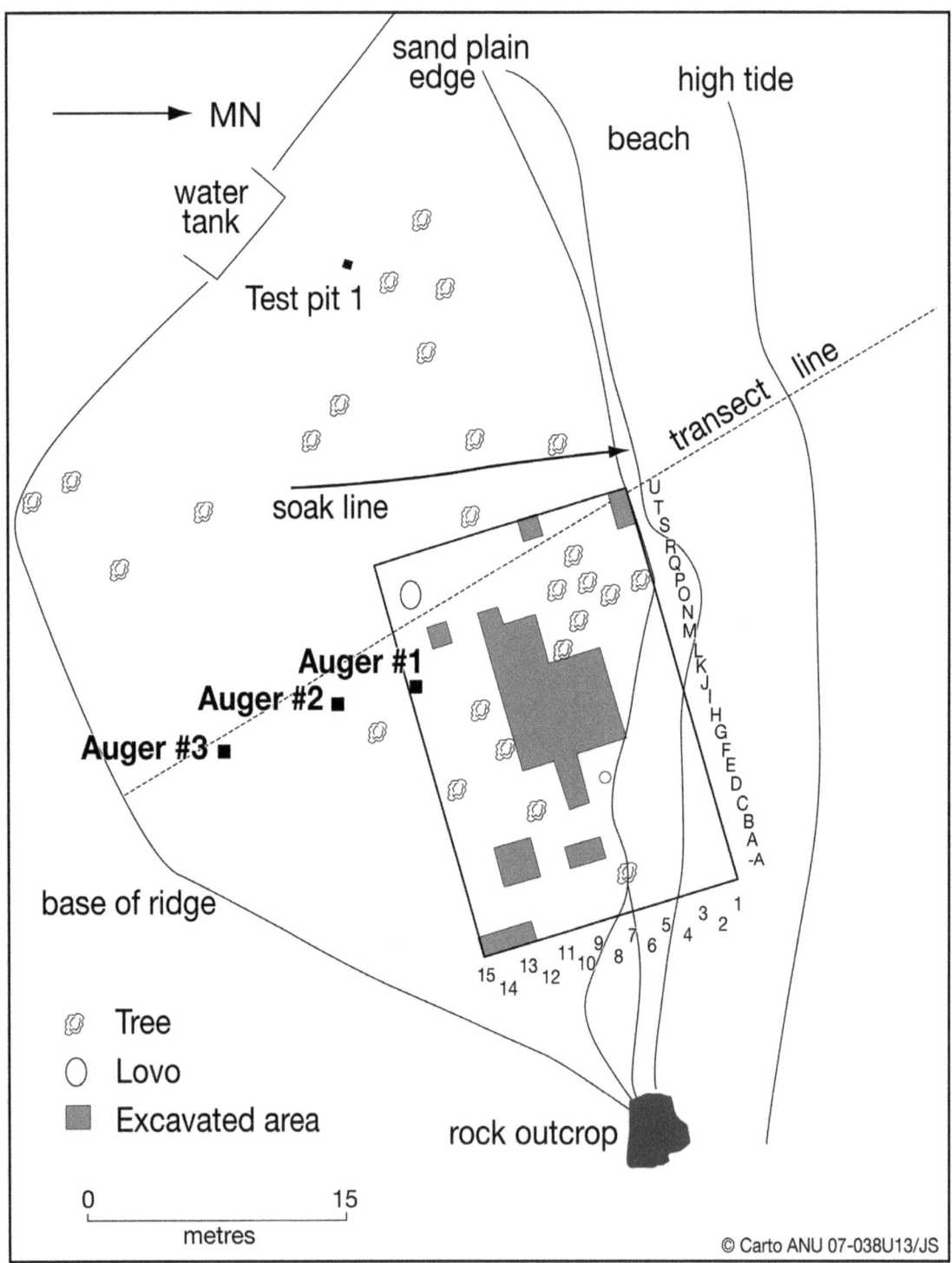

Figure 53. Ugaga Island, plan view of excavated area and environs.

Attention then focused on the eroding material exposed along the terrace-beach edge and a 1 m x 2 m rectangle (T/U-1) was excavated to determine the nature of the terrace-edge deposits. The excavation showed that ceramic sherds, marine shells and specks of charcoal were located to a depth of 60 cm. However, the major concentration of cultural material lay between 30 cm and 40 cm. To examine the sand-plain deposits excavation squares were positioned on a reference grid. The east–west baseline was labelled -A to Z and the north–south line labelled numerically from 1 to 15, with Square 1 the northernmost point. Thus, each 1 m square (except Test Pit 1) had an alphabetical and numerical code describing its location on the sand plain (Figure 53).

A total of 57 sq. m was excavated, with a main area comprising 43 sq. m providing a central sample of the sand-plain deposits (Figure 54). Eastern excavations outside the main area consisted of squares C/D12–13 (2 m x 2 m), -A13–15 (1 m x 3 m) and C8–9 (1 m x 2 m). Western excavations were T/U-1 (1 m x 2 m), U6 (1 m x 1 m), Q13 (1 m x 1 m) and Test Pit 1 (1 m x 1 m).

Material was extracted in 10 cm spits and by natural layer using trowels and sieved through 3 mm and 6 mm mesh. Cultural material (marine shell, pottery, bone and charcoal) was retained for further analysis from the surface to 50 cm depth. At the end of the excavation a final 50–60 cm spit was sieved to ensure basal deposits had been reached. In addition, Squares C/D12–13 were excavated down to 80 cm, and Squares -A13 to -A15, Q13, U6 and C8, I8 and L8 were taken down to 70 cm.

Stratigraphy

The stratigraphy of Ugaga Island was relatively simple, consisting of an upper layer containing the majority of the prehistoric material and three lower layers where cultural remains were sparse or absent. The two upper-layer descriptions were determined from the excavations, while the stratigraphy of the lower layers was identified by test pits and augering (Figures 55–57).

Figure 54. Ugaga Island, view of excavated area.

Layer 1: Was the principal cultural layer of the site. It consisted of a brownish-black silty clay with variable amounts of sand, abundant whole and fragmented marine shells, ceramics, oven stones and coral. The colour ranged from 7.5YR 2/2 near the surface to 10YR 2/2 at 40 cm depth, where it was a very dark-brown silty clay. Layer 1 pH levels showed little variation (pH 6.75 to 7.0) over the site. Layer 1 was generally around 30–40 cm in depth and had been disturbed by root penetration from surrounding coconut palms and earth-oven construction. After shellfish remains, ceramics were the most abundant evidence of prehistoric activity. Sherds decorated with dentate stamping, lip notching and different types of paddle relief were found throughout the Layer 1 deposit. Charcoal was relatively common in this layer with individual fragments of more than 100 g. Hermit crabs using the shells of *Nerita* sp. were abundant along the beach edge zone and frequently burrowed into Layer 1, illustrating their potential for site mixing by turning over deposits and introducing non-midden shell into a site. Two fragments of bottle glass (T/U-1), a piece of ceramic plate (K7), a metal bottle cap and a roofing nail (C13) were found in the top spit.

In the eastern part of the site (-A13–15, C/D12–13) a thin lens underlaid Layer 1.

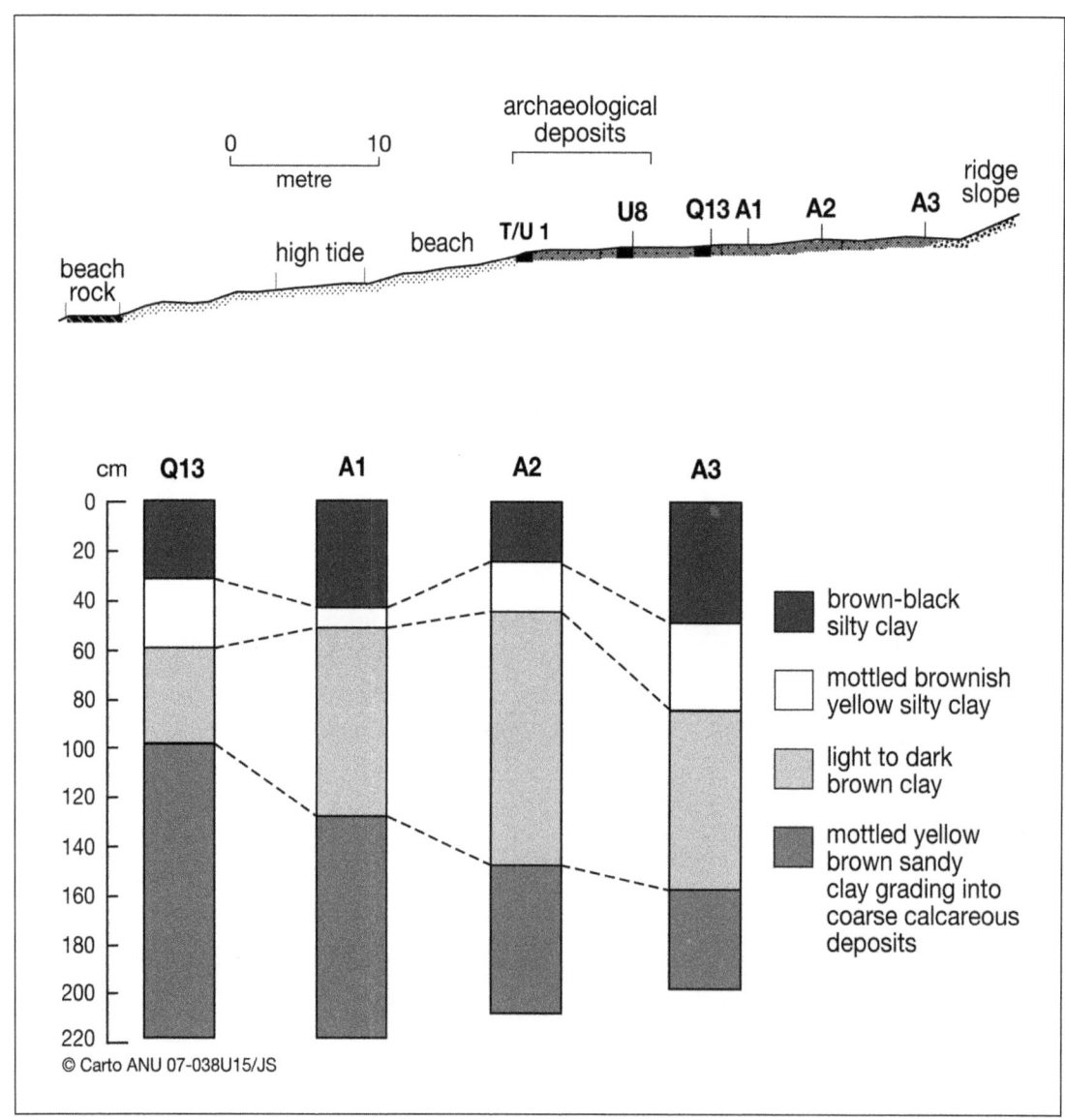

Figure 55. Ugaga Island, stratigraphy of auger transect.

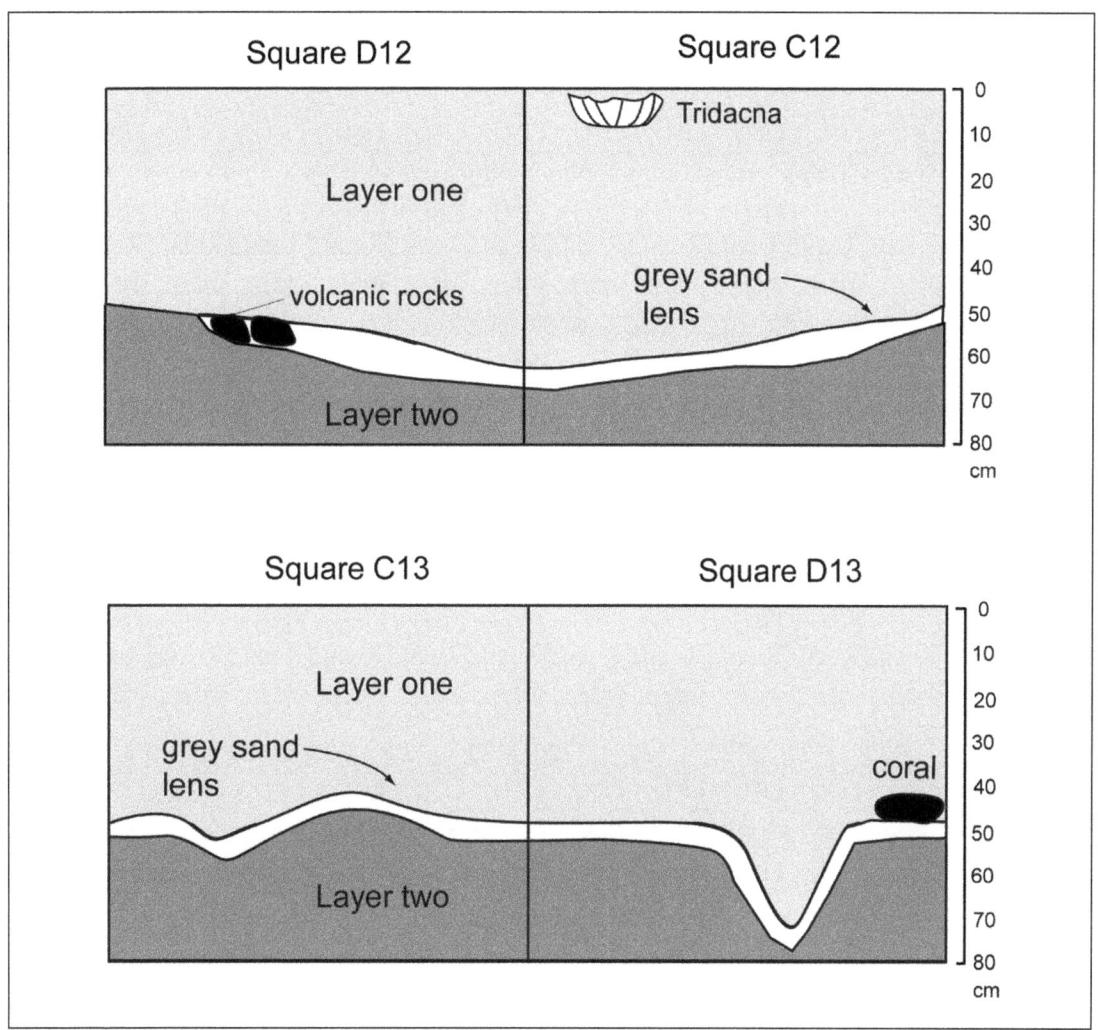

Figure 56. Ugaga Island, stratigraphy of CD12 (north) and CD13 (south).

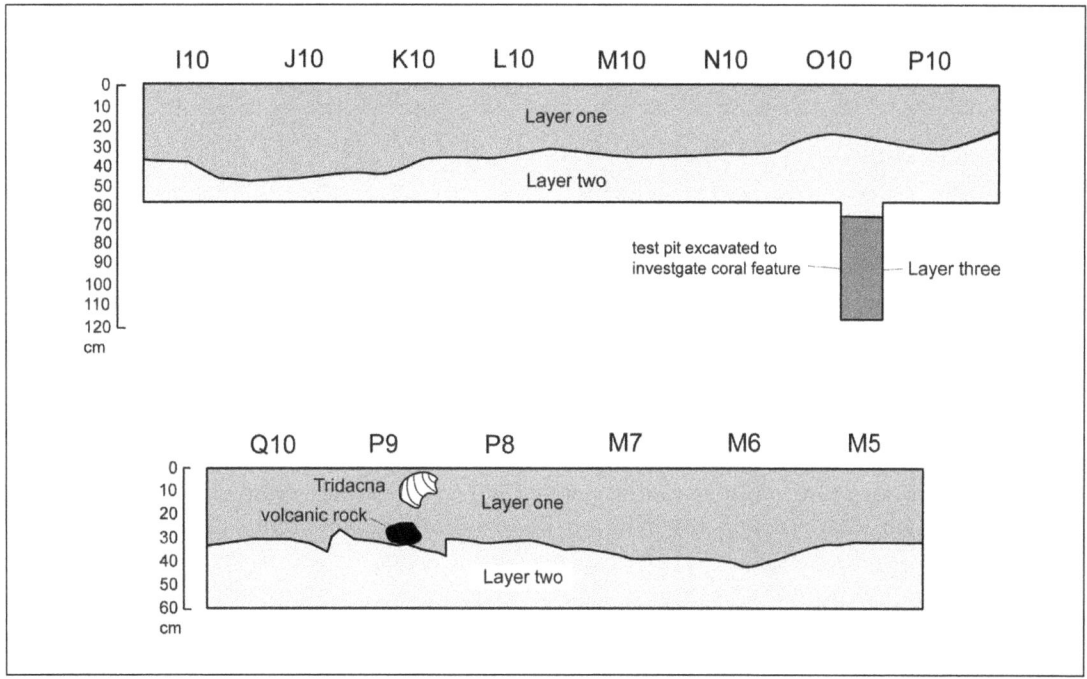

Figure 57. Ugaga Island, stratigraphy of Squares I10 to P10 (south) and Q10, P9–8, M7–5 (west).

It consisted of a mottled dark-greyish silty sand (10YR 4/2, pH=7.0) that contained a few plain pot sherds and marine shellfish (Figure 56).

Layer 2: A mottled brownish-yellow silty clay (10YR 4/4, pH=7.0) that was mixed with coarse calcareous grains. Along the terrace edge this layer contained a greater proportion of sand, but south and west of the edge the clay content increased, making the deposits wet and sticky. Layer depth was variable from 6 cm to 21 cm. The difference in layer depth over the site was probably due to cultural activities (i.e. oven building), the amount of vegetation disturbance, and the proximity to colluvium transported from adjacent slopes. Ceramics from squares with high clay contents were weathered, particularly those with shell temper. However, there was little cultural material in this layer, most of which was found at the interface between Layers 1 and 2. Charcoal existed as small and dispersed flecks.

Layer 3: Was differentiated from Layer 2 by the increasing quantity of clay. The colour of this layer ranged from light yellow-brown to dark-brown (10YR 4/4 to 7.5YR 4/4, pH=7.0). Calcareous sand and small nodules of rotted pumice and coral occurred throughout this layer. No cultural material was identified in the auger-hole spoil or in test pits dug into the layer from excavated squares. Layer depth in the auger holes varied from 37 cm to 100 cm. This layer was prominent to the south and west of the site but was difficult to distinguish towards the front of the site.

Layer 4: Consisted of a mottled brownish-yellow sandy clay (10 YR 6/6, pH=7.0) that became wetter as depth increased. In the lower part of the layer the silty-clay content decreased, grading into a coarse grit of shell and coral fragments. Large blocks of coral were found towards the base of Layer 4 and the water table was reached at 2.5 m depth (Figure 55).

Features were apparent across the site, the majority consisting of concentrations of fire-cracked rocks (Figures 58–59). Large quantities of charcoal near some of these stone concentrations indicated that many represented the remains of oven building and rake out. These features were mostly found between the surface and 30 cm depth. Throughout the deposits shellfish remains were prominent. Clusters of *Trochus niloticus* shells were found in Square C12 and five *Tridacna maxima* shells in Square O9 (Figures 58–59).

An oval-shaped group of coral cobbles was found on the surface of Layer 2 in Square P10 (Figure 59). The cobbles ranged in size from 12 cm to 27 cm. A test pit was dug through the feature to 120 cm but the feature did not extend below 45 cm depth. This feature most likely represents the base of an oven, an interpretation backed up by other findings in Fiji and the Pacific. For example, Best (1984:74) records the ethnographic use of coral ovens in sennit (*magimagi*) manufacture. Coral heating stones are also known from New Caledonia, Reef/Santa Cruz and the Talepakemalai site on Mussau (Kirch 1997:213; Spriggs 1997:136).

The edge of a large 2.0 m diameter oven was identified in Squares -A13/-A14 The oven deposits consisted of a dark charcoal-stained sand and numerous fragments of burnt shell (Figure 58).

The basal deposits at Ugaga are calcareous and form a low ridge parallel to the beach terrace near the front of the site. The Layer 4 beach material was probably laid down during a period of higher and relatively stabilised sea level from 6000 to 4000–3000 BP. During this time lateral shoreline erosion was significant and closure of what Nunn (1990:351) terms the 'Holocene high energy window' occurred after coral reefs had reached sea level and reef flats had developed.

Sea level fell by about 0.6 m (Shepherd 1990) from 3000 BP to the present. Nunn (1990) suggests a maximum Holocene sea level of 1–2 m above present sea level. Behind the low ridge, silty clays from the hill slopes overlay, and to a certain extent became integrated with, the Layer 4 deposits. The original surface when people first arrived on Ugaga probably varied from a relatively clean silty sand to the east, to a compact silty clay with calcareous inclusions in the west. Although on a smaller scale, the processes outlined above for Ugaga Island have also been noted at other prehistoric sites in the Pacific (Kirch and Hunt 1997).

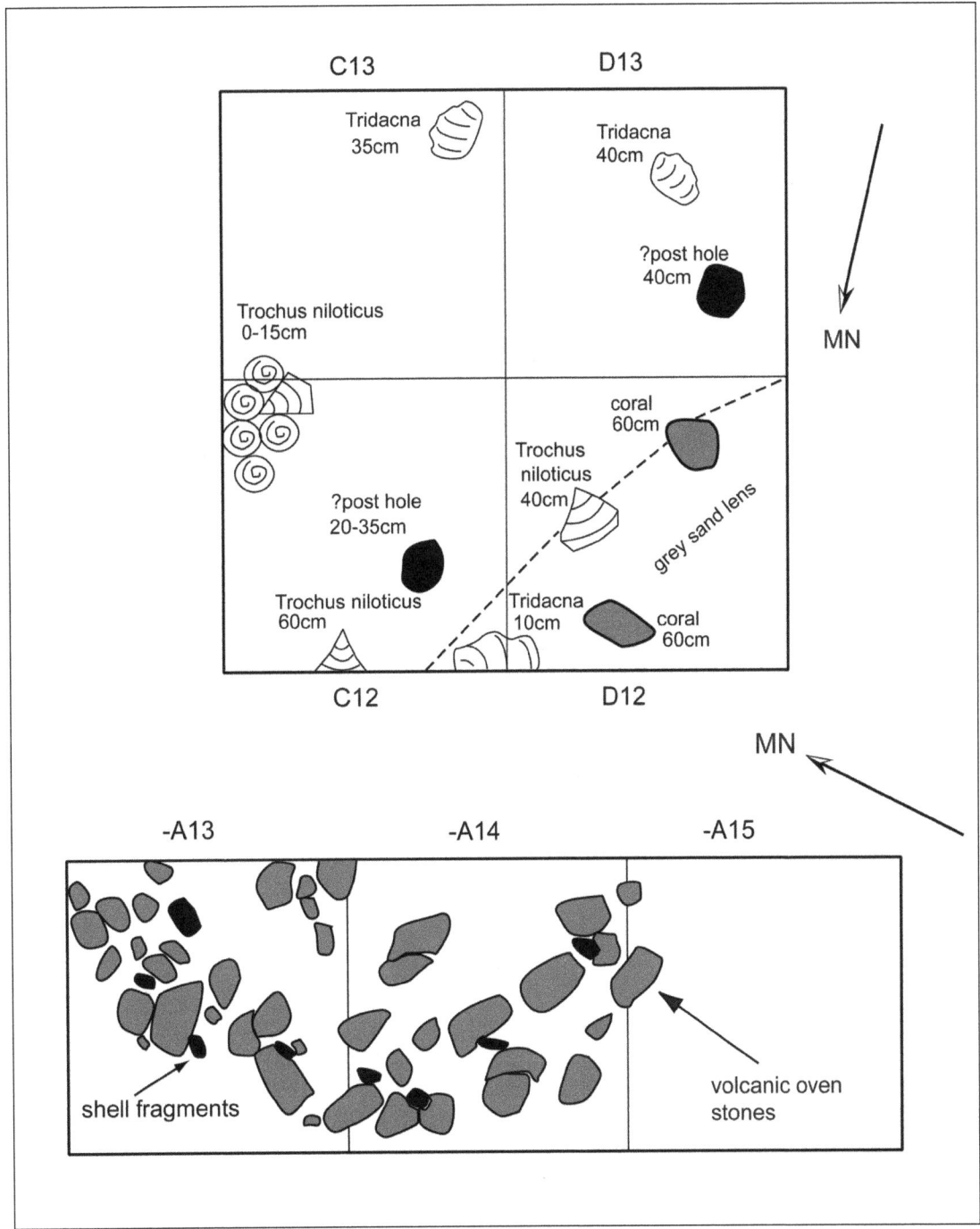

Figure 58. Ugaga Island, plan view of features in CD 12–13 (top) and -A13–15.

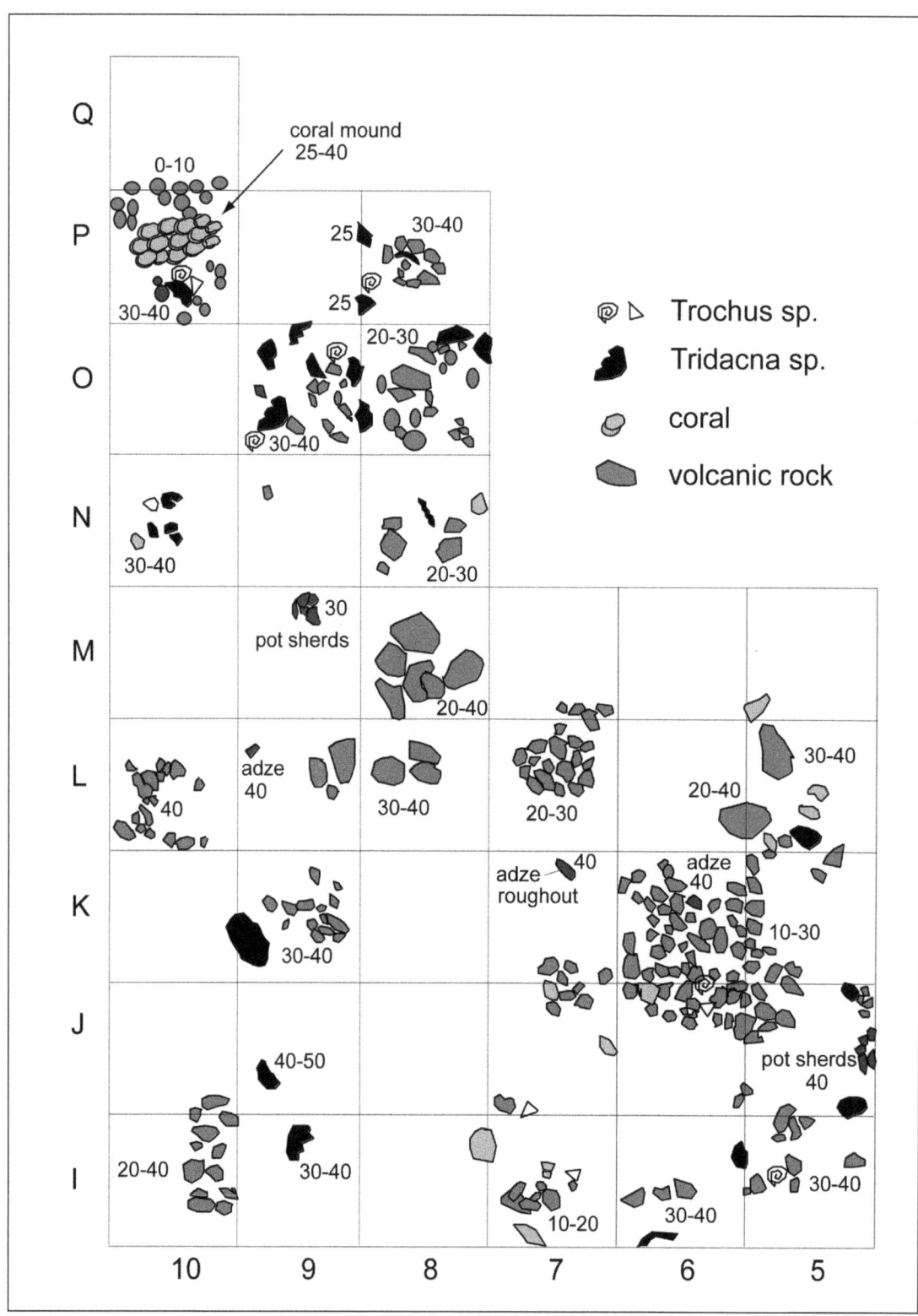

Figure 59. Ugaga Island, plan view of features exposed in main excavation area. Depths are spot heights below ground surface in cm.

References

Anderson, A., Clark, G. and Worthy, T. 2000. An inland Lapita site in Fiji. *Journal of the Polynesian Society* 109: 311–316.

Anderson, A., Roberts, R., Dickinson, W., Clark, G., Burley, D., De Biran, A., Hope, G. and Nunn, P. 2006. Times of sand: Sedimentary history and archaeology at the Sigatoka Dunes, Fiji. *Geoarchaeology* 21: 131–154.

Band, R.B. 1968. *The geology of southern Viti Levu and Mbengga*. Geological Survey of Fiji, Bulletin No. 15.

Best, S. 1984. Lakeba: The prehistory of a Fijian island. Unpublished PhD thesis, Department of Anthropology, University of Auckland.

Best, S.B. 1987a. A preliminary report on the Sigatoka burials. *Domodomo* 3: 2–15.

Best, S.B. 1987b. Sigatoka dune burials Site VL 16/1. A preliminary report. Unpublished report, Anthropology Department, University of Auckland.

Best, S.B. 1989. The Sigatoka dune burials Site VL 16/1. Unpublished report to the Fiji Museum, Suva.

Birks, L. 1973. Archaeological excavations at Sigatoka dune site, Fiji. Suva: *Bulletin of the Fiji Museum*, No. 1.

Burley, D.V. 1997. Archaeological research Sigatoka sand dune national park. Unpublished report to the Fiji Museum, Suva.

Burley, D.V. 2003. Dynamic landscapes and episodic occupations: Archaeological interpretation and implications in the prehistory of the Sigatoka Sand Dunes. In: Sand, C. (ed), *Pacific Archaeology: Assessments and prospects*, pp. 307–315. Les Cahiers de l'Archéologie en Nouvelle-Calédonie, Noumea.

Burley, D.V. 2005. Mid-sequence archaeology at the Sigatoka Sand Dunes with interpretive implications for Fijian and oceanic culture history. *Asian Perspectives* 44: 320–348.

Burley, D.V. and Dickinson, W.R. 2004. Late Lapita occupation and its ceramic assemblage at the Sigatoka Sand Dune site, Fiji and their place in oceanic prehistory. *Archaeology in Oceania*, 39: 12–25.

Burley, D. and Shortland, R. 1999. Report on 1998 field work activities Sigatoka Dunes National Park Viti Levu, Fiji. Department of Archaeology, Simon Fraser University, Burnaby B.C., Canada.

Crosby, A. 1988. Beqa: Archaeology, structure and history in Fiji. Unpublished MA thesis, Department of Anthropology, University of Auckland.

Crosby, A.D. 1991. Proposal for archaeological survey of Sigatoka Sand Dunes. Unpublished report, Fiji Museum, Suva.

Crosby, A.D. 1992. Further burials at the Sigatoka Sand Dunes Site VL 16/1. Unpublished report, Fiji Museum, Suva.

De Biran, A. 2001. The Holocene geomorphic evolution of the Sigatoka Delta, Viti Levu, Fiji Islands. Unpublished PhD thesis, University of the South Pacific, Suva, Fiji.

Dickinson, W.R. 1968. Sigatoka Sand Dunes, Viti Levu Fiji. *Sedimentary Geology* 2: 115–124.

Dickinson, W.R., Burley, D.V., Nunn, P.D., Anderson, A., Hope, G., de Biran, A., Burke, C. and Matararaba, S. 1998. Geomorphic and archaeological landscapes of the Sigatoka Dune Site, Viti Levu, Fiji: Interdisciplinary investigations. *Asian Perspectives* 37: 1–31.

Field, J.S. 2004. Environmental and climatic considerations: a hypothesis for conflict and the emergence of social complexity in Fijian prehistory. *Journal of Anthropological Archaeology* 23: 79–99.

Frost, E.L. 1979. Fiji. In: Jennings, J.D. (ed), *The prehistory of Polynesia*, pp. 61–81. Australian National University Press, Canberra.

Gibbons, J. 1985. A brief environmental history of Fiji. II. The Ice Ages and human habitation before European contact. *Domodomo* 3: 110–123.

Gifford, E.W. 1951. Archaeological excavations in Fiji. *University of California Anthropological Records* 13: 189–288.

Gilbert, T. 1984. Limestone and volcanic caves of the Fiji Islands. *Transactions of the British Cave Research Association* 11: 105–118.

Golson, J. 1974. Both sides of the Wallace Line: New Guinea, Australia, Island Melanesia and Asian prehistory. In: Barnard, N. (ed), *Early Chinese art and its possible influence in the Pacific Basin*.

pp. 533–595. Proceedings of a symposium arranged by the Department of Art History and Archaeology, Columbia University, New York City, Taiwan.

Green, R.C. 1963. A suggested revision of the Fiji sequence. *Journal of the Polynesian Society* 72: 235–253.

Green, R.C. and Palmer, J.B. 1964. Fiji sequence: Corrections and additional notes for Sigatoka. *Journal of the Polynesian Society* 73: 328–332.

Hudson, E. 1994. Sigatoka Sand Dune site archaeological rescue project 1993. Unpublished report, Auckland Uniservices Limited, Auckland.

Hunt, T.L. 1986. Conceptual and substantive issues in Fijian prehistory. In: Kirch, P.V. (ed), *Archaeological approaches to evolution and transformation*, pp. 20–32. Cambridge University Press, Cambridge.

Hunt, T.L. 1987. Patterns of human interaction and evolutionary divergence in the Fiji Islands. *Journal of the Polynesian Society* 96: 299–334.

Kirch, P.V. 1997. *The Lapita peoples. Ancestors of the oceanic world*. Blackwell Publishers, Cambridge and Oxford.

Kirch, P.V. and Hunt, T.L. (eds) 1997. *Historical ecology in the Pacific islands: Prehistoric environmental and landscape change*. Yale University Press, New Haven.

Marshall, Y., Crosby, A., Matararaba, S. and Wood, S. 2000. *Sigatoka the shifting sands of Fijian prehistory*. Oxbow Books, Oxford.

Matthews, P.J. and Gosden, C. 1997. Plant remains from waterlogged sites in the Arawe Islands, west New Britain province, Papua New Guinea: Implications for the history of plant use and domestication. *Economic Botany* 51: 121–133.

Nunn, P.D. 1990. Coastal geomorphology of Beqa and Yanuca Islands, South Pacific Ocean, and its significance for the tectonic history of the Vatulele–Beqa ridge. *Pacific Science* 44(4): 348–365.

Palmer, B. 1965. Excavations at Karobo, Viti Levu. *New Zealand Archaeological Association Newsletter* 8: 26–33.

Palmer, J.B., Shaw, E., Dickinson, P. and Sykes, M. 1968. Pottery making in Sigatoka, Fiji. *Records of the Fiji Museum* 13.

Parry, J. 1987. The Sigatoka valley – pathways into prehistory. *Bulletin of the Fiji Museum* No. 9.

Petchey, F. 1994. Pottery and stone analysis. In: Hudson, E. (ed), Sigatoka Dune Site archaeological rescue project 1993, pp. 28–39. Auckland Uniservices Limited, Auckland.

Petchey, F. 1995. Archaeology of Kudon: Archaeological analysis of Lapita ceramics from Mulifanua, Samoa and Sigatoka, Fiji. Unpublished MA thesis, University of Auckland, New Zealand.

Rajotte, F. and Bigay, J. (eds) 1981. *Beqa: Island of firewalkers*. Institute of Pacific Studies, University of the South Pacific, Suva.

Sawyer, B and Andrews, E.C. 1901. Notes on the caves of Fiji, with special reference to Lau. *Proceedings of the Linnean Society of New South Wales* 26: 91–106.

Shepherd, M.J. 1990. The evolution of a moderate energy coast in Holocene time, Pacific Harbour, Viti Levu, Fiji. *New Zealand Journal of Geology and Geophysics* 33: 547–556.

Smith, J.M.B. 1990. Drift disseminules on Fijian beaches. *New Zealand Journal of Botany* 28: 13–20.

Southern, W. 1986. The late Quaternary environmental history of Fiji. Unpublished PhD thesis, Australian National University, Australia.

Spriggs, M. 1997. *The island Melanesians*. Blackwell Publishers, Oxford and Massachusetts.

Visser, E.P. 1988. Hotel Masa Survey – Sigatoka. Unpublished report.

Visser, E. 1994. The prehistoric people from Sigatoka: An analysis of skeletal and dental traits as evidence of adaptation. Unpublished PhD thesis, University of Otago, New Zealand.

Whelan, P.W., Gill, J.B., Kollman, R., Duncan, R. and Drake, R. 1985. Radiometric dating of magmatic stages in Fiji. In: Scholl, D.W. and Vallier, T.L. (eds), *Geology and offshore resources of Pacific Island arcs – Tonga Region*, pp. 415–440. American Association of Petroleum Geologists Special Report 12.

Wood, S., Marshall, Y. and Crosby, A. 1998. Mapping Sigatoka Site VL 16/1: The 1992 field season and its implications. Unpublished report, Fiji Museum, Suva.

6

Fieldwork in northern Viti Levu and Mago Island

Geoffrey Clark
Archaeology and Natural History, The Australian National University

Atholl Anderson
Archaeology and Natural History, The Australian National University

Introduction

This chapter outlines fieldwork in north Viti Levu and on Mago Island in the Lau Group. Major investigations were made at two already known north-coast Viti Levu sites: the Lapita site of Natunuku, in Ba Province, and Navatu 17A, in Rakiraki Province. On Mago Island, a Lapita site at Votua was discovered and excavated in 1997 and 2000. A rock shelter known as Sovanibeka, inland from the Votua site, was also briefly examined. The research history and fieldwork involving these sites in our project is described below.

The north coast of Viti Levu is predominantly volcanic and, being on the leeward side, coastal zones have both a relatively low rainfall (<1800 mm per annum) and a propensity to drought. The highland core of Viti Levu exerts a powerful orographic effect on the southeast trade winds and the north coast experiences marked rain shadow in both wet and dry seasons relative to southern Viti Levu. The difficult environmental conditions were alleviated in prehistory by the construction of numerous fish traps (*moka*) on the coast and offshore islands and extensive irrigated terracing, particularly on the flanks and flood plains of the Nakauvadra Range (Kuhlken and Crosby 1999). Nonetheless, the lower economic productivity of the north coast is suggested by Parry (1997:147) to be manifested in the absence of very large sites and the lack of a site hierarchy in his aerial-photo site analysis, indicating general equality of status and the existence of a simple prehistoric polity compared with the large and complex socio-political entities that developed in southern and southeastern Viti Levu (Parry 1987).

Gifford's (1951) archaeological reconnaissance turned up 12 coastal sites between Lautoka and Rakiraki. One was Navatu 17A, which became the type site for the Navatu phase proposed by Green (1963), lasting from about 2100 to 900 BP. An older site, Natunuku (VL 1/1), found in 1967, contained Lapita pottery with early decorative styles. Both sites have been important in constructing and revising the first half of the archaeological sequence of Fiji (Green 1963; Best 1984, 2002; Clark and Murray 2006). Our aim was to locate previous excavations and obtain new sets of cultural remains, as the antiquity, nature and context of prehistoric materials at both sites was unclear, despite previous analyses of excavated material and reinterpretation of the deposits (Green 1963; Shaw 1967; Davidson et al. 1990; Davidson and Leach 1993). In short, archaeological uncertainty regarding the Natunuku and Navatu 17A sites has fed through to the entire Fiji sequence, hindering debate on the age of human colonisation in Fiji (e.g. Kirch and Hunt 1988; Spriggs 1990) and preventing a close comparison of ceramics and other artefacts, necessary to evaluate the extent of cultural variation within the archipelago and potential linkages between Fiji and other islands (Wahome 1995; Burley 2005).

A second project on Mago Island was centred on a late-Lapita site found in 1996 during a joint USP–Fiji Museum–ANU survey of archaeological deposits coordinated by Professor Patrick Nunn (Geography Department, USP). Some linguistic and archaeological data points to an early cultural divide between west Fiji and east Fiji (Geraghty 1983; Best 1984), which may have occurred as a result of Lapita groups from Tonga colonising parts of the Lau Group (Best 1984; Clark and Murray 2006). The issue of significant variation in the intra-archipelagic rate of prehistoric colonisation is one that could be tested by a comparison of Votua ceramics with pottery of late-Lapita age in west Fiji (i.e. Sigatoka, Level 1) and Tonga. During investigations at Votua, the small shelter of Sovanibeka was investigated and a few ceramics of Lapita and mid-sequence antiquity were recovered.

Fieldwork at Natunuku, VL 1/1

Natunuku is the name of a village and its immediate district near the mouth of the Ba River (Figure 60). A low peninsula of Pliocene volcanics projects westward for 1 km towards the river mouth from the northerly trending coastline. On the north side of the peninsula, facing a shallow, muddy estuary that merges into the broad northern lagoon of Viti Levu, is situated site VL 1/1. The existence of a Lapita site there was first evident to Bruce Palmer, Director of the Fiji Museum, in the mid 1960s when he saw sherds from the beach front, then actively eroding, and collected by Peter Bean. A rescue excavation was carried out by Elizabeth Shaw and Moce Qalo in August–September 1967, as part of a two-year program on Fijian archaeology, 1965–1967, funded by the National Science Foundation. Palmer (1968:24), writing during the period of excavation, observed that the Lapita-style pottery was more profusely decorated than at Sigatoka and probably earlier, making it, at that time, the oldest site in Fiji. This proposition was strengthened by an initial radiocarbon date from Layer 6, the basal cultural level, of 3240±100 BP (GaK-1218), and subsequent analyses of the Lapita assemblage, notably by Mead et al. (1973), led to the conclusion that at least part belonged to Green's (1974) Early Eastern Lapita Phase.

Subsequent research on the Natunuku pottery assemblage from Location C, where Lapita ceramics had been prominent, by Davidson et al. (1990), showed that while dentate-stamped Lapita wares were concentrated proportionately in the basal layer, they also occurred throughout the Natunuku stratigraphy and thus within ceramic contexts that spanned the full Fijian prehistoric sequence. In fact, the largest number and weight of dentate-stamped, unshaped body sherds at Location C occurred very near the surface, in Layer 3, together with the highest

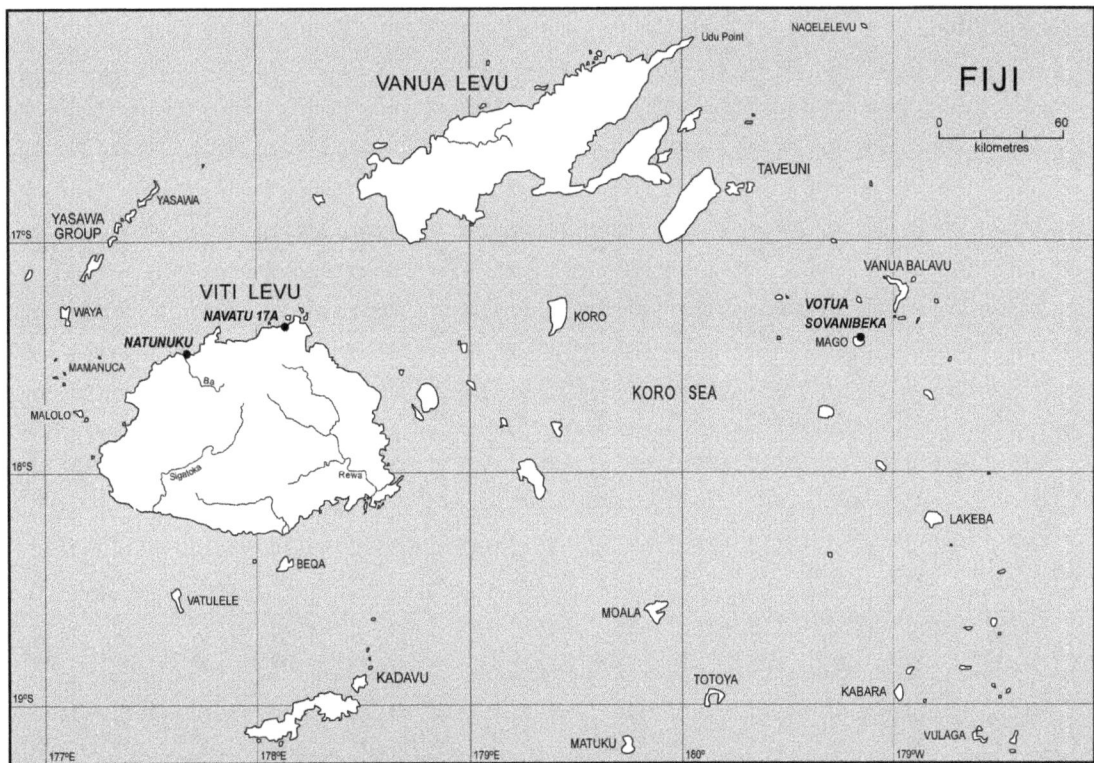

Figure 60. Map of Fiji showing research locations.

density of paddle-impressed sherds. To what extent this might be explained by disturbance was uncertain, and as the details of excavation had not been published by the excavators, and only so far as was necessary to put their analyses in context by Davidson et al. (1990), further research was called for. There had been a small test excavation, east of the main Lapita site, by Terry Hunt (1980:128), which produced a plainware vessel, but otherwise no additional fieldwork at Natunuku.

When our fieldwork took place in 1996, the evidence seemed to be that the site was probably not as old as the initial radiocarbon date had suggested, and the distribution of Lapita materials was very restricted. Revised correction of GaK-1218 by Davidson et al. (1990:131) indicated that a better estimate of its conventional age would be about 2800±90 BP. Additional dates on marine shell by Davidson and Leach (1993) showed that Layer 5, including 5b, probably dated to about 350 BC, i.e. post Lapita. They went on to say that the Lapita assemblage had probably been confined originally to Layer 6 in Location C and that Lapita sherds were absent from the other areas tested in the 1967 excavations (Locations A and B). They doubted that any of Layer 6 remained, due to coastal erosion.

Fieldwork objectives

Our research set out, nevertheless, to establish whether there was still a Lapita level at Natunuku, and whether it was possible to recover more from it than the exclusively ceramic assemblage that had been excavated in 1967, and to obtain additional samples for dating from Layer 6. As at Sigatoka, we wanted to establish whether the Natunuku Lapita horizon represented the first occupation of a coastline that had been available for settlement for a substantial period, or merely the settlement of a surface which had recently become available. For various reasons, these objectives turned out to be more difficult than we anticipated.

Site location

The major problem was the most basic – where, in fact, was Location C? Davidson et al. (1990:Figure 3) showed the localities excavated in 1967 in relation to a sketch of the coastline and the disposition of the old coastal village and cemetery. In advance of fieldwork this seemed sufficiently precise to find Location C. However, as soon as the shape of the shoreline and the position of the drain and creek mouths were understood, and approximate measurements taken by pacing and tape measure, it became apparent that there was a substantial error.

In the 1990 map, the main identifiable features of the shoreline (which is about 700 m long between mangrove stands at either end) are the mouth of the swale that runs behind and parallel to the shore (it runs much further west than shown in the 1990 map), and indentations which approximate the location of a creek mouth about 40 m east of Location C in the 1990 map and a drain mouth adjacent to Location B (Davidson et al. 1990:Figure 3). Both watercourse mouths can be seen very clearly on the 1967 aerial photo (Figure 61). The 1990 map makes Location B about 330 m west of the swale mouth, while our measurements put this position at about 260 m west. Similarly, the 1990 map makes Location C about 445 m west of the mouth of the swale. This was particularly difficult to understand. According to the site description (Davidson

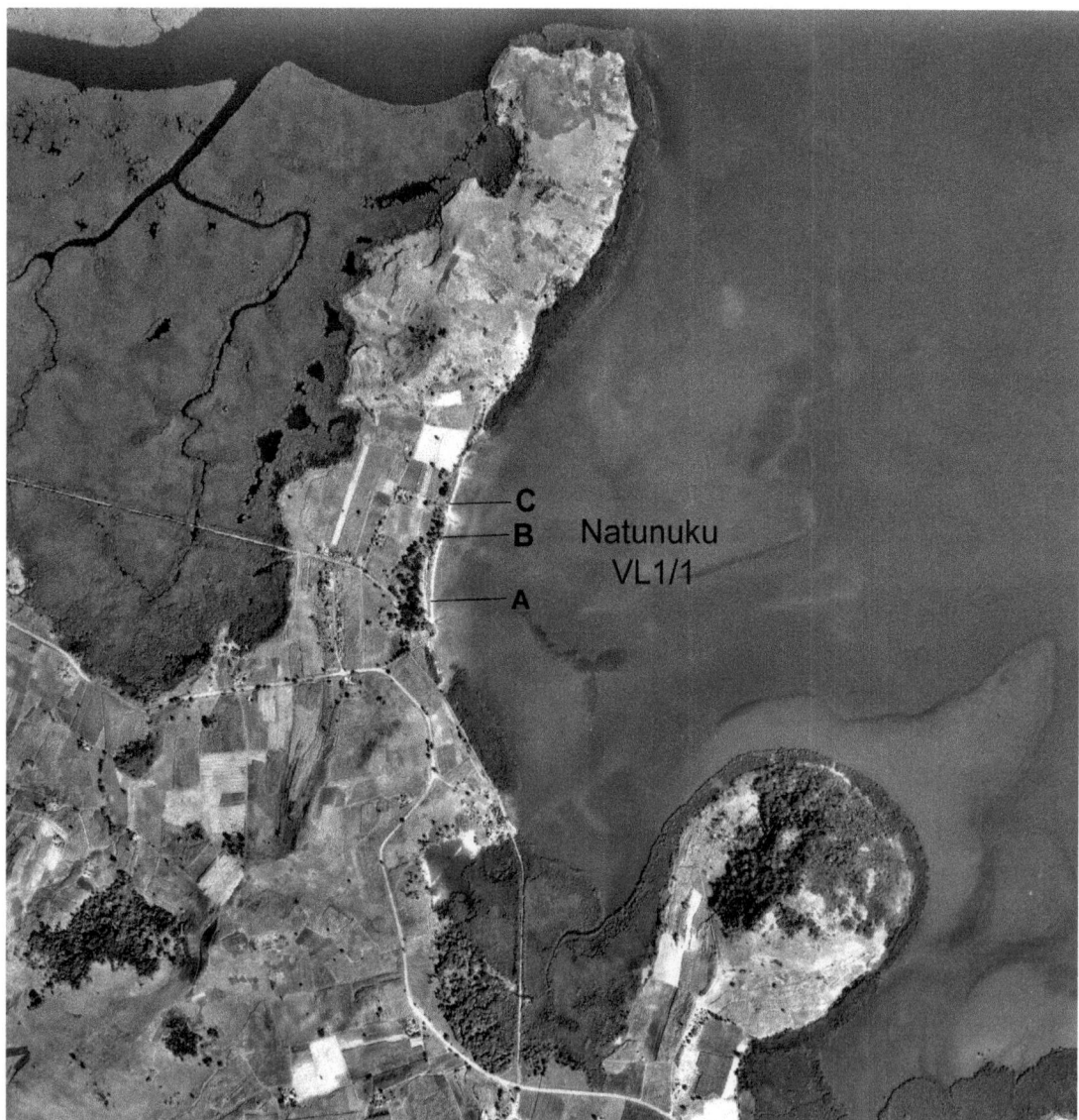

Figure 61. A 1967 aerial photo of Natunuku (courtesy of Elizabeth Hinds), showing the area of the site, on the coast between Locations A and C. The old village site extends approximately between Locations A and B.

et al. 1990), Location C lay on the front beach ridge, within the cemetery and (contrary to its accompanying map), east of the creek mouth and cane fields. On our measurements, a locality 445 m west of the swale mouth was well into the cane fields where neither beach ridge nor cemetery exists and the land slopes gently to the shore. Our initial impression of a substantial locational problem was substantiated by a total station survey of the beachfront and its salient features (Figure 62).

The one certainty was that Location C lay within the old cemetery, which extends about 115 m between the drain mouth and the creek mouth, to a maximum distance of about 360 m west of the mouth of the swale. Location C must have been in that area, but where? Inspection of the coastal area and discussion with Natunuku village elders, including the former Headman, Mr Penaia Natanu, who had worked on the 1967 excavations, reached the conclusion that Location C had been located immediately west of the exposed beach rock platform that lies on the west side of the drain, and therefore quite close to Location B.

The grounds for this were: (1) Mr Natanu recalled that our Trench 3 and Location C were essentially adjacent and both close to the grave of his grandfather. In fact, his recollection was that Location C lay between our Trench 3 position and the drain to the east, and he said that the excavations were about 1.2 m deep through brown sand and terminated in yellow sand – a plausible description of the Location C stratigraphy; (2) the exposed beach rock platform, above which Trench 3 is located, is a prominent feature along the shoreline, and it appears to be shown in Davidson (1990:Figure 4) as extending into Location C; (3) at no other place along the shoreline, at least as it could be observed in 1996, was there beach rock exposed so high in the section – in fact at 1 m high it was still lower than the estimated 1.5 m beach rock face which lay beneath Location C; (4) the beach ridge above the beach rock platform is well within the surface distribution of Lapita sherds.

Against this hypothesis were the following considerations: (1) Mr Natanu also recalled that two pits were excavated in 1967 about 50 m west of the beach rock platform, near the creek mouth. No sherds were recovered but a skeleton was found and it had a diamond-shaped shell pendant associated with it. He thought it was a modern burial and the pendant chain had rusted away. We cored and dug a spade hole in this area (under the ST4 point in Figure 62), but it is just low ground close to the water table (at 0.5 m depth) and has no archaeological remains; (2) although the grave shapes and disposition in the Location C plan (Davidson 1990:Figure 4) are quite distinctive, we could not match this arrangement on the ground; (3) the consensus of local opinion was that the shoreline had receded about 5–6 m in the centre of the bay since 1967, which on the face of it would have removed Location C almost entirely.

Subsequent to fieldwork, Dr E. Hinds (neé Shaw), now deceased, kindly provided copies of some unpublished plans of Natunuku (E. Hinds, pers. comm., Dunedin). A small-scale sketch map of the site (distances converted by us from imperial to decimal) shows Location B at about 280 m west of the swale mouth and area C, about 365 m west of that point. These figures are closer to our own than to those in Davidson (1990:Figure 3), but still different (e.g. our surveyed map puts the drain near location B at 260 m west of the swale mouth). More importantly, the Hinds map has Location B marked *east* of the drain, by about 35–50 m, and Location C midway between the drain and creek mouths, both of which are noted on the plan. This would put Location C within the approximate position shown in our Figure 62. Simon Best (pers. comm., Auckland) had reached the same conclusion about Location C in discussion of our surveyed map of the site.

As the Hinds map is the only original document we have seen which marks the positions of Location B and C in relation to the shape of the coast and the positions of the stream mouths, we are inclined to accept it. The important implication would be that our Trench 3 was, after

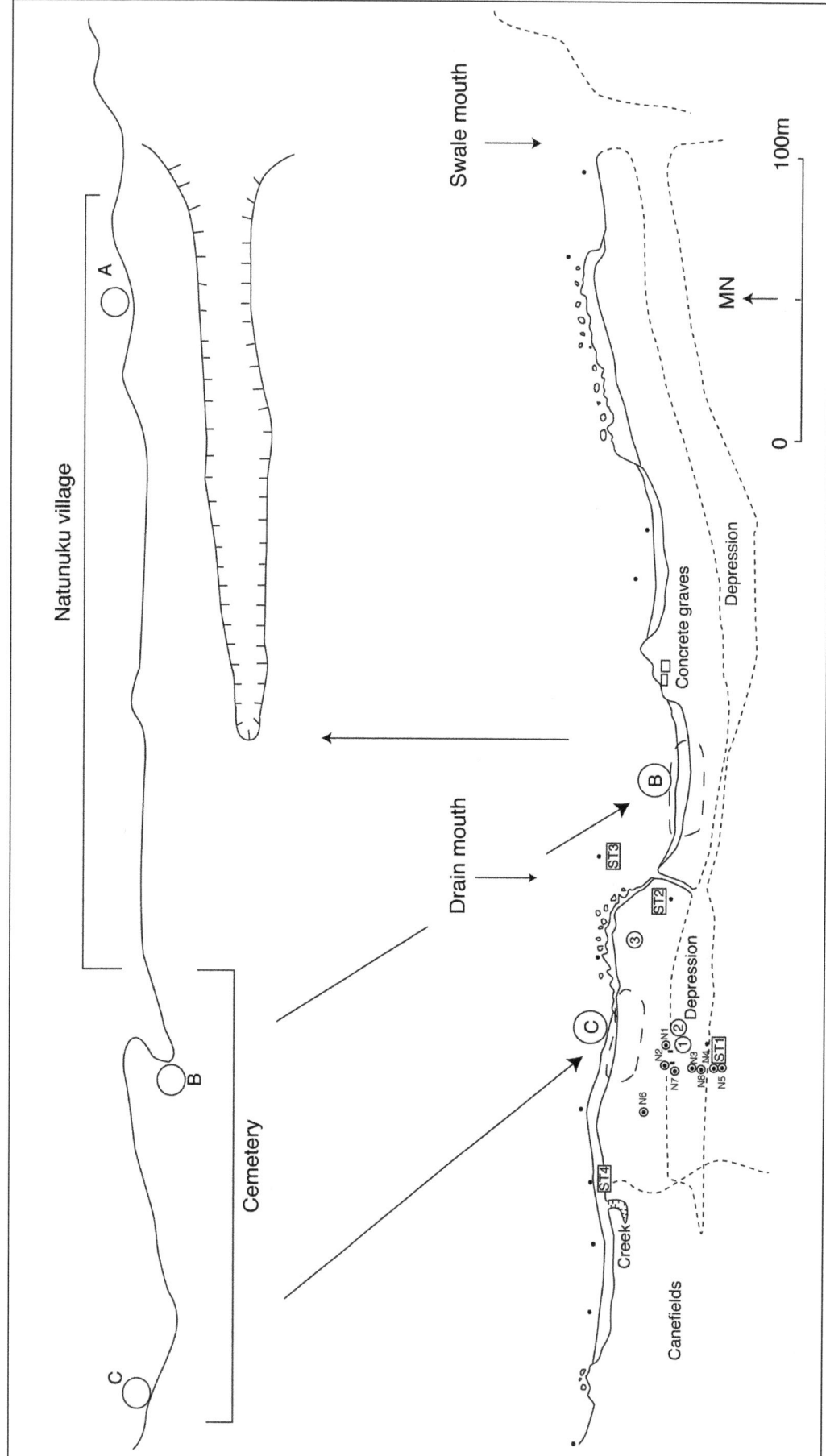

Figure 62. Natunuku, showing (above) the excavated locations from 1967 as plotted by Davidson et al. (1990:Figure 3); and (below), at the same scale, the surveyed map from 1996, indicating the main topographical features, the core transect, excavation trenches 1, 2, 3, survey station points (ST), and the probable areas of Locations B and C, relative to the 1990 plan.

all, significantly east of Location C, probably by at least 20 m, and it could not be expected to disclose the same stratigraphy and contents. Nevertheless, the distribution of Lapita ceramics extended well outside Location C and included the areas of our excavations. In fact, Lapita pottery can be picked up on the surface along approximately 100 m of the coastline west of the drain and for 20 m back to the northern slope of the swale. It is probable, therefore, that Location C and our excavations both sample the same ca. 2000 sq. m Lapita site.

Geomorphological investigation

Behind the shoreline beach ridge the swale extends much further west than is shown in the 1990 map or the Hinds sketch map. As indicated in our surveyed map (Figure 62), there are two basins to the swale, and they are linked by a narrow channel, running through beach rock, which also occurs in the sides of the swale, especially on the south side. While the eastern basin of this feature might have been dug in the 1920s (Davidson et al. 1990:122), there is no reason to think this was also true of the western basin or the connecting channel. Geomorphologically, these appear to be natural features. The western basin holds some depth of water quite often, according to local residents. It can spill out through the creek or through the cut drain when that is cleaned out. Assuming the western basin of the swale existed in the Lapita era, it would have been a useful source of freshwater on a coastline where creeks are often dry, and possibly a significant locational attraction.

In order to investigate the relationship of the Lapita site to the surface on which it was deposited, we cored on a transect through the swale and on to the top of the first beach ridge, although several core holes, notably N6, were displaced from the transect line to avoid beach rock or graves (Figure 62). This exercise showed that the basic sedimentary sequence, bottom to top, is as follows (Figure 63):

1. Dark-grey to blue, and occasionally rust-red, estuarine mud of a type found in mangrove environments. This is commonly encountered at 2.0–2.5 m below the beach ridges where it generally corresponds in depth with the water table. In some core holes this deposit appeared to keep on going and became so wet that the core could no longer recover any sediment. In N1–2, the estuarine mud bottoms out on an indurated shelly surface with large shells and coral. Elsewhere (N5, N4, N3 and shoreward of N6) there is beach rock at the base of the penetrable sediments.

2. Compact, orange-brown, gritty, shell hash, with small pieces of coral, some basalt cobbles.

3. Grey-white granular sand, often quite loose, with abundant shell, large lumps of rock and large pieces of coral and beach rock. It appears to have formed in a relatively high-energy beach environment.

4. Light-brown to grey-yellow, fairly compact, calcareous sand, originally a beach deposit, but with significant quantities of fragmented shell, silt and clay. No pottery was recovered but there were some large, unbroken shells. The sand becomes coarser with depth, and silt and clay are in higher proportions towards the top.

5. Dark-brown silty sand which appears to have been a forest soil. This is rich in archaeological remains. In core N6, this is overlain by a deposit of the light-brown calcareous sand which probably arose from grave-digging. Also in that core was a layer of orange-brown silty sand and clay, which contained large shell pieces, whole shells and beach rock. It was not found elsewhere.

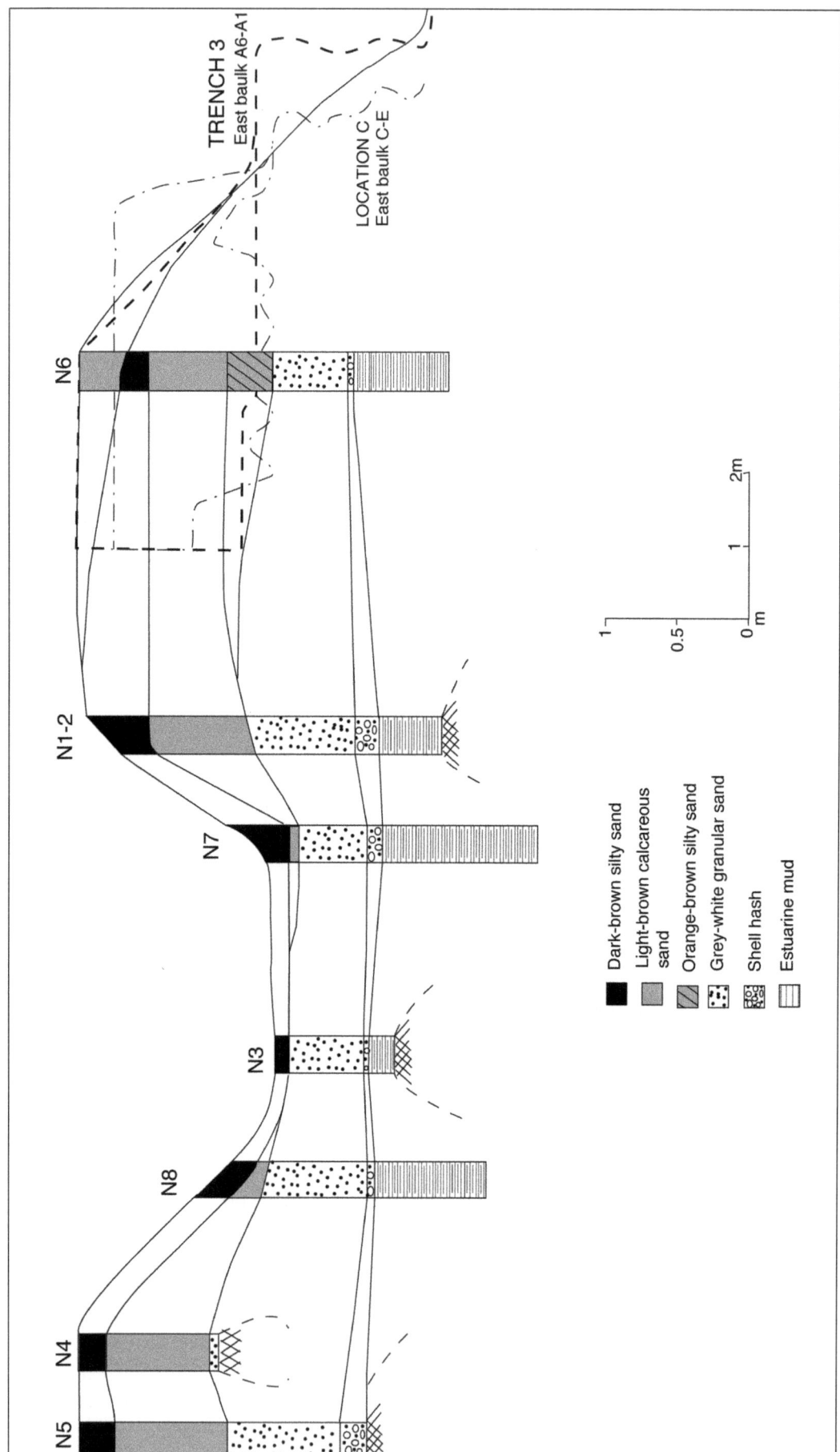

Figure 63. The results of coring at Natunuku, also showing the approximate cross-sectional relationships of Location C and Trench 3 excavations to each other and the transect.

In summary, it appears there was a higher and more active beach level than today, formed above an estuarine mud. The beach extended to at least 2 m above present high-tide level (consistently with Nunn's (1990) observations on the coral stacks to the east of Natunuku Bay). As sea level fell, the highest sediments were washed out to form the swale behind the present shoreline beach ridge; that being protected, perhaps, by a substantial underlying platform of beach rock. Key (n.d.) suggests there are two successive beach-rock levels at Natunuku. One, outcropping at the shore, is 1–1.3 m thick, and the other outcrops on the south side of the swale. It follows from this geomorphological history that the shoreline beach ridge and swale probably existed for some time before human habitation.

Turning to the Location C stratigraphy (Davidson et al. 1990:126), Layers 1 and 2 appear to have been deposited recently about the graves and along a path between them. These units are localised and were not found in our excavations. Layer 3 is the dark-brown silty sand and clay, seemingly a forest soil, which occurs at the top of the natural sedimentary sequence. Layer 4 is the light-brown calcareous sand and silt that underlies it in the natural sequence. Layer 5 appears, by description, to have been dune sand and it overlies apparent beach sand filled with cemented coral sand and beach rock (Layer 6), which, in turn lies on an irregular surface of the beach-rock platform. Layers 5 and 6 do not occur in our core transect and it is difficult, therefore, to understand them in relation to a broader coastal sequence. However, Layer 5 is at the same relative elevation as the light-brown calcareous sand in the natural section and is, we assume, a variation of it. Layer 6 appears to have been a clean yellow beach sand and cemented material, which contains only Lapita pottery and no other cultural material beyond a few flecks of charcoal. It might be equivalent to the orange-brown sand found in core N6 and further coring might have shown that this increases in depth and lightens in colour shorewards. Certainly a similar coarse, yellow sand with cemented lumps lies at the base of the Trench 3 excavation. It is possible pottery was re-deposited into Layer 6 by wave surge at some point during the Lapita era.

Excavations in 1996

Observing the wider than expected surface distribution of Lapita sherds, we set out two small excavations on the north slope of the swale (Trenches 1 and 2) and one (Trench 3) on the seaward face of the beach ridge (Figure 62). Excavation was by 10 cm spits within natural layers and material was sieved to 3 mm in the sandy layers, but often to only 6 mm in the stiff, blocky clay and loam layers, although material was well broken up to try to ensure that cultural material was not missed.

Trench 1 (Figure 64)

Layer 1: Light-brown sandy loam containing abundant shell and pottery. The shell was mostly oyster and *Anadara*, but also included *Tridacna*. Among the midden was some bottle glass and cattle bone. Lapita pottery was especially prominent and there were also pieces of shell armband and paddle-impressed ware.

Layer 2: Blocky, stiff, dark-brown sandy loam which was damp to excavate and dried very hard. Almost no midden or pottery was recovered.

Layer 3: Pale-yellow to grey compact sand, shell and coral. No cultural material was found.

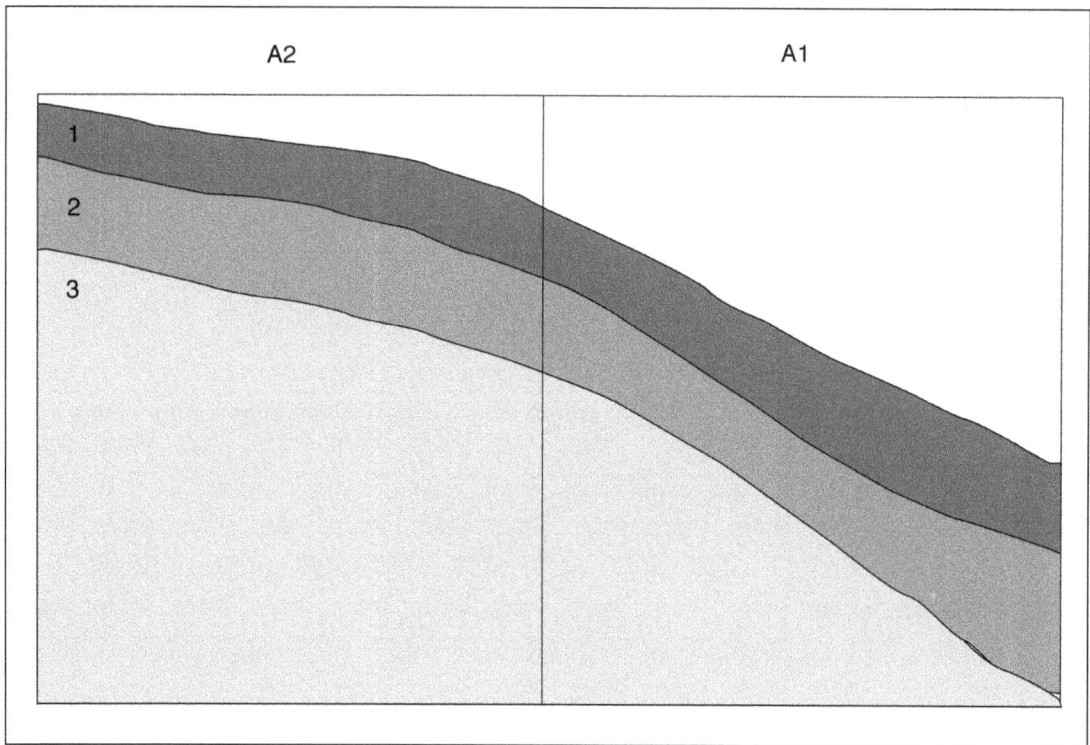

Figure 64. Stratigraphy of east baulk of Trench 1 (see text for layer descriptions).

Trench 2 (Figure 65)

Layer 1: Light-brown sandy loam containing abundant shell and pottery, again with Lapita sherds prominent. There were also pieces of shell armband, drilled shell pieces and plates, notched shell and other worked shell. Shell midden was less abundant than in Trench 1, but Lapita sherds were correspondingly more abundant. In Square 2, at 20 cm depth, a Lapita-style ceramic handle was found in association with two brass tap fittings.

Layer 2: Yellow-brown sandy loam full of shell midden and some pottery.

Layer 3: Blocky, stiff, dark-brown-to-black sandy loam which was damp to excavate but dried very hard. Very little midden or pottery and nearly all of it near the top.

Layer 4: Coarse, pale-yellow to light-brown calcareous sand with natural shell fragments and coral. No cultural material.

Layer 5: Damp grey-yellow coarse sand with much broken shell.

Trenches 1 and 2 appeared to contain, at the surface, re-deposited layers of the light-brown calcareous sand, presumably from grave-digging on the top of the beach ridge. This unit contained most of the cultural material and in Trench 2 a thin layer of it also occurred beneath the original forest soil, which was essentially bereft of cultural items. Excluding the probable re-deposition by natural down-slope movement and grave digging, the stratigraphy in this area suggests it is right on the margins of the Lapita site. Disturbance was clearly extensive, including by land crabs.

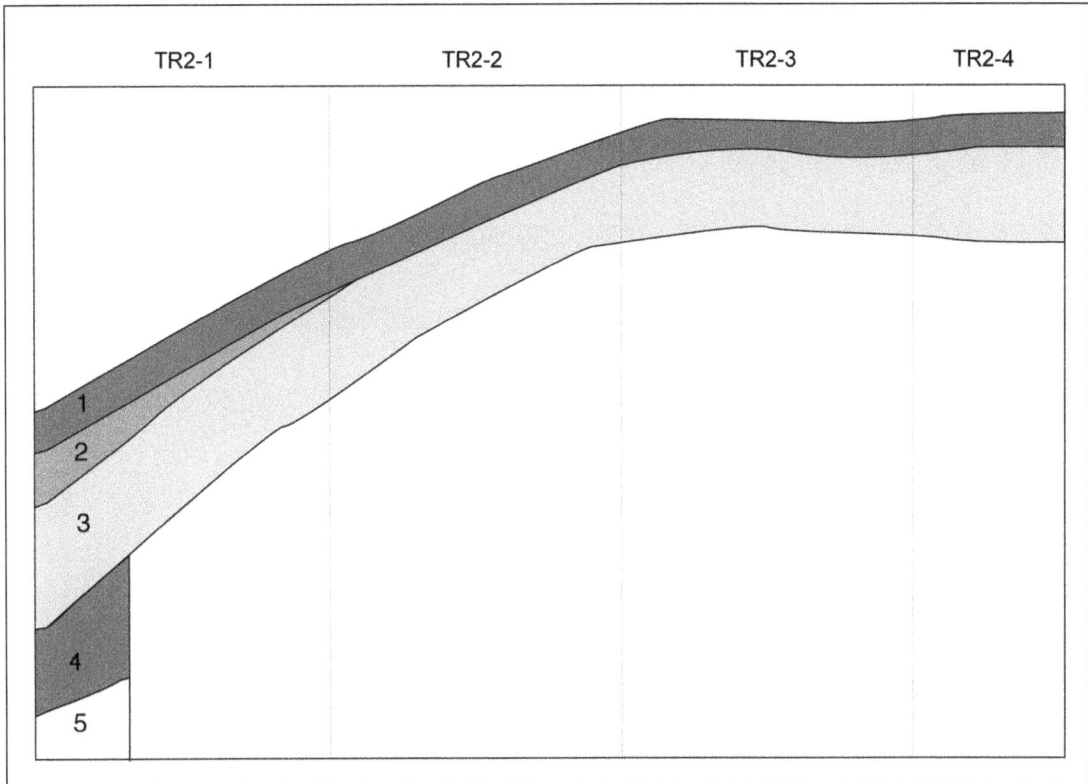

Figure 65. Stratigraphy of west baulk of Trench 2 (see text for layer descriptions).

Trench 3

This was an 8 sq. m excavation set out on the top and seaward slope of the beach ridge. In areal extent, it was the same size as the combined rectangles which were fully excavated in Location C (Davidson et al. 1990:125), and so far as can be judged from the description of Location C, and the published and unpublished (E. Hinds, pers. comm., Dunedin) sections, both Trench 3 and Location C represent essentially the same cross-sectional positions across the beach ridge and above the beach-rock platform (Figure 62). Nevertheless, they differ in cultural levels and content. The stratigraphy of Trench 3 from the top of the beach ridge was as follows; here from the west baulk of Square B6 (Figure 66).

Layer 1: 0–10 cm of weakly developed turf on friable light-brown sandy loam. Small quantities of shell and pottery.

Layer 2: 10 cm to 40–50 cm of a slightly sandy, compact dark-brown silt loam. Abundant shell and other midden, burned and cracked basalt and pottery. Decorated sherds of the latter were nearly all Lapita.

Layer 3: From base of Layer 2 to 50–70 cm depth of yellow-brown, humus-stained sand, with very little midden or pottery, and that mostly near the top.

Layer 4: This is a coarse, yellow, calcareous beach sand with much coral and broken shell. It closely resembles the description of Layer 6 in Location C (Davidson et al. 1990), but it contains no cultural material.

Other squares in Trench 3 were variations on this pattern, thinning seaward to Square A1 which had, under a thin turf, just a 1–3 cm layer of coarse, pale-yellow to grey sand above the

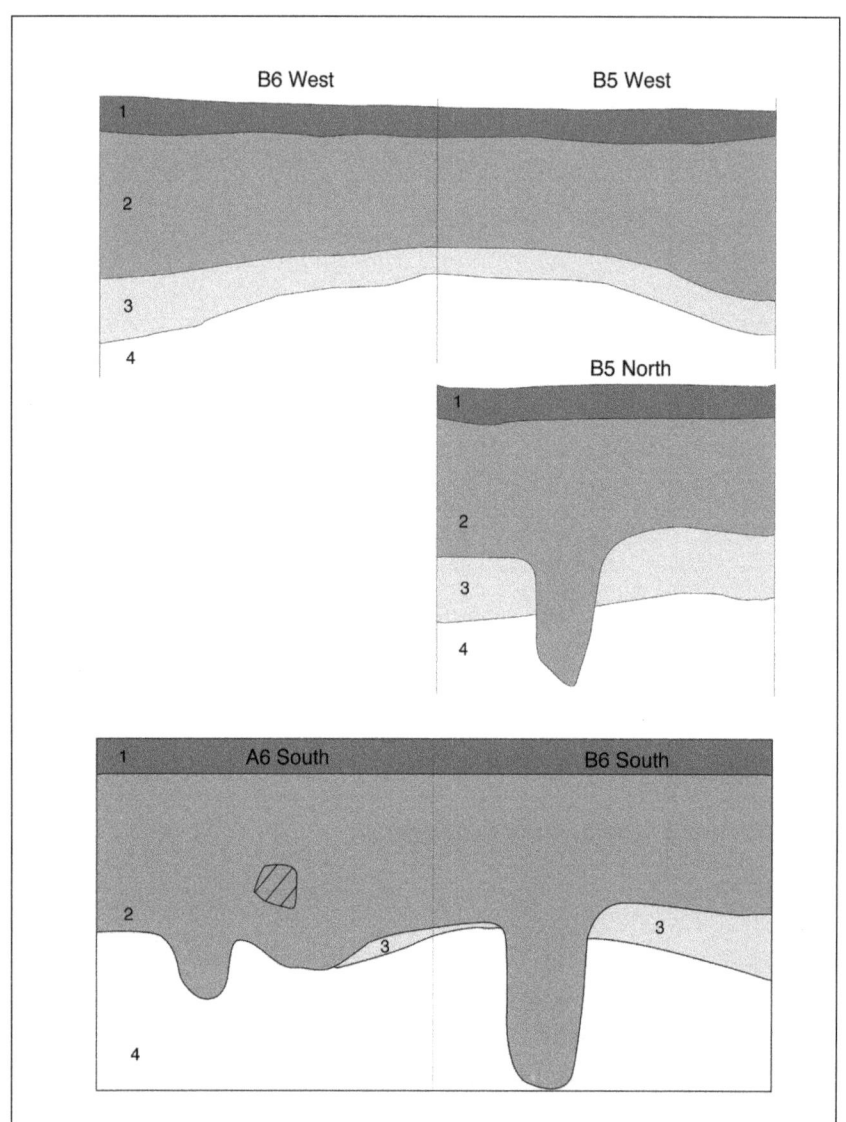

Figure 66. Stratigraphy of west baulk of Squares B5 and B6 (above), and south baulk of A6, B6 (below) in Trench 3 (see text for layer descriptions).

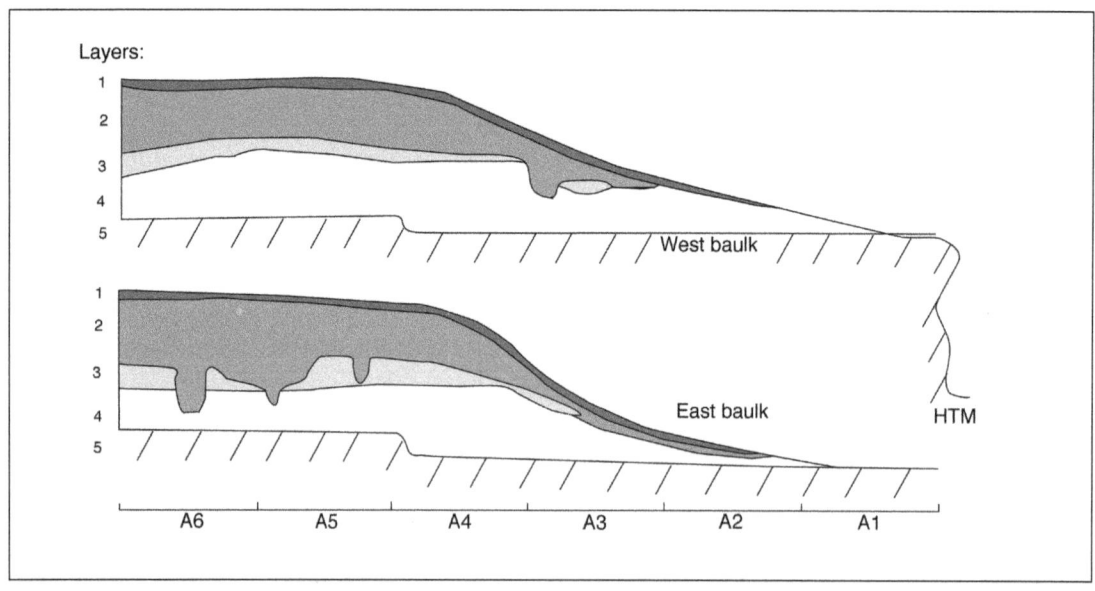

Figure 67. Stratigraphy of west (above) and east (below) baulks of the Trench 3 excavation (see text for layer descriptions). Both lie on a beach-rock platform at approximately 1 m above high tide mark.

beach-rock platform (Figure 67). Trench 3 stratigraphy had been substantially disturbed by ovens and post holes, cut from within Layer 2 and reaching to the base of the site (Figure 68), and also by land crabs. No post butts remained and it is impossible to be certain of the agency involved in each feature, but Feature A, which was packed with broken rock (although almost no charcoal), had probably been an oven. Features B, D, E, F, M and O seem to have been post holes. The others are enigmatic. They may have been post holes that were exploited subsequently by burrowing crabs.

Overall, the stratigraphy could be regarded as combining Layers 1–4 and 6 of Location C (Davidson et al. 1990), but with Layer 5 absent. It is possible that both the existence of Layer 5, an apparent dune sand, and the deposition of Lapita sherds in Layer 6, are quite localised phenomena. Now that it is possible to define the area of Location C more precisely, those issues need to be tested.

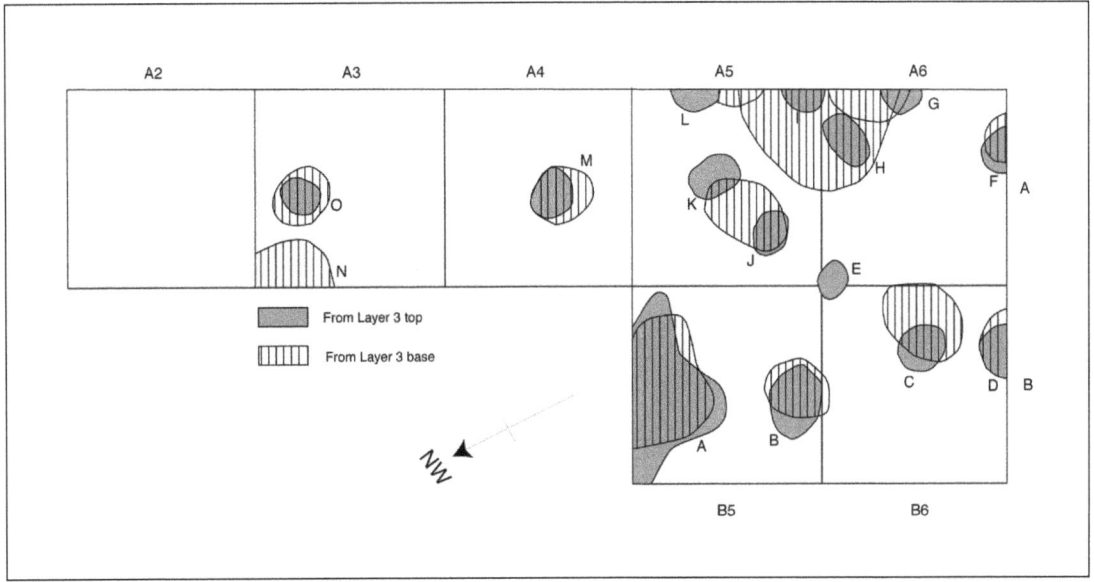

Figure 68. Features in Trench 3 at Natunuku, as seen at the top of Layer 3, and at the base of Layer 3. See text for suggested interpretation.

Fieldwork at Navatu, 17A

Navatu 17A was first excavated in 1947 by Edward Gifford, then aged 63 and Director of the Museum of Anthropology at the University of California. In a landmark paper published in 1963, Roger Green re-evaluated Gifford's material and divided Fiji's past into four phases, the longest of which (100 BC to 1100 AD) was called the Navatu phase after the site located in northern Viti Levu. Navatu 17A was re-excavated in 1996 as part of a wider investigation into the post-Lapita period of Fiji, and focused on obtaining pottery and dating samples to refine the chronology and stylistic content of the Navatu phase. Geomorphological investigations of the slope deposit and alluvial flat were made during recovery of a core for pollen analysis (Chapter 4).

The eponymous site for the Navatu phase is located on the western side of a volcanic plug, known as Uluinavatu (head of the rock), in the province of Ra, on the north coast of Viti Levu (Figure 69). In traditional history, Uluinavatu is one of the jumping-off places for spirits and was a famous refuge. In 1876 when Sir Arthur Gordon visited, there were three 'villages' on the plug, with the uppermost used as a refuge during warfare (Derrick 1951:195). Traditional and historical information concerning the area is summarised by Gifford (1951, 1952a), Frazer

(1963) and Parry (1997). Their accounts suggest that within Ra Province the movement of people was frequent due to the expansion of the Colo tribes from the interior as well as feuding among coastal *vanua* (group of related *yavusa*).

The volcanic plug has a maximum height of 198 m and is 0.8 km in diameter. It is composed of hornblende andesite of Pliocene age (Seeley and Searle 1970; Rodda 1976), and separates the coastal villages of Narewa to the west and Vitawa to the east. To its north, the plug is bordered by the mangrove-fringed coast, along which runs the light rail line built by the Colonial Sugar Refining Company. South of the plug, the King's Road divides the rocky and steep slopes of the volcanic plug from the low-lying alluvial flats used for cropping and grazing (Figure 70), with the steep Nakauvadra Range (altitude 750 m) lying 6 km behind the plug.

Vegetation covering the plug is dominated by *vaivai* (*Leucaena glauca*), an introduced legume. In recent years, the lower slope of the plug has been cleared for a variety of economic plants, especially cassava (*Maniot utilissima*), coconut (*Cocos nucifera*), banana (*Musa* sp.) and breadfruit (*Artocarpus altilis*). The flat area between the base of the western plug slopes and the Narewa creek is used for growing sugar cane (*Saccharum officinarium*) and grazing horses, cattle and goats. Small plots of taro (*Colocasia esculenta*) are grown along the sheltered sides of the Narewa stream.

Figure 69. Aerial photograph (pre-1970) showing the location of Navatu 17A on the flank of Uluinavatu.

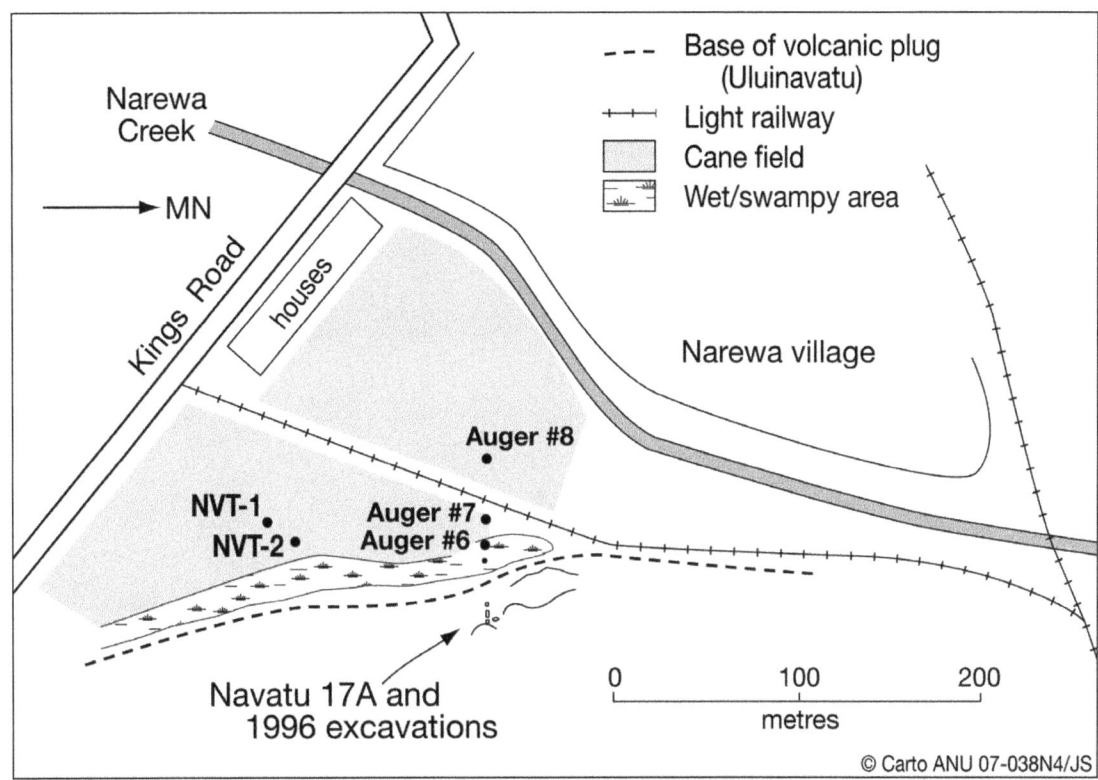

Figure 70. Navatu 17A, plan view of site location and environs showing auger and pollen core holes.

Excavation

The site of the 1947 investigations was located by reference to Gifford's site map (1951:Diagram 1) (Figure 71). Visible signs of the earlier excavations were found inside the small rock shelter, where the eastern extant of squares U3–5 could still be seen, and possibly on the slope surface, where an east–west depression corresponds with the difference in slope height recorded by Gifford (1951:Diagram 2).

A 1 m x 15 m transect was set out roughly parallel to the previous excavations. Isikeli Donu of Narewa village, who had worked with Gifford (Figure 72) in 1947 (Gifford 1951:Plate 14a), confirmed that the 1996 excavation transect was broadly parallel to and slightly north of the 1947 transect. Three trenches were laid out along the transect and positioned approximately east–west so as not to overlap with the earlier excavations (Figure 71).

Trench A was immediately in front and north of the rock-shelter entrance. The trench consisted of a 1 m x 3 m rectangle. The top (eastern) metre square was designated A1 and the bottom A3 (Figure 71).

Trench B was just over 3 m down-slope from Trench A and was originally 1 m x 3 m in size. This trench was later extended by 1 m, as large boulders occupied much of Squares B2 and B3. The eastern 1 m x 1 m square was designated B1 and the western square, B4 (Figures 71 and 73).

Trench C was situated on relatively flat ground near the marshy zone which lay between the plug slope and the cane fields. However, the amount of water at that location, either from a spring or the natural water table, halted investigations at 80 cm depth and Trench C was abandoned. It is possible that water-logged archaeological deposits occur in the vicinity of Trench C as there was apparently no diminution in cultural material in a core taken down to 1.2 m depth.

Excavation was by 10 cm and 20 cm spits within each natural layer. Two 20 cm spits were used for the first 40 cm of the deposit, and then consecutive 10 cm spits were taken. Matrix

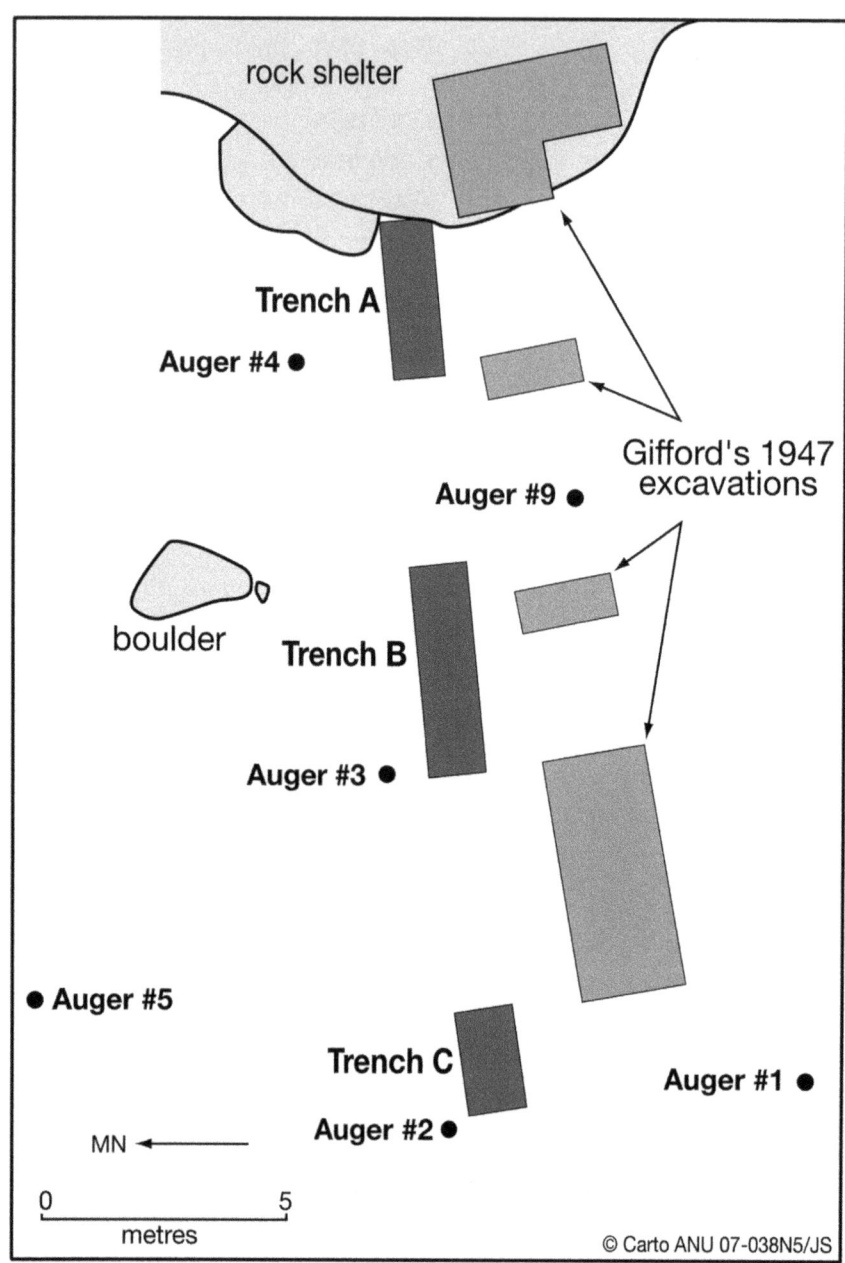

Figure 71. Navatu 17A, plan view of previous (1947) and recent (1996) excavations.

material was sieved using 3 mm and 6 mm mesh. However, the lowest deposits consisted of a wet, sticky clay that required washing and some hand-sorting to separate cultural material from sediment. Layer 4 (see below) was excavated as two units (B1+2 and B3+4) because of large andesite boulders in Squares B2 and B3 (Figures 74–75). A 50 cm x 50 cm column from the northeast corner of Trenches A and B was retained as bulk sample.

Four layers were identified during excavation of Trench B. Three of these contained cultural materials, while Layer 3 did not. The layers were not found in all excavated areas and the lowest cultural deposit, Layer 4, was identified in Trench B only (Figure 73 and Figure 75).

Layer 1: Consisted of a very dark-brown silty clay (10YR 3/1, pH=6.75). The depth of this layer varied due to the slope angle, the presence of large boulders and the effects of recent gardening. In general, Layer 1 was around 1–1.5 m in depth. Cultural material included large quantities of pottery sherds, marine shells, boulders and fragments of andesite, and charcoal. Several concentrations and horizontal lenses of shellfish remains were found at

Figure 72. Edward Gifford and work crew at Navatu-Narewa (see Gifford 1951:Plate13c). Photo courtesy of David DeGusta.

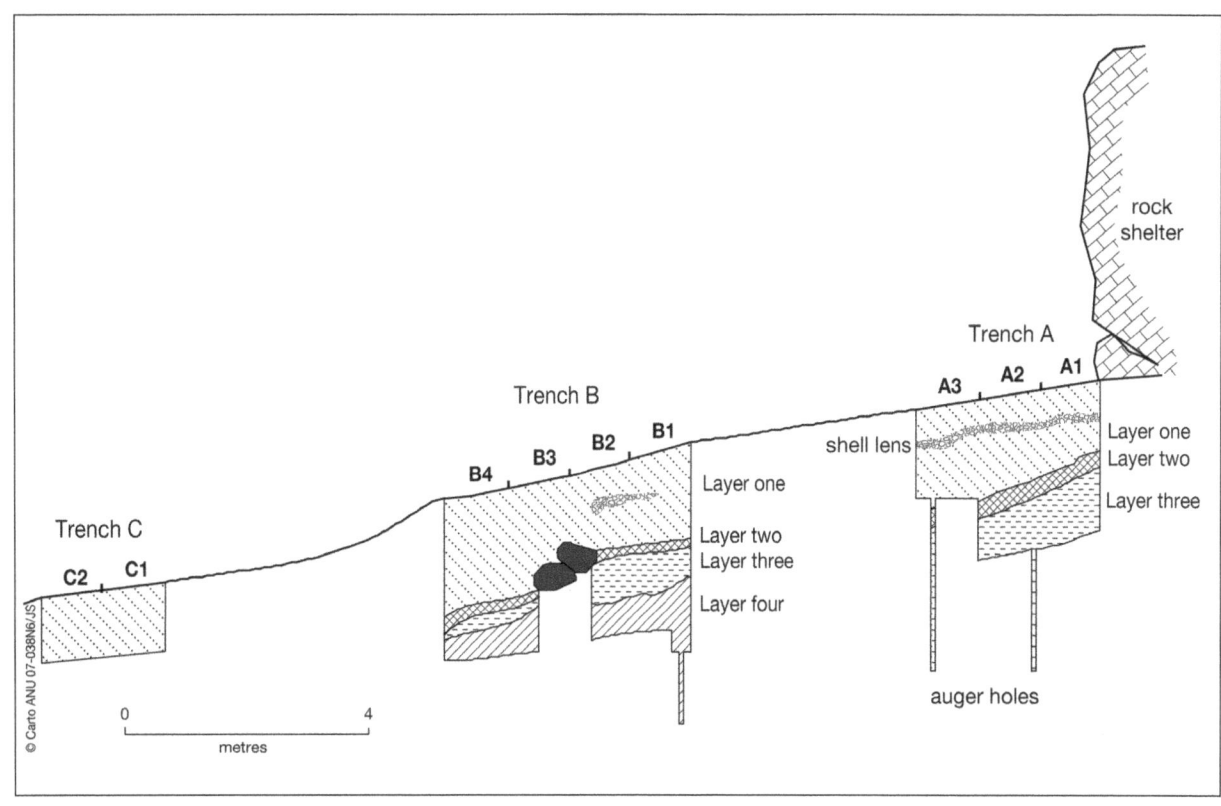

Figure 73. Navatu 17A, north section of 1996 excavation trenches.

Figure 74. Navatu 17A, Trench B excavation east baulk of B1.

50–80 cm (Figure 73 and Figure 75). Distinctive comb-incised sherds, which occur on the slope and circumference of the Navatu plug, were primarily confined to the first metre of this layer.

Layer 2: A dark-brown silty clay. The layer was found in Trenches A and B, and also identified in a nearby auger hole. The colour of this layer varied from a dark yellowish-brown (10YR 6/6) at its base to a dark brown (10YR 3/3, pH=6.75) where it merged with Layer 1. The layer depth varied from 10–50 cm. There was a low density of cultural remains, which were primarily shellfish and ceramics, with small quantities of bone and charcoal flecks. Ceramic sherds were mostly plain but included small and eroded specimens marked with wavy, parallel and cross-hatch paddle relief.

Layer 3: A mottled yellowish-brown material (10YR 5/8, pH=7.0). There was a gradual transition between this layer and Layer 2, suggesting development from Layer 3, whereas the Layer 3 boundary with Layer 4 was abrupt and consistent with an episode of very sudden deposition. No pottery, shell or charcoal was identified during excavation, and pollen and phytolith analysis of the Layer 3 sediments were also negative. The layer had a variable depth that was generally about 20–50 cm thick. In Trench A, coring into this layer showed that it graded into greyish-white silty clay below 3 m depth. The water table was struck at 3.8 m, where the deposits had an increasing quantity of coarse sand. At the western end of Trench B, Layer 3 became less defined, possibly due to the placement of a linear stone feature.

Microscopic analysis of the Layer 3 sediment revealed a dominance of angular feldspars with accessory mica and ferromagnesian grains. No volcanic glass was observed, suggesting that significant weathering of the material occurred since deposition. John Chappell (pers. comm., ANU) identified this material as a reworked tephra that has been deposited downslope from the plug flanks.

Layer 4: A dark greyish-brown clay (2.5YR 5/2, pH=6.75) that graded into a light grey-brown silty clay (10YR 4/2, pH=7.0) between 2.8 m and 3.0 m depth. The top of this layer contained quantities of weathered and often fragmentary marine shell. Small shell scatters occurred in the eastern part of Trench B and on the surface of Layer 4 (B1 and

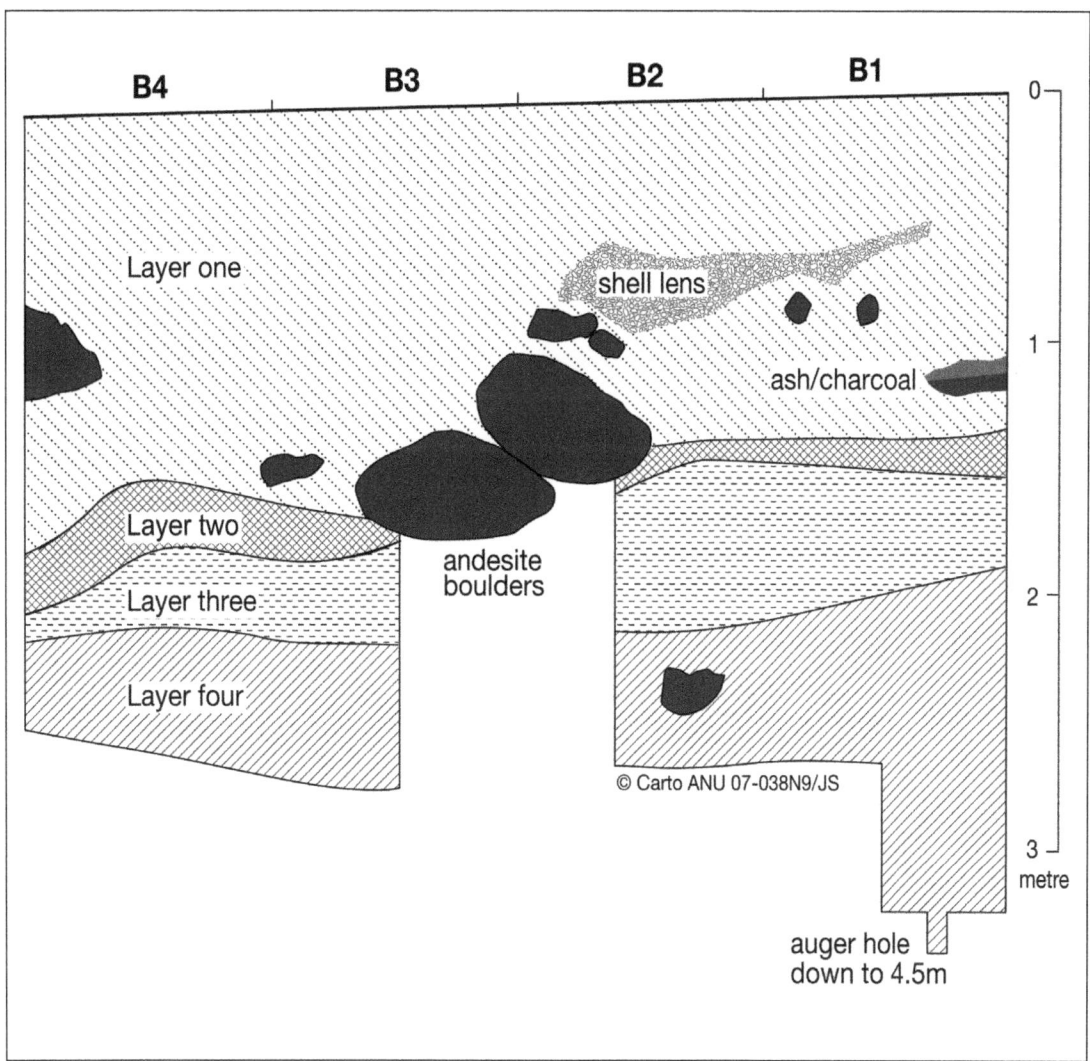

Figure 75. Navatu 17A, Trench B north profile (Squares B1 to B4).

B2). Associated with the shell were ceramic sherds decorated with varieties of paddle- and tool-impressed decoration. No structural features or non-ceramic artefacts were recovered. Bones from fish, turtle, shark and human were present in small amounts.

Features included several small hearths recognised by concentrations of ash and charcoal in Layer 1 of Trenches A and B. Other Layer 1 features included clusters of marine shells, and a post hole was dug from Layer 1 or 2 into Layer 3 (Figure 76). The stone alignment found in the western end of Trench B at a depth of 70 cm could be a natural or a cultural feature. Evidence for the latter is suggested by Gifford, who noted two stone lines, which were identified as buried house-mound foundations in rectangles EF3–4 (Gifford 1951:Diagram 1 and Plate 13e). The feature found in Trench B (Figure 76) lies in the same line as that found by Gifford (i.e. the eastern end of Gifford's A3–4 to F3–4 rectangles). While most features were found in Layer 1, smaller patches of shellfish remains occurred in Level 4.

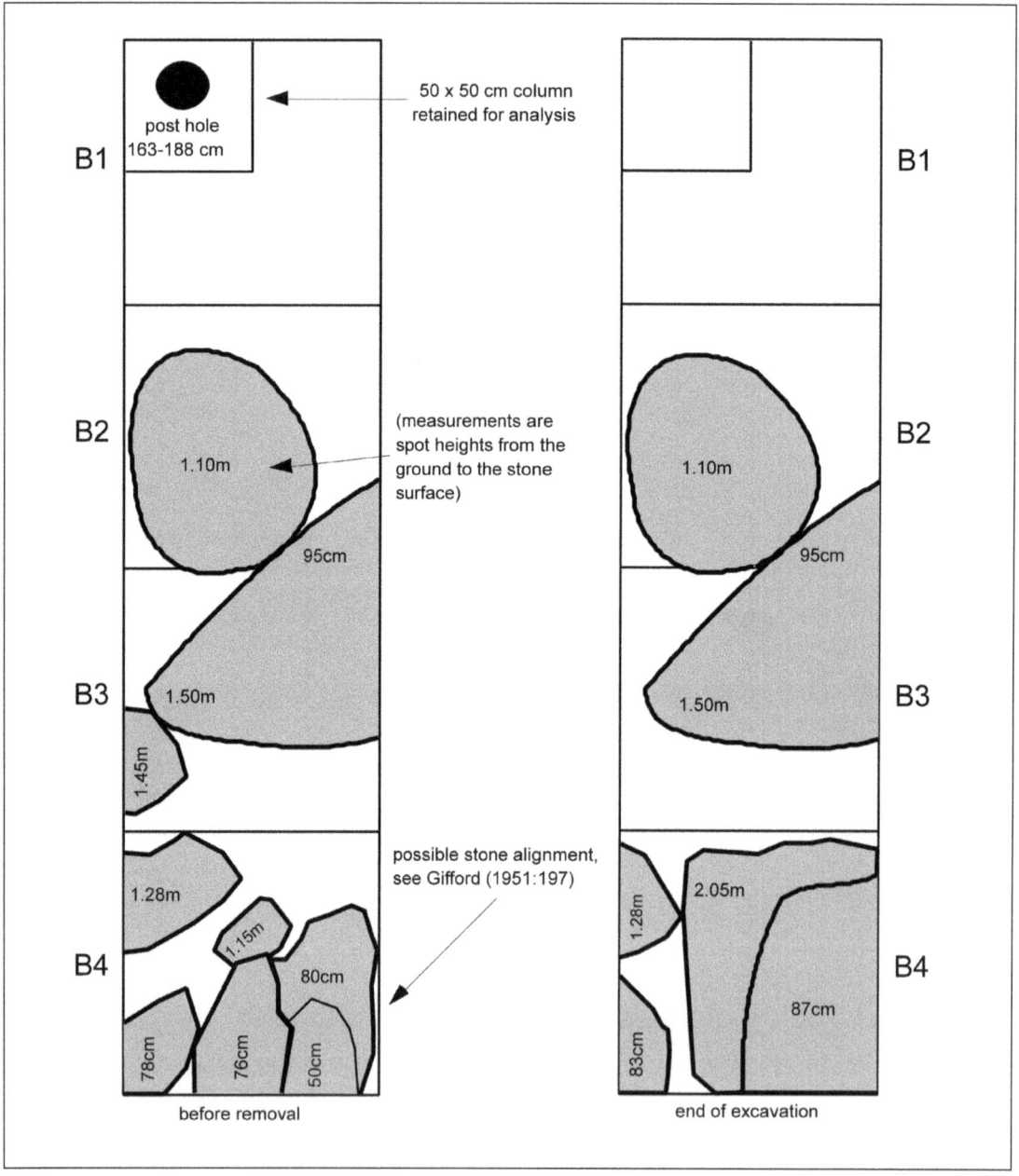

Figure 76. Navatu 17A, Trench B plan view before and after removal of stone feature.

Geomorphological investigations

A transect line of four auger holes was taken to examine whether the heavy cultural deposits on the plug flank extended west to the alluvial flat (Figures 70–71). Holes were made with a manual auger equipped with soil and sand barrels (10 cm diameter), and their stratigraphy is described below and is summarised in Figure 77.

> **Hole #5.** Location 9.2 m north of the northeast corner of Trench C.
> 0–41 cm: Dark-brown silty clay with abundant marine shell and pottery.
> 41–57 cm: Dense concentration of burned and fragmented marine shellfish in ash.
> 57–100 cm: Light-to-medium brown damp soil with little shell or cultural material, except flecks of charcoal.
> 100–142 cm: Grey mud with inclusions of a brown moist soil. Small quantities of pottery, fish bone and a few small marine shells. Core finished on rock (basement or boulder?).
>
> **Hole #6.** Location 22 m west of the northeast corner of Trench C, on the edge of the swampy area near the base of the volcanic plug.
> 0–67 cm: Dark-brown puggy soil with orange-brown fragments of rotted rock.
> 67–107 cm: Dark-grey soil with a plain pot sherd at 86 cm.
> 107–110 cm: Thin lens of grey sand.
> 110–197 cm: Grey-brown clay with orange fragments of rotted rock. Charcoal fragment at 1.42 m and water table reached at 1.70–1.80 m.
> 197–274 cm: Dark-grey sandy silt with flecks of charcoal and two plain pot sherds. Material too wet to remove below 274 cm.
>
> **Hole #7.** Location 42 m west of the northeast corner of Trench C, in the sugar-cane field.
> 0–83 cm: Dark-brown soil with a pot sherd at 37 cm depth.
> 83–121 cm: Grey-blue clay mixed with brown soil. Ground water at 100 cm depth.
> 121–230 cm: Grey-brown fine silty mud. Some charcoal at 180 cm.
> 230–235 cm: Grey-brown sand.
> 235–255 cm: Thin layer of brown soil with water-logged wood and charcoal.
> 255–344 cm: Black sandy-silt layer with inclusions of rock, clay and roots. Hole finished when wet sediments could not be collected.
>
> **Hole #8.** Location 72 m west of the northeast corner of Trench C, in the sugar-cane field.
> 0–81 cm: Dark-brown soil with flecks of charcoal.
> 81–167 cm: Light-brown soil with orange fragments of basalt and groundwater at 90 cm.
> 167–197 cm: Blue-grey clay with fragments of charcoal.

The lowest deposit in Holes #6–8 was an organic sandy silt, consistent with a swampy estuarine environment. Around 2 m depth this changes to a silty clay or mud with basalt clasts indicating that terrigenous sediments from the plug slopes, or more likely alluvium transported from the Nakauvadra catchment, had infilled the estuary. Except for a few fragments of charcoal, there is little evidence of prehistoric activity, other than in Hole #6, near to the plug flanks, where cultural material was found below 2 m depth in waterlogged conditions.

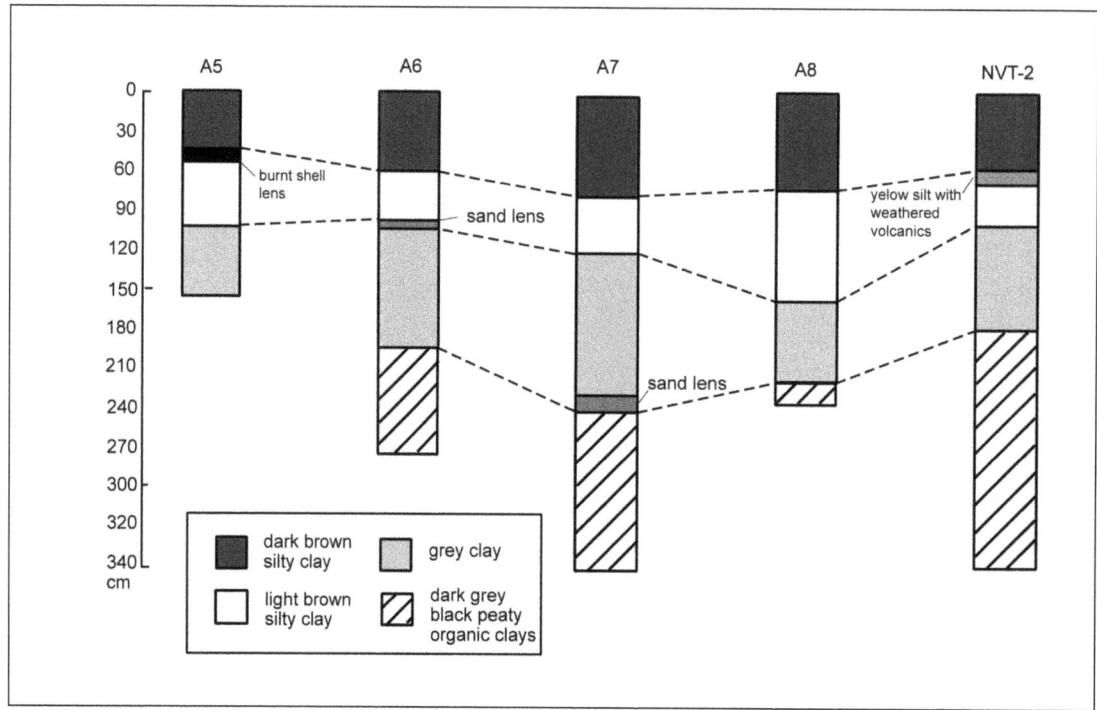

Figure 77. Navatu 17A, stratigraphy of auger and pollen core holes.

Navatu 17A: Reassessment

Two areas (A and B) at Navatu (Site 17) were excavated by Gifford in 1947. The main area studied by him was 17A. Navatu 17A is below a large boulder of hornblende andesite. The boulder lies on the western side of the plug about 25 m from the edge of the cane field and ca. 4.5 m above the cane field. The boulder overhang forms a small 3.7 m deep shelter. Gifford staked 6 ft x 3 ft rectangles from the base of the slope up to the overhang. Stakes were labelled alphabetically in the east-to-west line and numerically north to south. Fourteen rectangles were opened up but the presence of andesite boulders and the high water table near the slope base meant that some rectangles were only partially excavated or were abandoned. The excavation transect included five rectangles within the boulder overhang, two separate rectangles on the mid-slope region and the major excavation region of five adjoining rectangles near the slope base (A3–4 to F3–4). Gifford's excavation measurements are given in metric units to allow comparison with the 1996 excavation details (Figure 71).

The cultural remains recovered by Gifford from Navatu 17A have been influential in interpreting Fiji's and the Pacific's prehistory, and the site's remains continue to be used to examine Fiji's past (e.g. Wahome 1995; DeGusta 1999). The longevity of Gifford's classic 1951 report, *Archaeological Investigations in Fiji*, ensued from several factors, particularly the high standard of analysis and reportage. Of note was the presentation of excavated material, particularly pottery attributes by depth (decoration type and weight), the identification of fauna, the first petrographic analysis of pottery (Curtis 1951; Dickinson 1971), and subsequently the first radiocarbon dates for Fiji and the first identification of fish remains from an archaeological site in the Pacific (Gifford 1952b, 1955; Fowler 1955). Surprisingly, at the time of the EFP investigations, Gifford's report contained the only published information about prehistoric fauna from a Viti Levu site.

The 1996 excavations demonstrated, however, that Navatu 17A is, like many archaeological sites in the Pacific, a complicated deposit and the new data allows substantial revision of its stratigraphy. The Navatu deposits were interpreted by Gifford through cultural content rather than by natural layer. Thus, the presence and amount of shell and the type of pottery decoration indicated significant temporal and cultural differences between 'Early' and 'Late' materials. This approach meant that a layer described by Gifford (1951:195) as a 'sterile volcanic ash' was not recorded as a separate stratigraphic unit although its upper surface was plotted (Gifford 1951:198). This layer clearly corresponds to Layer 3 identified in the 1996 excavations. However, while showing that this layer was found over the transect area, nowhere in the original report is there mention of an underlying cultural deposit that would correspond to Layer 4. However, as the 1947 excavations went down to 3.7 m depth in some areas, like the rectangle EF3–4, Gifford must have gone through the 'yellow-volcanic ash substratum' and recovered material from a layer equivalent to Layer 4 identified in the 1996 investigations.

The 'yellow volcanic ash' deposit – now identified as a redeposited tephra and called Layer 3 – is an enigmatic layer that is the basal deposit in the Trench A excavation but lies above Layer 4 in Trench B only 3 m down-slope. Because the transition between Layers 4 and 3 was abrupt, while the transition between Layers 3 and 2 was gradual, it is likely that Layer 3 was deposited suddenly. Such an interpretation is reliant on a nearby tephra source that remained *in situ* for some time. Gifford (1951:198) found the tephra layer over the length of his transect area (18.3 m), but did not record its presence from Site 17B some 400 m northeast of 17A. It seems probable that the tuff was deposited on the plug slopes some millennia ago, converting to a tephra over time. Near the plug base the tephra level was excised, possibly during periods of higher sea level or episodes of river flooding, but human activities might also have been responsible. Around 1000 years ago the tephra bank slumped on to Layer 4 for reasons that are currently unclear but which could include clearance of slope vegetation (natural or anthropogenic), severe storm events or human modification of the area.

The Layer 4 cultural deposits had a lower density than those from Layer 1. Ceramic sherds were not as abundant and the marine-shell remains had an eroded appearance that was similar to weathered shellfish fragments on the Layer 1 surface, suggesting a period of site abandonment. Cooking and consumption of marine foods and cannibalism were represented in Layer 4, but no evidence of ceramic production, artefact manufacture or structural remains was identified. The number of double-spouted vessels, the presence of decorated bowls and, if historical observations from the 19th century are germane, the presence of prestige food remains (human and turtle) in Layer 4 could result from a high-status occupation.

Following the deposition of the tephra Layer 3 deposit, cultural and faunal remains were even sparser in Layer 2, suggesting a period of relative abandonment. The development of a soil profile on the surface of Layer 3 supports this idea. The greatest concentration of archaeological remains came from Layer 1. Surface remains (ceramics and shellfish) from this layer covered the entire area surrounding the lower elevations of the volcanic plug, and penetrated into the estuary. The deposits appear to have built up relatively quickly and were associated with the construction of house platforms on the flanks of Uluinavatu. Thus, while the quantity of the Layer 1 cultural deposits suggests a more intensive use of the area than had previously taken place, the areal extent of the Layer 1 deposits indicates the involvement of a greater number of people than represented in Layers 2 and 4.

Fieldwork at Votua and Sovanibeka, Mago Island

Mago Island (Figure 78) consists of raised limestone on a submarine ridge, through which Miocene and Pliocene eruptions have deposited volcanic rocks over the limestone. The island lies 220 km northeast of Viti Levu and 90 km east of Taveuni, but several islands in northern

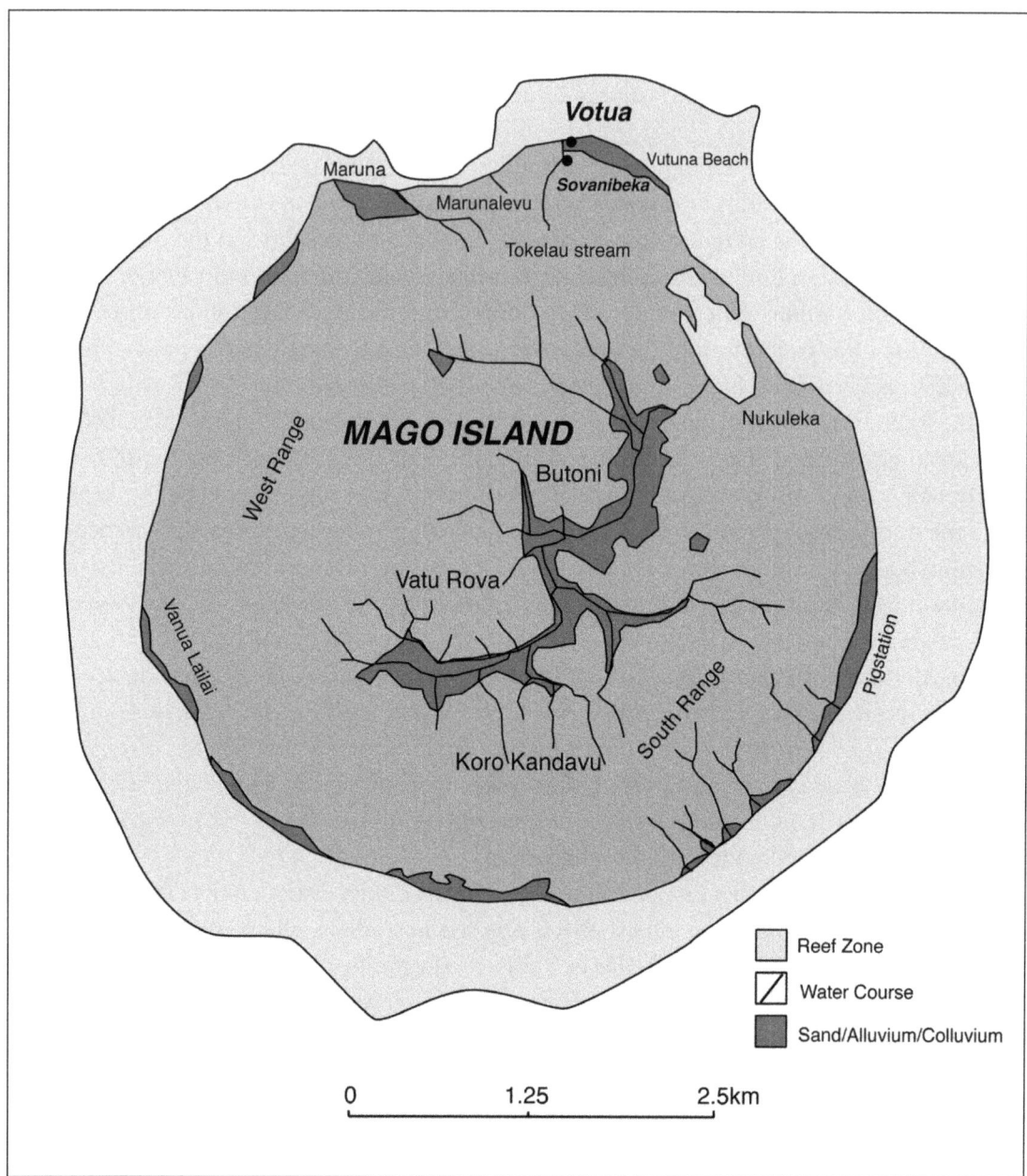

Figure 78. Mago Island and location of Votua and Sovanibeka.

Lau are visible from it, including Vanuabalavu. The physiography consists of steep weathered limestone ridges and plateaux bordering the coast, except in the north and southeast of the island, where volcanics have replaced limestone. Narrow coastal sand plains with a depth of up to 120 m are composed of carbonate sand and gravel of Holocene age, and are present discontinuously around the island (Ladd and Hoffmeister 1945; Woodhall 1985).

Excavations at Votua in late 1996 revealed an apparently single-phase late-Lapita site, which was first recognised from surface exposures of shell midden and red-slipped pottery, some with dentate stamping, at the west end of Vutuna beach (Figure 78). Because of time constraints, only 3 sq. m of the site was excavated – 2 m from a shell midden adjacent to Tokelau stream at the base of a natural volcanic-boulder mound (Figures 79–80), and a single unit called Test Pit 1, 60 m southeast of the midden. The analysis of the excavated materials and preliminary interpretation of the site were published by Clark et al. (2001:142), who concluded that: 'Although the site might extend to 3000 square metres, and bearing in mind the very small

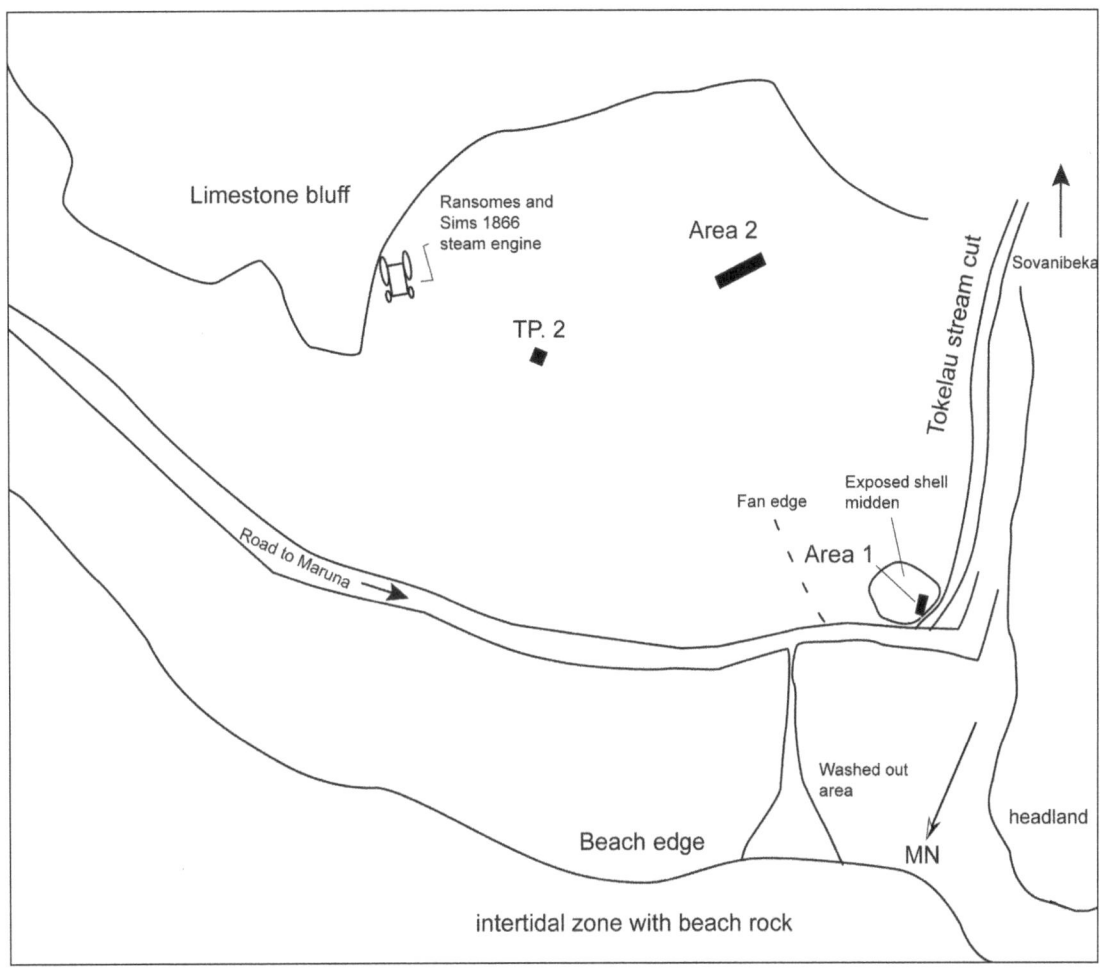

Figure 79. Votua, plan view of 1996 and 2000 excavations. Compass and tape map by G. Hope.

Figure 80. South view up the Tokelau stream bed. The Area 1 shell midden is behind the figure in the foreground.

size of the excavated sample, Votua can be considered nonetheless as an example of the mobile or encampment mode of Lapita settlement primarily sustained by marine and terrestrial wild foods, rather than the hamlet or village mode which is represented elsewhere.'

The conclusion was necessarily qualified due to the small size of the 1996 excavations, the dry sieving of the clayey soils, which can lead to the recovery of unrepresentative samples of material culture, and the restricted understanding of the site's extent and its past environmental setting. Clearly, better information from more detailed investigations could significantly change the interpretation of the Votua site, and thus of the variation in settlement pattern suggested for Lapita settlement in the Fiji Islands, for which Votua offered some preliminary evidence.

New work at the Votua site was undertaken in December 2000 during a research visit to Vanuabalavu organised by Professor Patrick Nunn (USP). The research aims were threefold. First, to determine the site limits with greater accuracy. In 1996, plain pottery had been identified some 250 m from Vutuna stream, but the main Lapita occupation zone at Votua was thought to cover only about 1000 to 3000 sq. m of the small sand plain to the east of Tokelau stream. Was this estimate reliable or did Votua extend over a much larger area? Second, would water sieving of the Votua deposits increase the faunal and artefactual remains to a point where the proposed 'mobile or encampment mode' of settlement might be challenged? Last, what was the environmental setting of the Lapita occupation at Votua?

The Votua site is located at the west end of Vutuna Beach on an indented limestone-backed sand plain, approximately 1.5–2.0 m above sea level, adjacent to Tokelau stream – a small and impermanent water course (Figures 79–80). The stream follows the boundary between the late Pleistocene volcanics and older limestone deposits and a mound of rounded basalt and limestone boulders lies immediately east of the stream, with the base of the mound on its seaward edge defined by the plantation road to Maruna. The sand plain is bordered in the east by limestone ridges and outcrops and in the south and east by a slope deposit containing soil, limestone and weathered volcanic boulders. The Vutuna sand plain was planted in coconut palms (*Cocos nucifera*) by at least 1882 (G. Ward, pers. comm., ANU), when it was owned by the Ryder brothers who used about 300 labourers from the Solomon Islands, Vanuatu, Tokelau, Tuvalu and Kiribati to work their plantations (Gordon Cumming 1885:333).

A trench 1 m x 4 m called Area 2 was laid out beside the 1996 Test Pit 1 excavation (Figure 79). Area 2 was about 75 m from the beach edge and the south square of Area 2 was placed near the top of a small rise, with other excavation squares down-slope. A single 1 m x 1 m square called Test Pit 2 was placed 19 m northeast of Area 2 and near a limestone cleft containing the remains of an 1866 'Ransomes and Sims' portable steam engine. The sand plain was tested with shovel holes and a soil/sand auger to identify the extent of the Lapita cultural deposits.

Area 2 and Test Pit 2 excavations were by 10 cm spit using a trowel. In contrast to the 1996 excavations, all the excavated deposits were water sieved through 3 mm mesh using water pumped from the fringing reef, or directly in the sea itself when the water pump broke down. Pot sherds and marine shell were bagged and taken to Maruna and recorded before the majority of plain sherds and shells were dumped at the garden edge at the back of the Maruna sand plain. Rim, neck and carinated sherds were retained and voucher specimens of all shell taxa collected for identification at the ANU. Field processing of the ceramics and particularly the shellfish was necessary because of weight limitations on the plane flight from Vanuabalavu to Viti Levu. As the total marine-shell weight was over 50 kg for each 1 m square excavated at Area 2, we were obliged to identify, count and weigh marine-shellfish remains in the field. The loss of information resulting from this procedure was partially offset by the presence of complete shellfish samples analysed from the 1996 excavations, particularly Test Pit 1, which was immediately beside the

Area 2 trench. Other cultural remains, such as fauna, charcoal, and artefacts of stone, coral and shell, represent complete samples that were bagged separately and returned to the ANU.

Votua Area 2

The stratigraphy of Area 2 is similar to that recorded from Test Pit 1 in 1996, where three layers were identified, but the more recent work added extra detail to the original layer descriptions (Figure 81).

Layer 1: Varied in depth from 22 cm to 30 cm. It consisted of a black to very dark-brown clay silt (10YR 2/1–2/2, pH=8.5–9.0), with tree roots and dispersed and fragmented remains of marine shells, small flakes of silicious material and patches of charcoal.

Layer 2: The main cultural layer. It varied from hard-packed brown to dark-brown silty clay containing sand (10YR 2/2 to 10YR 4/3, pH=8.0–9.5). Within Layer 2 were thin lenses of weathered ash varying in colour from purple/brown to yellow/white. At 42 cm depth there was a thin discontinuous lens of clean beach sand. From 40 cm to 60 cm the deposit consisted of a compact shell midden dominated by *Anadara* and *Gafrarium*.

The base of the cultural deposit was reached at 60 cm, except where small amounts of cultural material were deposited in small depressions penetrating Layer 3. At the bottom of the shell midden were valves of a large oyster (*Crassostrea* sp.). Large and small basalt rocks occurred throughout Layer 2 and while some appeared to be slope or human derived, others were clearly in original position, as shown by the position of ash lenses abutting some large rocks. This layer yielded a variety of shell artefacts, including ornaments, a fish hook, stone flakes, an adze, coral abraders and remains of fish, bird and turtle.

Layer 3: A brown compact clay (10YR 4/3, pH=8.0–8.5) with no charcoal, marine shell, or any other cultural remains. It was tested down to 120 cm depth with no change in the nature of the matrix recorded.

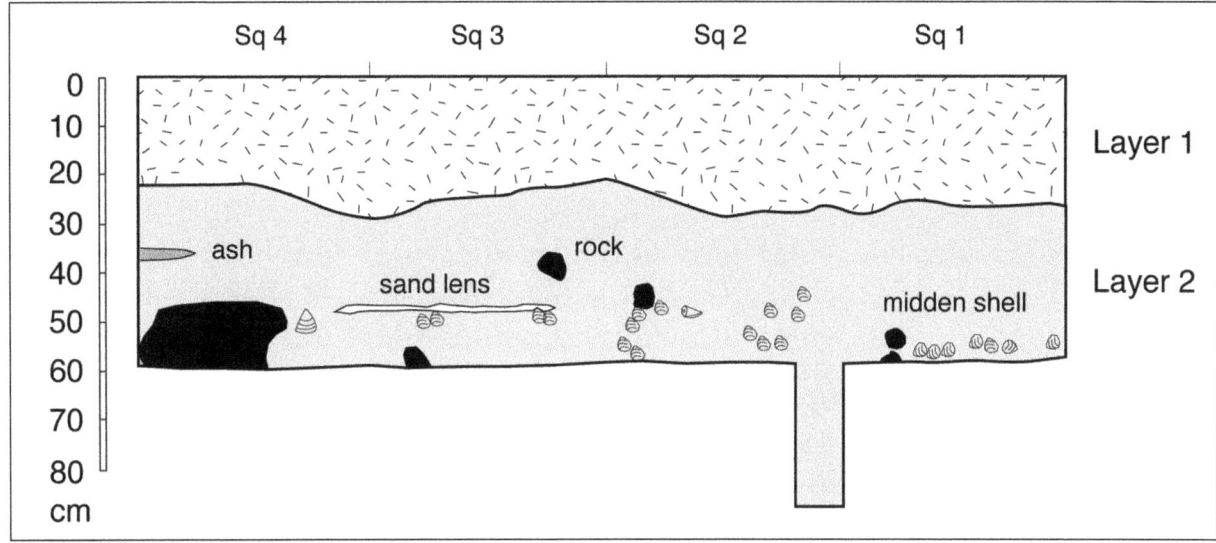

Figure 81. Votua, Area 2 stratigraphy (see Clark et al. 2001 for details of Area 1).

Votua Test Pit 2

The upper 20–30 cm of Test Pit 2 contained small marine bivalves fragmented in a reddish-brown sandy sediment with limestone and basalt rubble. Below this, shell and pottery fragments and pottery were more abundant, but the ceramic sherds were small, most less than 3 cm². The sand lens noted in Area 2 was also present in Test Pit 2 at a depth of ca. 35 cm and sterile cultural deposits of a dark-brown clay were reached at 50–60 cm depth. It seems likely that material from Test Pit 2 represents a disturbed deposit derived from the main deposit of prehistoric material on the old beach edge, as there was significantly less shell midden and pottery in Test Pit 2 than in Area 2 and it was significantly more fragmented, and it contained little bone or charcoal and only a few stone flakes.

The ash lenses in Layer 2 were usually about 1–3 cm thick and were present in patches over the entire area of Area 2, especially in the southern part towards the top of the small rise. It was difficult to separate out defined hearth zones due to the thinness of the ash deposits and the evidence for multiple small cooking fires in Area 2. Beside a few large basalt rocks a stratigraphic sequence of ash lenses was identified, but no stone-edged hearths or defined fire places were evident. Dug into the surface of Layer 3 were several round depressions that might have been stake or post holes. However, these were generally shallow, only 10–15 cm deep, and could conceivably result from the removal of rocks or be the base of shallow fire pits.

Site extent

Renewed investigations at Votua, including excavations, test pitting, augering and walk-over survey of the area, suggest the following. First, the main band of concentrated cultural deposits appears to be closely associated with the slope that marks the western and southern edge of the sand plain. This feature probably corresponds to the edge of an old shoreline that was available for human settlement during, or slightly after, a drop in sea level. Although the site might have extended further east beyond the limestone point containing the portable steam engine (Figure 79), surface collection of sherds from areas to the east of the point included spot-impressed and other late styles of Fijian pottery. This suggests Votua is probably around 1000 sq. m in extent and might occupy only 500 sq. m if the primary band of cultural debris is relatively narrow and restricted to the confines of the old shoreline, as suggested by the Test Pit 2 excavation.

Second, the restriction of settlement to the western end of Vutuna appears to be tied to the presence of a deeply indented bay whose limits are shown by the contour of the old shoreline. The bay was subsequently infilled by slope and reef-derived deposits. The small embayment would have been sheltered from prevailing southeast trade winds and appears to have fostered the kind of protected intertidal environment that supported concentrations of *Anadara* and *Gafrarium* bivalves. The sheltered position also supported mangroves, which is evidenced by the round cross-sections found on the back of *Crassostrea* sp. shells as a result of their attachment to aerial mangrove roots. In addition to the intermittent freshwater stream and number of nearby small springs along the limestone cliffs east of Votua, the site is at the base of a natural access route to Maruna and also to the interior of the island. Jasper flakes, calcareous-tempered pottery and a piece of dentate-stamped pottery were recovered from beach-rolled deposits at Maruna, and a dentate-stamped sherd was found at Sovanibeka (see below). This suggests that Lapita people were travelling to areas other than the coastal zone of Mago Island, perhaps for the purposes of hunting terrestrial birds and gardening.

Finally, the water sieving of deposits did result in the recovery of a larger set of artefacts and fauna than was found in the 1996 excavations and these are described elsewhere in this volume. Compact shell midden and ash from cooking fires mixed with pottery and other artefacts suggest that Area 2 was a multipurpose cooking/consumption/refuse dumping area. It is sufficient to note here that evidence for artefact manufacture, other than siliceous stone flakes, while present, is not particularly abundant or diverse, while the faunal deposits appear to represent a relatively brief period of activity, consistent with the earlier interpretation of the site. The reduction in the estimate of site size is also consistent with the 'mobile or encampment mode' of settlement proposed by Clark et al. (2001). Votua is one of the few single-phase Lapita sites known in the Fiji Islands, and unlike Level 1 of Sigatoka, it has well-preserved fauna and artefactual remains. Further work at this site is required to identify whether there is any evidence for substantial structures, perhaps of houses, above or in front of the old shoreline, or whether formal structures were not, apparently, part of the colonising strategy employed during the late-Lapita occupation of the Lau Islands.

Sovanibeka, Mago Island

A complex of caves and chambers was located in the *makatea* cliff at ca. 40 m altitude and about 300 m southwest of Vutuna Beach by Mr Mani Prasad. The complex, called Sovanibeka by S. Matararaba in 1996, appears to be one of those explored and briefly described by Sawyer and Andrews (1901), who did not record the presence of prehistoric remains. The cave complex includes substantial underground passages and an eroded former chamber now accessible through two sides, with a further high-level entrance allowing natural light to enter (Figure 82). The chamber is about 10 m long and 7 m wide, with a gently sloping dry-earth floor. On its southeast side is a raised shelf 5 m in length and 2 m broad which has scatters of marine shellfish and charcoal. Fine, grey, silty sands on this shelf extend to about 40 cm depth and partly derive from the droppings of a resident group of white-rumped swiftlets (*Collocalia spodiopygia*).

The chamber was investigated in 1996 (Clark and Hope 1997), and was subsequently visited briefly in 2000 during the second season of excavations at Votua, but material from test pits was collected during the first visit only. The chamber was initially targeted because it seemed a likely place in which subfossil remains of birds and other fauna might be found, and the discovery of pottery and midden material was therefore unexpected.

Test Pits

A small 30 cm x 30 cm test pit called Test Pit 1 was dug in the middle of the main open area (Figure 82). The top 20 cm of the deposit contained marine shells, charcoal, plain pottery, fire-cracked rock, and at 20 cm depth, large fragments of turtle bone. Below this the deposit was composed of a light reddish-brown fine silt containing shell and rock fragments and pot sherds.

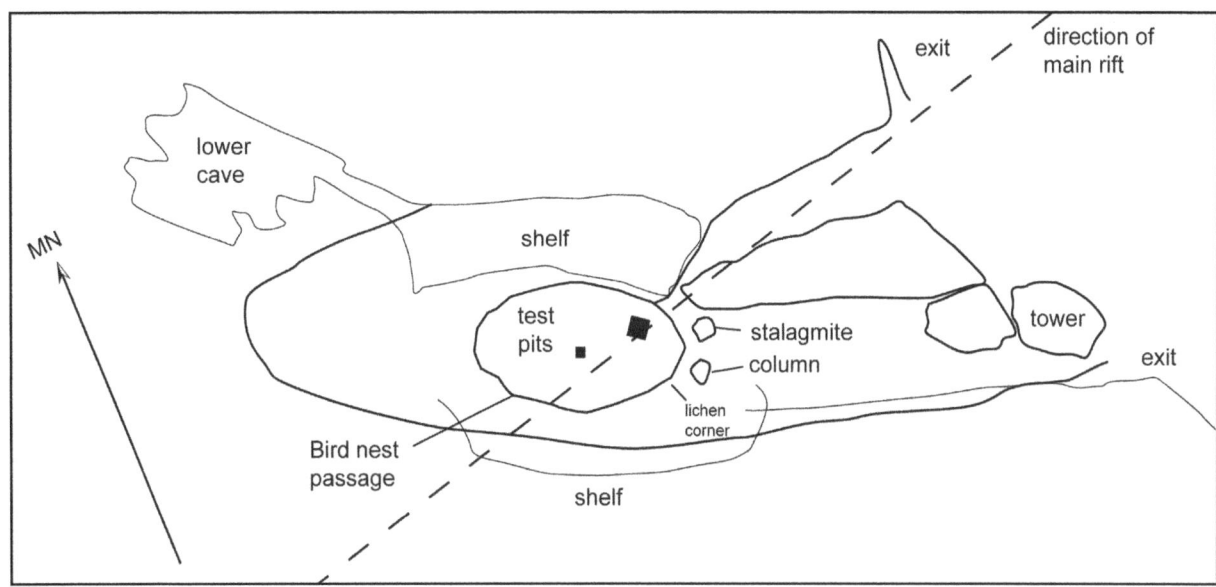

Figure 82. Sovanibeka rock shelter and location of test excavations.

Mixed through the upper and lower deposits to a depth of ca. 50 cm was a large amount of rat bone.

A second excavation, called Test Pit 2, was made to further sample the floor deposits. This was a 50 cm x 50 cm square excavated on the floor of the cave, approximately 2 m from the northern wall (Figure 82). The second test pit confirmed the stratigraphic picture obtained from Test Pit 1, but made important pottery finds. These consisted of a sherd decorated with an intersecting line of dentate stamping, at approximately 40–50 cm depth, and above it a rim-neck sherd decorated with oval rim notching and cross-hatch paddle relief, and body sherds marked by curvilinear relief, also called 'wavy' relief.

Test Pit 2 stratigraphy

0–10 cm: Brown clayey silt with abundant leaf and wood debris and rat bones.

10–42 cm: Grey ashy clayey silts with numerous pieces of limestone and some basalt rocks. Scattered lenses of ash and marine shell were abundant from about 20–40 cm depth, with pottery frequent at 30–40 cm depth, including a few large sherds, some of which were marked with different kinds of paddle relief. Rat bone became sparser as depth increased, while land snails became more abundant.

42–60 cm: Reddish-brown clay with many land-snail shells, but very sparse marine shell, pot sherds, charcoal or rat bone below 55 cm.

The limited data from Test Pits 1 and 2 indicates human use of Sovanibeka was infrequent and perhaps non-intensive, although the presence of turtle bone could suggest ceremonial or ritual activity in the small concealed chamber space. The loose and friable chamber deposits of Sovanibeka have been heavily disturbed and the small size of the test-pit excavations only hints at the range of prehistoric activities that might have been carried out in the chamber. Pottery, midden shell and small amounts of fish bone show that the location was used for cooking and food consumption, but a better understanding of the site requires further archaeological investigations.

References

Best, S. 1984. Lakeba: The prehistory of a Fijian Island. Unpublished PhD thesis, Department of Anthropology, University of Auckland.

Best, S. 2002. *Lapita: A view from the east.* New Zealand Archaeological Association Monograph 24.

Burley, D.V. 2005. Mid-sequence archaeology at the Sigatoka Sand Dunes with interpretive implications for Fijian and oceanic culture history. *Asian Perspectives* 44: 320–348.

Clark, G. and Hope, G. 1997. Archaeological and palaeoenvironmental investigations in northern Lau (Mago, Yacata-Kaibu and Vatuvara). Unpublished report to the Fiji Museum, Suva.

Clark, G., Anderson, A. and Matararaba, S. 2001. The Lapita site at Votua, northern Lau Islands, Fiji. *Archaeology in Oceania* 36: 134–145.

Clark, G. and Murray, T. 2006. Decay characteristics of the eastern Lapita design system. *Archaeology in Oceania* 41: 107–117.

Curtis, G.H. 1951. Appendix I. Petrography of pottery. In: Gifford, E.W. Archaeological excavations in Fiji, pp. 239–241. *University of California Anthropological Records* 13: 189–288.

Davidson, J., Hinds, E., Holdaway, S. and Leach, F. 1990. The Lapita site of Natunuku, Fiji. *New Zealand Journal of Archaeology* 12: 121–155.

Davidson, J. and Leach, F. 1993. The chronology of the Natunuku site, Fiji. *New Zealand Journal of Archaeology* 15: 99–105.

DeGusta, D. 1999. Fijian cannibalism: Osteological evidence from Navatu. *American Journal of Physical Anthropology* 110: 215–241.

Derrick, R. 1951. *The Fiji Islands: A geographical handbook.* Government Printing Office, Suva.

Dickinson, W.R. 1971. Petrography of some sand tempers in prehistoric pottery from Viti Levu, Fiji. Final report No. 2. *Records of the Fiji Museum* 1: 108–121.

Fowler, H.W. 1955. Archaeological fishbones collected by E.W. Gifford in Fiji. *Bernice P. Bishop Museum Bulletin* 214.

Frazer, R.M. 1963. A social and economic history of Ra Province. *Transactions and Proceedings of the Fiji Society* 9: 93–112.

Geraghty, P.A. 1983. The history of the Fijian languages. *Oceanic Linguistics Special Publication* No. 19. University of Hawaii Press, Honolulu.

Gifford, E.W. 1951. Archaeological excavations in Fiji. University of California *Anthropological Records* 13: 189–288.

Gifford, E.W. 1952a. *Tribes of Viti Levu and their origin places.* University of California Press, Berkeley.

Gifford, E.W. 1952b. A carbon-14 date from Fiji. *Journal of the Polynesian Society* 61: 327.

Gifford, E.W. 1955. Six Fijian radiocarbon dates. *Journal of the Polynesian Society* 64: 240.

Gordon Cumming, C.F. 1885. *At home in Fiji.* William Blackwood and Sons, Edinburgh and London.

Green, R.C. 1963. A suggested revision of the Fiji sequence. *Journal of the Polynesian Society* 72: 235–253.

Green, R.C. 1974. Sites with Lapita pottery: Importing and voyaging. *Mankind* 9: 253–259.

Hunt, T.L. 1980. Toward Fiji's past; archaeological research on southwestern Viti Levu. Unpublished MA thesis, University of Auckland.

Key, C.A. n.d. The geological structure at Natunuku. Unpublished manuscript in possession of the authors. Department of Archaeology and Natural History, Australian National University.

Kirch, P.V. and Hunt, T.L. 1988. The spatial and temporal boundaries of Lapita. In: Kirch, P.V. and Hunt, T.L. (eds), *Archaeology of the Lapita cultural complex: A critical review,* pp. 9–32. Thomas Burke Memorial Washington State Museum Research Report No. 5. The Burke Museum, Seattle.

Kuhlken, R. and Crosby, A. 1999. Agricultural terracing at Nakauvadra, Viti Levu: A late prehistoric irrigated agrosystem in Fiji. *Asian Perspectives* 38: 62–89.

Ladd, H.S. and Hoffmeister, J.E. 1945. Geology of Lau, Fiji. *Bernice P. Bishop Museum Bulletin* 181.

Mead, S., Birks, L., Birks, H. and Shaw, E. 1973. The Lapita pottery style of Fiji and its associations. *Journal of the Polynesian Society Memoir* 38: 1–98.

Nunn, P.D. 1990. Coastal processes and landforms of Fiji: Their bearing on Holocene sea level changes in the south and west Pacific. *Journal of Coastal Research* 6: 279–310.

Palmer, J.B. 1968. Recent results from the Sigatoka archaeological program. In: Yawata, I. and Sinoto, Y.H. (eds), *Prehistoric culture in Oceania*, pp. 19–27. B.P. Bishop Museum Press, Honolulu.

Parry, J. 1987. *The Sigatoka valley – pathways into prehistory*. Fiji Museum Bulletin No. 9. The Fiji Museum, Suva.

Parry, J.T. 1997. The north coast of Viti Levu Ba to Ra. Air photo archaeology and ethnohistory. *Bulletin of the Fiji Museum* No. 10.

Rodda, P. 1976. Geology of northern and central Viti Levu. *Fiji Mineral Resources Division Bulletin* 3.

Sawyer, B. and Andrews, E.C. 1901. Notes on the caves of Fiji, with special reference to Lau. *Proceedings of the Linnean Society of New South Wales* 29: 91–106.

Seeley, J.B. and Searle, E.J. 1970. Geology of the Rakiraki district, Viti Levu, Fiji. *New Zealand Journal of Geology and Geophysics* 13: 52–71.

Shaw, E. 1967. A reanalysis of pottery from Navatu and Vuda, Fiji. Unpublished MA thesis, Department of Anthropology, University of Auckland.

Spriggs, M. 1990. Dating Lapita: Another view. In: Spriggs, M. (ed), *Lapita design, form and composition*, pp. 83–122. Occasional Papers in Prehistory, No. 20. Department of Prehistory, Australian National University, Canberra.

Wahome, E.W. 1995. Ceramic and prehistoric exchange in the Admiralty Islands, Papua New Guinea. Unpublished PhD thesis, Australian National University.

Woodhall, D. 1985. Geology of the Lau Ridge. In: Scholl, D.W. and Vallier, T.L. (eds), *Geology and offshore resources of Pacific Island arcs – Tonga region*. Circum-Pacific Council for Energy and Mineral Resources Earth Science Series, Volume 2, pp. 351–378. Houston, Texas.

7

Site chronology and a review of radiocarbon dates from Fiji

Geoffrey Clark
Archaeology and Natural History, The Australian National University

Atholl Anderson
Archaeology and Natural History, The Australian National University

Introduction

The earliest radiocarbon dates from the Central Pacific were obtained by Edward W. Gifford, on charcoal recovered from excavations at Vunda and Navatu on Viti Levu (Gifford 1951a, b), and the results were later used to outline the first culture sequence proposed for Fiji, by Roger Green (1963). Subsequent investigations by Frost (1970, 1979) and Best (1984) substantially increased the number of ^{14}C results from the archipelago, and allowed a wider range of cultural attributes, such as settlement location, interaction pattern, subsistence economy and stone-tool types, to be age-correlated.

This chapter is divided into two sections, with the first section reporting the radiocarbon and thermoluminescence dates obtained by the Early Prehistory of Fiji project (the EPF) between 1996 and 2000. There were 68 radiocarbon determinations from 13 prehistoric sites. Most dated deposits were from coastal or near-coast locations on Viti Levu (n=9), two sites were from Beqa Island, and two excavations were on Mago Island in the Lau Group. Six sites contained ceramics of Lapita style (some mixed with pottery of post-Lapita age), two sites had deposits of mid-sequence antiquity, and five sites had pottery and other items common in late-prehistoric sites dating to the last millennium. Results were used to construct a chronology for each site by assessing the reliability of each determination. In several deposits, the age of the oldest cultural remains was not able to be determined with radiocarbon because of extensive reworking of Lapita remains with more recent cultural materials.

There are now more than 300 radiocarbon determinations from prehistoric sites in Fiji, and the second section of this chapter presents age results identified in a review of the archaeological literature. In listing the ^{14}C results from Fiji our purpose is to provide a comprehensive overview of archaeological determinations, and to illustrate the geographic locations and points in the Fiji culture sequence that have been the focus of chronometric research. Recent investigations with a significant dating component have greatly altered the temporal dimensions of key sections of the Fijian sequence. These include, in addition to the EPF, the work of Nunn, Kumar and colleagues at Lapita sites (2004a, 2004b), the analysis of mid-sequence ceramic change at the Sigatoka Sand Dunes (Burley 2005), and the study of fortifications (Field 2004, 2005). Our review concludes with a discussion of these parts of the sequence in light of new chronological data.

Site chronology

Radiocarbon determinations were obtained on samples from two north-coast Viti Levu sites (Natunuku, Navatu 17A), seven southwest Viti Levu sites (Karobo, Malaqereqere, Tuvu, Volivoli II, Volivoli III, Qaranioso I and Qaranioso II), Beqa Island and Ugaga Island (Kulu and Ugaga), and two sites on Mago Island in the Lau Group (Votua and Sovanibeka). There were 68 determinations, two AMS and the rest radiocarbon, and nine samples were 'modern' (Table 17). Two thermoluminescence determinations were obtained on pottery excavated from the Navatu 17A site (Table 18). At the Sigatoka Sand Dunes, an intact cultural deposit was not located, and optically stimulated luminescence (OSL) age results were obtained on the dune sediments (see Anderson et al. 2006). New radiocarbon dates from the Yanuca Lapita site excavated in the 1960s by Lawrence and Helen Birks have been reported previously (Clark and Anderson 2001b), and are listed in the review of archaeological dates (see below).

Radiocarbon samples of marine shell, terrestrial shell, bone, palm wood and charcoal were analysed at the Quaternary Dating Research Centre (QDRC) at the Australian National University (n=45), the Waikato Radiocarbon Dating Laboratory at the University of Waikato (n=15), the Beta Analytic Inc. Radiocarbon Dating Laboratory (BETA) in Florida (n=7), and the Australian Nuclear Sciences and Technology Organisation (ANSTO) at Lucas Heights (n=1). Two thermoluminescence dates were determined at the Department of Physics at the University of Adelaide. Sample pretreatment and calibration are outlined below. Radiocarbon results from the EPF are given in Table 17 and Figure 83, with the conventional radiocarbon age (CRA), ^{13}C value (estimated and measured), calendar age at 2SD (cal. BP), sample material/species, excavation context and sample weight.

Sample pretreatment

Charcoal

Clay, rootlets, shell fragments and other adhering non-charcoal materials were removed with tweezers from excavated charcoals before samples were submitted. Dating laboratories also physically removed possible contaminants before samples were washed in distilled water and crushed, or chopped to increase the surface area for subsequent pretreatment. Chemical pretreatment at the QDRC involved washing the charcoal in 10% HCl, whereas Waikato and Beta Analytic Inc. used the ABA method, in which the sample is heated with dilute HCl followed by dilute NaOH, and given a final treatment in dilute hot HCl. Identification of wood charcoals used in radiocarbon dating is routinely carried out in New Zealand, and at some contract archaeology companies working in the Pacific, such as the International Archaeological Research Institute, Inc. (IARII). Charcoal from twigs or shortlived taxa is preferred for radiocarbon dating since it is unlikely to incorporate a high 'inbuilt' age (Anderson 1991).

Table 17. Radiocarbon results from EPF archaeological investigations.

Lab. Number	Conventional Age (BP)	Calibrated Age BP (2 SD)	$\Delta^{13}C$	Sample type	Species	Unit and Depth below surface (cm)	Total weight (grams)
Ugaga							
ANU-10774	1720 ± 70	1150–1390	0.0 ± 2.0E	Marine shell	*Tridacna maxima*	Sq. I5: 20–30	81.0
ANU-10776	1900 ± 60	1310–1590	0.0 ± 2.0E	Marine shell	*Turbo argyrostromus*	Sq. M8: 20–30	111.9
Beta-107951	2130 ± 50	1580–1850	2.0	Marine shell	*Tridacna maxima*	Sq. -A13: 30–-40	117.8
ANU-10772	2140 ± 70	1550–1890	0.0 ± 2.0E	Marine shell	*Trochus niloticus*	Sq. I5: 30–40	443.3
ANU-10773	2490 ± 70	1970–2320	0.0 ± 2.0E	Marine shell	*Tridacna maxima*	Sq. O9: 30–40	206.6
ANU-10777	2530 ± 70	2000–2340	0.0 ± 2.0E	Marine shell	*Tridacna maxima*	Sq. J9: 40–50	137.0
ANU-10778	2600 ± 70	2090–2470	0.0 ± 2.0E	Marine shell	*Tridacna maxima*	Sq. T/U-1: 40–50	131.9
ANU-10775	2620 ± 60	2130–2470	0.0 ± 2.0E	Marine shell	*Tridacna maxima*	Sq. I9: 30–40	180.3
Beta-107952	2690 ± 60	2260–2650	2.0	Marine shell	*Tridacna maxima*	Sq. P10: 30–40	132.7
Beta-107953	3150 ± 70	2760–3140	3.2	Marine shell	*Trochus niloticus*	Sq. C12: 50–60	278.2
ANU-10734	97.7 ± 0.8%M	Modern	-24 ± 2.0E	Charcoal	–	Sq. I9: 20–30	100.0
Wk-5553	98.5 ± 0.7%M	Modern	-27.7 ± 0.2	Charcoal	–	Sq. K5: 30–40	18.2
Wk-5554	98.3 ± 0.5%M	Modern	-26.9 ± 0.2	Charcoal	–	Sq. J9: 20–30	11.0
Wk-5555	98.8 ± 0.5%M	Modern	-26.8 ± 0.2	Charcoal	–	Sq. K7: 20–30	100.0
Wk-5556	98.2 ± 0.5%M	Modern	-25.3 ± 0.2	Charcoal	–	Sq. P8: 20–30	56.1
Kulu							
Beta 107947	2590 ± 50	2120–2380	1.8	Marine shell	*Tridacna* sp.	C11: 60–70	–
Beta 107948	2590 ± 50	2120–2380	1.5	Marine shell	*Cerithium* sp.	C11: 130–140	–
Beta 107949	180 ± 40	0–280	-29.0	Charcoal	Candle nut	C11: 110–120	–
Beta 107950	220 ± 50	0–310	-24.0	Charcoal	Candle nut	C11: 140–150	–
ANU-10727	820 ± 100	560–910	-24 ± 2.0E	Charcoal	–	C9: 40–50	3.0
ANU-10743*	117.2 ± 2.7%M	Modern	-24 ± 2.0E	Charcoal	–	C11: 100–110	0.32
Karobo							
ANU-10781	300 ± 70	0–500	-24 ± 2.0E	Charcoal	–	Square Y, L3: 33	9.5
ANU-10780	1780 ± 80	1420–1830	-24 ± 2.0E	Charcoal	–	Square Ab-1, L7: 122	7.3
ANU-11067	1680 ± 70	1370–1700	-24 ± 2.0E	Charcoal	–	Square A2, L5: 100	6.2
ANU-11068	2130 ± 120	1740–2340	-24 ± 2.0E	Wood	Palm cf. *Cocos nucifora*	Square A2, L5: 137	15.9
Malaqereqere							
ANU-10453	830 ± 90	560–910	-24 ± 2.0E	Charcoal	–	Sq. A2: 60–70	5.5
ANU-10452	460 ± 60	330–420	-24 ± 2.0E	Charcoal	–	Sq. A1: 10–20	78.3
ANU-10454	670 ± 70	520–680	-24 ± 2.0E	Charcoal	–	Sq. A1: 40–50	11.0
Tuvu							
ANU-11020	1570 ± 100	1260–1700	-24 ± 2.0E	Charcoal	–	TP 1, Spit IV	3.0
Volivoli II							
ANU-10449	1120 ± 70	810–1170	-24 ± 2.0E	Charcoal	–	TR. 1: 20–30	5.6
ANU-10450	1960 ± 70	1630–2040	-24 ± 2.0E	Charcoal	–	TR. 1: 40–50	11.5
ANU-10451	1080 ± 190	580–1300	-24 ± 2.0E	Charcoal	–	TR.1: 50–60	4.6
Volivoli III							
ANU-11018	290 ± 60	0–490	-24 ± 2.0E	Charcoal	–	TP. 1, Spit 2	7.0
ANU-11016	1100 ± 90	770–1170	-24 ± 2.0E	Charcoal	–	TP. 1, Spit 5	2.2
ANU-11019	1060 ± 80	740–1070	-24 ± 2.0E	Charcoal	–	TP. 1, Spit 8	4.5
Qaranioso 1							
ANU-11015	1280 ± 120	920–1350	-24 ± 2.0E	Charcoal	–	TP. 1: 30	–

Continued on nexxt page

Table 17 continued

Lab. Number	Conventional Age (BP)	Calibrated Age BP (2 SD)	Δ13C	Sample type	Species	Unit and Depth below surface (cm)	Total weight (grams)
Qaranioso II							
ANU-11014	660 ± 60	530–670	-24 ± 2.0E	Charcoal	–	TP. 1: 30	–
Natunuku							
ANU-10382	98.4 ± 1.0%M	Modern	-24 ± 2.0E	Charcoal	–	Tr.3, Sq.6: 25–40	7.0
ANU-10699	1160 ± 70	600–890	0.0 ± 2.0E	Marine shell	Tridacna sp.	Tr.3, Sq.A5: 30–40	65.9
ANU-10381	99.7 ± 0.8%M	Modern	-24 ± 2.0E	Charcoal	–	Tr.3, Sq.A5: 10–20	20.4
ANU-10700	380 ± 70	160–230	0.0 ± 2.0E	Marine shell	Trochus sp.	Tr.3, Sq.A5: 10–20	172.8
ANU-10698	2780 ± 90	2310–2720	0.0 ± 2.0E	Marine shell	Tridacna sp.	Tr.3, Sq.A5: 20–30	95.8
ANU-11307	2600 ± 60	2110–2440	0.0 ± 2.0E	Marine shell	Species ?	Tr. 3, no context	–
ANU-11306	1170 ± 50	630–840	0.0 ± 2.0E	Marine shell	Species ?	Tr. 3, no context	–
ANU-11305	2900 ± 50	2490–2770	0.0 ± 2.0E	Marine shell	Species ?	Tr. 3, no context	–
Navatu 17A							
ANU-10385	350 ± 70	150–500	-24 ± 2.0E	Charcoal	–	Tr. A1, L1: 100	40.7
ANU-10388	104.0 ± 1.1%M	Modern	-24 ± 2.0E	Charcoal	–	Tr. B2, L1: 20	5.0
ANU-10710	720 ± 70	250–500	0.0 ± 2.0E	Marine shell	Anadara sp.	Tr. B2, L1: 50	116.8
ANU-10389	330 ± 60	150–490	-24 ± 2.0E	Charcoal	–	Tr. B1, L1: 86	20.7
ANU-10709	980 ± 70	480–670	0.0 ± 2.0E	Marine shell	Gafrarium sp.	Tr. B1, L2: 120	51.7
ANU-10384	870 ± 70	660–910	-24 ± 2.0E	Charcoal	–	Tr. B1, L2: 140	6.0
ANU-10387	1240 ± 140	800–1350	-24 ± 2.0E	Charcoal	–	Tr. B1+2, L4: 215	2.4
ANU-10390	1010 ± 140	660–1180	-24 ± 2.0E	Charcoal	–	Tr. B1+2, L4: 220	2.1
ANU-10386	1670 ± 70	1360–1690	-24 ± 2.0E	Charcoal	–	Tr. B3+4, L4: 230	7.3
ANU-10708	1980 ± 70	1360–1710	0.0 ± 2.0E	Marine shell	Tridacna sp.	Tr. B3+4, L4: 230	78.8
Votua							
Wk-5366	2970 ± 50	2620–2870	-0.3 ± 0.2	Marine shell	Anadara antiquata	Testpit 1, 60–70	133.3
Wk-5367	2930 ± 50	2540–2830	-0.2 ± 0.2	Marine shell	Anadara antiquata	Testpit 1, 30–40	198.8
ANU-10706	2520 ± 120	2170–2790	-24 ± 2.0E	Charcoal	–	Testpit 1, 40–50	7.1
Wk-5368	2940 ± 50	2570–2840	-0.4 ± 0.2	Marine shell	Anadara antiquata	Area 1: 20–30	157.7
Wk-5369	2950 ± 50	2600–2850	-0.2 ± 0.2	Marine shell	Anadara antiquata	Area 1: 10–20	183.4
ANU-10707	2670 ± 70	2460–2880	-24 ± 2.0E	Charcoal	–	Area 1: 20–30	4.6
ANU-11069 A	2490 ± 60	1990–2300	0.0 ± 2.0E	Marine shell	Trochus niloticus	Area 1: 20–30	68.0
ANU-11069 B	2990 ± 60	2650–2930	0.0 ± 2.0E	Marine shell	Trochus niloticus	Area 1: 10–20	40.0
ANU-11528	2680 ± 70	2470–2920	-26.4± 0.2	Charcoal	–	Area 2, Sq. 4: 60	8.1
ANU-11527	2850 ± 50	2440–2730	-1.5 ± 0.1	Marine shell	Anadara antiquata	Area 2, Sq. 1: 60–70	43.6
Sovanibeka							
OZF882*	840 ± 40	670–770	-20.0	Bone	Rattus praetor	Test Pit 1: 50–60	1.7
ANU-10779	2820 ± 70	2360–2720	0.0 ± 0.2E	Marine shell	Anadara antiquata	Test Pit 2: 30–50	7.3
ANU-11246	4290 ± 60	4540–4960	-2.5 ± 0.2	Land snail	Gonatorhaphe lavens	Test Pit 2: 55–58	34.1

* = AMS determination.
'E' in the delta ^{13}C column indicates the use of an estimated ^{13}C value.

Table 18. Navatu 17A thermoluminescence results (Trench B, Square 1).

TL No.	Unit/Depth (cm)	Equivalent dose (Gy)	a-value	Total dose rate (Gy ka-1)	Age	Age range
98001	Tr. B, Sq. 1: 140	1.59±0.3	0.22±0.03	1.22 ± 0.11	1300 ± 275	1575–1025
98002	Tr. B, Sq. 1: 230	2.44±0.3	0.28±0.03	1.10 ± 0.13	2230 ± 380	2610–1850

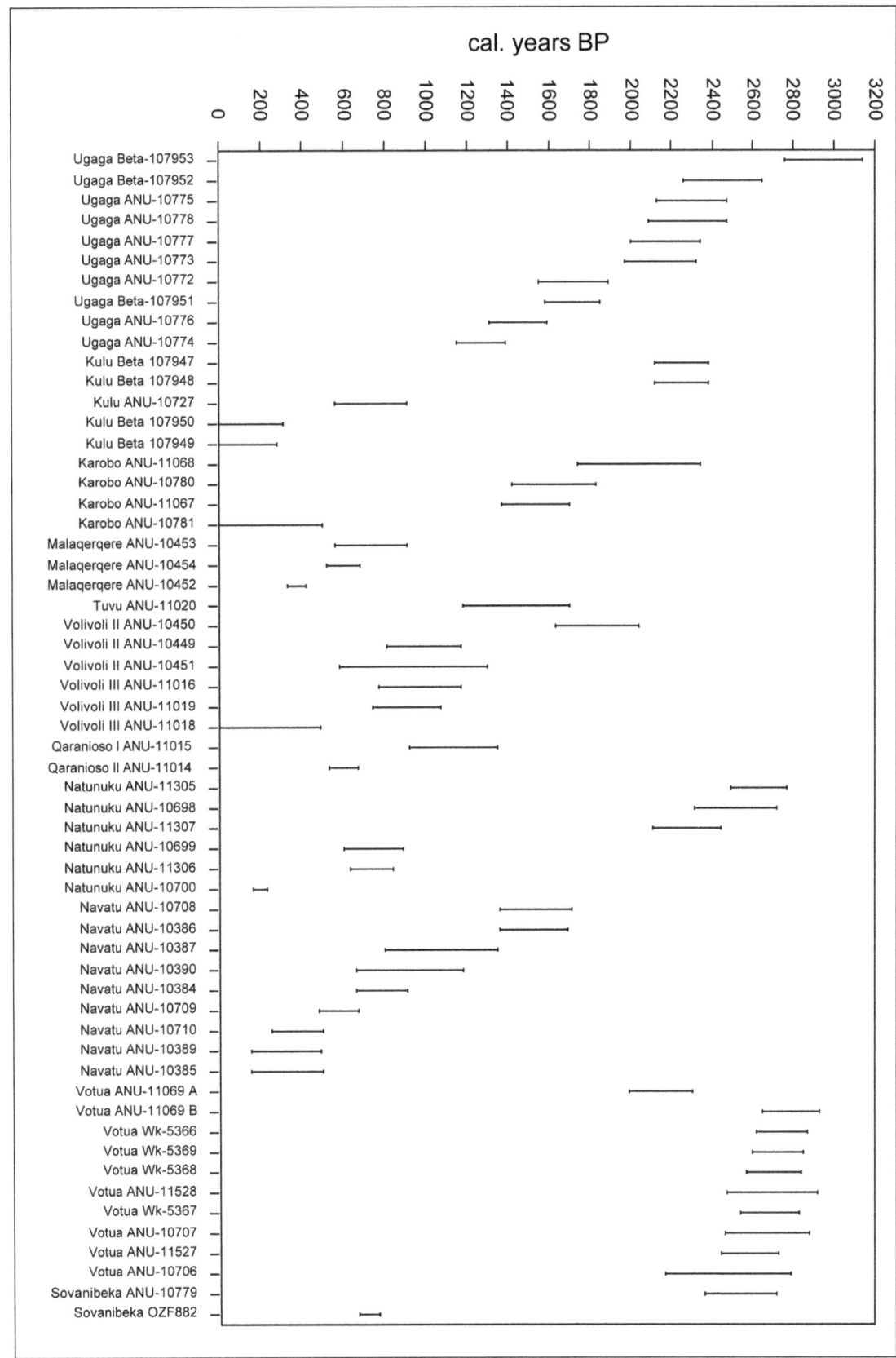

Figure 83. EPF calibrated age determinations at 2SD.

Radiocarbon laboratories do not currently identify archaeological charcoals from the tropical Pacific. Consequently, ages on charcoal from Fiji and from elsewhere in the West and Central Pacific may be older than the cultural activity associated with the sample.

Palm wood

The surfaces of a palm-wood sample dated at the QDRC were scraped clean and the wood was chopped into small splinters and milled. The sample was washed in hot 10% HCl, rinsed and dried. The sample was soxlet extracted with ethanol, ethanol/chloroform (2:1) and water, bleached with sodium perchlorate, rinsed and dried.

Marine and terrestrial shell

Marine-shell samples were identified using a reference collection at the ANU, and cleaned with a dental drill (QDRC) or acid etched (Beta Analytic Inc., Waikato). The Waikato laboratory tests marine shells for recrystallisation before dating, but this procedure was not standard for marine shell dated at the QDRC and Beta Analytic Inc. Marine shells from the Votua site were examined for recrystallisation with X-ray diffraction, which identified the samples as 100% aragonite, indicating that the prehistoric shell samples were not affected by the transformation of biogenic aragonite to calcite. Land snails were identified by Winston Ponder (Australian Museum), with samples of a single species sorted and pretreated by gently crushing the shell and repeatedly washing the residue in an ultrasonic bath filled with distilled water until adhering cave sediments had been removed from the surface shell.

Bone

Macroscopic contaminants attached to the bone sample were removed with tweezers at ANSTO, the dry bone was crushed in a mortar and pestle, and the fragments were washed in an ultrasonic bath filled with Milli-RO water until clean. The fragments were placed in a freeze dryer for one to two days, then ground to powder with a particle size of less than 200 μm. Chemical pretreatment involved removal of the inorganic bone component with an acid-alkali wash and gelatin extraction in heated 0.01M HCl, followed by separation of the collagen in solution with a centrifuge, and two to three days of freeze drying to dry the gelatin.

CRA and calibration

Isotopic fractionation refers to the difference in the proportion of ^{14}C to ^{12}C in a living organism or sample, and the proportion of ^{14}C to ^{12}C in the carbon reservoir. The conventional radiocarbon age (CRA) is corrected for fractionation by measuring the delta^{13}C of a sample with a mass spectrometer, or by using an estimated value for marine and terrestrial carbon reservoirs. Some CRA ages from the QDRC had measured delta^{13}C values, but most incorporated estimated values of –24±2.0‰ for charcoal and 0±2.0‰ for marine shell relative to VDPB. For Fijian charcoal samples the measured delta^{13}C varied from –29.0‰ to –24.0‰ (delta^{13}C range=5.0‰). The majority of marine shells had a similar range of 5.7‰ (3.2‰ to –2.5‰), suggesting that in most cases the use of estimated delta^{13}C values would not have made a significant change to the CRA. However, a *Trachycardium* shell from the Yanuca site on Viti Levu was measured at –12.3‰ (Clark and Anderson 2001b), indicating that some marine shellfish from locations adjacent to freshwater sources can have delta^{13}C values significantly different from the estimated marine reservoir value. CRAs and standard errors (1SD) were rounded to the nearest decade.

Calibrations were by CALIB 5.0 (Stuiver and Reimer 1993), with terrestrial samples calculated with the Southern Hemisphere curve (McCormac et al. 2004), marine samples with the Marine curve of Hughen et al. (2004), and mixed terrestrial-marine samples with the Southern Hemisphere combined curves of Hughen et al. (2004) and McCormac et al. (2004). DeltaR was set at 0 for marine samples. DeltaR values of +25 years (Petchey 1995) and +45±30 years (Stuiver and Braziunas 1993) have been used to calibrate radiocarbon determinations from Fiji, and a marine reservoir value of 38±16 years has been calculated for Viti Levu on coral rings (Toggweiler et al. 1991). In the absence of marine-reservoir values for specific locations, we prefer to use the 0 value, given the diversity of marine and coastal environments in Fiji. Marine-shell-charcoal pairs from archaeological sites in Viti Levu and the Lau Group (Clark 2000; Thomas et al. 2004) also suggest that the value of DeltaR is relatively small. Samples of human bone (Table 19) were calibrated with the terrestrial-marine Southern Hemisphere calibration curve, with DeltaR set at 50% because of the likelihood of marine carbon in the diet (Leach et al. 2001). Calibrated results are reported at two standard deviations and rounded to the nearest decade.

Ugaga Island

Four charcoal samples were sent to the Waikato Radiocarbon Dating Laboratory and one to the QDRC. Modern results were obtained, necessitating a new sample submission strategy (Wk-5553, Wk-5554, Wk-5555, Wk-5556, ANU-10734). Graphing the weight of charcoal recovered from each square and spit at the site revealed that the samples came from squares with abundant charcoal that was probably introduced by recent ovens dug into the site. Because of the difficulty of identifying prehistoric charcoal samples in the mixed stratigraphy at Ugaga, marine shells were selected for radiocarbon dating instead of charcoal.

Two factors supported the use of marine shell for dating the site. First, large and heavy shells are less susceptible to profile migration through the digging activities of crabs, people and other agents. Second, local informants said shellfish were not plentiful on the island's small reef, and had not been collected from Ugaga in recent times. This suggested much of the marine shell on Ugaga could have been deposited in prehistoric times. Ten marine-shell samples were dated, three at Beta Analytic, Inc. and seven at the QDRC.

In contrast to the charcoal results, all of the marine-shell samples gave prehistoric ages, with CRA results ranging from 1720–3150 BP. Five of the calibrated dates lay between 1970 and 2650 cal. BP (ANU-10773, ANU-10777, ANU-107778, ANU-10775, Beta-107952), and four between 1150 and 1890 cal. BP (ANU-10774, ANU-10766, Beta-107951, ANU-10772). A large unbroken *Trochus niloticus* shell from Square D12 had an age of 2760–3140 cal. BP (Beta-107953). The sample was collected from a grey sand at 60 cm depth that contained a few plain sherds and several large fragments of coral.

Considering the amount of disturbance at Ugaga (Chapter 5), there is a reasonable age-depth relationship over the site, with the most recent shell determinations from the 20–30 cm spit, and the oldest ^{14}C dates from lower spits. Square I5 had stratigraphically consistent dates from upper and lower spits (ANU-10774, ANU-10772). Modern determinations (ANU-10734, Wk-5554) on charcoal from squares I9 (20–30 cm) and J9 (20–30 cm) were contradicted by much older ages on shell from the same squares (ANU-10775, ANU-10775), emphasising the capacity for earth ovens (*lovo*) to introduce large amounts of modern charcoal into prehistoric levels.

Radiocarbon dates from Ugaga show the small island was used in the Lapita era and for the following two millennia, with only limited evidence in the ceramics and radiocarbon results for human use in the past 1000 years.

Table 19. An inventory of radiocarbon results from archaeological sites in Fiji.

Island	Site	Lab Code	CRA	CRA SE	C13	Cal. BP	Sample Type	Identification	Context	Reference
Aiwa Lailai	DR:1	Beta-172192	1510	40	–	1290–1410	Bone	*Pteropus* sp.	IIIb/4	O'Day et al. (2007)
Aiwa Lailai	DR:2	Beta-172191	2300	50	–	2140–2350	Bone	*Gallus gallus*	IV/5	O'Day et al. (2007)
Aiwa Levu	AC2:1	Beta-165465	2380	40	–	2160–2490	Bone	*Gallus galllus*	II/2	O'Day et al. (2007)
Aiwa Levu	AC2:2	Beta-165466	960	40	–	750–920	Bone	*Pteropus* sp.	I/1	O'Day et al. (2007)
Aiwa Levu	AC2:3	Beta-165467	1630	40	–	1370–1550	Bone	*Pteropus* sp.	II/2	O'Day et al. (2007)
Aiwa Levu	AR1:2	Beta-164251	280	40	–	150–450	Bone	*Pteropus* sp.	I/1	O'Day et al. (2007)
Aiwa Levu	AR1:2	Beta-164252	2310	40	–	1970–2290	Bone	Human	III/13	O'Day et al. (2007)
Aiwa Levu	AR1:2	Beta-164260	200	40	–	0–300	Charcoal	–	II/5	O'Day et al. (2007)
Aiwa Levu	AR1:2	Beta-164261	570	40	–	500–630	Charcoal	–	III/10	O'Day et al. (2007)
Aiwa Levu	AR1:4	Beta-164258	360	40	–	310–490	Bone	*Pteropus* sp.	II/3	O'Day et al. (2007)
Aiwa Levu	GR1	Beta-165469	370	40	–	310–490	Bone	*Ducula* sp.	II/5	O'Day et al. (2007)
Beqa	Kulu	ANU-10727	820	100	$-24 \pm 2.0E$	560–910	Marine shell	–	C9: 40–50 cmbs	ANU-EPF
Beqa	Kulu	Beta 107947	2590	50	1.8	2120–2380	Marine shell	*Tridacna* sp.	C11, 60–70 cmbs	ANU-EPF
Beqa	Kulu	Beta 107948	2590	50	1.5	2120–2380	Marine shell	*Cerithium* sp.	C11, 130–140 cmbs	ANU-EPF
Beqa	Kulu	Beta 107949	180	40	-29.0	0–280	Charcoal	Candle nut	C11, 110–120 cmbs	ANU-EPF
Beqa	Kulu	Beta 107950	220	50	-24.0	0–310	Charcoal	Candle nut	C11, 140–150 cmbs	ANU-EPF
Beqa	Nacuromoce	?	626	60	–	104–430	Marine shell	*Trochus niloticus*	Layer 1	Crosby (1988: Appendix)
Beqa	Rukua	?	1670	60	–	1370–1690	Charcoal	–	Layer 3	Crosby (1988: Appendix)
Beqa	Rukua	?	1676	60	–	1090–1340	Marine shell	*Atactodea striata*	Layer 3	Crosby (1988: Appendix)
Beqa	Kulu	ANU-10743*	$117.2 \pm 2.7\%M$	–	$-24 \pm 2.0E$	–	Chacoal	–	C11: 100–110	ANU-EPF
Beqa	Natunuku	ANU-10382	$98.4 \pm 1.0\%M$	–	$-24 \pm 2.0E$	–	Charcoal	–	Tr.3, Sq.6: 25–40	ANU-EPF
Lakeba	Kedeke	NZ-4042	690	50	–	550–670	Charcoal	–	Sq A, Layer J7	Best (1984: 146)
Lakeba	Kedeke	NZ-4043	110	60	–	0–280	Charcoal	–	Sq D, Layer 2	Best (1984: 146)
Lakeba	Laselase	NZ-4039	80	70	–	–	Charcoal	–	B.E	Best (1984: 87)
Lakeba	Laselase	NZ-4040	2000	100	–	1620–2150	Charcoal	–	L,M	Best (1984: 87)
Lakeba	Laselase	NZ-4041	2280	100	–	1950–2490	Charcoal	–	S-U	Best (1984: 87)
Lakeba	Laselase	NZ-4903	1515	60	–	1280–1520	Charcoal	–	J2	Best (1984: 87)
Lakeba	Laselase	NZ-5182	1200	40	–	660–850	Marine shell	*Turbo chrysostomus*	J1	Best (1984: 87)
Lakeba	Qaranipuqa	NZ-4588	1790	40	–	1260–1430	Marine shell	*Tridacna maxima*	Layer F3	Best (1984: 75)
Lakeba	Qaranipuqa	NZ-4589	2600	50	–	2130–2400	Marine shell	*Lambis lambis*	Layer T	Best (1984: 75)
Lakeba	Qaranipuqa	NZ-4590	2830	60	–	2390–2730	Marine shell	*Conus leopardus*	Layer W	Best (1984: 75)
Lakeba	Qaranipuqa	NZ-4591	2230	50	–	1700–1960	Marine shell	*Turbo bruneus*	Layer K4	Best (1984: 75)
Lakeba	Qaranipuqa	NZ-4592	1770	90	–	1410–1860	Charcoal	–	Layer F3	Best (1984: 75)
Lakeba	Qaranipuqa	NZ-4593	2110	90	–	1820–2310	Charcoal	–	Layer K1	Best (1984: 75)
Lakeba	Qaranipuqa	NZ-4594	2960	70	–	2860–3320	Charcoal	–	Layer N	Best (1984: 75)
Lakeba	Qaranipuqa	NZ-4595	1120	90	–	780–1230	Charcoal	Coconut	Layer W	Best (1984: 75)
Lakeba	Qaranipuqa	NZ-4596	2620	100	–	2360–2850	Charcoal	–	Layer T	Best (1984: 75)

Continued on next page

Table 19 continued

Island	Site	Lab Code	CRA	CRA SE	C13	Cal. BP	Sample Type	Identification	Context	Reference
Lakeba	Qaranipuqa	NZ-4808	2260	80	–	2000–2350	Charcoal	–	Layer N	Best (1984: 75)
Lakeba	Qaranipuqa	NZ-4810	4010	620	–	2530–5580	Bone	Turtle	Layer W	Best (1984: 75)
Lakeba	Qaranipuqa	NZ-4904	394	84	–	160–540	Charcoal	–	Layer A2	Best (1984: 75)
Lakeba	Qaranipuqa	NZ-4905	892	60	–	670–910	Charcoal	–	Layer E2	Best (1984: 75)
Lakeba	Qaranipuqa	NZ-4906	2960	160	–	2330–3130	Bone	Turtle	Layer W	Best (1984: 75)
Lakeba	Ulunikoro	NZ-4044	1020	90	–	690–1060	Charcoal	–	Sq 3, Layer B	Best (1984: 129)
Lakeba	Ulunikoro	NZ-4581	930	40	–	480–620	Marine shell	*Turbo chrysostomus*	Sq 15, Layer B2	Best (1984: 129)
Lakeba	Ulunikoro	NZ-4582	970	40	–	500–640	Marine shell	*Turbo chrysostomus*	Sq 17, Layer B3	Best (1984: 129)
Lakeba	Ulunikoro	NZ-4583	980	40	–	510–640	Marine shell	*Turbo chrysostomus*	Sq 12, Layer B1	Best (1984: 129)
Lakeba	Ulunikoro	NZ-4584	340	50	–	290–490	Charcoal	–	Sq 8, Layer B5	Best (1984: 129)
Lakeba	Ulunikoro	NZ-4585	900	90	–	650–950	Charcoal	–	Sq 15, Layer B3	Best (1984: 129)
Lakeba	Ulunikoro	NZ-4586	1010	90	–	690–1060	Charcoal	–	Sq 12/13, Layer B1	Best (1984: 129)
Lakeba	Ulunikoro	NZ-4587	1030	90	–	690–1070	Bone	Turtle	Sq 12, Layer B1	Best (1984: 129)
Lakeba	Ulunikoro	NZ-5179	984	50	–	500–650	Marine shell	*Turbo crassus*	Sq 12, Layer A	Best (1984: 129)
Lakeba	Ulunikoro	NZ-5180	1315	40	–	760–940	Marine shell	*Turbo chrysostomus*	Sq 8, Layer B5	Best (1984: 129)
Lakeba	Ulunikoro	NZ-5181	411	40	–	0–130	Marine shell	*Turbo chrysostomus*	Sq 10, Layer B	Best (1984: 129)
Lakeba	Wakea	NZ-4807	2701	120	–	2360–3060	Charcoal	–	Sq 25, Layer B18, approx: 225 cmbs	Best (1984)
Lakeba	Wakea	NZ-4809	2604	80	–	1050–2520	Marine shell	*Trochus niloticus*	Sq 19, Layer B20a, approx: 225 cmbs	Best (1984)
Mago	Sovanibeka	ANU-10779	2820	70	0.0 ± 2.0E	2360–2720	Marine shell	*Anadara antiquata*	Test Pit 2, 30–50 cmbs	ANU-EPF
Mago	Sovanibeka	ANU-11246	4290	60	-2.5 ± 0.2	4540–4960	Land snail	*Gonatorhaphe lavens*	Test Pit 2, 55–58 cmbs	ANU-EPF
Mago	Sovanibeka	OZF882	840	40	-20.0	670–770	Bone	*Rattus praetor*	Test Pit 1: 50–60 cmbs	ANU-EPF
Mago	Votua	ANU-10706	2520	120	-24 ± 2.0E	2170–2790	Charcoal	–	Testpit 1, 40–50 cmbs	ANU-EPF
Mago	Votua	ANU-10707	2670	70	-24 ± 2.0E	2460–2880	Charcoal	–	Area 1, 20–30 cmbs	ANU-EPF
Mago	Votua	ANU-11069 A	2490	60	0.0 ± 2.0E	1990–2300	Marine shell	*Trochus niloticus*	Area 1, 20–30 cmbs	ANU-EPF
Mago	Votua	ANU-11069 B	2990	60	0.0 ± 2.0E	2650–2930	Marine shell	*Trochus niloticus*	Area 1, 10–20 cmbs.	ANU-EPF
Mago	Votua	ANU-11527	2850	50	-1.5 ± 0.1	2440–2730	Marine shell	*Anadara antiquata*	Area 2, Sq. 1, 60–70 cmbs	ANU-EPF
Mago	Votua	ANU-11528	2680	70	-26.4± 0.2	2470–2920	Charcoal	–	Area 2, Sq. 4, 60 cmbs	ANU-EPF
Mago	Votua	Wk-5366	2970	50	-0.3 ± 0.2	2620–2870	Marine shell	*Anadara antiquata*	Testpit 1, 60–70 cmbs	ANU-EPF
Mago	Votua	Wk-5367	2930	50	-0.2 ± 0.2	2540–2830	Marine shell	*Anadara antiquata*	Testpit 1, 30–40 cmbs	ANU-EPF
Mago	Votua	Wk-5368	2940	50	-0.4 ± 0.2	2570–2840	Marine shell	*Anadara antiquata*	Area 1, 20–30 cmbs	ANU-EPF
Mago	Votua	Wk-5369	2950	50	-0.2 ± 0.2	2600–2850	Marine shell	*Anadara antiquata*	Area 1, 10–20 cmbs	ANU-EPF
Moturiki	Naitabale	NUTA2-5198a	2492	70	-15.4	2110–2650	Bone	Human	T1: 150 cmbs	P. Nunn, pers. comm., USP
Moturiki	Naitabale	NUTA2-5198b	2547	90	-15.4	2160–2690	Bone	Human	T1: 150 cmbs	P. Nunn, pers. comm., USP
Moturiki	Naitabale	NUTA2-5198c	2550	80	-15.4	2630–2690	Bone	Human	T1: 150 cmbs	P. Nunn, pers. comm., USP
Moturiki	Naitabale	NUTA2-5200a	2664	70	-15.1	2360–2720	Bone	Human	T1: 150 cmbs	P. Nunn, pers. comm., USP
Moturiki	Naitabale	NUTA2-5200b	2637	70	-15.1	2345–2710	Bone	Human	T1: 150 cmbs	P. Nunn, pers. comm., USP

Continued on next page

Table 19 continued

Island	Site	Lab Code	CRA	CRA SE	C13	Cal. BP	Sample Type	Identification	Context	Reference
Moturiki	Naitabale	NUTA2-5200c	2576	80	-15.1	2190–2710	Bone	Human	T1: 150 cmbs	P. Nunn, pers. comm., USP
Moturiki	Naitabale	Wk-11474	339	40	-27.2	300–470	Charcoal	–	T1: 75 cmbs	P. Nunn, pers. comm., USP
Moturiki	Naitabale	Wk-11475	2438	50	-27.4	2330–2700	Charcoal	–	T1: 75 cmbs	P. Nunn, pers. comm., USP
Moturiki	Naitabale	Wk-11476	2650	40	-26.8	2500–2790	Charcoal	–	T1: 145 cmbs	P. Nunn, pers. comm., USP
Moturiki	Naitabale	Wk-11477	2519	40	-25.6	2360–2710	Charcoal	–	P3: 85 cmbs	P. Nunn, pers. comm., USP
Moturiki	Naitabale	Wk-11478	2644	40	-26.3	2500–2780	Charcoal	–	P3: 115 cmbs	P. Nunn, pers. comm., USP
Moturiki	Naitabale	Wk-11479	295	40	-27.4	2890–3210	Charcoal	–	R2: 55 cmbs	P. Nunn, pers. comm., USP
Moturiki	Naitabale	Wk-11480	2576	40	-24.4	2370–2750	Charcoal	–	R2: 105 cmbs	P. Nunn, pers. comm., USP
Moturiki	Naitabale	Wk-11481	2854	50	-28.0	2780–3060	Charcoal	–	R2: 115 cmbs	P. Nunn, pers. comm., USP
Moturiki	Naitabale	Wk-11482	2456	40	-28.4	2340–2700	Charcoal	–	R2: 125 cmbs	P. Nunn, pers. comm., USP
Moturiki	Naitabale	Wk-13402	2974	40	2.1± 0.2	2680–2840	Marine shell	*Anadara* sp.	T1: 150 cmbs	P. Nunn, pers. comm., USP
Moturiki	Naitabale	Wk-13403	2951	40	3.0 ± 0.2	2650–2840	Marine shell	*Tectus pyramis*	T1: 150 cmbs	P. Nunn, pers. comm., USP
Moturiki	Naitabale	Wk-13404	2931	40	3.0 ± 0.2	2600–2840	Marine shell	*Trochus niloticus*	T1: 150 cmbs	P. Nunn, pers. comm., USP
Moturiki	Naitabale	Wk-13405	2483	50	-27.1	2350–2710	Charcoal	–	P3: 135 cmbs	P. Nunn, pers. comm., USP
Naigani	Naigani	NZ-5615	3142	50	–	2780–3080	Marine shell	*Tridacna maxima*	Sq 7, extension, 2.92 m below datum	Best (1981)
Naigani	Naigani	NZ-5616	3152	50	–	2790–3100	Marine shell	*Tridacna maxima*	Sq 13, 2.6 m below datum	Best (1981)
Naigani	Naigani	NZ-5617	3052	50	–	2730–2950	Marine shell	*Saccostrea cucullata*	Sq 7, extension, 2.37 m below datum	Best (1981)
Naigani	Naigani	NZ-5618	3082	70	–	2720–3050	Marine shell	*Trochus niloticus*	Sq 4, extension, 1.72 m below datum	Best (1981)
Viti Levu	Natunuku	ANU-10381	99.7 ± 0.8%M	–	-24 ± 2.0E	–	Charcoal	–	Tr.3, Sq.A5: 10–20	ANU-EPF
Viti Levu	Navatu	ANU-10388	104.0 ± 1.1%M	–	–	–	Charcoal	–	Tr. B2, L1: 20	ANU-EPF
Qoqo	Qoqo	Wk-16208	2925	40	3.2 ± 0.2	2570–2790	Marine shell	*Trochus niloticus*	F1: 188	Nunn et al. (2006)
Qoqo	Qoqo	Wk-16209	2990	40	0.0	2700–2850	Marine shell	*Anadara* sp., *Codakia punctata*, *Gafrarium tumidum*	R2: 87	Nunn et al. (2006)
Qoqo	Qoqo	Wk-16218	2790	40	-24.5	2760–2940	Charcoal	–	R2: 118	Nunn et al. (2006)
Qoqo	Qoqo	Wk-16219	402	40	-24.0	330–500	Charcoal	–	P1: 185	Nunn et al. (2006)
Qoqo	Qoqo	Wk-16220	393	40	-24.0	320–500	Charcoal	–	P1: 205	Nunn et al. (2006)
Taveuni	Navolivoli	GaK-2411	710	80	–	530–730	Charcoal	–	Structure #11	Frost (1970: 132)
Taveuni	Navolivoli	GaK-2412	2050	150	–	1620–2330	Charcoal	–	Trench #14, 30 cm below Layer A	Frost (1970: 137,141)
Taveuni	Nawa	GaK-2414	710	80	–	530–730	Charcoal	–	Component E	Frost (1970: 113–114)
Taveuni	Nayalayala	GaK-2507	340	80	–	0–510	Charcoal	–	Structure #8, 40 cmbs	Frost (1970: 97)
Taveuni	Qalau	GaK-2510	280	90	–	0–490	Charcoal	–	Structure #5	Frost (1970: 119)
Taveuni	Taveuni	GaK-2413	740	70	–	550–740	Charcoal	–	Trench #6, 40–70 cmbs	Frost (1970: 99,102)
Taveuni	Taveuni	GaK-2508	Modern	–	–	–	Charcoal	–	Trench #2	Frost (1970: 68)
Taveuni	Taveuni	GaK-2509	620	90	–	470–720	Charcoal	–	Trench #2, Layer A	Frost (1970: 76)
Totoya	Lawaki Levu	Beta-67623	2480	60	–	1980–2300	Marine shell	*Tridacna* sp.	TP-3, Layer III, 40cm cmbs	Clark and Cole (1997)

Continued on next page

Table 19 *continued*

Island	Site	Lab Code	CRA	CRA SE	C13	Cal. BP	Sample Type	Identification	Context	Reference
Totoya	Lawaki Levu	Beta-67624	2370	60	–	1840–2150	Marine shell	*Tectus* sp.	TP-1, Layer II, 40cm cmbs	Clark and Cole (1997)
Ugaga	Ugaga	ANU-10772	2140	70	0.0 ± 2.0E	1550–1890	Marine shell	*Trochus niloticus*	I5: 30–40 cmbs	ANU-EPF
Ugaga	Ugaga	ANU-10773	2490	70	0.0 ± 2.0E	1970–2320	Marine shell	*Tridacna maxima*	O9: 30–40 cmbs	ANU-EPF
Ugaga	Ugaga	ANU-10774	1720	70	0.0 ± 2.0E	1150–1390	Marine shell	*Tridacna maxima*	I5: 20–30 cmbs	ANU-EPF
Ugaga	Ugaga	ANU-10775	2620	60	0.0 ± 2.0E	2130–2470	Marine shell	*Tridacna maxima*	I9: 30–40 cmbs	ANU-EPF
Ugaga	Ugaga	ANU-10776	1900	60	0.0 ± 2.0E	1310–1590	Marine shell	*Turbo argyrostromus*	M8: 20–30 cmbs	ANU-EPF
Ugaga	Ugaga	ANU-10777	2530	70	0.0 ± 2.0E	2000–2340	Marine shell	*Tridacna maxima*	J9: 40–50 cmbs	ANU-EPF
Ugaga	Ugaga	ANU-10778	2600	70	0.0 ± 2.0E	2090–2470	Marine shell	*Tridacna maxima*	T/U-1: 40–50 cmbs	ANU-EPF
Ugaga	Ugaga	Beta-107951	2130	50	2.0	1580–1850	Marine shell	*Tridacna maxima*	minus A13: 30–40 cmbs	ANU-EPF
Ugaga	Ugaga	Beta-107952	2690	60	2.0	2260–2650	Marine shell	*Tridacna maxima*	P10: 30–40 cmbs	ANU-EPF
Ugaga	Ugaga	Beta-107953	3150	70	3.2	2760–3140	Marine shell	*Trochus niloticus*	C12: 50–60 cmbs	ANU-EPF
Ugaga	Ugaga	Wk-5554	98.3 ± 0.5%M	–	-24 ± 2.0E	–	Charcoal	–	Sq. K7: 20–30	ANU-EPF
Ugaga	Ugaga	Wk-5555	98.8 ± 0.5%M	–	-24 ± 2.0E	–	Charcoal	–	Sq. K7: 20–30	ANU-EPF
Ugaga	Ugaga	Wk-5556	98.2 ± 0.5%M	–	-24 ± 2.0E	–	Charcoal	–	Sq. P8: 20–30	ANU-EPF
Vanuabalavu	Qaranilaca	ANU-11536H	980	80	0.0 ± 2.0	460–690	Marine shell	*Anadara* sp.	Layer III: 80 cmbs	Nunn et al. (2004a)
Vanuabalavu	Qaranilaca	ANU-11537H	1140	80	0.0 ± 2.0	550–870	Marine shell	*Anadara* sp.	Layer IV: 105 cmbs	Nunn et al. (2004a)
Vanuabalavu	Qaranilaca	ANU-11538H	1060	60	-24 ± 2.0E	790–1060	Charcoal	–	Layer III: 75–85 cmbs	Nunn et al. (2004a)
Vanuabalavu	Qaranilaca	ANU-11539H	1180	60	-24 ± 2.0E	930–1220	Charcoal	–	Layer IV: 104–109 cmbs	Nunn et al. (2004a)
Viti Levu	Bourewa	Wk-14235	2896	40	-27.4	2810–3140	Charcoal	–	Pit 3: 123 cmbs	P. Nunn, pers. comm., USP
Viti Levu	Bourewa	Wk-14236	2867	40	-25.0	2790–3060	Charcoal	–	Pit 3: 109 cmbs	P. Nunn, pers. comm., USP
Viti Levu	Bourewa	Wk-14237	3259	40	-12.8	2950–3220	Marine shell	Tellinidae	Pit 4: 53 cmbs	P. Nunn, pers. comm., USP
Viti Levu	Bourewa	Wk-14238	2740	40	2.5 ± 0.2	2330–2640	Marine shell	*Fimbria fimbriata, Codakia punctata*	Pit 2: 55 cmbs	P. Nunn, pers. comm., USP
Viti Levu	Bourewa	Wk-14239	3027	40	3.5± 0.2	2720–2900	Marine shell	*Trochus niloticus*	Pit 1: 71 cmbs	P. Nunn, pers. comm., USP
Viti Levu	Bourewa	Wk-14594	2944	40	2.9± 0.2	2610–2830	Marine shell	*Codakia punctata*	Pit 3: 105 cmbs	P. Nunn, pers. comm., USP
Viti Levu	Bourewa	Wk-14595	2915	40	-23.5	2860–3140	Charcoal	–	Pit 4: 54 cmbs	P. Nunn, pers. comm., USP
Viti Levu	Bourewa	Wk-14597	2717	40	-23.6	2730–2860	Charcoal	–	Pit 2: 57 cmbs	P. Nunn, pers. comm., USP
Viti Levu	Bourewa	Wk-14598	2612	40	-23.1	2490–2760	Charcoal	–	Pit 1: 54 cmbs	P. Nunn, pers. comm., USP
Viti Levu	Bourewa	Wk-14599	2894	40	-24.7	2800–3140	Charcoal	–	Pit 1: 85 cmbs	P. Nunn, pers. comm., USP
Viti Levu	Bourewa	Wk-16206	1590	40	3.6 ± 0.2	1050–1250	Marine shell	*Strombus gibberulus, Strombus labiatus, Fimbria fimbriata, Vasum turbinellus*	Pit L4: 82 cmbs	P. Nunn, pers. comm., USP
Viti Levu	Bourewa	Wk-16207	2940	40	2.9 ± 0.2	2610–2730	Marine shell	*Anadara* sp., *Codakia* sp.	Pit B3: 90 cmbs	P. Nunn, pers. comm., USP
Viti Levu	Bourewa	Wk-16216	164	40	-24.4	0–280	Charcoal	–	Pit B4: 134 cmbs	P. Nunn, pers. comm., USP
Viti Levu	Bourewa	Wk-17539	383	30	-25.1	320–490	Charcoal	–	Pit X8: 95 cmbs	P. Nunn, pers. comm., USP
Viti Levu	Bourewa	Wk-17540	133	30	-26.7	0–260	Charcoal	–	Pit X2: 196 cmbs	P. Nunn, pers. comm., USP
Viti Levu	Bourewa	Wk-17541	2506	30	-26.1	2360–2710	Charcoal	–	Pit X1: 105 cmbs	P. Nunn, pers. comm., USP
Viti Levu	Bourewa	Wk-17542	2920	30	-24.4	2870–3140	Charcoal	–	Pit X3: 135 cmbs	P. Nunn, pers. comm., USP

Continued on next page

Table 19 *continued*

Island	Site	Lab Code	CRA	CRA SE	C13	Cal. BP	Sample Type	Identification	Context	Reference
Viti Levu	Bourewa	Wk-17543	3006	40	4.1 ± 0.2	2710–2870	Marine shell	*Trochus niloticus*	Pit X24E: 52 cmbs	P. Nunn, pers. comm., USP
Viti Levu	Bourewa	Wk-17544	3474	40	3.2 ± 0.2	3250–3450	Marine shell	*Conus* sp.	Pit X25: 140 cmbs	P. Nunn, pers. comm., USP
Viti Levu	Bourewa	Wk-17545	2851	40	2.9 ± 0.2	2470–2720	Marine shell	*Codakia punctata*	Pit X23: 98 cmbs	P. Nunn, pers. comm., USP
Viti Levu	Bourewa	Wk-17546	2951	40	2.4 ± 0.2	2650–2840	Marine shell	*Codakia punctata, Gafrarium tumidum, Turbo* sp.	Pit X3: 124 cmbs	P. Nunn, pers. comm., USP
Viti Levu	Bourewa	Wk-17547	3006	40	4.5 ± 0.2	2710–2870	Marine shell	*Trochus niloticus*	Pit X6: 94 cmbs	P. Nunn, pers. comm., USP
Viti Levu	Bourewa	Wk-17548	2938	40	1.6 ± 0.2	2610–2820	Marine shell	*Anadara* sp.	Pit X2: 120 cmbs	P. Nunn, pers. comm., USP
Viti Levu	Bourewa	Wk-17549	3046	40	4.4 ± 0.2	2730–2920	Marine shell	*Trochus niloticus*	Pit X3: 104 cmbs	P. Nunn, pers. comm., USP
Viti Levu	Bourewa	Wk-17967	198	30	-19.4	0–130	Bone	*Sus scrofa*	Pit X8: 55 cmbs	P. Nunn, pers. comm., USP
Viti Levu	Bourewa	Wk-17968	3107	40	2.4 ± 0.2	2760–3000	Marine shell	*Atactodea striata*	Pit X6: 68 cmbs	P. Nunn, pers. comm., USP
Viti Levu	Bourewa	Wk-17969	1740	30	2.9 ± 0.2	1230–1360	Marine shell	*Strombus gibberulus*	Pit X8: 68 cmbs	P. Nunn, pers. comm., USP
Viti Levu	Bourewa	Wk-17970	2866	30	2.3 ± 0.2	2610–2730	Marine shell	*Tridacna squamosa*	Pit X10: 78 cmbs	P. Nunn, pers. comm., USP
Viti Levu	Bourewa	Wk-17971	2831	40	3.8 ± 0.2	2450–2710	Marine shell	*Turbo chrysostomus*	Pit X20: 60 cmbs	P. Nunn, pers. comm., USP
Viti Levu	Bourewa	Wk-17972	2824	40	3.0 ± 0.2	2430–2710	Marine shell	*Turbo* sp.	Pit X20: 69 cmbs	P. Nunn, pers. comm., USP
Viti Levu	Bourewa	Wk-17973	2870	30	-25.8	2800–3060	Charcoal	–	Pit X3: 121 cmbs	P. Nunn, pers. comm., USP
Viti Levu	Bourewa	Wk-17974	891	30	-25.2	680–900	Charcoal	–	Pit X21E: 45 cmbs	P. Nunn, pers. comm., USP
Viti Levu	Bourewa	Wk-20281	3038	40	3.6 ± 0.2	2730–2910	Marine shell	*Trochus niloticus*	Pit X2: 90 cmbs	P. Nunn, pers. comm., USP
Viti Levu	Bourewa	Wk-20282	3014	40	3.6 ± 0.2	2710–2880	Marine shell	*Trochus niloticus*	Pit X2: 20 cmbs	P. Nunn, pers. comm., USP
Viti Levu	Bourewa	Wk-20283	2976	40	4.3 ± 0.2	2690–2850	Marine shell	*Trochus niloticus*	Pit X3: 70 cmbs	P. Nunn, pers. comm., USP
Viti Levu	Bourewa	Wk-20284	3044	40	3.6 ± 0.2	2730–2920	Marine shell	*Trochus niloticus*	Pit X3: 30 cmbs	P. Nunn, pers. comm., USP
Viti Levu	Bukusia	AA-50303	189	50	-28.3	0–300	Charcoal	–	TU 1, 30–40 cmbs	Field (2004: 90)
Viti Levu	Bukusia	AA-50304	259	40	-24.3	0–440	Charcoal	–	TU 2, 40–50 cmbs	Field (2004: 90)
Viti Levu	Bukusia	Wk-11135	202	60	-29.6	0–300	Charcoal	–	TU 2, 80–90 cmbs	Field (2004: 90)
Viti Levu	Korohewa	AA-50305	210	40	-27.9	0–300	Charcoal	–	TU 1, 60–70 cmbs	Field (2004: 90)
Viti Levu	Korovatuma	AA-50300	527	50	-27.2	460–630	Charcoal	–	TU 1, 60–70 cmbs	Field (2004: 90)
Viti Levu	Korovatuma	AA-50301	188	40	-27.2	0–290	Charcoal	–	TU 1, 20–30 cmbs	Field (2004: 90)
Viti Levu	Korovatuma	AA-50310	338	50	-26.0	160–490	Charcoal	–	TU 2, 60 cmbs	Field (2004: 90)
Viti Levu	Madraya	AA-50296	398	40	-28.7	320–500	Charcoal	–	TU1, 20–30 cmbs	Field (2004: 90)
Viti Levu	Malaqerqere	ANU-10452	460	60	-24 ± 2.0E	320–540	Charcoal	–	Sq. A1: 10–20 cmbs	ANU-EPF
Viti Levu	Malaqerqere	ANU-10453	830	90	-24 ± 2.0E	560–910	Charcoal	–	Sq. A2: 60–70 cmbs	ANU-EPF
Viti Levu	Malaqerqere	ANU-10454	670	70	-24 ± 2.0E	520–680	Charcoal	–	Sq. A1: 40–50 cmbs	ANU-EPF
Viti Levu	Malua	AA-50290	159	30	-26.5	0–280	Charcoal	–	TU1, 50–60 cmbs	Field (2004: 90)
Viti Levu	Malua	AA-50295	624	30	-26.3	530–640	Charcoal	–	TU2, 10–20 cmbs	Field (2004: 90)
Viti Levu	Nadroga	AA-50297	224	50	-24.6	0–320	Charcoal	–	TU1, 50–60 cmbs	Field (2004: 90)
Viti Levu	Nasilai	Beta-22096	Modern	–	–	–	Wood	Post	Level IV	Rosenthal (1995: 97)
Viti Levu	Nasilai	Beta-22097	330	70	–	150–230	Wood	Canoe mast	?	Rosenthal (1995: 97)
Viti Levu	Natunuku	ANU-10698	2780	90	0.0 ± 2.0E	2310–2720	Marine shell	*Tridacna* sp.	Tr.3, Sq.A5: 30–40 cmbs	ANU-EPF

Continued on next page

Table 19 *continued*

Island	Site	Lab Code	CRA	CRA SE	C13	Cal. BP	Sample Type	Identification	Context	Reference
Viti Levu	Natunuku	ANU-10699	1160	70	0.0 ± 2.0E	600–890	Marine shell	*Tridacna* sp.	Tr.3, Sq.A5: 30–40 cmbs	ANU-EPF
Viti Levu	Natunuku	ANU-10700	380	70	0.0 ± 2.0E	0–230	Marine shell	*Trochus* sp.	Tr.3, Sq.A5: 20–30 cmbs	ANU-EPF
Viti Levu	Natunuku	ANU-11305	2900	50	0.0 ± 2.0E	2490–2770	Marine shell	? Species	Trench 3	ANU-EPF
Viti Levu	Natunuku	ANU-11306	1170	50	0.0 ± 2.0E	630–840	Marine shell	? Species	Trench 3	ANU-EPF
Viti Levu	Natunuku	ANU-11307	2600	60	0.0 ± 2.0E	2110–2440	Marine shell	? Species	Trench 3	ANU-EPF
Viti Levu	Natunuku	GaK-1218	3240	100	–	3080–3680	Charcoal	–	Layer 6, Rectangle E, Location C	Davidson et al. (1990: 131)
Viti Levu	Natunuku	NZ-7863	2640	30	0.7	2210–2440	Marine shell	*Tridacna maxima*	Layer 5, Rectangle D, Location C	Petchey (1995: 94)
Viti Levu	Natunuku	NZ-7864	2750	30	0.3	2340–2610	Marine shell	*Tridacna maxima*	Layer 5b, Rectangle D, Location C	Petchey (1995: 94)
Viti Levu	Natunuku	NZ-7865	2622	30	-0.3	2180–2390	Marine shell	*Gafarium tumidum*	Layer 5b, Rectangle D, Location C	Petchey (1995: 94)
Viti Levu	Natunuku	NZA-2117	2676	60	1.8	2200–2600	Marine shell	*Gafarium tumidum*	Layer 5, Rectangle D, Location C	Petchey (1995: 94)
Viti Levu	Natunuku	NZA-2512	1896	90	-14.8	1400–1820	Bone	Human	Rectangle C, Layer above 5, Location C	Davidson et al. (1990: 131)
Viti Levu	Navatu	M-5810	950	300	–	320–1390	Charcoal	–	24–30 inches bs	Gifford (1951b)
Viti Levu	Navatu	M-5879	1200	500	–	150–2150	Charcoal	–	90 inches bs	Gifford (1951b)
Viti Levu	Navatu	M-6342	1300	500	–	310–2310	Charcoal	–	96–104 inches bs	Gifford (1951b)
Viti Levu	Navatu	M-351	2000	500	-24 ± 2.0E	850–3140	Charcoal	–	104–110 inches bs	Gifford (1951b)
Viti Levu	Navatu 17A	ANU-10384	870	70	-24 ± 2.0E	660–910	Charcoal	–	Tr. B1: L2, 140 cmbs	ANU-EPF
Viti Levu	Navatu 17A	ANU-10385	350	70	-24 ± 2.0E	150–500	Charcoal	–	Tr. A1: L1, 100 cmbs	ANU-EPF
Viti Levu	Navatu 17A	ANU-10386	1670	70	-24 ± 2.0E	1350–1690	Charcoal	–	Tr. B3+4: L4, 230 cmbs	ANU-EPF
Viti Levu	Navatu 17A	ANU-10387	1240	140	-24 ± 2.0E	800–1350	Charcoal	–	Tr. B1+2: L4, 215 cmbs	ANU-EPF
Viti Levu	Navatu 17A	ANU-10389	330	60	-24 ± 2.0E	150–490	Charcoal	–	Tr. B1: L1, 86 cmbs	ANU-EPF
Viti Levu	Navatu 17A	ANU-10390	1010	140	-24 ± 2.0E	660–1180	Charcoal	–	Tr. B1+2: L4, 220 cmbs	ANU-EPF
Viti Levu	Navatu 17A	ANU-10708	1980	70	0.0 ± 2.0E	1360–1710	Marine shell	*Tridacna* sp.	Tr. B3+4: L4, 230 cmbs	ANU-EPF
Viti Levu	Navatu 17A	ANU-10709	980	70	0.0 ± 2.0E	480–670	Marine shell	*Gafrarium* sp.	Tr. B1: L2, 120 cmbs	ANU-EPF
Viti Levu	Navatu 17A	ANU-10710	720	70	0.0 ± 2.0E	250–500	Marine shell	*Anadara* sp.	Tr. B2: L1, 50 cmbs	ANU-EPF
Viti Levu	Nokonoko	AA-50283	1311	40	-25.0	1080–1280	Charcoal	–	TU 1, 95–105 cmbs	Field (2004: 90)
Viti Levu	Nokonoko	AA-50284	674	40	-8.7	440–550	Riparian shell	? Species	TU 3, 10–20 cmbs	Field (2004: 90)
Viti Levu	Nokonoko	AA-50287	1492	40	-26.7	1290–1400	Charcoal	–	TU 5, 20–30 cmbs	Field (2004: 90)
Viti Levu	Nokonoko	AA-50288	212	40	-24.5	0–310	Charcoal	–	TU 6, 30–40 cmbs	Field (2004: 90)
Viti Levu	Nokonoko	AA-50289	135	30	-24.9	0–260	Charcoal	–	TU 10, 10–20 cmbs	Field (2004: 90)
Viti Levu	Nokonoko	AA-50299	185	60	-27.4	0–290	Charcoal	–	TU 7, 30–40 cmbs	Field (2004: 90)
Viti levu	Qara-I-Oso I	ANU-11015	1280	120	-24 ± 2.0E	920–1350	Charcoal	–	TP. 1: 30 cmbs	ANU-EPF
Viti Levu	Qara-I-Oso II	ANU-11014	660	60	-24 ± 2.0E	530–670	Charcoal	–	TP.1, Layer 2: 30 cmbs	ANU-EPF
Viti Levu	Qaramatatolu	Wk-16214	297	40	–	150–450	Charcoal	–	Pit M4: 160 cmbs	Nunn et al. (2005)
Viti Levu	Qaramatatolu	Wk-16213	970	40	–	750–920	Charcoal	–	Pit M4: 145 cmbs	Nunn et al. (2005)

Continued on next page

Table 19 continued

Island	Site	Lab Code	CRA	CRA SE	C13	Cal. BP	Sample Type	Identification	Context	Reference
Viti Levu	Qoroqoro	AA-50307	974	40	-29.4	750–930	Charcoal	–	TU1, 90–100 cmbs	Field (2004: 90)
Viti Levu	Qoroqoro	AA-50308	182	40	-29.1	0–290	Charcoal	–	TU3, 20–30 cmbs	Field (2004: 90)
Viti Levu	Qoroqoro	Wk-11134	259	100	-28.2	0–460	Charcoal	–	TU4, 50–70 cmbs	Field (2004)
Viti Levu	Rove	Wk-14240	155	30	-25.2	0–280	Charcoal	–	Pit 1: 65 cmbs	P. Nunn, pers. comm., USP
Viti Levu	Rove	Wk-14241	187	60	-24.9	0–290	Charcoal	–	Pit 1: 95 cmbs	P. Nunn, pers. comm., USP
Viti Levu	Rove	Wk-14242	95	40	-24.6	–	Charcoal	–	Pit 1: 75 cmbs	P. Nunn, pers. comm., USP
Viti Levu	Rukuruku	Beta 64460	210	60	–	–	Marine shell	*Trochus niloticus*	Surface	Kuhlken and Crosby (1999)
Viti Levu	Rukuruku	Beta 64461	160	70	–	0–290	Charcoal	–	Trench 3/4, Layer 3: 60 cmbs	Kuhlken and Crosby (1999)
Viti Levu	Sigatoka	CAMS 32251	230	40	-27.8	0–310	Charcoal	–	West Dunes	Dickinson et al. (1998)
Viti Levu	Sigatoka	CAMS 32252	510	60	-25.9	330–630	Charcoal	–	Open field	Dickinson et al. (1998)
Viti Levu	Sigatoka	CAMS 48565	2470	50	-23.7	2350–2700	Charcoal	–	Level 1	Burley (2003, 2005)
Viti Levu	Sigatoka	CAMS 48566	2490	50	-21.4	2350–2710	Charcoal	–	Level 1	Burley (2003, 2005)
Viti Levu	Sigatoka	CAMS 68191	1550	40	-27.4	1300–1520	Charcoal	–	Level 2	Burley (2003, 2005)
Viti Levu	Sigatoka	CAMS 68192	1540	40	-26	1300–1520	Charcoal	–	Level 2	Burley (2003, 2005)
Viti Levu	Sigatoka	CAMS 68194	1620	40	-25.5	1360–1540	Charcoal	–	Level 2	Burley (2003, 2005)
Viti Levu	Sigatoka	CAMS 68195	1310	40	24.5	1080–1280	Charcoal	–	Level 2	Burley (2003, 2005)
Viti Levu	Sigatoka	CAMS 68196	2510	40	-24.3	2360–2710	Charcoal	–	Level 1	Burley (2003, 2005)
Viti Levu	Sigatoka	CAMS 70090	1400	40	-28.3	1180–1330	Charcoal	–	Level 2	Burley (2003, 2005)
Viti Levu	Sigatoka	CAMS 70091	1430	40	-27.4	1180–1360	Charcoal	–	Level 2	Burley (2003, 2005)
Viti Levu	Sigatoka	CAMS 70920	1480	40	-25.5	1280–1390	Charcoal	–	Level 2	Burley (2003, 2005)
Viti Levu	Sigatoka	CAMS 70921	1410	40	-24.6	1180–1340	Charcoal	–	Level 2	Burley (2003, 2005)
Viti Levu	Sigatoka	GaK-1206	1720	80	–	1380–1810	Charcoal	–	Level 2, Sq. 52C, 12–15 inches	Birks (1973:57)
Viti Levu	Sigatoka	GaK-946	2460	90	–	2190–2740	Charcoal	–	Level 1, Sq. 45A, bottom 6 inches	Birks (1973:57)
Viti Levu	Sigatoka	NZ-7599	1680	60	–	1380–1690	Charcoal	–	Level 2	Best (1988)
Viti Levu	Sigatoka	NZA-4789	2627	80	-25.8	2360–2840	Charcoal	–	Level 1', 53 cm below datum	Petchey (1995)
Viti Levu	Sigatoka	Wk 8239	2740	80	–	2500–3000	Charcoal	–	Level 1	De Biran (2001)
Viti Levu	Sigatoka	Wk 8328	1410	150	–	960–1550	Charcoal	–	Level 2	De Biran (2001)
Viti Levu	Sigatoka	Wk 8900	690	50	–	550–670	Charcoal	–	Level 3	De Biran (2001)
Viti Levu	Sigatoka	Wk 9030	1400	40	–	1180–1330	Charcoal	–	Level 2	De Biran (2001)
Viti Levu	Sigatoka	WK 996a	Modern	–	-7.6	–	Bone	Human	Mound south of Sq. B4	Best (1988: 6,14)
Viti Levu	Sigatoka	WK 996b	1870	70	-15.9	1390–1770	Bone	Human	Mound south of Sq. B4	Best (1988: 6,14)
Viti Levu	Sigatoka	Wk-5333	590	60	-26.3	500–650	Charcoal	–	West Dune Field: Level 3?	Dickinson et al. (1998)
Viti Levu	Tatuba Cave	AA-50291	207	30	-28.1	0–300	Charcoal	–	TU1, 190–200 cmbs	Field (2004: 90)
Viti Levu	Tatuba Cave	AA-50292	1802	30	-25.5	1550–1770	Charcoal	–	TU1, 140–150 cmbs	Field (2004: 90)
Viti Levu	Tatuba Cave	AA-50293	339	40	-20.6	0–260	Bone	Human	TU 1, 130–140 cmbs	Field (2004: 90)
Viti Levu	Tatuba Cave	AA-50294	1993	40	-26.0	1740–1990	Charcoal	–	TU1, 80–90 cmbs	Field (2004: 90)
Viti Levu	Tatuba Cave	AA-50298	1294	40	-25.6	1070–1270	Charcoal	–	TU1, 50–60 cmbsr	Field (2004: 90)

Continued on next page

Table 19 *continued*

Island	Site	Lab Code	CRA	CRA SE	C13	Cal. BP	Sample Type	Identification	Context	Reference
Viti Levu	Tatuba Cave	Wk-11137	968	50	-28.0	740–930	Charcoal	–	TU1, Ft. 1, 45–55 cmbs	Field (2004: 90)
Viti Levu	Tomato patch	Wk-16205	1720	30	3.5 ± 0.2	1210–1340	Marine shell	*Trochus* sp.	Surface: 88 cmbs	P. Nunn, pers. comm., USP
Viti Levu	Tomato patch	Wk-16215	370	40	-26.9	310–490	Charcoal	–	Surface: 90 cmbs	P. Nunn, pers. comm., USP
Viti Levu	Tuvu	ANU-11020	1570	100	-24.0	1260–1700	Charcoal	–	TP 1, Spit IV	ANU-EPF
Viti Levu	Vitoga	AA-50302	198	60	-24.9	0–300	Charcoal	–	TU1, 60–77 cmbs	Field (2004: 90)
Viti Levu	Vitoga	AA-50306	175	40	-25.0	0–280	Charcoal	–	TU1, 20–30 cmbs	Field (2004: 90)
Viti Levu	Vitoga	AA-50309	261	50	-25.1	0–450	Charcoal	–	TU2, 40–50 cmbs	Field (2004: 90)
Viti Levu	Volivoli II	ANU-10449	1120	70	-24.0	810–1170	Charcoal	–	TR. 1: 20–30 cmbs	ANU-EPF
Viti Levu	Volivoli II	ANU-10450	1960	70	-24.0	1630–2040	Charcoal	–	TR. 1: 40–50 cmbs	ANU-EPF
Viti Levu	Volivoli II	ANU-10451	1080	190	-24.0	580–1300	Charcoal	–	TR.1: 50–60 cmbs	ANU-EPF
Viti Levu	Volivoli III	ANU-11016	1100	90	-24.0	770–1170	Charcoal	–	TP. 1, Spit 5	ANU-EPF
Viti Levu	Volivoli III	ANU-11018	290	60	-24.0	0–490	Charcoal	–	TP. 1, Spit 2	ANU-EPF
Viti Levu	Volivoli III	ANU-11019	1060	80	-24.0	740–1070	Charcoal	–	TP. 1, Spit 8	ANU-EPF
Viti Levu	Vunda	?6349	700	300	–	0–1170	Charcoal	–	24–30 inches bs	Gifford (1951b)
Viti Levu	Vunda	?6353	650	300	–	0–1060	Charcoal	–	12–18 inches bs	Gifford (1951b)
Viti Levu	Yanuca	ANU-11413	2650	50	-12.3 ± 0.2	2170–2490	Marine shell	*Trachycardium* cf. *reeveanum*	Trench 4, Zone 3, Spit 2, 152.4 cmbs	Clark and Anderson (2001)
Viti Levu	Yanuca	ANU-11414	3150	60	-12.3 ± 2.0	2780–3120	Fresh water shell	*Batissa violacea*	Trench 2A, Zone 3, Spit 4, 167.6 cmbs	Clark and Anderson (2001)
Viti Levu	Yanuca	ANU-11415	2300	50	1.5 ± 2.0	1790–2060	Marine shell	*Tonna sulcosa*	Trench 3A, Zone 3, Spit 4, 167.6 cmbs	Clark and Anderson (2001)
Viti Levu	Yanuca	ANU-11416	2940	60	3.8 ± 2.0	2520–2850	Marine shell	*Anadara antiquata*	Trench 3, Zone 3, Spit 7, 190.5 cmbs	Clark and Anderson (2001)
Viti Levu	Yanuca	ANU-11417	3050	80	2.7 ± 5.7	2680–3050	Marine shell	*Cyprea tigris*	Trench 2-2A, Zone 3, Spit 3, 160.0 cmbs	Clark and Anderson (2001)
Viti Levu	Yanuca	GaK-1226	2980	90	–	2860–3340	Charcoal	–	Zone 3, 66 inches bs	Birks and Birks (1978)
Viti Levu	Yanuca	GaK-1227	2660	90	–	2360–2880	Charcoal	–	Zone 2, 48 inches bs	Birks and Birks (1978)
Viti Levu	Yanuca	GaK-1228	2060	100	–	1710–2300	Charcoal	–	Zone 2, 30 inches bs	Birks and Birks (1978)
Viti Levu	Yanuca	GaK-1229	Modern	–	–	–	Charcoal	–	Zone 2, 10 inches bs	Birks and Birks (1978)
Viti Levu	Karobo	ANU-10780	1780	80	-24 ± 2.0E	1420–1830	Charcoal	–	Square Ab-1: L7, 122 cmbs	ANU-EPF
Viti Levu	Karobo	ANU-10781	300	70	-24 ± 2.0E	0–500	Charcoal	–	Square Y: L3, 33 cmbs	ANU-EPF
Viti Levu	Karobo	ANU-11067	1680	70	-24 ± 2.0E	1370–1700	Charcoal	–	Square A2: L5, 100 cmbs	ANU-EPF
Viti Levu	Karobo	ANU-11068	2130	120	-24 ± 2.0E	1740–2340	Wood	cf. *Cocos nucifera*	Square A2: L5, 137 cmbs	ANU-EPF
Wakaya	Delaini	Beta 45789	300	70	-26.0	0–490	Charcoal	–	Unit 2-D4, 40 cmbs	Rechtman (1992: 202)
Wakaya	Delaini	Beta 46438	140	50	-17.5	0–130	Bone	?Species	Unit 3-C3, 120 cmbs	Rechtman (1992: 202)
Wakaya	Delaini	Beta 46439	410	60	-26.5	310–510	Charcoal	–	Unit 2-D4, 60 cmbs	Rechtman (1992: 202)
Wakaya	Delaini	Beta 46440	190	70	-25.5	0–300	Charcoal	–	Unit 3-C3, 100 cmbs	Rechtman (1992: 202)
Wakaya	Delaini	Beta 46441	210	50	-26.6	0–310	Charcoal	–	Unit 3-B4, 52 cmbs	Rechtman (1992: 202)
Wakaya	Delaini	Beta 46442	350	80	-28.7	150–520	Charcoal	–	Unit 2-D2, 50 cmbs	Rechtman (1992: 202)
Wakaya	Delaini	Beta 46444	210	50	-27.8	0–310	Charcoal	–	Unit 4-C4, 80 cmbs	Rechtman (1992: 202)

Continued on next page

Table 19 continued

Island	Site	Lab Code	CRA	CRA SE	C13	Cal. BP	Sample Type	Identification	Context	Reference
Wakaya	Delaini	Beta 46445	Modern	–	-26.2	–	Charcoal		Unit EP-5, depth 40 cmbs	Rechtman (1992: 202)
Wakaya	Delaini	Beta 46446	120	50	-24.9	0–280	Charcoal	–	Unit 4-C4, 70 cmbs	Rechtman (1992: 202)
Wakaya	Delaini	Beta 49824	420	90	-18.5	0–430	Bone	?Species	Unit 2-C3, 30 cmbs	Rechtman (1992: 202)
Wakaya	Delaini	Beta 49825	40	50	-22	–	Bone		Unit EP-11, depth 30 cmbs	Rechtman (1992: 202)
Wakaya	Delaini	Beta 49826	120	50	-18.3	0–60	Bone	?Species	Unit 3-C3, 70 cmbs	Rechtman (1992: 202)
Wakaya	Korolevu A	Beta 45785	610	60	-24.3	510–650	Charcoal	–	Unit 1, 60 cmbs	Rechtman (1992: 202)
Wakaya	Korolevu A	Beta 45786	440	60	-25.8	320–530	Charcoal	–	Unit 2, 85 cmbs	Rechtman (1992: 202)
Wakaya	Korolevu A	Beta 45787	410	60	-25.7	310–510	Charcoal	–	Unit 3, 85 cmbs	Rechtman (1992: 202)
Wakaya	Korolevu A	Beta 45790	540	80	-19.0	150–510	Bone	?Species	Unit 5, 40 cmbs	Rechtman (1992: 202)
Wakaya	Korolevu A	Beta 49827	60	50	3.3	–	Marine shell	?Species	Unit EPA, 20 cmbs	Rechtman (1992: 202)
Wakaya	Korolevu A	Beta 49828	160	50	3.4	–	Marine shell	?Species	Unit EPA, 20 cmbs	Rechtman (1992: 202)
Wakaya	Korolevu B	Beta 45788	80	60	-27.3	–	Charcoal	–	Unit 2a, 36 cmbs	Rechtman (1992: 202)
Wakaya	Korolevu B	Beta 45791	190	60	-18.9	0–240	Bone	?Species	Unit 1, 100 cmbs	Rechtman (1992: 202)
Wakaya	Korolevu B	Beta 46443	1950	70	-27.7	1630–2000	Charcoal		Unit 5, 122 cmbs	Rechtman (1992: 202)
Wakaya	Korolevu B	Beta 50522	40	70	-19.6	–	Bone	?Species	Unit 5, 35 cmbs	Rechtman (1992: 202)
Wakaya	Korolevu B	Beta 50523	210	80	-20.2	0–260	Bone	?Species	Unit 1, 20 cmbs	Rechtman (1992: 202)
Yacata	Nadrodrodro	ANU-10811	1040	90	-24.0 E	690–1080	Charcoal	–	Layer 2: 52–60 cmbs	Clark and Hope (2001)
Yadua	Vagairiki-1	Wk-15423	870	30	3.1 ± 0.2	440–540	Marine shell	Trochus niloticus	Pit T1:130–140 cmbs	Nunn et al. (2004)
Yadua	Vagairiki-2	Wk-15424	760	40	3.3 ± 0.2	300–480	Marine shell	Trochus niloticus	Pit T1:140–150 cmbs	Nunn et al. (2004)
Yadua	Denimanu	Wk-15425	2427	40	-26.0 ± 0.2	2320–2700	Charcoal	–	Pit T3:120–130 cmbs	Nunn et al. (2004)
Yasawa	Y1-12	AA-60257	156	30	-24.2	0–280	Charcoal	–	TU1, L.I, lvl. 2	Cochrane (2004: 191)
Yasawa	Y1-15	AA-60255	2207	40	-25.6	2000–2310	Carbonised residue	–	TU 5, L.III, lvl. 14	Cochrane (2004: 191)
Yasawa	Y1-15	AA-60256	607	30	-27.1	520–630	Carbonised residue	–	TU 5, L.I, lvl. 7	Cochrane (2004: 191)
Yasawa	Y2-22	Wk-6482	500	50	–	0–240	Marine shell	Trochus sp.	Surface	Cochrane (2004: 191)
Yasawa	Y2-25	Beta-86839	2540	50	-28.2	2360–2730	Charcoal	–	TU3, L.II base	Cochrane (2004: 191)
Yasawa	Y2-25	Beta-86840	2570	90	-28.7	2360–2760	Charcoal	–	TU3, pit feature1	Cochrane (2004: 191)
Yasawa	Y2-25	CAMS-24946	2530	50	–	2160–2650	Bone	Human	L.II	Cochrane (2004: 191)
Yasawa	Y2-39	Beta-174986	780	40	-26.4	570–730	Charcoal	–	TU3, L.III	Cochrane (2004: 191)
Yasawa	Y2-39	Beta-52221	2260	90	-28.2	1950–2430	Charcoal	–	TU1, L.IV, lvl. 22	Cochrane (2004: 191)
Yasawa	Y2-39	Beta-53193	2790	260	-28.0	2160–3470	Charcoal	–	TU1, L.IV, lvl. 23	Cochrane (2004: 191)
Yasawa	Y2-39	Beta-53194	2870	110	-27.2	2740–3250	Charcoal	–	TU1, L.IV, lvl. 21	Cochrane (2004: 191)
Yasawa	Y2-39	Beta-53195	2400	80	-27.2	2160–2710	Charcoal	–	TU1, L.IV, lvl. 17	Cochrane (2004: 191)
Yasawa	Y2-39	Beta-53196	1160	80	-26.6	820–1260	Charcoal	–	TU1, L.III, lxl. 12	Cochrane (2004: 191)
Yasawa	Y2-39	Beta-53197	330	70	-27.4	150–500	Charcoal	–	TU1, L.II, ivl 6	Cochrane (2004: 191)
Yasawa	Y2-45	Wk-6485	480	50	–	0–230	Marine shell	Trochus sp.	Surface	Cochrane (2004: 191)
Yasawa	Y2-46	Beta-93971	360	90	-25.7	0–530	Charcoal	–	TU1, L.I, lvl. 1	Cochrane (2004: 191)

Kulu Bay

The Lapita site at Kulu Bay is in swampy terrain behind a low beach ridge that had been affected by stream cutting and mixing of beach materials with a fine, sticky clay-soil from nearby hill slopes. The six radiocarbon determinations clearly demonstrate extensive site disturbance, as three charcoal samples have a modern or recent age regardless of sample depth (ANU-10743, ANU-107949, ANU-107950), and one result on charcoal has a recent age of 560-910 (ANU-10727) that is too recent considering the presence of early pottery. Results indicate substantial mobilisation and deposition of slope sediments on to the Kulu beach flat in the last millennium. In contrast, two marine-shell dates with identical results of 2120–2380 cal. BP (Beta-107947, Beta-107948) indicate the redeposition of cultural material of Lapita and post-Lapita age in the stream-affected back-beach deposits.

Karobo

Adequate provenance information was available for one wood and three charcoal samples and these were submitted to the QDRC (Table 17). The first sample listed was collected from the base of Layer 3 in Square Y, and dated an earth oven (ANU-10781). The excavation notes mention the possibility that Square Y ceramics were not associated with the oven as most were found below Layer 3. The recent age of the oven (0–500 cal. BP) suggests this was probably the case. The remaining two determinations on charcoal came from a ceramic 'horizon' where Palmer and Golson had recorded abundant remains of flat-bottomed dishes, relief-marked ceramics and oven stones. The dates range from 1370 to 1830 cal. BP (ANU-10780, ANU-11067), similar to Level 2 determinations from Sigatoka where cognate ceramics have been recorded (Birks 1973; Burley 1997:Table 2).

The fourth date (ANU-11068) from Layer 5 is older and barely overlaps with charcoal determinations from the same layer (1740–2340 cal. BP). The sample is a rectangular piece of cut palm wood, thought to be coconut (Palmer 1965:56). At Karobo, the excavators recorded no evidence for an occupation below the 'horizon' containing platter fragments, lenses of charcoal and oven stones.

Introduction of the worked palm wood might have occurred at an earlier time during the formation of the sand ridge, perhaps by flooding and channel cutting of the sand ridge by swamp water. Alternatively, the date itself might be questioned in view of the difficult pre-treatment required to extract cellulose from wood samples (A. Alimanovic, pers. comm., QDRC).

Malaqereqere

Three determinations on charcoal from the highly stratified cultural sediments in the Malaqereqere rock shelter gave consistent age-depth results. The shelter is dated by ANU-10453 immediately above the limestone floor with an age of 560–910 cal. BP, and a date in the overlying level 10–20 cm below the surface extending to 330 cal. BP (ANU-10452). The stratigraphy and radiocarbon dates show that the relatively small and low shelter was first used late in prehistory around 750 cal. BP and was regularly visited from then on.

Volivoli II and III

The excavation in the narrow chamber of Volivoli II produced three samples of charcoal, which were dated. Two dates on samples from 30–40 cm and 50–60 cm were similar and had a range of 580–1300 ca. BP (ANU-10449, ANU-10451), while the other from 40–50 cm was older 1630–2040 cal. BP. (ANU-10450). It appears that despite the relatively clear stratigraphy recorded in excavation, the cultural deposit in the enclosed shelter space has been disturbed significantly.

Similar to other rock shelters, like Malaqereqere, Qaranioso I and II, and Tuvu, three age results from the Volivoli III site point to human use in the period 1200–1000 cal. BP. Two dates have almost identical CRAs and span 740–1170 cal. BP, although the charcoal was collected from 80–90 cm and 50–60 cm respectively (ANU-11019, ANU-11016), indicating either rapid deposit build-up, or the mixing of archaeological charcoals with older and younger deposits. The remaining result on charcoal collected from 20–30 cm depth had an age of 0–460 cal. BP (ANU-11018).

Tuvu

A single result on charcoal from a thin lens in Spit IV (30–40 cm) returned a calibrated age of 1180–1700 cal. BP (ANU-11020), with the large standard error of ±100 responsible for the substantial age range. The single date suggests people were using rock shelters in the middle reaches of the Sigatoka Valley towards the middle of the first millennium AD.

Qaranioso I and II

At the large cave known as Qaranioso I, a single ^{14}C date was obtained on charcoal collected from a small hearth at 30 cm depth. The result (ANU-11015) was an age of 920–1350 cal. BP. Excavation in the nearby but smaller cave called Qaranioso II revealed paddle-impressed and shell-stamped pottery in Layer 2 (14–49 cm), with bone of the extinct giant iguana in Layer 3 (50–65 cm). Giant-iguana bone was submitted for ^{14}C AMS dating to the Oxford University Radiocarbon Accelerator Unit. However, it proved to contain too little collagen for dating. A single result on charcoal from 30 cm depth had a recent age of 530–670 cal. BP (ANU-11014).

Natunuku

Excavations at Natunuku were in a disturbed area where early and late prehistoric remains had been mixed together in the surface zone of the coastal site. Species and context information for three samples (ANU-11305, ANU-11306, ANU-11307) was misplaced, and a sample origin in Trench 3 is the only provenance information available. Two dates on charcoal were modern (ANU-10382, ANU-10381), while six marine-shell determinations were prehistoric, similar to Ugaga, where ovens had introduced recent charcoal into the deposit, and the marine-shell ages were prehistoric. The oldest shell dates (ANU-11305, ANU-10698, ANU-11307) extend to the terminal phase of the Lapita era, but no determinations appear to date the earliest cultural remains reported from Natunuku (Davidson et al. 1990; Davidson and Leach 1993), which were encountered by us only in displaced contexts. The other three marine-shell results have a span of 160–890 cal. BP (ANU-10699, ANU-10700, ANU-11306). Pottery from the site is stylistically varied, with diagnostic sherds from all periods of the sequence.

Navatu 17A

Six charcoal and three marine-shell samples from Trench B, and one charcoal sample from Trench A were dated at the QDRC. Radiocarbon results given in Table 17 have a consistent age-with-depth relationship. Median dates from the upper Layer 1 indicate an age of 150–500 cal. BP (ANU-10385, ANU-10710, ANU-10389). Layer 2 has an age spread of approximately 480–910 cal. BP (ANU-10709, ANU-10384). Basal dates on charcoal and marine shell from Layer 4 indicate deposition between 1360 and 1710 cal. BP (ANU-10708, ANU-10386), but two charcoal dates from levels slightly above these dates are more recent and overlap with the Layer 2 determinations. These dates (ANU-10390, ANU-10387) are from the eastern B1+2 squares, while the earlier dates are from the down-slope B3+4 squares. It appears that cultural remains from the oldest Layer 4 occupation, dating to ca. 1500 cal. BP, were mixed, at least in the B1+2 area, with more recent remains with an age of 660–1350 cal. BP.

Thermoluminescence results

Six pot sherds and samples of surrounding soil were sent to Gillian Robertson (Department of Physics, University of Adelaide). Two plain sherds were found to be suitable for dating with the fine-grain thermoluminescence (TL) technique. Dose rates from radioactive elements in the sherds and surrounding soils were calculated from thick-source alpha counting of uranium and thorium, and from X-ray spectrometer analysis of potassium (Table 18). A contribution from cosmic rays was included in the calculation of total dose. The uranium and thorium concentrations are very low, as expected from previous experiences with South Pacific pottery. The potassium levels are also similar to other Fijian samples (Prescott et al. 1982). In calculating the dose rate it is necessary to take into account the water content of the site. At Navatu the samples were high in water content (22–24%). A decrease in water content would increase the dose rate, and thus the estimated age could be lower by a few percent than that quoted.

Even so, the TL ages appear too old compared with calibrated marine-shell and charcoal radiocarbon ages from similar contexts which do not overlap at two standard deviations. The discrepancy between the two dating techniques could be caused by the small quantity of quartz often present in Navatu and Fijian ceramics (Dickinson 1971; Prescott et al. 1982), and uncertainty over the water content of the Navatu 17A deposits during the period of burial. Whatever the reason for the discrepancy, the radiocarbon results are considered the more reliable age estimates.

Votua

Eight radiocarbon determinations on marine shell and charcoal from the 1996 excavations at Votua were reported in Clark et al. (2001), and another two dates were obtained on samples from Area 2 excavated in 2000. Table 17 lists the full set of Votua age results, which comprises seven marine shell and three charcoal dates. Determinations were on two shellfish species with different environmental preferences – with *Anadara antiquata* a common inhabitant of intertidal coral sand and *Trochus niloticus* associated with intertidal reef flats, and on unidentified wood charcoal. Seven ^{14}C ages indicate Lapita occupation at Votua between 2650 and 2800 cal. BP.

Two determinations have longer spans, with lower ranges extending to the period 2170–2470 cal. BP, but ANU-10706 on charcoal has a large standard error (±120 years), while ANU-11527 on *Anadara* intercepts a plateau on the marine calibration curve (Stuiver and Braziunas 1993:Figure 17F). Neither provides reliable evidence that occupation at Votua lasted several centuries. A third date on *Trochus niloticus* (ANU-11069A) has an age of 1900–2300 cal. BP. The sample came from within the Area 1 shell midden and is suspected to have been contaminated by younger carbonates that were not removed by the pretreatment process (A. Alimanovic, pers. comm., QDRC). The difference is not related to the effects of dietary variation between species because a 'B' sample of *Trochus* shell from the spit above ANU-11069A gave a CRA of 2990±60 BP (ANU-11069B).

The pooled mean for six marine-shell dates was 2940 BP, which has a calibrated range of 2680–2760 cal. BP. Two charcoal ages have a pooled mean of 2690 BP, and an age span of 2690–2850 cal. BP (p=0.83), which is almost identical to the calibrated age of the pooled marine-shell age.

Sovanibeka

There are three radiocarbon dates for Sovanibeka on three different types of material. The first was on a sample of *Anadara antiquata* taken from a bulk sample of Test Pit 2 material collected at 30–50 cm depth, which also produced a dentate-stamped sherd. This date (ANU-10779) has a calibrated age of 2360–2720 cal. BP, which overlaps with determinations from the nearby Votua site. The association of the shell sample with Lapita materials is unclear from the context and it might indicate later use of the cave after abandonment of the Votua site.

The second determination (ANU-11246) was on land-snail shell (*Gonatorhaphe lavensis*) from a Test Pit 1 bulk sample at the interface between an upper cultural-material/rat-bone deposit and the lower deposit of red silt with abundant land snails. The small number of land snails in the upper sediment suggests either that human activity impacted the local vegetation, or that the introduction of rats (*Rattus praetor* and *Rattus exulans*) in prehistory caused a decline in the number of land snails.

If the land-snail result was post-Lapita in age it might suggest the Votua occupation caused only minor vegetation modification in areas close to the Lapita occupation. Alternatively, an age result coterminous with Lapita settlement might indicate that widespread vegetation change occurred during the phase of initial settlement and extended beyond the immediate zone of occupation, indicating widespread clearing.

The sample of land-snail shell gave a CRA of 4290±60 BP, which does not provide a useful estimate for dating human impact on local vegetation. It is feasible that the age is too old because land snails living in the limestone chamber were absorbing old carbon in their diet. Dating of modern and prehistoric land snails suggests that species living in limestone areas are more likely to absorb old carbon than those living in non-limestone areas (e.g. Rafter et al. 1972; Goodfriend and Stipp 1983). The explanation for the early land-snail age advanced here is that either prehistoric human and rat activity in the chamber caused sediment compaction and mixing of cultural remains with those of land snails deposited in the mid-Holocene, or the land snails were absorbing old carbon from limestone.

The third determination was on a purified bone collagen from a rat humerus identified as *Rattus praetor*, the large spiny rat (K. Aplin, pers. comm., CSIRO). The humerus was recovered from Test Pit 1 at 50–60 cm depth in the transition zone between sediments containing cultural material and the underlying natural deposit. Rat bone in the size range of *Rattus praetor* was also found in the Votua excavations, but two samples submitted to ANSTO had insufficient collagen after pretreatment to obtain an AMS date. The calibrated result for OZF882 of 670–770 cal. BP is considerably later than anticipated and, if accurate, might suggest that *Rattus praetor* was a relatively late prehistoric arrival to Fiji, or that it was introduced in the Lapita phase and survived until the arrival of European rats in the early 19th century. An attempt to clarify whether rat arrival was coincident with Lapita expansion by AMS dating of two *Rattus praetor* bones recovered from the basal levels of the Navaprah site in Vanuatu (Bedford 2000) also failed due to low collagen yields. In short, although *Rattus praetor* remains have been identified in New Ireland, Reef/Santa Cruz Islands, Tikopia, Vanuatu and Fiji (White et al. 2000), it is unclear when the species first arrived in Fiji, how long it persisted, what impact the rat had on native fauna and flora, and when it became extinct.

Review of radiocarbon dates from Fiji

A goal of the EPF dating program was to establish whether evidence of human occupation older than Lapita culture could be identified in open sites and caves/rock shelters, and if it could not, to accurately date the Lapita phase in Fiji. A second objective examined the change from

Lapita-influenced ceramic assemblages to those with a distinctive Fijian character during the first millennium AD. The stylistic boundary between Lapita and post-Lapita pottery assemblages has been viewed as a formative period when traits characteristic of the late prehistoric period emerged in nascent form. These include an explicit concern with defence and territory, manifested by the development of constructed fortifications, cannibalism, agricultural intensification, craft specialisation and the movement of populations inland.

These topics have been to the forefront of archaeological research in the archipelago. They were first set out as three distinct issues in the 1960s by Bruce Palmer, Director of the Fiji Museum, and they continue to be important to prehistorians working in the Central Pacific. This is illustrated by considering the population of radiocarbon dates recovered from Fijian archaeological sites since the 1950s, a list compiled by recording the ^{14}C ages listed in theses, reports and publications. We recorded all results, including modern determinations, ages which have large standard errors, and dates on material of potentially high inbuilt age such as turtle bone, and have not evaluated the cultural association of the analysed samples, an issue we return to in our discussion of the Fiji radiocarbon sequence. Determinations on bulk palaeosol humin were omitted, as sediment antiquity may be different from the age of cultural material found in it.

The results reported in Table 19 include the majority of ^{14}C determinations from Fiji, and although a few results have no doubt been missed, the dates demonstrate a continuing concern with major aspects of Bruce Palmer's research agenda. When examined by geographic location, most of the CRAs are from the large island of Viti Levu. Elsewhere, there is a reasonable number of determinations from the Yasawa Islands, Taveuni and parts of the Lau Group. Island size is not correlated with the amount of research activity, and there are no age results from Vanua Levu and Kandavu, respectively the second and third-equal largest landmasses, or from substantial islands such as Vatulele. Within Viti Levu most determinations are from the southwest coast area where several Lapita and mid-sequence ceramics sites, in addition to fortifications in the Sigatoka Valley, were recorded by Palmer (1965, 1966, 1967, 1969). An absolute chronology for human occupation of the interior of large islands of Fiji in prehistory has received little attention, with the exception of Field's (2004) study of fortifications in the Sigatoka Valley.

Thesis and published research also divide neatly into Palmer's three research subjects, with the study of warfare, fortifications and socio-political complexity (Frost 1970; Clunie 1977; Best 1984; Parry 1987; Rechtman 1992; Cochrane 2004; Field 2004), mid-sequence ceramic and social change (Hunt 1980; Best 1984; DeGusta 1999; Clark 2000; Burley 2003, 2005), and the excavation and analysis of Lapita sites (Birks 1973; Mead et al. 1973; Best 1981, 1984; Kay 1984; Anderson and Clark 1999, Clark and Anderson 2001a). The radiocarbon results from the EPF, along with age determinations obtained in recent investigations, now make it practicable to revisit the chronology of these recognised inflection points in the Fijian sequence. Calibrated ages at 2SD for the ^{14}C results listed in Table 19 are shown in Figure 84. Excluded dates were those with a standard error larger than ±100 years, 'modern' results, CRAs with an age less than 110 BP, and land-snail shell dates. Removing these leaves a total of 281 radiocarbon results.

Lapita settlement of Fiji

The chronology of Lapita expansion is controlled at the regional level by the age of the oldest site on an island or archipelago, since colonising populations are by definition inherently mobile, and uninhabited landscapes, even those relatively poor in natural food resources, appear to offer few impediments to the spread of Neolithic populations (Clark et al. 2006). Kirch and Hunt (1988:24) argued that 'frequency distributions for dates from the eastern and westernmost

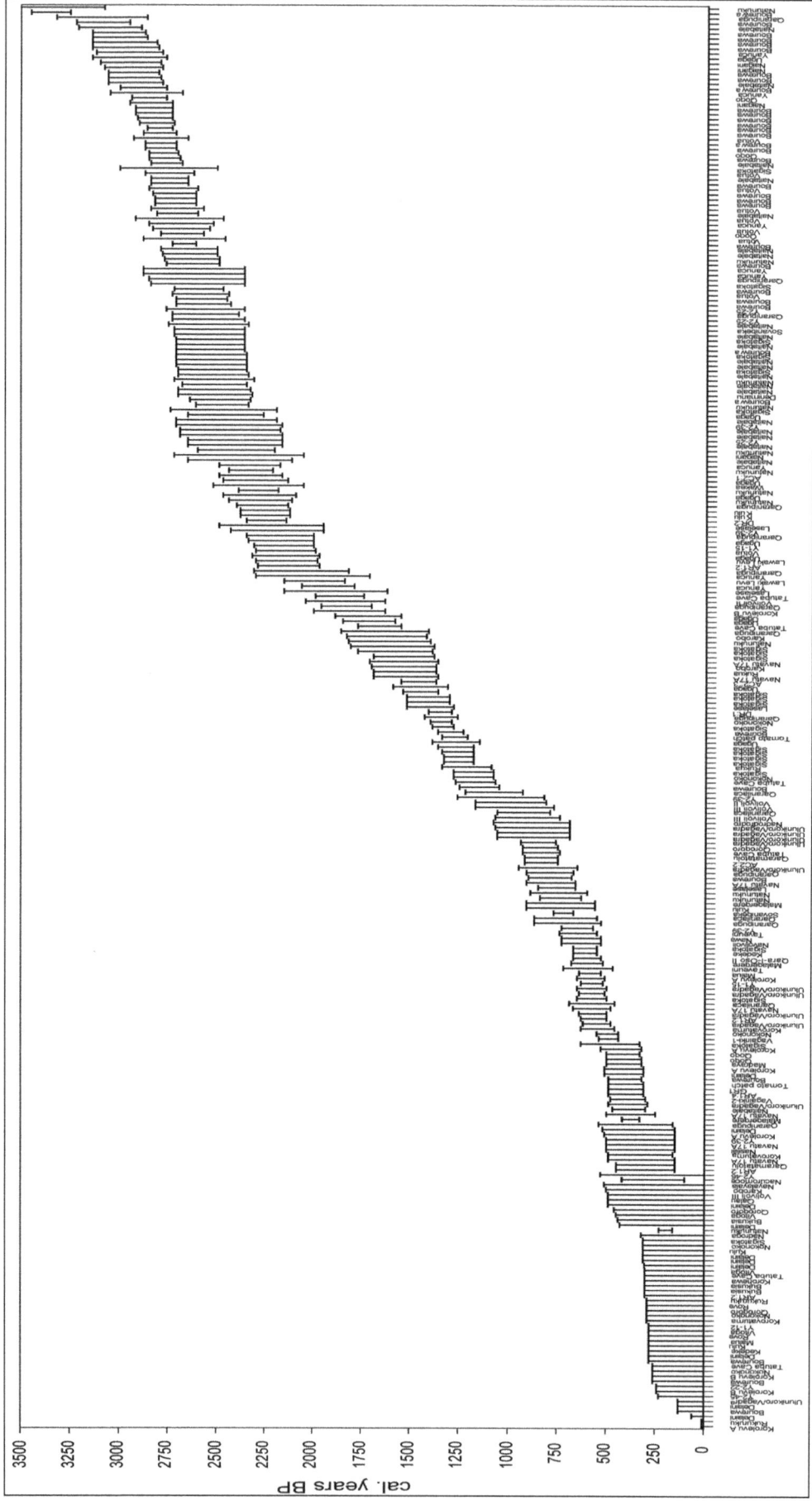

Figure 84. Calibrated ¹⁴C ages from archaeological sites in Fiji. Labels identify determination to a site, but the large number of analyses mean that site labels may be difficult to read. See Table 19 for further details of plotted radiocarbon results.

regions (Bismarcks and Fiji–Western Polynesia) displayed nearly identical ranges and modes', and that the Fijian radiocarbon ages on Lapita sites extended to about 3500 cal. BP. Spriggs (1990:19–20) in a critical review of available dates suggested that Fiji–West Polynesia was not occupied earlier than 3050 cal. BP, with the colonisation of Fiji later revised to 2800–2900 cal. BP from a survey of screened dates from Lapita sites (Anderson and Clark 1999).

The trend towards a more recent colonisation age reflected in the literature from the 1980s to the end of the 1990s began almost immediately to reverse, with the Yanuca Lapita site dated to 2950 cal. BP or older (Clark and Anderson 2001b), and reports that the newly discovered Lapita sites of Bourwea and Naitabale might date to 3220 cal. BP (Kumar et al. 2004; Nunn et al. 2004b). Such claims were given support by the revision of the age of the Nukuleka (TO.2) site in Tonga to ca. 2900 cal. BP (Burley and Dickinson 2001), and the possibility that the Teouma site in Vanuatu dated to 3200–3000 cal. BP (Bedford et al. 2006). The revised colonisation age for Fiji and neighbouring island groups to the east and west was intriguing, as the age of Lapita sites in the Bismarck Archipelago was previously argued to be no older than 3300–3200 cal. BP (Specht and Gosden 1997). If Lapita occupation of Fiji began at 3200 cal. BP, it would imply a very rapid spread of Lapita groups eastward to Vanuatu and Fiji by 3200 cal. BP, followed by a substantial and puzzling hiatus of around 200–300 years before settlement of New Caledonia and Tonga at 3000–2900 cal. BP (Sand 1997; Burley and Dickinson 2001).

Inspection of the oldest ^{14}C results from Fiji has determinations from eight locations with calibrated spans extending to 3000 cal. BP or older. Rejected from this set are Gak-1218 (3240±100 BP) from Natunuku (see Clark and Anderson 2001a), NZ-4594 (2960±70 BP) from Qaranipuqa, as it is out of sequence with other results, and Wk-17544 (3480±40 BP) from Bourewa which is significantly older than all other age results from the site. Single determinations on marine shell and charcoal from Ugaga Island, Sigatoka and Naitabale (Beta-107953, Wk-8239, Wk-11481) are also excluded, along with ANU-11414 (3150±60 BP) on *Batissa violacea*, a freshwater shellfish that may incorporate old carbon from dissolved limestone in its shell. The last five dates may in fact be accurate determinations, but individual results on material known to produce unreliable results, and samples of uncertain cultural association, are inadequate to establish the antiquity of human colonisation.

Remaining dates are ANU-11417 (3050±60 BP) from Yanuca on *Cyprea tigris*, excavated by Birks and Birks (1978), with a calibrated age span of 2680–3050 cal. BP, and four marine-shell dates from Naigani with a pooled CRA of 3110 BP, and a calibrated age of 2790–2980 cal. BP. The results suggest human arrival in the period ca. 3000–2900 cal. BP. Evidence for older occupation has recently been recorded from Bourewa, where there are eight dates indicating Lapita occupation in Fiji began before 3000 cal. BP. These include paired dates on charcoal from Unit 3 (Wk-14235, Wk-14236) and Unit X3 (Wk-17542, Wk-17937), and paired charcoal-marine shell results from Unit 4 (Wk-14237, Wk-14595). Although two early ages on marine shell were on small species (*Tellinidae* sp. and *Atacodea striata*) that are often found naturally deposited on beaches, the oldest CRA (Wk-14237) from Unit 4 is supported by Wk-14595 on charcoal from the same level. The six oldest charcoal determinations from Bourewa have a pooled CRA of 2894 BP and a 2SD age span of 2870–3080 cal. BP. The two oldest marine-shell dates have a pooled CRA of 3180 BP, and an almost identical range to the combined charcoal result of 2870–3090 cal. BP. A conservative interpretation of these dates, considering that the charcoal has not been identified to taxa, and the possibility that some marine shellfish have been wave deposited, suggests Lapita colonisation of Fiji in the period 2950–3050 cal. BP, rather than 3200 cal. BP.

Mid-sequence ceramic change

The three sites where some of the most important mid-sequence deposits in Fiji have been found – Sigatoka VL 16/1, Yanuca VL 16/81 and Natunuku VL 1/1 – were excavated initially because of the discovery of Lapita ceramics, and the mid-sequence materials recovered were used only to aid the establishment of a ceramic sequence. Initially described by Green (1963) as the Navatu phase (2100–900 BP), the mid-sequence was distinguished by a high proportion of relief-marked sherds (up to 50%), including cross-hatch or diamond relief, parallel rib and 'wavy' impressed sherds, with the proportion of relief-marked pottery declining by the end of the phase to approximately 20% of the assemblage.

Differences between Lapita and mid-sequence ceramics in vessel form and decoration were linked by Palmer (1965:33) to the Sa-Huynh-Kalanay ceramics of Southeast Asia. The makers of relief pottery were therefore identified as proto-Polynesians. Previously, Gifford and Shutler (1956) had noted the similarity between parallel-rib and cross-hatch relief sherds from New Caledonia and sherds from Fiji, and Garanger (1971:58) linked cord-impressed ceramics found on the Mele Plain on Efate Island in Vanuatu with two Fijian sherds impressed with woven fibre and excavated from Navatu 17A (Gifford 1951a). However, recent work has shown that the Mele Plain sherds were made in Japan and belong to the early Jomon tradition (Dickinson et al. 1999). Until the past decade, there have been few well-dated archaeological sites in Fiji, New Caledonia and Vanuatu with which to compare the antiquity of widespread decorative traits, and examine the similarities and differences among regional ceramic sequences.

A chronology of mid-sequence ceramic change was first proposed by Best (1984), who identified two points of stylistic change in Lakeba ceramics, which he interpreted as evidence for population movements from New Caledonia and Vanuatu. The first, emanating from New Caledonia at ca. 2100 cal. BP, introduced an ovoid vessel with sharply everted rims and square lips that was decorated with parallel-rib or cross-hatch relief markings. The second, at 1700 cal. BP, correlated with the appearance of minor decorative techniques such as asymmetric and fingernail incision, finger pinching, cord-wrapped paddle impressing and rim notching. These traits were seen as characteristic of Vanuatu ceramic traditions that had been introduced to Fiji.

Radiocarbon results from the EPF at the mid-sequence sites of Natatu 17A, Karobo and Ugaga also suggested a major ceramic change took place around 2300–1900 cal. BP, when the Lapita-derived ceramic trajectory was altered when jars and bowls marked with heavy parallel-relief impressions, dents and deep wiping appeared (Clark 2000). The dating of the transition was poorly focused, however, due to substantial site disturbance at Ugaga (Table 17), although the presence of mid-sequence ceramics dating to around 1500 cal. BP at Navatu 17A and Karobo indicated that ceramic change had occurred somewhat earlier.

Investigations at the Sigatoka Sand Dune by Burley (2003, 2005) revealed two distinct mid-sequence ceramic assemblages separated by a thin sand layer. The lower, termed 'Fijian Plainware', includes ovoid jars and decorative techniques of parallel and cross-hatch relief, punctate and lip notching. This assemblage is seen as having continuity in vessel form and technology with Lapita ceramics (Burley 2005:321). The upper ceramics, called 'Navatu', comprise globular jars with highly everted rims, lip notching, end-tool and side impressions, and fingernail pinching/gouging (see Chapter 12).

The 'Navatu' deposit at Sigatoka was dated by three ^{14}C results (CAMS-70090, CAMS-70091, CAMS-70920), with a pooled CRA of 1437 BP, calibrating to 1275–1340 cal. BP. Five results date the lower Fijian Plainware levels, with two determinations (CAMS-68195 and CAMS-70921) considered to be outliers (Burley 2005:325). The three oldest ^{14}C ages have a pooled age of 1570 BP, and an age range of 1335–1516 cal. BP, indicating a rapid transition to 'Navatu' pottery over a century. The presence of 'Navatu' pottery traits on Lakeba in east Fiji at 1700–1600 cal. BP, and the later arrival of these traits in north and south Viti Levu at about 1300 cal. BP is suggested to be the result of gradual east-to-west movement of 'Navatu'-related groups, or ceramic transmission from the Lau Group (Burley 2005:342). Additional examination of stylistic phases and ceramic transformation through ^{14}C dating mid-sequence deposits is particularly important for identifying the direction and extent of population movements within and beyond the Fiji Islands.

Fortifications and defensive sites

Studies have shown that the development of social complexity in Fiji was associated with the appearance of fortifications and horticultural intensification (Palmer 1969; Frost 1970; Parry 1987), with population growth and control over horticultural resources being key attributes that led to the 'classic' Fijian chiefdoms (Parry 1987; Field 2004). Establishing an absolute chronology for defensive sites provides a proxy for the broader socio-political and economic transformations in Fiji prehistory.

Radiocarbon dating of fortified sites suggests that most of those on Taveuni, Wakaya and Lakeba date to the past 700 years or less. On Taveuni, defensive sites like Navolivoli and Nawa were probably first used about 500–700 cal. BP (Gak-2411, Gak-2414), while those on Wakaya (Delaini and Korolevu) date slightly later to 500–300 cal. BP (Beta-45787, Beta-45790). The massive hill fort of Ulunikoro, located on a limestone plateau on Lakeba in the Lau Group, is older still, with CRAs on charcoal and marine shell (NZ-4044, NZ-4585, NZ-4586, NZ-4587, NZ-5180) indicating occupation at 800–1000 cal. BP. On Beqa Island, a very large fortification, also known as Korolevu, has been recorded, but according to Crosby (1988:236), it is probably less than 500 years old.

Fortifications, like most prehistoric structures built of earth and stone in the Central Pacific such as house mounds, tombs, walls and roads, are difficult to radiocarbon date because construction, use and reuse can incorporate samples of different ages in a structure. In addition, unmodified strategic locations used for defence and refuge are likely to have lower site visibility than sites associated with constructed defences. In a nuanced study of sites in the Sigatoka Valley, Field (2004, 2005) showed that natural defences such as large caves and remote peaks (Tatuba, Nokonoko) were used as territorial strongholds and refuges by 1400 cal. BP (AA-50287, AA-50283, AA-50298). The establishment of sites with constructed features on highly visible outcrops (Malua, Korovatuma) began at 500–600 cal. BP (AA-50295, AA-50300), with the emergence of new ring-ditch sites on the valley floor (Bukusia and Vitonga) at 150–350 cal. BP (AA-50309, AA-50302, AA-50304, Wk-11135).

The EPF dating program, while not aimed specifically at defensive sites, nonetheless investigated several rock shelters and deposits with a potential refuge/defensive aspect. Chief among these is the Navatu 17A site on the flanks of a volcanic plug, which was used as a refuge in the 19th century. The lowest cultural deposit included cannibalised human bone from the B3+4 square, and is dated to 1360–1710 cal. BP. The site position is not strongly defensive, but might have been chosen due to its proximity to a high refuge. The presence of cannibalism at Navatu supports Field's hypothesis that inter-group conflict was becoming more prevalent, and as a result, defensive considerations began to influence site location and position in the period 1000–1500 cal. BP. Interestingly, this is the period when Burley (2003, 2005) identifies a significant mid-sequence change in the ceramics and economy at the Sigatoka Sand Dunes, and Dickinson (2006:117–119) records several examples of long-distance ceramic transfer from Fiji to islands outside the archipelago.

Conclusion

The EPF resulted in reliable radiocarbon dates for the late-Lapita site at Votua, but at Natunuku, Ugaga and Kulu Bay, the antiquity of the oldest remains could not be determined due to redeposition and mixing of cultural material of different ages and the absence of dateable material at Qaranioso II. Deposits of mid-sequence age at Navatu 17A and Karobo were better delineated, and at Ugaga the majority of ^{14}C dates spanned 2500–1200 cal. BP, suggesting that many of the cultural remains from the island covered the late-Lapita to mid-sequence transition. Several rock shelters on Viti Levi (Malaqereqere, Volivoli II and III, Tuvu and Qaranioso II) were mainly used in the past 1000 years, with several of the cultural deposits including evidence for occasional use in late-Lapita (Qaranioso II) and mid-sequence (Volivoli II) times.

Combining the EPF determinations with those from recent and earlier studies showed that the earliest evidence for Lapita colonisation is at Bourewa in western Viti Levu, which is dated to 2950–3050 cal. BP. Other results from sites on Viti Levu and nearby islands such as Ugaga, Naigani, Yanuca and Naitabale suggest that Lapita groups were either highly mobile or relatively numerous, and both attributes may have been in play. While the size of the migrant population entering Fiji was sufficient to leave a presence on Viti Levu and nearby islands, the population does not appear to have reached the Lau Group until 2850–2900 cal. BP.

The intra-archipelago colonisation interval is significant, as it suggests that the presence of large islands like Viti Levu (10,947 sq. km) diverted human movement, for a time, away from long-distance expansion and instead towards coastal and inland exploration of a large island. One means of testing this hypothesis is to look at the southernmost islands of the Lau Group that are roughly equidistant from Viti Levu and Tonga. For instance, the ceramic and material-culture assemblages of Lapita sites on islands like those in the Ono-i-lau Group and Vatoa could show, when examined, a closer affinity to Tongan Lapita materials than to Lapita ceramics from western Fiji. Such a finding would be consistent with the independent colonisation of Tonga from a location like the Reef Santa Cruz Islands (Burley and Dickinson 2001), and the expansion of Lapita groups in Tonga to neighbouring and possibly unoccupied islands in the Lau Group. Similarly, if the oldest Lapita ceramics in southern Lau were shown to have an affinity with ceramics from other parts of Fiji, but dated 100–200 years later, it would indicate a noticeable decline in the dispersal rate of Lapita groups after human arrival in west Fiji. One outcome of such a finding would be that very different social and demographic conditions characterised the colonisation of west Fiji than the colonisation of east Fiji.

Dating the mid-sequence transition at the Sigatoka Sand Dunes indicates that stylistic change can occur rapidly over about century from ca. 1400–1300 cal. BP, which is significant, as the rate of ceramic change is frequently correlated in archaeology with major social change, particularly the arrival or influence of new populations (Hunt 1986). The ceramic record of the Fiji Islands, located on the ethnological border between Melanesia and Polynesia, has been scrutinised particularly for evidence of cultural intrusion (Clark 2003) because the people of Fiji have different physical characteristics from nearby populations in West Polynesia. It is important to note that while the rate of ceramic change appears to be rapid, radiocarbon dating of fortifications and habitation sites indicates that wider changes were occurring in Fijian society during the mid-sequence. These include the expansion of populations to the interior of large and small islands, the use of naturally defended locations, and the presence of cannibalism at ca. 1400 cal. BP. A significant episode of external population arrival and impact in Fiji has not been identified convincingly in the archaeological record, and several researchers have rejected migration as an explanation for the advent of fortifications, or the cause of stylistic change in pottery (Clark 2000; Cochrane 2004; Field 2004). This is an issue yet to be resolved (e.g. Chapter 12; Burley 2005).

The chronology of the Fiji sequence, although based on a relatively large number of ^{14}C results, has long focused on clarifying the temporal boundaries of three parts of the sequence (colonisation/mid-sequence/social complexity). As the above review shows, refinements to the absolute chronology have raised new questions about the pattern of Lapita dispersal, and have closed the gap between the timing of mid-sequence ceramic change and the advent of population expansion and territoriality, previously seen as distinct events separated by 500 or more years. Several major geographical and temporal gaps remain, with few intact assemblages from the interval 2500–1500 cal. BP adequately dated, and the possibility of regional variation in Fijian material culture still to be examined by the recovery of well-dated sequences from Vanua Levu and several other large islands that have yet to receive even cursory archaeological research. A number of recognised site types have also to be dated, such as the enigmatic *naga* enclosures (Palmer 1971), agricultural field systems (e.g. Kuhlken and Crosby 1999) and adze and flake quarries (see Chapter 14).

References

Anderson, A. and Clark, G. 1999. The age of Lapita settlement in Fiji. *Archaeology in Oceania* 34: 31–39.

Anderson, A., Roberts, R., Dickinson, W., Clark, G., Burley, D., De Biran, A., Hope, G. and Nunn, P. 2006. Times of sand: Sedimentary history and archaeology at the Sigatoka Dunes, Fiji. *Geoarchaeology* 21: 131–154.

Anderson, A., Clark, G. and Worthy, T. 2000. An inland Lapita site in Fiji. *Journal of the Polynesian Society* 109: 311–316.

Bedford, S.H. 2000. Pieces of the Vanuatu puzzle: Archaeology of the North, South and Centre. Unpublished PhD thesis, Australian National University, Canberra.

Bedford, S., Spriggs, M. and Regenvanu, R. 2006. The Teouma Lapita site and the early human settlement of the Pacific Islands. *Antiquity* 80: 812–828.

Best, S. 1981. Excavations at Site VL 21/5 Naigani Island, Fiji, a preliminary report. Department of Anthropology, University of Auckland.

Best, S. 1984. Lakeba: The prehistory of a Fijian Island. Unpublished PhD thesis, Department of Anthropology, University of Auckland.

Best, S. 1987. The Sigatoka dune burials (Site VL 16/1). Unpublished report to the Fiji Museum, Suva.

Birks, L. 1973. Archaeological excavations at Sigatoka dune site, Fiji. *Bulletin of the Fiji Museum* No.1.

Birks, L. and Birks, H. 1978. Archaeological excavations at site VL16/81, Yanuca Island, Fiji. *Oceanic Prehistory Records* No. 6. University of Auckland.

Burley, D. 1997. Archaeological research Sigatoka Sand Dune National Park. Unpublished report to the Fiji Museum, Suva.

Burley, D.V. 2003. Dynamic landscapes and episodic occupations: Archaeological interpretation and implications in the prehistory of the Sigatoka Sand Dunes. In: Sand, C. (ed), Pacific Archaeology: Assessments and prospects, pp. 307–315. Les Cahiers de l' Archéologie en Nouvelle-Calédonie Number 15, New Caledonia.

Burley, D.V. 2005. Mid-sequence archaeology at the Sigatoka Sand Dunes with interpretive implications for Fijian and oceanic culture history. *Asian Perspectives* 44: 320–348.

Burley, D.V. and Dickinson, W.R. 2001. Origin and significance of a founding settlement in Polynesia. *Proceedings of the National Academy of Sciences of the USA* 98: 11829–11831.

Clark, G. 2000. Post-Lapita Fiji: Cultural transformation in the Mid-sequence. Unpublished PhD thesis, Australian National University, Canberra.

Clark, G. 2003. Shards of meaning: Archaeology and the Melanesia–Polynesia distinction. *Journal of Pacific History* 38: 197–213.

Clark, G. and Sorovi-Vunidilo, T. 1999. Fijian double-spouted vessels. *Domodomo* 11: 6–14.

Clark, G. and Anderson, A. 2001a. The pattern of Lapita settlement in Fiji. *Archaeology in Oceania* 36: 77–88.

Clark, G. and Anderson, A. 2001b. The age of the Yanuca Lapita site, Viti Levu, Fiji. *New Zealand Journal of Archaeology* 22: 15–30.

Clark, G., Anderson, A. and Matararaba, S. 2001. The Lapita site at Votua, northern Lau Islands, Fiji. *Archaeology in Oceania* 36: 134–145.

Clark, G and Hope, G. 2001. Archaeological and palaeoenvironmental investigations on Yacata Island, northern Lau, Fiji. *Domodomo* 13: 29–47.

Clark, G., Anderson, A. and Wright, D. 2006. Human colonization of the Palau Islands, western Micronesia. *Journal of Island and Coastal Archaeology* 1: 215–232.

Clark, J.T. and Cole, A.O. 1997. Environmental change and human prehistory in the Central Pacific: Archaeological and palynological investigations on Totoya Island, Fiji. Report to the Fiji Museum, Suva.

Clunie, F. 1977. Fijian weapons and warfare. *Bulletin of the Fiji Museum* No. 2.

Cochrane, E.C. 2004. Explaining cultural diversity in ancient Fiji: The transmission of ceramic variability. Unpublished PhD thesis, University of Hawaii.

Crosby, A. 1988. Beqa: archaeology, structure and history in Fiji. Unpublished MA thesis, Department of Anthropology, University of Auckland.

Davidson, J., Hinds, E., Holdaway, S. and Leach, F. 1990. The Lapita site of Natunuku, Fiji. *New Zealand Journal of Archaeology* 12: 121–155.

Davidson, J. and Leach, F. 1993. The chronology of the Natunuku site, Fiji. *New Zealand Journal of Archaeology* 15: 99–105.

De Biran, A. 2001. The Holocene geomorphic evolution of the Sigatoka Delta, Viti Levu, Fiji Islands. Unpublished PhD thesis, University of the South Pacific, Suva, Fiji Islands.

DeGusta, D. 1999. Fijian cannibalism: Osteological evidence from Navatu. *American Journal of Physical Anthropology* 110: 215–241.

Dickinson, W.R. 1971. Petrography of some sand tempers in prehistoric pottery from Viti Levu, Fiji. Final report No. 2. *Records of the Fiji Museum* 1: 108–121.

Dickinson, W.R. 2006. *Temper sands in prehistoric Oceanian pottery: Geotectonics, sedimentology, petrography, provenance*. The Geological Society of America Special Paper 406.

Dickinson, W.R., Burley, D.V., Nunn, P.D., Anderson, A., Hope, G., De Biran, A., Burke, C. and Matararaba, S. 1998. Geomorphic and archaeological landscapes of the Sigatoka Dune site, Viti Levu, Fiji: Interdisciplinary investigations. *Asian Perspectives* 37: 1–31.

Dickinson, W.R., Sinoto, Y. H., Shutler, R. Jr., Shutler, M.E., Garanger, J. and Teska, T.H. 1999. Japanese Jomon sherds in artifact collections from Mele Plain on Efate in Vanuatu. *Archaeology in Oceania* 34: 15–24.

Field, J.S. 2004. Environmental and climatic considerations: A hypothesis for conflict and the emergence of social complexity in Fijian prehistory. *Journal of Anthropological Archaeology* 23: 79–99.

Field, J.S. 2005. Land tenure, competition and ecology in Fijian prehistory. *Antiquity* 79: 586–600.

Frost, E.L. 1970. Archaeological excavations of fortified sites on Taveuni, Fiji. Unpublished PhD thesis, University of Oregon.

Frost, E.L. 1979. Fiji. In: Jennings, J.D. (ed), *The prehistory of Polynesia*, pp. 61–81. Australian National University Press.

Garanger, J. 1971. Incised and applied-relief pottery, its chronology and development in southeastern

Melanesia, and extra areal comparisons. In: Green, R.C. and Kelly M. (eds), *Studies in Oceanic Culture History volume 2*, pp. 53–99. Pacific Anthropological Records No. 12.

Gifford, E.W. 1951a. Archaeological excavations in Fiji. *University of California Anthropological Records* 13: 189–288.

Gifford, E.W. 1951b. Six Fijian radiocarbon dates. *Journal of the Polynesian Society* 64: 240.

Gifford, E.W. and Shutler, D. Jr. 1956. Archaeological excavations in New Caledonia. *Anthropological Records* 18, No. 1. University of California Press, Berkeley and Los Angeles.

Green, R.C. 1963. A suggested revision of the Fiji sequence. *Journal of the Polynesian Society* 72: 235–253.

Goodfriend, G.A. and Stipp, J.J. 1983. Limestone and the problem of radiocarbon dating land-snail shell carbonate. *Geology* 11: 575–577.

Hughen, K.A., Baillie, M.G.L., Bard, E., Bayliss, A., Beck, J.W., Bertrand, C., Blackwell, P.G., Buck, C.E., Burr, G., Cutler, K.B., Damon, P.E., Edwards, R.L., Fairbanks, R.G., Friedrich, M., Guilderson, T.P., Kromer, B., McCormac, F.G., Manning, S., Bronk Ramsey, C., Reimer, P.J., Reimer, R.W., Remmele, S., Southon, J.R., Stuiver, M., Talamo, S., Taylor, F.W., Plicht, J. van der and Weyhenmeyer C.E. 2004. Marine04 marine radiocarbon age calibration 26–0 ka BP. *Radiocarbon* 46: 1059–1086.

Hunt, T.L. 1980. Toward Fiji's past; archaeological research on southwestern Viti Levu. Unpublished MA thesis, University of Auckland.

Hunt, T.L. 1986. Conceptual and substantive issues in Fijian prehistory. In: Kirch, P.V. (ed), *Archaeological approaches to evolution and transformation*, pp. 20–32. Cambridge University Press, Cambridge.

Jones, S., Steadman, D.W. and O'Day, P.M. 2007. Archaeological investigations on the Small Islands of Aiwa Levu and Aiwa Lailai, Lau Group Fiji. *Journal of Island and Coastal Archaeology* 2: 72–98.

Kay, R. 1984. Analysis of archaeological material from Naigani. Unpublished MA thesis, University of Auckland.

Kirch, P.V. and Hunt, T.L. 1988. The spatial and temporal boundaries of Lapita. In: Kirch, P.V. and Hunt, T.L. (eds), *Archaeology of the Lapita cultural complex: A critical review*, pp. 9–32. Thomas Burke Memorial Washington State Museum Research Report No. 5. Seattle: The Burke Museum.

Kuhlken, R. and Crosby, A. 1999. Agricultural terracing at Nakauvadra, Viti Levu: A late prehistoric irrigated agrosystem in Fiji. *Asian Perspectives* 38: 62–89.

Kumar, R., Nunn, P.D., Katayama, K., Oda, H., Matararaba, S. and Osborne, T. 2004. The earliest-known humans in Fiji and their pottery: The first dates from the 2002 excavations at Naitabale (Nartururuku), Moturiki Island. *South Pacific Journal of Natural Science* 22: 15–21.

Kumar, R., Nunn, P.D., Field, J. and De Biran, A. 2006. Human response to climate change around AD 1300: A case study of the Sigatoka Valley, Viti Levu Island, Fiji. *Quaternary International* 151: 133–143.

Leach, F., Quinn, C., Morrison, J. and Lyon, G. 2001. The use of multiple isotope signatures in reconstructing prehistoric human diet from archaeological bone from the Pacific and New Zealand. *New Zealand Journal of Archaeology* 23: 31–98.

McCormac, F.G., Hogg, A.G., Blackwell, P.G., Buck, C.E., Higham, T.F.G. and Reimer, P.J. 2004. SHCal04 Southern Hemisphere Calibration 0–11.0 cal kyr BP. *Radiocarbon* 46: 1087–1092.

Mead, S.M., Birks, L., Birks, H. and Shaw, E. 1973. The decorative system of the Lapita potters of Sigatoka, Fiji. *Journal of the Polynesian Society Memoir Supplement* 82: 1–43, 44–98.

Nunn, P.D., Matararaba, S., Ishimura, T., Kumar, R. and Nakoro, E. 2004a. Reconstructing the Lapita-era geography of Northern Fiji: A newly discovered Lapita site on Yadua Island and its implications. *New Zealand Journal of Archaeology* 26: 41–55.

Nunn, P.D., Kumar, R., Matararaba, S., Ishimura, T., Seeto, J., Rayawa, S., Kuruyawa, S., Nasila, A., Oloni, B., Ram, A.R., Saunivalu, P., Sing, P and Tegu, E. 2004b. Early Lapita settlement site at Bourewa, southwest Viti Levu Island, Fiji. *Archaeology in Oceania* 39: 139–143.

Nunn, P.D., Pepe, C., Matararaba, S., Kumar, R., Sing, P., Nakoro, E., Gwilliam, M., Heorake, T., Kuilanisautabu, L., Nakoro, E., Narayan, L., Pastorizo, M.A., Robinson, S., Saunivalu, P. and Tamani, F. 2005. Human occupations of caves of the Rove Peninsula, southwest Viti Levu Island, Fiji. *South Pacific Journal of Natural Science* 23: 16–23.

Nunn, P.D., Matararaba, S., Kumar, R., Pene, C., Yuen, L., Pastorizo, M.A. 2006. Lapita on an island in the mangroves? The earliest human occupation at Qoqo Island, Southwest Viti Levu, Fiji. *Archaeology in New Zealand* 49: 205–212.

O'Day, S. Jones, O'Day, P., and Steadman, D.W. 2003. Defining the Lau context: Recent findings on Nayau, Lau Islands, Fiji. *New Zealand Journal of Archaeology* 25: 31–56.

Palmer, B. 1965. Excavations at Karobo, Viti Levu. *New Zealand Archaeological Association Newsletter* 8: 26–33.

Palmer, B. 1966. Lapita style potsherds from Fiji. *Journal of the Polynesian Society* 75: 373–377.

Palmer, B. 1967. Sigatoka research project. *New Zealand Archaeological Association Newsletter* 10: 2–15.

Palmer, B. 1969. Ring-ditch fortifications on windward Viti Levu, Fiji. *Archaeology and Physical Anthropology in Oceania* 4: 181–197.

Palmer, B. 1971. Naga ceremonial sites in the Navosa Upper Sigatoka valley. Final Report No. 1. *Records of the Fiji Museum* 5: 92–106.

Parry, J. 1987. The Sigatoka valley – pathways into prehistory. *Bulletin of the Fiji Museum* No. 9.

Petchey, F. 1995. Archaeology of Kudon: Archaeological analysis of Lapita ceramics from Mulifanua, Samoa and Sigatoka, Fiji. Unpublished MA thesis, Department of Anthropology, University of Auckland.

Prescott, J.R., Robertson, G.B. and Green, R.C. 1982. Thermoluminescence dating of Pacific island pottery: Successes and failures. *Archaeology in Oceania* 17: 142–147.

Rafter, T.A., Jansen, H.S., Lockerbie, L. and Trotter, M.M. 1972. New Zealand radiocarbon reference standards. In: Rafter, T.A. and Grant-Taylor, T. (eds), *Proceedings of the Eighth International Radiocarbon Dating Conference*, pp. 625–668. Royal Society of New Zealand, Wellington.

Rechtman, R.B. 1992. *The evolution of socio-political complexity in the Fiji Islands*. PhD thesis, Ann Arbor, Michigan.

Rosenthal, M.E. 1995. The archaeological excavation of an outrigger canoe from the Nasilai site, Rewa Delta, Viti Levu, Fiji. *Asian Perspectives* 34: 91–118.

Sand, C. 1997. The chronology of Lapita ware in New Caledonia. *Antiquity* 71: 539–547.

Sand, C. and Valentin, F. 1997. Cikobia et Naqelelevu. Programme archeologique et anthropologique sur deux iles de Fidje. Resultats preliminaires de la mission 1997. Noumea, New Caledonia.

Specht, J. and Gosden, C. 1997. Dating Lapita pottery in the Bismarck Archipelago, Papua New Guinea. *Asian Perspectives* 36(2): 175–199.

Spriggs, M. 1990. Dating Lapita: another view. In Spriggs, M. (ed), *Lapita design, form and composition*, pp. 83–122. Occasional Papers in Prehistory, No. 20. Canberra, Department of Prehistory, Australian National University.

Stuiver, M. and Braziunas, T.F. 1993. Modeling atmospheric 14C influences and 14C ages of marinesamples to 10,000 BC. *Radiocarbon* 35: 137-189.

Stuiver, M. and Reimer, P.J. 1993. Extended 14C data base and revised CALIB 3.0 14C age calibration program. *Radiocarbon* 35: 215–230.

Thomas, F.R., Nunn, P.D., Osborne, T., Kumar, R., Areki, F., Matararaba, S., Steadman, D. and Hope G. 2004. Recent archaeological findings at Qaranilaca Cave, Vanuabalavu Island, Fiji. *Archaeology in Oceania* 39: 42–49.

Toggweiler, J.R., Dixon, K. and Broecker, W.S. 1991. The Peru upwelling and the ventilation of the South Pacific thermocline. *Journal of Geophysical Research* 96: 467–497.

White, P.J., Clark, G. and Bedford, S. 2000. Distribution, present and past, of *Rattus praetor* in the Pacific and its implications. *Pacific Science* 54: 105–117.

8

Molluscan remains from Fiji

Katherine Szabó
Archaeology and Natural History, The Australian National University

Introduction

Shell recovered from archaeological sites can give valuable insight to issues of site formation, taphonomy, subsistence, the nature of the environment and environmental change over time. Here, I present a series of shell analyses that can assist in the investigation of several research issues, focusing primarily on ecological issues.

The primary concern is the interaction of prehistoric Fijians with their environment. Firstly, the shell assemblages will be used to give a general idea of the structure and nature of exploited ecological zones. Once this has been established, the species diversity of each assemblage, coupled with an assessment of the relative importance of various exploited species, is used to understand how Fijians went about selecting and procuring molluscs in the past. Approaches to harvesting wild resources have wide-ranging and varied impacts on local environments that may in turn force change in human exploitation tactics. However, change in patterns of environmental exploitation need not stem from an environmental stimulus. These issues will be considered on an assemblage-by-assemblage basis.

Background to the samples

The molluscan remains discussed in this chapter derive from 11 sites. These are Natunuku, Votua (1996), Kulu, Navatu, Malaqereqere, Ugaga, Qaranioso I and II, Volivoli II and III, and Tuvu. Archaeological sediments were screened through 3 mm or 4 mm mesh, and, at all but two sites (Qaranioso I and II), all recovered shell material was retained for further analysis. The first exception is the sample derived from the Qaranioso II rock shelter, where most marine shell was discarded (Anderson et al. 2000:312). The second site where shell was not retained was Qaranioso I, where excavations recovered only sparse *Anadara* and *Turbo*, with only two shell fragments present in the analysed sample (see below).

The sites analysed are of different types and ages, and are located within varied landscapes.

It cannot be expected that assemblages will be patterned in the same way or reflect the same approach to mollusc exploitation. In each case, the surrounding environment and the nature of the site itself (e.g. open/rock shelter, coastal/inland) were taken into account. There are also considerable differences in sample size (Table 20), and some differences in sample retention that require further discussion. Each sample is briefly reviewed below.

Natunuku

The molluscan assemblage from the Lapita site of Natunuku is one of the largest under discussion, totalling 58.2 kg. Unlike many of the other samples considered, Natunuku is located near a muddy estuary and this location is clearly reflected in the nature of the shell sample. Three excavations were made at Natunuku, with the first two showing clear signs of disturbance through grave-digging and other processes (see Chapter 6). Trench 3 was a larger excavation with a correspondingly larger shell sample. Despite localised disturbance, it most likely provides the best sample of Lapita-age shellfish from Natunuku, and shell material from Trench 3 is used in the following discussions. Preliminary results of shell analysis for this site were presented in Szabó (2001), but have been revised and expanded.

Votua

Molluscan shell samples were analysed from both Test Pit 1 and Area 1 adjacent to the Tokelau Stream, excavated in 1996. As previously pointed out by Clark et al. (2001:138), Area 1 has very dense deposits of shellfish, and despite only reaching a maximum depth of 70 cm in this area, more than 109 kg of shell was recovered. A second season of excavation in 2000 recovered more than 50 kg of shell for each 1 m square excavated in Area 2. These samples were processed on-site and this assemblage is not discussed further.

Kulu Bay

The Kulu Bay open site produced a total shell sample of 11.6 kg. As discussed in Chapter 5, the material excavated at Kulu has probably been redeposited and represents multiple prehistoric phases. Nevertheless, the Kulu sample remains interesting in its diversity, although shell preservation is extremely poor. Despite an interpretation of redeposition, it is interesting

Table 20. Total shell sample weights recovered from EPF archaeological sites.

Site	Weight (g) rounded to nearest gram	Number of species represented
Natunuku	58,235	143
Ugaga (sub-sample)	17,255	121
Malaqereqere	13,669	110
Volivoli II	6,399	107
Votua (first season only)	109,092	100
Kulu	11,569	92
Navatu	11,034	56
Volivoli III	920	29
Qaranioso I	23	Selective sample only
Qaranioso II	786	23
Tuvu	21	1

Navatu

All shell material for Navatu derives from the Trench B excavations, with a total sample weight of just over 11 kg. A complete sequence is represented from the surface to a depth of 260 cm. This maximum depth for shellfish remains within the sample was in the basal Layer 4 deposit but shell from this layer was 'chalky' and did not survive. Molluscan remains are generally sparse and highly fragmentary below 90 cm depth, and discussion necessarily centres on the shell recovered from Layers 1 and 2. As at Natunuku, the closest coast is mangrove-dominated and this is reflected in the molluscan sample.

Volivoli II and III

No shell from Volivoli I was analysed, but samples were examined from the Volivoli II and III rock shelters. Volivoli II was the larger of the two samples, with 6.4 kg of shell, much of which was composed of fragile land-snail remains. The Volivoli III shell sample totalled 920 g, but land-snail remains were absent. While details of the substantial land-snail component in the Volivoli II sample will be discussed in greater detail below, the major question concerning the presence of land snails is whether they represent natural introductions or cultural refuse. Most of the land-snail species in Volivoli II remain unidentified for want of comparative material, but the three major species were identified from comparison with material held at the Netherlands Museum of Natural History (Naturalis) in Leiden.

Malaqereqere

The Malaqereqere rock shelter excavations yielded a 13.7 kg sample of molluscan remains, along with plentiful remains of decapod crustacea and echinoderm spines. While the crab remains, including dactyls, chelipeds and fragments of carapace and legs, were not analysed in any detail, initial sorting identified at least 27 different crab taxa. The absence of reference material precluded further serious analysis. It should also be noted that the abundance of crab holes through the Malaqereqere deposits (see Chapter 5) makes it likely that at least some of the crab remains relate to post-depositional disturbance, rather than being evidence of prehistoric subsistence.

Ugaga

The large shell sample from the Ugaga site corresponds to the scale of excavations conducted at the site (see Chapter 5). Although total weights for the shell sample were not taken, it is safe to say the Ugaga sample is the largest within this project. For the sake of practicality, the shell was sub-sampled, with a total of 17.26 kg studied. This total represents all excavated shell from squares -A13, C12, D12, I5 and P10, with C12 and D12 being contiguous squares. As outlined in Chapter 5, squares -A13, C12 and D12 were excavated to below cultural levels to ensure the base of the cultural layer had been reached.

Qaranioso I and II

As outlined in Chapter 5, excavations at Qaranioso I yielded sparse molluscan remains, with the presence of *Anadara* and *Turbo* being noted on site. Only two fragments of shell were retained from these excavations: a fragment of unidentified *Strombus* sp. and a single *Batissa violacea* valve. This being the case, the shell sample from this site will not be discussed further. Qaranioso II yielded 786 g of shell, which seems to be a selective sample. Five fragments of unidentified crab were also present in the sample.

Tuvu

Only four fragments of shell, all deriving from the freshwater bivalve *Batissa violacea*, were recovered from the excavations at Tuvu. Whether these fragments represent subsistence refuse, discarded expedient tools, or both is unclear. Due to the small sample size, this site will not be discussed further.

Methodology and approach

The level and extent of identifications were considered important for this study, as ecological differences within families and even genera can affect overall interpretations of human gathering practices. Shells were identified using the personal collection of the author, as well as a range of literature sources, including Cernohorsky (1972, 1978), Abbot and Dance (1982), Hinton (1972), Dance (1977), Kira (1965) and Habe (1964). All shells and shell fragments were identified to the lowest possible taxonomic level. However, care was also taken not to over-identify, so that where a fragment itself only had defining characteristics to genus level, it was not assumed that this was part of a dominant species group already identified within the sample. For example, although *Lambis lambis* was the only species from genus *Lambis* readily identifiable within the samples, fragments that were clearly genus *Lambis* but, due to factors such as size or condition, did not carry specific diagnostic traits of *Lambis lambis*, were only identified to genus level. This was done so as to record ambiguities within the datasets and to minimise methodological assumptions.

An effort was made to identify all shell within the samples, with no assumptions made about the size or condition of the fragment or assumed 'edibility' of the species. Given that the interest was in the range of species collected rather than establishing economic species *per se*, even species represented only by a single individual were not assumed at the outset to be unimportant or incidental. From a gathering-strategy perspective, even specimens collected secondarily or unintentionally can contribute to an understanding of how gatherers interacted with the environment. In addition, analysis of anything less than every shell in the sample would necessarily prohibit questions regarding whether a gathering strategy was fine or coarse grained.

Three modes of quantification were used for all samples: minimum number of individuals (MNI); number of identified specimens present (NISP) and shell weights. There has been considerable discussion in the literature regarding the relative merits of MNI and NISP techniques (e.g. Mason et al. 1998, 2000; Claassen 2000; Glassow 2000), with a number of important issues raised. NISP is essentially a fragment count of all identifiable pieces of shell, regardless of size or completeness. Thus, issues attached to this quantification method include differential fragmentation between taxa caused by varying degrees of shell robustness, meat-extraction techniques applied to particular taxa, fragmentation associated with shell reduction for artefact production, and variable responses to the action of taphonomic processes.

In short, differences between the gross abundance of fragments of identified taxa may mean a number of things. The MNI technique overcomes these issues by counting a single, non-repetitive element consistently throughout a site or stratigraphic layer. The single major problem with MNI quantification – as outlined by Grayson (1984:29–49) – is termed 'division in aggregates'. This applies when arbitrary spits are treated as stratigraphic units by the analyst, and the consistently counted element selected is different between spits, which can serve to inflate counts. For example, if nine spires and four apertures of a *Turbo setosus* are counted in one spit, and two spires and eight apertures in the next spit, the MNI is not 17 unless these two spits represent separate stratigraphic units. If the division between spits is simply arbitrary, the MNI will be 12 on the basis of the higher aperture count.

With fewer parts, the 'division into aggregates' argument is less of an issue with molluscan shell than it is with the quantification of vertebrate faunas, but it is nevertheless desirable to quantify within stratigraphic units. In the assemblages discussed here, details of stratigraphy were not always known at the time of analysis. Thus, quantified elements for particular species remained constant throughout the analysis of shell from each site. In choosing elements for counting, a number of factors were taken into account. For gastropods, apertures tend to be more identifiable than spires, thus for the majority of gastropods, MNI counts refer to aperture frequencies. However, if assemblages are highly fragmented, apertures are frequently broken. In light of this, *whole* apertures did not form the basis of quantification, but rather the sturdy inner edge of the aperture that represents the anterior portion of the columella. For bivalves, both left and right hinges were counted, and the higher number was taken for either stratigraphic units (where known), or the entire assemblage (where stratigraphic units were unknown). This approach to MNI could well have resulted in the underestimate of abundance, but cannot have overestimated species abundance.

NISP counts were also made for a variety of reasons. Firstly, species represented by one or a few fragments may be simply reduced to 'present' within MNI counts – particularly if only body fragments are present, or there are otherwise few or no easily countable elements. Secondly, the comparison of MNI and NISP totals can give clear insights into differential fragmentation between taxa. If specimens are whole, ratios will be 1:1 for gastropods and 1:2 for bivalves. However, high levels of fragmentation will result in a high NISP count relative to the MNI count. Such situations may point to deliberate cultural fragmentation of particular taxa, related to processes such as meat extraction or shell working.

Quantification by weight is problematic with shell for two main reasons. The first is that shell robusticity is not necessarily tied either to shell size or meat weight. Thus, some large meaty molluscs (e.g. *Tonna perdix*) have very frail shells, and smaller shells (e.g. *Drupa morum*, *Cantharus undosus*) may be robust and relatively heavy. Secondly, processes such as burning and leaching can drastically reduce the weight of a shell. Although weights have been taken for all taxa/spit categories here, the only weight values discussed are total assemblage weights relative to each other, and even these should be treated with some caution.

For all assemblages, condition of the shell was noted. This not only relates to the condition of preservation, but to human variables such as burning and observed meat-extraction patterns. It further includes the alteration of shells by natural processes. Any shells that were observed to be introduced to deposits post-mortem, through the recording of indicators such as beach-rolling and sponge-boring and epibiont adhesions (such as worm-casts and barnacles) on the inner surfaces, were excluded from quantifications.

Given the geographic spread of the samples under consideration here, investigating issues of change over time seemed unviable, although where clearly stratified sequences exist (e.g. Volivoli II), such issues receive consideration. Rather, the overall thrust of the questioning here relates to how ancient Fijians – at different times and in different locales – interacted with the aquatic environment through shellfish gathering. It has often been assumed that shell-gathering practices target the largest individuals or species (e.g. Kress 2000: 295–296; see Allen 2003 for a general discussion). While there have been occasions where this has been demonstrated (e.g. Anderson 1981), results have also sometimes diverged from this expectation (e.g. Szabó 1999). I am reluctant to follow Allen's (2003) suggestion that a prey-choice model (*sensu* Broughton

1999) be applied at the outset, as experience suggests that assumptions often lead to an analytical, or indeed on-site sampling, bias where smaller or seemingly insignificant taxa are sidelined or ignored altogether.

Taking a different starting point, the principal question asked here of each assemblage is *how* ancient Fijians exploited molluscan resources, without underlying assumptions or expectations as to what is expected according to a particular model. Is there a noticeable focus on particular taxa, size or age classes? Do these patterns change over time or between collecting environments? Are multiple niches being exploited simultaneously? Through an analysis of the samples treated here, the aim is to examine the selectiveness or otherwise of Fijian shellfish-gathering strategies.

Results

The results of shell analysis for each site will be presented first, as many have their own particular issues and complexities. Following this, the results will be considered in the discussion.

Natunuku

As outlined above, the discussion of molluscan remains recovered from the Natunuku site relies largely on results from the major Trench 3 excavations. Trench 3 yielded a total of 5978 individuals (MNI) across 109 different molluscan species. A further 34 species were identified from areas other than Trench 3, bringing the total number of species for Natunuku to 143. Figure 85 shows the spread of all taxa represented by 20 or more individuals (MNI) within the Trench 3 sample. While *Anadara antiquata* is dominant, both *Gafrarium tumidum* and the small upper-intertidal rocky shore gastropod *Planaxis sulcatus* are strongly represented. A range of hard and soft-shore species are represented in much lower numbers. The spread of individuals derived from different niches is shown in Figure 86.

When the results of analysis for the Natunuku molluscan sample were originally published (Szabó 2001), the spread and relative proportions of taxa were interpreted within a framework of 'target species'. These included *primary species* that were interpreted as being the major focus of interest in gathering forays, *secondary species* that would be collected if encountered in the search for primary species, and *incidental species* that were seen as being the 'by-catch' or those species accidentally gathered or introduced into deposits. In light of additional analysis of shell-midden material from Fiji and elsewhere, this remains one of two likely interpretations for the wide diversity of species that contribute to overall assemblages. The other interpretation is that there was very low selectivity in the gathering process. This latter interpretation is now considered more likely, for one reason in particular: in addition to a high level of species diversity, all the Fijian middens studied showed little discrimination as to the size of individuals selected. Thus, even in early sites such as Natunuku where very large individuals of various species are present, juvenile and sub-adult specimens are also a notable component of the assemblage. There appears to be no chronological patterning to size-classes represented, with large and small specimens being taken simultaneously throughout the prehistoric sequence. This is amply demonstrated in Figures 87 and 88, which show the anterior-posterior measurements for all *Anadara antiquata* and *Gafrarium tumidum* valves complete along this axis from Trench 3.

When the results of quantification for Trench 3 and the Natunuku site as a whole are compared, it is apparent that there is some level of intra-site variation in the distribution of molluscan taxa (compare Figure 89 with Figure 85). Rocky-shore taxa, such as *Saccostrea cucullata*, *Planaxis sulcatus* and *Clypeomorus traillii*, are better represented in areas outside Trench 3, while, correspondingly, soft-shore taxa are slightly more prevalent in Trench 3. Also,

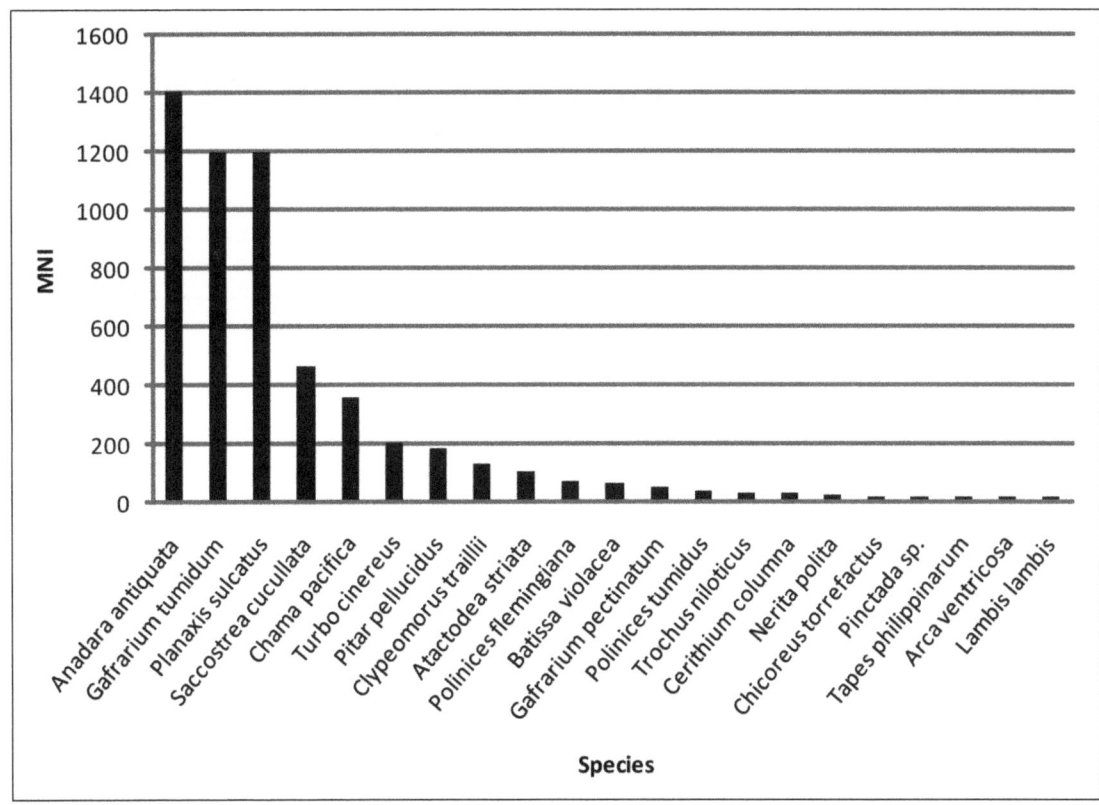

Figure 85. Mollusc species from Natunuku, Trench 3, represented by 20 or more individuals (MNI).

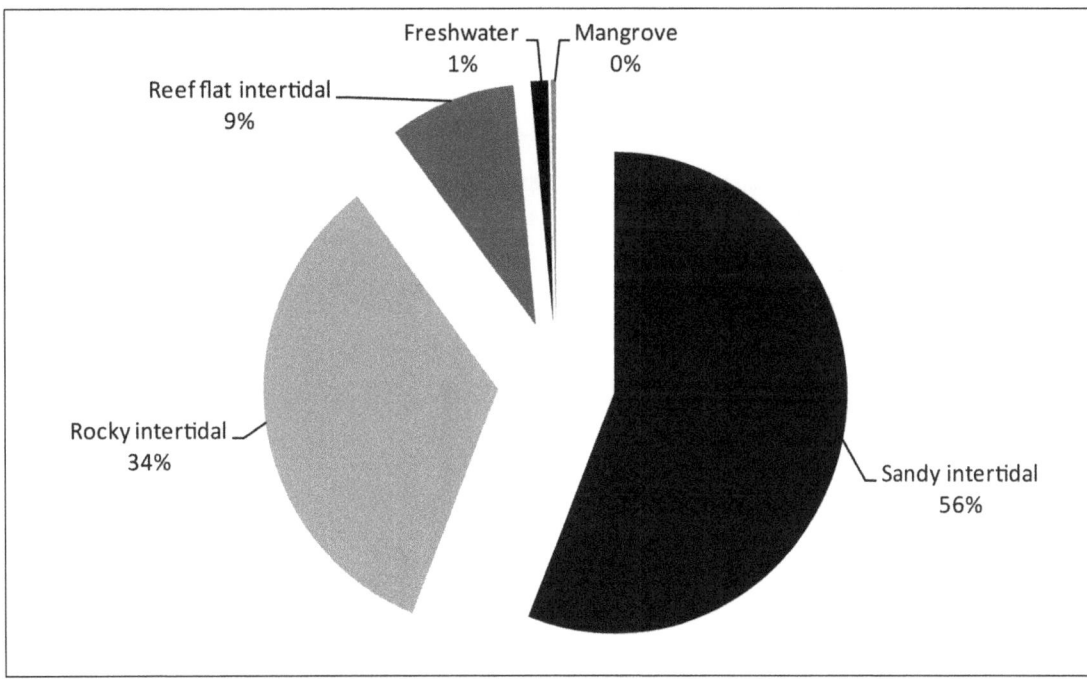

Figure 86. Proportions of different environments represented in the Natunuku shell assemblage as calculated through MNI values.

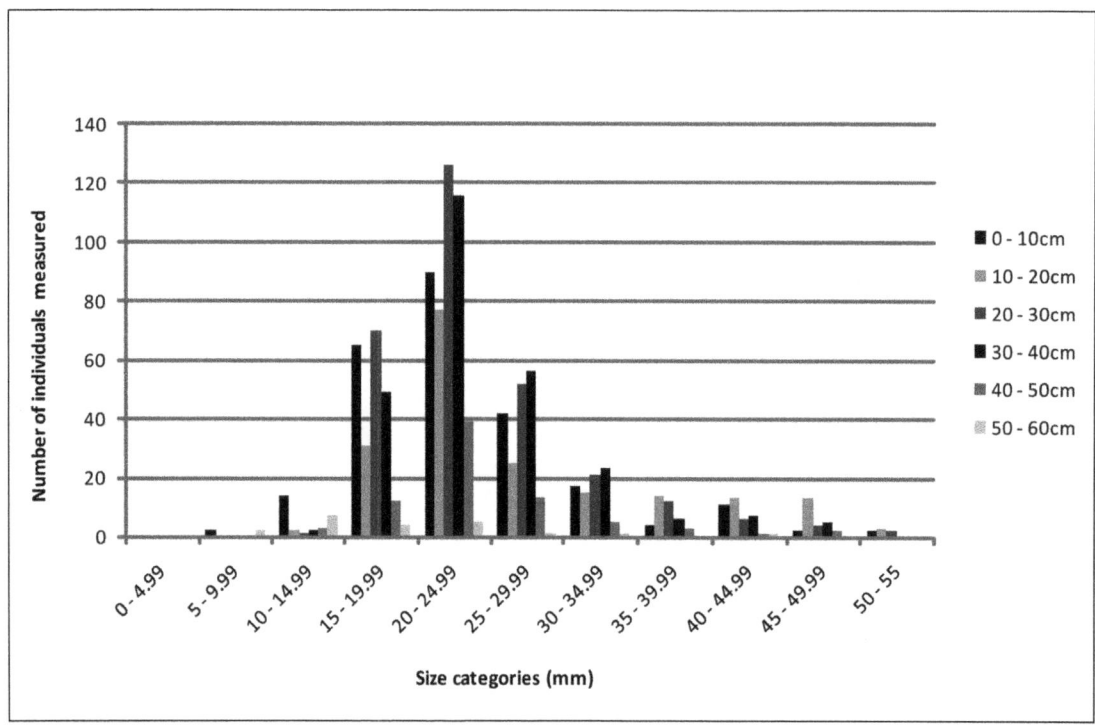

Figure 87. Frequency of various size-classes of *Anadara antiquata* within the Trench 3 sample from Natunuku.

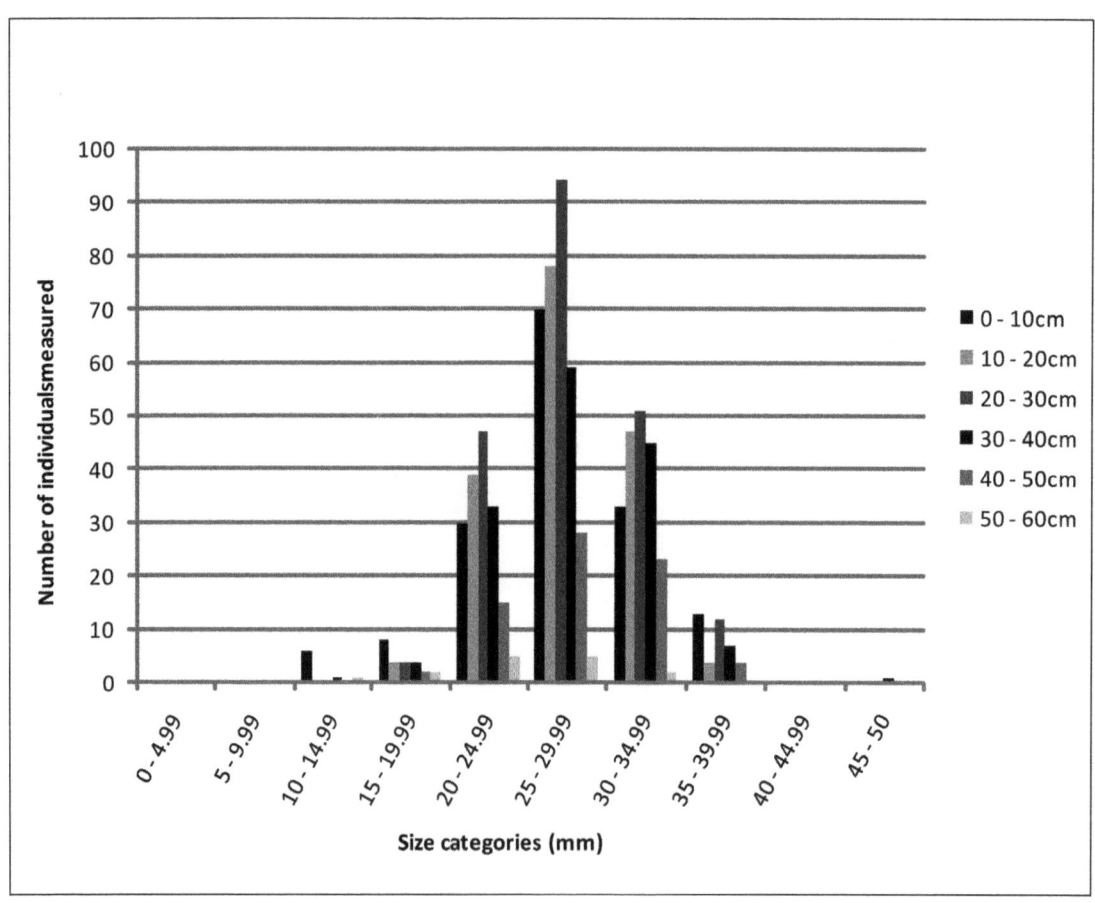

Figure 88. Frequency of various size-classes of *Gafrarium tumidum* within the Trench 3 sample from Natunuku.

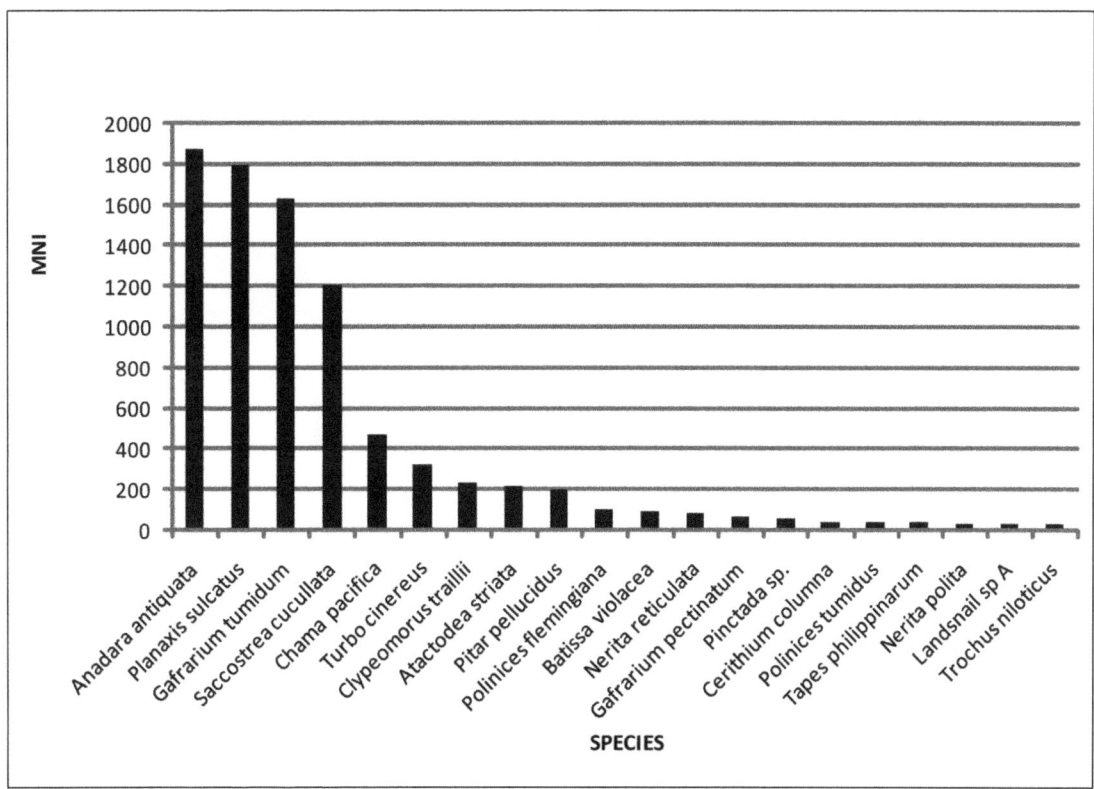

Figure 89. The 20 highest ranking species (MNI) in the complete Natunuku shell sample.

freshwater gastropods, such as neritids within the genus *Clithon*, and coastal vegetation-dwelling gastropods, such as *Cassidula nucleus*, are restricted to areas outside Trench 3. The mangrove pearl oysters *Melina ephippium* and *Isognomon* sp. are likewise absent from Trench 3. Observations such as these suggest, unsurprisingly, that molluscan remains from different gathering forays are being deposited in different areas of the site, and in all likelihood are being deposited closer to the niches from which they were originally collected. Thus, despite the large size of the Trench 3 sample, it is clear that additional information can be derived from drawing samples from different areas of large sites such as Natunuku.

Votua

The Votua 1996 shell sample contains 4533 individuals (MNI) from a minimum of 100 different molluscan species. Square A1 contained the most shell, with a total of 2297 individuals, with A2 having 1902 individuals and the remaining 334 individuals deriving from TP 1. The dominant species in all locales is *Anadara antiquata*, being supplemented by lesser numbers of *Turbo chrysostomus* and *Gafrarium tumidum* (see Figure 90). Despite the individual dominance of soft-shore bivalve species, diverse reef-flat and rocky-shore taxa represented by smaller numbers of individuals combine to make these zones important gathering areas too. Figure 91 shows that the reef-flat intertidal zone contributes 23% of all individuals, while the rocky shore contributes a further 4%. The freshwater species *Batissa violacea* and *Clithon brevispina* (n=6) are present in low numbers, but nevertheless demonstrate occasional exploitation of freshwater habitats.

There would appear to be little difference in species composition by depth across TP 1, Area 1 and Area 2. The oyster-rich layer noted for the lower reaches of Area 2 (see Chapter 6) is not apparent in the final quantifications for the 1996 sample. If this is the case, it would appear that either human preference or the nature of the littoral zone near the site changed substantially before deposition of the main midden.

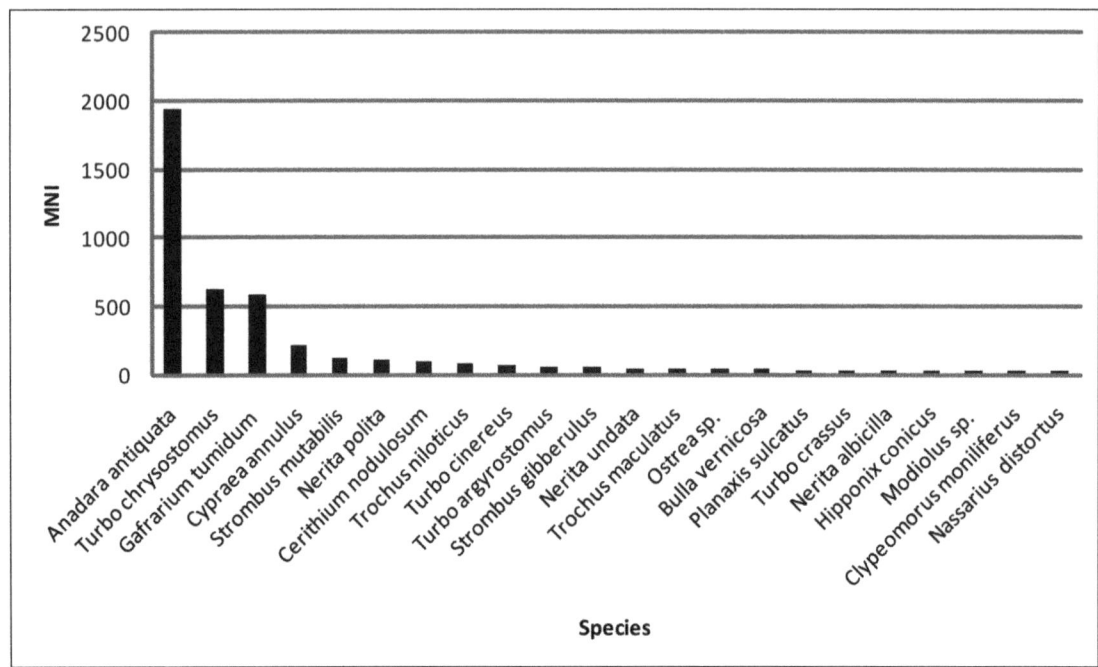

Figure 90. Mollusc species from Votua represented by 20 or more individuals (MNI).

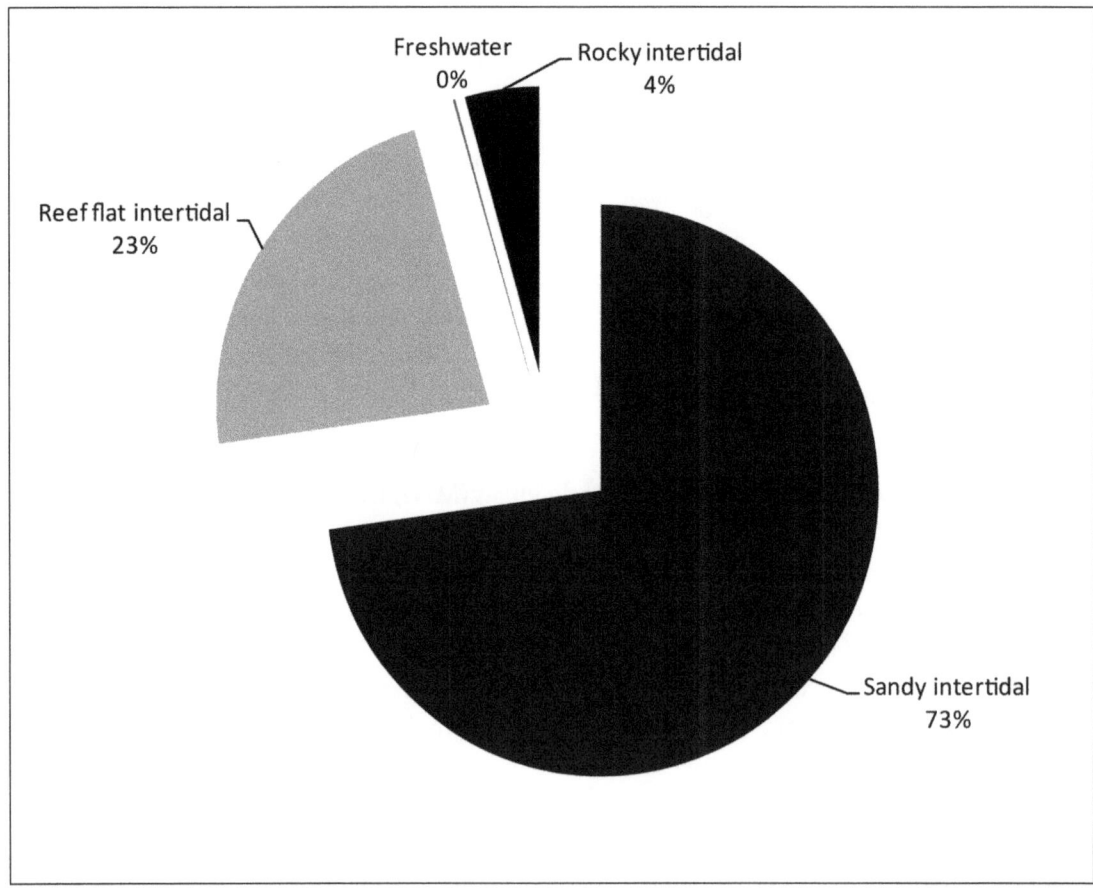

Figure 91. Proportions of different environments represented in the Votua shell assemblage as calculated through MNI values.

Kulu Bay

The most noticeable feature of the Kulu assemblage is the diversity of taxa present: 92 species in a total of less than 1000 (n=903 MNI) individual specimens. Figure 92 graphs the taxa represented by 10 or more individuals, and it can be seen that no particular taxon dominates. Opercula of various species of *Turbo*, at least five of which are represented within the Kulu Bay I sample, dominate the assemblage. However, the numbers of opercula (n=516) greatly outnumber the combined MNI for all species of *Turbo* represented by shells alone (n=114). This may be an issue of preservation, as all shell recovered from Kulu I was chalky and highly deteriorated, although many smaller and frail taxa survive in identifiable condition.

The 160 cm sequence deriving from Square C11 shows a trend that accords well with on-site observations regarding stratigraphy, but diverges in terms of observations on shell concentrations. Figure 93 shows the abundance by depth of the major species represented within the Kulu Bay assemblage: *Turbo* spp. opercula, *Cerithium nodulosum*, *Turbo chrysostomus* and both left and right valves of the small bivalve *Atactodea striata*. There are two noticeable peaks in shell frequencies. The first is within Layer 2 from about 40 cm to 110 cm, in association with animal bone, lithic flakes and fragments of various types of pottery. The second is a smaller peak associated with the sticky clay Layer 3, from around 120 cm, dropping off at 170 cm. Excavation of the latter layer was associated with large *Turbo* and other shells, but, in fact, only two *Turbo* spp. shells (one *Turbo chrysostomus* and one *Turbo argyrostomus*) were recorded for this layer, as opposed to 29 individuals from medium-large *Turbo* spp. in Layer 2. There is little difference in the species composition of the two peaks, and the fact that some species (such as the freshwater *Batissa violacea*) only occur in Layer 2 is just as likely to be a reflection of differential sample size as environmental or behavioural change.

One of the most striking features of the Kulu Bay molluscan assemblage is the diversity of niches from which the sample was drawn. Figure 94 shows that the majority of shellfish

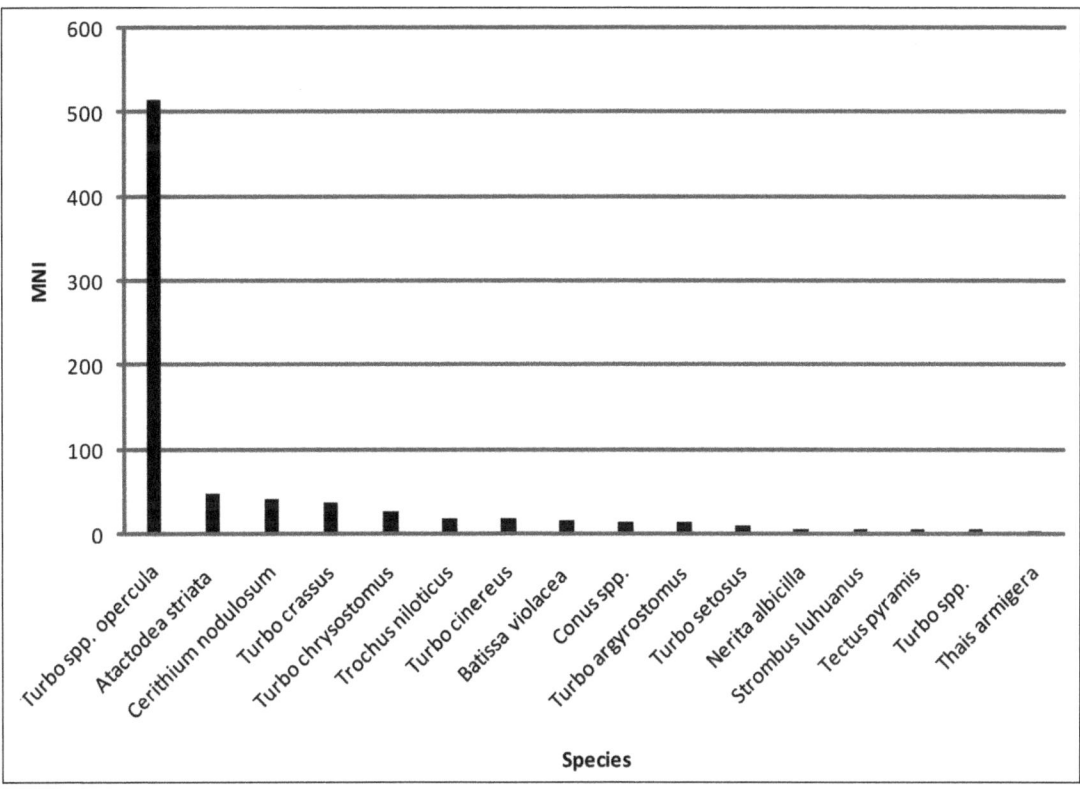

Figure 92. Mollusc species from Kulu Bay 1 represented by 10 or more individuals (MNI).

represented within the sample derive from either sandy intertidal or hard reef-flat intertidal niches, with a further 9% being drawn from the rocky upper-shore zone, 4% from the subtidal rocky zone and 6% from freshwater habitats. Given the redeposited nature of the Kulu assemblage, it cannot be said whether this diversity in environmental composition reflects similar diversity within the original donor assemblage, or whether it represents a composite of different deposits focused on distinct niches.

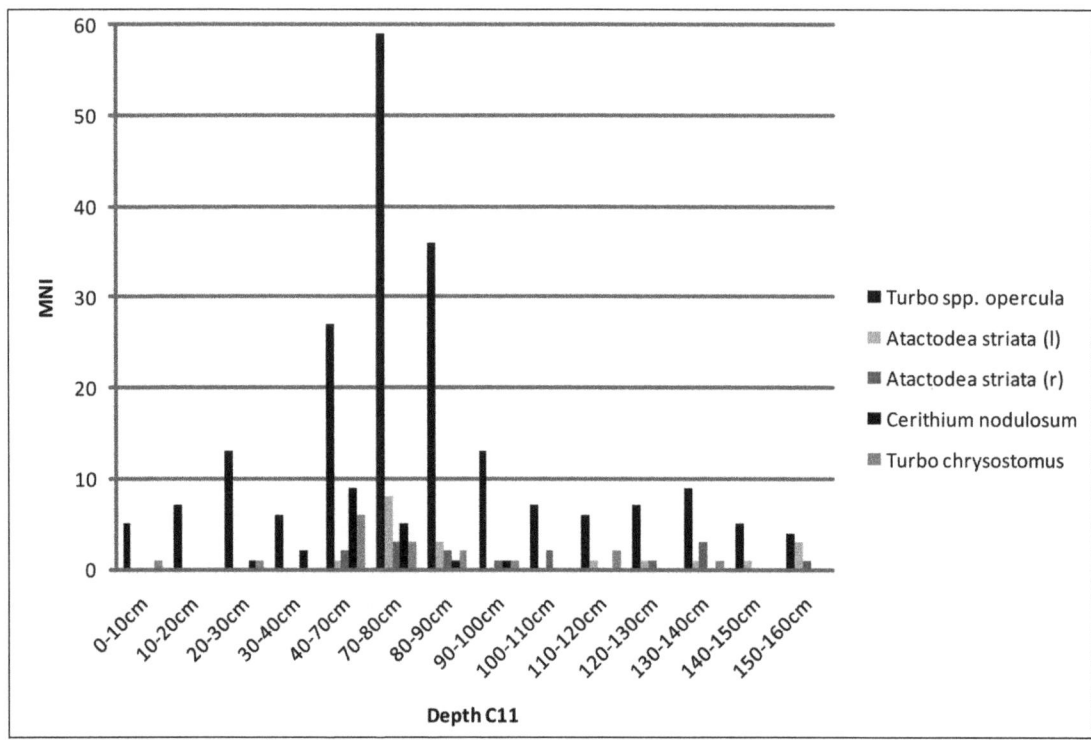

Figure 93. Distributions of major molluscan taxa by depth within Square C11, Kulu Bay 1.

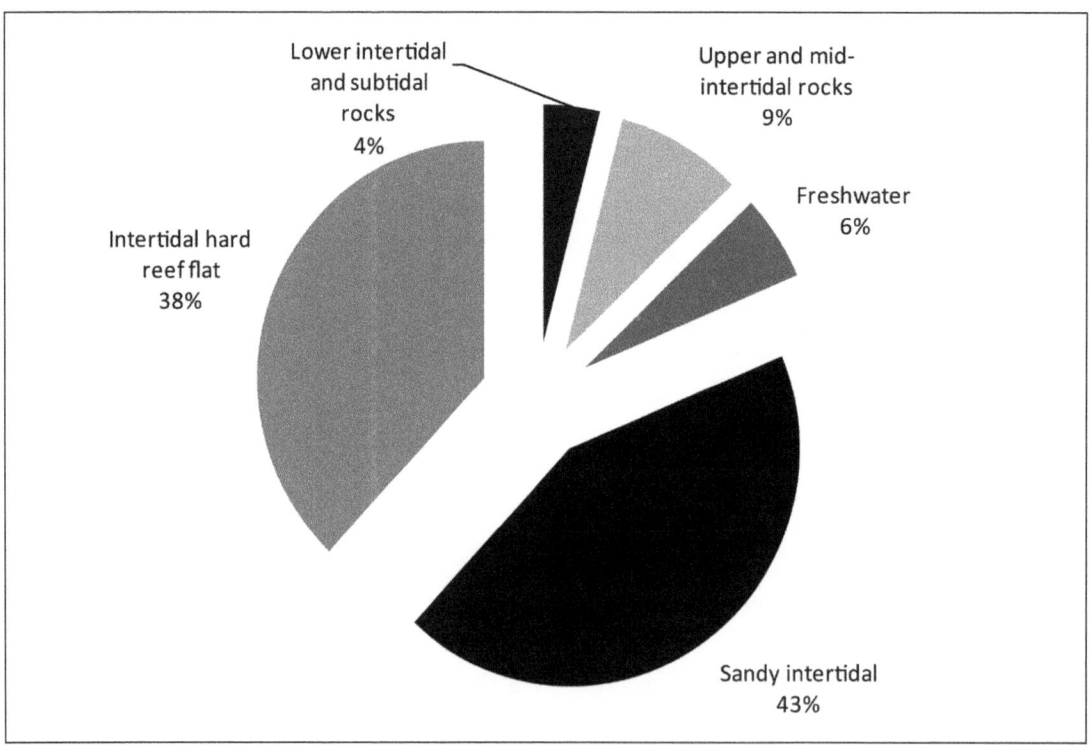

Figure 94. Proportions of different environments represented in the Kulu shell assemblage as calculated through MNI values.

Navatu

As mentioned above, shell was sparse below a depth of 90 cm, meaning that the bulk of Navatu molluscan remains relate to Layers 1 and 2. These have been treated as one sample in light of various problems to do with separating the two analytically. Species represented by five or more individuals are shown in Figure 95. With only 556 individuals (MNI) within the Navatu sample, it is questionable how much can be concluded from the contribution of various species relative to each other. Nevertheless, the dominance of bivalves is noteworthy, with most deriving from the soft-shore zone (e.g. *Gafrarium tumidum*, *Anadara antiquata* and *Fragum unedo*), supplemented by species from the rocky intertidal and subtidal niches (e.g. *Saccostrea cucullata*, *Chama iostoma*). Clean reef environments are not especially well represented, with four *Tridacna* spp. specimens (one *Tridacna maxima* and one *Tridacna squamosa*, one *Tridacna gigas* and one specimen identifiable only to genus level) and only two *Trochus niloticus* specimens. Apart from the rocky-shore-dwelling *Turbo cinereus*, there are no turbinid shells. However, despite a paucity of molluscs deriving from the clean reef-flat environment, the gathering spectrum is far from homogenously silty sand. Figure 96 shows that 68% of individuals derive from soft intertidal substrates, grading from muddy to weedy sand. Of the remaining 32%, 25% come from rocky substrates, with a further 4% from clean reef flats and 2% from freshwater environments. The freshwater component is not composed simply of *Batissa violacea* valves, which are frequently transported as expedient tools, but consists also of the gastropods *Melanoides tuberculata* and an unidentified species of freshwater Neritidae (*Neritina* sp.).

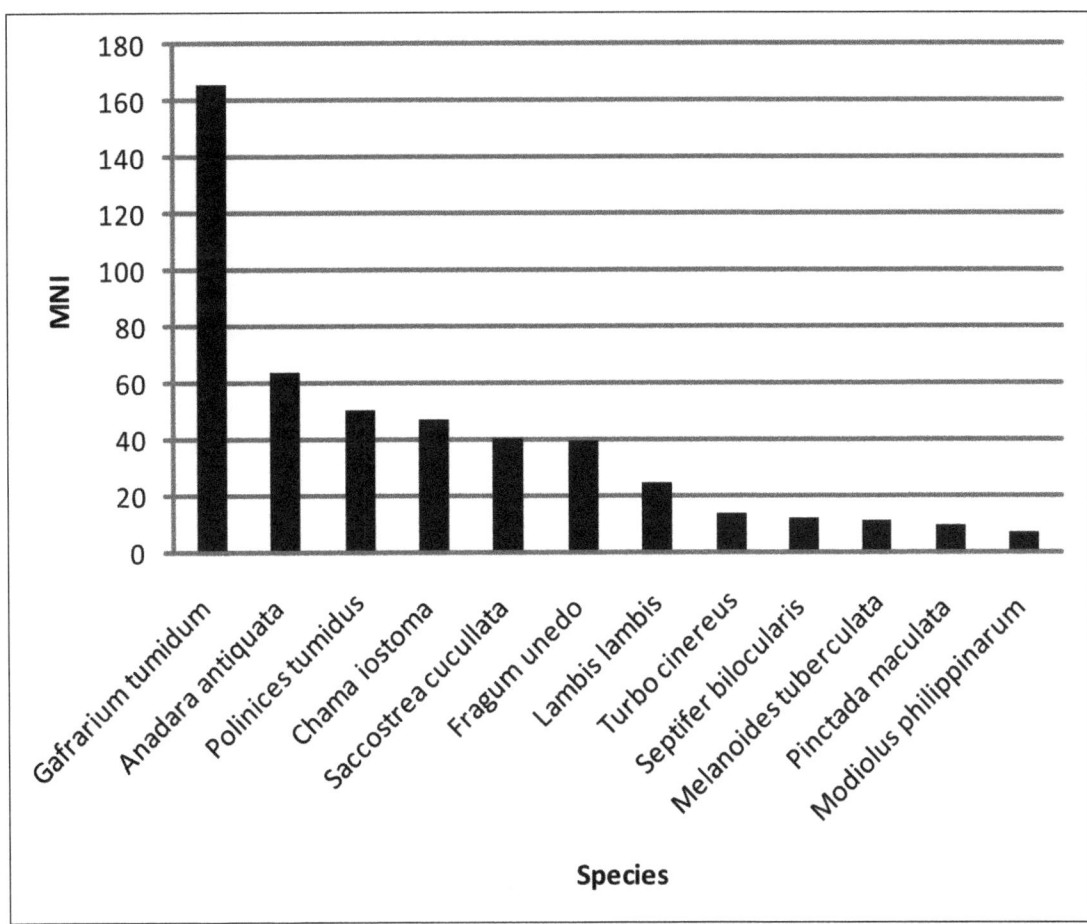

Figure 95. Mollusc species at Navatu represented by five or more individuals (MNI).

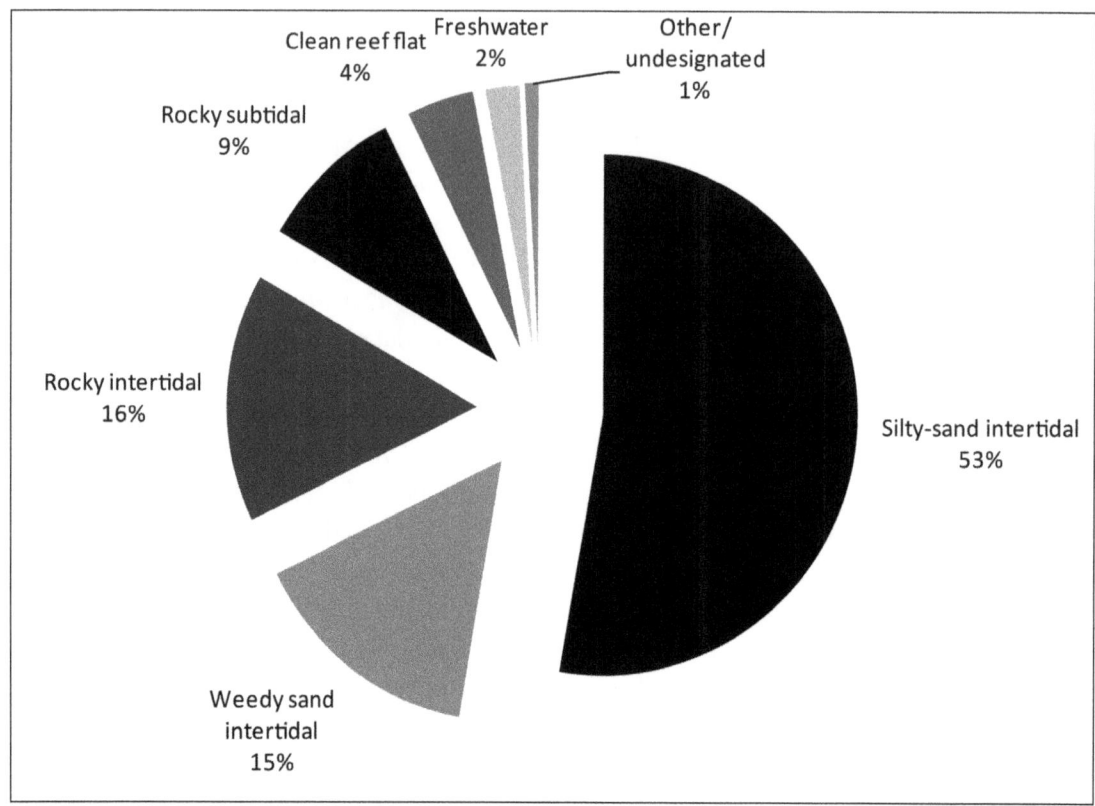

Figure 96. Proportions of different environments represented in the Navatu shell assemblage as calculated through MNI values.

Volivoli II and III

The Volivoli II shell assemblage is one of the more intriguing of the EPF sites, not least for its terrestrial snail component. The well-stratified nature of the sample, coupled with clear differences in molluscan composition within this stratigraphy, means that more questions can viably be posed of the Volivoli II assemblage than of many of the open middens.

Molluscan shell was recovered to a depth of 130 cm, which represents the base of the shelter. However, as observed in Chapter 5, cultural material largely disappears at 80 cm depth. This discrepancy between the molluscan vertical spread and cultural stratigraphy makes sense only when the shell component is scrutinised in greater detail. Volivoli II is the only site excavated as part of this project that has a sizeable terrestrial-snail component. Land snails occur throughout the sedimentary sequence, but distinct changes can be observed stratigraphically. There is only one land-snail species, *Naninia pfeifferi*, which occurs in numbers throughout the cultural layers. Indeed, it is the most abundant species from the surface to a depth of 70 cm. Within the 70–80 cm spit a distinct change is seen, with *N. pfeifferi* falling off, and disappearing completely below a depth of 90 cm. In its stead, a group of other terrestrial snail taxa appears, dominated by two other ariophantid snails: *Naninia* cf. *ornata* and an unidentified species of *Naninia*. Land-snail abundances by depth are shown in Figure 97.

The land-snail assemblage from below 80 cm depth is composed of a variety of species, including some very small (>1 cm) taxa, and represents a natural-death assemblage, in line with the stratigraphic distribution of cultural materials in the site. The dominance of *N. pfeifferi* above 80 cm presents another issue. This species is not represented in the natural-death assemblage from 90–130 cm depth, implying it was not part of the land-snail community located in close proximity to the site before human occupation. While its sudden appearance may be to do with vegetational change around the rock-shelter area, its dominance over culturally associated taxa and the virtual disappearance of all other taxa found in the lowest layer of the site suggest another explanation.

It has rarely been considered that terrestrial snails can be food resources, and indeed, given the low occurrences of medium-large land snails in coastal Pacific sites, there is little reason why they generally should be considered. Inland sites present different resource opportunities, and a local abundance of reasonably sized land snails may, in these circumstances, appear an attractive resource. With regards to Volivoli II, if land snails were entirely self-introduced, one would expect to see a cross-section of the local land-snail population within the site, including various taxa, size and age classes. This is, indeed, what is present towards the base of the site. However, it is not what is present above 80 cm. In sum, the presence of *N. pfeifferi* in the upper 80 cm to the exclusion of other land snails and this species' dominance over marine taxa point to human agency (see Figure 98). The fact that the lower levels of the deposit do suggest that *N. pfeifferi* was a major taxon in the natural land-snail fauna around the site supports the view that the species was a resource deliberately gathered by humans.

Looking at the rest of the cultural molluscan assemblage, *Turbo* spp. opercula are abundant (n=496), and as at Kulu Bay, occur in considerably greater numbers than remains of the shells themselves (n=80). While this is feasibly related to taphonomic issues and loss of shell fragments, unlike Kulu Bay, the preservation of shell remains at Volivoli II is excellent. The difference in *Turbo* spp. shell and opercula representation is more likely due to the distance of the Volivoli II shelter from the coast (ca. 1.5 km). *Turbo* spp. shells are relatively heavy and bulky, and if the shells were processed at or near the point of collection, and only the animal and adherent operculum transported back to the site, one would expect a refuse pattern such as that witnessed at Volivoli II. If this interpretation is correct, we might expect other clean reef-flat species with bulky or heavy shells to have been processed in a similar way. It is possible that heavy species such as *Trochus niloticus* (n=12) and *Tridacna* spp. (n=1) are under-represented at Volivoli II.

It is clear that environments other than clean reef flats and terrestrial locales were being exploited by the inhabitants of Volivoli II. The freshwater bivalve *Batissa violacea* occurs in relatively high numbers (n=297), and is supplemented by various fresh/brackish-water neritids

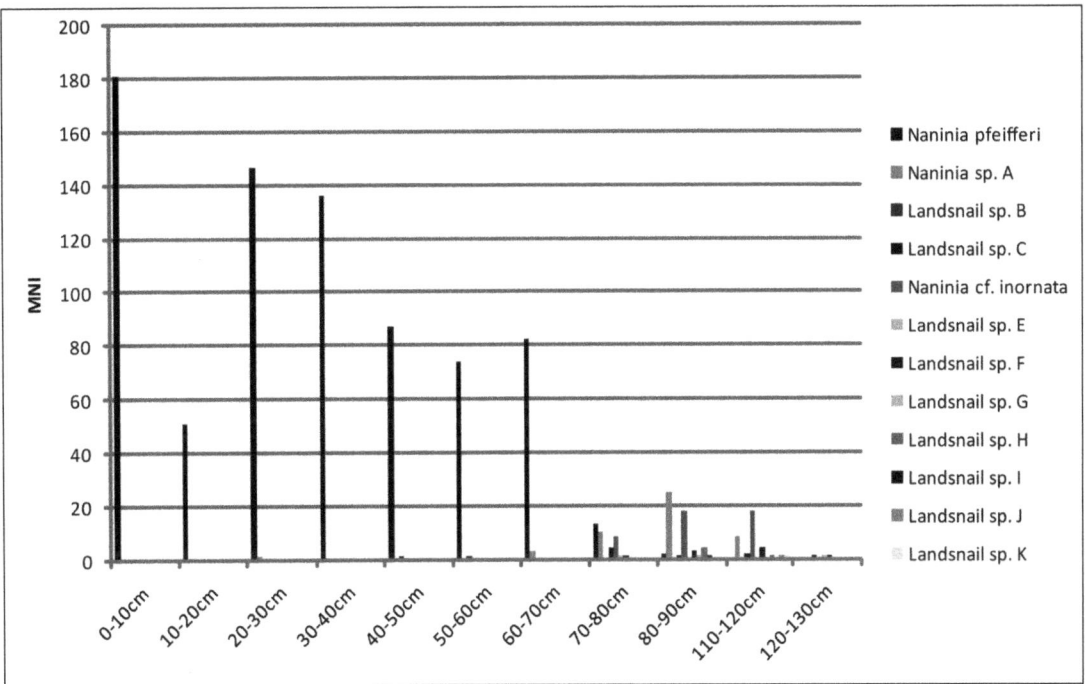

Figure 97. Land-snail abundances (MNI) by depth at Volivoli II.

(*Neritina turrita*, *Neritodryas dubia*), freshwater thiarids (*Melanoides tuberculata* and *Thiara* sp.) and an unidentified freshwater bivalve. The lack of clearly mangrove/estuarine-associated bivalves and gastropods suggests that such freshwater environments were not located in the immediate vicinity of the coast.

Figure 99 shows the proportions of the overall mollusc assemblage that derive from various environmental niches. In addition to the terrestrial, reef-flat intertidal and freshwater environments already discussed, 27% derive from weedy-sand environments. There is a strong focus on gastropods, and in particular *Strombus mutabilis* (n=190), supplemented by smaller contributions from *Strombus gibberulus gibbosus* (n=39), *Tellina palatum* (n=48) and various cypraeids, cerithids and naticids.

As mentioned above, the Volivoli III molluscan sample is much smaller, reflecting the lower frequency of shell in these deposits. Unlike Volivoli II, there were no land snails identified within the Volivoli III sample, although in terms of the marine component, there are strong similarities between the two shelters. Twenty-nine species are represented, with the most common species being *Strombus mutabilis* (n=39), followed by the freshwater bivalve *Batissa violacea* (n=16). Species represented by more than a single individual are graphed in Figure 100. The absence of land snails from Volivoli III reinforces the interpretation of a cultural introduction for Volivoli II, while the exploitation of freshwater, reef-intertidal and weedy-sand environments remains constant (see Figure 101).

Aside from the terrestrial-snail component, the only notable difference between the Volivoli II and III molluscan shell samples is the predominance of *Turbo* spp. shells over opercula at Volivoli III. It is possible that the smaller volumes of shell transported to Volivoli III made feasible the transport of whole unprocessed shells, rather than simply the flesh and opercula.

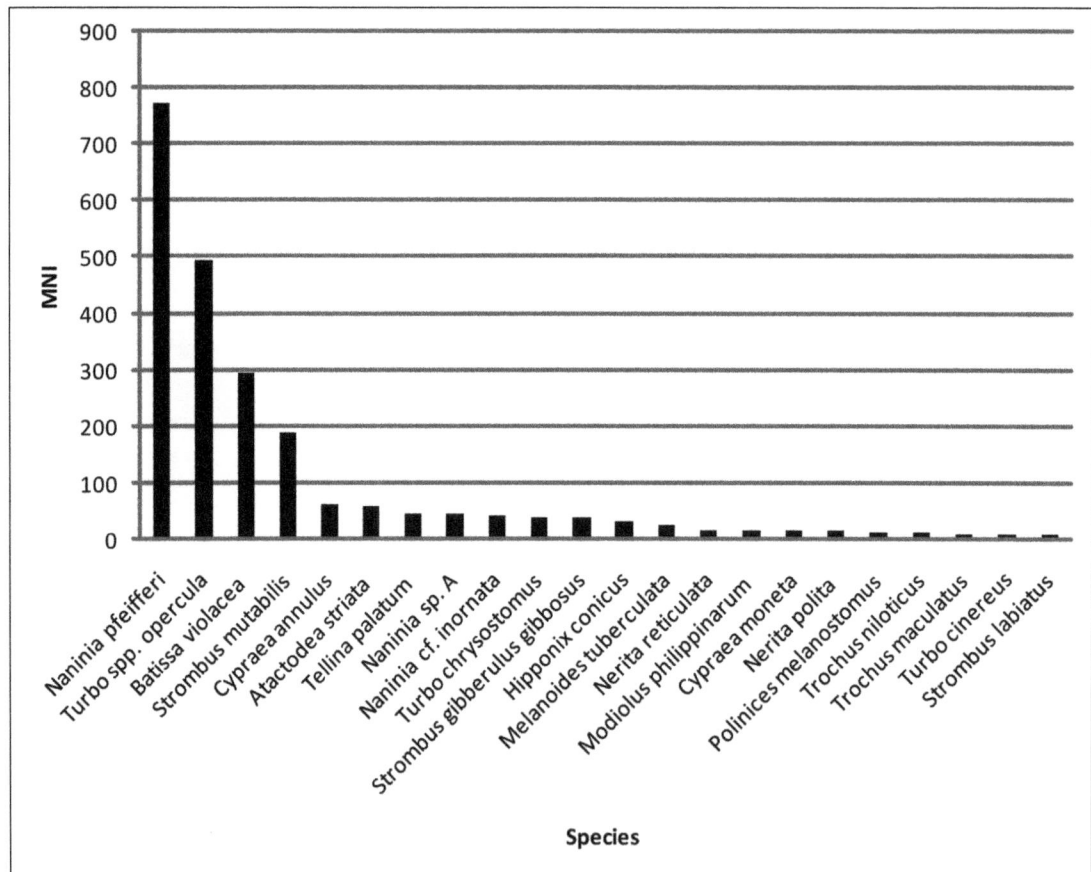

Figure 98. Molluscan taxa represented by 10 or more individuals at Volivoli II.

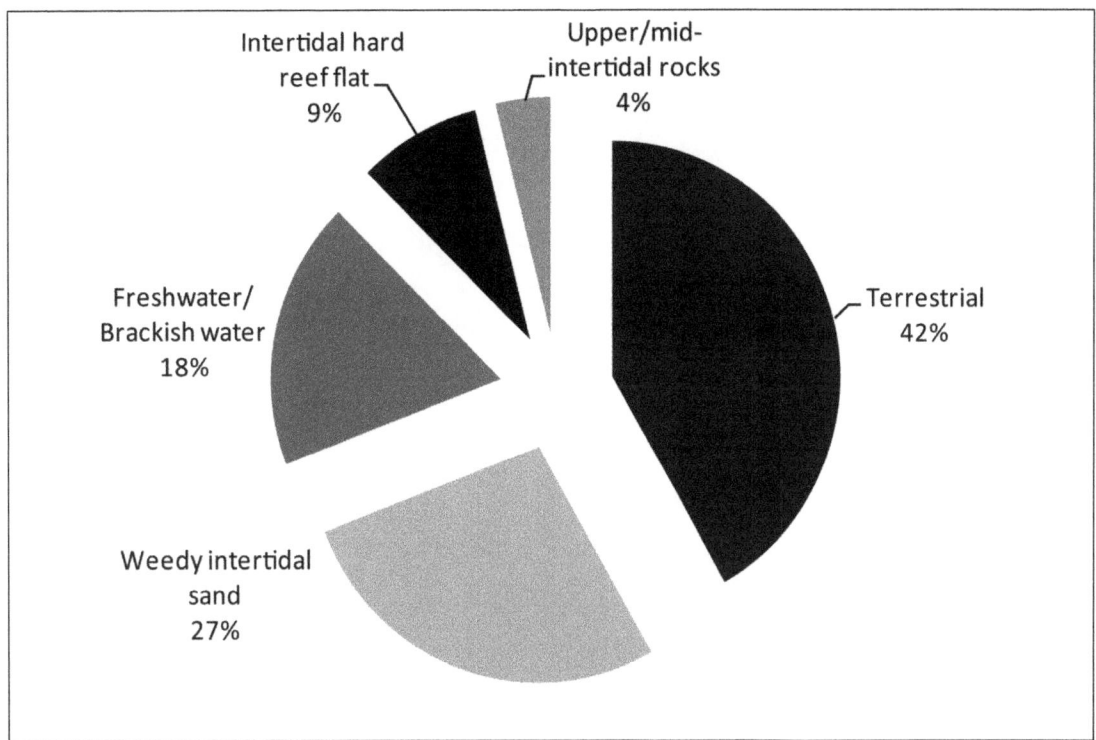

Figure 99. Proportions of different environments represented in the Volivoli II shell assemblage as calculated through MNI values. The only land snail included within these calculations is *Naninia pfeifferi*. Opercula values for *Turbo* spp. and *Nerita* spp. have been omitted as, without species information, ecological attribution is not feasible.

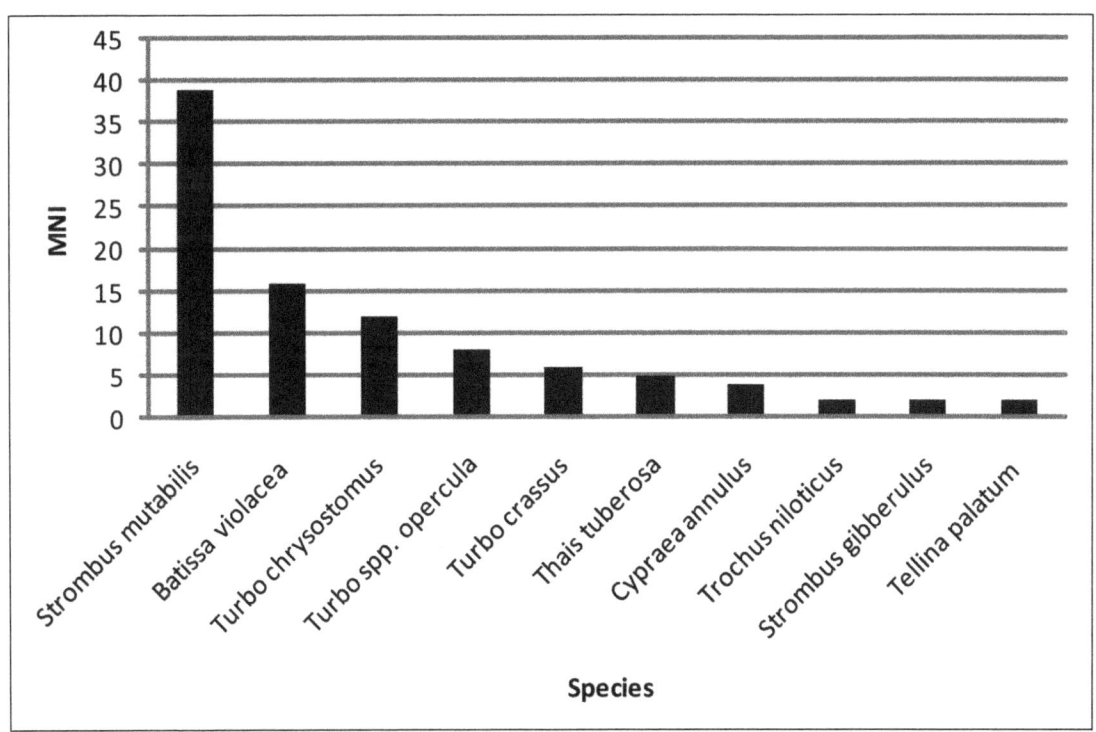

Figure 100. Mollusc species from Volivoli III represented by more than one individual (MNI).

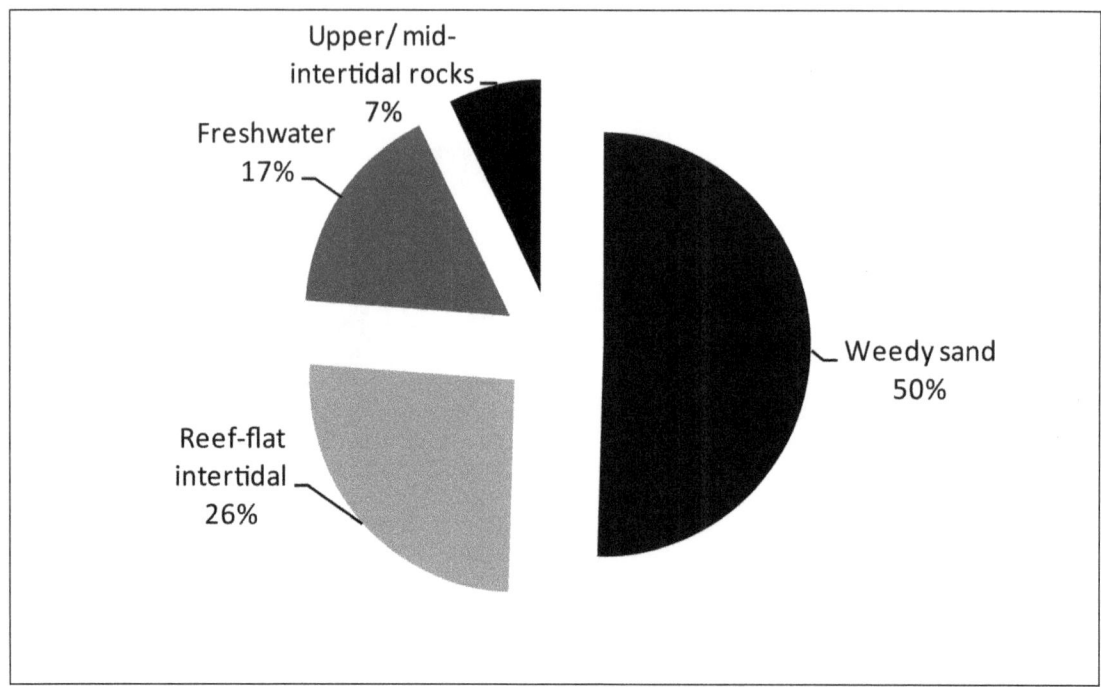

Figure 101. Proportions of different environments represented in the Volivoli III shell assemblage as calculated through MNI values. *Turbo* spp. operculum values have been omitted from these calculations so as not to inflate the importance of *Turbo*.

Malaqereqere

The shell sample from Malaqereqere is relatively large and diverse, with a total of 6071 individuals (MNI), deriving from at least 110 species. This latter total does not include specimens identified only to genus level, except where such fragments are the only one/s identified for that genus. As outlined in Chapter 5, the Malaqereqere shelter had a complex stratigraphy in which five major layers were recognised. The difficulty in dealing with the shell sample is that it was retrieved according to 10 cm spits and, given that most layer divisions fall halfway between spits, the sample cannot be reconciled back into layers. Despite these difficulties, an investigation of change in taxonomic frequency per spit offers some insight into changing gathering patterns. These are discussed further below.

Malaqereqere follows the pattern seen in Volivoli II and Kulu Bay, whereby *Turbo* spp. opercula dramatically outnumber the combined total of individual shells identified within the genus (see Figure 102). This does not necessarily represent a focus on intertidal reef-flat exploitation, given the dominance of the rocky-shore *Turbo cinereus* over reef-intertidal taxa such as *Turbo setosus*, *T. chrysostomus* and *T. crassus* in the assemblage. Indeed, the most well-represented taxa give some idea as to the overall pattern of niche exploitation by Malaqereqere shellfish gatherers (see Figure 103). *Strombus mutabilis* can be found in sheltered, sandy intertidal environments (Demond 1957:296), while *Batissa violacea* is an occupant of fresh or slightly brackish-water environments (van Bentham Jutting 1953:47, 53). *Nerita undata*, on the other hand, is most often associated with rocky-shore environments (Morton and Raj n.d.:11; Demond 1957:288), but has also been recorded in association with littorinid snails within the mangrove zone (Demond 1957:288–289). The latter habitat is an unlikely zone of origin in the case of Malaqereqere, given the absence of other mangrove-associated species.

Considering the whole shell assemblage as an aggregate unit, molluscs deriving from the sandy intertidal zone, supplemented by those sourced from the upper-to-mid-intertidal rocky shore, contribute the greatest numbers. However, there are variables that may distort this picture. As outlined above in the case of Volivoli II, the lack of fit between *Turbo* spp. opercula and *Turbo* spp. shells suggests processing at/near the point of collection. If many of these opercula are associated with reef-flat intertidal *Turbo* species, then it is likely that other medium-large intertidal reef-flat gastropods will be underrepresented or absent. However, this line of reasoning appears less likely for Malaqereqere than for Volivoli II, as even smaller reef-flat intertidal species are uncommon. In addition, it should be pointed out many of the more common species grouped under 'reef-flat intertidal' in Figure 103 can also be found in the sandy intertidal zone (e.g. *Cypraea annulus, C. tigris*) or the rocky shore (e.g. *Nerita chamaeleon, Nerita albicilla*), thus probably overestimating the contribution of the reef-flat intertidal zone at Malaqereqere.

Again following the pattern seen in several of the other Fijian sites, freshwater niches are consistently represented. Comprising 11% (MNI) of the overall Malaqereqere assemblage, the large bivalve *Batissa violacea* (n=357) dominates, supplemented by *Melanoides tuberculata* (n=9) and various freshwater neritid taxa (*Neritina turrita* and *Neritodryas cornea*). The lack of mangrove-associated taxa once more indicates that freshwater environments are being specifically targeted, rather than being a peripheral zone abutting estuarine areas.

While the Malaqereqere shell sample cannot be broken down into stratigraphic layers to assess change over time, a spit-based comparison sheds some light on temporal patterning. Four taxa were selected for comparison for various reasons. *Strombus mutabilis* is the most common species associated with the intertidal sandy niche, while *Nerita undata* can be considered the equivalent species representing the rocky upper-to-mid-intertidal zone. *Modiolus philippinarum* is not as common as the preceding species, but gives an alternate picture of rocky-shore exploitation when compared with *Nerita undata* distributions. As discussed above, the case of *Turbo* spp. opercula is more complicated, with associated species deriving from both the rocky and reef-flat intertidal zones in unknown proportions.

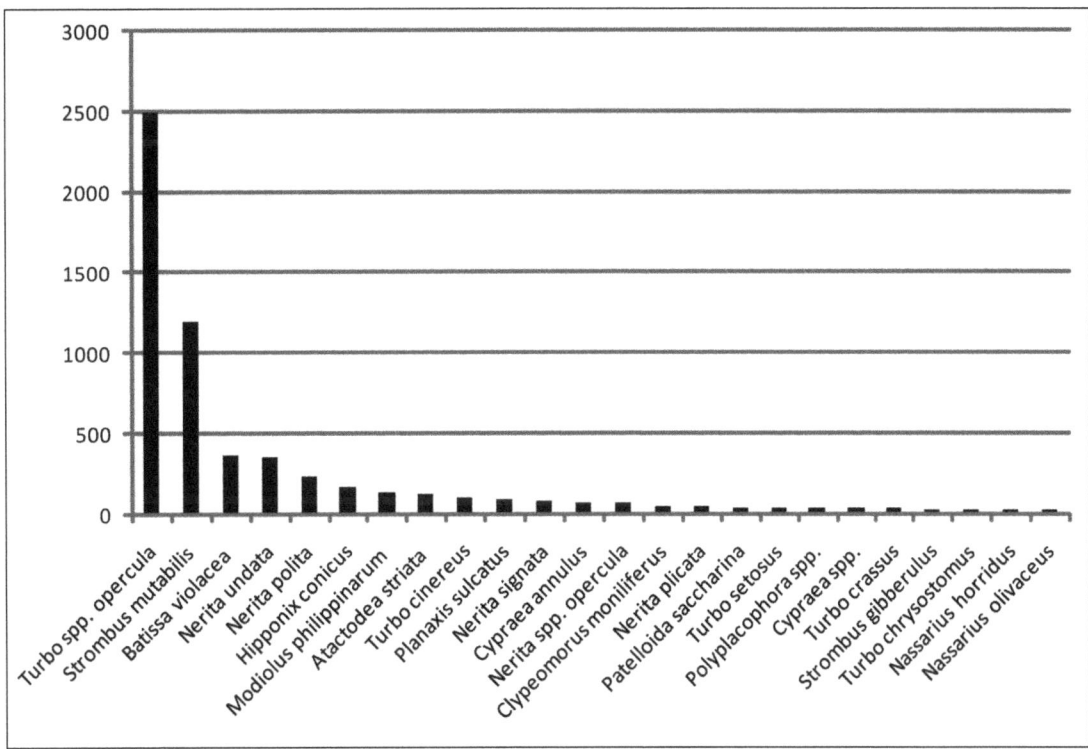

Figure 102. Mollusc species at Malaqereqere represented by 20 or more individuals (MNI).

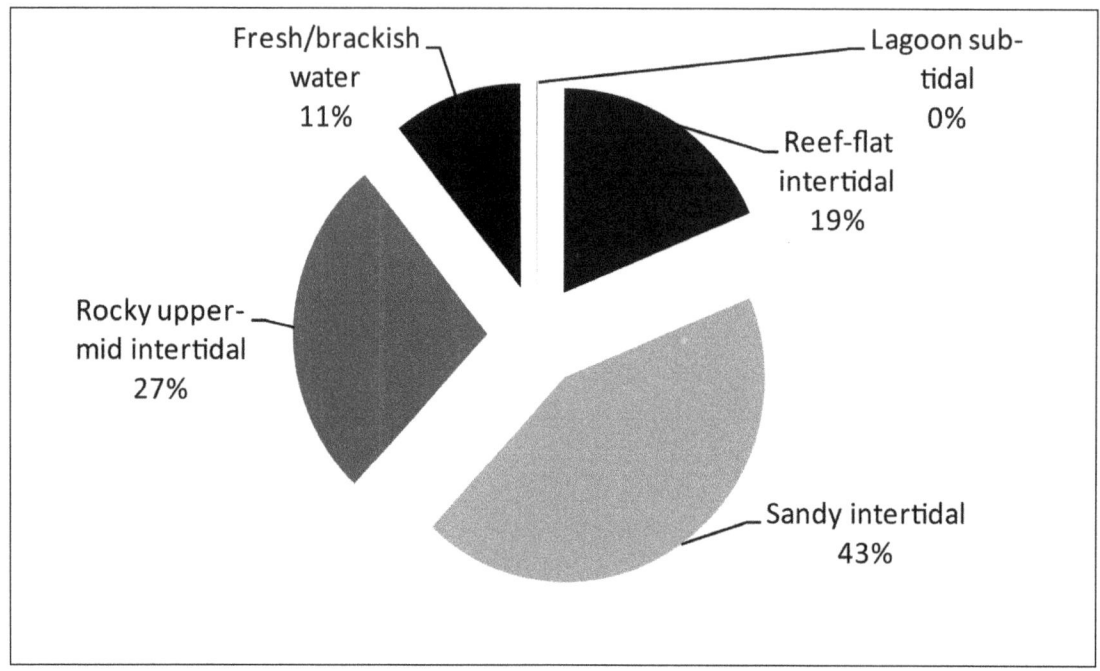

Figure 103. Proportions of different environments represented in the Malaqereqere shell assemblage as calculated through MNI values. Opercula values for *Turbo* spp. and *Nerita* spp. have been omitted.

Figure 104 shows the different relative frequencies of the indicator taxa through time at Malaqereqere, while Figure 105 gives absolute frequencies. The *Strombus mutabilis* values indicate that sandy intertidal environments are locally present and exploited throughout the sequence, and although relative frequencies would suggest this niche was most important mid-sequence, absolute frequencies show this is a feature of sample size. *Batissa violacea* is also present throughout the sequence, representing the exploitation of freshwater environments. Both relative and absolute frequencies show that this niche received greater focus in the lowest spits of Malaqereqere.

The relationship between *Nerita undata* and *Modiolus philippinarum* is intriguing. As mentioned above, *Nerita undata* is most often associated with rocky-shore environments and a mangrove association is unlikely in the case of Malaqereqere. *Modiolus philippinarum* is likewise associated with rocky shores, although as pointed out by Gosliner et al. (1996:179), it is sometimes found in association with live coral heads. It is perhaps this more subtle difference in ecology that explains the inverse relationship between the two species shown in both Figures 104 and 105, with *Modiolus philippinarum* more prevalent towards the bottom of the sequence and *Nerita undata* only becoming an important contributor in upper levels. However, the rocky-shore gastropod *Planaxis sulcatus* shows spikes in abundance at both the 10–20 cm and 50–60 cm levels. There are perhaps subtle ecological factors at play with rocky-shore environments in the vicinity of Malaqereqere, but what can certainly be said is that this broad niche was exploited for molluscan resources throughout the sequence.

Finally, while it cannot be determined how far *Turbo* spp. opercula indicate either rocky intertidal or reef-flat intertidal environments, what can be said is that the upper two spits show the decreasing importance of hard-shore environments in favour of sandy habitats.

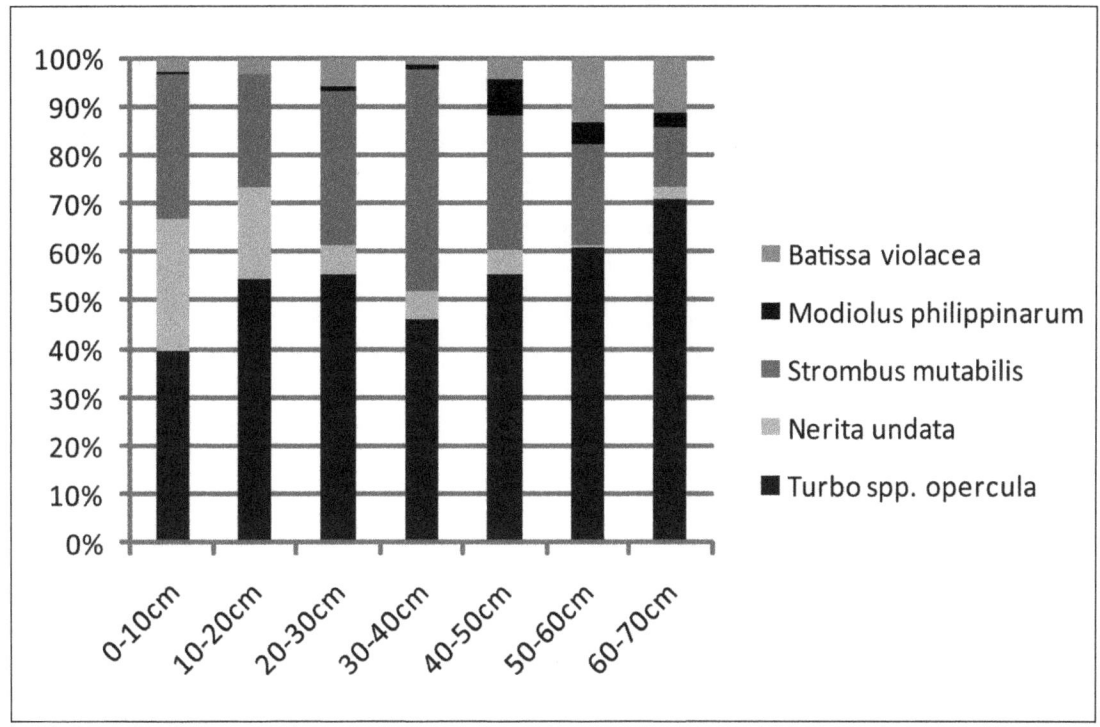

Figure 104. Relative frequencies of major molluscan indicator taxa through time at Malaqereqere shelter – Squares A1 and A2 combined.

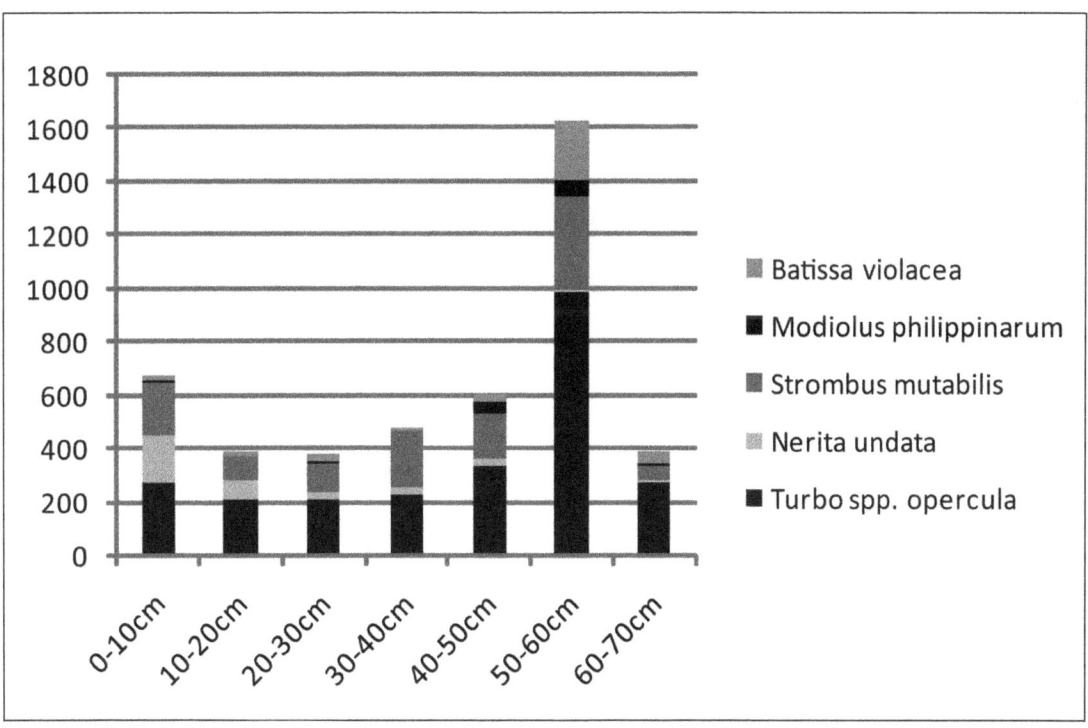

Figure 105. Absolute frequencies of major molluscan indicator taxa through time at Malaqereqere shelter – Squares A1 and A2 combined.

Ugaga

In total, 121 species of mollusc were identified within the Ugaga sub-sample, which comprised 2061 individuals (MNI). This is a rather high level of diversity when compared with the overall sample size, though it should be noted that the majority of the shell (1320 MNI) comes from four species alone: *Nerita polita, Nerita albicilla, Turbo chrysostomus* and *Turbo cinereus*. Figure 106 shows this pattern, along with the totals of other species that contribute 10 or more individuals to the overall sample. In keeping with the ecological proclivities of the four dominant taxa, 75% of the shell studied from Ugaga derives from the intertidal reef platform, with smaller numbers deriving from upper to mid-intertidal rocks and the sandy intertidal zone (see Figure 107). Eight fragments of *Batissa violacea*, together with a single *Neritina violacea*, represent freshwater habitats, which are absent on Ugaga Island, and so must be human introductions. Although there is no apparent use-wear, it is possible that *Batissa violacea* valves were transported as expedient tools. A single *Placostylus* sp. shell represents the input of terrestrial habitats, but it is unclear whether *Placostylus*-bearing habitats were/are present on Ugaga Island.

Before drawing too many conclusions regarding the patterning of molluscan remains at Ugaga, it should be stated that the majority of the shell sample studied does *not* represent direct human-food refuse. Rather, distinctive patterns of wear around the aperture and body whorl indicate that many univalve shells were used and deposited by terrestrial hermit crabs in the genus *Coenobita*, and most probably the species *Coenobita rugosa*. The potential of coenobitid hermit crabs to not only disturb deposits, but to remove midden shell in exchange for worn, hermitted specimens of unknown original provenance, has been theoretically acknowledged in

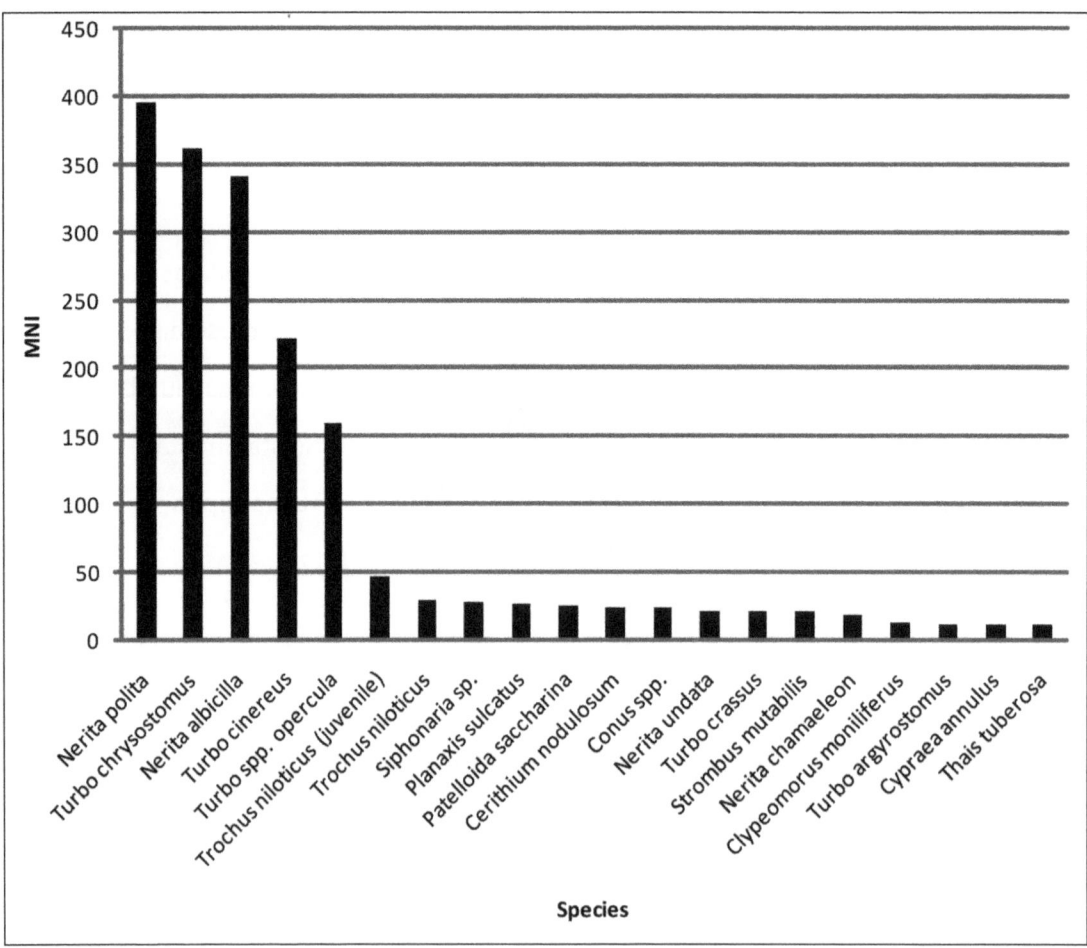

Figure 106. Mollusc species at Ugaga represented by 10 or more individuals (MNI).

the archaeological literature (Carucci 1992; Reitz and Wing 1999:65–66), and recognised and enfolded into interpretation rarely (but see Walker 1994, 1995 and Scudder and Quitmyer 1998 for palaeontology). Precise ways to recognise shell deposited by terrestrial hermit crabs are outlined in Szabó and Yang (In prep.).

In the case of Ugaga, Figure 108 demonstrates the extent of hermit-crab interference with the archaeological deposits. Such interference goes far beyond the normal bioturbation processes often associated with crabs (e.g. Palmer 1965; Green et al. 1967; Specht 1968, 1985), and has the potential to affect not only the interpretation of human shell-gathering practices, but also a site chronology based on radiocarbon dates obtained on gastropod marine shell. Of the 10 radiocarbon dates on marine shellfish from Ugaga, seven were on the bivalve *Tridacna maxima* not used by hermit crabs, and two of the univalves (Beta-107953 and ANU-10776) were examined for evidence of aperture damage/modification before sample submission. It should be noted that identification of hermit-crabbed specimens using wear and shell modification indicators was conservative, and actual hermit-crab usage rates are likely to be higher than recorded.

The common Pacific species *Coenobita rugosus* is the most likely species responsible for shell removal at Ugaga. Depending on the local ecology, different species of *Coenobita* will favour different shell species. In the case of the ground-dwelling *C. rugosus*, robust, globose shells with a large interior cavity and circular or D-shaped aperture are preferred (Barnes 1999, 2001), translating to a common preference for species within the Turbinidae and Neritidae (Barnes 1999; see also Kinosita and Akira 1968 and Osorno et al. 1998). Unlike marine hermit crabs (Decapoda: Diogenidae), coenobitid hermit crabs are primarily nocturnal and require freshwater which is held in the shell (Hazlett 1981:4–5; Small and Thacker 1994:171; De Wilde 1973 in Walker 1994; Barnes 1997:138–139), and as such are unlikely to have been the hermit-crab taxa noted during excavation. They have been noted to be strongly attracted to coastal human settlements, which provide a variety of food sources attractive to scavengers as well as dumps of whole shells

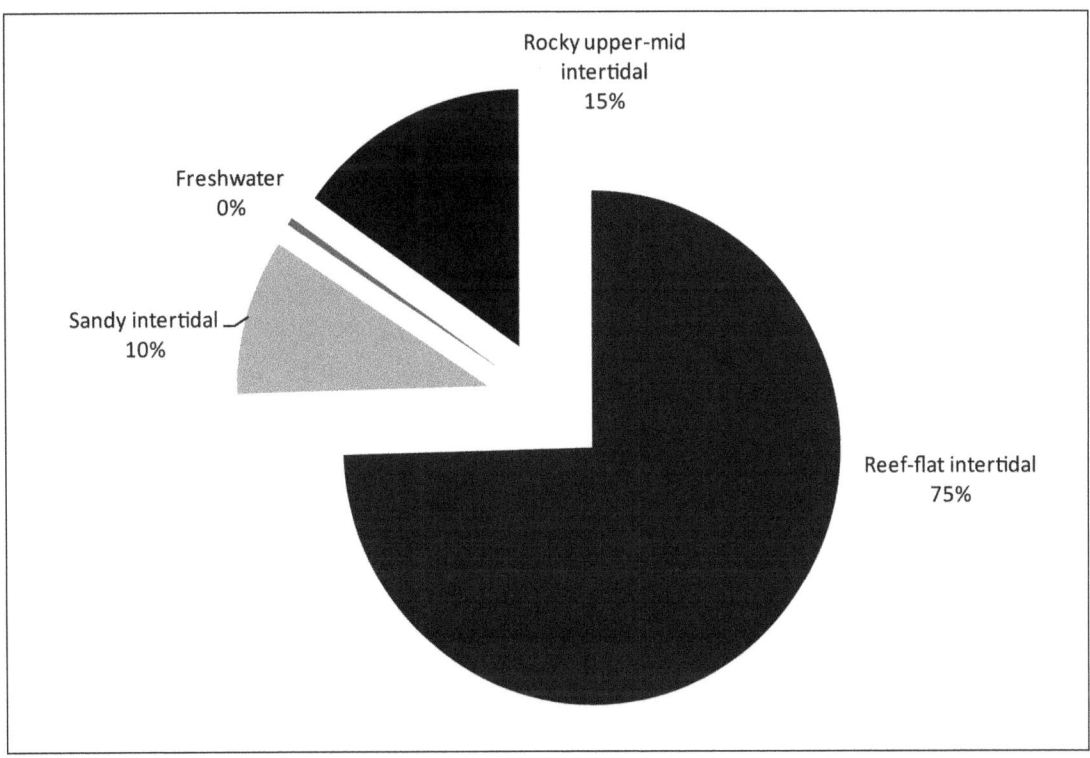

Figure 107. Proportions of different environments represented in the Ugaga shell assemblage as calculated through MNI values. Opercula and shell values for *Turbo* spp. have been omitted.

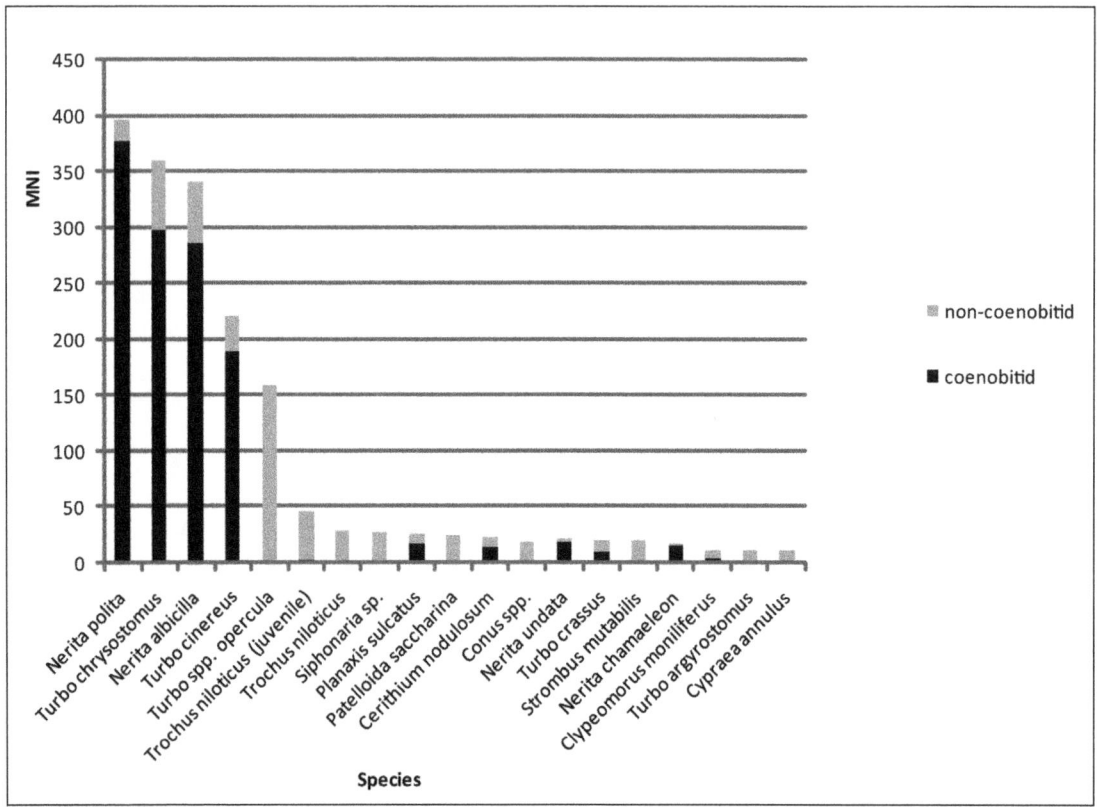

Figure 108. Graph showing the extent of coenobitid hermit-crab shell deposition noted for the major taxa represented at Ugaga.

– a common limiting factor on coenobitid populations in nature (Hazlett 1981:11–13; Barnes 2001). Furthermore, research suggests that *C. rugosus* only approaches shells that have a suitably shaped and sized aperture visible at its eye level (Kinosita and Akira 1968:310, 355). This means that partially buried shells or shells lying with the aperture at a visual angle which precludes size assessment will not be approached, and thus buried or partly buried midden shells are unlikely to be targeted by *C. rugosus* (see also Hazlett 1981; Barnes 1999).

All of these factors make plain that the shell replacement witnessed for Ugaga is not only a recent activity, but that univalve shell exchange was most likely going on as the midden was being formed.

Few definite conclusions can be drawn about *human* shell-gathering practices at Ugaga. There is no guarantee that coenobitid crabs deposited shells of the same species they removed. Nevertheless, it has been demonstrated that coenobitids will not cast off a more preferred species of shell for a less preferred one (Thacker 1994; Osorno et al. 1998). Given the preference of *C. rugosus* for turbinids and neritids, and its dominance within the Ugaga deposits, it can be reasonably safely assumed that these taxa had the highest removal rates. The relatively high incidence of *Turbo* spp. opercula also attests to the original presence of *Turbo* spp. within the midden.

Qaranioso II

The small shell sample from Qaranioso II contains a total of 111 individuals (MNI) spread across 23 different species. Soft-shore bivalves are strongly dominant, with *Gafrarium tumidum*, *Anadara antiquata* and *Atactodea striata* all well represented, supplemented by *Codakia tigerina*, *Tellina palatum* and *Fragum unedo* (see Figure 109). Occasional specimens derive from reef-platform intertidal or rocky-shore environments, but soft-shore species account for 89% of the total shell sample (see Figure 110).

The majority of shell was associated with Layers 1 and 2, with only two fragments (*Tellina palatum* and *Gafrarium tumidum*) being found in Layer 3. There is little apparent difference in molluscan concentrations or representation between Layers 1 and 2.

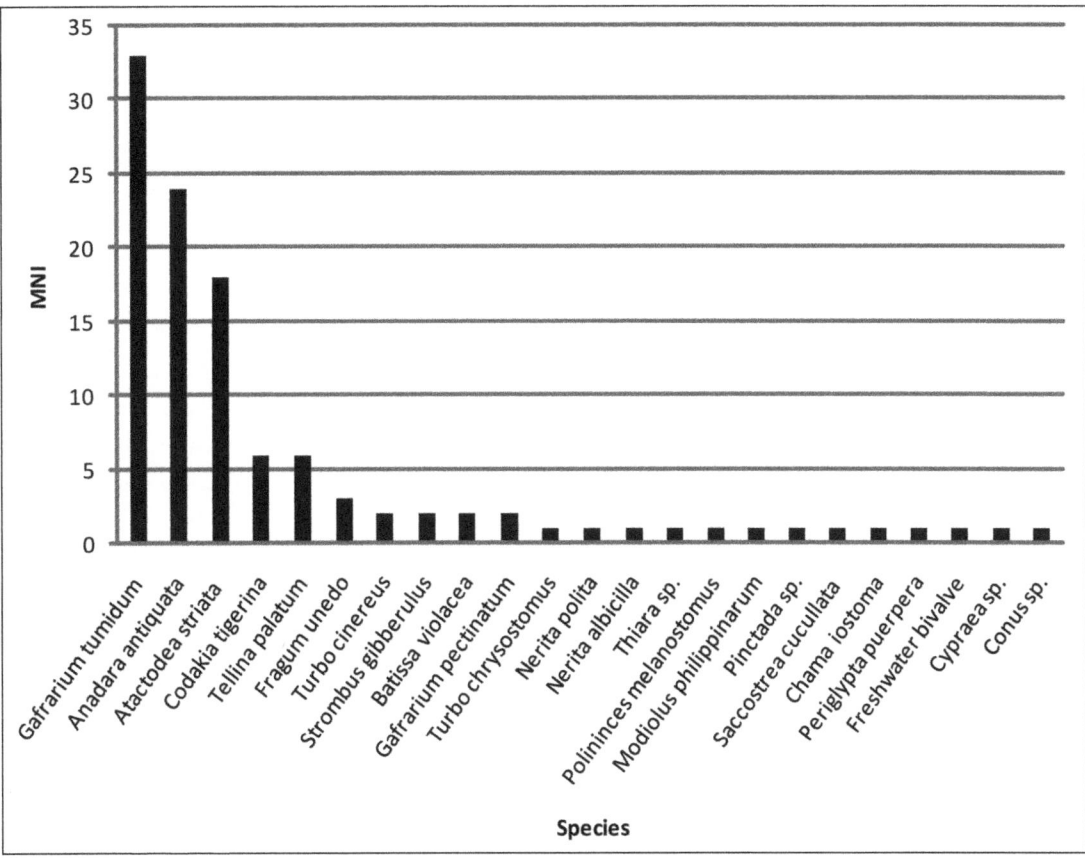

Figure 109. Abundances of all molluscan remains recovered from the Qaranioso II (MNI).

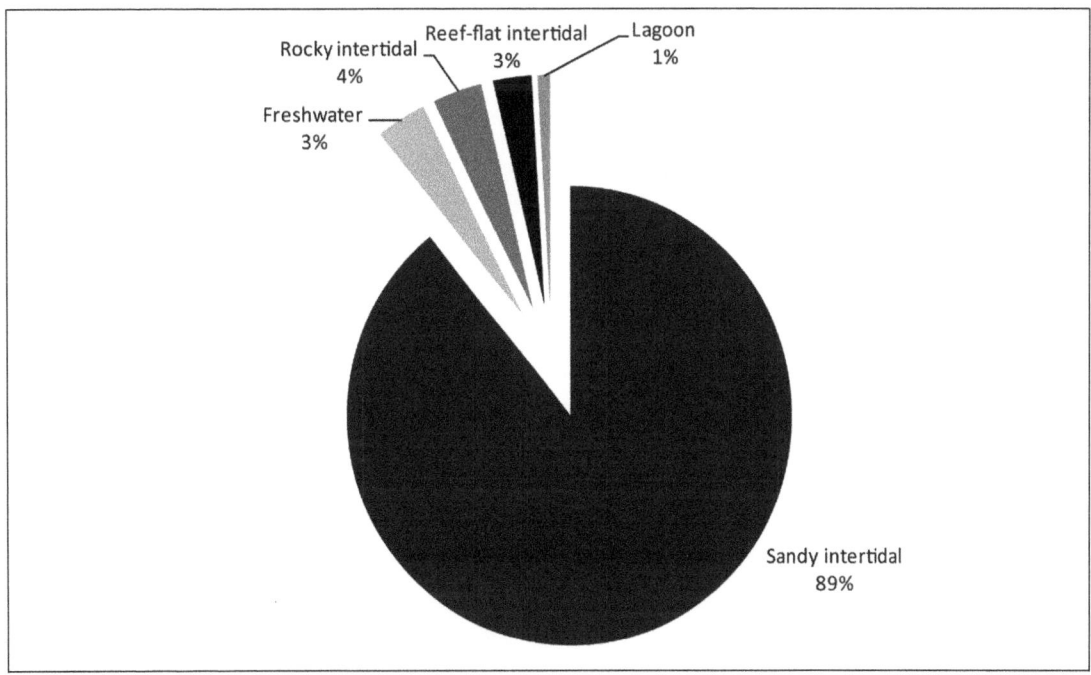

Figure 110. Proportions of different environments represented in the Qaranioso II shell assemblage as calculated through MNI values. Opercula values for *Turbo* spp. have been omitted.

Discussion

When all the samples discussed above are considered as a whole, the most notable feature is the sheer diversity of species represented. Figure 111 shows the relationship between sample size and species diversity for all samples bar Tuvu and Qaranioso I. Given that species richness is closely correlated with sample size, it is unsurprising that some of the most diverse samples are the larger ones: Ugaga, Votua and Natunuku. However, Figure 111 also shows that some of the smaller samples are more diverse than their larger counterparts.

Although the Votua Lapita sample was the largest analysed, it falls behind Ugaga and Natunuku in terms of species diversity, but also behind the much smaller assemblages from Malaqereqere and Volivoli II. This would appear to be at least partially attributable to the spread of mollusc-bearing niches used by ancient shell-gatherers. Nearly 75% of the Votua assemblage derives from the sandy intertidal zone, with a strong focus on the collection of the muddy-sand bivalve *Anadara antiquata*. The only other assemblages that show such a strong collecting focus on a single littoral niche are Qaranioso II, with 89% of specimens derived from the sandy intertidal, and Ugaga, where 75% of individuals are drawn from the reef-flat intertidal zone. At Ugaga, the reef-flat niche is represented by a variety of species, with the representation being skewed to an unknown degree by hermit-crab shell deposition.

At Qaranioso II, three species (*Gafrarium tumidum*, *Anadara antiquata* and *Atactodea striata*) combine to elevate the soft shore to a position of prominence within the overall collecting structure. Thus, Votua is unique among the assemblages studied in having such a concerted focus on a single species, and it is the only site for which a premeditated, focused collecting strategy can be argued. It is also the only single-phase Lapita site excavated, and other EPF sites with Lapita age materials, such as Natunuku, Kulu Bay and Ugaga, contain evidence of disturbance that might have obscured the pattern of shellfish gathering during the colonisation phase.

All other sites show a collecting pattern that is considerably more fine-grained. Species are taken from the environment in the relative proportions in which they naturally occur. This appears to be as true of species representation as it is of size classes within a population. This approach to mollusc collection diverges not only from the focused approach seen at Votua, but also from other recorded patterns, where large individuals are taken regardless of species (e.g. Anderson 1981). Indeed, the strategy manifest for the bulk of the Fijian shell-midden samples can be fairly categorised as 'reef-sweeping'.

This observation has important implications for the discussion of potential human impact on mollusc populations, and for statements that link a decrease in average size over time with predation pressure (e.g. Bedford 2007:189 for Lapita, contrasted with Allen 2000:149 and references therein for Pleistocene Near Oceania). Certainly, a gathering strategy that focuses on the removal of only the largest (and most fecund) individuals of a population will display a different final structure from a strategy in which large and small, mature and immature specimens have been harvested more or less equally. Exactly what such strategies may produce in terms of a final demographic structure will depend not only on the particular behaviours and population dynamics of the species under discussion, but also the local environmental variables.

There seems to be no major temporal trend apparent in the data, nor particular differences between open and shelter sites. Rather, notable tendencies such as high species diversity and multiple coastal niche exploitation seem to be reflected across all samples to a greater or lesser degree. Occasional specimens indicate that molluscan-bearing freshwater environments were generally accessible, but barring the regular occurrence of the bivalve *Batissa violacea*, were not exploited to any great degree. The same can be said of exploitation of terrestrial molluscs, with the possible exception of Volivoli II.

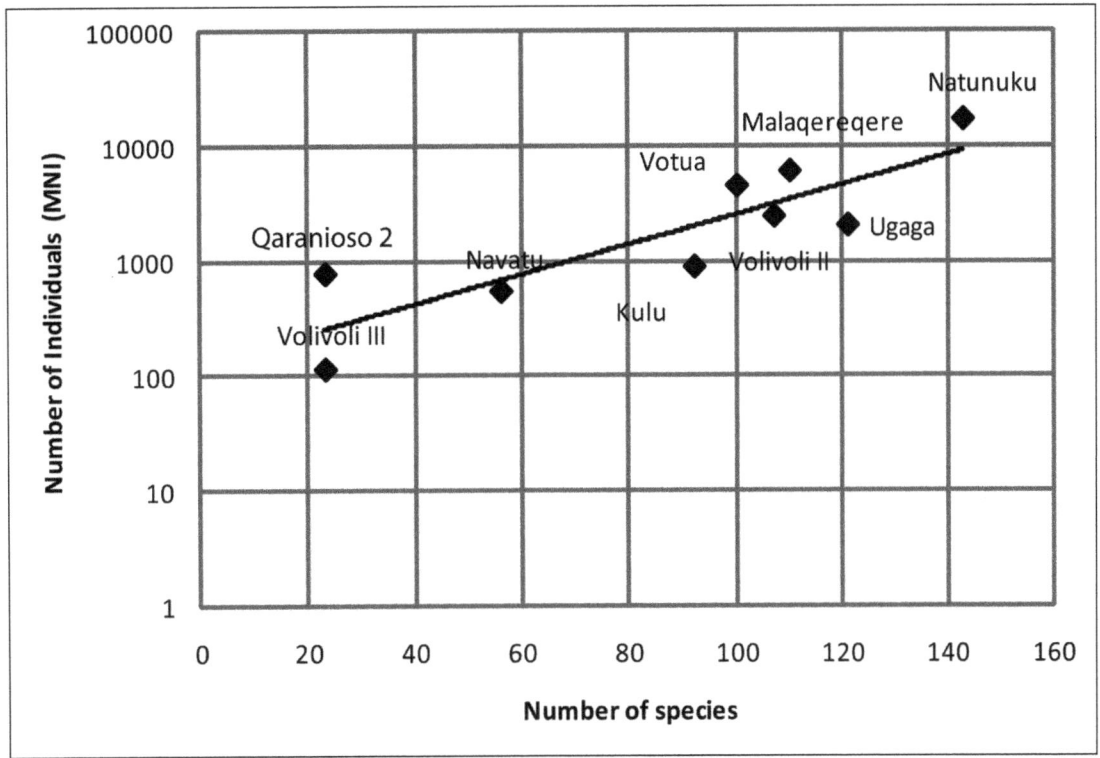

Figure 111. Graph to show the relationship between sample size (total MNI) and species diversity for all samples except Tuvu and Qaranioso I. Note that the Y-axis is a log scale.

Conclusion

The broad picture presented by the results of analysis of the molluscan remains from the EPF sites is a consistent one. A general low level of selectivity for particular species or size classes, combined with exploitation of a range of littoral habitats, has resulted in very diverse samples. Interestingly, diversity is the key point stressed by Burrows (1940:12) regarding mollusc-gathering strategies in Fiji in the ethnographic present: '. . . it would be wrong to say that any [molluscs] are exempt from finding their way into the cooking pot.' Burrows (1940:12) goes on to state that various species are particularly prized, but close reading indicates that these are species (e.g. *Anadara antiquata, Batissa violacea* and *Gafrarium tumidum*) gathered for sale at the markets, rather than for family consumption.

Perhaps it is the common assumption that molluscs represent a labour-intensive and poor source of food that leads to the presupposition of a high level of selectiveness (see Erlandson (2001) for a review of the status of molluscs in archaeological subsistence arguments). What the Fijian assemblages clearly demonstrate is that all molluscs, large and small, were collected, and that selectivity cannot be assumed at the outset. This conclusion indicates that analysts of archaeological shell must completely identify their samples, and that field archaeologists should sample shell midden to a sufficient degree and not discard shell in the field.

References

Abbot, R.T. and Dance, S.P. 1982. *Compendium of seashells*. E.P. Dutton, New York.

Allen, J. 2000. From beach to beach: The development of maritime economies in prehistoric Melanesia. In: O'Connor, S. and Veth, P. (eds), *East of Wallace's Line: Studies of past and present maritime cultures of the Indo-Pacific region*, pp. 139–176. A.A. Balkema, Rotterdam and Brookfield.

Allen, M.S. 2003. Human impact on Pacific nearshore marine ecosystems. In: Sand, C. (ed), *Pacific archaeology: Assessments and prospects*, pp. 317–325. Service des Musées et du Patrimoine, Nouméa.

Anderson, A. 1981. A model of prehistoric collecting on the rocky shore. *Journal of Archaeological Science* 8: 109–120.

Anderson, A., Clark, G. and Worthy, T. 2000. An inland Lapita site in Fiji. *Journal of the Polynesian Society* 109: 311–316.

Barnes, D.K.A. 1997. Ecology of tropical hermit crabs at Quirimba Island, Mozambique: Distribution, abundance and activity. *Marine Ecology Progress Series* 154: 133–142.

Barnes, D.K.A. 1999. Ecology of tropical hermit crabs at Quirimba Island, Mozambique: Shell characteristics and utilisation. *Marine Ecology Progress Series* 183: 241–251.

Barnes, D.K.A. 2001. Hermit crabs, humans and Mozambique mangroves. *African Journal of Ecology* 39: 241–248.

Bedford, S. 2007. Crucial first steps into Remote Oceania. In: Chiu, S. and Sand, C. (eds), *From Southeast Asia to the Pacific: Archaeological perspectives on the Austronesian expansion and the Lapita Cultural Complex*, pp. 185–213. Center for Archaeological Studies, Academia Sinica, Taipei.

Broughton, J.M. 1999. *Resource depression and intensification during the Late Holocene, San Francisco Bay: Evidence from the Emeryville shellmound vertebrate fauna*. University of California Publications, Anthropological Records No. 32. University of California, Berkeley.

Burrows, Commander W. 1940. Notes on molluscs used as food by the Fijians. *Transactions and Proceedings of the Fiji Society* 2(1): 12–14.

Carucci, J. 1992. *Cultural and natural patterning in prehistoric marine foodshell from Palau, Micronesia*. Unpublished PhD thesis, Southern Illinois University at Carbondale.

Cernohorsky, W.O. 1972. *Marine shells of the Pacific, Volume II*. Pacific Publications, Sydney.

Cernohorsky, W.O. 1978. *Tropical Pacific marine shells*. Pacific Publications, Sydney and New York.

Claassen, C. 2000. Quantifying shell: Comments on Mason, Peterson and Tiffany. *American Antiquity* 65(2): 415–418.

Clark, G., Anderson, A. and Matararaba, S. 2001. The Lapita site at Votua, northern Lau Islands, Fiji. *Archaeology in Oceania* 36: 134–145.

Dance, S.P. 1977. *The encyclopedia of shells*. Australia and New Zealand Book Company, Sydney.

Demond, J. 1957. Micronesian reef-associated gastropods. *Pacific Science* XI(3): 275–341.

Erlandson, J. 2001. The archaeology of aquatic adaptations: Paradigms for a new millennium. *Journal of Archaeological Science* 9(4): 287–350.

Glassow, M.A. 2000. Weighing vs. counting shellfish remains: A comment on Mason, Peterson and Tiffany. *American Antiquity* 65(2): 407–414.

Gosliner, T.M., Behrens, D.W. and Williams, G.C. 1996. *Coral reef animals of the Indo-Pacific*. Sea Challengers, Monterey CA.

Grayson, D.K. 1984. *Quantitative zooarchaeology: Topics in the analysis of archaeological faunas*. Academic Press, Orlando FL and London.

Green, R.C., Green, K., Rappaport, R.A., Rappaport, A. and Davidson, J. 1967. Archaeology on the island of Mo'orea, French Polynesia. *Anthropological Papers of the American Museum of Natural History* 51(2).

Habe, T. 1964. *Shells of the Western Pacific in color, Volume 2*. Hoikusha Publishing Company, Osaka.

Hazlett, B.A. 1981. The behavioural ecology of hermit crabs. *Annual Review of Ecology and Systematics* 12: 1–22.

Hinton, A. 1972. *Shells of New Guinea and the Central Pacific Indo-Pacific*. Robert Brown and Associates and Jacaranda Press, Port Moresby and Milton QLD.

Kinosita, H. and Akira O. 1968. Analysis of shell-searching behaviour of the land hermit-crab, *Coenobita rugosus* H. Milne Edwards. *Journal of the Faculty of Science, University of Tokyo: Section IV Zoology* 11(3): 293–358.

Kira, T. 1965. *Shells of the Western Pacific in color, Volume 1*. Revised edition. Hoikusha Publishing Company, Osaka.

Kress, J.H. 2000. The malacoarchaeology of Palawan Island. *Journal of East Asian Archaeology* 2(1): 285–328.

Mason, R.D., Peterson, M.L. and Tiffany, J.A. 1998. Weighing vs. counting: Measurement reliability and the California school of midden analysis. *American Antiquity* 63(2): 303–324.

Mason, R.D., Peterson, M.L. and Tiffany, J.A. 2000. Weighing and counting shell: A response to Glassow and Claassen. *American Antiquity* 65(4): 757–761.

Morton, J. and Raj, U. n.d. *The shore ecology of Suva and South Viti Levu*. University of the South Pacific. Introduction to Zoning and Reef Structures – Soft Shores, Book One. Suva, Fiji.

Osorno, J-L., Fernández-Casillas, L. and Rodríguez-Juárez, C. 1998. Are hermit crabs looking for light and large shells?: Evidence from natural and field-induced shell exchanges. *Journal of Experimental Marine Biology and Ecology* 222(1998): 163–173.

Palmer, B. 1965. Excavations at Karobo, Viti Levu. *New Zealand Archaeological Association Newsletter* 8: 26–33.

Palmer, J.B. 1968. Excavations at Karobo, Viti Levu. *New Zealand Archaeological Association Newsletter* 8(2): 26–34.

Reitz, E.J. and Wing, E.S. 1999. *Zooarchaeology*. Cambridge University Press, Cambridge, New York and Melbourne.

Scudder, S.J. and Quitmyer, I.R. 1998. Evaluation of evidence for pre-Columbian occupation at Great Cave, Cayman Brac, Cayman Islands. *Caribbean Journal of Science* 34(1–2): 41–9.

Small, M.P. and Thacker, W.T. 1994. Land hermit crabs use odors of dead conspecifics to locate shells. *Journal of Experimental Marine Biology and Ecology* 182(1994): 169–182.

Specht, J. 1968. Preliminary report of excavations on Watom Island. *Journal of the Polynesian Society* 77(2): 117–134.

Specht, J. 1985. Crabs as disturbance factors in tropical archaeological sites. *Australian Archaeologist* 21: 11–18.

Szabó, K. 1999. Shellfish gathering and foraging behaviour: An investigation into optimality and mollusc remains from prehistoric Motutapu Island. Unpublished BA(hons) thesis, Department of Anthropology, University of Auckland.

Szabó, K. 2001. The reef, the beach and the rocks: An environmental analysis of mollusc remains from Natunuku, Viti Levu, Fiji. In: Clark, G.R., Anderson, A.J. and Vunidilo, T. (eds), *The Archaeology of Lapita Dispersal in Oceania*, pp. 159–166. Pandanus Books, Canberra.

Szabó, K. and Yang, H-Y. S. In prep. Terrestrial hermit crab interference in archaeological shell deposits.

Thacker, R.W. 1994. Volatile shell-investigation cues of land hermit crabs: Effect of shell fit, detection of cues from other hermit crab species, and cue isolation. *Journal of Chemical Ecology* 20(7): 1457–1482.

Van Benthem Jutting, W.S.S. 1953. Systematic studies on the non-marine mollusca of the Indo-Australian Archipelago; part IV: Critical revision of the freshwater bivalves of Java. *Treubia* 21(1): 19–73.

Walker, S.E. 1994. Biological remanie: Gastropod fossils used by the living terrestrial hermit crab, *Coenobita clypeatus*, on Bermuda. *Palaios* 9: 403–412.

Walker, S.E. 1995. Taphonomy of modern and fossil intertidal gastropod associations from Isla Santa Cruz and Isla Santa Fe, Galápagos Islands. *Lethaia* 28: 371–382.

terra australis 31

9

The fish bone remains

Geoffrey Clark
Archaeology and Natural History, The Australian National University

Katherine Szabó
Archaeology and Natural History, The Australian National University

Introduction

Fisheries are a fundamental part of Remote Oceanic economies and lifeways, used for different types of fishing, invertebrate capture and collection, and the gathering of marine plants. Where no bones or calcareous parts remain, these activities are invisible to archaeologists, but modern studies of marine exploitation in Fiji and elsewhere in the Pacific (e.g. Rawlinson et al. 1994; Dalzell et al. 1996) indicate that a good portion of activities should leave traces in the archaeological record. As with marine mollusca, tropical Indo-Pacific fish species diversity is high. However unlike the mollusca, our inability to identify remains beyond the family level limits our ability to talk in any sensitive manner about ecology, niche exploitation, or often capture techniques. Nevertheless, through attention to ethnographic strategies and generalised family ecology, archaeologists have attempted to gain insight into prehistoric fishing strategies (e.g. Coutts 1975; Kirch and Dye 1979; Butler 1994), and we continue to build on this approach here, drawing in modern studies of subsistence and artisanal fishing in Fiji and elsewhere.

In a review of fish assemblages recovered from Lapita sites, Butler (1988:109–110) highlighted the dominance of inshore fish taxa by eight families (Serranidae, Lutjanidae, Lethrinidae, Labridae, Scaridae, Acanthuridae, Balistidae, Diodontidae), which accounted for more than 85% of archaeological fish remains. The predominance of these taxa has been used to characterise Lapita fishing as 'near shore' or 'inshore' (Green 1976, 1986; Kirch and Dye 1979; Kirch and Yen 1982; Kirch 1988). Despite the focus on inshore families, Butler (1994) argued there were important differences between the fishing strategies of Lapita groups in Near Oceania and those in Remote Oceania, including Fiji. In particular, fish assemblages in western Lapita sites such as Mussau indicated a generalised fishing strategy involving angling for carnivores and a range of techniques, such as traps, netting, spearing and poisoning, to capture herbivores/omnivores. In Remote Oceania, Lapita fishing concentrated on herbivore/omnivore families and capture strategies other than angling. Further afield, early Austronesian fishing at the Bukit Tengkorak site in Sabah, Borneo Island, had a pattern similar to that of Lapita fishing in Remote Oceania: a focus on inshore herbivores/omnivores taken with nets, traps, poison and spears; the secondary importance of angling to catch Labridae and some species of Lethrinidae and Serranidae; and the relative unimportance of fishing in the pelagic zone with a hook or trolling lure (Ono 2003).

In contrast, fish remains from the Naigani Lapita site in Fiji, analysed by Hawkins (2000), had an atypical emphasis on reef-edge/reef-flat families, with the top five taxa consisting of Lethrinidae, Scaridae, Serranidae, Lutjanidae and Diodontidae. Three of the five taxa are carnivores that can be taken by angling, suggesting an emphasis on hook and line fishing, although no fish hooks or lure parts were found at the site (Best 1981; Hawkins 2000). The possibility that Lapita fishing strategies in Remote Oceania were flexible and able to be tailored to a local environment is supportive of a 'generalist' subsistence colonising strategy (Dye and Steadman 1990) in which a range of basic techniques were suitable for fishing a variety of inshore environments. Such flexibility suggests the pelagic zone could also have been used in Lapita times (see Szabó and Summerhayes 2002:95; Szabó 2007). Burley and Shutler (2007) record rotating and jabbing shell fish hooks from early sites in Tonga, along with a composite trolling lure suitable for capturing pelagic species made in *Trochus* shell, which is dated by a charcoal determination to 2620±50 BP (CAMS 41531). Szabó (2007) records a near-identical *Trochus niloticus* lure shank of presumed Lapita age from Bourewa, Fiji.

Allen (1992:448–450) considers that Lapita subsistence patterns were not structurally different from those of post-Lapita Polynesian groups, but for Fiji it has been difficult to evaluate the variability of Lapita fishing in the archipelago, as well as the possibility of a post-Lapita change in fish-capture strategies due to technological developments and/or environmental factors. In this chapter, we present fish-bone identifications from six EPF sites (Figure 112) and consider prehistoric fish-capture strategies based on the dietary preference of taxa and ethnographic observations of traditional fishing (Masse 1986; Ono 2003). Results are compared with other archaeological fish-bone assemblages from Fiji to assess capture methods during the colonisation phase and whether different fishing strategies were used in the post-Lapita era. The effect of different collection methods on a fish-bone assemblage is examined from the Votua Lapita site excavated with dry sieving in 4 mm and 6 mm mesh, and an assemblage recovered from the same site by wet sieving with 3 mm mesh. Fish bone was analysed from the sites of Natunuku, Navatu, Kulu Bay, Malaqereqere, Volivoli II and Votua (1996 and 2000 excavations). The six assemblages yielded a Minimum Number of Individuals (MNI) of 406 fish from a total of 5231 identified bones. Bones were identified using a reference collection at the Australian National University, and the Navatu assemblage was identified by B.F. Leach at the Archaeozoology Laboratory (Wellington, New Zealand). Fish bone was absent or present in only trace amounts at Volivoli III, Qaranioso II and III, Ugaga Island and Karobo, and was not analysed from those sites.

Methodology

Following Leach (1997), the term fish 'type' or 'taxon/taxa' will be used, rather than 'species', as the identification of EPF assemblages has been made to the family level (e.g. Leach 1986; Nagaoka 1994; Hawkins 2000). Identification of taxa was with diagnostic head bones and

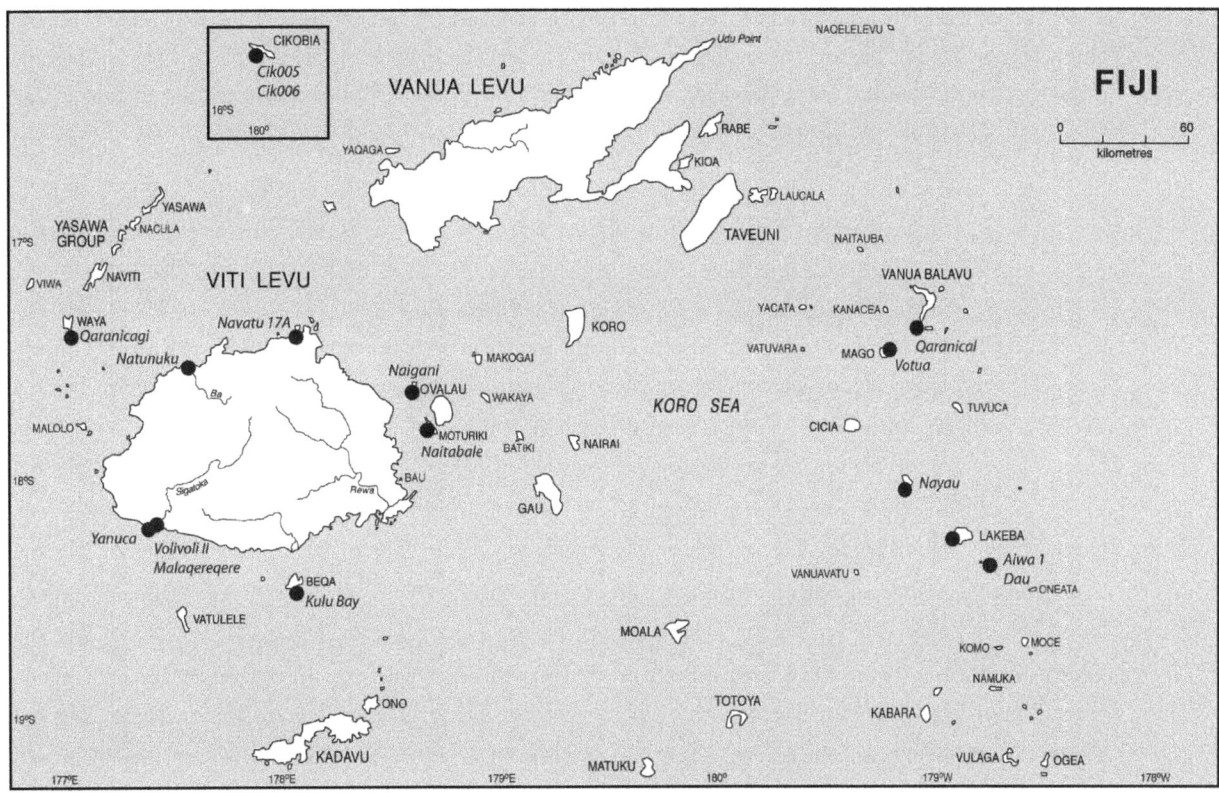

Figure 112. Map of Fiji showing the location of EPF and other fish-bone assemblages mentioned in the text.

'special' bones, following the methodology outlined in Leach (1986, 1997), using the fish reference collection in the Department of Archaeology and Natural History (ANU) established by Barnett (1978). Vogel (2005) has clearly demonstrated the utility of expanding the number of bones traditionally used for identification, identifying significant numbers of rarely or hitherto unrecorded families, such as Chaetodontidae (butterflyfishes) and Pomacentridae (damselfishes) for sites in south-central Polynesia. Unfortunately, the analyses presented here were largely completed before Vogel's study, and the identification of bones beyond the standard roster requires that the reference collection used has such additional bones present and correctly identified – a problem also encountered by Vogel (2005).

The abundance of different taxa in each assemblage was assessed by calculating NISP (Number of Identified Specimens) and MNI (Minimum Number of Individuals). The calculation of MNI follows the methodology of Chaplin (1971) as discussed in Leach (1986, 1997). In accordance with this, no attempt was made to increase the MNI results by adjusting for observed size difference in diagnostic head bones (e.g. Leach et al. 1997). In the comparison of site assemblages, the effects of different collection and aggregation strategies on the results are discussed, including assemblage sampling, and the effect of screen size and sieving method (e.g. Grayson 1984; Masse 1989).

An assessment of the relative importance of each taxon to the prehistoric diet is not attempted here, as the amount of food represented by a fish varies from species to species, and depends on the size of the individual fish caught, which could not be determined due to the absence of complete and measurable cranial bones (e.g. Leach et al. 1997). The ecological preference for each identified taxa along with the main types of capture technology have been discussed by several authorities (Kirch and Dye 1979; Butler 1994; Hawkins 2000; Ono 2003). Masse (1986, 1989) outlines the methodological problems of determining fish-capture technology in the Pacific where identification is at the family level. Within a family, a number of strategies are used to catch different species and often more than one technique is used to harvest a single species. The missionary Thomas Williams (1858[1985]:89–90) observed the diversity of Fijian fishing techniques in the 19th century:

> Various means are employed for taking fish, including nets and a sort of weir formed like the creels and crab-pots used along the British coasts, and baited and secured in the same way. Another kind has two apertures; a third contrivance is an intricate fence, either fixed or portable. Stone pens, hooks, and fish spears, are in use throughout Fiji. Some drowsy fish of the shark family are taken by passing a noose over their heads, and a vegetable poison from a climbing glycine is employed to stupify smaller kinds. In some parts the *rau* is used, which is a fringe formed by winding split cocoa-nut leaves round a number of vines, to the length of hundreds or even thousands of feet. This being stretched in a straight line, the canoes to which the ends are attached approach until they meet, thus making a vast enclosure within which the fish are then speared or netted. One kind of net is used in the same way. The native seines are like our own, and are well made.

Despite the potential diversity of ethnographically documented fishing strategies, consideration of 'preferred' fish-capture technology is considered helpful in illustrating potential inter-site differences in capture technology, which can be tested to some extent by archaeological remains of fishing gear (sinkers, net weights and fish hooks). These approaches will be coupled here with studies and creel surveys derived from modern studies of Fijian fisheries (e.g. Rawlinson et al. 1994). While there are important technological differences, and introduced species such as jungle perch (*Kuhlia rupestris*) and tilapia (*Oreochromis mossambicus*) form an important component of the overall fisheries effort, these studies still highlight important links between fish behaviour and capture techniques, as well as giving a clear overview of important nearshore species available to Fijians.

Kulu Bay

At Kulu Bay 863 g of fish bone was recovered, with a NISP of 2907, including 15 identifiable taxa and a minimum of 240 individuals (Table 21). Based on MNI%, seven taxa were responsible for 84% of the total – Scaridae (24.2%), Labridae (15.0%), Acanthuridae (10.4%), Lethrinidae (9.6%), Serranidae (9.2%), Diodontidae (7.5%) and Lutjanidae (7.5%). Inspection of bone provenience shows that by weight, the amount of fish bone increased below 40 cm depth in all excavations, with the deepest excavation in square C11 returning quantities of fish bone down to 130–140 cm depth. This depth-density distribution is also seen with the Kulu Bay 1 shell sample (see Chapter 8).

The most commonly represented family in the Kulu assemblage was the Scaridae, followed by the Labridae and the Acanthuridae. The first-ranked taxon is a coral grazer that inhabits shallow reef waters. Masse (1986) argued that the most common method for harvesting herbivorous reef fish was by netting. However, in principle, any non-hook method is viable, with scarids being a major component of modern spearfish catches in Fiji and significant amounts also taken in gillnets (Gillett and Moy 2006:16). It should be noted that spearfishing has become both more commonly practised and able to quickly take a larger range of fish following the introduction of goggles, spearguns and scuba gear during the 20th century (Johannes 1981:67; Gillett and Moy 2006:11). Nevertheless, these observations, coupled with scarid ecology, demonstrate the effectiveness of spearing technologies for parrotfish. Adding the Diodontidae, Ostraciidae and Acanthuridae totals to the Scaridae, 46% of the identified MNI elements belong to taxa that are most likely to have been taken by non-hook technology (Table 22).

Table 21. Identified fish families recovered from Kulu Bay.

Family	NISP	NISP%	MNI	MNI%
Acanthuridae	27	0.9	25	10.4
Balistidae	7	0.2	7	2.9
Carangidae	3	0.1	2	0.8
Elasmobranchi	2	0.1	2	0.8
Diodontidae	70	2.4	18	7.5
Holocentridae	2	0.1	2	0.8
Labridae	78	2.7	36	15.0
Lethrinidae	36	1.2	23	9.6
Lutjanidae	30	1.0	18	7.5
Nemipteridae	21	0.7	14	5.8
Ostraciidae	14	0.5	10	4.2
Scaridae	171	5.9	58	24.2
Thunnidae/Katsuwonidae	2	0.1	2	0.8
Serranidae	37	1.3	22	9.2
Sphyraenidae	1	0.0	1	0.4
Unidentified	2406	82.8	0	0.0
Total	**2907**	**100.0**	**240**	**100.0**

Table 22. Ethnographic capture methods and fish family representation (MNI%) at Kulu Bay.

Family	MNI%	Baithook	Trolling lure	Net	Basket trap	Handspear	Poisoning	Preferred method
Acanthuridae	10.4	X		X	X	X	X	Net
Balistidae	2.9	X		X		X	X	Net
Carangidae	0.8	X	X	X		X		Hook
Elasmobranchi	0.8	X	X	X		X		Spear
Diodontidae	7.5			X		X		Net
Holocentridae	0.8	X	X			X		Hook
Labridae	15.0	X		X	X	X	X	Hook
Lethrinidae	9.6	X		X	X		X	Hook
Lutjanidae	7.5	X	X	X		X	X	Hook
Nemipteridae	5.8	X						Hook
Ostraciidae	4.2			X				Net
Scaridae	24.2	X		X	X	X	X	Net
Thunnidae/Katsuwonidae	0.8	X	X			X		Lure
Serranidae	9.2	X		X				Hook
Sphyraenidae	0.4	X	X					Lure

The labrids are the second-largest reef-fish family, and are diverse in habits, size and food preference (Masse 1986). The Balistidae are also complex in a Fijian context. Although often cited as herbivorous (e.g. Carcasson 1977:266), the most-targeted balistid in Fiji (*Pseudobalistes flavimarginatus* or yellowmargin triggerfish) (Carcasson 1977:268) is omnivorous, feeding on coral tips, gastropods, foraminiferans, crustaceans and tunicates (Froese and Pauly 2009), and nowadays is generally caught using a handline (see data in Rawlinson et al. 1994:50). It is possible that up to 54% of the Kulu fish assemblage could have been harvested using angling methods, but diverse techniques are used to capture fish species within all of these families, with even sphyraenids and emperors featuring in simple bamboo-spear catches by fishers wading in shallow water on the receding tide (Gillett and Moy 2006:15). Even the Spanish mackerel (*Scomberomorus commerson*), characteristic of modern Fijian troll-fisheries catches, is inquisitive and vulnerable to spearing (Rawlinson et al. 1994:415).

Ethno-archaeological studies of fishing (Kirch and Dye 1979; Masse 1986) suggest that a combined netting/angling strategy is a common fishing strategy among Pacific communities. A combined strategy using hook and non-hook technologies is suggested at Kulu Bay. While netting may well have been important at Kulu Bay, it is interesting to note the lack of species from the Siganidae (rabbitfishes) and Mugilidae (mullets) families, and the absence of the small mackerel *Rastrelliger kanagurta* (Scombridae), which feature very strongly in lagoon net catches in Fiji (Rawlinson et al. 1994:50; Dalzell et al. 1996:453). This may be an issue of identification or preservation, or may speak directly to the nature of the capture technologies employed.

The effects of element survival must also be considered at Kulu Bay, where the cultural materials have been redeposited. Of the surviving remains, the majority are the most robust bones in the fish skeleton, particularly the pharyngeal plates of the scarids and dorsal spines from large individuals. These are the main elements that have been assigned to a family. The dominance in the Kulu Bay assemblage of coral grazers might not accurately represent the prehistoric fish take, through under-representing individuals and taxa with small and fragile skeletal elements.

Volivoli II

From the identifiable fish-jaw elements recovered from Volivoli II, five taxa were identified. Members of the class Elasmobranchii (sharks, skates and rays) were identified from their distinctive vertebrae and teeth. The percentage of each taxa is given in Table 23, which shows that the small assemblage (NISP=106, MNI=9) also contained acanthurids, lethrinids, serranids and lutjanids. These three families (Acanthuridae, Lethrinidae and Serranidae) inhabit different niches and have different feeding strategies, suggesting that several capture strategies were employed (Butler 1994). Studies of fish feeding behaviour (Kirch and Dye 1979; Masse 1986; Butler 1994) indicate that the most effective way to catch acanthurids is with nets, spears or poison, as the taxa will not readily take a baited hook. Lethrinids and serranids are mainly caught by hook and line techniques. The different capture preferences for each taxon represented at Volivoli II are listed in Table 24. Due to the small size of the assemblage, it can only be suggested that a combination of non-hook and angling fishing strategies was employed.

Table 23. Identified fish families recovered from Volivoli II.

Taxa	NISP	NISP%	MNI	MNI%
Acanthuridae	6	5.7	3	33.3
Elasmobranchi	1	0.9	1	11.1
Lethrinidae	2	1.9	2	22.2
Lutjanidae	1	0.9	1	11.1
Serranidae	5	4.7	2	22.2
Unidentified	91	85.8	0	0
Total	**106**	**100.0**	**9**	**100.0**

Table 24. Ethnographic capture methods and fish family representation (MNI%) at Volivoli II.

Family	MNI%	Baithook	Trolling lure	Net	Basket trap	Handspear	Poisoning	Preferred method
Acanthuridae	33.3	X		X	X	X	X	Net
Elasmobranchi	11.1	X	X	X		X		Spear
Lethrinidae	22.2	X		X	X		X	Hook
Lutjanidae	11.1	X	X	X		X	X	Hook
Serranidae	22.2	X		X				Hook

Malaqereqere

The Malaqereqere fish-bone assemblage had a NISP of 754 and an MNI of 54 from eight taxa. The site is a small coastal rock shelter that may have been used by fishing parties, resulting in a relatively high density of fish bone. The proportion of each taxon recovered from the Malaqereqere rock shelter is listed in Table 25, which shows the dominance of the Acanthuridae, comprising 37% of the total assemblage, followed by the Serranidae (14.8%), Diodontidae (14.8%) and Lethrinidae (13%). The different capture methods for each of the taxa are listed in Table 26. As mentioned previously, acanthurids are algal grazers mainly taken by netting, diodontids are taken by netting or spearing, and serranids are often caught by hook and line techniques. The combination of the techniques of angling and netting suggests a mixed strategy of inshore fishing on and around the reef.

Table 25. Identified fish families recovered from Malaqereqere.

Taxa	NISP	NISP%	MNI	MNI%
Acanthuridae	20	2.7	20	37.0
Balistidae	1	0.1	1	1.9
Diodontidae	18	2.4	8	14.8
Labridae	3	0.4	3	5.6
Lethrinidae	8	1.1	7	13.0
Lutjanidae	8	1.1	5	9.3
Scaridae	2	0.3	2	3.7
Serranidae	13	1.7	8	14.8
Unidentified	681	90.3	0	0
Total	**754**	**100.0**	**54**	**100.0**

Table 26. Ethnographic capture methods and fish family representation (MNI%) at Malaqereqere.

Family	MNI%	Baithook	Trolling lure	Net	Basket trap	Handspear	Poisoning	Preferred method
Acanthuridae	37.0	X		X	X	X	X	Net
Balistidae	1.9	X		X		X	X	Net
Diodontidae	14.8			X		X		Net
Labridae	5.6	X		X	X	X	X	Hook
Lethrinidae	13	X		X	X		X	Hook
Lutjanidae	9.3	X	X	X		X	X	Hook
Scaridae	3.7	X		X	X	X	X	Net
Serranidae	14.8	X		X				Hook

Navatu

Fish bone from Trench B of the Navatu site was analysed by B.F. Leach, and the remains have been divided into two assemblages (Tables 27–30). The first assemblage contains the fish remains from Layer 1 and Layer 2, which date to around 600–500 cal. BP, while the second assemblage consists of the Layer 4 fish bone, dating to about 1000–1500 cal. BP. The sticky nature of the deposit at Navatu did not sieve well and the Navatu fish-bone assemblage is likely to over-represent large and robust elements compared with small and fragile bone remains. The upper (Layer 1 and Layer 2) and lower (Layer 4) assemblages have the same number of taxa, with individuals in the Scaridae and Lethrinidae families dominant by MNI% in Layer 4, and the Tetraodontidae and Lethrinidae in Layers 1–2. A shark tooth from 80–90 cm depth was identified as mako (*Isurus glaucus*), and may represent shark fishing. In 19th century Fiji, sharks were caught by noosing, spearing or poisoning (Williams 1858[1985]:90). Although both of the Navatu fish-bone assemblages are small, the mixed netting-angling-spearing strategy (Table 30) suggests continuity in fish capture from the post-Lapita period through to the second millennium AD.

Table 27. Identified fish families recovered from Navatu (Layers 1 and 2).

Family name	NISP	NISP%	MNI	MNI%
Balistidae	1	5.9	1	10.0
Diodontidae	3	17.6	1	10.0
Elasmobranchi	1	5.9	1	10.0
Labridae	2	11.8	1	10.0
Lethrinidae	4	23.5	2	20.0
Lutjanidae	1	5.9	1	10.0
Scaridae	2	11.8	1	10.0
Tetraodontidae	3	17.6	2	20.0
Total	17	100.0	10	100.0

Table 28. Ethnographic capture methods and fish family representation (MNI%) at Navatu (Layers 1 and 2).

Family	MNI%	Baithook	Trolling lure	Net	Basket trap	Handspear	Poisoning	Preferred method
Balistidae	10.0	X		X		X	X	Net
Diodontidae	10.0			X		X		Net
Elasmobranchi	10.0	X	X	X		X		Spear
Labridae	10.0	X		X	X	X	X	Hook
Lethrinidae	20.0	X		X	X		X	Hook
Lutjanidae	10.0	X	X	X		X	X	Hook
Scaridae	10.0	X		X	X	X	X	Net
Tetraodontidae	20.0			X	X	X	X	Net

Table 29. Identified fish families recovered from Navatu (Layer 4).

Family name	NISP	NISP%	MNI	MNI%
Diodontidae	1	3.4	1	9.1
Elasmobranchi	4	13.8	1	9.1
Lethrinidae	5	17.3	2	18.2
Lutjanidae	1	3.4	1	9.1
Scaridae	12	41.4	4	36.3
Tetraodontidae	2	6.9	1	9.1
Total	**29**	**100.0**	**11**	**10.0**

Table 30. Ethnographic capture methods and fish family representation (MNI%) at Navatu (Layer 4).

Family	MNI%	Baithook	Trolling lure	Net	Basket trap	Handspear	Poisoning	Preferred method
Diodontidae	9.1			X		X		Net
Elasmobranchi	9.1	X	X	X		X		Spear
Lethrinidae	18.2	X		X	X		X	Hook
Lutjanidae	9.1	X	X	X		X	X	Hook
Scaridae	36.3	X		X	X	X	X	Net
Serranidae	9.1	X		X				Hook
Tetraodontidae	9.1			X	X	X	X	Net

Natunuku

The fish-bone assemblage from the Natunuku Lapita site (NISP=215) was compromised by its small size, high degree of fragmentation and general lack of identifiable elements (Table 31). The only family that could be firmly identified was the Scaridae. Elasmobranchii or cartilaginous fishes were represented in the deposits by small vertebrae, along with the pharyngeal plate of a diodont. The lack of fishing gear in the artefact assemblage from Natunuku (Davidson et al. 1990) could indicate that angling was not used at the site and that fish capture was with nets/spears/traps/poison, but robust conclusions about the nature of Lapita fishing cannot be drawn from the Natunuku assemblage.

Table 31. Identifiable elements in the Natunuku fish bone assemblage (NISP=215).

Provenance	Taxa	Element	NISP
TP1:0–10	Unidentified	vertebrae	3
TP1:0–10	Unidentified	premaxilla	1
TP1/2:0–10	Unidentified	vertebrae	1
TP1/2:0–10	Unidentified	fragment	1
TP1/2:10–20	Unidentified	vertebrae	1
TP1/2:20–30	Unidentified	vertebrae	4
TP2:0–10	Unidentified	vertebrae	2
TP2:10–20	Elasmobranchi	tooth	1
TP2/2: 0–10	Unidentified	vertebrae	6
TP2/2: 0–10	Elasmobranchi	vertebrae	1
TP2/2:10–20	Unidentified	vertebrae	4
Tp2/2:10–20	Unidentified	fragments	2
TP2/3: 0–10	Unidentified	vertebrae	2
TP2/3:10–20	Unidentified	vertebrae	1
T3/A3/Layer 2a	Unidentified	fragment	1
T3/A3/Layer 2	Unidentified	vertebrae	2
T3/A4:10–20	Elasmobranchi	vertebrae	1
T3/A4:10–20	Unidentified	quadrate	1
T3/A4:20–30	Unidentified	vertebrae	1
T3/A4:20–30	Unidentified	fragment	1
T3/A5:0–10	Unidentified	vertebrae	1
T3/A5:0–10	Diodontidae	pharyngeal plate	1
T3/A5:20–30	Elasmobranchi	vertebrae	2
T3/A5:30–40	Elasmobranchi	vertebrae	1
T3/A5:30–40	Scaridae	dentary	1
T3/A6:10–20	Scaridae	dentary	1
T3/A6:10–20	Unidentified	vertebrae	5
T3/A6:20–30	Unidentified	vertebrae	1
T3/B5:10–20	Elasmobranchi	vertebrae	2
T3/B6:20–30	Scaridae	premaxilla	1
T3/B6:40–50	Unidentified	vertebrae	2
T3/B6:50–60	Elasmobranchi	vertebrae	1
T3/B6:50–60	Unidentified	vertebrae	4
Total			**60**

Votua

The Votua Lapita site was discovered in 1996 and test excavations in a shell midden (Area 1) and test pit (TP1) recovered small amounts of fish bone (Clark et al. 2001) from dry sieving of the clay sediments through 4 mm and 6 mm mesh. The possibility that a coarse collection strategy in 1996, necessitated by the nature of the deposits and available equipment, had led to the loss of faunal remains, especially of fish, from the Lapita deposit was tested in 2000 when Area 2 (1 m x 4 m) was excavated and all sediments were water sieved through 3 mm mesh. A low NISP of 16 representing an MNI of 11 from five taxa was found in the 1996 investigations (Tables 32–33), compared with a NISP of 1343 and MNI of 57 from six taxa in 2000 (Tables 34–36). A breakdown of identified taxa elements relative to the number of vertebra and spines is shown in Table 34. The two assemblages differ in the presence of individuals from the Lethrinidae and Monocanthidae families in Area 1/TP1 and Acanthuridae and Carangidae in Area 2, but both assemblages were dominated by scarids (1996=54.5%, 2000=40.4%), and the number of taxa did not change significantly, in spite of the larger sample obtained in 2000 (Tables 32 and 34–35). Despite the significant difference in sample size, both of the Votua assemblages suggest a major focus on non-hook technologies, in tandem with some angling (Tables 33 and 36).

Artefacts from the Votua 2000 excavations support the view that angling was undertaken, as there were several fragments from small pearl-shell fish hooks (tab and shank), similar to those recorded by Best (1984:450) from early deposits on Lakeba (see Chapter 14 Appendix:Figure 155). Votua also contained pieces of coral abraded with semi-circular linear grooves that might have been used to shape the shaft of arrows or spears for use in fishing (Best 1984:445; Chapter 14 Appendix:Figure 159). The diameter of nine coral grooves ranged from 5.8 mm to 11.8 mm, and traditional wooden arrow shafts used today have a diameter of 6.5 mm to 9.2 mm. At Votua, fishing with spears/bow and arrow was a potentially important capture strategy during the Lapita era.

Table 32. Identified fish families recovered from Votua 1996 excavations.

Family	NISP	NISP%	MNI	MNI%
Labridae	1	6.3	1	9.1
Lethrinidae	4	25.0	2	18.2
Monocanthidae	1	6.3	1	9.1
Scaridae	7	43.7	6	54.5
Serranidae	3	18.7	1	9.1
Total	**16**	**100.0**	**11**	**100.0**

Table 33. Ethnographic capture methods and fish family representation (MNI%) at Votua (Area 1 and TP1).

Family	MNI%	Baithook	Trolling lure	Net	Basket trap	Handspear	Poisoning	Preferred method
Labridae	9.1	X		X	X	X	X	Hook
Lethrinidae	18.2	X		X	X		X	Hook
Monocathidae	9.1			X	X	X	X	Net
Scaridae	54.5	X		X	X	X	X	Net
Serranidae	9.1	X		X				Hook

Table 34. Fish bone recovered from Votua 2000 excavations (Area 2, Squares 1–4).

Spit	ID NISP	ID (g)	Vertebra (NISP)	Vertebra (g)	Spine (NISP)	Spine (g)	Residue (NISP)	Residue (g)	NISP Total	Spit weight (g)
0–10	5	5.4	23	5.1	13	3.2	27	4.0	68	17.7
10–20	8	5.3	58	14.2	29	2.5	76	10.0	171	32.0
20–30	11	5.2	52	23.0	56	5.6	93	12.8	212	46.6
30–40	16	9.0	70	16.9	103	14.2	126	21.9	315	62.0
40–50	20	6.9	73	23.5	95	9.4	166	19.6	354	59.4
50–60	12	9.0	71	22.3	27	3.6	87	10.5	197	45.4
60–70	1	2.4	12	3.0	3	0	10	1.2	26	6.6
Total	73	27.3	359	108.0	326	38.5	585	80.0	1343	269.7

Table 35. Identified fish families recovered from Votua 2000 excavations.

Family	NISP	NISP %	MNI	MNI%
Acanthuridae	14	1.1	12	21.0
Carangidae	5	0.4	3	5.3
Diodontidae	40	3.0	5	8.8
Labridae	10	0.7	8	14.0
Scaridae	42	3.1	23	40.4
Serranidae	13	1.0	6	10.5
Unidentified	1219	90.7	0	0
Total	1343	100.0	57	100.0

Table 36. Ethnographic capture methods and fish family representation (MNI%) at Votua 2000 excavations (Area 2, Squares 1–4).

Family	MNI%	Baithook	Trolling lure	Net	Basket trap	Handspear	Poisoning	Preferred method
Acanthuridae	21.0	X		X	X	X	X	Net
Carangidae	5.3	X	X	X		X		Hook
Diodontidae	8.8			X		X		Net
Labridae	14.0	X		X	X	X	X	Hook
Scaridae	40.4	X		X	X	X	X	Net
Serranidae	10.5	X		X				Hook

Prehistoric fishing in Fiji

A hierarchical cluster analysis of family MNI% was made with SPSS (16.0) to examine relationships among the EPF fish assemblages (Figure 113). The two south-coast Viti Levu assemblages of Volivoli II and Malaqereqere dating to the past 2000 years group together, as they have low proportions of Scaridae and contain a balance of other herbivores/omnivores (Acanthuridae, Diodontidae) and carnivores (Lethrinidae, Lutjanidae, Serranidae). In the main cluster, fish bone from the two Lapita deposits of Votua (2000) and Kulu Bay are placed together away from the Votua 1996 and Navatu Layers 1–2 and Layer 4 assemblages. Interestingly,

Kulu Bay and Votua 2000 were the only assemblages recovered by water sieving, and although Kulu Bay has a greater number of taxa than Votua 2000 (Kulu Bay=15 families, Votua 2000=6 families), they both have a primary emphasis on herbivores/omnivores (Scaridae, Acanthuridae, Diodontidae) and a secondary focus on carnivores (Labridae, Lethrinidae, Serranidae). The Navatu and Votua 1996 excavations sampled sediments that did not sieve easily, and the grouping of these two assemblages might indicate a potential bias against remains from small individuals, especially those of Scaridae. An alternative is that environmental differences were responsible for the low proportion of Scaridae at Volivoli II and Malaqereqere, pointing to the absence of shallow reef environments along the south coast of Viti Levu, compared with the prehistoric marine environment at Votua, Kulu Bay and Navatu. However, such potential environmental differences are not clearly reflected in the molluscan remains (see Chapter 8). Although Volivoli II is complicated by the dominance of terrestrial snails and opercula from an unidentified species of *Turbo* which may derive from either a rocky or reef-flat environment, Malaqereqere has a wide range of shellfish species from rocky and reef-flat environments that occur in some numbers.

The EPF fish-bone results were also compared with other Lapita and post-Lapita fish assemblages from Fiji to examine geographic and temporal variation in prehistoric fishing. Although Fowler (1955) recorded fish bone from 20 species and several genera from the Navatu site, his identifications require verification as in most instances Pacific fish bone can currently be reliably attributed only to the family level (Leach 1986; Nagaoka 1994). At the Yanuca rock-shelter site (VL 16/81), Hunt (1980) recorded 18 individuals and three families (Scaridae, Diodontidae, Serranidae), while at Naigani (VL 21/5), an approximate MNI of 18 was dominated by the Lethrinidae at 60%, with the Scaridae at only 5% (Best 1981:17). On Lakeba Island, fish bone analysed from sites 197, 196 and 47 suggests an early Lapita emphasis on the Lethrinidae (carnivores) and the Balistidae (omnivores), followed by an increase in the MNI of the Scaridae (herbivores), Diodontidae (omnivores) and Labridae (carnivores) and a decrease in the Lethrinidae and Balistidae (Best 1984). The view of prehistoric fishing from Lakeba is one of little change in the main taxa taken, but this is combined with an increase in the number of taxa taken over time. In the three lowest levels of the Lakeba 197 site, dating to ca. 2850–2900 cal. BP, there were only nine fish families, compared with 21 families in the three uppermost levels, dating to the past 500 years. At the Qaranicagi rock shelter (Y2-39) on Waya Island in the Yasawas, Hunt et al. (1999) report a fish-bone assemblage consisting of 70

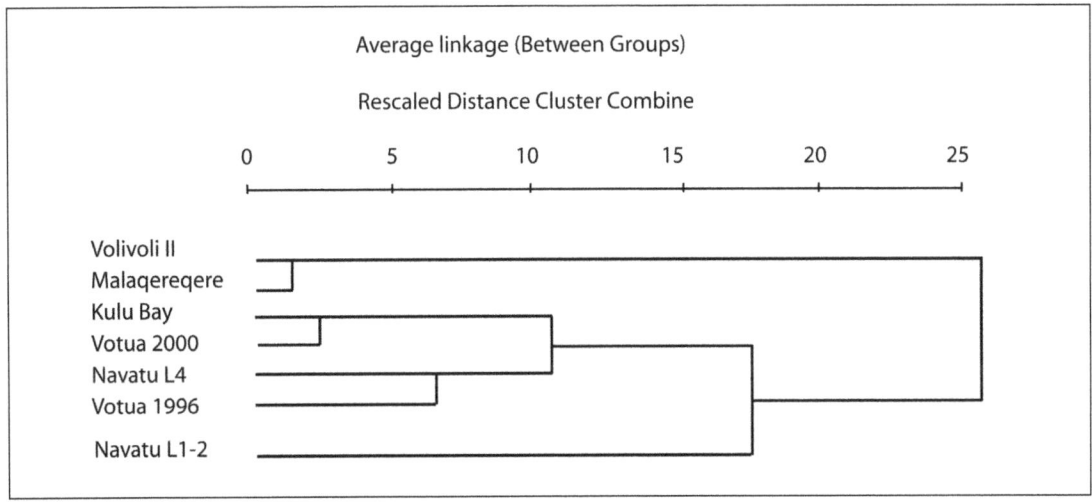

Figure 113. A hierarchical cluster analysis (HCA) of EPF fish-bone assemblages based on MNI%.

bones that were identified to 14 families, dominated by the Acanthuridae, Scaridae, Balistidae, Diodontidae and Labridae, repeating the mix of omnivores/herbivores and carnivores found in several EPF sites.

Lapita-era fish bone identified from Naitabale on Moturiki Island, reported by Nunn et al. (2007), was, in decreasing order of abundance, from the Scaridae, Lethrinidae, Serranidae, Diodontidae and Lutjanidae families. The Lapita levels of sites on Cikobia reported by Leach et al. (2000) were reanalysed by Hawkins (2000:46), and showed an emphasis on the Scaridae, Acanthuridae, Ostraciidae and Diodontidae, which can all be caught with non-angling techniques, along with a minor emphasis on carnivorous fish such as the Labridae, Lethrinidae and Serranidae, often caught by angling. However, in the two Aiwa Islands in the Lau Group, the Aiwa 1 site fish bone NISP of 2111 represented 19 families, dominated, in order, by the Serranidae, Acanthuridae, Balistidae, Scaridae, Diodontidae, Labridae and Lethrinidae, which was different from the Dau rock shelter (NISP=1575, 14 families) and Cave 2 assemblage (NISP=1180, 17 families), where the Scaridae and Acanthuridae were the main taxa taken (O'Day et al. 2003). A summary of fish bone from 12 sites on Nayau Island in the Lau Group based on %NISP (Jones et al. 2007) indicates that the Scaridae (8%) were less important than the Acanthuridae (34%), Balistidae (19%) and Diodontidae (16%). Another site in the Lau Group, the Qaranilaca Cave on Vanuabalavu dating to the second millennium BP, had a fish bone NISP of 1073 from at least 16 families, with the Scaridae and Carangidae having the highest MNI, followed by the Labridae, Balistidae, Lethrinidae and Serranidae.

The main fish taxa in each assemblage vary widely in the proportion of carnivores relative to omnivores/herbivores, with several sites of Lapita and post-Lapita age containing a significant proportion of carnivores (Lakeba site 197 (basal levels), Aiwa 1, Naitabale). Such sites contrast with those where the Scaridae are dominant (Votua 2000, Kulu Bay, Navatu Layer 4) and those where there is a relatively even balance of carnivores and herbivores/omnivores (Volivoli II and Malaqereqere). The Qaranilaca site in northern Lau is unusual for the proportion of carangids, which combined with individuals of the Lethrinidae, suggests targeting of these taxa (Thomas et al. 2004).

The proportions of carnivores and omnivores/herbivores vary between Lapita sites, and geographic location and the local marine environment are the most likely causes (see Davidson et al. 2002; O'Day et al. 2003:47). The Votua 2000 assemblage was dominated by the Scaridae (40.4%), while at Naigani, lethrinids were the main taxon caught (42.8%), as at Lakeba site 197, where the basal levels were dominated by the Lethrinidae. It is notable that despite the difference in the main taxa taken (Scaridae versus Lethrinidae), the same shell fish hooks and arrow/spear smoothing coral abraders were found at Votua (Mago Island) and Lakeba, suggesting the technology was suitable for taking the variety of taxa common to nearshore environments. Over time, there is evidence for a greater number of fish taxa being taken, which could represent the increasing use of traps, nets and community fishing strategies in the post-Lapita period, as well as the targeting of families found at particular locations (e.g. Aiwa 1, Qaranilaca).

Given the results of shell-midden analysis in which freshwater species figure consistently in low numbers, as well as data from modern Fijian fisheries (e.g. see Rawlinson et al. 1994:Chapter 5), the lack of freshwater and/or estuarine fish and eels is perhaps surprising. However, there may be several interlocking factors at play here. Firstly, the Archaeology and Natural History fish-bone reference collection is focused on marine taxa, meaning that freshwater fish bones may not have been identified. Secondly, some of the freshwater fish that contribute so strongly to modern catches, such as the jungle perch (*Kuhlia rupestris*) and tilapia (*Oreochromis mossambicus*), are modern introductions to Fiji. Thirdly, many of the native fish species common to freshwater/

estuarine niches fall into predominantly marine families that *have* been identified (e.g. *Lutjanus argentimaculatus* in the Lutjanidae). Thus, without species-level identifications, the potential importance of this ecological zone may have been obscured. Lastly, the use of different capture methods appears to strongly influence catch composition, with a creel survey conducted by Rawlinson et al. (1994:47) demonstrating that although the eel *Anguila obscura* was a preferred and apparently targeted taxon, the predominant use of gillnetting meant it did not feature strongly in actual catch data.

There is no doubt that an ability to identify fish bones beyond family level would greatly enhance our ability to discuss capture strategies, patterning in the exploitation of different environmental zones, economic structure and any tendency towards specialisation. Studies conducted elsewhere certainly demonstrate the utility of a more fine-grained, identification-driven approach (e.g. Cooke 1992 for the tropical Pacific coast of the Americas; Leach and Boocock 1995; Leach et al. 1996, 1997 for New Zealand). There are clearly many obstacles to achieving this, given the variety of fish in the tropical Indo–West Pacific and the fact that species within some families (such as the Scaridae) can be difficult to accurately identify, even when alive. In addition, as pointed out above as well as by Vogel (2005), our reference collections need to be able to support these refinements.

Modern-day studies derived from fisheries and resource management can give insights, especially by pin-pointing species common at particular Pacific locales, thereby indicating a 'first port of call' in a reference collection. Johannes and MacFarlane (1991:120), in their study of traditional fishing in the Torres Strait Islands, point out that although they recorded the capture of more than 75 species during the course of their study, only five species contributed nearly 86% of overall catches. Similar conclusions are presented throughout Dalzell et al. (1996), who also observe that different species within the same family can dominate catches from island to island. For example, Dalzell et al. (1996:415) note that modern lethrinid catches from inshore fisheries around Fiji are dominated by *Lethrinus nebulosus*, while at Tikehau Atoll in French Polynesia, the dominant lethrinid is *L. miniatus*. Such geographic patterning is noted for the Lutjanidae, Acanthuridae and Serranidae, as well (Dalzell et al. 1996).

Despite the family-level identifications, what the various EPF assemblages tell us very clearly is that a range of capture techniques were employed from the Lapita period onwards. What remains of the actual prehistoric fishing technologies also suggests that generalised, versatile fishing gear was used. These results are in strong agreement with the molluscan remains, which point to a generalist gathering strategy involving taking a range of species from a variety of littoral niches. Further refinement of fish-bone identifications would allow us to explore issues of change and patterning in capture techniques, economic specialisation and the targeting of various niches, and is a clear agenda for the future.

References

Allen, G. 2002. *Marine fishes of tropical Australia and South-East Asia.* Third edition. Western Australian Museum, Perth.

Allen, M.S. 1992. Temporal variation in Polynesian fishing strategies: The Southern Cook Islands in regional perspective. *Asian Perspectives* 31: 183–204.

Barnett, L.A. 1978. *Manual for the identification of fish bones: A guide to the comparative skeletal collection in the Department of Prehistory.* Department of Prehistory, Research School of Pacific Studies, Australian National University, Canberra.

Best, S. 1981. Excavations at Site VL 21/5 Naigani Island, Fiji, a preliminary report. Unpublished report, Department of Anthropology, University of Auckland.

Best, S. 1984. Lakeba: The prehistory of a Fijian Island. Unpublished PhD dissertation. Department of Anthropology, University of Auckland.

Burley, D.V. and Shutler, R. Jr. 2007. Ancestral Polynesian fishing gear: Archaeological insights from Tonga. In: Anderson, A., Green, K. and Leach, F. (eds), *Vastly ingenious: The archaeology of Pacific material culture in honour of Janet M. Davidson*, pp. 155–172. University of Otago Press, Dunedin.

Butler, V.L. 1988. Lapita fishing strategies: The faunal evidence. In: Kirch, P.V. and Hunt, T.L. (eds), *Archaeology of the Lapita cultural complex: A critical review*, pp. 99–115. Thomas Burke Memorial Washington State Museum research report No. 5. Burke Museum, Seattle.

Butler, V.L. 1994. Fish feeding behaviours and fish capture: The case for variation in Lapita fishing strategies. *Archaeology in Oceania* 29: 81–90.

Carcasson, R.H. 1977. *A field guide to the coral reef fishes of the Indian and West Pacific Oceans.* William Collins and Sons, Glasgow.

Chaplin, R.E. 1971. *The study of animal bones from archaeological sites.* Seminar Press, London.

Clark, G., Anderson, A. and Matararaba, S. 2001. The Lapita site at Votua, northern Lau Islands, Fiji. *Archaeology in Oceania* 36: 134–145.

Cooke, R. 1992. Prehistoric nearshore and littoral fishing in the eastern tropical Pacific: An ichthyological evaluation. *Journal of World Prehistory* 6(1): 1–49.

Coutts, P.J.F. 1975. Marine fishing in archaeological perspective: Techniques for determining fishing strategies. In: Casteel, R.W. and Quimby, G.I. (eds), *Maritime adaptations of the Pacific.* Moulton Publishers, The Hague and Paris.

Dalzell, P., Adams, T.J.H. and Polunin, N.V.C. 1996. Coastal fisheries in the Pacific Islands. *Oceanography and Marine Biology: An Annual Review* 34: 395–531.

Davidson, J., Hinds, E., Holdaway, S. and Leach, F. 1990. The Lapita site of Natunuku, Fiji. *New Zealand Journal of Archaeology* 12: 121–155.

Davidson, J., Leach, F. and Sand, C. 2002. Three thousand years of fishing in New Caledonia and the Loyalty Islands. In: Bedford, S., Sand, C. and Burley, D. (eds), *Fifty years in the field*, pp. 153–164. New Zealand Archaeological Association Monograph.

Dye, T. and Steadman, D.W. 1990. Polynesian ancestors and their animal world. *American Scientist* 78: 207–215.

Fowler, H.W. 1955. Archaeological fish bones collected by E.W. Gifford in Fiji. *Bernice P. Bishop Museum Bulletin* 214.

Froese, R. and Pauly, D. (eds) 2009. *Pseudobalistes flavimarginatus.* In: *FishBase World Wide Web Electronic Publication;* www.fishbase.org, version (03/2009) URL: http://www.fishbase.org/Summary/speciesSummary.php?ID=6027&genusname=Pseudobalistes&speciesname=flavimarginatus

Gillett, R. and Moy, W. 2006. *Spearfishing in the Pacific Islands: Current status and management issues.* Secretariat of the Pacific Community, Noumea.

Grayson, D.K. 1984. *Quantitative Zooarchaeology.* Academic Press, New York.

Green, R.C. 1976. Lapita sites in the Santa Cruz Group. In: Green, R.C. and Cresswell, M.M. (eds), *Southeast Solomon Islands cultural history: A preliminary survey.* pp. 181–191. Royal Society of New Zealand Bulletin No. 11.

Green, R.C. 1986. Lapita fishing: The evidence of site SE-RF-2 from the main reef islands, Santa Cruz Group, Solomons. In: Anderson, A.J. (ed), *Traditional fishing in the Pacific*, pp. 119–135. Pacific Anthropological Records 37. Honolulu, Hawaii.

Hawkins, S.C. 2000. Voyagers and fishermen: Early prehistoric fishing on Naigani Island, Fiji. Unpublished MA thesis, University of Auckland.

Hunt, T.L. 1980. Towards Fiji's past: Archaeological research on southwestern Viti Levu. Unpublished MA Thesis. Department of Anthropology, University of Auckland.

Hunt, T.L., Aronson, K.F., Cochrane, E.E., Field, J.S., Humphrey, L. and Rieth, T.M. 1999. A preliminary report on archaeological research in the Yasawa Islands, Fiji. *Domodomo* 12(2): 5–43.

Johannes, R. 1981. *Words of the lagoon: Fishing and marine lore in the Palau District of Micronesia*. University of California Press, Berkeley.

Johannes, R. E. and MacFarlane, J. W. 1991. *Traditional fishing in the Torres Strait Islands*. CSIRO Division of Fisheries Hobart, Australia.

Jones, S., Steadman, D. and O'Day, P. 2007. Archaeological investigations on the small island of Aiwa Levu and Aiwa Lailai, Lau Group, Fiji. *Journal of Coastal and Island Archaeology* 2: 72–98.

Kirch, P.V. and Dye, T. 1979. Ethno-archaeology and the development of Polynesian fishing strategies. *Journal of the Polynesian Society* 88: 53–76.

Kirch, P.V. and Yen, D.E. 1982. Tikopia: The prehistory and ecology of a Polynesian outlier. *Bernice P. Bishop Museum Bulletin* 238. Honolulu, Hawaii.

Kirch, P.V. 1988. Niuatoputapu: The prehistory of a Polynesian chiefdom. *Thomas Burke Memorial Washington State Museum Monograph* No. 5. The Burke Museum, Seattle.

Leach, B.F. 1986. A method for the analysis of Pacific Island fish bone assemblages and an associated data base management system. *Journal of Archaeological Science* 13(2): 147–159.

Leach, B.F. 1997. A guide to the identification of fish remains from New Zealand Archaeological Sites. *New Zealand Journal of Archaeology Special Publication*.

Leach, B.F. and Boocock, A. 1995. The estimation of live fish catches from archaeological bone fragments of the New Zealand snapper *Pagrus auratus*. *Tuhinga: Records of the Museum of New Zealand* 3: 1–28.

Leach, B.F., Davidson, J.M., Horwood, L.M., and Anderson, A.J. 1996. The estimation of live fish size from archaeological cranial bones of the New Zealand barracouta *Thyrsites atun*. *Tuhinga: Records of the Museum of New Zealand* 6: 1–25.

Leach, B.F., Davidson, J.M. and Horwood, L.M. 1997. The estimation of live fish size from archaeological cranial bones of New Zealand blue cod *Parpercis colias*. *International Journal of Osteoarchaeology* 7: 481–496.

Leach, B.F., Davidson, J.M., Fraser, K. and Budec-Piric, A. 2000. Analysis of faunal material from several archaeological sites on Cikobia, Fiji. Technical Report 28. Museum of New Zealand Te Papa Tongarewa.

Masse, B. 1986. A millennium of fishing in the Palau Islands, Micronesia. In: Anderson, A.J. (ed), *Traditional fishing in the Pacific: Ethnographical and archaeological papers from the 15th Pacific Science Congress* pp. 85–117. Pacific Anthropological Records No. 37, B.P. Bishop Museum, Honolulu.

Masse, B. 1989. *The archaeology and ecology of fishing in the Belau Islands*. PhD thesis, Ann Arbor Press, Michigan.

Nagaoka, L. 1994. Differential recovery of Pacific fish remains: Evidence from the Motrakau Rockshelter, Aitutaki, Cook Islands. *Asian Perspectives* 33: 1–17.

Nunn, P.D., Ishimura, T., Dickinson, W.R., Katayama, K., Thomas, F., Kumar, R., Matararaba, S., Davidson, J. and Worthy, T. 2007. The Lapita occupation at Naitabale, Moturiki Island, Central Fiji. *Asian Perspectives* 46(1): 96–132.

Ono, R. 2003. Prehistoric Austronesian fishing strategies: A comparison between Island Southeast Asia and the Lapita cultural complex. In: Sand, C. (ed), *Pacific archaeology: Assessments and prospects*.

Proceedings of the New Caledonia 2002 conference, pp. 43–52. Les Cahiers de l'Archéologie en Nouvelle-Calédonie 15.

O'Day, S. Jones, O'Day, P., and Steadman, D.W. 2003. Defining the Lau context: Recent findings on Nayau, Lau Islands, Fiji. *New Zealand Journal of Archaeology* 25: 31–56.

Rawlinson, N.F.J., Milton, D.A., Blaber, S.M.J., Sesewa, A. and Sharma, S.P. 1994. *A survey of the subsistence and artisanal fisheries in rural areas of Viti Levu, Fiji.* Australian Centre for International Agricultural Research (ACIAR), Canberra.

Szabó, K. and Summerhayes, G. 2002. Worked shell artefacts – new data from early Lapita. In: Bedford, S., Sand, C. and Burley, D. (eds), *Fifty years in the field*, pp. 91–100. New Zealand Archaeological Association Monograph.

Szabó. K. 2007. An assessment of shell fishhooks of the Lapita cultural complex. In: Anderson, A., Green, K. and Leach, F. (eds), *Vastly ingenious: The archaeology of Pacific material culture in honour of Janet M. Davidson*, pp. 227–241. University of Otago Press, Dunedin.

Thomas, F.R., Nunn, P.D., Osborne, T., Kumar, R., Areki, F., Matararaba, S., Steadman, D. and Hope, G. 2004. Recent archaeological findings at Qaranilaca Cave, Vanuabalavu Island, Fiji. *Archaeology in Oceania* 39: 42–49.

Vogel, Y. 2005. Ika. Unpublished MA thesis. Department of Anthropology, University of Otago.

Walter, R. 1989. Lapita fishing strategies: A review of the archaeological and linguistic evidence. *Pacific Studies* 13: 127–149.

Walter, R. 1998. Fish and fishing. In: Walter, R. *Anai'o: The archaeology of a fourteenth century Polynesian community in the Cook Islands*, pp. 64–73. New Zealand Archaeological Association Monograph 22.

Williams, T. 1858[1985]. *Fiji and the Fijians. The islands and their inhabitants*. Fiji Museum, Suva.

10

Bird, mammal and reptile remains

Trevor H. Worthy
School of Biological, Earth and Environmental Sciences, The University of New South Wales

Geoffrey Clark
Department of Archaeology and Natural History, The Australian National University

Introduction

This chapter reports the non-fish remains from 10 archaeological excavations on Viti Levu and the Lau Group, including the reanalysis of a bird-bone assemblage from Lakeba Island excavated previously by Simon Best (1984). Bone remains from Natunuku and Ugaga were uncommon and the small assemblages were misplaced during collection relocation after bushfires destroyed the ANU archaeological storage facility in 2003, and these assemblages are not considered further. Three of the non-fish faunal assemblages are from the Lau Group (Qaranipuqa, Votua, Sovanibeka), one is from the north coast of Viti Levu (Navatu 17A), and the remainder are from the southwest Viti Levu region (Malaqereqere, Tuvu, Volivoli II, Volivoli III, Qaraninoso II) and Beqa Island (Kulu). This chapter presents the non-fish fauna from the Lau Group, followed by that from Viti Levu and Beqa Island.

Faunal analysis began early in Fiji, with bone remains identified at Navatu and Vuda on Viti Levu by Gifford (1951:208–213). Gifford's excavations demonstrated that pig, dog, chicken, turtle, fruit bat and humans were consumed during the 'early period' of Fiji. The study of archaeofauna declined after this promising start due to the absence of prehistoric fauna in sites such as Sigatoka and Karobo (Palmer 1965; Birks 1973), and the cursory identification of bone remains at sites like Yanuca and Natunuku (Birks and Birks 1978; Davidson et al. 1990), which was, in part, a result of the intense focus on the decorative system found on Lapita ceramics. Although a detailed analysis of prehistoric fauna from Lakeba was made by Best (1984), it is notable that Gifford's (1951) faunal identifications were the only detailed archaeofaunal record available for the large island of Viti Levu before the EPF investigations in the 1990s. As Viti

Levu and Vanua Levu are significantly larger and older landforms than the islands of the Lau Group, it was thought probable that west Fiji contained different taxa than east Fiji, and human arrival and transformation of the environment may have followed a different path on the two large islands than on the small islands of the Lau Group.

Consequently, it was anticipated that the non-fish fauna from prehistoric sites in Fiji would shed light on the nature and variability of Lapita subsistence systems – in particular, the effect Lapita people had on Fiji's native birds and reptiles through predation and the introduction of commensal species such as the pig, dog, chicken and rat. The status of these species as Lapita imports has been unclear for many years, with a pig bone from basal levels of Yanuca (Hunt 1980) now identified as turtle, and a dog bone from Naigani (Best 1981) now regarded as questionable (Worthy pers. obs.). In Tonga, only the domestic fowl (*Gallus gallus*) and commensal Pacific rat (*Rattus exulans*) are unequivocally identified as Lapita-era introductions, raising the possibility that Lapita economies in Fiji–West Polynesia were initially less reliant on transported plants and animals for subsistence than those in the west (as outlined in Clark and Anderson 2001; Burley 2007). The second issue concerned the nature of post-Lapita subsistence and whether it involved a broadening of diet items, perhaps as a response to the loss of large and readily available wild-food resources, coupled with the increasing food demands of a growing population. Such conditions could result in food stress and relate to social adaptations in the Fiji sequence, including settlement pattern change and increased investment in horticultural production systems, as well as greater inter-group conflict and cannibalism.

Methods

Bird, reptile and mammal remains were identified by THW and GC using archaeozoology reference collections held at the ANU and the Museum of New Zealand. Worthy borrowed from the Fiji Museum the collection of bird bones excavated from the Qaranipuqa rock shelter (Best 1984). He identified them in the Museum of New Zealand Te Papa Tongarewa, with reference to the extensive collection of modern material housed there, augmented by study of loaned skeletal material from the Fiji Museum, the Smithsonian Institution (USNM), and the Canterbury Museum (CM). NISP and MNI were calculated for all assemblages, but only NISP is reported due to the degree of deposit mixing and the small amount of non-fish fauna in most sites. The exception is the bird remains from a stratified site on Lakeba for which an MNI and a maximum MNI were calculated for each level of the Qaranipuqa rock shelter. A recent study has found unexpected diversity amid Fijian iguanas and has named a third species *Brachylophus bulabula* for populations in the wet forests of Viti Levu, Vanua Levu and Kadavu, formerly known as *B. fasciatus* (Keogh et al. 2008). Populations in the Lau Group remain as *B. fasciatus*. We follow this nomenclature here.

The Lau Group

Reanalysis of Lakeba avifauna: The Best collection

In the late 1970s, Simon Best directed excavations at two adjacent sites on the northwest coast of Lakeba, and recovered a still unparalleled collection of Fijian archaeofauna, particularly bird remains, spanning Lapita and subsequent cultural phases (Steadman 2006a). The sites were Qaranipuqa (101/7/197), a large rock shelter eroded out of the limestone cliffs 220 m from the sea, and Wakea (101/7/196), a raised sand plain at the base of the limestone cliffs, just east of Qaranipuqa. The excavations recovered 1225 bird bones and fragments, most of which came from the three lowest layers of the Qaranipuqa rock shelter in association with Lapita pottery.

In total, 21 species from 11 families were identified by P. Millener, G. van Tets, S. Olsen and D. Steadman. Identifications were reported in Best's PhD thesis (Best 1984:Table 7.7), and included an extinct megapode attributed to *Megapodius freycinet* and an extinct large pigeon (*Ducula* sp.).

The great advantage of the Lakeba collection of late-Holocene avifauna is that it derives from one of the few well-stratified, carefully excavated and adequately radiocarbon-dated Lapita sites in Fiji. However, the initial identifications given in Best's 1984 thesis now require revision. Best (1984:528–532, 2002) noted that the comparative material available to identify pigeons, doves and rails was restricted and in some cases attribution to species/family was 'fairly general'. The lack of detailed comparative material with which to compare the Lakeba bird bones resulted in the tentative identification of two pigeons, two parrots and the barred-wing rail, and raised the possibility that two specimens of *Gallus gallus* in Lapita levels might belong to *Megapodius freycinet*. The last point is significant, as an incorrect *Gallus* identification might favour the view of a colonising population without domestic animals, in line with Groube's (1971:312) much contested view of Lapita people as 'oceanic strandloopers' who had a restricted maritime/lagoonal economy (see Davidson and Leach 2001).

Recent work has obtained an enlarged fossil record for Fiji (Worthy 2000, 2001a, 2001b; Worthy and Anderson 1999; Worthy et al. 1999; see Chapters 2–3). These palaeofaunal investigations and a larger set of modern reference specimens have allowed a more accurate species list for the Lakeba avifauna. The revised list includes records of several species previously unknown in Fiji and returns a significant increase in the number of species (see below). The principal archaeological benefit of the revision lies in its contribution to understanding the nature of the Lapita economy in east Fiji. For several reasons, such as a high degree of deposit disturbance and the relatively coarse excavation techniques used in the past, this aspect of the Fijian sequence is not well understood on Viti Levu (see Clark and Anderson 2001). Thus the Lakeba cultural sequences excavated by Best are currently the best example of the marked impact of prehistoric people on Fiji's land-bird populations during the colonisation phase.

Skeletal elements and descriptive terms

The following abbreviations apply to single and plural usage of the elements: cmc, carpometacarpi; cor, coracoids; fem, femora; fib, fibulae; hum, humeri; pt, part; quad, quadrates; rad, radii; scap, scapulae; stern, sterna; tmt, tarsometatarsi; and tib, tibiotarsi. When listing material, bones are sometimes identified as left (L) or right (R) elements. L or R prefixed by 'p', 's', or 'd' indicates 'proximal', 'shaft', or 'distal' part of the element respectively, e.g. pR fem means the proximal part of a right femur.

Anatomical nomenclature for specific bone landmarks follows Baumel and Witmer (1993), but terms are Anglicised after first mention. Some common terms are abbreviated as follows: *proc.* for *processus*; *artic.* for *articularis*.

Systematics

The Best collection from Lakeba contained many fragmentary bones, however 304 bones were identified to a taxon as recorded below (each element and catalogue number separated by semicolon), with comments on their identification if necessary. In the catalogue number (recorded on the bones), the first three digits refer to the site (197). The excavation at this site had two squares called Square 1 and Square 3, identified in the following digit after 197. The alphanumeric (e.g. W or T) refers to the layer (top is A1, bottom is X, in total 34 layers). Layer T1 and T2 are about 4 m below surface, and Layers W1 and W2 are approximately 4.5 m below the surface and are the earliest cultural layers of the site. Best (1984) divided the layers into parts, such as T1 or T2, and so the digit after the letter in the catalogue number is assumed to be the layer part, which can be as high as 7 for layer M or 10 for layer K. Here, the specimens are tabulated into layers A to U only (Table 37), and even then, single bones had constituent parts in adjacent layers, so finer tabulation is not warranted for faunal analysis.

While most bones (300) are from Qaranipuqa, a few are from other sites, and for completeness they are listed with the rest of the Lakeba fauna. Two bones are from Site 196, or Wakea, which is adjacent to the Qaranipuqa site. They are the single bone of *Egretta sacra* and one of the two *Limosa lapponica* bones, so are significant additions to the total fauna. One bone of *Columba vitiensis* is from Site 47, which is the fortified site Ulunikoro or Vagadra above Qaranipuqa. One bone of *Porphryio porphyrio* (135.1.3.C+D) is from a ring-ditch settlement known as Liqau on the northwest coast. All are listed below as a complete listing of identified Lakeba material from Best's excavations (Table 37).

Class Reptilia

Family Boidae
Candoia bibroni Pacific boa
Material: vertebra, 197.1.X.2,7.

Class Aves

Family Phaethontidae
Phaethon lepturus White-tailed tropicbird
Material: R cmc, 197.3.A.5(a), 1; R cor, 197.3.N.1(e), 3; L scap, 197.3.N.1(e), 7; L tib, 197.1.A.3.4, 1; pL cor, 197.1.N.1.3, 4; R rad, 197.1.M.10.4, f96, 1; L cmc, 197.1.M.8.3, f80, 1; d+sL rad, 197.3.M.10(a), 9; dL ulna, 197.3.M.8(e), 1; (total 9 bones).

Family Fregatidae
Fregata ariel Lesser frigatebird
Material: pR cor, 197.3.K.10(a), 1; (total 1 bone).

Family Ardeidae
Egretta sacra Reef heron
Material: pR hum, 196.18.A.3, 1; (total 1 bone).
Butorides striatus Mangrove heron
Material: dL tib, 197.3.W.1.7, 10; (total 1 bone)

Family Anatidae
Anas superciliosa Black duck
Material: sternal end L cor, 197.3.V.7, 1; dR ulna, 197.1.L.f18, 4; (total 2 bones).

Family Megapodiidae
Megapodius alimentum Extinct scrubfowl
Material: A total of 49 bones. The elements and their catalogue numbers are listed in Worthy (2000), except the sL cmc (197.1.U.2,4) that was subsequently identified. Nearly all were from layer W, with one from Layer U, two from Layer V and three from Layer X.

This species, first described on bones from Tonga by Steadman (1989), was redescribed by Worthy (2000) using the Lakeba material.

Family Phasianidae

Gallus gallus Domestic fowl
Material: dR hum, 197.3.M.1, 1; dL tib, 197.3.W.1.4, 12; dL tib, 197.3.U.1(E), 4; dL tib, 197.3.W.2E, 10; (total 4 bones).

Family Rallidae

Gallirallus philippensis Banded rail
Material: sL tib, 197.1.A.14.4, 1; R cor, 197.1.E.4,f1,f19, 32, 1 (medial length = 22.9 mm); sternum, 197.1.M.4.3, 2; L cor, 197.2.M.1, 2 (medial length = 24.4 mm); pR tib, 197.3.H.4(e), 3; dR tib, 197.3.F.1.f171(d).a, 4; d+sR tmt, 197.3.F.f171(d).a, 2; R cor, 197.1.L.1.3, 2 (medial length = 22.4 mm; R cor, 197.1.A.11.4, 1 (medial length = 21.5 mm); (total 9 bones).

These bones are listed by Steadman (2006a) as a flightless taxon '*Gallirallus* undescribed sp. D', which was assumed to be endemic to Lakeba and nearby Aiwa Levu and Aiwa Lailai. However, the material listed here provides no evidence for the bones having been derived from a flightless taxon, or that they differed significantly from the widespread *Gallirallus philippensis*. Medial lengths for coracoids of two specimens of *Gallirallus philippensis sethsmithi* from Fiji are: FM8 22.2 mm; FM19 23.7 mm, well within the range of the fossils.

Porphyrio porphyrio Purple swamphen
Material: dL fem, 197.3.K.5(1), f226, 4; sR tib, 197.3.F.1, f171(6), 2; pt pR ulna, 197.3.M.7(2), 1; s+dR tmt, 135.1.3.C+D, leve SW; R fem, 197.1.L.4(a).1, 1; dR tib, 197.3.W.1.1, 29; pR hum, 197.3.K2.1.L4 NE extn, 1; sR tib, 197.3.M.7(a), 2; dR tmt, 197.1.x.1, 31; dR tmt, 197.3.K.10(L1.4), 2; dL tib, 197.1.L.3a.4; s+pL tib, 197.3.E.2+3(a), 1; R cor, 197.3.M.6(a), 1; dR tib 197.1.L.3a.4, 3; pR cor, 197.3.W.1.2, 21; sR tib, 197.1.M.1.3, 1; dR tib, 197.1.J.2.1, 1; pR fem, 197.1.N.1.3, 3; pR cor, 197.1.C.3a.4, 2; dL tib, 197.3.K.10(L1–4), 4; sR hum, 197.3.M.10, f238, 1; dL cmc, 197.1.N.1.3(b), 1; dR tib, 197.1.L.3(c).1, 2; pt pR hum, 197.1.L.3a.4, 1; L cor, 197.3.W.1.1, 9; R cor, 197.3.K.2(a), 2; dL ulna, 197.3.W.1.1, 18; dL rad, 197.3.W.1.1, 27; dR tib, 197.3.W.2(E), 31; L scap, 197.3.W.1.4, 17; sR tmt, 197.3.K.10(L1–4), 5; dR tmt, 197.3.W.3(w), 2; sR tmt, 197.3.K.10(L1–4), 4; dR tmt, 197.1.M.9.1, 8; dL fem, 197.1.M.9.1, 10; sternal end L cor, 197.3.W.2, 26; pR ulna, 197.3.O.1(E), 1; d+sR tib, 197.3.E.5, 4; sL tib, 197.3.H.2(f), 1; sR fem, 197.3.F.1(a), 2; L cor, 197.1.M.9.2, 1; (total 41 bones).

These bones are of the small Pacific form of *Porphyrio*, often listed in the subspecies *P. p. vitiensis* or *P. p. samoensis*. They are distinct from the Australasian *P. melanotus*. The smaller examples of this species from this site were listed previously by Best (1984) as *Nesoclopeus poicilopterus*.

Porzana tabuensis Spotless crake
Material: L hum, 197.3.E.2+3, 1; (total 1 bone).

Family Charadriidae

Pluvialis fulva Pacific golden plover
Material: L cor, 197.1.E.4.3, 1; (total 1 bone).

Family Scolopacidae

Limosa lapponica Bar-tailed godwit
Material: pt sternum, 196.17.B.4, f14; dR hum, 197.3.A.5, 3; (total 2 bones).

Family Columbidae

Gallicolumba stairii Friendly ground dove
Material: L scap, 197.3.W.1.8, 45; L scap, 197.3.W.1.8, 12; R cor, 197.1.T.6, 2; dR ulna, 197.3.?; sR tib, 197.1.W.1(e), 6; dL tmt, 197.3.T.6, 1;pL hum, 197.3.W.1.6, 2; dR cmc, 197.1.T.6, 3; (total 8 bones).

These bones conform well with a large series from Vatulele.

Didunculus strigirostris Tooth-billed pigeon
Material: L quad 197.1.W.2, 30; pR cmc, 197.3.W.1.8; pL tmt, 197.3.W.1.8, 39; (total 3 bones).

These bones are good matches for CM Av7160. The carpometacarpus has a more upturned and pointed *proc. extensorius* than in *Ducula*, and it is grooved proximally between the minor and major *os metacarpales* on the dorsal surface. The tarsometatarsus is more elongate than *Ducula* or *Columba* and has a characteristic very small *foramina vascularia proximalia lateralis*.

?*Didunculus* sp.
Material: pR cor, 197.3.W.1.2, 10; dL cor, 197.3.w?, 11; L hum, 197.1.v.1(c), 13; dR cor, 197.3.W.3, 2; pR cor, 197.3.W.7.3, 29; (total 5 bones).

The proximal coracoids are tentatively referred to *Didunculus* because they are highly pneumatic under the acrocoracoid, and the distal coracoid has a large dorsal pneumatic fossa, but they are not *Caloenas*. These features exclude *Ducula* and *Columba* and the bones are of the expected size for *Didunculus*. CM Av7160 lacks comparable elements, precluding certain identification of these fossils.

Ducula lakeba Lakeba pigeon
Material: total 92 bones. The elements and their catalogue numbers are listed in Worthy (2001b). Most specimens are from Layer W. Two are from Layer X, 13 from Layer V, and one from Layer T, i.e. in the basal Lapita layers of the site. This species was described by Worthy (2001b) and named for the island from which it was first identified. However, it is a volant pigeon and is expected to have occurred on all the larger islands of the Lau Group. A similar, if not the same species, occurred on Viti Levu as well. It is slightly larger and more gracile than *Ducula david* described from Wallis Island by Balouet and Olson (1987).

Ducula pacifica Pacific pigeon
Material: d+sR hum, 197.3.W.1(a), 2; pR cmc, 197.1.L.3(c).1, 1; pL cmc, 197.1.W.2, 38; L tmt, 197.1.W.1, 24 + 197.1.V.2, 1; pR cor, 197.3.W.1(a), 5; pR cor, 197.3.U.2, 7; (total 6 bones).

The tarsometatarsus of *D. pacifica* is longer than *Columba vitiensis*, and has a large lateral vascular foramen (much reduced in *Columba*). On the coracoid, the acrocoracoid is not dorsally expanded to markedly overhang the *sulcus supracoracoidei* as in *Columba*. Carpometacarpus with *proc. alularis* more distad than internal rim of *trochlea carpalis* (equal in *Columba*).

Ducula pacifica or *Columba* sp.
Material: dR cmc, 197.3.W.1.8, 22; R scap, 197.3.W.1(a), 6; sR ulna, 197.3.V.1(E), 2; (total 3 bones). Bones were not sufficiently complete for further identification.

Columba vitiensis White-throated pigeon
Material: dR tib, 197.1.W.1, 11; pelvis, 197.3.K.6+7(a), 1; pR cmc, 197.3.W.1.B; dL tmt, 197.1.W.2, 1; dR tib, 197.1.W.1, 31; sR tib, 197.3.V.1(E), 1; pL cor, 197.1.W.1, 16; pR scap, 47.10.B(5-), 1; (total 8 bones).

Bones of *Columba vitiensis* are smaller than *Ducula pacifica* and otherwise differ by: tarsometatarsi with straight lateral margin of shaft (not concave), and a more pointed *trochlea metatarsi II* (medial trochlea). Carpometacarpus with alular process and internal rim of carpal trochlea of equal distal extent (not with alular process more distad as in *Ducula*). Tibiotarsus with lateral condyle more rounded cranio-proximally. Coracoid with acrocoracoid markedly overhanging the supracoracoidal sulcus (does not in *Ducula*). Scapula with pneumatic *acromion* (not in *Ducula*).

Columbid sp. Unidentified pigeon
Material: L cmc, 197.3.W.1.8, 1 (length = 39.44 mm, proximal width = 10.6 mm); pR cmc, 197.3.W.1.1, 2; dL cmc, 197.1.W.1, 10; pt sL tib 197.3.K2 to L4 NE ext, 7; L rad 197.3.W.1.6; pR rad, 197.3.W.1.6, 117; dL cor 197.3.W.2, 27; pt head of R hum, 197.3.W.1.5, 41; L scap, 197.3.W.2(E), 9; sL hum, 197.1.w, 1; dL cor 197.3.W.1.8, 2; dR hum 197.3.W.1.6, 26; sR hum 197.3.A.15(a), 1; dL fem 197.1.W.B1, 11 (distal width = 9.16 mm); sL fem 197.1.W.2, 41; pL scap 197.1.W.1, 35; L scap 197.3.v.3(w), 2; (total 17 bones).

Most of these specimens are bigger than the available *Ducula pacifica* reference skeletons, or the same size or bigger than the larger *D. latrans* skeleton at hand (FM28). It is probable they represent larger specimens of one or both these species. There is insufficient skeletal material of *D. latrans* to adequately define the size range of elements and no qualitative differences in post-cranial elements were noted. Steadman (2006a) lists *D. latrans* from his excavations on Aiwa Levu and Aiwa Lailai.

Ptilinopus porphyraceus Crimson-crowned fruit dove
Material: dL ulna, 197.1.S.3.2, 1; L cmc, 197.3.W.1.1, 17; dR cor, 197.1.x.1, 6; dL fem, 197.3.W.1.1, 11; sL hum, W.3(w); R tmt, 197.3.V.3, 1; pR hum, 197.1.W.1, 4; dR tib, 197.3.W.1.4; dL tib, 197.3.W.1, 33; sL cor, 197.3.T.7, 8; R cmc, 197.3.W.1(a), 3; dR ulna, 197.3.W.1.1, 59; R ulna, 197.3.W.1(a), 8; (total 13 bones).

Ptilinopus sp. Undetermined dove species
Material: R tmt, 197.3.W.1.5, 23; (total 1 bone).

The specimen lacks the distal trochlea but with a length of 22.5 mm to the middle of the distal foramen and an estimated length of 26 mm, it is much longer than *P. porphyraceus* or *P. perousii*, and any members of the golden dove (*P. lutiovirens, P. victor, P. layardi*) group of Fiji. However, measurements given by Steadman (1992) show that both *P. rarotongensis* of Rarotonga and *P. purpuratus* of the Society Islands–Tuamotu Group have similar sized tarsometatarsi.

Family Psittacidae

Prosopeia sp. Undetermined species of musk parrot
Material: sL tmt, 197.1.X.1, 30; dL ulna, 197.3.T.6(E), 1; dL hum, 197.1.V.1(a), 1; (total 3 bones).

These bones were bigger than *P. tabuensis splendens* (USNM 614998), but this sub-species from Kadavu may be smaller than other subspecies (*P. t. atrogularis* from Vanua Levu and offshore islands, *P. t. taviunenesis* from Taveuni and Qamea, *P. t. koroensis* from Koro, and *P. t. tabuensis* from Gau and Tonga), for which no skeletons were available.

Vini solitarius Collared lory
Material: pL ulna, 197.3.W.1.4, 4; dL hum, 197.3.T.7, 1; R tmt, 197.3.W.1.6, 33; R cmc, 197.3.W.1.6, 7; pR ulna, 197.3.W.1.4, 7; L cor, 197.3.W.1.6, 41; R rad, 197.3.T.6, 11; R scap, 197.3.W.2; (total 8 bones).

?*Charmosyma amabilis* ?Red-throated lorikeet
Material: L tib, 197.3.F.1; f189; 5 (length = ca. 28.3 mm, proximal width = 3.26 mm, shaft width = 1.39 mm.); (total 1 bone).
No reference specimen available.

Family Tytonidae

Tyto alba Barn owl
Material: pt L cor, 197.1.L.4(a).1, 3; pR fem, 197.1.A.8.2, 1; dL tib, 197.3.E.4, 2; dR fem, 197.1.E.3+4, 1; (total 4 bones).

Family Alcedinidae

Halcyon chloris White-collared kingfisher
Material: L cmc, 197.1.A.12.1; dR ulna, 197.1.A.4.2, 2; (total 2 bones).

Family Meliphagidae

Foulehaio carunculata Wattled honeyeater
Material: L tib, 197.3.K.2(a).1, 1; R cmc, 197.1.V.1(e), 14; L hum, 197.1.A.4.2, 1; (total 3 bones).

Family Sturnidae

Aplonis tabuensis Polynesian starling
Material: R ulna, 197.1.A.6.4, 2 ; R tmt, 197.1.E.9, 32, (L=26.05 mm); dR tib, 197.3.M.11, E; R rad, 197.1.A.6.4, 3; L hum, 197.1.A.6.4, 1; (total 5 bones).

Table 37. The faunal list derived from 302 identified bones from the adjacent sites Qaranipuqa (site 197) and Wakea (site 196) on Lakeba. Only the single *Egretta sacra* bone and one *Limosa* bone are from Site 196. Data is shown as NISP (number of specimens), MNI (minimum number of individuals for whole assemblage), NISP within Layers A–U, and Max MNI (MNI maximised by assuming sets of layers come from single units, as follows U–X, and H–O, E–F, and A–C).

Species	Common Name	NISP	MNI	A	B	C	D	E	F	G	H	I	J	K	L	M	N	O	P	Q	R	S	T	U	V	W	X	?	Max MNI
Candoia bibroni	Pacific boa	1	1																								1		1
Phaethon lepturus	White-tailed tropicbird	9	1	2												4	3											2
Fregata ariel	Lesser frigate bird	1	1											1															1
Egretta sacra	Reef heron	1	1	1																									1
Butorides striatus	Mangrove heron	1	1																								1			1
Anas superciliosa	Grey duck	2	1											1													1			2
Megapodius alimentum	Extinct megapode	49	5																						1	2	43	3		5
Gallus gallus	Domestic fowl	4	3				2							1													1			4
Gallirallus philippensis	Banded rail	9	3	2			1	2		1				1	2															3
Porphyrio porphyrio	Purple swamphen	40	6			1		2	2		1		1	7	5	8	2	1									9	1		8
Porzana tabuensis	Spotless crake	1	1					1																						1
Pluvialis fulva	Pacific golden plover	1	1					1																						1
Limosa lapponica	Bar-tailed godwit	2	1	1	1																									1
Gallicolumba stairii	Friendly ground dove	8	2																					3			4		1	3
Didunculus strigirostris	Tooth-billed pigeon	3	1																								3			1
? Didunculus strigirostris	?Tooth-billed pigeon	5	2																							1	4			2
Ducula lakeba	Lakeba pigeon	92	6																					1		13	76	2		6
Ducula pacifica	Pacific pigeon	6	2											1												1	4			3
Columbid sp. *D. latrans* or *D. pacifica*	Peale's pigeon or large Pacific pigeon	17	3	1										1												1	14			5
Columba vitiensis	White-throated pigeon	7	1											1												1	5			2
Columbid sp. *Ducula* or *Columba*	Pigeon spp.	3																								1	2			0
Ptilinopus porphyraceus	Crimson-crowned fruit-dove	13	2																				1	1		1	9	1		3
Ptilinopus sp.	Unknown dove	1	1																								1			1
Prosopeia sp.	Musk parrot	3	1																							1	1		1	1
Vini solitarius	Collared lory	8	1																							2	6			1
?Charmosyma amabilis	Red-throated lorikeet	1	1							1																				1
Tyto alba	Barn owl	4	1	1			2							1																3
Halcyon chloris	White-collared kingfisher	2	1	2																										1
Foulehaio carunculata	Wattled honeyeater	3	1	1								1															1			3
Aplonis tabuensis	Polynesian starling	5	1	3			1							1																3
Total		**302**	**53**																											**70**

Votua and Sovanibeka (Mago Island, Lau Group)

The Votua Lapita site was re-excavated in 2000, and the water-sieved sediments from the Area 2 trench excavation (1 m x 4 m) yielded small amounts of identifiable bird, rat and turtle bone (Table 38). Land birds were hunted at Votua by Lapita people, as at Lakeba, with remains recovered from an extinct megapode, *Megapodius alimentum*, banded rail and Polynesian starling. The passerine, *Gymnomyza viridis* (giant forest honeyeater), has been recorded in modern times on Viti Levu, Vanua Levu and Taveuni, but is not found in the Lau Group today (Steadman 2006a). As it occurs at Votua, it may have been more widely distributed in the Fiji Islands in the past. A humerus from a young sea turtle (*Chelonia mydas*) and rat bones from *Rattus exulans* and *Rattus praetor* were also recovered. Two *R. praetor* bones were sent for AMS analysis to determine whether the spiny rat arrived in Fiji in Lapita times, or was introduced from the west at a later date (see White et al. 2000). However, after pre-treatment, both the rat bones failed to provide sufficient material for an age determination, and as the burrowing propensity of this rat is unclear (Taylor et al. 1982), the remains could post-date the Lapita occupation at Votua.

Fauna from the Sovanibeka Test Pit 2 excavation derived from an owl-roost deposit and prehistoric human activity (Table 38). The remains of *R. exulans* and *R. praetor* were abundant, along with very small bones from the swiftlet (*Collocalia spodiopygia*) and the Oceanic gecko (*Gehyra oceanica*), both residents of the limestone complex today. An AMS date on a well-preserved *R. praetor* bone had an age of 670–770 cal. BP (OZF882), evidence that the spiny rat lived in Fiji during the second millennium AD, before apparently becoming extinct. Land snails were common in the lower part of the Sovanibeka deposit, but diminished in number in the upper stratigraphy, with four species identified using the comparative collection of the Australian Museum (*Gonatorhaphe lavensis*, *Helicina tectiformis*, *Truncatella* cf. *clathrata* and *Omphalotropsis* sp.) A ^{14}C result on land-snail shell (*Gonatorhaphe lavensis*) from Test Pit 1 had an age of 4290±60 BP (ANU-11246). Owl predation is almost certainly responsible for the sheath-tailed bat (*Emballonura semicaudata*) and banded iguana (*Brachylophus bulabula*) remains, while burnt turtle bone and bone from the domestic fowl probably result from prehistoric human use of the shelter. Sparse dentate-stamped and paddle-impressed sherds and occasional food debris, along with use of the shelter as an owl roost, suggest intermittent use of the Sovanibeka site in prehistory.

Viti Levu and Beqa Island

Navatu 17A (north Viti Levu)

The non-fish bone assemblage from the 1996 excavation of Trench B (Squares 1–4) had a NISP of 252 (Table 39). The bird bone was small and broken, consisting of shaft fragments from limb bones, and only two bones from the barn owl (*Tyto alba*) were able to be identified. Barn owls are primarily birds of open country or forest edges, and are specialist rodent predators. Prehistoric human colonisation of the Pacific was responsible for introducing rats (*Rattus exulans* and *Rattus praetor*) and vegetation clearance, both of which would have enabled owls to expand their range after human colonisation. The presence of owl at Navatu suggests relatively open country surrounding the volcanic plug by 800 BP (ANU-10384). Bird bone from the upper levels (0–70 cm depth) of the 1947 excavation was identified as black duck (*Anas superciliosa*), barred-wing rail (*Gallirallus* (=*Nesoclopeus*) *poicilopterus*) and swamp harrier (*Circus approximans*) (Gifford 1951:211). None of the turtle or lizard bone was identifiable to species and both were present in small amounts.

Table 38. Votua and Sovanibeka non-fish remains.

Provenience	Taxa	Common name	Element	NISP
Votua: Area 2				
Square 3: 0–10 cm	*Gallirallus philippensis*	Banded rail	distal femur (L)	1
Square 2: 10–20 cm	*G. philippensis*	Banded rail	distal femur (R)	1
Square 4: 10–20 cm	*Gallus ?species*	Scrub fowl	proximal manus phalange (R)	1
Square: 3: 10–20 cm	*G. philippensis*	Banded rail	shaft tarsometatarsus (R)	1
Square 3: 30–40 cm	*Megapodius alimentum*	Extinct scrubfowl	proximal ulna (L)	1
Square 1: 30–40 cm	*Halcyon sancta*	White-collared kingfisher	distal humerus (R)	1
Square 2: 30–40 cm	*Chelonia mydas*	Green turtle	radius (L)	1
Square 3: 30–40 cm	*Rattus praetor*	Spiny rat	femur (R)	1
Square 2: 40–50 cm	*Megapodius ?species*	Scrub fowl	proximal radius (R)	1
Square 4: 50–60 cm	cf. *Gymnomyza viridis*	?Giant forest honeyeater	proximal carpometacarpus (R)	1
Square 4: 50–60 cm	*Pteropus cf tonganus*	Large fruit bat	distal humerus	1
Square 3: 50–60 cm	*Rattus praetor*	Spiny rat	tibia (L)	1
Square 4: 50–60 cm	*Megapodius ?species*	Banded rail	distal pelvis	1
Square 3: 50–60 cm	*G. philippensis*	Banded rail	coracoid (L)	1
Square 4: 50–60 cm	*Ratus exulans*	Pacific rat	mandible (L)	1
Square 2: 50–60 cm	*Megapodius alimentum*	Extinct scrubfowl	distal ulna (R)	1
Square 4: 50–60 cm	cf. *Aplonis tabuensis*	Polynesian starling	proximal ulna (L)	1
Square 4: 60–70 cm	*Megapodius ?species*	Scrub fowl	shaft femur (L)	1
NISP Total				18
Sovanibeka Test Pit 2				
TP 2: 0–50 cm	*Collocalia spodiopygia*	Swiftlet	all elements present	>60
TP 2: 0–50 cm	*Rattus exulans*	Pacific rat	all elements present	>60
TP 2: 0–50 cm	*Rattus praetor*	Spiny rat	all elements present	>40
TP 2: 0–30 cm	*Porphyrio porphyrio*	Purple swamphen	proximal carpometacarpus (R)	1
TP 2: 0–30 cm	*Columbid species*	Pigeon sp.	sacrum	1
TP 2: 0–30 cm	*Halcyon chloris*	White-collared kingfisher	humerus (R)	1
TP 2: 0–30 cm	*Aplonis tabuensis*	Polynesian starling	humerus (L+R), tarsometatarsus (R), ulna (R), tibiotarsus (L)	5
TP 2: 0–30 cm	?*Gallicolumba*	Dove species	proximal tibia (R)	5
TP 2: 0–30 cm	*Porzana tabuensis*	Spotless crake	proximal humerus (L), tarsometatarsus (R), femur (R), distal tibia (R+L)	5
TP 2: 0–30 cm	*Gehyra oceanica*	Oceanic gecko	maxilla (2R+2L), dentary (7L+1R)	12
TP 2: 0–30 cm	*Chelonia mydas*	Green turtle	humerus	1
TP 2: 0–30 cm	*Gecko ?species*	Gecko species	dentary (3L+1R), scapulocoracoid (1R), femur (4), humerus (1), maxilla (L+R)	12
TP 2: 0–30 cm	?*Emballonura semicaudata*	Pacific sheath-tailed bat	dentary	1
TP 2: 30–50 cm	*Brachylophus fasciatus*	Banded iguana	maxilla (L)	1
TP 2: 30–50 cm	*Halcyon chloris*	White-collared kingfisher	humerus (L)	1
TP 2: 30–50 cm	*Gallus gallus*	Domestic fowl	humerus (R), shaft ulna	2
TP 2: 30–50 cm	*Porphyrio porphyrio*	Purple swamphen	proximal humerus (R), distal femur (R), scapula (L)	3
TP 2: 30–50 cm	*Gallus gallus*	Domestic fowl	distal tarsometatarsus (R), coracoid (R)	2
TP 2: 30–50 cm	*Aplonis tabuensis*	Polynesian starling	shaft humerus (L), distal ulna (R+L), tibiotarsus (R), tarsometatarsus (L)	5
NISP Total				>218

Table 39. Navatu 17A, Trench B, non-fish remains.

Provenience	Taxa	Common name	Element	NISP
1: 0–20 cm	*Homo sapiens*	human	crania-vault	2
1: 20–40 cm	Mammal ?species		fragment (2 burnt)	3
1: 20–40 cm	Mammal ?species		fragment	4
2: 20–40 cm	Mammal ?species		fragment	1
3: 20–40 cm	*Sus scrofa*	pig	calcaneum (R)	1
3: 20–40 cm	*Homo sapiens*	human	metatarsal-5 (R)	1
1: 40–50 cm	?Mammal		long bone	1
2: 40–50 cm	*Homo sapiens*	human	capitate	1
1: 40–50 cm	Mammal ?species		metatarsal	1
1: 50–60 cm	*?Homo sapiens*		fragment	1
2: 50–60 cm	Turtle		plastron	4
2: 50–60 cm	*Homo sapiens*	human	*Homo sapiens*	1
2: 50–60 cm	Mammal ?species		fragment	1
3: 50–60 cm	Mammal		long bone fragment	1
1: 60–70 cm	Mammal ?species.		fragment	2
3: 60–70 cm	Bird ?species		long bone fragment	1
3: 60–70 cm	*Homo sapiens*	human	crania-parietal	3
3: 60–70 cm	*Pteropus* sp.	fruit bat	mandible	1
1: 70–80 cm	Mammal ?species		proximal rib	1
1: 70–80 cm	Mammal ?species		long bone	2
2: 70–80 cm	Turtle		plastron	1
2: 70–80 cm	*Homo sapiens*	human	proximal radius	1
2: 70–80 cm	*Homo sapiens*	human	tooth-M^1	1
2: 70–80 cm	Reptile ?sp.		epiphysis	1
2: 70–80 cm	Bird ?species		long bone fragment	1
3: 70–80 cm	Mammal ?species		shaft rib	2
4: 70–80 cm	*Homo sapiens*	human	proximal ulna	1
2: 80–90 cm	Lizard ? Sp		long bone fragment	1
2: 80–90 cm	Turtle?		metatarsal	1
2: 80–90 cm	Turtle		plastron	1
2: 80–90 cm	Mammal ?species		fragment	1
3: 80–90 cm	Bird ?species		long bone fragment	1
3: 80–90 cm	*?Homo sapiens*	human	shaft rib	1
3: 80–90 cm	Mammal ?species		fragment	1
1: 90–100 cm	*Homo sapiens*	human	shaft ulna/radius	1
2: 90–100 cm	Turtle		plastron	2
2: 90–100 cm	Bird ?species		long bone fragment	1
3: 90–100 cm	Turtle		plastron	1
3: 90–100 cm	*Rattus exulans*	Pacific rat	humerus (L)	1
3: 90–100 cm	*Homo sapiens*	human	phalange-5	1
3: 90–100 cm	Mammal ?species		fragment	1

Continued on next page

Table 39 *continued*

Provenience	Taxa	Common name	Element	NISP
3: 100–110 cm	*Pteropus* sp.	fruit bat	mandible (R)	1
3: 100–110 cm	Mammal ?species		fragment	5
1: 100–110 cm	*Tyto alba*	barn owl	distal tarsometatarsus (L)	1
2: 100–110 cm	Bird ?species		long bone fragment	2
3: 110–120 cm	*Tyto alba*	barn owl	distal ulna (R)	1
3: 110–120 cm	Bird ?species		long bone fragment	1
3: 110–120 cm	Bird ?species		distal tarsometatarsus	1
1: 120–160 cm	*Homo sapiens*	human	tooth-M_1 (caries)	1
1: 120–160 cm	Mammal ?species		long bone	1
1: 180–190 cm	Mammal ?species		fragment	2
1: 180–190 cm	?Turtle		metatarsal/carpal	1
1+2: 200–210 cm	*Homo sapiens*	human	crania-vault	1
1+2: 210–220 cm	Mammal ?species		fragment	1
1+2: 210–220 cm	Bird ?species		long bone fragment	1
1+2: 210–220 cm	Turtle		plastron	2
1+2: 210–220 cm	Mammal ?species		fragment	4
1+2: 220–230 cm	Turtle		plastron	4
1+2: 220–230 cm	Mammal ?species		plastron	10
1+2: 230–240 cm	Turtle		plastron	4
1+2: 230–240 cm	Mammal ?species		long bone fragment	7
1+2: 230–240 cm	Mammal ?species		shaft rib	2
1+2: 230–240 cm	Mammal ?species		vertebra	10
1+2: 230–240 cm	Mammal ?species		fragment	4
3+4: 230–240 cm	Bird ?species		long bone fragment	4
3+4: 230–240 cm	Bird ?species		fragment	1
3+4: 230–240 cm	*Homo sapiens*	human	shaft tibia	3
3+4: 230–240 cm	Mammal ?species		fragment	60
1+2: 240–250 cm	*Homo sapiens*	human	zygomatic	1
1+2: 240–250 cm	*Homo sapiens*	human	crania-vault	1
1+2: 240–250 cm	Turtle		plastron	3
1+2: 240–250 cm	Bird ?species		long bone fragment	1
1+2: 240–250 cm	Mammal ?species		fragment	41
3+4: 240–250 cm	Mammal ?species		shaft rib	1
3+4: 240–250 cm	Mammal ?species		fragment	5
1+2: 250–260 cm	*Rattus exulans*	Pacific rat	distal radius	1
1+2: 250–260 cm	*Rattus exulans*	Pacific rat	vertebra	1
1+2: 250–260 cm	Turtle		plastron	4
3+4: 250–260 cm	Lizard ?species		proximal humerus	1
3+4: 250–260 cm	*Homo sapiens*	human	proximal phalange-I/II	1
NISP Total				252

Most of the small collection of mammal bone was from human, with pig and flying fox in Layer 1 and the Pacific rat (*Rattus exulans*), only in Layer 4. A single rib fragment in Layer 4 was identified as belonging to a medium-sized mammal, possibly pig, but no unequivocal evidence for the mammalian commensals, pig and dog, was recorded from the pre-1000 BP deposit. Gifford (1951) recorded pig bone in his excavations, at a depth of about 2.6 m. The human bone from earlier and recent excavations consisted of fragments from the cranium, mandible, arm, hand and leg. The remains do not appear to be from a disturbed primary or secondary burial. Analysis by David DeGusta (pers. comm., University of California) of human remains from the 1947 and 1996 excavations identified cut marks and modification (burning, ancient breaks, crushing, percussion pits), consistent with cannibalism (Figure 114), which supports Gifford's (1951:108) assessment that: 'it seems clear that human flesh was eaten in the Early period'. Redating of the Layer 4 deposit indicates that cannibalism was present in Fiji before 1000 BP (see also Best 1984:562, 592).

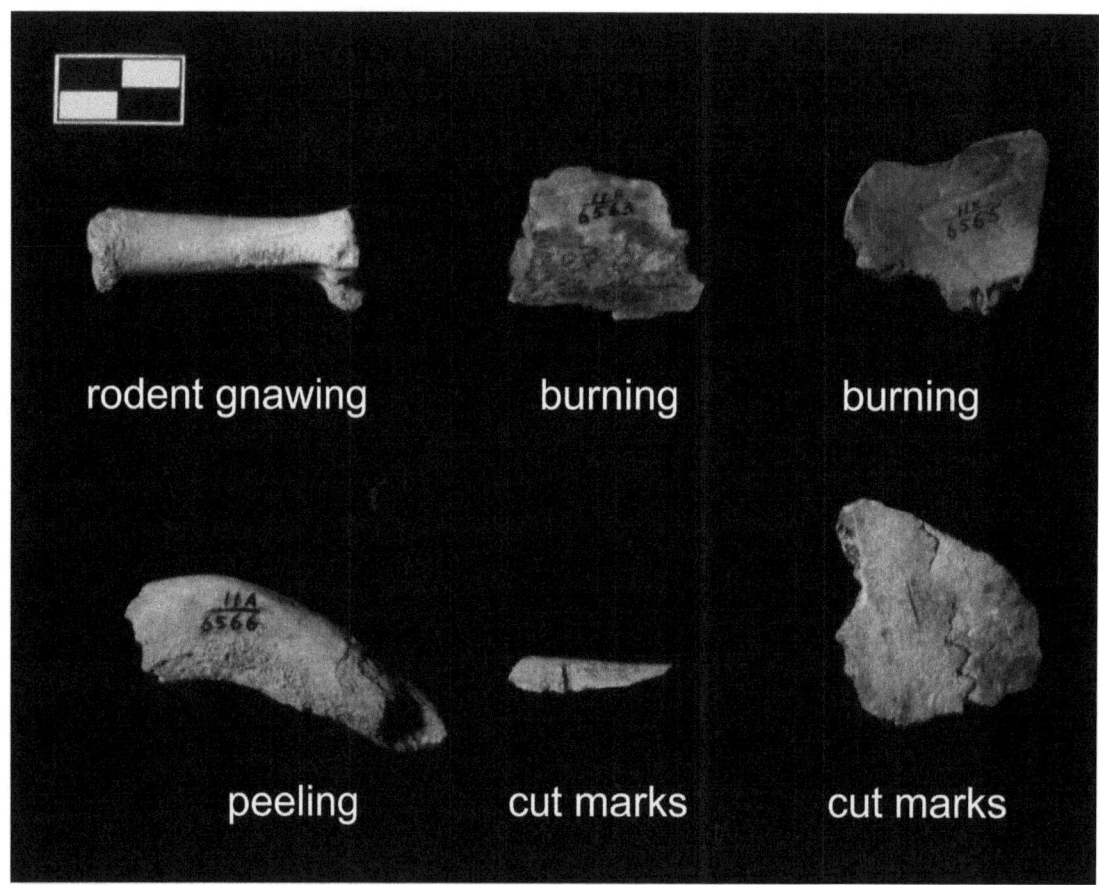

Figure 114. Modification of human bone at the Navatu 17A site. Photo courtesy of David DeGusta.

Kulu Bay (Beqa Island)

The non-fish fauna from Kulu contained remains from three domestic species (pig, dog and chicken), in addition to a large species and a small species of *Rattus* (Table 40). The large species had remains of comparable size to bones from *R. praetor*, and the smaller species was comparable in size to *R. exulans*. Kulu is one of the few Lapita deposits in Fiji that might contain the full suite of animal species that were transported to the Pacific in prehistory (see also Nunn et al. 2007). However, the Kulu sediments were water-transported and the deposit contains ceramics of post-Lapita age along with Lapita sherds. Without directly dating the remains of domestic

Table 40. Kulu Bay non-fish remains.

Provenience	Taxa	Common name	Element	NISP
C9: 10–20 cm	Mammal ?species		fragment vertebra	1
C9: 10–20 cm	Mammal ?species		metatarsal	1
C9: 20–30 cm	Mammal ?species		fragment	1
C9 30–40 cm	Turtle sp.		plastron	3
C9: 30–40 cm	*Gallus gallus*	Domestic chicken	proximal tarsometatarsus (L)	1
C9: 30–40 cm	*Sus scrofa*	Pig	vertebra	1
C9: 40–50 cm	*Canis familiaris*	Dog	tooth-incisor	1
C9: 40–50 cm	Turtle sp.		plastron	3
C9: 40–50 cm	Bird ?species		long bone fragment	1
C9: 40–50 cm	Bird ?species		long bone fragment	1
C9: 50–60 cm	Turtle sp.		plastron	4
C9: 50–60 cm	*Pteropus* cf. *tonganus*	Large fruit bat	mandible	1
C9: 50–60 cm	Bird ?species		fragment long bone	3
C10: 10–20 cm	Mammal ?species		long bone fragment	1
C10: 30–50 cm	Mammal ?species		fragment	3
C10: 50–70 cm	Turtle sp.		plastron	2
C10: 60–80 cm	*Canis familiaris*	Dog	tooth-canine	1
C10: 60–80 cm	*Gallus gallus*	Domestic chicken	proximal tarsometatarsus (L)	1
C10: 70–80 cm	Mammal ?species		fragment vertebra	1
C10: 90–100 cm	*Canis familiaris*	Dog	tooth-incisor	2
C10: 90–100 cm	Mammal ?species		fragment	2
C10: 90–100 cm	*Homo sapiens*	Human	tooth-molar	1
C11: 0–10 cm	Mammal ?species		long bone fragment	1
C11: 20–30 cm	Turtle sp.		fragment	2
C11: 20–30 cm	Mammal ?species		fragment	1
C11: 30–40 cm	*Canis familiaris*	Dog	tooth-premolar	1
C11: 30–40 cm	*Rattus* sp.	Rat	distal tibia	1
C11: 30–40 cm	Mammal ?species		fragment	5
C11: 60–70 cm	Mammal ?species		long bone fragment	1
C11: 70–80 cm	Mammal ?species		fragment	5
C11: 70–80 cm	*Rattus* sp.	Rat	mandible (L)	1
C11: 70–80 cm	*Sus scrofa*	Pig	tooth-incisor	1
C11: 70–80 cm	*Ducula* cf. *lakeba*	Lau imperial pigeon	distal coracoid (R)	1
C11: 80–90 cm	Turtle sp.		plastron	3
C11: 80–90 cm	*Rattus* sp.	Rat	humerus (R)	1
C11: 80–90 cm	Mammal ?species		fragment	7
C11: 80–90 cm	cf. *Puffinus pacificus*	Wedge-tailed shearwater	shaft humerus (R)	1
C11: 90–100 cm	*Rattus* sp.	Rat	vertebra	1
C11: 90–100 cm	*Canis familiaris*	Dog	tooth-incisor	2
C11: 90–100 cm	*Sus scrofa*	Pig	tooth-incisor	1
C11: 90–100 cm	Mammal ?species		fragment	6
C11: 100–110 cm	Turtle sp.		fragment	4
C11: 100–110 cm	*Rattus* sp.	Rat	shaft humerus	1
C11: 100–110 cm	*Rattus* sp.	Rat	shaft tibia	1
C11: 100–110 cm	*Rattus* sp.	Rat	pelvis (L)	1

Continued on next page

Table 40 *continued*

Provenience	Taxa	Common name	Element	NISP
C11: 100–110 cm	Mammal ?species		fragment	4
C11: 110–120 cm	Canis familiaris	Dog	tooth-incisor	1
C11: 110–120 cm	Sus scrofa	Pig	tooth-incisor	1
C11: 110–120 cm	Rattus sp.	Rat	femur (R)	2
C11: 110–120 cm	Rattus sp.	Rat	femur (L)	1
C11: 110–120 cm	Rattus sp.	Rat	tibia	2
C11: 110–120 cm	Rattus sp.	Rat	humerus (R)	1
C11: 110–120 cm	Rattus sp.	Rat	pelvis (R)	2
C11: 110–120 cm	Rattus sp.	Rat	pelvis	1
C11: 110–120 cm	Rattus sp.	Rat	caudal vertebra	2
C11: 110–120 cm	Mammal ?species		vertebra	1
C11: 110–120 cm	Mammal ?species		fragment	11
C11: 110–120 cm	Bird ?species		fragment long bone	1
C11: 120–130 cm	Rattus sp.	Rat	humerus (R)	1
C11: 120–130 cm	Canis familiaris	Dog	tooth-incisor	1
C11: 120–130 cm	Mammal ?species		fragment	2
C11: 130–140 cm	Homo sapiens	Human	tooth-molar fragment	1
C11: 130–140 cm	Canis familiaris	Dog	tooth-incisor	1
C11: 130–140 cm	Mammal ?species		long bone fragment	1
C11: 130–140 cm	Bird ?species		fragment long bone	1
C11: 150–160 cm	Mammal ?species		long bone fragment	2
NISP Total				**125**

species, we cannot be certain that the Lapita occupation at Kulu involved the husbandry of introduced animals. Only a few identifiable bird bones were recovered from the excavations, with remains of *Gallus gallus* and a Procellarid, probably the wedge-tailed shearwater. Shearwaters are medium-sized pelagic birds that nest mostly in ground burrows and are mainly nocturnal on their breeding grounds (Pratt et al. 1987:51). Interestingly, the middle levels of the site had a single bone from the extinct volant pigeon (*Ducula lakeba*) that is otherwise known from the early-Lapita deposits on Lakeba Island, and the pigeon probably existed on many Fiji Islands in the past (Worthy 2001b; Steadman 2006a). The small amount of human bone did not exhibit any evidence of cannibalism and may represent a redeposited early burial.

Volivoli II, Volivoli III and Malaqereqere (south Viti Levu)

Volivoli II

The fauna from Volivoli II consisted mainly of bones from *Rattus* sp., along with sparse amounts of bird, turtle, fruit bat, pig and goat bone (Table 41). The small amount of bird bone is significant in that it contains bones from the small collared petrel (*Pterodroma brevipes*), which might have bred in large numbers on the inland hills of Viti Levu before human activity and the arrival of introduced predators such as rats.

Volivoli III

The site contained remains of the fruit bat and unidentified gecko and bird species (Table 41).

Malaqereqere

In contrast to the numerous fish bones in the coastal rock shelter, the non-fish bone component included sparse remains from fruit bat and a *Rattus* sp., probably *R. exulans*. An unidentified rail (cf. *Gallirallus philippensis*) was present, along with two reptiles (Table 41). One of these is the Pacific boa (*Candoia* sp.), which is currently widespread in Fiji, while the other is the extinct giant ground frog (*Platymantis megabotoniviti*) that is assumed to have become extinct after the arrival of people and rodents to Fiji (Worthy 2001a).

Table 41. Volivoli II, Volivoli III and Malaqereqere non-fish remains.

Provenience	Taxa	Common name	Element	NISP
0–10 cm	*Sus scrofa*	Pig	tooth-incisor	3
0–10 cm	*Sus scrofa*	Pig	phalange	1
0–10 cm	Mammal ?species		long bone fragments	22
10–20 cm	*Capra hircus*	Domestic goat	tooth-molar	1
10–20 cm	*Rattus* sp.	Rat	tibia (R)	1
10–20 cm	?Species		fragments	6
20–30 cm	Turtle sp.		plastron	33
20–30 cm	*Rattus* sp.	Rat	mandible (R)	2
20–30	*Rattus* sp.	Rat	tooth-incisor	1
20–30	*Rattus* sp.	Rat	femur (L)	7
20–30	*Rattus* sp.	Rat	femur (R)	4
20–30	*Rattus* sp.	Rat	ulna (R)	2
20–30	*Rattus* sp.	Rat	humerus (L)	1
20–30	*Rattus* sp.	Rat	humerus (R)	1
20–30	*Rattus* sp.	Rat	pelvis (R)	1
20–30	*Rattus* sp.	Rat	tibia (R)	5
20–30	*Rattus* sp.	Rat	tibia (L)	2
20–30	*Gallirallus philippensis*	Banded rail	proximal humerus (R)	1
20–30	?Species		fragments	9
30–40	*Rattus* sp.	Rat	femur (L)	12
30–40	*Rattus* sp.	Rat	femur (R)	6
30–40	*Rattus* sp.	Rat	humerus (L)	1
30–40	*Rattus* sp.	Rat	humerus (R)	1
30–40	*Rattus* sp.	Rat	vertebrae	1
30–40	*Rattus* sp.	Rat	mandible (R)	3
30–40	*Rattus* sp.	Rat	mandible (L)	1
30–40	*Rattus* sp.	Rat	maxilla (R)	1
30–40	*Rattus* sp.	Rat	pelvis (R)	2
30–40	*Rattus* sp.	Rat	pelvis (L)	3
30–40	*Rattus* sp.	Rat	tibia (L)	5
30–40	*Rattus* sp.	Rat	tibia (R)	7
30–40	*Pterodrama* cf. *brevipes*	Small collared petrel	proximal humerus (L)	1
30–40	?Species		fragments	7
40–50	Turtle sp.	Turtle	plastron	7
40–50	*Rattus* sp.	Rat	tibia (L)	4

Continued on next page

Table 41 *continued*

Provenience	Taxa	Common name	Element	NISP
40–50	*Rattus* sp.	Rat	tibia (R)	2
40–50	*Rattus* sp.	Rat	femur (R)	4
40–50	*Rattus* sp.	Rat	femur (L)	3
40–50	*Rattus* sp.	Rat	humerus (L)	2
40–50	*Rattus* sp.	Rat	ulna (L)	1
40–50	*Pterodrama* cf. *brevipes*	Small collared petrel	distal humerus (L), radius	2
40–50	?Species		fragments	16
50–60	Turtle sp.	Turtle	plastron	2
50–60	*Rattus* sp.	Rat	mandible (L)	1
50–60	*Rattus* sp.	Rat	mandible (R)	1
50–60	*Rattus* sp.	Rat	pelvis (?)	1
50–60	*Rattus* sp.	Rat	tibia (L)	1
50–60	*Rattus* sp.	Rat	scapula	1
50–60	?Species		fragments	7
60–70	*Rattus* sp.	Rat	humerus (L)	1
60–70	?Species		long bone fragments	1
Posthole fill	?Species		fragments	2
Posthole fill	?Species		tooth	1
NISP Total				**214**
Volivoli III				
Spit V	*Pteropus* cf. *tonganus*	Large fruit bat	mandible	1
Spit VIII	*Pteropus* cf. *tonganus*	Large fruit bat	long bones	4
Spit VIII	Gecko sp.	Gecko	fragment	1
Spit VIII	Bird ?species		long bone	1
NISP Total				**7**
Malaqereqere				
A1: 10–20 cm	*Pteropus* cf. *tonganus*	Large fruit bat	long bones	5
A1: 20–30 cm	*Pteropus* cf. *tonganus*	Large fruit bat	long bones	4
A1: 30–40 cm	*Pteropus* cf. *tonganus*	Large fruit bat	long bones	5
A1: 30–40 cm	*Rattus* sp.	Rat	long bone	1
A1: 30–40 cm	*Candoia bibroni*	Pacific boa	vertebra	1
A1: 40–50 cm	*Pteropus* cf. *tonganus*	Large fruit bat	long bone	1
A1: 40–50 cm	*Rattus* sp.	Rat	long bone, pelvis	1
A2: 10–20 cm	*Pteropus* cf. *tonganus*	Large fruit bat	long bones	5
A2: 10–20 cm	Rail ?species	Rail	proximal tarsometatarsus	1
A2: 50–60 cm	*Porphyrio porphyrio*	Purple swamphen	shaft tibiotarsus (R)	1
A2: 50–60 cm	*Platymantis megabotoniviti*	Giant Fiji ground frog	vertebra	1
A2: 50–60 cm	*Rattus* sp.	Rat	long bones	2
NISP Total				**28**

Qaranioso II and Tuvu (west Viti Levu)

Qaranioso II

The inland shelter produced small amounts of pottery and faunal material (Table 42), which is significant for two reasons. First, a decorated ceramic rim of late-Lapita age showed that people were using the interior regions of Viti Levu early in prehistory and affecting the environment (Anderson et al. 2000). Evidence for this at Qaranioso II is suggested by the remains of a large extinct iguana (*Lapitiguana impensa*). This iguana had an estimated snout-to-vent length of 500 mm (Pregill and Worthy 2003), and it was much larger than either of the three iguanas in Fiji today (*Brachylophus fasciatus, B. bulabula* and *B. vitiensis*). In Tonga, bones from a large iguana (*Brachylophus gibbonsi*) have been found in several Lapita sites and direct radiocarbon dating of iguana bones suggests it became extinct there within a century or two of human arrival (Steadman et al. 2002). Although radiocarbon dating of the iguana bone from Qaranioso II failed due to a lack of adequate dateable material, the co-occurrence of the remains of *Lapitiguana impensa* with pottery of late-Lapita age suggests a similar pattern of human predation to that witnessed on Tonga. The rock shelter also contained bat remains (microbat, *Notopterus macdonaldi*), Pacific boa and banded rail, as well as three species of *Rattus* (*R. exulans, R. praetor, R. rattus*). The rat-bone sequence includes *R. praetor* bone found in the 10–20 cm level of the shelter, while the

Table 42. Qaranioso II and Tuvu non-fish remains.

Provenience	Taxa	Common name	Element	NISP
Qaranioso II				
TP 1: 0–10 cm	*Gallirallus philippensis*	Banded rail	long bone	1
TP 1: 0–10 cm	*Rattus* cf. *rattus*	Black rat	long bones	6
TP 1: 0–10 cm	*Rattus* cf. *exulans*	Pacific rat	long bone	1
TP 1: 10–20 cm	*Rattus exulans*	Pacific rat	long bones	4
TP 1: 10–20 cm	*Rattus* sp. (large)	Rat	long bones	5
TP 1: 10–20 cm	*Rattus praetor*	Spiny rat	mandible	1
TP 1: 10–20 cm	*Gallus* sp.		proximal radius, phalange	2
TP 1: 10–20 cm	Microchiroptera	Microbat	long bone	1
TP 1: 20–30 cm	*Rattus praetor*	Spiny rat	maxilla	1
TP 1: 40–50 cm	Bird ?species		fragments	2
TP : 50–60 cm	*Notopteris macdonaldi*	Long-tailed fruit bat		11
TP 1: 50–60 cm	*Rattus* cf *exulans*	Pacific rat	long bones	2
TP 1: 50–60 cm	*Candoia* cf. *bibroni*	Pacific boa	vertebra	3
TP 1: 50–60 cm	?*Platymantis vitianus*	Fiji ground frog	fragment	1
TP 1: 50–60 cm	Bird ?species		fragment	1
TP 1: 60–70 cm	*Lapitiguana impensa*	Fiji giant iguana	shaft scapulacorocoid (R), chevron bone	2
TP 1: 60–70 cm	*Rattus* sp. (large)	Rat	long bone	1
NISP Total				45
Tuvu				
Spit 3	*Rattus* sp.	Rat	tibia	1

European-introduced *R. rattus* was found above it, in the top 0–10 cm level. A radiocarbon date from 30 cm depth has an age of 530–670 cal. BP (ANU-11014), indicating that *R. praetor* survived until recent times and became extinct after the arrival of European species of *Rattus*.

Tuvu

A single bone of *Rattus* sp. was recovered from the Tuvu deposit (Table 42).

Discussion

The prehistoric fauna from archaeological sites in Fiji includes several extinct species found in deposits containing material culture of Lapita age. Two extinct reptiles and a frog – the giant iguana (*Lapitiguana impensa*), endemic crocodilian (*Volia athollandersoni*) and giant ground frog (*Platymantis megabotoniviti*) – have all been found on Viti Levu or on nearby islands, but not as yet in the Lau Group. Extinct reptile remains were found in cultural deposits at Qaranioso II and Malaqereqere, but whether the reptile remains result from human predation or natural deposition is unclear. Bone from turtle and fruit bat is found in small amounts in many Lapita and post-Lapita sites, with the Qaranipuqa Lapita levels having greater amounts of both than post-Lapita levels. Extinct land birds have been identified at sites with Lapita ceramics, such as Kulu (Beqa Island), Votua (Mago Island), Qaranipuqa (Lakeba Island) and Naigani Island, but not in a late-Lapita deposit on Waya Island (Steadman 2006a:166, Tables 6–8). A site on Aiwa Levu Island (ALR1) in the Lau Group with extinct bird bone appears to contain avifauna from pre-human deposits, as well as those of post-Lapita age. The association of the extinct species with the post-Lapita cultural deposit is unclear (Steadman 2006a:178).

Elsewhere in Fiji, bone from extinct bird species, however, is absent from post-Lapita deposits on Viti Levu (e.g. Sigatoka, Navatu, Malaqereqere, Volivoli II) and the Lau Group (Aiwa Lailai Island, Nayau Island, Lakeba Island) (Steadman 2006a). This suggests that Fiji's avifauna, especially its endemic species, was significantly depleted during the first centuries of Lapita occupation. The effect of human arrival on Fiji's native birds is most clearly seen at the Lakeba site of Qaranipuqa excavated by Simon Best in the 1970s, and the bird remains are discussed further below.

The Lakeba avifauna sequence

At least 26 native species of birds are represented in the fauna from Qaranipuqa and Wakea. A striking feature of the fauna is that it is dominated by land birds and poorly represents sea birds. For example, petrels, terns, and boobies, which are prominent in the extant fauna of the region today (Watling 1982), are entirely lacking. Both groups are often very common in tropical Pacific archaeological sites (Steadman 1995, 2006a), e.g. on Niue (Worthy et al. 1998), American Samoa (Steadman 1994), Mangaia (Steadman 1985; Steadman and Kirch 1990), and Henderson Island (Wragg and Weisler 1994; Wragg 1995). It may be that these colonial nesting birds were not available in the near vicinity of Qaranipuqa, as those sea birds that were taken would have been available nesting in the forest (e.g. white-tailed tropicbird) or on the adjacent coast as individuals (e.g. the herons and godwit).

When the fauna is analysed by depth, as in Table 37, it is obvious most of the fauna came from the lower layers T–X, with a lesser accumulation in H–O, and scattered bones in A–F. Layers A–F date largely to the past 1000 years, and there is a discontinuity in the Qaranipuqa deposits between Layers A–F and underlying layers (Best 1984:Table 2.2).

It is likely that all fauna from Layers A and B, at least, and possibly as deep as Layer F, is derived, not from cultural activity, but from the middens of barn owls (*Tyto alba*) that lived in the shelter. All of the species recorded in these upper layers would be able to be taken by barn owls. Faunas from modern barn-owl middens on Viti Levu and Vatulele (see Chapter 3) indicate that barn owls regularly take *Egretta* and shore birds when available, in addition to small forest birds. Therefore, in the Qaranipuqa fauna, both waders and the heron are almost certainly owl-caught species. Similarly, the small passerines, the kingfisher and the lorikeet bones are also probably from the owl midden.

The fauna from the middle part of the sequence (Layers H–O) represents a comparatively depauperate fauna being taken by the human inhabitants of Qaranipuqa. These layers are radiocarbon dated to between about 2300 cal. BP (Layer O) and 1800 cal. BP (Layer H). The hunted species were mainly rails, a few pigeons and a few sea birds (white-tailed tropicbird and frigate bird). In contrast, the Lapita people, represented in the earliest layers, T–X, hunted a diverse range of species that included no sea birds.

The Qaranipuqa fauna reveals that the following taxa have gone extinct on Lakeba, and did so during deposition of the lower layers of the site, as none occurs above Lapita horizons: the megapode *Megapodius alimentum* (as *M. freycinet* in Best 1984), a large pigeon (*Ducula lakeba*), the tooth-billed pigeon (*Didunculus strigirostris*), and the musk parrot (*Prosopeia* sp.). *Porphyrio porphyrio* has since become extinct on the island (Steadman and Franklin 2000).

Several taxa await reference material for certain identification. For example, the lorikeet *Charmosyma amabilis* is probably represented in the Lakeba fauna, which would be a significant extension of its present range in Viti Levu, Taveuni and Ovalau (Watling 1982). Several pigeon bones bigger than *Ducula pacifica* and smaller than the large extinct *Ducula lakeba* also await more extensive reference material for certain identification, but are likely to be *Ducula latrans*. This large-bodied fruit pigeon is currently restricted to the large Fiji Islands and its range includes Lakeba (Watling 1982). One tarsometatarsus represents a *Ptilinopus* sp. that is larger than any of the species of *Ptilinopus* extant in Fiji. However, both *P. rarotongensis* of Rarotonga and *P. purpuratus* of the Society Islands–Tuamotu Group have similar-sized tarsometatarsi (Steadman 1992). The fossil may indicate that a dove larger than those in the golden dove group or *P. porphyraceus* and *P. perousii* and similar in size to these more eastern taxa formerly lived on the Lau Group.

Of the extinct pigeons, *Ducula lakeba* has not yet been recorded from elsewhere, although a similar-sized pigeon (perhaps the same taxon) is known from Viti Levu and Beqa (Worthy 2001b). *Ducula lakeba* and *D. david* (Balouet and Olson 1987) are the largest fruit pigeons described from the Pacific, and are only a little smaller than the large New Zealand *Hemiphaga novaeseelandiae*. Steadman (1989, 1997) recorded *Ducula david* from Foa and Lifuka in the Ha'apai Group and 'Eua, all in the Kingdom of Tonga, and provisionally lists this species from Lakeba (Steadman 1997). The species *D. david* was based on a partial tarsometatarsus, and the only described Tongan bone, a coracoid, was referred by Steadman (1989) to *D. david*, based on its size. Steadman (1997) did not mention whether comparable material is included in the other sites. Steadman (1997) also listed a *Ducula* new sp. from Lifuka and 'Eua, which is presumed to be the same as that described in Steadman (1989) and as such is a much larger pigeon. However, following the distinction of *D. lakeba* from *D. david* (Worthy 2001b), the Tongan large *Ducula* bones were listed as an undescribed species (Steadman 2006a). The tooth-billed pigeon *Didunculus strigirostris* survives only in American Samoa, so the certain identification of several bones from Lakeba is a major extension of its range. Steadman (1993, 1997) reported a new species of *Didunculus* from two caves on 'Eua. It has recently been named (Steadman 2006c).

The presence of a megapode on Lakeba and in Votua on Mago (see Clark et al. 2001) elsewhere in the Lau Group is not unexpected as various species have been reported previously from island groups to the east of their main extant distribution in the western Pacific (Jones et al. 1995), as far as Niue (Steadman et al. 2000). At least four species of megapodes are known from Tonga (Steadman 1999, 2006a). Of these, the medium-sized scrubfowl *M. alimentum* (Steadman 1989) is here confirmed as that from Lakeba, as suggested by Steadman (1999). This species is also reported from Mago Island, but contra Steadman (1999), it has not been found on Naigani off Viti Levu. That megapode was the very large *Megavitiornis altirostris* (Worthy 2000). *Megapodius alimentum* was a volant species and so was probably widespread in the Lau Group and east to Tonga. On Viti Levu and probably on Vanua Levu, however, the larger and probably flightless *Megapodius amissus* (Worthy 2000) replaced *M. alimentum*.

The age of the older Lapita fauna from Qaranipuqa (Layer W to Layer R/S) has been re-evaluated by Anderson and Clark (1999) as about 2700–2900 cal BP. It is within this period that the extinctions occurred. The composition of the original fauna included the black duck *Anas superciliosa*, which is still widespread in the Pacific and common on the island today (Steadman and Franklin 2000), occupying both freshwater wetlands and coastal habitats. Of the rails, *Porphyrio porphyrio* was present in the early and middle parts of the sequence and has probably gone extinct historically as it has elsewhere in the Fiji archipelago following the impact of mammalian predation. The banded rail *Gallirallus philippensis* may have been a more recent arrival, as all bones were only recorded from upper horizons. Perhaps either habitat changes or faunal extinctions after human arrival enabled the banded rail to establish populations on Lakeba. The revised identification confirms the presence of *Gallus gallus* in the Lapita levels of the site, although secure evidence of the pig and dog in sites of Lapita age in Fiji and Tonga has yet to be recovered (Burley 1998; Clark and Anderson 2001).

All the *Tyto* bones come from upper layers in the site, conforming with a suggested post-human expansion by this owl into the Pacific (see Chapter 3) following the introduction of rodents. There are no prehuman records of these owls known from Fiji (data herein), Niue (Worthy et al. 1998), or elsewhere in Polynesia (Steadman 2006a), so far as the authors are aware.

The modern fauna of Lakeba includes 21 land and freshwater birds (Steadman and Franklin 2000). Their survey shows that both *Gallirallus philippensis* and *Gallicolumba stairii* are present, although rare, due probably to the presence of abundant feral cats. The pigeons include the two doves *Ptilinopus porphyraceus* and *P. perousii*, in addition to the fruit pigeons *D. pacifica* and *C. vitiensis*. The modern fauna contains several species not found in the archaeological fauna: *Circus approximans* harrier, *Collocalia spodiopygia* swiftlet, and the small passerines *Lalage maculosa*, *Mayrornis lessoni*, *Myiagra vanikorensis* and *Myzomela jugalis*. These six species plus *P. perousii* are likely to have been former inhabitants of Lakeba and so add to the 20 land and freshwater species in the archaeological fauna for a total of at least 27 land and freshwater species (33 in total) in the original fauna. This fauna is likely to be extended by the addition of extinct flightless rails such as have been found in the Cook Islands (Steadman 1987) and Niue (Steadman et al. 2000).

Commensal introduction and post-Lapita subsistence

The extinction of land birds and probably several taxa of reptile appears to have taken place during the Lapita phase in Fiji and involved heavy human predation in the case of land birds. The impact that commensal species had on the demise of Fiji's native fauna during the colonisation era is unclear because a Lapita association for the three domesticates, pig, dog and chicken, and two species of *Rattus* (*R. praetor* and *R. exulans*) in disturbed sites is questionable. This is an important issue since domestic animals often serve as a proxy marker of a horticultural society, and if a transported economic system of flora and fauna underwrote, to some extent, Lapita subsistence, then human impact on Fiji's indigenous taxa might have, in the short term, been less harmful, and secondary to the negative effects of introduced commensal species. Conversely, an absence of commensal species in Lapita times could favour a scenario involving the colonists' early reliance on Fiji's wild foods, with the subsequent introduction of domesticates and the increased probability of additional migrants arriving in Fiji during the Lapita era.

The two species of *Rattus* introduced to Fiji in prehistory (*R. exulans* and *R. praetor*) both appear to be early introductions and have been found in several Lapita sites, such as Votua and Qaranipuqa in the Lau Group, and on Viti Levu, although *R. praetor* has not so far been reported from the Yasawas or Aiwa Islands (Cochrane 2006; Jones et al. 2007). At the Qaranipuqa site on Lakeba, both *R. praetor* and *R. exulans* were found together in Layers P–T, which overlie Layers U–X (White et al. 2000) that contain abundant remains of extinct land birds, especially *Megapodius alimentum* and *Ducula lakeba*. It is feasible that the two species of *Rattus* reached the Lau Group shortly after initial human arrival. The geographic distribution of *R. praetor* is intriguing, as it was evidently introduced to Vanuatu, but is not recorded from Lapita sites in New Caledonia or Tonga (White et al. 2000; Grant-Mackie et al. 2003). Attempts to establish the dispersal chronology of *R. praetor* by AMS dating its remains from New Ireland (Buang Merabak), Vanuatu (Navaprah) and Fiji (Votua and Sovanibeka) failed, with only one AMS determination able to be made on a *R. praetor* bone from the Sovanibeka deposit, with an age of 670–770 cal. BP (OZF882). The remains of *R. praetor* were common in the 'Navatu' levels at the Sigatoka Sand Dune on Viti Levu by 1340–1275 cal. BP (Burley 2005) and were found in upper levels of the Qaranioso II site, which indicates that *R. praetor* was sympatric with *R. exulans* for some time before becoming extinct in Fiji. The arrival of European rats probably caused the demise of *R. praetor* in Vanuatu and Fiji.

Like the two species of *Rattus*, the domestic fowl (*Gallus gallus*) was evidently brought to Fiji in Lapita times, with a single *Gallus gallus* bone in Layer W of the Qaranipuqa site and two chicken bones from Aiwa Levu and Aiwa Lailai that are AMS dated to 2000–2500 cal. BP, confirming its early presence in the Lau Group (Jones et al. 2007). The rarity of chicken bone from Lapita and post-Lapita sites in Fiji (Thomas et al. 2004; Burley 2005; Cochrane 2006; Jones et al. 2007; Nunn et al. 2007) contrasts with its frequency in archaeological deposits in Tonga, Niue and Rapa Nui, suggesting that *Gallus gallus* may have been semi-domesticated in Fiji, with feral populations present on many islands.

Both pig and dog have been recorded from mixed Lapita sites (e.g. Nunn et al. 2007) and occur at Kulu where the sediments have been redeposited. The restudy of suspected pig and dog remains from Yanuca and Naigani (Hunt 1980; Best 1981) has not been able to confirm their presence at these sites (T. Worthy pers. obs.; Figure 115). In well-preserved Lapita deposits such as Votua these species do not occur, and at the Qaranipuqa site they are found only in the uppermost layers (A–E1) dating to the last 1000 years, which is also the case for the pig at Navatu 17A (1996 excavations). In the Yasawas, there is pig bone from Level 15 of Qaranicagi (Site Y2–39), which has an estimated age range of 1000–2500 cal. BP (Cochrane 2006), while rare pig and dog bone is recorded from 'Navatu' and 'Plainware' levels at Sigatoka dated to ca. 1280–1520 cal. BP (Burley 2005). The age of the pig and dog remains found at two sites on Aiwa Levu and Aiwa Lailai is not reported (Jones et al. 2007). Thus, it is still uncertain when the pig and dog were introduced to Fiji, and whether these species had a major role in the decline of native species in Fiji. However, the relative absence of pig and dog remains in early archaeological sites suggests these animals played a minor role in Lapita subsistence, particularly in east Fiji. This also appears to be the case in Tonga and in New Caledonia where pigs seem

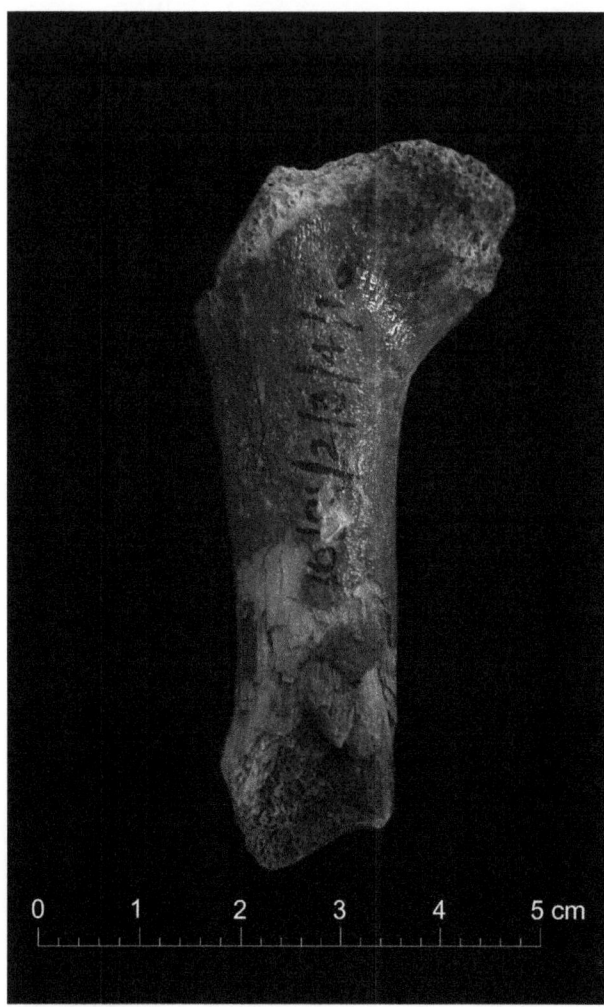

Figure 115. A small 'pig' femur found in the Lapita levels at the Yanuca site (Trench 2/Zone 3/Spit 4, see Hunt 1980:185-188) was re-examined by T.H. Worthy (University of New South Wales) and E.S. Gaffney (American Museum of Natural History) who identified it as turtle (Cheloniiade).

not to have been introduced in prehistory, but contrasts with some parts of Vanuatu where significant amounts of pig bone occurs in Lapita and early post-Lapita contexts. In Fiji, it is feasible that pigs were introduced to west Fiji, and were not initially taken to east Fiji. Direct dating of pig and dog bone from sites such as Naitabale and Bourewa (Nunn 2007; Nunn et al. 2007) is required to establish whether these animals were Lapita introductions to west Fiji.

If pig and dog had a limited role in Lapita subsistence in Fiji, as the current and admittedly scarce data suggests, then terrestrial sources of protein such as endemic reptiles and land bird taxa would likely have been sought during the colonisation era, leading to the extinction of vulnerable taxa in many parts of the archipelago within 200 to 300 years. The decline in native fauna would have necessitated a change in subsistence behaviour, particularly in foraging mobility in the immediate post-Lapita period, but archaeological sites and faunal assemblages from this period with which to evaluate this proposition are currently inadequate. Mobility was clearly greater during the colonisation phase than afterward, as shown by the evidence for significant early interaction on Lakeba (Best 1984; Green 1996; Clark 2000), but it is unclear whether early mobility relates, in part, to the ongoing exploitation of native fauna, or was primarily directed towards social interaction.

It has been argued that during the first millennium AD food stress is seen in the 'Navatu' faunal assemblage from Sigatoka that contains small fish and shellfish, along with Pacific boa, iguana and lizard, and several human remains from the burial area have enamel hypoplasia, possibly the result of food stress (Burley 2005). However, Pietrusewsky et al. (1994:32) note that in the Sigatoka human remains: 'overall very few teeth (20/885, or 2.3%) exhibit hypoplastic defects', suggesting the majority of Sigatoka people during the 'Fijian Plainware-Navatu' period did not suffer food stress.

Evidence for increasing inter-group competition from the occupation of naturally defended hilltops by 1500 BP has been proposed in the Sigatoka Valley by Field (2004), and cannibalism is evident from Navatu 17A by ca. 1400 BP, Vuda at ca. 1000 BP (DeGusta 2000), Qaranicagi (Y2–39) at ca. 750 BP (Cochrane et al. 2004), and Waya Island at ca. 500 BP (Rechtman 1992). On Lakeba, Best (1984:534–535) identified scattered human remains as food debris in several rock shelters. At Qaranipuqa, human bone is a consistent component of the deposits from Layer O, which suggests that cannibalism was an early cultural trait in Fiji from 2500 BP that co-occurred with a population movement inland and the occupation of easily defendable hilltops (Best 1984:562). It is apparent, though, that most fortified sites were utilised post-1500 BP, and became common after 600 BP. Measured archaeologically, both conflict and cannibalism became increasingly prevalent in the past 500 years. Some support for this is in the skeletal record of conflict that shows it is absent-to-rare in human remains from Sigatoka dating to the first millennium AD (Pietrusewsky et al. 1994), but cannibalism is frequent in human remains associated with fortified sites on Waya Island that date to the past 300 years (Rechtman 1992).

References

Anderson A.J. and Clark, G.R. 1999. The age of Lapita settlement in Fiji. *Archaeology in Oceania* 34: 31–39.

Anderson, A., Clark, G. and Worthy, T. 2000. An inland Lapita site in Fiji. *Journal of the Polynesian Society* 109(3): 311–316.

Balouet, J.C. and Olson, S.L. 1987. An extinct species of giant pigeon (Columbidae: *Ducula*) from archaeological deposits on Wallis (Uvea) Island, South Pacific. *Proceedings of the Biological Society of Washington* 100(4): 769–775.

Baumel, J.J. and Witmer, L.M. 1993. Osteologia. In: Baumel, J.J., King, A.S., Breazile, J.E., Evans, H.E. and Vanden Berge, J.C. (eds), *Handbook of avian anatomy: Nomina Anatomica Avium*, Second Edition. *Publications of the Nuttall Ornithological Club* 23: 45–132. Cambridge, Massachusetts.

Best, S. 1981. Excavations at Site VL 21/5 Naigani Island, Fiji, a preliminary report. Department of Anthropology, University of Auckland.

Best, S. 1984. Lakeba: The prehistory of a Fijian island. Unpublished PhD thesis, University of Auckland, Auckland.

Birks, L. 1973. Archaeological excavations at Sigatoka dune site, Fiji. *Bulletin of the Fiji Museum* No.1.

Birks, L. and Birks, H. 1978. Archaeological excavations at site VL 16/81, Yanuca Island, Fiji. *Oceanic Prehistory Records* No. 6. University of Auckland.

Burley, D.V. 1998. Tongan archaeology and the Tongan past, 2850–150 B.P. *World Archaeology* 12(3): 337–392.

Burley, D.V. 2005. Mid-sequence archaeology at the Sigatoka Sand Dunes with interpretive implications for Fijian and Oceanic culture history. *Asian Perspectives* 44: 320–348.

Burley, D.V. 2007. In search of Lapita and Polynesian Plainware settlements in Vava'u, Kingdom of Tonga. In: Bedford, S., Sand, C. and Connaughton, S.P. (eds), *Oceanic explorations: Lapita and Western Pacific settlement*, pp. 187–198. Terra Australis 26. ANU EPress, Australian National University.

Clark, G.R. and Anderson, A.J. 2001. The pattern of Lapita settlement in Fiji. *Archaeology in Oceania* 36: 77–88.

Clark, G.R., Anderson, A.J. and Matararaba, S. 2001. The Lapita site at Votua, northern Lau Islands, Fiji. *Archaeology in Oceania* 36: 134-145.

Clark, G. 2000. Mid-sequence isolation in the Fijian archipelago 2500–1000 BP. *Bulletin of the Indo-Pacific Prehistory Association* 19(3): 152–158.

Cochrane, E.E. 2006. Archaeology in the Yasawa Islands, Western Fiji: A report on fieldwork from 1978 to 2003. *Domodomo* 18(1–2): 1–67.

Cochrane, E.E., Pietrusewsky, M. and Douglas, M.T. 2004. Culturally modified human remains recovered from an earth oven internment on Waya Island, Fiji. *Archaeology in Oceania* 39: 54–59.

Davidson, J., Hinds, E., Holdaway, S. and Leach, F. 1990. The Lapita site of Natunuku, Fiji. *New Zealand Journal of Archaeology* 12: 121–155.

Davidson, J.M. and Leach. B.F. 2001. The strandlooper concept and economic naivete. In: Clark, G.R., Anderson, A.J. and Vunidilo, T. (eds), *The archaeology of Lapita dispersal in Oceania*, pp.115–123. Terra Australis 17, Pandanus Press, Canberra.

DeGusta, D. 1999. Fijian cannibalism: Osteological evidence from Navatu. *American Journal of Physical Anthropology* 110: 215–241.

DeGusta, D. 2000. Fijian cannibalism and mortuary ritual: Bioarchaeological evidence from Vunda. *International Journal of Osteoarchaeology* 10: 76–92.

Field, J.S. 2004. Environmental and climatic considerations: A hypothesis for conflict and the emergence of social complexity in Fijian prehistory. *Journal of Anthropological Archaeology* 23: 79–99.

Gifford, E.W. 1951. Archaeological excavations in Fiji. *University of California Anthropological Records* 13: 189–288.

Grant-Mackie, J.A., Bauer, A.M. and Tyler, M.J. 2003. Stratigraphy and herpetofauna of Me Aure cave (site WMD007), Mondou, New Caledonia. In: Sand, C. (ed), *Pacific archaeology: Assessments and prospects*, pp. 295–306. Les Cahiers de l' Archéologie en Nouvelle-Calédonie Number 15, New Caledonia.

Green, R.C. 1996. Prehistoric transfers of portable items during the Lapita horizon in remote Oceania: A review. *Bulletin of the Indo-Pacific Prehistory Association* 15: 119–130.

Groube, L.M. 1971. Tonga, Lapita pottery, and Polynesian origins. *Journal of the Polynesian Society* 80(3): 278–316.

Jones, D.N., Dekker, R.W.R.J. and Roselaar, C.S. 1995. *The megapodes, Megapodiidae. Bird families of the world.* Oxford University Press, Oxford.

Jones, S., Steadman, D.W. and O'Day, P.M. 2007. Archaeological investigations on the small islands of Aiwa Levu and Aiwa Lailai, Lau Group Fiji. *Journal of Island and Coastal Archaeology* 2: 72–98.

Keogh, J.S., Edwards, D.L., Fisher, R.N., and Harlow, P.S. 2008. Molecular and morphological analysis of the critically endangered Fijian iguanas reveals cryptic diversity and a complex biogeographic history. *Philosophical Transactions of the Royal Society of London B* 363: 3413–3426.

Hunt, T.L. 1980. Toward Fiji's past; archaeological research on southwestern Viti Levu. Unpublished MA thesis, University of Auckland.

Nunn, P.D. 2007. Echoes from a distance: Research into the Lapita occupation of the Rove Peninsula, southwest Viti Levu, Fiji. In: Bedford, S., Sand, C. and Connaughton, S.P. (eds), *Oceanic explorations: Lapita and Western Pacific settlement*, pp. 163–176. Terra Australis 26. ANU EPress, Australian National University.

Nunn, P.D., Ishimura, T., Dickinson, W.D., Katayama, K., Thomas, F., Kumar, R., Matararaba, S., Davidson, J. and Wothy, T. 2007. The Lapita occupation at Naitabale, Motiriki Island, Central Fiji. *Asian Perspectives* 46: 96–132.

Palmer, B. 1965. Excavations at Karobo, Viti Levu. *New Zealand Archaeological Association Newsletter* 8: 26–33.

Pietrusewsky, M., Douglas, M.T. and Ikehara-Quebral, R.M. 1994. The human osteology of the Sigatoka dune burials (Site VL 16/1) Viti-Levu, Fiji Islands. Unpublished report, University of Hawaii.

Pratt, H.D., Bruner, P.I., and Berrett, D.G. 1987. *A field guide to the birds of Hawaii and the tropical Pacific*. Princeton University Press, Princeton, New Jersey.

Pregill, G.K. and Worthy, T.H. 2003. A new iguanid lizard (Squamata, Iguanidae) from the late Quaternary of Fiji, Southwest Pacific. *Herpetologica* 59: 57–67.

Rechtman, R.B. 1992. *The evolution of socio-political complexity in the Fiji Islands*. Unpublished PhD thesis, Ann Arbor, Michigan.

Steadman, D.W. 1985. Fossil birds from Mangaia, southern Cook Islands. *Bulletin of the British Ornithologists Club* 105(2): 58–65.

Steadman, D.W. 1987. Two new species of rails (Aves: Rallidae) from Mangaia, Southern Cook Islands. *Pacific Science* 40: 27–43.

Steadman, D.W. 1989. New species and records of birds (Aves: Megapodiidae, Columbidae) from an archaeological site on Lifuka, Tonga. *Proceedings of the Biological Society of Washington* 102(3): 537–552.

Steadman, D.W. 1992. New species of *Gallicolumba* and *Macropygia* (Aves: Columbidae). *Los Angeles County Museum of Natural History, Science Series* 36: 329–348.

Steadman, D.W. 1993. Biogeography of Tongan birds before and after human impact. *Proceedings of the National Academy of Sciences USA* 90: 818–822.

Steadman, D.W. 1994. Bird bones from the To'aga site, Ofu, American Samoa: Prehistoric loss of seabirds and megapodes. *University of California Archaeological Research Facility, Contributions* 51: 217–228.

Steadman, D.W. 1995. Prehistoric extinctions of Pacific island birds: Biodiversity meets zooarchaeology. *Science* 267: 1123–1131.

Steadman, D.W. 1997. The historic biogeography and community ecology of Polynesian pigeons and doves. *Journal of Biogeography* 24: 737–753.

Steadman, D.W. 1999. The biogeography and extinction of megapodes in Oceania. In: Dekker, R.W.R.J., Jones, D.N. and Benshemesh, J. (eds), Proceedings of the Third International Megapode symposium. *Zoologische Verhandelingen Leiden* 327: 7–21.

Steadman, D.W. 2006a. *Extinction and biogeography of tropical Pacific birds*. University of Chicago Press, Chicago and London.

Steadman, D.W. 2006b. A new species of extinct parrot (Psittacidae: *Eclectus*) from Tonga and Vanuatu, South Pacific. *Pacific Science* 60: 137–145.

Steadman, D.W. 2006c. An extinct species of tooth-billed pigeon (*Didunculus*) from the Kingdom of Tonga, and the concept of endemism in insular landbirds. *Journal of Zoology* 268: 233–241.

Steadman, D.W. and Franklin, J. 2000. A preliminary survey of landbirds on Lakeba, Lau Group, Fiji. *Emu* 100: 227–235.

Steadman, D.W. and Kirch, P.V. 1990. Prehistoric extinction of birds on Mangaia, Cook Islands, Polynesia. *Proceedings of the National Academy of Sciences USA* 87: 9605–9609.

Steadman, D.W., Worthy, T.H., Anderson, A.J. and Water R. 2000. New species and records of birds from prehistoric sites on Niue, Southwest Pacific. *Wilson Bulletin* 112: 165–186.

Steadman D.W., G.K. Pregill and Burley, D.V. 2002. Rapid prehistoric extinction of iguanas and birds in Polynesia. *Proceedings of the National Academy Sciences USA* 99: 3673–3677.

Taylor, J.M., Calaby, J.H. and van Deusen, H.M. 1982. A revision of the genus *Rattus* (Rodentia: Muridae) in the New Guinea region. *Bulletin of the American Museum of Natural History* 173: 177–336.

Thomas, F.R., Nunn, P.D., Osborne, T., Kumar, R., Areki, F., Matararaba, S., Steadman, D. and Hope G. 2004. Recent archaeological findings at Qaranilaca Cave, Vanuabalavu Island, Fiji. *Archaeology in Oceania* 39: 42–49.

Watling, D. 1982. *Birds of Fiji, Tonga and Samoa*, Millwood Press, Wellington, New Zealand.

White, P.J., Clark, G. and Bedford, S. 2000. Distribution, present and past, of *Rattus praetor* in the Pacific and its implications. *Pacific Science* 54(2): 105–117.

Worthy, T.H. 2000. The fossil megapodes (Aves: Megapodiidae) of Fiji with descriptions of a new genus and two new species. *Journal of the Royal Society of New Zealand* 30: 337–364.

Worthy, T.H. 2001a. A new species of Platymantis (Anura: Ranidae) from Quaternary deposits on Viti Levu, Fiji. *Palaeontology* 44: 665–680.

Worthy, T.H. 2001b. A giant flightless pigeon gen. et sp. nov. and a new species of *Ducula* (Aves: Columbidae), from Quaternary deposits in Fiji. *Journal of the Royal Society of New Zealand* 31: 763–794.

Worthy, T.H. and Anderson, A.J. 1999. *Research on the caves of Viti Levu, Fiji, June 1997 – October 1998, and their significance for palaeontology and archaeology*. Report to the Fiji Museum, ANH, RSPAS, ANU, Canberra, ACT 0200, Australia.

Worthy, T.H., Anderson, A.J. and Molnar, R.E. 1999. Megafaunal expression in a land without mammals – the first fossil faunas from terrestrial deposits in Fiji (Vertebrata: Amphibia, Reptilia, Aves). *Senckenbergiana biologica* 79(2): 237–242.

Worthy, T.H., Walter, R. and Anderson, A.J. 1998. Fossil and archaeological avifauna of Niue. *Notornis* 45: 177–190.

Wragg, G.M. and Weisler, M.I. 1994. Extinctions and new records of birds from Henderson Island, Pitcairn Group, South Pacific Ocean. *Notornis* 41: 61–70.

Wragg, G.M. 1995. The fossil birds of Henderson Island, Pitcairn Group: Natural turnover and human impact, a synopsis. *Biological Journal of the Linnean Society* 56: 405–414.

11

Ceramic assemblages from excavations on Viti Levu, Beqa-Ugaga and Mago Island

Geoffrey Clark
Department of Archaeology and Natural History, The Australian National University

Introduction

This chapter describes the ceramic collections from Navatu 17A, Karobo, Votua (1996), Natunuku, Malaqereqere, Volivoli II, Volivoli III, Ugaga Island and Kulu Bay. The EPF ceramics from the nine sites consisted of 54,522 sherds, weighing 295.8 kg. The ceramics were analysed at different intensities, with Navatu, Karobo and Ugaga reported in a PhD thesis (Clark 2000), and those from Votua, Natunuku and Qaranioso II published, although not always in detail, in several papers (Anderson and Clark 1999; Anderson et al. 2000; Clark and Anderson 2001; Clark et al. 2001). Details of the ceramics from the nine sites are discussed further below, with assemblage descriptions divided in two.

First, each assemblage is described in terms of sherd type (number of plain body, decorated body, rims, necks) and weight by excavation level, along with the occurrence and distribution of decoration and surface modification. Where assemblages could be identified by stratigraphy/age, the ceramic assemblages are considered separately, as at Navatu 17A, where three assemblages were defined. At sites such as Kulu Bay, Ugaga Island and Natunuku, where ceramics were mixed and contained older and more recent pottery, the entire ceramic assemblage is described. When the size of rim fragments allows, an attempt is made to identify sherds to a particular vessel form, with a description of reconstructed vessels from Navatu, Ugaga, Votua and Karobo in Clark (2000) and Clark et al. (2001). Selected sherds are figured in line drawings and photographs, but the large size of the collection precludes full depiction of all diagnostic sherds in the EPF collections.

Vessel forms

Rim sherds were classed into one of 10 generalised vessel forms (Figure 116, see Clark 2000:61–64).

Jars – Form 1

1A. Everted-direct rim – indirect body contour
1B. Abruptly thickened then thinning rim – indirect body contour

Jars were the main vessel form identified in the EPF collection's assemblages. They are characterised by a small to significant degree of rim eversion (0–85°) and have a restricted orifice (indirect rim-body contour). Form 1B jars are distinguished by abruptly thickened rims, and include the important collar-rim vessels associated with Lapita assemblages.

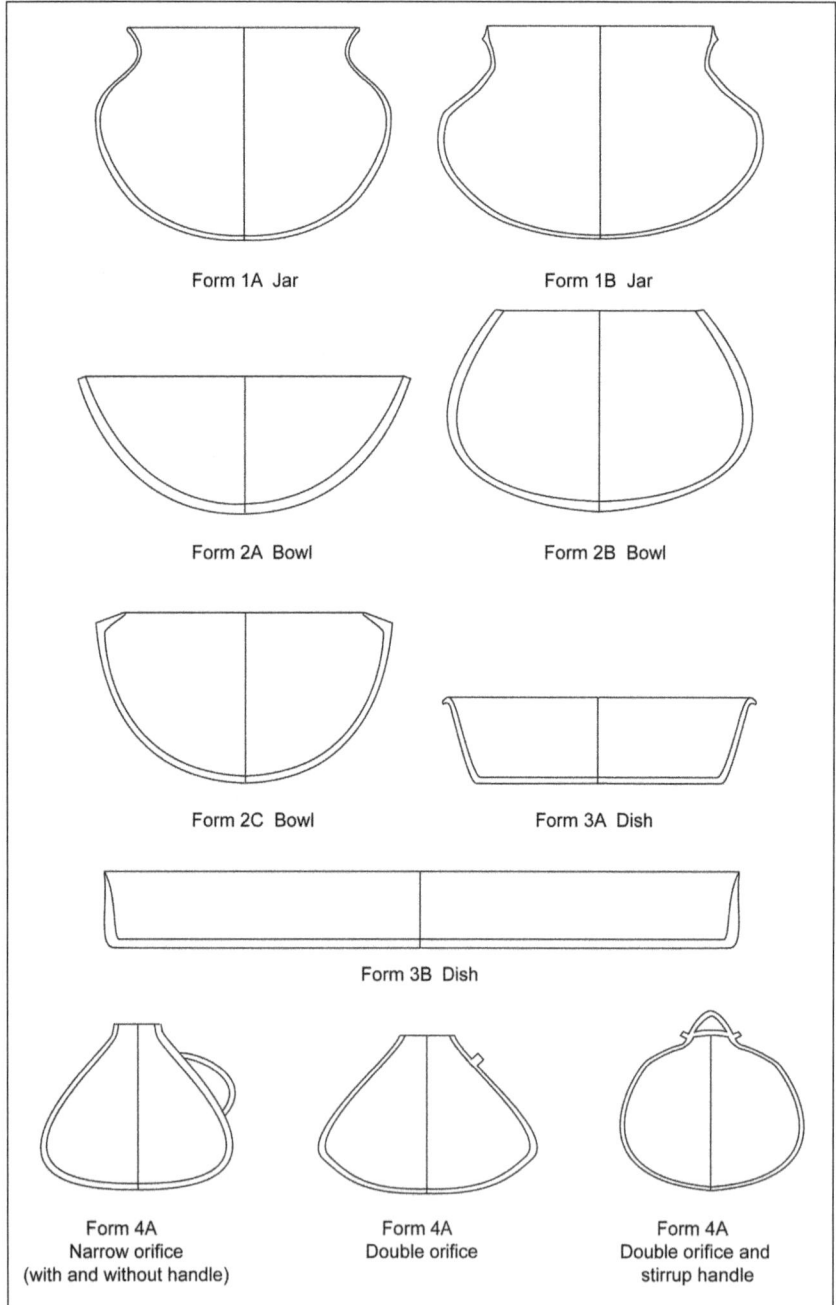

Figure 116. Generalised vessel forms. Form 1 Jars, Form 2 bowls, Form 3 dishes and platters, Form 4 narrow orifice.

Bowls – Form 2

2A. Everted rim – direct rim-body contour

2B. Inverted rim – direct rim-body contour

2C. Inverted rim – indirect rim-body contour

These bowls have a direct or indirect rim-body contour, but do not have necks (Rice 1987:216). Three vessel sub-forms varying in rim orientation and rim contour were identified. Bowls were the second most common vessel form, although they were substantially fewer in number than Form 1 vessels.

Flat-based vessels (dishes) – Form 3

3A. Flat-based – small diameter (<30 cm)

3B. Flat-based – large diameter (>45 cm)

Vessels with flat bases were divided into two sub-forms to distinguish between temporally and morphologically distinct forms. Few flat-based vessels were present in any assemblage.

Narrow orifice (10 cm diameter or less) – Form 4

4A. Single orifice and indirect rim-body contour (with and without a handle)

4B. Double orifice

4C. Double orifice and stirrup handle

The fourth vessel form includes vessels with narrow apertures/orifices. Three sub-forms were established to encompass the range of vessels present. Vessels with double apertures emerging from a stirrup handle dominate this group.

Navatu ceramics

Navatu Layer 1 ceramics (Table 43)

Of the 5070 sherds recovered from Layer 1, 4.2% are decorated. Carved paddle-impressed sherds (cross-hatch, parallel rib, curvilinear) occurred throughout Layer 1 in low frequencies (n=39). These sherds almost certainly derived from Layers 2 or 4, as they are small and eroded in comparison to other Layer 1 sherds, and surface modification of this kind was otherwise restricted to Layer 4. Other decorated sherds likely to be intrusive include an applied fillet with end-tool impressing, and a body sherd with two rows of diagonal fingernail impressions; both sherds from basal Layer 1 contexts. The most frequent kind of vessel decoration consists of shell impressions (2.2%). The impressions appear to have been made with marine-shell valves, but other tools could produce similar results. Four kinds of shell impression are included in the 'shell-impressed' category. These are wavy comb, linear comb, vertical comb and angled comb (see Figure 117).

Wavy comb refers to the curvilinear pattern imparted from a toothed comb, possibly with the valve edge from a marine bivalve such as *Anadara* or *Gafrarium*. The sinusoidal patterns have a short amplitude of 1 cm or less and were placed on the interior/exterior rim and body of Form 1A jars. On the interior of the rim, wavy comb is bordered by horizontal bands of linear incising. On the exterior vessel, surface wavy comb occurs on the shoulder, where it was bordered by horizontal bands of linear-comb or angled-comb incising. The most frequent type of linear comb are bands of incised lines. The incising consists of three to seven lines that circle the neck, shoulder or inner rim. Linear-comb incising was also used to border a geometric area that was left undecorated or was filled with vertical or angled comb. Vertical comb was applied in two ways. In the first, the toothed shell edge penetrated the clay, leaving a set of small and irregular wedge-shaped impressions (Gifford 1951:Plate 22m). The impressions were stacked in linear

Table 43. Navatu, Trench B, Layer 1 ceramics: Sherd type and decoration by depth.

Depth (cm)	Plain body	Decorated body	Rim	Neck	Narrow orifice	Number	Weight (g)
0–20	182	31	17	7		237	2549
20–40	174	14	20	4		212	2311
40–50	220	22	6	4	1	253	2487
50–60	667	26	14	5		712	3893
60–70	341	11	5	1		358	1873
70–80	602	15	15	7		639	2986
80–90	621	5	22	6		654	3351
90–100	616	18	4	9	1	648	2361
100–110	599	20	12	6		637	2551
110–120	674	17	15	14		720	2294
Total	**4696**	**179**	**130**	**63**	**2**	**5070**	**26656**

Depth (cm)	CPI-X	CPI-//	CPI-wavy	Side tool	Shell impressed	Appliqué	Incised symm.	End-tool impressed
0–20				1	36	2	4	1
20–40				3	19	1	1	1
40–50	1				11		3	
50–60		1		2	21	3	1	1
60–70				2	10			
70–80	2		2	1	6	1	2	
80–90			2	2	3	2		
90–100	1	1	4		5	2	2	
100–110	2	7	2	3			1	1
110–120	7	6	1	1	2	1	1*	
Total	**13**	**15**	**11**	**15**	**113**	**12**	**15**	**4**

CPI=carved paddle impressed, //=parallel-rib, X=cross-hatch, wavy=curvilinear. *=sherd with asymmetric incision.

columns and bordered by linear-comb incision on the shoulder and neck. By pushing the shell deeper into the vessel surface, a short undulating line was formed and these impressions were applied in columns and diagonal rows (Figure 117). This was a common method for decorating the lip of Form 1A vessels. Angled comb was similar to vertical comb, except the valve edge was pressed into the clay at an angle, rather than vertically. This created a strongly textured surface, which was applied in block form as columns, rows and other geometric shapes.

Only 12 cases (0.2%) of appliqué were found in Layer 1. These consist of fillets, buttons, buttresses, small ovals and clay crescents (1.2 cm long). Buttresses consist of an applied clay band around the neck that were finger gouged or modelled. Buttons and fillets were placed on neck and shoulder regions, but the designs cannot be determined. Of the 15 cases of side-tool notching, three are likely to derive from Layer 4, as indicated by their distinctive oval form. The remaining side-tool notching is on rims from medium-to-large Form 1A vessels. The notching consists of deep serrations on outer and inner-lip circumferences. Outer-edge serrations are usually deeper and wider spaced (0.3–0.5 cm) than those on the inner lip. The

Figure 117. Navatu 17A, Layer 1 sherds decorated with shell impression, appliqué and incision.

serrations were made with the toothed edge of a shell valve. There are 14 sherds (0.3%) with symmetric incision. Thin 'V' shaped incisions were found on the lip of a Form 1A jar and Form 4A vessel. Cross-hatch incisions occur on a Form 1A vessel and on the rim of an unknown vessel form with a thick rim and round lip. Incised hatching in the form of large (2 cm) and small (0.4 cm) diamond patterns was found on two body sherds. The remaining sherds have incised chevrons or partial chevrons. These were placed on the inner-rim surface of Form 1A vessels and on an unknown vessel form with a thin wall, where the incisions were bordered by horizontal fillets and oval buttons.

> **Form 1A jars:** Almost 93% of rims identifiable to a vessel form are assessed as coming from Form 1A vessels. Rim courses are concave (70%) or straight, and the rim profile is parallel (37%) or gradually thinning (44%). Remaining rims thicken towards the lip (n=9). Lip shape is limited, with most having flat/flat-rounded form (89%) and the balance

round/pointed. Decoration was identified on 26 rims. Shell impressing, either across the lip surface or vertically against the lip edge, is the most common decoration (n=19). Incision (chevron and hatching) and appliqué make up the remainder. Mean rim eversion is 30° (range 11–72°) and average rim course thickness is 7.3 mm. Rim height varies from 16 mm to 85 mm, with a mean of 37 mm. The neck inclination from 17 sherds has a mean of 103°. The average diameter of 44 rims is 24 cm (range 12–36 cm). There are two forms of Form 1A jar. The first has a rim profile that is parallel or thinned/thickened gradually. Two of the rims belong to large vessels and have interior and exterior rim decoration. The other rim form is a thickened and inwardly bevelled lip, marked by crescent notching or incising.

Form 2A bowls: Two Form 2A vessels were identified. The rims have parallel profiles and flat/flat-rounded lips, with rim eversion angles of 31° and 42°. Lip decoration consists of a raised modelled ridge and a faint central groove. Estimated bowl diameters are 24 cm and 30 cm, and it is likely that these vessels represent the ethnographically known *dari* used in the *kava (yaqona)* ceremony. Both vessel sherds were in the 0–20 cm spit.

Form 4 narrow-orifice vessels: Sherds from two narrow-orifice vessels were found in Layer 1 at depths of 40–50 cm and 80–90 cm. These vessels have short everted rims, with external lip diameters of ca. 10 cm. Lips are flat-rounded and 1 cm wide. The vessels are decorated with incised chevrons on the lips and fingernail impressions on the buttressed necks. The body shapes were difficult to determine due to the small neck-body portion, and could be ovoid or globular.

Navatu Layer 2 ceramics (Table 44)

Only 281 sherds were found in Layer 2 and most of these (90%) are undecorated body sherds. Relief decoration identical to that found in Layer 4 was found on five relatively small and eroded sherds. Side-tool notching on two rims from Form 1A vessels and on a carinated sherd is also similar to decoration found in Layer 4 (see below). Buttressing below the neck of a Form 1A vessel and hatched incising on a rim have parallels with decorated sherds found in Layer 1.

Table 44. Navatu, Trench B, Layer 2 ceramics: Sherd type and decoration by depth.

Depth (cm)	Plain body	Decorated body	Rim	Neck	Carinated	Number	Weight (g)
120–140~	254	13	9	4	1	281	1363
Depth (cm)	CPI-X	CPI-//	CPI- wavy	Side tool	Appliqué	Incised symm.	End-tool impressed
120–140~	2	2	1	1	1	1	1

Navatu Layer 4 ceramics (Table 45)

The highest frequency of sherds with surface modification (24%) was found in the Layer 4 assemblage. Paddle relief of various kinds (cross-hatch, parallel rib and curvilinear) is dominant, and smaller numbers of sherds are decorated with other techniques (symmetric incising, end tool and side tool). The cross-hatch group includes relief of diamond, square and rectangular shapes. The combined grouping is necessary, as many Navatu sherds have overlapping or faint impressions that obscure the original form. Sherds with cross-hatch relief make up 7.2% of the Layer 4 assemblage. The width and height dimensions of the cross-hatch patterns are 3–11.4 mm, with most impressions 7–8 mm in size (Figure 118). The depth of the pattern varies from faint surface markings to raised ridges 3–4 mm high. Vessel forms marked with cross-hatch relief include Form 1A and Form 2B vessels (Gifford 1951:Plate 22x). Sherds with parallel relief total

5.0% of the Layer 4 assemblage. Like other kinds of relief applied with a carved paddle, parallel ribs varied in size, depth and location on a vessel. The spacing of parallel ridges ranges from 0.3 cm to 1.5 cm and ridge width from 1 mm to 4 mm (Figure 118).

Carinated sherds are decorated above or below the carination line at an angle of 40–65° to the vertical (Figure 119). Linear relief was applied in horizontal and diagonal lines to Form 2A and 2B vessels. The body of Form 1A vessels might have been marked by parallel ribs but, except for the presence of thick body sherds with parallel relief, there is little evidence, either in the 1996 assemblage or in Gifford's excavation report, to support this. Of 1852 sherds found in Layer 4, 5.3% are marked with a raised sinusoidal or curvilinear pattern, a pattern referred to as wavy or zig-zag by previous researchers (Gifford 1951; Shaw 1967; Frost 1970). The wavy impressions are most regular when applied to the shoulder of Form 1A jars (Gifford 1951:Plate 26) and Form 2 bowls. These display shallow to deep impressions 1 mm to 4 mm in height, with spacing between ridges of 0.8 cm to 1.5 cm (Figure 118). Reverse impressions from shoulder sherds indicate that flat-rounded grooves about 5.2 mm to 7.5 mm in width were carved into the paddle in a smooth curvilinear pattern.

Shaw (1967) suggested that the curvilinear impressions could have been made by pressing the subdermal plates from a large turtle into the vessel. This appears unlikely, as the depressions on subdermal bones are much smaller (see Harrisson 1965) than most wavy designs and have

Table 45. Navatu, Trench B, Layer 4 ceramics: Sherd type and decoration by depth.

Depth (cm)	Plain body	Decorated body	Rim	Neck	Carinated	Narrow orifice	Total	Weight (g)
180–190	63	6	8				77	383
190–200		7	7				14	125
200–210	10	36	15	2	1		64	571
210–220	354	57	13	11	2	1	438	2001
220–230	255	111	24	4	1	4	399	3609
230–240	268	89	16	7	2	2	384	3022
240–250	207	83	28	3	4		325	2452
250–260	119	16	10	2			147	1330
260–280		4					4	9
Total	1276	409	121	29	10	7	1852	13493

Depth (cm)	CPI-X	CPI-//	CPI- wavy	Spot impressed	Side tool	Appliqué	Incised symm.	End-tool impressed	Finger pinching
180–190	2		2		1				
190–200	2	1	1		1			1	
200–210	11	4	14		2	1		8	
210–220	16	12	16	2	4	3	3	3	
220–230	35	20	24	1	5		1	14	
230–240	34	14	27	1	5		2	7	
240–250	30	28	14	1	5			9	1
250–260	3	8	6		1			1	
260–280	1		1						
Total	134	87	104	5	24	4	6	43	1

a dispersed and dimpled surface. Body sherds decorated by wavy impressions exhibit greater variability in pattern. They include chevrons (lines angled at 35–55°) and shallow ridges of uncertain form. Often the relief is faint or heavily superimposed and it is unclear whether a carved paddle was used to apply all of the surface modification classed as wavy relief. For example, the curvilinear shape on some sherds could have resulted from denting the pot with the edge of a carved paddle or other tool to create an uneven rippled surface. A wavy surface could also have been made with natural materials such as bark to impress wavy ridges or tool/finger gouging followed by smoothing.

Form 1A jars: The majority of Layer 4 rims (71%) are from 'jars'. The rims have straight or slightly curving rim courses that are parallel (50%), slightly thickened (29%) or gradually thinning towards the lip (16%). Two kinds of lip form were identified – flat/flat-rounded (91%) and a few rounded/pointed. Side-tool lip treatment was found on 16% of Form 1A rims and 3.5% were marked with an end tool. Rim eversion varies from 2° to 32° with a mean of 16°. The thickness of the rim course is 4.3–11.0 mm (mean 7.4 mm), while the rim height is 17–56 mm, with an average of 30 mm. Inclination angles from 22 rim sherds have a mean of 129° (range 110–151°). Vessel diameters (41 sherds) are mostly in the 18–26 cm range (mean of 22 cm), with a maximum recorded vessel diameter of 38 cm and a minimum of 12 cm. Seven Form 1A jars were identified in the Layer 4 assemblage.

Figure 118. Navatu 17A, Layer 4 sherds decorated with curvilinear, parallel-rib, spot and cross-hatch relief.

Figure 119. Navatu 17A, Layer 4 sherds decorated with end and side-tool impression, finger-gouging, incision and modelling.

The diameter of these vessels is 17–29 cm. Two of the vessels have notched lips and one has rows of oval end-tool impressions on the neck. Lips are flat/flat-rounded and the mean rim eversion is 24°. No paddle-relief markings were found on the rim or neck and few of these sherds from the Layer 4 assemblage have attached body-sherd portions. It is likely that some of these vessels had paddle relief, given the presence of paddle-relief vessels in Gifford's (1951) much larger sample.

Form 2 bowls

Form 2A everted rim/direct rim-body contour: A single Form 2A vessel, with parallel relief, a flat-rounded lip and a diameter of 20 cm, was identified.

Form 2B inverted rim/direct rim-body contour: There are three vessels with rims inverted from 2° to 43°. The vessel with the high inversion angle has an inturned lip and otherwise would have a much smaller degree of rim inversion. The lip forms are flat-rounded and two are marked with paddle relief (curvilinear and parallel rib).

Form 2C inverted rim/indirect body contour: Three Form 2C vessels have an inversion angle range of 38° to 40° and gradually thinning rims, terminating in pointed lips. Decoration consists of deep finger gouges/pinching on the circumference, diagonal incision and circular punctate on the rim. Their diameters are between 22 cm and 30 cm. These vessels have finger impressions below the rim-body corner point and comprise a distinct vessel form at Navatu 17A.

Form 4 narrow-orifice vessels

Form 4A single orifice/indirect rim-body contour: The only single-orifice vessel has a neck height of 17 mm and internal orifice dimensions of 17 mm x 21 mm. It is decorated with oval end-tool impressions and appears to have had an ovoid or flask-shaped body.

Form 4C double orifice and stirrup handle: Two forms of double-spouted vessel were identified. The first has a stirrup handle, with an interior handle diameter of 17–31 mm. The orifices exit the dorsal surface of the handle (internal orifice diameter 10–15 mm). Spout openings are angled 0–10°. In the second form, the spouts are oriented horizontally, and it is possible that a small handle bridged the spouts. The internal spout diameter range is 7.6–13.0 mm. The body of the double-orifice vessel appears to have been oval-to-globular, with the housing containing the vessel openings protruding above the body. The handle-orifice component is probably centered over the body. Decoration is limited to the application of applied nubbins around the circumference of the handle base and modelling of the stirrup handle (Gifford 1951:Plate 23jk).

Carinated vessels: The vessel forms associated with the carinated sherds are unclear. Sherd curvature and thickness suggests that carinated sherds came from small to mid-sized vessels. Shaw (1967:82) identified two carinated forms at Navatu 17A. The first belonged to an inverted bowl. Lips were described as rounded and bevelled and vessel size was similar to the ethnographically known *vuluvulu* or finger bowl. Carinated sherds from Layer 4 are commonly decorated below the carination line with paddle markings (parallel rib and curvilinear) and punctation, and on the carination line with end-tool impressions. Other carinated forms have everted indirect rims approximately 4 cm in length and flat-rounded lips.

Ugaga Island ceramics

The Ugaga Island ceramic collection, from an excavated area of 55 sq. m (Test Pit 1 and U6 ceramics were not analysed), consists of 20,793 sherds weighing a total of 115.4 kg (Table 46). More than 80% of sherds (by number and weight) occurred between 10 cm and 40 cm depth. Plain body sherds comprise the majority of the assemblage, at 91.2%, with smaller numbers of decorated body sherds (4.3%), rims (3.8%) and necks (0.6%). Spouts, carinations, '?lugs', '?stands' and handles are present in small numbers (0.1%) and the majority were found in the large excavation area. Eastern excavation squares had low-to-medium sherd numbers and weights, while squares in the main excavation area such as M6, O7–O8, O10 and P8, and T/U-1 in the west, had the largest sherd numbers.

The main types of surface modification found in the assemblage are shown in Table 47, along with the percentage of plain sherds. Plain sherds make up more than 90% of the ceramics in all but two squares. Squares I9 and I10 had large numbers of shell-impressed and incised sherds that derived from a single vessel (see below). Crosby (1988:125) recorded decorated sherd percentages at Ugaga of 40–55%, but his small sample was not representative of the site. Sherds with surface modification were more abundant in the central excavation area than the smaller eastern areas

Sherds with dentate stamping were present in the main excavation area but not in the smaller areas to the east and west. The 91 sherds with dentate stamping (0.4% of the assemblage) were dispersed in rows K–M and there was no evidence for concentrations of dentate sherds by square or area within the main excavation zone. Stratigraphically, the majority of dentate sherds occurred in the 20–30 cm (n=25) and 30–40 cm (n=46) spits. Fifteen sherds initially recorded as dentate stamped were later identified under low-power magnification as having a crenate edge consistent with stamping the edge of a shell valve edge in the clay vessel.

The majority of sherds with dentate stamping have single or double lines of impressions. Recognisable design elements and motifs (e.g. Anson 1983; Best 1984) are shown in Figures 120 and 121. The limited number of motifs and the 'exploded' or open dentate-stamped patterns have a parallel in eastern Lapita assemblages (Sigatoka, Mulifanua and Niuatoputapu), as well as in what Summerhayes (1996) termed 'Late Lapita' assemblages from Near and Remote Oceania.

At Ugaga, dentate stamping is associated with appliqué fillet, symmetric incision, shell impression and a red slip. It is probable that many of the dentate-stamped sherds were red slipped, but the delicate layer of soluble iron oxide was subject to chemical and physical weathering and has not survived in the shallow and disturbed Ugaga deposits. The dentate tools are variable in width, number of teeth and amount of wear. For example, on some sherds the corners of the tooth surface were irregularly rounded, producing uneven oval or circular punctations. In contrast, the tool used to decorate several other vessels was sharp edged, with almost twice the number of teeth per centimetre.

Fifteen rims and four carinations are dentate stamped. The rims are from Form 1 vessels with flaring rims. Dentate stamping is commonly applied to the lip surface and 11 rims have transverse rows of stamping (2–3 teeth). Dentate stamping of interior and exterior rim surfaces is often associated with lip stamping.

Sherds with fine striations make up 0.3% of the assemblage. They occurred in the eastern, central and western excavation areas and 73% of them were found at 20–40 cm depth. Wiping as a form of surface modification is variable in the Ugaga assemblage with some sherds showing faint, and others deep, striations. However, the striations were always applied horizontally and they are almost exclusively on the rim and neck. It seems likely that wipe marks were produced

Table 46. Ugaga Island ceramics: Sherd type by excavation square and depth.

Square/depth (cm)	Plain body	Decorated body	Rims	Necks	Other	Total	Weight (g)
-A13							
0–10	35		2	1		38	195.6
10–20	37	2	1			40	269.7
20–30	34		2			36	229.9
30–40	11					11	38.8
Total						**125**	**734**
-A14							
0–10	79		1	1		81	306.3
10–20	43					43	223.7
20–30	37	1	2			40	164.7
30–40	44	4	3	1		52	322.2
Total						**216**	**1016.7**
-A15							
0–10	23		1			24	169.4
10–20	56	2	4	1		63	423.6
20–30	30		1			31	102.3
30–40	41		1			42	164.0
Total						**160**	**859.3**
C8							
0–10	58	2		1		61	335.3
10–20	123	2	2	2		129	740.7
20–30	94		2	3		99	584.9
30–40	134	5	12	6		157	787.0
40–50	1					1	22.0
50–60			1			1	3.6
Total						**448**	**2473.5**
C9							
0–10	34	1				25	175.4
10–20	120	4	5	1		130	710.6
20–30	224	18	6	2		224	1279.5
30–40	64	6	3	3		76	548.6
Total						**455**	**2714.1**
C12							
0–10	30					30	94.1
10–20	74	2	3	3		82	542.8
20–30	52	5	2	2		61	301.6
30–40	88	8	8		1 handle	105	584.5
40–50	63	3	4	3		73	320.3
Total						**351**	**1843.3**
C13							
0–10	57	2				61	298.7
10–20	117	2	2	1		129	545.0
20–30	131		2	2		99	846.9
30–40	81	5	12	3		157	323.9
40–50	21			6		1	146.8
50–60							
Total						**447**	**2161.3**

Continued on next page

Table 46 continued

Square/depth (cm)	Plain body	Decorated body	Rims	Necks	Other	Total	Weight (g)
D12							
0–10	22					22	134.4
10–20	80		3			83	541.7
20–30	74	2	1	1	1 ?stand	79	447.0
30–40	70	6	9			85	528.7
40–50	82			2		84	323.7
Total						**353**	**1975.5**
D13							
0–10	54		1	1		56	235.2
10–20	102		5	3		110	737.4
20–30	123	4		1		128	553.1
30–40	74	1	5			80	426.7
40–50	52					52	201.1
50–60	23	2	2			27	96.7
Total						**453**	**2250.2**
F8							
0–10	14					14	37.2
10–20	78	3	6			87	494.5
20–30	72	6	4	3		85	554.5
30–40	62	9	10	1		82	639.6
40–50	81	2				83	257.5
50–60	49		2	3		54	189.9
60–70	28	3				31	131.4
Total						**436**	**2304.6**
G8							
0–10	20					20	47.8
10–20	100	3	4	1		108	379.2
20–30	112	15	2			129	820.6
30–40	94		9	1		104	646.4
40–50	64	7	1	1		73	319.3
Total						**434**	**2213.3**
H8							
0–10	8					8	25.6
10–20	53	3	1			57	263.4
20–30	87	4		2		93	657.6
30–40	69	3	3	1		76	421.9
40–50	65		4			69	192.2
Total						**303**	**1560.7**
I5							
0–10	26					26	104.9
10–20	55		1	2		58	312.9
20–30	60	1	3	1		65	403.4
30–40	177	7	6			190	1690.0
40–50	46		4	1		51	285.4
Total						**390**	**2796.6**

Continued on next page

Table 46 *continued*

Square/ depth (cm)	Plain body	Decorated body	Rims	Necks	Other	Total	Weight (g)
I6							
0–10	25	3	1			29	140.7
10–20	38	3	2			43	382.0
20–30	137		6		1 ?stand	144	966.7
30–40	74		4			79	565.2
40–50	60		5			65	255.1
Total						360	2309.7
I7							
0–10	3		2			5	343.9
10–20	94	3	8			105	616.0
20–30	104	2	5	2		113	400.0
30–40	37		2			39	78.0
40–50							
Total						262	1437.9
I8							
0–10	41	3				44	181.5
10–20	8					8	70.1
20–30	60	3	1	3		67	298.9
30–40	151	8	4	1		164	755.3
40–50	57	1	3			61	236.7
50–60	23	1	4			28	141.7
60–70	7					7	10.5
Total						379	1694.7
I9							
0–10	22	2	1			25	106.4
10–20	18	14				32	152.9
20–30	69	2				71	312.2
30–40	103	5	4		1 handle	113	679.3
40–50	36		2			38	213.9
Total						279	1464.7
I10							
0–10	40	1				41	172.7
10–20	107	18	3			128	632.4
20–30	118	5	5	1		129	777.9
30–40	64		3			67	294.7
40–50	51		2			53	178.4
Total						418	2056.1
J5							
0–10	29	2	1	1		33	234.7
10–20	42	10		2		54	401.1
20–30	56	5	7	1		69	550.7
30–40	125	4	3	1		133	1371.5
40–50	77	3	4	2		86	670.7
Total						365	3228.7

Continued on next page

Table 46 *continued*

Square/ depth (cm)	Plain body	Decorated body	Rims	Necks	Other	Total	Weight (g)
J6							
0–10	21	1				22	201.1
10–20	26					26	243.7
20–30	55	1	3	2		61	476.9
30–40	103	2	7	1		113	1107.5
40–50	72	1	4			77	430.1
Total						**299**	**2459.3**
J7							
0–10	21		1			22	106.8
10–20	51	3				54	325.6
20–30	72	6	3			81	392.9
30–40	142	3	8		1 handle	154	1037.7
40–50	43		3	1		47	221.3
Total						**358**	**2084.3**
J8							
0–10	16	1				17	174.9
10–20	30					30	163.2
20–30	39	6	6			51	479
30–40	86	4	13			103	780.6
40–50	38	2	7			47	256
Total						**248**	**1853.7**
J9							
0–10	40		1			41	48.4
10–20	77		1			78	291.6
20–30	99	8	2	1	2 ?lug	112	666.4
30–40	98	6	3			107	452
40–50	17		4			21	132.4
Total						**359**	**1590.8**
J10							
0–10	4					4	13.1
10–20	70	3				73	430.6
20–30	70	6	6	2		84	575.1
30–40	103	16	3			122	667.5
40–50	36	1	2			39	231.0
Total						**322**	**1917.3**
K5							
0–10	25		1			26	108.9
10–20	62	4	3			69	357
20–30	46	5	2			53	316
30–40	116	9	4		carination	129	1007.8
40–50	57		4		carination	63	264.4
Total						**340**	**2054.1**
K6							
0–10	34					34	113.7
10–20	56	1				57	222
20–30	132	5	2			139	648.4
30–40	108	6	4			118	550.3
40–50	73	8	6			87	462.3
Total						**435**	**1996.7**

Continued on next page

Table 46 *continued*

Square/depth (cm)	Plain body	Decorated body	Rims	Necks	Other	Total	Weight (g)
K7							
0–10	25					25	102.7
10–20	31					31	190.6
20–30	39					39	222.6
30–40	141	2	7	1	1 ?lug	152	767.6
40–50	51	4				55	247.1
Total						**302**	**1530.6**
K8							
0–10	18	1				19	97.8
10–20	42	5				47	242
20–30	33	11	3			47	441.1
30–40	61		6			67	465.8
40–50	56					56	146.1
Total						**236**	**1392.8**
K9							
0–10	39					39	162.9
10–20	105	3	2			110	570.2
20–30	69	3	1	1		74	426.5
30–40	78	4	2		carination	85	541.7
40–50	58	1	1			60	296.3
Total						**368**	**1997.6**
K10							
0–10	27					27	82.8
10–20	84	2	7			93	445.9
20–30	85	2		2		90	391.9
30–40	110	9	7		1 handle	126	610.6
40–50	68	1	1			70	182.4
Total						**406**	**1713.6**
L5							
0–10	39	3	2			44	254.2
10–20	99	5	4	1		109	530.3
20–30	140	15	5	2		162	940.7
30–40	171	13	11	1	1 ?stand	197	1117.2
Total						**512**	**2842.4**
L6							
0–10	12					12	42.9
10–20	39		4	1		44	302.9
20–30	103	12	4			119	758.6
30–40	95		10	1	1 handle	107	503.7
40–50	26	4	3			33	160.9
Total						**315**	**1769**
L7							
0–10	22		1			23	83
10–20	47					47	180.9
20–30	25	1	4		1 handle	31	336.7
30–40	88	12	9			109	989.5
40–50	49		3			52	169.4
Total						**262**	**1759.5**

Continued on next page

Table 46 continued

Square/ depth (cm)	Plain body	Decorated body	Rims	Necks	Other	Total	Weight (g)
L8							
0–10	5	1				6	35.3
10–20	20					20	66.4
20–30	62		1			63	372
30–40	71	6	7		1?lug	86	671.8
40–50	48		8			56	465.4
50–60	9	1				10	19.7
Total						**241**	**1630.6**
L9							
0–10	17	1				18	60.3
10–20	96	4	3			103	299.6
20–30	149	8				157	658.6
30–40	7	6	6			19	153.9
40–50	21	1	1			23	178.6
Total						**320**	**1351**
L10							
0–10	100	3	1			104	508.5
10–20	74	2				76	357.6
20–30	83	4	3			90	538.4
30–40	73	4	2			79	417.1
40–50	25		2			27	96.6
Total						**376**	**1918.2**
M5							
0–10	40	2	1	1		44	150.5
10–20	92	7	6			105	316.9
20–30	151	17	7	2		177	876.7
30–40	138				carination	139	583.2
40–50	62	1			carination	64	206.3
Total						**424**	**2133.6**
M6							
0–10	26		1			27	86.5
10–20	110	8		1		119	366.3
20–30	153	19	7	2	carination	182	1495.6
30–40	137	5	6	1		149	875.6
40–50	40	3				43	222.2
Total						**520**	**3046.2**
M7							
0–10	27	4				31	157.9
10–20	89	5	1			95	290.3
20–30	110	4	2			116	638.5
30–40	52	1	7	1		61	472
40–50	32		2			34	192.9
Total						**337**	**1751.6**
M8							
0–10	16	2				18	100.3
10–20	37	1				38	277.4
20–30	72	8	1			81	378.1
30–40	124	2	2		1 ?stand	129	599.5
40–50	41	1		1		43	264.1
50–60							
Total						**309**	**1619.4**

Continued on next page

Table 46 continued

Square/ depth (cm)	Plain body	Decorated body	Rims	Necks	Other	Total	Weight (g)
M9							
0–10	20					20	92.7
10–20	121	6	4			131	665.3
20–30	128	7	2			137	599.4
30–40	134	1	9		carination	145	888.4
40–50	37	1	3			41	203.1
Total						474	2448.9
M10							
0–10	74	1				75	324.8
10–20	119	1	5			126	374.4
20–30	106	7	3		1 handle	117	499.8
30–40	232	7	10			249	936.2
40–50	24					24	56.1
Total						591	2191.3
N8							
0–10	11					11	60.2
10–20	75	4	3	1		83	479.8
20–30	92	9	3			104	677.9
30–40	90	3	11	1	carination	106	614.3
40–50	56	2	2			60	395.2
50–60	1					1	17.1
Total						365	2244.5
N9							
0–10	112		5			117	552.2
10–20	132	4	7			143	937.4
20–30	79	12	5	1	carination	98	621.1
30–40	129	4	6	1		140	755.3
40–50	18	5	2			25	76
Total						523	2942
N10							
0–10	68	1	1	1		71	590.3
10–20	155	3	2			160	727.2
20–30	92	12	9			113	820.9
30–40	147	1	6			154	670.4
40–50	10	1				11	61.6
Total						509	2870.4
O8							
0–10	49	2				51	233.2
10–20	118	4	3			125	722
20–30	220	14	13			247	1581.3
30–40	156	12	15			183	1276
40–50	30	2	2			34	337.5
50–60						5	50.6
Total						645	4200.6
O9							
0–10	46	1	1			48	241.9
10–20							
20–30	102	9	6			117	559.5
30–40	56	4	11			71	556.3
40–50	4		2			6	14.5
Total						242	1372.2

Continued on next page

Table 46 continued

Square/ depth (cm)	Plain body	Decorated body	Rims	Necks	Other	Total	Weight (g)
O10							
0–10	142	6	6			154	696.5
10–20	205	22	5			232	1236.3
20–30	109	4	3			116	569.7
30–40	58	1				59	280.1
40–50	3					3	15.3
Total						**564**	**2797.9**
P8							
0–10	24					24	177.4
10–20	47					57	332.3
20–30	138		10		1 ?lug	149	976.5
30–40	176		7		1 ?lug	184	967.9
40–50	28					28	122.4
Total						**442**	**2576.5**
P9							
0–10	110		2			112	466.8
10–20	213	2	3			218	900.8
20–30	145	8	5	1		159	1363.0
30–40	9	10	2			21	47.6
40–50	8					8	32.5
Total						**518**	**2810.7**
P10							
0–10	81	2	1			84	373.1
10–20	108	6	2			116	549.5
20–30	92	5	5			102	753.5
30–40	46	1	3			50	306.9
40–50	6		1			7	49.0
Total						**359**	**2031.8**
Q10							
0–10	102					102	413.3
10–20	82	5	8			95	514.9
20–30	87	2	2			91	492
30–40	40					40	185.9
Total						**328**	**1606.1**
Q13							
0–10	9	2				10	46.4
10–20	8					9	43
20–30							
30–40	90	3	5			98	443.9
Total						**117**	**533.3**
T/U-1							
0–10	40	6	1			47	325.5
10–20	47	8	9		2 handles	66	713.6
20–30	442	32	18	10		502	3214.6
30–40	357	3	10		carination	371	2217
40–50	74					74	480.1
50–60	83		1			84	320.9
Total						**1144**	**7271.7**

Table 47. Ugaga Island ceramics: Sherd decoration by excavation square and depth.

Square/depth (cm)	Plain sherds	Dentate stamped	Wiped	Side tool	Shell imp.	Dents	CPI-//	CPI-X	Incision	End-tool imp.
-A13										
0–10	38			1						
10–20	40									
20–30	36									
30–40	11									
%Plain	98.4									
-A14										
0–10	81									
10–20	43									
20–30	39								1	
30–40	49					1		1	1	
%Plain	97.6									
-A15										
0–10	24									
10–20	62			1				1		
20–30	31									
30–40	42									
%Plain	98.7									
C8										
0–10	59							1		
10–20	128								1	
20–30	99									
30–40	148		3	1				6		
40–50	1									
50–60	1									
%Plain	97.0									
C9										
0–10	24							1		
10–20	126							4		
20–30	208							12	3	1	1
30–40	70							5	1	
40–50										
50–60										
%Plain	93.2									
C12										
0–10	30									
10–20	80							2		
20–30	56		1			1		3		
30–40	97		2			2		4		
40–50	68							5		
%Plain	94.0									

Continued on next page

Table 47 continued

Square/depth (cm)	Plain sherds	Dentate stamped	Wiped	Side tool	Shell imp.	Dents	CPI-//	CPI-X	Incision	End-tool imp.
C13										
0–10	60									
10–20	120			1						
20–30	135				1	1	5			
30–40	87						1			
40–50	23									
%Plain	98.6									
D12										
0–10	22									
10–20	83									
20–30	76				1		1	1		
30–40	79					1	4	1		
40–50	84									
%Plain	97.4									
D13										
0–10	56									
10–20	110									
20–30	125					1	2			
30–40	79						1			
40–50	52									
50–60	26						1		1	
%Plain	98.7									
F8										
0–10	14									
10–20	85						1	1		
20–30	80						3	2		
30–40	77	2	1		1	2	2		1	
40–50	81						2			
50–60	54									
60–70	28						1	2		
%Plain	95.2									
G8										
0–10	20									
10–20	106						2		1	
20–30	115						12	2	1	
30–40	104			1						
40–50	68			1			4	1		
%Plain	94.7									
H8										
0–10	8									
10–20	55						2			
20–30	88						5			
30–40	75							1		
40–50	69									
%Plain	96.6									

Continued on next page

Table 47 continued

Square/depth (cm)	Plain sherds	Dentate stamped	Wiped	Side tool	Shell imp.	Dents	CPI-//	CPI-X	Incision	End-tool imp.
I5										
0–10	26									
10–20	58									
20–30	62						2	2		
30–40	183		2				3	2		
40–50	50				1					
%Plain	96.8									
I6										
0–10	28								1	
10–20	40						1	2		
20–30	141						3			
30–40	77		1	1				1		
40–50	65									
%Plain	97.4									
I7										
0–10	5			1						
10–20	103			2			1	1		
20–30	111			1				2		
30–40	39									
40–50										
%Plain	98.0									
I8										
0–10	40				1			2	1	
10–20	8									
20–30	64	1						3		
30–40	158	3	1	1			4	2		
40–50	60		1					1		
50–60	27			1				1		
I60–70	7									
%Plain	95.8									
I9										
0–10	22				1				2	
10–20	7				12			1	13	
20–30	68				1			1	1	
I30–40	108					1	2	2		
40–50	38									
%Plain	85.2									
I10										
0–10	39		1		1				1	
10–20	102				10		1	6	10	
20–30	124				1		2	1	1	
30–40	67			1						
40–50	51		1		1					
%Plain	89.6									

Continued on next page

Table 47 continued

Square/depth (cm)	Plain sherds	Dentate stamped	Wiped	Side tool	Shell imp.	Dents	CPI-//	CPI-X	Incision	End-tool imp.
J5										
0–10	20			1				2	1	
10–20	45		1				3	5	1	
20–30	62						5	1	1	
30–40	128		1				2		2	
40–50	83			1			1	2		
%Plain	92.0									
J6										
0–10	21							1		
10–20	26									
20–30	60			1			1			
30–40	110					1	2			
40–50	76			1			1			
%Plain	98.0									
J7										
0–10	21			1						1
10–20	51	3								
20–30	73		4		1		2		1	
30–40	151	1		1			2			
40–50	47			1						
%Plain	95.6									
J8										
0–10	16							1		
10–20	30									
20–30	44	1	1	1		3	2			
30–40	98	2		3	2	1				
40–50	46	1	1	2						
%Plain	93.2									
J9										
0–10	40									1
10–20	78									
20–30	104	2					2	3	1	
30–40	102						2	3		
40–50	20		1							
%Plain	95.3									
J10										
0–10	4									
10–20	70						2	1		
20–30	77		2	1		1	3	1		
30–40	107	1		1		1	7	6		
40–50	38							1		
%Plain	90.5									

Continued on next page

Ceramic assemblages from excavations on Viti Levu, Beqa-Ugaga and Mago Island   281

Table 47 *continued*

Square/depth (cm)	Plain sherds	Dentate stamped	Wiped	Side tool	Shell imp.	Dents	CPI-//	CPI-X	Incision	End-tool imp.
K5										
0–10	26									
10–20	65						1	2	1	
20–30	48						3	3		
30–40	120	1				2	2	4		
40–50	63			2						
%Plain	94.4									
K6										
0–10	34									
10–20	56						1			
20-30	133	1		1		1	3	1		
30-40	111			1		1	4	2		
40-50	80	2		2	1		4			
%Plain	94.9									
K7										
0-10	25									
10-20	31									
20-30	39									
30-40	150			3				2		
40-50	52		1				1	1		
%Plain	98.0									
K8										
0-10	18			1						
10-20	47									
20-30	44	1					1	1		
30-40	55	4	1	1			2	3	2	
40-50	56									
%Plain	90.5									
K9										
0-10	39									
10-20	106			1			2	1		
20-30	70				1			1	2	
30-40	79			2				4		
40-50	59							1		
%Plain	95.8									
K10										
0-10	27									
10-20	92						1			
20-30	87						1	1		
30-40	117			1	1		4	3	1	
40-50	69		1	1						
%Plain	96.2									
L5										
0-10	40	1		1			1	1		
10-20	104	1					1	3		
20-30	147	3	3		1		6	2		
30-40	183	1	4	2		1	3	4		
%Plain	91.1									

Continued on next page

Table 47 continued

Square/depth (cm)	Plain sherds	Dentate stamped	Wiped	Side tool	Shell imp.	Dents	CPI-//	CPI-X	Incision	End-tool imp.
L6										
0-10	12									
10-20	44									
20-30	107						5	7		
30-40	102	1			2					1
40-50	28	2		2			1			
%Plain	92.2									
L7										
0-10	23									
10-20	47									
20-30	29			1				1		
30-40	97	3	1	1		1	2	4		
40-50	52									
%Plain	94.4									
L8										
0-10	5							1		
10-20	20									
20-30	63									
30-40	80	3					3			
40-50	51	1	1	1	3					
50-60	9							1		
%Plain	93.9									
L9										
0-10	18								1	1
10-20	99	1		1			1	1		
20-30	151		1				5		1	
30-40	11	5		1		1	1			
40-50	22					1				
%Plain	93.0									
L10										
0-10	101							2	1	
10-20	67						1	1		
20-30	90		2				2	2		
30-40	73	1		1			3	1		
40-50	27									
%Plain	95.0									
M5										
0-10	42						2			
10-20	97	2	2	2			1	1		
20-30	159	2	2	1			8	5		
30-40	138				1					
40-50	62	1					1			
%Plain	93.2									

Continued on next page

Table 47 *continued*

Square/depth (cm)	Plain sherds	Dentate stamped	Wiped	Side tool	Shell imp.	Dents	CPI-//	CPI-X	Incision	End-tool imp.
M6										
0-10	27									
10-20	112						2	5		
20-30	164	2					9	7		
30-40	141	2	1	1	1		1	2		
40-50	40	2					1			
%Plain	91.7									
M7										
0-10	28						1	2		
10-20	95									
20-30	112						1	3		
30-40	54		1	1			3	2		
40-50	33			1						
%Plain	94.4									
M8										
0-10	16							2		
10-20	37							1		
20-30	73	1		1			3	2	1	
30-40	125	1		1	1		1			
40-50	42							1		
50-60										
%Plain	94.2									
M9										
0-10	20									
10-20	124		1	1	1	1	2	1		
20-30	127	2	1				4			
30-40	141	2			1		1			
40-50	41									
%Plain	94.9									
M10										
0-10	74							1		
10-20	122			1	1			1		
20-30	112	3					1	1		
30-40	239	1	2	1			4	2		
40-50	24									
%Plain	96.1									
N8										
0-10	11									
10-20	81			1				1		
20-30	96	1	1				1	5		
30-40	97	2		3	1		2	1		
40-50	56	1		1			2			
50-60	1									
%Plain	91.8									

Continued on next page

Table 47 continued

Square/depth (cm)	Plain sherds	Dentate stamped	Wiped	Side tool	Shell imp.	Dents	CPI-//	CPI-X	Incision	End-tool imp.
N9										
0-10	111	1		1			3	1		
10-20	128	4	1	1	1		5	3		
20-30	92	1			1		2	2		
30-40	133	3					3	1		
40-50	23			2						
%Plain	92.2									
N10										
0-10	68	1	1	1						
10-20	157						2	1		
20-30	100	2	1	2	1		6	1		3
30-40	151			2			1			
40-50	10							1		
%Plain	95.3									
O8										
0-10	49						1	1		
10-20	121						2	2		
20-30	229	1	1	1	2	1	5	7		
30-40	164	1	1	2	4		4	6		1
40-50	31			1			1	1		
50-60	5									
%Plain	92.1									
O9										
0-10	46						2			
10-20										
20-30	109		1			1	4	2		
30-40	65			1	1		2	1		1
40-50	6									
%Plain	92.5									
O10										
0-10	148		1				4	1		
10-20	211		2	1		2	13	2		1
20-30	112		1				1	1		1
30-40	58							1		
40-50	3									
%Plain	93.4									
P8										
0-10	24									
10-20	55							2		
20-30	142		1				4	2		
30-40	173	2	1		1		5	2		
40-50	28									
%Plain	94.8									

Continued on next page

Table 47 *continued*

Square/depth (cm)	Plain sherds	Dentate stamped	Wiped	Side tool	Shell imp.	Dents	CPI-//	CPI-X	Incision	End-tool imp.
P9										
0-10	112									
10-20	206		2				5	5		
20-30	143	1	2	1	1	2	8			1
30-40	20		1							
40-50	8									
%Plain	93.7									
P10										
0-10	82							2		
10-20	110							6		
20-30	102							2		
30-40	45				1	1		2		
40-50	5			1						
50-60										
%Plain	95.3									
Q10										
0-10	102									
10-20	90						1	4		
20-30	90		1							
30-40	40									
%Plain	97.8									
Q13										
0-10	10								2	
10-20	7									
20-30										
30-40	96							2		
%Plain	95.6									
T/U-1										
0-10	41						5	1		
10-20	57						3	4	1	1
20-30	464		1	1		1	21	14		
30-40	366					1	2	2		
40-50	74									
50-60	84									
%Plain	94.5									

by the potter using a fibrous material, such as the inner husk of the coconut, on the outer rim during the finishing stages of vessel manufacture. Wiping was identified on 22 rims, of which 76% belong to Form 1A vessels with straight profiles and flat/flat-rounded lips. No wiped bowls were identified, although a plain collar rim has deep striations below the collar. Associated with exterior-rim wiping is one case of interior-lip notching with a side tool. The rim of this vessel is unusual for the depth of the striae and the irregularity of its rim profile and rim-body join.

The use of a side tool to make notches, ovals and cuts is evident on 0.4% of sherds. Almost 63% of such sherds were found below 30 cm depth, and the sherds were in most excavation areas. Two types of side tool were employed. The first had a thin sharp edge that was used to make cuts or apex-down triangular incisions. An impressed diamond shape resulted from moving the edge of the side tool from side-to-side on the lip edge or rim collar. The second tool was oval in cross-section and was used to make small oval impressions 3–8 mm wide on the lip.

Of the 91 sherds with side-tool impression, all but four are rims. The majority of these (n=64) belong to Form 1B vessels. In all cases, the side tool was applied along the thickest point of the rim and spaced from 0.6 cm to 1.2 cm. Collar rims were restricted to the main excavation area and like dentate-stamped sherds were not found in the smaller eastern and western excavations. Side-tool marking on Form 1A vessels consists of incised lines across the lip and on the interior or exterior lip edge. Form 2A and 2C vessels also have notching and incision on the lip, including one with a crenate-incised lip. Bivalve-edge impressing was found on 0.3%

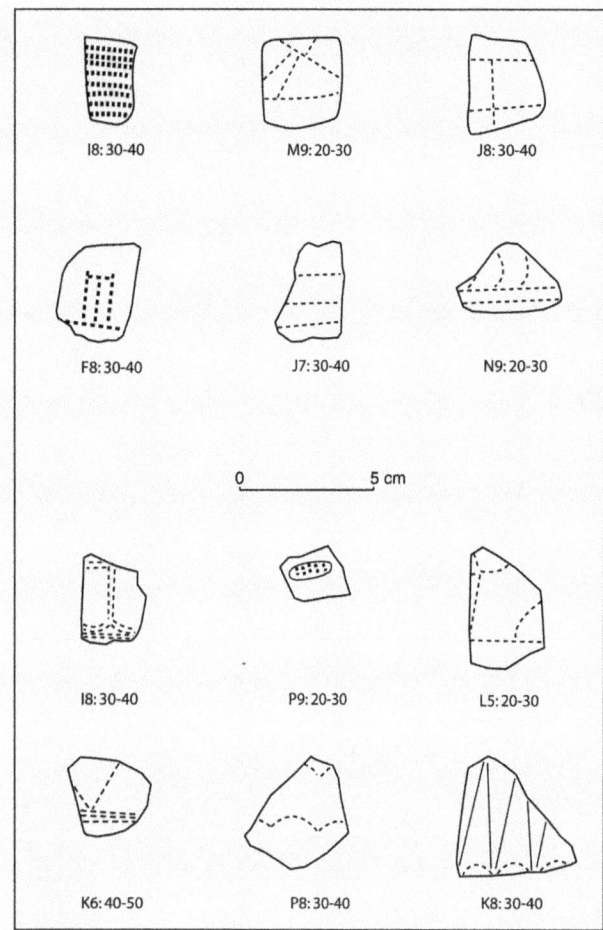

Figure 120. Ugaga Island dentate-stamped sherds (square and depth).

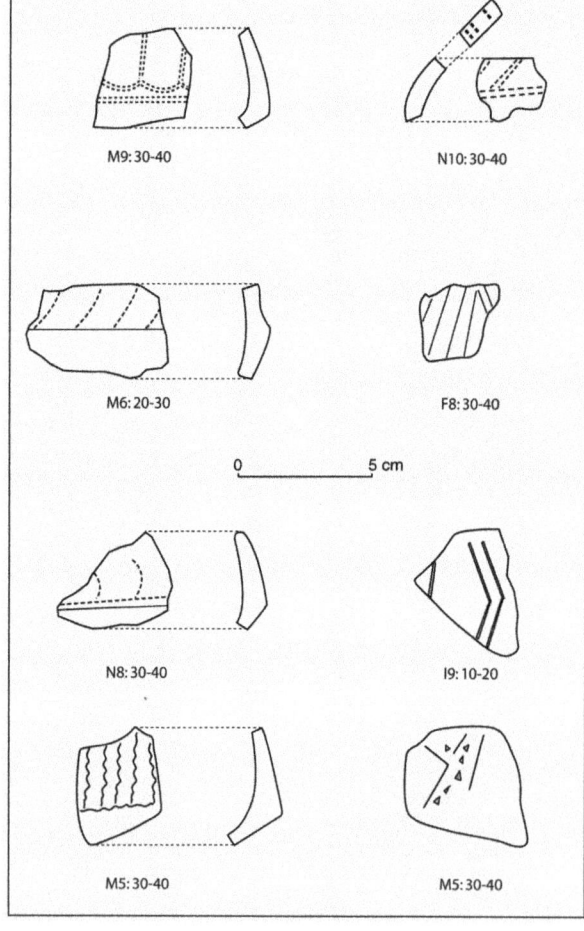

Figure 121. Ugaga Island dentate-stamped, carinated and incised sherds (square and depth).

of the assemblage. The length of the impression was usually less than 0.6 mm, although a length of 2.2 cm was recorded from a carinated sherd. Shell impressions were found on 24 Form 1B rims, where they are aligned vertically or diagonally along the widest point of the collar.

Other vessel forms with bivalve-edge impressions are a Form 1A jar and a Form 2C bowl with vertical shell crescents on the rim and small shell impressions on the lip. Most shell-impressed sherds (n=28) were located in the 10–20 cm spit of squares I9–I10 and are derived from one vessel. Very few sherds with dents were found (n=35) and the category is difficult to reliably separate from sherds with 'heavy ribs', especially when the sherds are small. Dented sherds were found in all of the excavated areas, mostly at 10–30 cm depth. In general, dents have straight parallel edges that gradually terminate at one end. The best explanation for this shape is that a flat-rounded or round-edged paddle was used against the vessel surface. Dents were identified on a Form 1A and a Form 2B vessel. Parallel-relief sherds have the highest frequency of any type of surface modification. However, their proportion in the Ugaga assemblage is still small, at 1.9% of the total assemblage. Sherd numbers were greatest in squares C9 and O10, and the sherds were found in all excavation areas, with 70% of them between 20 cm and 40 cm.

Nine Form 1A vessels have parallel relief on their rim or body. On four of these, the ribs were placed horizontally and are 1.8–2.3 cm in length. Diagonal parallel impressions of different lengths were found on several vessels. Heavy ribs more than 2 cm long occur on a Form 1A vessel. Diagonal and horizontal parallel impressions of different sizes were also found on Form 2A and 2B bowls. Sherds with cross-hatch relief make up 1.2% of the Ugaga assemblage. They were found in most squares and 78% were recovered from 20 cm to 40 cm depth. The majority of cross-hatch sherds are from the body and only one rim provides any indication of vessel form. Impressions from large shoulder sherds and body sherds indicate that diamond-shaped impressions are vertically orientated. Three size classes (height 3–5 mm, 5–8 mm, 8–12 mm) of square and diamond impressions were recorded from the Ugaga assemblage.

The interior surface of 12 body sherds with cross-hatching (5–8 mm size class) is rough and pitted. The texture is unlike that produced using a coral anvil (Birks 1973:Plate 36A and 44A). Similar impressions were identified on Level 2 vessels from Sigatoka, where unsmoothed stone anvils were thought to have been used (Birks 1973:42). Impressions from the Ugaga basalt breccia in modelling compound gave a comparable surface texture to that found on the sherds, supporting Birks' identification.

Of the 55 sherds (0.3%) with symmetric or asymmetric incision, 28 belong to one vessel. The remainder have single or multiple parallel lines (up to five), although no comb-incised sherds were identified. Crosby (1988:125) records that comb-incising was common in late-prehistoric sites on nearby Beqa. The incision depth ranges from light surface markings to 2 mm deep cuts. Incision is associated with dentate arcs on one sherd and with triangular end-tool impressions on another. A single sherd with asymmetric incision in an 'exploded' chevron pattern was recorded from I9: 10–20 cm.

There are 14 sherds marked by end tools and seven of these came from one vessel marked with circular impressions 2–3 mm in diameter. Other end-tool impressions include an example of finger-nail impressing and oval, square and triangular shapes. Oval to circular impressions, possibly made with a finger tip, were found on Form 1B vessels. A rim from a Form 1A vessel is unusual for its extremely thickened lip that was marked using a straight-sided tool with a chisel-shaped tip.

Form 1 jars: The majority of Ugaga rims for which the orientation and rim-body contour can be determined (63% of the assemblage) belong to Form 1 vessels. Rim course is straight

(47%) or concave (52%), with a single convave (highly everted) rim. Rim profile is divided relatively evenly between parallel (31%), gradually thickening (23%) and gradually thinning (20%) forms. Abruptly thickened rims from Form 1B vessels make up the remaining 26%. Flat/flat-rounded lips account for 72% and round/pointed lips 28% of the 462 undamaged lips. For rim sherds with surface modification, the decoration was most often applied to the rim (79%) and less frequently to the lip (14%), body (6%), or interior rim. Side tool (notching and cuts) is the most common type of surface modification (46%), followed by shell impressing (18%) and wiping (13%). Present at frequencies below 10% are paddle relief (8%), dentate stamping (7%), incision (6%), end tool (2%) and dents (1%).

The mean rim eversion of 282 Form 1 rims is 20°, with a large range, of 2–81°. A histogram plot shows that the data is positively skewed between 2° and 36°, with a single outlier at 81°. Rim-course measurements (n=474) are normally distributed, with a mean of 7 mm and a range of 3–14 mm. The height of the rim to the corner point varies from 7 mm to 63 mm, with a mean of 26 mm. Neck-body inclination angles (n=107) are 58–150° (mean 121°). The average external rim diameter is 22 cm. Clearly, there is considerable size and shape variation within the Form 1 group.

Form 1B jars with abruptly thickened rims and thinning lips: Eighteen vessels have collar rims (a clay band was applied to the exterior rim surface) or abruptly thickened rims (sharp edged and asymmetric to the exterior). All rim courses are concave. Collar rims vary from thin applied and rounded additions, to large and small applied bands that are triangular or sub-triangular in cross-section. The interior of some Ugaga Form 1B vessels has a rim-body join below the collar rim, suggesting separate manufacture of the thickened rim and body. Lips are mostly round-pointed (58%), with roughly equal numbers of flat/flat-rounded and flat/sharp edged. All vessels, except one, are decorated with side-tool notching, shell impressing, or round/oval end-tool impressing at the point of maximum rim thickness. Dentate stamping was found on one vessel with a thickened rim. Form 1B vessels are not strongly everted (mean 16°), have a mean rim height of 26 mm, and have an average diameter of 21 cm.

Form 1A jars with aperture diameter 10–20 cm: The majority of the 25 vessels with aperture diameters 10–20 cm have concave rim profiles (68%). The most common rim profile is gradual thinning (44%), with the remainder almost evenly divided between parallel and gradual thickening shapes. Lips are flat/flat-rounded (72%). Five vessels are decorated on the lip, rim or body. Lip decoration is varied, with side-tool cuts, shell impression, dentate stamping and end tool applied to the lip surface. Two vessels have horizontal parallel relief on the rim and body. Lips are flat/flat-rounded (72%) or round/pointed. The mean rim eversion is 25° and the maximum eversion angle for any vessel in the Ugaga assemblage, of 81°, was found in this group. The average rim height is 24 mm.

Form 1A jars with aperture diameter 21–29 cm: The largest group of Form 1A vessels has aperture diameters of 21–29 cm (n=37). In contrast to previous vessel groups, the majority of rim courses are straight (70%), with convex (24%) and concave (6%) courses in the minority. The distribution of rim profiles is spread fairly evenly between parallel, and gradually thickening or thinning forms. Most lips are flat/flat-rounded (72%). Sixteen vessels have surface modification, divided between those with modification on the rim or body (n=8) and vessels where the lip and/or rim is marked. The former group has paddle relief (cross hatch and parallel rib), and the latter group wiping, dentate stamping and side-tool notching. Two sorts of side-tool notching were recorded. The first was applied across or diagonally to the lip surface, while the second involves notches on the interior lip-rim surface. Rim eversion is 3–40° (mean 20°). Rim height (mean 37 mm) is greater than that of Form 1A vessels, with diameters of 10–20 cm, and of Form 1B vessels.

Form 1A jars with aperture diameters ≥30 cm: Only eight vessels have rim diameters equal to, or greater than, 30 cm. These vessels have straight and concave rim courses and parallel or gradually changing profiles. Most lips are flat or flat-rounded and only one is round/pointed. The body and rim of two vessels are modified by paddle relief and denting. The average rim eversion is 19°. Mean values for rim-course thickness (7.5 mm) and rim height (39 mm) are the largest of any sub-group.

Form 2 bowls: There are 72 rims from Form 2 vessels. The number almost certainly under-represents their real abundance, as larger sherd sizes are required to differentiate Form 2A and 2B rims from Form 1A rims. The majority of rims are Form 2A (70%), with Forms 2B and 2C contributing the balance. The main rim profile is parallel (44%), with gradually expanding or contracting profiles present in roughly equal amounts. Lips are flat/flat-rounded (81%), with a few round/pointed specimens. Surface modification was found on 15 sherds, either on the lip (interior, upper surface, exterior) or body. The limited surface-modification inventory consists of side-tool cuts (n=8), parallel rib (n=5), shell impressions and dents. The mean eversion angle is 14° and for inverted rims 21°. The mean diameter is 24 cm, which is similar to that of the total Form 1 sample.

Form 2A everted rim/direct rim-body contour: There are 13 Form 2A vessels. These have straight rim courses and gradually changing or parallel rim (n=5) profiles. Most lips are flat/flat-rounded (77%). Five vessels have surface modification that was placed on the lip (interior and exterior) and body. The surface modification consists of parallel-rib relief and side-tool cuts (n=3). Eversion angles range from 5° to 31°, with a mean of 20°, and the average rim diameter is 25 cm.

Form 2B inverted rim/direct rim-body contour: Five of six Form 2B vessels have evenly inverted rim courses and one is straight. Rim profiles are parallel (n=5) or gradually thickened. Surface modification of parallel relief and dents occurs on the bodies of five vessels. Four of these vessels are similar to one another in shape, diameter (19–20 cm) and rim inversion angle (31–37°).

Form 2C inverted rim/indirect rim-body contour: Three Form 2C bowls with pointed/rounded lips are decorated on the exterior or interior lip. Decoration consists of shell impressions and side-tool cuts. The diameter range is 18–34 cm.

Form 3 flat-based vessels

Form 3A flat-based vessel diameter <30 cm: Eight sherds from a dentate-stamped dish with outcurving sides and a flat base were found in Squares J10, K6, K8, L6, L8 and L9 at depths between 30 cm and 50 cm. The base diameter is calculated at 20 cm and the estimated diameter of the exterior rim is 22 cm. Anson motifs 314 and 366, both previously found in Reef/Santa Cruz assemblages (Anson 1983), are evident between single and double horizontal rows of dentate stamping. The tools used were thin (approximately 1 mm wide) and had up to six toothed projections per centimetre.

Form 4 narrow-orifice vessels

Form 4B double orifice: A single double-spouted vessel has a central orifice 23 mm in diameter and a small spout with an estimated opening of 5 mm above or on the vessel shoulder. This thin-walled vessel is decorated with a horizontal applied band and shell impressing within radiating incised lines. This vessel is similar to the historically known *gusui rua* (Palmer 1971:Fig. 1; Rossitto 1990).

Form 4C double orifice and stirrup handle: Two of the three vessels with spouts belong to double-spouted and stirrup-handled forms also identified at Navatu. Internal spout diameters are 7–10 mm.

Carinations, handles, ?lugs and ?stands: A mean angle of 132° was found for 10 carinated sherds (range 108–155°). Five are decorated with dentate stamping or shell impressing. Three kinds of handles are tentatively identified. The first is a vertical handle with a height of 30 mm, a flat top and a diameter of 15–30 mm. Side-tool markings are visible on two specimens. It is possible that what have been identified as 'handles' are, in fact, legs or other kinds of vessel projection. However, in one case the sherd thickness below the handle is only 4.5 mm, suggesting a lid function. Two handles with narrow oval cross-sections are likely to derive from the apex of stirrup handles from double-spouted vessels. Two ?handle fragments might be from narrow-orifice Form 4A vessels with strap handles similar to those found at Sigatoka Level 1 (Birks 1973:119). Sherds identified as 'lugs' are most frequently 'tongue' or oval shaped in plan view and vary significantly in thickness. Irregularly shaped sherds provisionally classified as ?stands could also be fragments from vessels with thick and uneven rims, or from vessels with currently unrecognised morphology.

Karobo ceramics

More than 82% of sherds from the Karobo assemblage have some form of surface modification (Tables 48–49). Just over 70% of sherds identifiable to Form 1A jars or Form 2 bowls have relief surface modification, indicating that most of the non-platter ceramics were marked with cross hatch or parallel relief. Side tool, end tool and incision are extremely rare in the collection. Sherds with cross-hatch relief comprise the largest group, at 42% of the decorated sherds (Figure 122). Three size classes of diamond-shaped impression are recorded. The largest of these has a length of 1.2 cm and width of 0.6 cm, the next size class has a length of 1.0 cm and width of 0.4–0.5 cm, and the smallest diamond impressions from the assemblage have a length of 0.7 cm and width of 0.3–0.4 cm. Dimensions of square impressions are ca. 0.8 cm, 0.5 cm and 0.2 cm. Sherds with linear relief (Figure 123) comprise 18.9% of the Karobo assemblage. Parallel impressions are divided into three forms on the basis of their width and interval spacing. Thin ribs – 0.5–1 mm wide separated by 0.5–3 mm gaps – are lightly impressed on a vessel, and on one sherd the impressions are vertically positioned. Medium ribs – with a spacing of 2–4 mm and a variable width of 1.5–3.7 mm – are unevenly aligned and inspection under low-power magnification suggests the tool used to groove the paddle had a straight or slightly curved edge. Long and irregular parallel impressions are rare, occurring on fewer than 15 sherds. These impressions have low and irregular borders that are 4–7 mm wide and spaced 4–6 mm apart. Rather than incisions on a paddle's surface, these impressions might have been created using the edge of a paddle or baton against the vessel.

Only 11 sherds, or 1.1% of the Karobo assemblage, are decorated by incision, or end or side tool. Incision is symmetric, and except in one case consists of single or parallel lines. Although

Table 48. Karobo ceramics: Sherd type by excavation square and depth.

Excavation/layer	Plain body	Decorated body	Rim	Neck	Platter rims	Platter body	Total	Weight (g)
A2: Layer 1	2					12	14	168
A2: Layer 2	9	7					16	161
A2: Layer 3		6				8	14	175
A2: Layer 4								
A2: Layer 5	136	415	24	45	62	372	1054	27979
Total	**147**	**428**	**24**	**45**	**62**	**392**	**1098**	**28483**
Aa: Layer 1								
Aa: Layer 2								
Aa: Layer 3	7	1				17	25	277
Aa: Layer 4	5	4		1		5	15	72
Aa: Layer 5						8	8	315
Aa: Layer 6					1	7	8	255
Aa: Layer 7	34	75	4	5		54	172	3536
Total	**46**	**80**	**4**	**6**	**1**	**91**	**228**	**4455**
Ab: Layer 1								
Ab: Layer 2								
Ab: Layer 3		18	1	1		28	48	542
Ab: Layer 4	1		2	1			4	25
Ab: Layer 5						22	22	178
Ab: Layer 6	5	1				5	11	104
Ab: Layer 7	10	28	8	8	17	157	228	6974
Total	**16**	**47**	**11**	**10**	**17**	**212**	**313**	**7823**
Y: Layer 3		19					19	102
Y: Layer 4	18	122	1	3			144	1135
Total	**18**	**141**	**1**	**3**			**163**	**1237**
Site Total	**227**	**696**	**40**	**64**	**80**	**695**	**1802**	**41998**

Table 49. Karobo ceramics: Sherd decoration by excavation square and depth.

Excavation/layer	CPI-X	CPI-//	CPI-?	Leaf imp.	Mat imp.	?Leaf/Mat	Incised symm.	End tool	Side tool
A2:Layer 1				12					
A2:Layer 2	6	1							
A2:Layer 3			3	7	1				
A2:Layer 4									
A2:Layer 5	277	103	45	393	7	35	3	2	1
Aa:Layer 1									
Aa:Layer 2									
Aa:Layer 3	1			17					
Aa:Layer 4	4			5					
Aa:Layer 5				8					
Aa:Layer 6				8					
Aa:Layer 7	46	21	9	54				1	2
Ab:Layer 1									
Ab:Layer 2									
Ab:Layer 3	8	6	4	28					
Ab:Layer 4									
Ab:Layer 5				22					
Ab:Layer 6	1								
Ab:Layer 7	26	2	4	168	6				
Y:Layer 3	6	5	8						
Y:Layer 4	52	56	14						
Site Total	**427**	**194**	**87**	**722**	**14**	**35**	**4**	**4**	**1**

superficially similar to comb incising, three of the four sherds have a smooth-rounded cross-section unlike the irregular and flat-bottomed channels made with a comb. A single case each of side-tool notching and finger impression was found on sherds of unknown vessel form. A rim sherd with a mat-impressed surface was also found, with the impressions similar to those made using a *Pandanus* sp. mat (see below). Almost all sherds (99.5%) from flat-based platters have leaf or mat impressions on their base. Leaf impressions are prominent (93%), with a smaller number of mat impressions (1.8%). Palmer (1965a:28) recorded two kinds of leaf impression from the Karobo platters, one from a banana leaf (*Musa* sp.), while the other was not identified. In a detailed study of the leaf impressions found on similar vessels from Level 2 of Sigatoka, Lambert (1971) identified *Hibiscus*, *Macaranga* and *Aleurites moluccana* impressions, using leaf shape and venation patterns from modern reference material. In that study, Lambert records that the Karobo leaf impressions were identified as *Macaranga magna*. Leaf impressions at Karobo occur on the base and rim but are often indistinct. The few sherds with clear leaf markings are compatible with Lambert's species attribution. The impressions have parallel, evenly spaced primary veins attached to a midrib, vein termination in a shallow deltoid shape at the laminal edge, and secondary veins that are rectangular and evenly spaced between the major veins. According to Parham (1964), *Macaranga magna* is a common forest tree in wet zones like the south Viti Levu coast.

Mat impressions on platter sherds are of two sizes and restricted to the exterior of platter bases. The stem width is 2.5–3.5 mm on the smaller and 4–6 mm on the larger. Lambert (1971:133) records that in some cases impressions from *Pandanus* mats can be identified. The

Figure 122. Karobo VL 18/1 sherds decorated with cross-hatch relief.

Figure 123. Karobo VL 18/1 sherds decorated with parallel-rib relief.

lower surface of the *Pandanus* leaf is marked by evenly spaced longitudinal ridges, while the upper surface is smooth. Other sedges used to make mats such as *Eleocharus* sp. have a different surface structure (Lambert 1971:Plate X). When mat impressions display alternating smooth and fine-ridged sections it is likely the mat was made from *Pandanus* sp. Impressions taken from mat-impressed sherds displayed alternating smooth and ridged surfaces, indicative of *Pandanus* mats.

Form 1A jars: Almost all rims from non-platter vessels (93%) belong to Form 1A vessels. The rim course is straight (57%) or slightly concave (43%), and the rim profile is parallel (55%) or gradual thinning (37%) or displays a small amount of proximal thickening (8%). There are two lip shapes: flat/flat-rounded forms, oriented normal to the rim axis, account for 88%, and round/pointed 12%. Rim decoration is limited to a single case of circular punctate on the dorsal lip and 18 sherds with cross-hatch and parallel relief on the rim. The mean eversion angle from 45 Form 1A rims is 21°, with a range of 14–33°. The rim-course thickness (n=49) varies from 4.4 mm to 13.8 mm, with a mean of 7.8 mm, and the rim height average is 33 mm (range 12–52 mm). The average neck inclination angle of 34 rims is 133° (range 100–156°). The vessel diameter (34 rims) is 18–32 cm, with a mean of 25 cm.

Form 2 bowls: Rims from three Form 2 vessel forms are identified. The first is from a Form 2B vessel with a flat lip normal to the rim axis and rounded edges. The vessel has cross-hatch relief and an estimated diameter of 29 cm. Another Form 2B represents a bowl with a flat lip and diameter of 32–35 cm. The final vessel form is an unusual Form 2C with a slightly inverted rim. Lip shape is flat and the diameter is 29 cm.

Form 3 flat-based vessels: As noted by Birks (1973:44), the rim height of flat-based vessels can vary by 50% on the same vessel. Lip form varies from gradual to sharply tapering points. An additional source of rim-form variation is found in corner sections that are shallow and rounded in cross-section. At Karobo, the base of these vessels appears to have been formed by rolling out slabs of clay on top of a leaf or mat covering (base thickness 6.7–23.4 mm). A slab or cylinder of clay was then shaped into a triangular-sectioned piece that was fixed and smoothed to the basal slab. In contrast to the irregular surface of the exterior base, the interior surface was smoothed. The rim to base height ranges from 2.7 mm to 6.6 mm, with a mean height of 40 mm. While platter form is difficult to determine, it is likely that in plan view they have straight or slightly curving sides and rounded corners. The diameter of four Karobo platters is estimated from large rim and base sections at approximately 50–53 cm. The estimate is consistent with plan dimensions from three platters from Level 2 at Sigatoka (ca. 52 cm, 67 cm, 76–78 cm). A minimum of three or probably four platters are present in the Karobo deposits.

Form 4 narrow-orifice vessels: A single example of a double-spouted vessel (Form 4A) was found at Karobo. The sherd has a flat handle and orifice diameters of 9 mm and 12 mm. The sherd does not have a provenance and was probably collected from the surface of the site. It has an internal spout diameter of 15 mm and a narrow handle diameter of 24 mm. Two spouts from Karobo are also unlocalised, but probably derive from surface collections. One of these might have been from a double-spouted vessel.

Perforated clay object: An unusual find at Karobo was a perforated clay fragment that would have been roughly circular when complete. Maximum dimensions of the piece are 8.5 cm x 8.2 cm (thickness 4.2 cm). The tapered perforation has a diameter of 20 mm at the top and 15 mm at the bottom. The function of this object is not known.

Votua ceramics

A total of 1400 sherds weighing 5.8 kg was recovered from the Area 1 shell midden excavation with more than 80% of the sherds, by weight and number, coming from the surface to 20 cm depth (Table 50). Plain body sherds make up 82% of the assemblage, and the mean sherd thickness of a sherd sub-sample is 6.8 mm. The incidence of surface modification is low, with 38, or 2.7%, of sherds marked, but the majority have traces of a red slip/wash. Seventeen sherds have coarse wipe marks made using coconut husk fibre or similar material. Dentate stamping on eight sherds consists of simple horizontal, diagonal and intersecting straight lines and arcs. The single motif (Figure 124) is a repeated loop, bordered above and below by a single horizontal line of dentate stamping, a motif similar to M46 of Mead et al. (1973). Remaining decorated sherds consist of single or double-impressed lines made using the edge of a shell bivalve, and a single notched and applied band. Several lug/handle sherds are also recorded (Figure 125). There are 157 rim sherds, most (54%) of which come from vessels with an everted rim and indirect body contour characteristic of 'jar' vessel forms. Vessels with inverted or direct rims and direct body contours ('bowls') make up 26% of all rims. The Area 1 vessel forms reconstructed from the largest rim sherds are shown in Figure 126, which shows a diverse but not uncommon Lapita assemblage composed of large and small diameter bowls, jars with strongly everted rims, rounded or flat lips and sub-globular bodies, jars with collar rims and shallow carinated dishes.

Table 50. Votua (1996) ceramics: Sherd type by excavation square and depth.

Excavation/ depth (cm)	Plain body	Decorated body	Rims	Necks	Carination	Handle/lug	Number	Weight (g)
A1:0–10	315	1	43	8	2	2	371	1510
A1:10–20	29	5	13	3			50	230
A1:20–30	1	10			1		82	340
Total	414	7	66	11	3	2	503	2080
A2:0–10	480	5	52	51	1	2	545	2290
A2:10–20	241	1	33		1	1	277	1110
A2:20–30	48	1	6				55	290
A2:30–40	20						20	50
Total	**789**	**7**	**91**	**5**	**2**	**3**	**897**	**3740**
TP1:0–10	122		10				132	510
TP1:10–20	140		6	2			148	530
TP1:20–30	152		11	1			164	740
TP1:30–40	190		18	2		1	211	980
TP1:40–50	447		57	3		4	511	2610
TP1:50–60	69		11	1	2		83	390
TP1:60–70	68	7					75	470
Total	**1188**		**120**	**9**	**2**	**5**	**1324**	**6230**

Malaqereqere ceramics

The small pottery assemblage from Malaqereqere was recovered from excavation units A1 and A2. The two units were excavated to a depth of 60–70 cm. The total collection consists of 1057 sherds weighing 3.2 kg (Table 51). Almost the entire ceramic assemblage shows signs of burning on the interior and exterior of sherds. This black discolouration makes the identification of burnishing or slip application difficult, and sherds are small, indicating substantial fragmentation. The distribution of plain body sherds shows a peak at 50–60 cm depth in both test pits. Ceramic

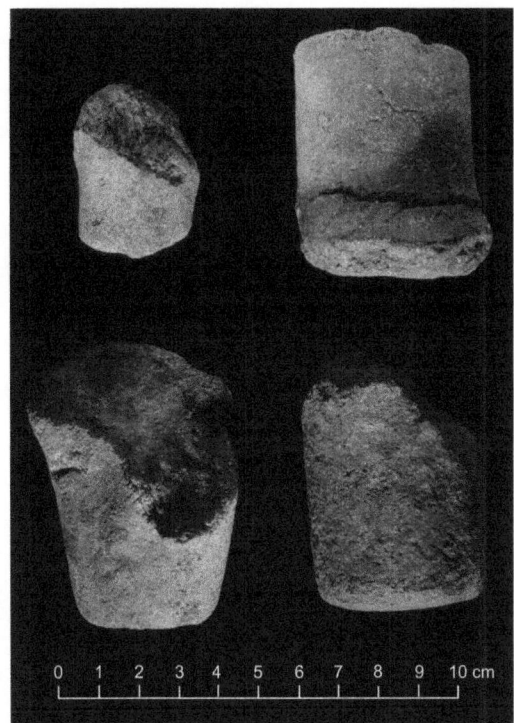
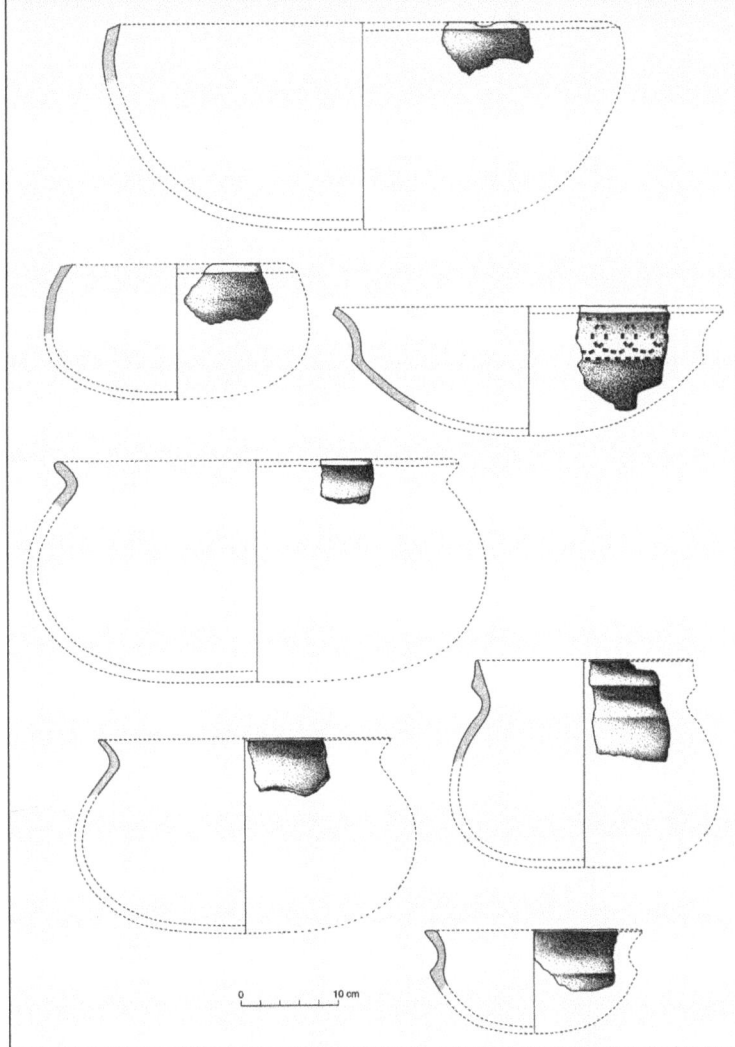

Figure 124. (Above left) Votua rim sherd from a carinated dish/bowl with coarse dentate stamping.

Figure 125. (Above right) Votua handle/lug sherds.

Figure 126. (Left) Votua reconstructed vessels.

decoration is rare, with examples of incision, end-tool impression and fingernail impression, which are all indicative of late prehistoric ceramics. However, a single dentate-stamped sherd was found at 50–60 cm depth in Square A1. Identifiable rim sherds are from Form 1A jars with parallel or thinning profiles and pointed and flat lips. One Form 1A is from a typical late-prehistoric *kuro* style cooking pot with a sharply everted rim and an aperture diameter of 28 cm.

Table 51. Malaqereqere ceramics: Sherd type by excavation square and depth.

Excavation/ depth (cm)	Plain body	Decorated body	Rim	Neck	Number	Weight (g)
A1:0–10	49		2		51	246.3
A1:10–20	36		1		37	179.7
A1:20–30	26				26	125.2
A1:30–40	17				17	55.6
A1:40–50	73	5		1	79	252.1
A1:50–60	228	6	1		235	603
A1:60–70	82		1		83	221.8
Total	**511**	**11**	**5**	**1**	**528**	**1683.7**
A2:0–10	34		3		37	167.5
A2:10–20	21				21	104.9
A2:20–30	23	1			24	84.8
A2:30–40	25				25	71.4
A2:40–50	59	1			60	176.1
A2:50–60	332	1	3		336	880.3
A2:60–70	26				26	41.8
Total	**520**	**3**	**6**		**529**	**1526.8**

Volivoli II ceramics

The pottery assemblage from Volivoli II is small, consisting of 1326 sherds, weighing 6.89 kg (Table 52). Most are plain body sherds (93.5%). The density of pottery was highest in the top 60 cm and declined below, with only a few possibly intrusive sherds found below 100 cm depth. Decoration consists of comb incised and tool incised (10–30 cm), with paddle impression (cross hatch, parallel rib and diamond) from 20–50 cm depth. Rims are from Form 1A jars (15 sherds from six vessels), Form 2A bowls (three sherds from three vessels) and a Form 2B bowl (one sherd from one vessel). Rims from all vessel forms have a profile that is parallel or thinning, and lip forms that are flat-sharp edged or flat-rounded.

Volivoli III ceramics

The small pottery assemblage from Volivoli III consists of 371 sherds, weighing 3.33 kg (Table 53). The vast majority of these (94.5%) are plain body sherds. Only two body sherds from Spit 3 are decorated, marked with end-tool impressions. The 13 rim sherds derive from a Form 1A jar, and from vertical and everted bowls (Form 2B). A possible collar rim from a small vessel was found in Spit 3. Rim profiles are parallel and thinning, and lips forms are flat, rounded and tapering. A single carination was present in Spit 6.

Table 52. Volivoli II ceramics: Sherd type by excavation square and depth.

Depth (cm)	Plain body	Decorated body	Rims	Necks	Number	Weight (g)
0–10	283		5		288	2023.2
10–20	310	1	4		315	1695.5
20–30	292	4	7	2	305	1371.1
30–40	38	1	1	1	41	249.5
40–50	158	25	11	8	202	923.7
50–60	81	7	5	2	95	376.4
60–70	42		1	1	44	135.2
70–80	24				24	75.6
80–90	5				5	21
90–100						
100–110						
110–120	2				2	3.5
120–130	2				2	8.6
Posthole fill	3				3	9.9
Total	**1240**	**38**	**34**	**14**	**1326**	**6893.2**

Table 53. Volivoli III ceramics: Sherd type by excavation square and depth.

Depth (cm)	Plain body	Decorated body	Rims	Carination	Number	Weight (g)
Surface	28		1		29	283.5
TP.1:Spit 1						
TP.1:Spit 2	50		2		52	480.2
TP.1:Spit 3	33	2	5		40	258.9
TP.1:Spit 4	141				141	1153.3
TP.1:Spit 5	15		1		16	161.4
TP.1:Spit 6	41		3	1	45	274.1
TP.1:Spit 7	14				14	66.7
TP.1:Spit 8	30		1		31	641.9
TP.1:Spit 9	3				3	14.2
Total	**355**	**2**	**13**		**371**	**3334.2**

Kulu Bay ceramics

A total of 11,398 sherds was recovered from the Kulu Bay excavations. Of these 10,353 (90.8%) are plain body sherds, with about half of the total assemblage coming from the C11 excavation (Table 54). Lapita-age sherds marked with dentate stamping were found in all deposits, along with post-Lapita pottery marked with parallel and cross-hatch paddle impression (Table 55). Late-prehistoric ceramics, such as *dari* and comb-incised vessels, are represented by a few sherds. Lapita-era rim forms are from Form 1B jars with abruptly thickened 'collar' rims, and Form 1A jars with everted rims, including highly everted 'rolled' rims. As at Sigatoka, collar-rim jars are decorated with side-tool impressions and shell impressing along the collar, and carinations carry linear incision and dentate stamping. Many sherds have traces of red slip and wiping on internal and external surfaces. As well as Form 1B jars with a sub-globular body, and everted jars with short necks and everted jars with thickened rims, additional vessels include a probable flat-based dish, everted direct bowls, inverted direct bowls and indirect inverted bowls (Forms 2A, 2B, 2C). High sherd fragmentation prohibited vessel reconstruction and examples of rim forms and decoration are shown in Figures 127–131.

Table 54. Kulu Bay ceramics: Sherd type by excavation square and depth.

Excavation/depth (cm)	Plain body	Decorated body	Rims	Carinations	Handles/ lugs	Number	Weight (g)
TP2:0–20	9	10	11			30	768.4
TP2:10–20	97	13	10			120	698.1
TP2:30–40	117	3	6			126	870.11
C9:0–10	128	10	9			147	530.2
C9:10–20	105	1	4			110	297.2
C9:20–30	220	7	18			245	1265.6
C9:30–40	395	12	27			434	1672.6
C9:40–50	703	15	38			756	2255.6
C9:50–60	418	11	24	2		455	1653.9
C10: 0–30	151	7	12			170	1082
C10:30–50	552	11	52		1	616	3519.2
C10:50–70	89	5	5			99	987.3
C10:60–80	291	15	13			319	994.5
C10:70–80	314	10	15			339	1243.6
C10:80–90	443	12	11			466	1621.6
C10:90–100	645	30	43		1	719	2309.4
C11:0–10	166	8	9	3	1	187	922.1
C11:10–20	234	10	10			254	1003.8
C11:20–30	453	17	41	3		514	2823.4
C11:30–40	135	6	14	1		156	873.5
C11:40–50	151	12	16			179	1278.5
C11:40–60	139	3	14			156	1006.6
C11:50–60	51	1	6		1	59	428.6
C11: 60–70	258	8	14	1	2	283	1463.8
C11:70–80	863	17	44	1	1	926	3668.4
C11:80–90	906	19	57		3	985	2878.4
C11:90–100	622	16	45		1	684	2613.8
C11:100–110	462	5	46	2		515	1964.8
C11:110–120	383	27	25			435	1477.6
C11:120–130	359	10	14			383	1236.3
C11:130–140	350	5	19			374	1194.9
C11:140–150	98	2	2			102	297.9
C11:150–160	46	5	4			55	230.6
Total	10353	343	678	13	11	11398	47132.3

Table 55. Kulu Bay ceramics: Sherd decoration by excavation square and depth.

Excavation/depth (cm)	Plain body	Dentate	Wiped	Side tool	Dents	CPI-//	CPI-X	Incision	End tool
T2:0–20	9	1	0	0	0	1	8	0	0
T2:10–20	97	0	0	0	0	0	13	0	0
T2:30–40	117	0	1	0	0	1	1	0	0
T2 Total	**223**	**1**	**1**	**0**	**0**	**2**	**22**	**0**	**0**
C9:0–10	128	2	3	0	0	0	5	0	0
C9:10–20	105	0	1	0	0	0	0	0	0
C9:20–30	220	1	1	0	0	2	3	0	0
C9:30–40	395	1	2	0	1	0	8	0	0
C9:40–50	703	4	4	1	0	1	5	0	0
C9:50–60	418	1	3	1	0	4	1	1	0
C9 Total	**1841**	**7**	**11**	**2**	**1**	**7**	**17**	**1**	**0**
C10: 0–30	151	0	1	0	1	2	3	0	1
C10:30–50	552	0	0	2	1	4	3	1	0
C10:50–70	89	1	1	1	0	0	2	0	0
C10:60–80	291	2	6	0	0	0	2	1	4
C10:70–80	314	2	3	2	1	1	1	0	0
C10:80–90	443	3	2	1	0	1	3	2	0
C10:90–100	645	2	6	1	0	3	14	2	2
C10 Total	**2485**	**10**	**19**	**7**	**3**	**11**	**28**	**6**	**7**
C11:0–10	166	0	0	1	0	0	4	3	0
C11:10–20	234	0	2	2	0	2	3	1	0
C11:20–30	453	0	5	1	0	2	8	0	1
C11:30–40	135	0	4	0	0	0	2	0	0
C11:40–50	151	0	4	2	0	0	4	1	1
C11:40–60	139	0	0	0	0	0	3	0	0
C11:50–60	51	0	1	0	0	0	0	0	0
C11: 60–70	258	2	2	0	0	1	3	0	0
C11:70–80	863	1	6	2	1	2	2	3	0
C11:80–90	906	1	13	1	0	0	3	0	0
C11:90–100	622	4	5	0	0	0	5	2	0
C11:100–110	462	0	2	0	0	0	3	0	0
C11:110–120	383	6	12	4	0	0	2	3	0
C11:120–130	359	0	3	3	0	1	3	0	0
C11:130–140	350	0	2	1	0	1	1	0	0
C11:140–150	98	0	0	1	0	0	0	1	0
C11:150–160	46	0	2	1	0	1	1	0	0
C11 Total	**5676**	**14**	**63**	**19**	**1**	**10**	**47**	**14**	**2**
Total	**10353**	**34**	**97**	**28**	**5**	**30**	**119**	**21**	**9**

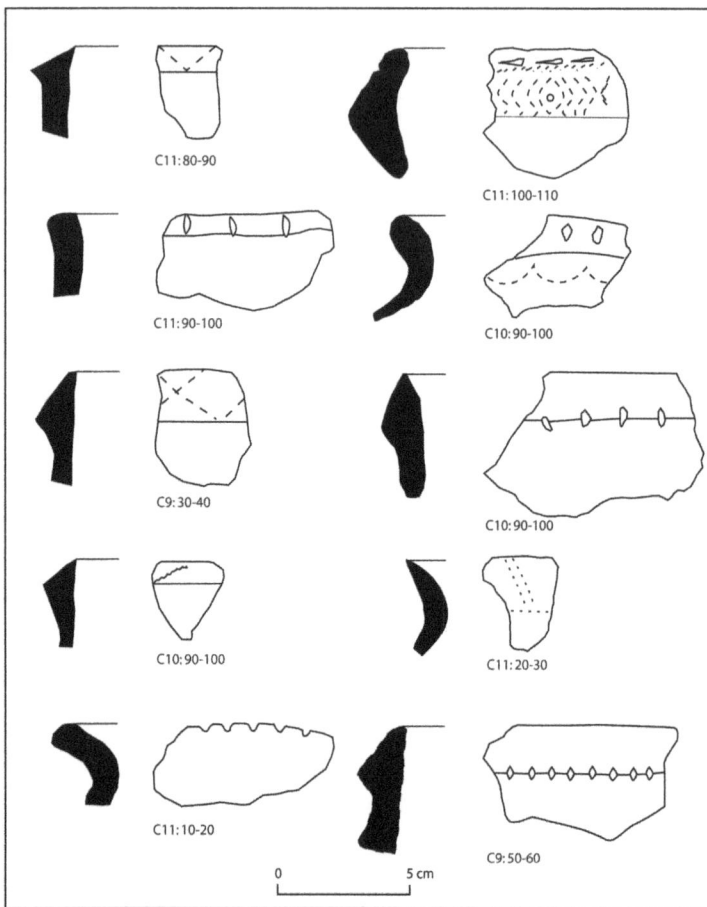

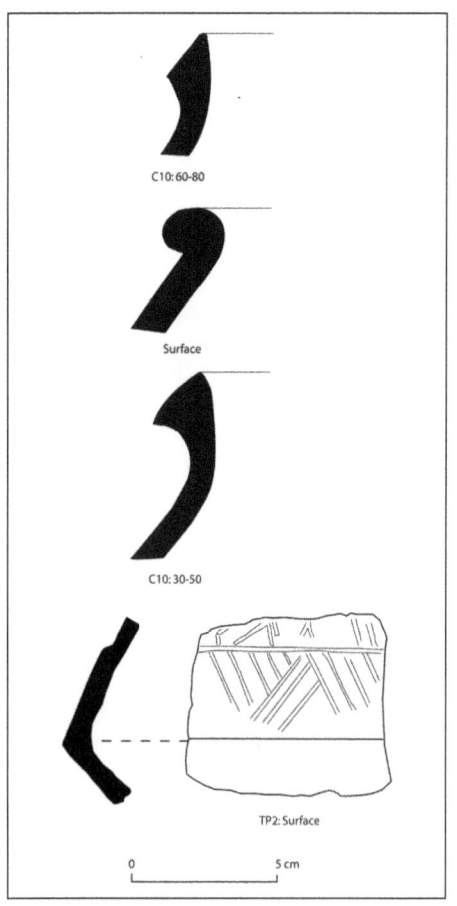

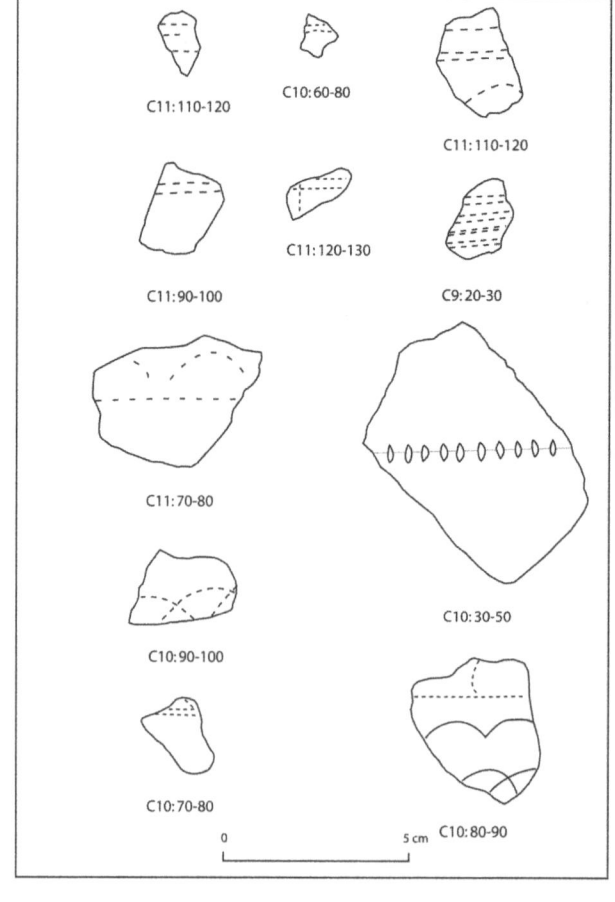

Figure 127. (Left) Kulu Bay decorated rim sherds.

Figure 128. (Below left) Kulu Bay rims and an incised carination.

Figure 129. (Below right) Kulu Bay decorated sherds.

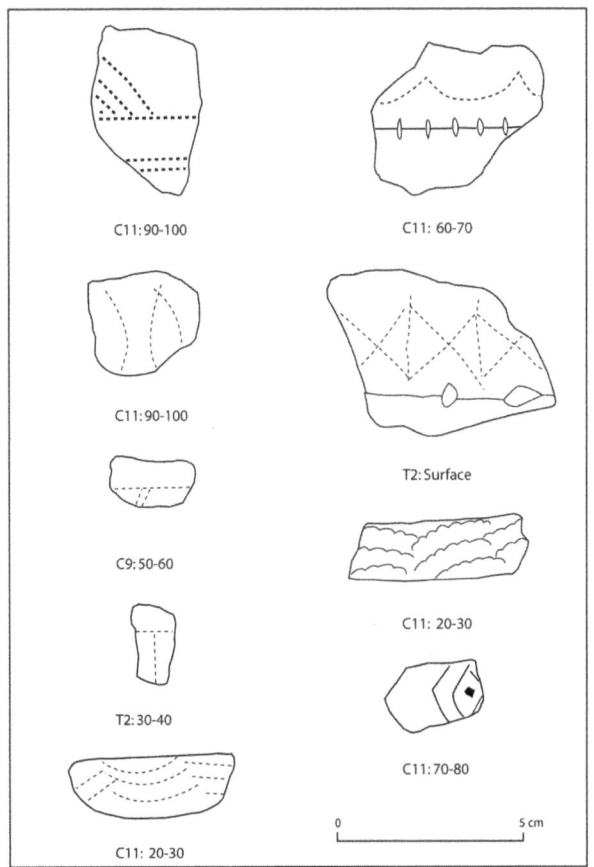

Figure 130. Kulu Bay decorated sherds.

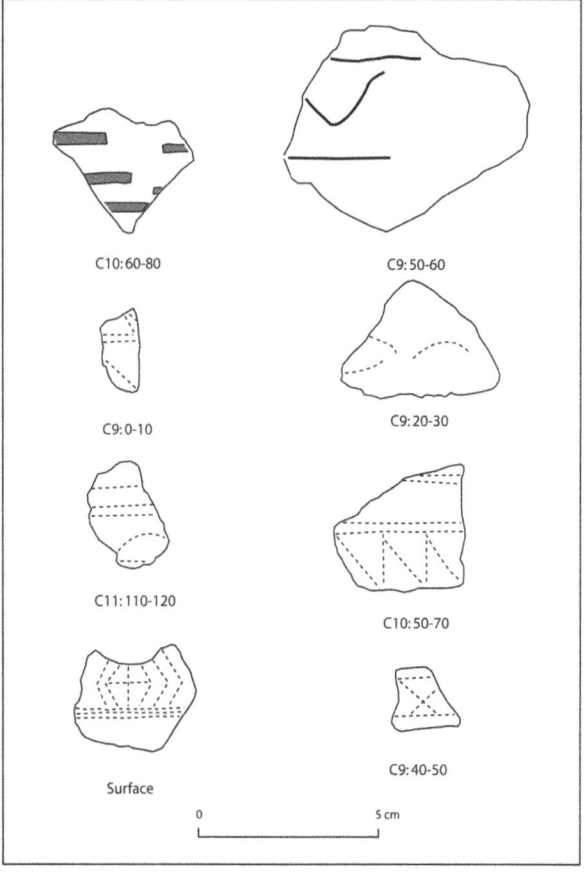

Figure 131. Kulu Bay decorated sherds.

Natunuku ceramics

The Natunuku investigations recovered 6318 sherds, weighing 17.13 kg, with the majority of sherds deriving from the Trench 3 excavation. Sherd density is highest in the upper levels of TP1, TP2 and TR3, and all units contain decorated sherds from Lapita, post-Lapita and late-prehistoric assemblages (Table 56). This is demonstrated by comb-incised sherds in the upper deposits of TP1 and TP2, and by carved-paddle-impressed sherds in all levels of the TR3 excavations (Table 57). The highest frequency of dentate-stamped sherds was in the top 20 cm of units, except in TR3 where there were more decorated sherds than plain sherds at 40–50 cm depth. However, carved-paddle-impressed sherds were found in the lower levels of TR3, indicating deposit mixing of Lapita with post-Lapita ceramics has taken place. Dentate-stamped decoration is similar to that reported by Davidson et al. (1990:Figures 12, 14, 15, 16) and examples are shown in Figure 132. Decorated sherds from the Natunuku assemblage were photographed and drawn, but after the 2003 Canberra bushfires, the Natunuku ceramics and a number of documentary records about the site could not be relocated, limiting the detail in which the collection can be described.

Nonetheless, it is possible from rim information to describe the main vessel forms and two complementary systems have been used. The first uses the lip shape and rim profile codes of Best (1984:161) for rims, while vessel-form categories follow those of previous work on Natunuku ceramics developed by Davidson et al. (1990). The latter study identified five vessel categories containing 15 vessel forms: Category i – flat-bottomed dish; Category ii – globular or ovoid-bodied pot or jar; Category iii – water jar (narrow aperture); Category iv – shouldered pot/jar;

Category v – direct bowl. Early vessels in the current study include Category i; Category ii – Form IV (collar rim), Form VI and Form VII (outward flaring rim), Form VII (thickened rim); Category iv – Form XI, Form XIV (carinated), Form XIII (double flange rim). Late vessel forms are category ii – Form III, characterised by straight everted rims like those of late prehistoric *kuro* pots. Selected rim sherds are identified to a vessel category in Table 58, with category i (flat-bottomed dish) and category ii (Form VI and Form VII) collar-rim vessels and flaring-rim vessels from the Lapita assemblage, and category ii (Form III) vessels with straight everted rims of post-Lapita age.

Table 56. Natunuku ceramics: Sherd type by excavation square and depth.

Excavation/depth (cm)	Plain body	Decorated body	Plain rims	Decorated rims	Handles/lugs	Weight (g)
TP1:Surface	11	0	2	0	1	140.9
TP1:0–10	416	27	14	7	0	1375.7
TP1:10–20	49	2	0	0	0	240.5
TP1/2:0–10	107	6	4	0	1	333.3
TP1/2:10–20	97	5	8	0	0	221.8
TP1/2:20–30	132	1	0	0	0	232.2
Total	**812**	**41**	**28**	**7**	**2**	**2544.4**
TP2:0–10	590	35	16	5	1	1943.6
TP2:10–20	628	13	11	2	2	1531.2
TP2-1:20–30	69	1	0	3	0	213.2
TP2-1:30–40	5	0	0	0	0	5.3
Total	**1292**	**49**	**27**	**10**	**3**	**3693.3**
TR3:0–10	1016	23	36	4	3	2482.9
TR3:10–20	879	14	32	7	0	2686.9
TR3:20–30	660	16	27	1	1	1965.5
TR3:30–40	604	9	35	1	1	1883.3
TR3:40–50	418	13	25	4	0	1274.9
TR3:50–60	141	2	7	0	0	422
TR3:Feature A	46	3	2	0	0	134.7
No depth	17	0	0	0	0	45
Total	**3781**	**80**	**164**	**17**	**5**	**10895.2**
Site Total	**5885**	**170**	**219**	**34**	**10**	**17132.9**

Table 57. Natunuku ceramics: Sherd decoration by excavation square and depth.

Excavation/depth (cm)	Plain	Dentate	Wiped	End tool	Appliqué	CPI-//	CPI-X	Incised	Comb Incised
TP1:Surface	11	0	0	0	0	0	0	0	1
TP1:0–10	416	12	2	2	1	3	2	4	8
TP1:10–20	49	0	0	0	0	0	1	0	1
TP1/2:0–10	107	3	0	0	1	0	1	0	1
TP1/2:10–20	97	2	0	1	0	0	1	0	1
TP1/2:20–30	132	0	0	0	0	0	0	0	1
TP2:0–10	590	31	2	3	0	1	0	2	1
TP2:10–20	628	10	0	1	1	1	1	0	1
TP2:20–30	69	2	0	2	0	0	0	0	0
TP2:30–40	5	0	0	0	0	0	0	0	0
TR3:0–10	1016	16	2	4	1	0	2	1	1
TR3:10–20	879	12	0	5	0	0	4	0	0
TR3:20–30	660	6	1	2	0	1	7	0	0
TR3:30–40	604	4	2	2	0	1	1	0	0
TR3:40–50	418	12	2	0	1	2	0	0	0
TR3:50–60	141	1	0	0	0	0	1	0	0
TR3:Feature A	46	1	0	0	0	2	0	0	0
TR3:No Depth	17	0	0	0	0	0	0	0	0
Site Total	**5885**	**112**	**11**	**22**	**5**	**11**	**21**	**7**	**16**

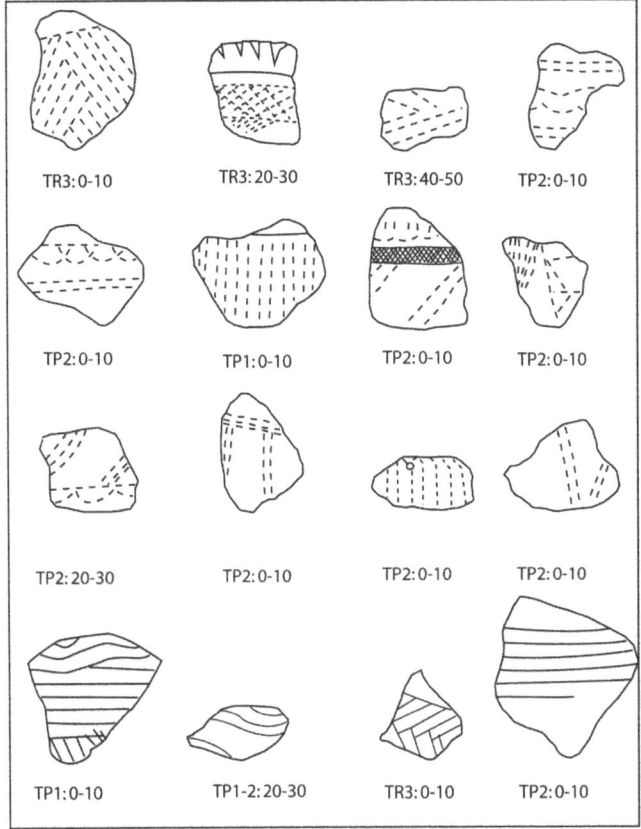

Figure 132. Natunuku decorated sherds.

Table 58. Natunuku ceramics: Selected vessel forms and rims by excavation square and depth.

Excavation/depth (cm)	Lip	Profile	Decoration	Vessel type	Weight (g)
TP1:0–10	39	30	CPI-X	?	4.2
TP1:0–10	40	42	Side tool	?	4.6
TP1:0–10	47	35	Dentate	Category iv	9.7
TP1:0–10	40	30	Dentate	Category i	6.1
TP1:0–10	39	30	Dentate	Category i	10.2
TP1:0–10	49	34	Side tool	Category iv	6.2
TP2:0–10	45	30	Side tool	?	7.2
TP2:0–10	39	30	Dentate	?Category i	2.8
TP2:0–10	40	30	Dentate	?Category i	3.3
TP2:0–10	39	30	Dentate	?Category i	4.8
TP2:10–20	40	33	End tool	?	4.7
TP2:10–20	39	30	Dentate	Category i	31.0
TP2/1:20–30	40	30	Dentate+Side tool	?Category i	5.5
TP2/1:20–30	40	30	Side tool	Category ii	6.7
TP2/2:0–10	42	34	Side tool	Category iv	72.9
TP2/2:20-30	39	30	Dentate+Side tool	?Category i	3.3
TR3/A3/2A	39	?	Side tool	?	1.7
TR3/A4:0–10	40	30	Side tool	?	3.9
TR3/A4:10–20	39	30	Dentate	?Category i	7.2
TR3/A4:20–30	40	30	Perforation	?	2.0
TR3/A5:0–10	39	31	Side tool	?	2.4
TR3/A5:0–10	44	30	Dentate	Category i	2.9
TR3/A6:10–20	44	30	Side tool	?	3.5
TR3/A6:10–20	39	31	Side tool	?	6.1
TR3/A6:10–20	39	30	Side tool	?	5.4
TR3/A6:20–30	39	30	Side tool	?	8.1
TR3/A6:30–40	39	30	Dentate+Side tool	Category i	2.5
TR3/A6:40–50	39	30	Side tool	?	9.9
TR3/A6:40–50	39	30	CPI-//	?	1.1
TR3/A6:40–50	44	30	Dentate	?Category i	2.6
TR3/A6:40–50	44	30	Side tool	?	2.7
TR3/B6:10–20	39	30	Side tool	?	2.4
TR3/B6:10–20	39	30	Side tool	?	3.3
TP1:0–10	39	30	Plain	Category v	2.4
TP1:0–10	49	30	Plain	Category v	2.7
TP1:0–10	40	30	Plain	Category v	5.5
TP1:0–10	49	30	Plain	Category v	7.1
TP1:0–10	39	30	Plain	Category v	11.0

Continued on next page

Table 58 continued

Excavation/depth (cm)	Lip	Profile	Decoration	Vessel type	Weight (g)
TP1:0–10	39	30	Plain	Category v	23.7
TP2:10–20	39	30	Plain	Category v	7.9
TR3/A5:0–10	40	30	Plain	Category v	2.6
TR3/A5:10–20	39	30	Plain	Category v	15.4
TR3/B5:10–20	39	30	Plain	Category v	11.2
TR3/B5:30–40	45	30	Plain	Category v	14.5
TR3/B5:40–50	39	30	Plain	Category v	3.9
TR3/B5:40–50	40	30	Plain	Category v	4.7
TR3/B6:50–60	40	30	Plain	Category v	6.4
TP1:Surface	39	30	Plain	Category ii–III	9.6
TP1:0–10	44	31	Plain	Category ii–III	4.9
TP2:10–20	39	32	Plain	Category ii–VII	14.7
TR3/A4:0–10	45	30	Plain	Category ii–III	2.5
TR3/A5:30–40	39	35	Plain	Category ii–III	14.4
TR3/A5:30–40	39	33	Plain	Category ii–VII	10.3
TR3/A5:30–40	39	30	Plain	Category ii–III	9.4
TR3/A6:20–30	45	30	Plain	Category ii–VI	5.7
TR3/A6:40–50	40	31	Plain	Category ii–III	3.5
TR3/A6:40–50	39	30	Plain	Category ii–III	6.5
TR3/B6:40–50	39	30	Plain	Category i	19.9

'Lip' and 'Profile' descriptions after Best (1984:170, Fig. 3.3). Vessel categories and forms after Davidson et al. (1990).

Qaranioso II ceramics

The small Qaranioso II pottery assemblage consists of 206 sherds, weighing 0.93 kg (Table 59). Most are plain-body sherds, with carved-paddle-impressed sherds present in the middle levels, along with one sherd marked with fingernail impressions. At the base of the site was a rim sherd from a small vessel (estimated aperture diameter 16–18 cm), marked on the lip from a section of bivalve shell arc containing seven teeth (Figure 133). The rim is thickened at the lip and is similar to rims found at Ugaga and at Sigatoka Level 1 (cf. Birks 1973:Vessels No. 37 and 38).

Table 59. Qaranioso II ceramics: Sherd type and decoration by excavation square and depth.

Depth	Plain body	Decorated body	Rims	Weight (g)	CPI-X	End tool – fingernail	Shell impressed
TP1:0–10	6			105.0			
TP1:10–20	30	2	1	130.7	1	1	
TP1:20–30	53	7		231.2	7		
TP1:30–40	40		4	234.7			
TP1:40–50	41		2	152.8			
TP1:50–60	18	1	1	73.9			1
Total	188	10	8	928.3	8	1	1

Figure 133. Qaranioso II rim sherd marked with a coarse dentate tool.

References

Anderson, A. and Clark, G. 1999. The age of Lapita settlement in Fiji. *Archaeology in Oceania* 34: 31–39.

Anson, D. 1983. Lapita pottery of the Bismarck Archipelago and its affinities. Unpublished PhD thesis, University of Sydney.

Best, S. 1984. Lakeba: The prehistory of a Fijian Island. Unpublished PhD thesis, Department of Anthropology, University of Auckland.

Birks, L. 1973. Archaeological excavations at Sigatoka dune site, Fiji. *Bulletin of the Fiji Museum* No.1.

Clark, G. 2000. Post-Lapita Fiji: Cultural transformation in the mid-sequence. Unpublished PhD thesis, Australian National University.

Clark, G. and Anderson, A. 2001. The pattern of Lapita settlement in Fiji. *Archaeology in Oceania* 36: 77–88.

Clark, G., Anderson, A. and Matararaba, S. 2001. The Lapita site at Votua, northern Lau Islands, Fiji. *Archaeology in Oceania* 36: 134–145.

Crosby, A. 1988. Beqa: Archaeology, structure and history in Fiji. Unpublished MA thesis, Department of Anthropology, University of Auckland.

Davidson, J., Hinds, E., Holdaway, S. and Leach, F. 1990. The Lapita site of Natunuku, Fiji. *New Zealand Journal of Archaeology* 12: 121–155.

Frost, E.L. 1970. Archaeological excavations of fortified sites on Taveuni, Fiji. Unpublished PhD thesis, University of Oregon.

Gifford, E.W. 1951. Archaeological excavations in Fiji. *University of California Anthropological Records* 13:189–288.

Harrisson, T. 1965. 'Turtle-ware' from Borneo caves. *The Sarawak Museum Journal* 12: 63–67.

Lambert, R. 1971. Botanical identification of impressions on archaeological potsherds from Sigatoka. Final Report No. 3. *Records of the Fiji Museum* 1: 124–148.

Mead, S., Birks, L., Birks, H. and Shaw, E. 1973. The Lapita pottery style of Fiji and its associations. *Journal of the Polynesian Society Memoir* 38: 1–98.

Palmer, B. 1971. Fijian pottery technologies: their relevance to certain problems of southwest Pacific history. In: Green, R.C. and Kelly, M. (eds), *Studies in Oceanic culture history volume 2*, pp. 77–103. Pacific Anthropological Records No. 12.

Parham, J. 1964. *Plants of the Fiji Islands*. Government Press, Suva.

Rossitto, R. 1990. Stylistic change of Fijian pottery. Part 1: form. *Domodomo* 8: 1–47.

Shaw, E. 1967. A reanalysis of pottery from Navatu and Vuda, Fiji. Unpublished MA thesis, Department of Anthropology, University of Auckland.

Summerhayes, G.R. 1996. Interaction in Pacific prehistory: An approach based on production, distribution and use of pottery. Unpublished PhD thesis, La Trobe University.

12

Post-Lapita ceramic change in Fiji

Geoffrey Clark
Department of Archaeology and Natural History, The Australian National University

Introduction

No ceramic sequence in the Pacific has been as closely examined for evidence of stylistic change and external influences as Fiji's. Such scrutiny stems from long-observed differences between the physical characteristics and social structures of 'Melanesian' Fiji and 'Polynesian' people who inhabit islands to the east of Fiji, and a search for historical explanations for the differences, which in due course began to incorporate archaeological data (Hunt 1986; Clark 2003). The data, methods and theories used to interpret the Fiji ceramic sequence are a litmus test for understanding prehistoric culture contact, and have implications for interpreting archaeological sequences elsewhere in the Pacific.

Binford (1972:119) noted that population contact and replacement is a frequent, but often incorrect, explanation when an expectation of gradual change in the prehistoric record is not met. This is evident in Fiji where differences between material-culture sets have been interpreted as contact/arrival of people from beyond Fiji, particularly from Vanuatu and New Caledonia. One major deficiency of such an assumption is that it is self-sufficient and does not require supporting evidence from rigorous testing of presumed 'intrusive' material-culture sets against the material culture from the putative place of origin, which is a logical corollary of the explanation. Second, the magnitude of sequence change and the similarity/dissimilarity of 'foreign' assemblages to earlier cultural material is seldom quantified in a rigorous manner.

As a result, claims of cultural arrival and intrusion frequently have a diffusionist character in which isolated cultural traits in the prehistoric record are combined with those from ethnology to form an overly simplistic and extravagant explanation of culture change through hypothetical migration and culture contact. In the Pacific, both migration and interaction among island groups certainly took place in the past, but hypotheses that invoke such movements – if they are to have a status above assertion – need first, to be tethered to secure evidence for inter-archipelago contact, and second, that evidence needs to be placed in a theory of culture contact that specifies why some culture traits were changed by contact while others were not, and why intra-archipelago development should be definitively ruled out.

Reliable evidence for prehistoric migration/contact includes geochemical sourcing of archaeological materials from different island groups, traces of language intrusion in historical linguistics (e.g. Schmidt 2003), independent traditions of culture contact in island societies, biological data for long-distance movement such as from osteology, ancient DNA and isotope studies, and clear stylistic similarities between local and foreign ceramic assemblages rather than selective use of a few traits/attributes to posit long-distance contact. If evidence for prehistoric contact is absent/minimal then it is reasonable to consider hypotheses that feature endogenous mechanisms of culture change (see below). The scale and scope of culture change from inter-archipelago mobility should also be defined, as should whether prehistoric contact modified material culture, language, biological systems, settlement patterns and architecture.

Pre-contact population estimates for Fiji range from a high of 300,000 (Hunt in Derrick 1974:48) to a more likely size of 150,000 (Wilkes 1985; Williams 1985:102), and while population size in the post-Lapita era is not known the local population was large enough to have spread inland (Chapter 4; Field et al. 2009) indicating that favourable coastal locations were already occupied. Was the magnitude of post-Lapita population movement between Vanuatu/New Caledonia and Fiji sufficient to shift the established 'Lapita' Fijian phenotype to a more 'Melanesian' form, implying that similar movements also altered the Lapita populations of Vanuatu and New Caledonia, and if migration-contact from the west was significant, is there linguistic or other evidence for it in Fiji and other parts of the West Pacific?

In archaeological theory, the attribution of sequence inflection to an external cause neglects the possibility of dynamic culture change stemming from internal archipelago developments such as subsistence activities, demography, interaction networks, social hierarchy and organisation, and the transformation of terrestrial and maritime landscapes as a result of anthropogenic activity and climate change. Invoking an external influence for prehistoric cultural change as the result of climate change or exogenous culture contact has the potential, therefore, to unduly simplify Pacific prehistory, most particularly by diminishing the complexity and importance of local processes to the evolution of human social systems.

The hypothesis that culture change in Fiji is due to population contact/migration in the post-Lapita period (ca. 2500–1000 BP) also diverts attention away from the significant issue of Lapita colonisation, especially the degree of variability among migrating groups. For example, were there minor or major cultural, biological and linguistic differences between the migrant streams which colonised Tonga–Samoa and those which settled in Fiji, which over 3000 years, resulted in the classification of 'Melanesian Fiji' and its separation from 'Polynesian Tonga–Samoa'? There is currently no definitive answer to this question, but it is important to outline the plausible alternatives, particularly the possibility that contemporary differences between the populations of Fiji and West Polynesia developed over three millennia of predominantly local development, rather than from a few centuries of inter-archipelago contact with island groups to the west of Fiji in the post-Lapita period, an explanation which is not supported by current archaeological data.

Historical development

The influential geocultural divisions of Melanesia and Polynesia were first instituted and hierarchically arranged on a socio-evolutionary scale by Dumont d'Urville in 1827, with

Polynesians at the top, Melanesians at the bottom and Micronesians in the middle (Clark 2003). Early ethnographers and anthropologists such as Horatio Hale, Abraham Fornander, Thomas Williams, Arthur Hocart and Alfred Kroeber developed historical sequences to account for the cultural separation of Melanesia from Polynesia that featured intrusive population waves arriving in the Pacific, rather than hypotheses featuring *in situ* culture change. Archaeologists employed the population-wave paradigm derived from anthropology and ethnology as a framework to interpret the emergent prehistoric record, with Edward Gifford (1951:189) commenting that the presence of ceramics at Navatu and Vuda in Fiji 'ruled out any likelihood that the first settlers at these two sites were Polynesians'. Solheim (1952a, b), Palmer (1974), Green (1972) and Golson (1974), among others, also found evidence in comparisons of prehistoric ceramics for population movements from Melanesia and Southeast Asia to Fiji.

The use by archaeologists of ceramic traits to examine past population movements in the Pacific was rapidly vindicated in the case of the Lapita culture, which was identified from the Bismarck Archipelago all the way to Tonga and Samoa from the similarity of dentate-stamped designs on pot sherds (Golson 1961). The presence of an early-Lapita ceramic culture with a distribution that spanned Dumont d'Urville's ethnological zones suggested that the cultural and biological separation of Melanesia from Polynesia had occurred in the post-Lapita period from a population movement from western Melanesia. This 'Melanesian' population extended to Fiji, but did not reach or affect the Polynesian archipelagos of Tonga and Samoa (Garanger 1971; Green 1972; Golson 1974). Since Fiji formed the eastern boundary of a Melanesian population movement, it was logical to examine the post-Lapita archaeological record for evidence of cultural arrival and replacement, especially from possible stratigraphic discontinuities in the pottery sequence and a comparison of Fijian ceramics with ceramics in island groups to the west. As a result, the recording and comparison of Fijian pottery has involved unusually detailed attribute recording and statistical analysis to identify points of dramatic change in ceramics that might represent the arrival of a new group or evidence of cultural contact (Frost 1970; Birks 1973; Best 1984; Hunt 1986; Crosby 1988; Clark 2000a). In recent years, questions of migration and culture change have broadened, with the application of transmission theory to ceramics (Clark and Murray 2006; Cochrane 2008) and the compositional study of prehistoric materials, particularly ceramic temper and fabric, to examine the timing and extent of intra-archipelago and inter-archipelago contacts (Best 1984, 2002; Green 1996; Clark 2000a, b; Cochrane and Neff 2006; Dickinson 2006).

Central questions about the affinities and meaning of change in the Fijian ceramic sequence remain, despite enhanced methodological sophistication in quantifying prehistoric interaction from sourcing archaeological materials. In this chapter, ceramic data from selected sites is used to examine the central issue of culture change in the post-Lapita period of Fiji. The EPF ceramic assemblages are described in Chapter 11 (see also Clark 2000a). The interpretation of Lapita ceramics in Fiji, including the possibility of an early division between west Fiji and east Fiji, has implications for understanding the colonisation pattern and diversity of Lapita groups entering Fiji (Burley and Dickinson 2001; Clark and Anderson 2001; Best 2002), an issue which cannot be examined using the EPF collections alone, and the topic is examined elsewhere (Chapter 16; Clark and Anderson 2001; Clark and Murray 2006; Clark and Bedford 2008).

Post-Lapita contact between Vanuatu and Fiji

Points of significant stylistic change in the Fijian ceramic sequence have been viewed as the result of a migration from Vanuatu to Fiji, primarily because of the identification of Vanuatu obsidian on Lakeba Island in east Fiji dating to ca. 1700 BP, but also because of the perceived stylistic similarities of Fijian pottery to ceramics found in Vanuatu (Wahome 1998; Best 2002:31; Spriggs 2003; Burley 2005; Cochrane 2008). A postulated Vanuatu migration to Fiji in the post-Lapita period is critical to the interpretation of the Fiji sequence as it supports an intrusionist explanation for the greater amount of biological, cultural and linguistic variation seen in West Pacific populations, which contrasts with the comparative biological and linguistic homogeneity of Polynesian groups in the East Pacific.

Recent work involving the reanalysis of obsidian flakes from several Lakeba sites in east Fiji that were sourced to Vanuatu (Best 1984:434) reveals that the obsidian does not originate from Vanuatu as previously thought. Geochemical analysis of 12 pieces of the 'Vanuatu' obsidian with LA-ICP-MC and MC-ICP-MS indicates the material most likely derives from a source in the Fiji–Tonga region, and it does not originate from any of the major obsidian sources in the West and Central Pacific (Reepmeyer and Clark 2009). This finding removes the only piece of physical evidence for contact between Vanuatu and Fiji in the post-colonisation era (ca. 2500–1000 cal. BP).

The absence of physical evidence for a connection between Fiji and Vanuatu in the post-Lapita period raises questions about the ceramic methods, evidence and models used to infer prehistoric migration and interaction within and beyond Fiji. For example, while a substantial migration to Fiji could reasonably be expected to result in the transmission of a large part of a Vanuatu ceramic complex – as shown by the similarity between ceramic assemblages found at migrant source and destination – the effects of inter-archipelago interaction, trade and exchange on a pottery assemblage is more complicated, as these might result in only the partial transmission of the ceramic repertoire. In the following sections, the evidence and methods used to hypothesise a Vanuatu–Fiji connection from the ceramic sequence of Fiji are critically reviewed, and data suggesting that changes in the ceramic sequence of Fiji originate primarily from socio-economic events within the archipelago is presented.

In Pacific ethnology and archaeology there is a long tradition of using individual ceramic traits/attributes to postulate a 'Melanesian' movement to Fiji that transformed the composition and culture of the founding population (see Clark 2000a; Bedford and Clark 2001; Bedford 2006). From such work, it was possible to postulate a widespread post-Lapita interaction network that connected Fiji with island groups to the west such as Vanuatu, New Caledonia and the Solomon Islands (Galipaud 1996; Spriggs 1997:161–162; Wahome 1997, 1998).

As knowledge has improved about prehistoric ceramics from Island Melanesia, particularly Vanuatu, the perceived similarities between Fijian pottery and that of other island groups to the west have diminished substantially. In the 1970s, Garanger (1971:62) said that the pottery of Fiji was 'exactly the same as the pottery of Mangaasi [in Vanuatu]', whereas in the more recent work of Best (2002:30) the stylistic similarities are reduced to three techniques (asymmetric incising, finger pinching and rim notching), and the source of these traits lies in the poorly known ceramic assemblages of northern Vanuatu. However, despite Best's (2002) claim, recent investigations by Bedford and Spriggs (2008) in northern Vanuatu indicate that Vanuatu ceramics are not related to the post-Lapita assemblages from Fiji. In addition, Sheppard and Walter (2006) have also failed to identify a widespread incised and applied ceramic tradition in pottery assemblages in the western Solomons.

West Pacific ceramic connections with Fiji

Archaeologists working in Fiji have elaborated a post-Lapita connection with Vanuatu from detailed ceramic investigations. The studies of Burley (2005) and Cochrane (2008) are reviewed because they involve new data and approaches that constitute the strongest case for prehistoric culture contact and interaction across the 850 km water gap separating Fiji from Vanuatu in the post-colonisation era.

Investigations at the Sigatoka Sand Dunes in south Viti Levu by Burley (2005) identified a sharp break within post-Lapita Level 2 ceramics, with the oldest assemblage labelled 'Fijian Plainware' because of its perceived affinities to late-Lapita pottery at the dune (Birks 1973). Above the Fijian Plainwares there was a more recent 'Navatu phase' assemblage thought to have been influenced by contact with Vanuatu.

The two assemblages were described as stylistically distinct, although radiocarbon dates indicate they were separated from one another by only a century or two (see Chapter 7). The Fijian Plainware ceramics contained subglobular jars with everted to slightly inverted flattened rims, cups and bowls, with the main decorative techniques comprising parallel rib and cross-hatch paddle impression, punctate, notched lip (single and alternate side). Navatu ceramics consisted of thin-walled globular jars with a flaring everted rim, along with jar forms similar to those in the Fijian Plainwares (Burley 2005:Table 2), cups, bowls and flat-based 'salt' trays. The Navatu assemblage was marked with tool impressions (end, side, fingernail) and incisions that did not occur in the Fijian Plainwares, although other techniques were common to both groups, like punctation, parallel-rib impression, and lip notching (single and alternate side).

The extent of the Plainware/Navatu ceramic 'break' described by Burley (2005) and the perceived relationship of Plainware ceramics to the late-Lapita pottery at Sigatoka is difficult to evaluate from the published data. Vessel-form identifications suggest that Plainware and Navatu assemblages share 60% of vessel forms and 46% of decorative applications (Burley 2005:Table 2 and Table 3), indicating a connection between the two ceramic groups, rather than rapid replacement of Plainware pottery by Vanuatu-influenced Navatu assemblages. An example is cross-hatch paddle impression, which was not reported from the smaller Navatu-phase assemblage excavated by Burley (Burley 2005:Table 3), yet is reported in the text as being a component of Navatu-phase assemblages (Burley 2005:Figure 5C, 336).

Given the presence of paddle-impressed and punctate-marked ceramics to the west of Fiji, Burley (2005:339, 342) argues for an intrusion of ceramic influences from central Melanesia (Vanuatu–New Caledonia). The intrusive ceramic traits occurred earlier on Lakeba Island, where the 'Vanuatu' obsidian was found, suggesting the Lau Group was influenced by contact with the 'Melanesian' west first, followed by the spread of exotic Navatu-phase ceramic techniques from east Fiji to west Fiji 200 years later. Not only are the dating of the obsidian and the 'exotic' ceramic stylistic traits at Lakeba uncertain (Bedford and Clark 2001), but the obsidian does not originate from northern Vanuatu (Reepmeyer and Clark 2009), and the hypothesis relies fundamentally on a questionable assumption that the stylistic differences between Fijian Plainware and Navatu-phase ceramics were the result of prehistoric contact with Vanuatu.

Whereas previous researchers have used numerical taxonomy to investigate and evaluate change in Fijian ceramics, Cochrane (2008) uses transmission theory to evaluate the relative likelihood of cultural transmission between Fiji and Vanuatu. Ceramics from the Yasawa Islands in west Fiji were described using units (classes) designed to track homologous similarity (similarity that is the result of shared ancestry) and these classes were compared with those obtained on published Vanuatu rim cross-sections (Bedford and Clark 2001; Bedford 2006). Ceramic dimensions and modes (cf. classes and attributes in numerical taxonomy) of shouldered rim sherds used in the study were rim curvature (8 modes), angle (3 modes), symmetry (7 modes), thickness (3 modes) and first temper abundance (5 modes). Cladistic analysis identified potential phylogenetic transmission patterns by using temporally defined ceramic classes (early and late prehistoric) which had the most members. Equally parsimonious phylogenetic trees generated ceramic classes that suggested possible cultural transmission between Fiji and Vanuatu before and after 2100 BP.

While transmission theory has several advantages over the *post hoc* evaluation of culture change in numerical taxonomy, the quality of the ceramic data (dimension and modes) is a major concern, as is the assertion that the ceramic dimensions measure homologous similarity due to prehistoric contact, rather than deriving from the ancestral ceramic assemblages introduced during the Lapita colonisation of Fiji and Vanuatu. In regard to the latter point, the inclusion of 'First temper abundance' is unlikely to track homologous similarity because the availability of different tempers is conditioned by local geological and environmental conditions, as well as by landscape change due to sea-level variation and anthropogenic impacts on the environment, rather than cultural preference for a type of temper sand. In Palau, the earliest ceramics were tempered with calcareous and volcanic sands, which were no longer readily available on Babeldoab after anthropogenic upland erosion, island subsidence and the ensuing expansion of mangroves over 80% of the coastline. As an alternative to increasingly scarce beach sand tempers (Clark 2005) potters instead turned to 'grog' (prefired clay).

Both 'early' and 'late' ceramic clades in the phylogenetic hierarchy contained Yasawa and Vanuatu ceramic classes representing 'transmission within a combined Vanuatu-Yasawa population' (Cochrane 2008:142). The three ceramic classes (12321, 22121, 12121) comprising five dimension modes suggested culture contact between Vanuatu and Fiji in the early prehistoric period, from the presence of vessels with an expanded rim, a rim angle between 70° and 90°, and calcium carbonate temper. The ceramic classes differ in their rim angle (as defined by Cochrane 2008) and thickness. Although ceramic transmission analysis is a promising avenue for investigating prehistoric migration and culture contact, the small number of generic ceramic dimensions/modes and the exclusion of crucial vessel size and decoration information in Cochrane's study mean that the results are not by themselves accurate enough to infer inter-archipelago voyaging between Vanuatu and Fiji, particularly now that the 'Vanuatu' obsidian from Lakeba has been reassessed as deriving from the Fiji–Tonga region (Reepmeyer and Clark 2009), and ceramic assemblages from several parts of Vanuatu have been explicitly described as being unlike the post-Lapita pottery of Fiji (Bedford 2006; Bedford and Spriggs 2008).

Ceramic diversification and vessel trajectories

Several observers have argued for a dramatic change in the ceramic sequence of the post-Lapita period of Fiji, with researchers divided over the timing and significance of stylistic change and whether change stems from internal or external events. In a multi-dimensional scaling analysis (MDS) of fixed and continuous attributes from jar rims from Ugaga, Karobo, Navatu and Sigatoka, the late-Lapita rims clustered together, while post-Lapita rim forms dating to ca. 1800–1000 BP had the greatest amount of stylistic variability (Clark 2000a:179–181, Figures 37a–b, 38a–b, 43). The main issue is whether a) this variability results from the replacement of Fijian Plainware assemblages with Navatu-phase ceramics, as suggested by Burley (2005), and b) Navatu-phase pottery can be demonstrated to be similar to prehistoric ceramics from Vanuatu. These two associations underpin the case for a sharp division between Lapita-derived Fiji Plainwares and the foreign-influenced Navatu-phase ceramics proposed by Burley (2005), and the case for ongoing Vanuatu–Fiji interaction put forward by Cochrane (2008).

Rim-sherd attributes are commonly used in empirical studies of pottery assemblages, but such comparisons can be problematic because the attributes derive from small portions of vessels and observations of vessel morphology may not be accurate. An alternative is to use observations from whole vessels, which have been determined from partial or complete parts of a prehistoric vessel. Overall, vessel morphology is likely to be culturally constrained when ceramics are made by household production or household industry modes (Rice 1987:184), which have been proposed in Fiji from physiochemical analyses showing local production (Clark 2000a:214). Under these production conditions, ceramics adhere to accepted forms as they are manufactured primarily by, and for, the local community, although in some instances pottery-making communities also export 'domestic' vessels to non-pottery making groups. An example of pottery with constrained vessel proportions is a sample of 59 utilitarian containers made for domestic use by the pottery-producing community on Mailu in island New Guinea, recorded by Irwin (1985), which have coefficients of variation for vessel height and maximum body diameter of 12–13% (R^2=0.657).

For Fiji, 'jars' from Sigatoka Level 1 (n=45) and Level 2 (n=11) published in Birks (1973) were scanned and resized in Adobe Illustrator to the tabulated vessel size. Two additional vessels from the Level 2 deposit at Sigatoka (Burley 2005:Figure 5d and Figure 6a), and reconstructed 'jars' from Vanuatu (n=25) dating from the first two millennia of occupation were scanned and resized (Bedford 2006), and four estimated vessel dimensions were recorded (exterior diameter, internal diameter, vessel height, maximum body width). The dimensions of whole vessels can be used to illustrate the morphological pattern of Fijian jar forms at different points in time, and the vessel dimensions can be compared with Vanuatu vessels to determine whether Fijian jars have similar vessel proportions, consistent with ceramic transmission.

In Figure 134, vessel height (cm) is plotted against a vessel-width index made by multiplying aperture diameter (cm) by the maximum body diameter (cm)/100. The plot separates Sigatoka late-Lapita jars, which are characterised by a subglobular body and a vessel height smaller than maximum body diameter. There is a very strong correlation (R^2=0.917) between vessel height and maximum body diameter, demonstrating that late Lapita potters at Sigatoka produced jars with highly consistent vessel proportions, despite substantial variability in container size.

In comparison, Fijian Plainware and Navatu-phase ceramics from Level 2 are significantly more variable, especially in their aperture dimensions, and are distinguished from Sigatoka Level 1 jars by their greater vessel height and volume. The R^2 value for maximum body diameter against vessel height for these vessels is 0.637, similar to domestic pots from Mailu. One Navatu vessel (Birks Vessel No. 237) has a subglobular body and similar vessel dimensions to some Level 1 jars, highlighting the variability among post-Lapita vessels.

It is clear that vessel proportions do not demonstrate a close relationship between Fijian Plainware jars and Sigatoka jars of late-Lapita age. Fijian Plainware vessel proportions are most like those of Navatu-phase ceramics, which supports the idea of some continuity between the two Sigatoka Level 2 assemblages, rather than ceramic replacement of Fijian Plainwares by Navatu-phase ceramics. This was also seen in the number of shared vessel forms and continuity in the main types of decoration (Burley 2005:Tables 2 and 3). Fijian Plainwares demonstrate a tendency towards a small aperture size relative to vessel height, which nonetheless is a trait also present in some Navatu-phase jars, and possibly relates to a functional change, as a small vessel aperture reduces evaporation when cooking (Rice 1987:241).

The dimensions of 25 reconstructed Vanuatu jars are plotted with the Sigatoka vessels in Figure 135. Compared with Sigatoka jars, those from Vanuatu are most like Sigatoka late-Lapita jars in their vessel proportions, but are less subglobular in having a slightly greater vessel height. The Vanuatu vessels are also distinct in their proportions from the Plainware and Navatu jars of Sigatoka Level 2, which have a greater vessel height. However, one Vanuatu vessel (6.18a) has some similarity to three Plainware/Navatu vessels (205, 217, 233) while a Navatu vessel (237) plots close to two Vanuatu vessels (6.17 318(2) and 6.2a).

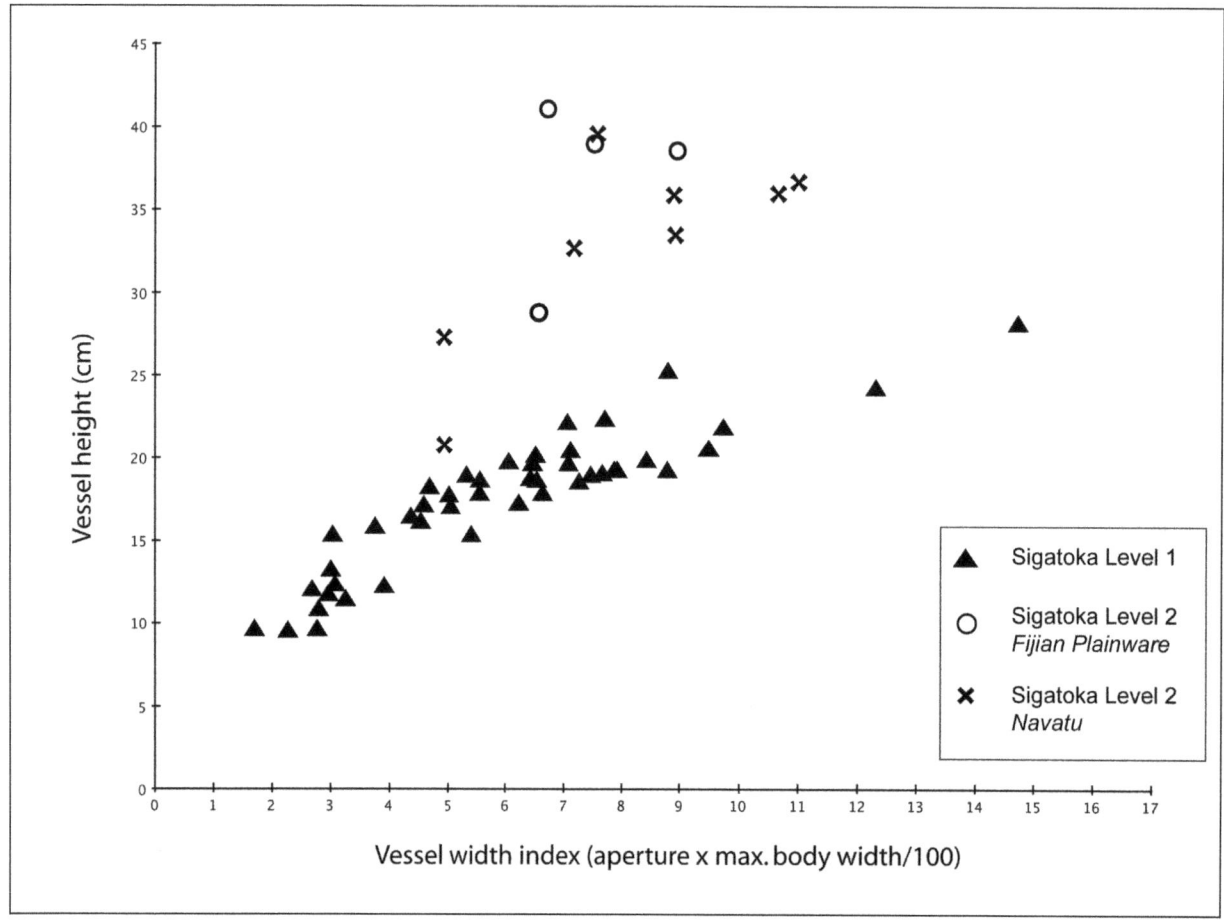

Figure 134. Late-Lapita and post-Lapita jar proportions. Triangles=Sigatoka Level 1 Birks (1973) vessels 120, 70, 10, 27, 26, 99, 29, 117, 23, 121, 92, 37, 122, 67, 66, 113, 72, 61, 90, 95, 25, 38, 4, 48, 88, 68, 40, 21, 57, 112, 86, 69, 87, 89, 94, 6, 50, 103, 71, 79, 91, 101, 111, 141, 82). Crosses=Sigatoka Level 2 Navatu phase Birks (1973) vessels 239, 237, 217, 276, 233, 233, 221, Burley (2005:vessel Figure 5b). Circles=Sigatoka Level 2 Fijian Plainware, Birks (1973) vessels 205, 271, 277, and Burley (2005) vessel shown in Figure 6a. Note the separation between Sigatoka Level 1 jars and Sigatoka Level 2 jars, and overlap in vessel proportions between Fijian Plainwares and Navatu phase jars, highlighting continuity in vessel form.

The great advantage of dealing with reconstructed vessel forms is that we can directly compare Fijian and Vanuatu vessels of similar proportions to see whether they are similar in other aspects, such as rim form, angle and decoration. The vessels plotting closest to Vanuatu 6.18a and Fiji 237 are shown at the same scale in Figure 136, along with details of decoration and surface markings on each. There is no convincing example of vessel similarity from inspection of lip and rim form and the type of decoration, although a larger comparison of reconstructed vessel forms could reveal stronger vessel analogues.

Nonetheless, the analysis of vessel proportions does indicate a significant break between the late-Lapita assemblages of Sigatoka dating to 2650 cal. BP and the later Fijian Plainware/Navatu-phase assemblages produced at 1300–1500 cal. BP. Since the stylistic 'break' between the Level 1 and Level 2 ceramics covers around 1000 years, there may well be pottery assemblages that when eventually described will form transitional assemblages between the late-Lapita and the post-Lapita ceramics (see Hunt 1986). It is also apparent that the vessel proportion analysis has upheld Burley's observation of increased stylistic diversity within post-Lapita assemblages relative to late-Lapita pottery. This has been ascribed to post-Lapita influence and contact with Vanuatu, but in fact New Caledonia has decorative traits such as parallel and cross-hatch paddle

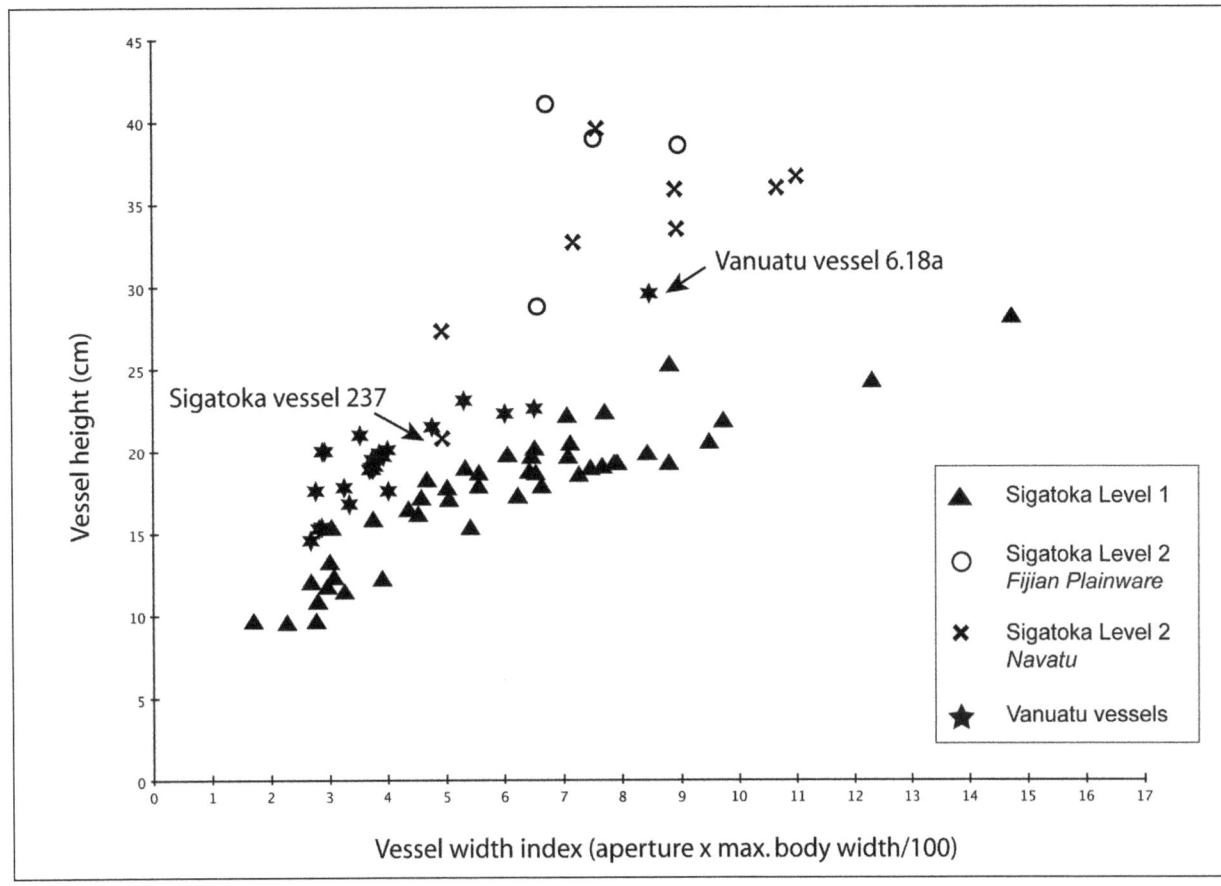

Figure 135. Fijian late-Lapita and post-Lapita jar proportions compared to reconstructed Vanuatu jars illustrated in Bedford (2006). Triangles=Sigatoka Level 1 jars, Crosses=Sigatoka Level 2 Navatu phase jars, Circles=Sigatoka Level 2 Fijian Plainware jars, Stars=Vanuatu jars.

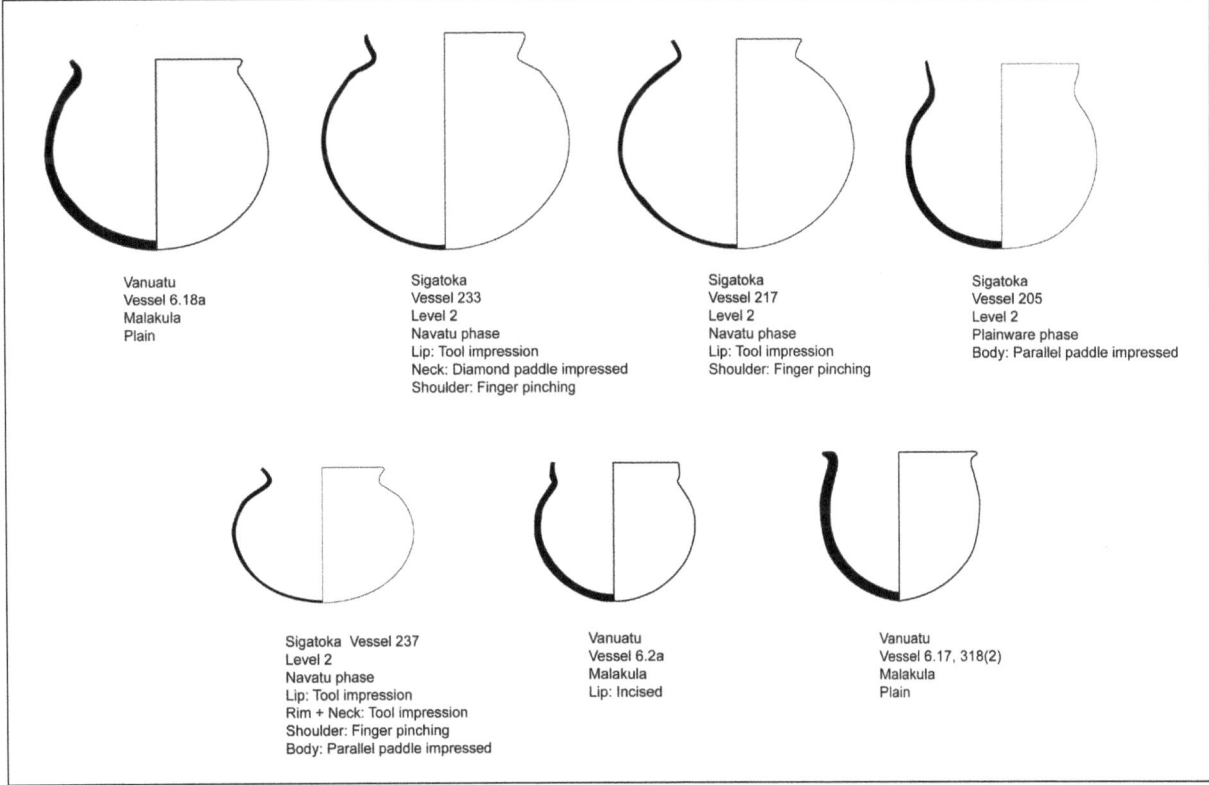

Figure 136. Comparison of Vanuatu vessel 6.18a with three Sigatoka Level 2 jars (top row) and Sigatoka Level 2 vessel 237 with Vanuatu vessels (see Figure 135). The Fijian jars are distinct in decoration and morphology from the Vanuatu jars.

impression, along with cord marking, that are also found in Fiji. The mistaken attribution of the post-Lapita obsidian from Lakeba as deriving from Vanuatu has been the main reason why the task of establishing the ceramic similarities between New Caledonian and Fiji has received less attention than a presumed Fij–Vanuatu connection, and this is a topic that remains to be properly explored (see Clark 2000a:240–241; Bedford 2006:181–182).

Mid-sequence ceramic change

If the evidence for external influences on the Fijian ceramic sequence is not convincing, as I have argued, then we are still left with the question about the cause of stylistic diversity and the meaning of ceramic change in the Fiji Islands in the post-Lapita period. Ceramic collections from many parts of Fiji have traits similar to those of the Sigatoka Level 2 assemblages described by Birks (1973) and Burley (2005). These include several types of paddle impression, tool impression, finger pinching and incision, along with distinctive vessel forms like the flat-based tray that Burley (2005:333) suggests was used in salt production. One important post-Lapita vessel is the double-spouted vessel (Figure 137), which has been found on Viti Levu (Sigatoka, Navatu, Vuda, Karobo), Beqa Island (Ugaga Island), Taveuni (Navolivoli) and Cikobia (CIK-021). The widespread distribution of this unique vessel form through much of the Fiji Group argues for a degree of post-Lapita intra-archipelago connectivity (Clark and Sorovi-Vunidilo 1999). At the same time, there is also significant variability at the intra-assemblage level, as demonstrated by the vessel proportions of Sigatoka Level 2 jars. What does this contradictory picture of stylistic association say about social interaction?

According to Lyman and O'Brian (2000), the richness of decorative types or styles is often correlated with social dynamics, especially the frequency of group interaction or intergroup transmission. As Davis (in Conkey 1992:12) puts it: '. . . if we interpret stylistic similarity as

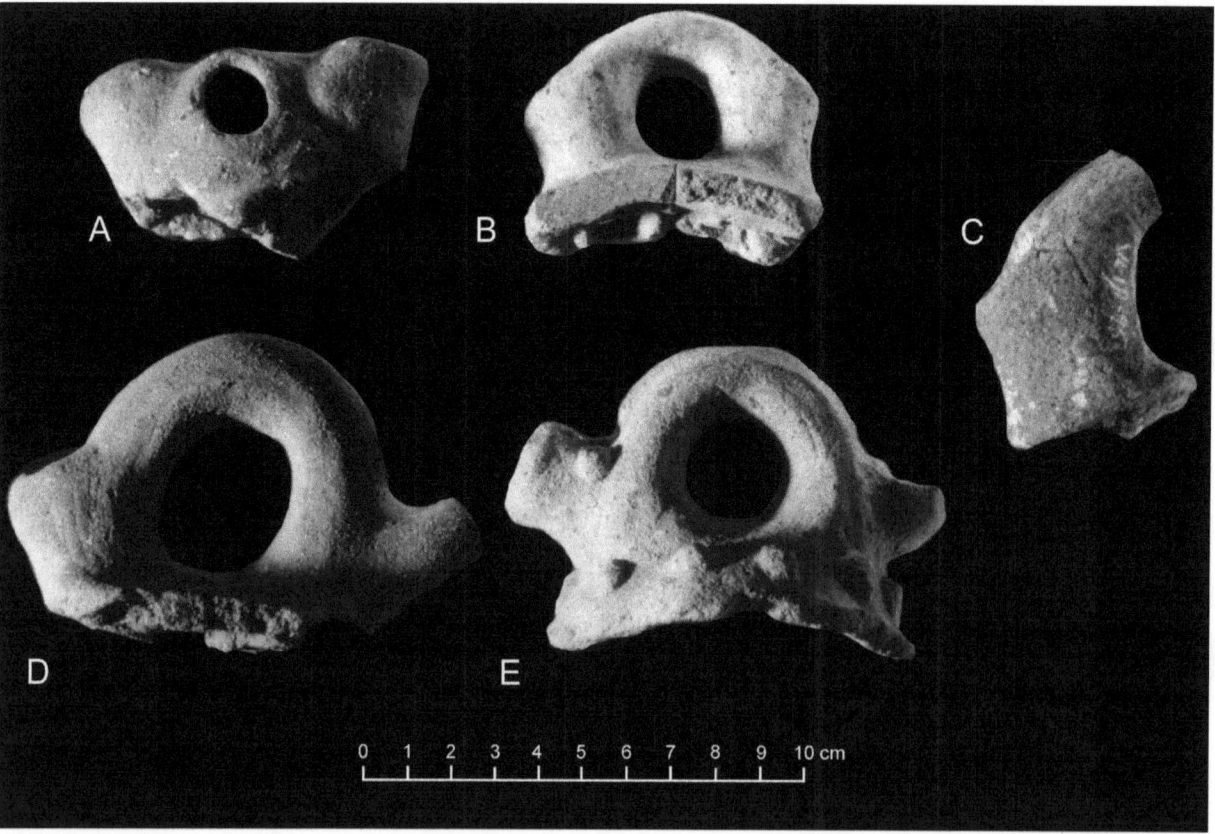

Figure 137. Fijian double-spouted vessels. A=Natunuku, B=Navatu, C=Natunuku, D=Sigatoka, E=Navatu.

indicating social interaction among the producers of artefacts, then we must simultaneously interpret it as also indicating a "social boundary" – for where similarity decreases, by hypothesis we are seeing less social interaction.' Increasing stylistic diversity between groups can come about because potters are increasing isolated, causing decorative styles and vessel proportions to evolve in independent directions. The known post-Lapita assemblages of Fiji, however, do not appear to be sufficiently independent of one another to argue for significant ceramic divergence as the result of social isolation (Best 1984). If ceramic divergence was a feature of the post-Lapita period then we should see significant differences between geographically distant assemblages, but this has not been proposed in any ceramic study, with researchers able to describe pottery assemblages from throughout Fiji using a common terminology (Frost 1970; Best 1984; Crosby 1988; Rechtman 1992; J. Clark and Cole 1997; Hunt et al. 1999; Clark 2000a).

An alternative proposed by Neiman (1995) is that within-assemblage ceramic diversity scales with the effective population size and the innovation rate. The innovation rate is controlled by the number of intergroup transmissions, with high stylistic diversity representing high levels of intergroup contact. Fiji is a large and dispersed archipelago and it is probable that some potting communities were more isolated than others and developed semi-localised pottery styles, and also that population increase contributed to increasing intra-assemblage diversity. However, there are sufficient similarities among post-Lapita ceramic assemblages to suggest that rates of interaction were sufficient for a distinctive Fijian ceramic complex to develop over much of the archipelago during the post-Lapita period, even though coastal potting groups may have had higher rates of intergroup contact compared with inland communities and potting groups on distant islands like those of southern Lau, which might have been relatively isolated from stylistic developments on the main islands. Along with the effect of population increase on the innovation rate, the extension of social and trade networks in post-Lapita times may well have enhanced stylistic diversity by increasing the frequency and intensity of intergroup contact as well as introducing stylistic variability from contact with communities whose ceramics had become partially 'localised'. Population increase is frequently accompanied by human dispersal to new environments, and during post-Lapita times palaeoecological and archaeological evidence demonstrates an increasing focus on the settlement of interior landscapes (Chapters 4 and 16). Such movements involved new adaptations, particularly economic emphasis on horticulture and new social configurations relating to land use, and trade and exchange networks with coastal groups. These social and economic changes, which remain to be investigated in detail, likely stimulated change in material culture, including the size, shape and decoration of ceramic containers.

In their panmictic characteristics, the post-Lapita ceramics of Fiji stand in contrast to the more regionalised ceramic assemblages known from New Caledonia and Vanuatu (Sand 1996, 1999; Bedford 2006; Bedford and Spriggs 2008). Environmental variability among the Fiji Islands may be a significant driver of archipelago interaction as it may have been advantageous for populations on the numerous small to medium-sized islands to have strong social and economic relationships with groups on the large islands of Viti Levu, Vanua Levu, Kadavu and Taveuni – a situation that would have encouraged the spread of stylistic traits. Webster (1975) suggested that juxtaposed zones of differing productive and demographic potential were important for the emergence of social complexity, of which the development of archipelago networks in the post-Lapita period of Fiji might be one manifestation. In contrast, the Grande Terre of New Caledonia and island-rich archipelago of Vanuatu (12 islands with a land area greater than 300 sq. m compared with Fiji which has three islands) have a potentially more even distribution of archipelagic resources that could have led to lower rates of inter-group contact, leading to greater stylistic independence and ceramic divergence. We require much more empirical data and new models to examine in detail the relationship between island geography, resource distribution and culture patterning, but one starting point would be to investigate whether archipelagic variability in language and material-culture diversity correlates with environmental and topographic variation. Although exogenous explanations for ceramic change in Fiji cannot be entirely ruled out given current knowledge of the prehistoric sequence, they now receive less archaeological support than at any time in the past (Sheppard and Walter 2006; Reepmeyer and Clark 2009), and models featuring culture change as the result of internal archipelago processes (e.g. Rechtman 1992; Field 2004, 2005) must also be considered.

References

Bedford, S. 2006. *Pieces of the Vanuatu puzzle: Archaeology of the north, south and centre*. Terra Australis 23. Pandanus Books, Canberra.

Bedford, S. and Clark, G.R. 2001. The rise and rise of the Incised and Applied Relief Tradition: A review and reassessment. In: Clark, G.R., Anderson, A.J. and Vunidilo, T. (eds), *The Archaeology of the Lapita Dispersal in Oceania*, pp. 61–74. Pandanus Books, Canberra.

Bedford, S. and Spriggs, M. 2008. Northern Vanuatu as a Pacific crossroads. The archaeology of discovery, interaction, and the emergence of the ethnographic present *Asian Perspectives* 47(1): 95–120.

Best, S. 1984. Lakeba: The prehistory of a Fijian Island. Unpublished PhD thesis, Department of Anthropology, University of Auckland.

Best, S. 2002. *Lapita: A view from the east*. New Zealand Archaeological Association Monographs 24, Auckland, New Zealand Archaeological Association.

Binford, L.R. 1972. Contemporary model building: Paradigms and the current state of Palaeolithic research. In: Clarke, D.L. (ed), *Models in Archaeology*, pp. 109–166. Methuen and Co Ltd, Great Britain.

Birks, L. 1973. Archaeological excavations at Sigatoka dune site, Fiji. *Bulletin of the Fiji Museum* No.1.

Burley, D. 2005. Mid-sequence archaeology at the Sigatoka Sand Dunes with interpretive implications for Fijian and Oceanic culture history. *Asian Perspectives* 44(2): 320–348.

Burley, D.V. and Dickinson, W.R. 2001. Origin and significance of a founding settlement in Polynesia. *Proceedings of the National Academy of Sciences USA* 98: 11829–11831.

Clark, G.R. 2000a. Post-Lapita Fiji: Cultural transformation in the mid-sequence, Unpublished PhD thesis, Australian National University, Canberra.

Clark, G.R. 2000b. Mid-sequence isolation in the Fijian archipelago 2500–1000 BP. *Bulletin of the Indo-Pacific Prehistory Association* 19(3): 152–158.

Clark, G.R. 2003. Shards of meaning: Archaeology and the Melanesia–Polynesia divide. *The Journal of Pacific History* 38(2): 197–215.

Clark, G. 2005. A 3000-year culture sequence from Palau, western Micronesia. *Asian Perspectives* 44: 349–380.

Clark, G. and Sorovi-Vunidilo, T. 1999. Double-spouted vessels from Fiji. *Domodomo* 11(2): 6–11.

Clark, G. and Anderson, A. 2001. The pattern of Lapita settlement in Fiji. *Archaeology in Oceania* 36: 77–88.

Clark, G.R. and Murray, T. 2006. Decay characteristics of the eastern Lapita design system. *Archaeology in Oceania* 41: 107–117.

Clark, G. and Bedford, S. 2008. Friction zones in Lapita colonisation. In: Clark, G.R. Leach, F. and

O'Connor, S. (eds), *Islands of Inquiry: Colonisation, seafaring and the archaeology of maritime landscapes*, pp. 59–73. Terra Australis 29. Canberra, ANU E Press.

Clark, J.T. and Cole, T. 1997. Environmental change and human prehistory in the Central Pacific: Archaeological and palynological investigations on Totoya Island, Fiji. Unpublished report to the Fiji Museum, Suva.

Cochrane, E.E. 2008. Migration and cultural transmission: Investigating human movement as an explanation for Fijian ceramic change. In: O'Brian, M.J. (ed), *Cultural transmission and archaeology: Issues and case studies*, pp. 132–145. Society for American Archaeology, The SAA Press, Washington, DC.

Cochrane, E.E. and Neff, H. 2006. Investigating compositional diversity among Fijian ceramics with laser ablation-inductively coupled plasma-mass spectrometry (LA-ICP-MS): Implications for interaction studies on geologically similar islands. *Journal of Archaeological Science* 33: 378–390.

Conkey, M.W. 1992. Experimenting with style in archaeology: some historical and theoretical issues. In: Conkey, M. and Hastorf, C. (eds), *The uses of style in archaeology*, pp. 5–17. Cambridge University Press, Cambridge.

Crosby, A. 1988. Beqa: archaeology, structure and history in Fiji. Unpublished MA thesis, Department of Anthropology, University of Auckland.

Derrick, R.A. 1974. *A history of Fiji*. Government Press, Suva.

Dickinson, W.R. 2006. *Temper sands in Prehistoric Oceanian pottery: Geotectonics, sedimentology, petrography, provenance*. Geological Society of America Special Papers 406. The Geological Society of America, Boulder, Colorado.

Field, J.S. 2004. Environmental and climatic considerations: A hypothesis for conflict and the emergence of social complexity in Fijian prehistory. *Journal of Anthropological Archaeology* 23: 79–99.

Field, J.S. 2005. Land tenure, competition and ecology in Fijian prehistory. *Antiquity* 79: 586–600.

Field, J.S., Cochrane, E.E. and Greenlee, D.M. 2009. Dietary change in Fijian prehistory: Isotopic analyses of human and animal skeletal material. *Journal of Archaeological Science* 36: 1547–1556.

Frost, E.L. 1970. Archaeological Excavations of fortified sites on Taveuni, Fiji. Unpublished PhD thesis, University of Oregon.

Galipaud, J-C. 1996. New Caledonia: some recent archaeological perspectives. In: Davidson, J.M., Irwin, G., Leach, B.F., Pawley, A. and Brown, D. (eds), *Oceanic culture history: Essays in honour of Roger Green*, pp. 297–305. New Zealand Journal of Archaeology Special Publication.

Garanger, J. 1971. Incised and applied-relief pottery, its chronology and development in southeastern Melanesia, and extra areal comparisons. In: Green, R.C. and Kelly, M. (eds), *Studies in Oceanic Culture History Volume 2*, pp. 53–99. Pacific Anthropological Records No. 12.

Gifford, E.W. 1951. Archaeological excavations in Fiji. *University of California Anthropological Records* 13: 189–288.

Golson, J. 1961. Report on New Zealand, Western Polynesia, New Caledonia, and Fiji. *Asian Perspectives* 5: 166–180.

Golson, J. 1974. Both sides of the Wallace Line: New Guinea, Australia, Island Melanesia and Asian prehistory. In: Barnard, N. (ed), *Early Chinese art and its possible influence in the Pacific Basin*, pp. 533–595. Proceedings of a symposium arranged by the Department of Art History and Archaeology, Columbia University, New York City and Taiwan.

Green, R.C. 1972. Aspects of the Neolithic in Oceania. In: N. Barnard (ed), *Early Chinese art and its possible influences in the Pacific Basin, Volume 3*, pp. 655–691. Proceedings of a symposium arranged by the Department of Art History and Archaeology, Columbia University, New York City and Taiwan

Green, R.C. 1996. Prehistoric transfers of portable items during the Lapita horizon in Remote Oceania: A review. *Bulletin of the Indo-Pacific Prehistory Association* 15: 119–130.

Hunt, T.L. 1980. Towards Fiji's Past: Archaeological research on southwestern Viti Levu. Unpublished MA Thesis. Department of Anthropology, University of Auckland.

Hunt, T.L. 1986. Conceptual and substantive issues in Fijian prehistory. In: Kirch, P.V. (ed), *Archaeological approaches to evolution and transformation*, pp. 20–32. Cambridge University Press, Cambridge.

Hunt, T.L., Aronson, K.F., Cochrane, E.E., Field, J.S., Humphrey, L. and Rieth, T.M. 1999. A preliminary report on archaeological research in the Yasawa Islands, Fiji. *Domodomo* 12(2): 5–43.

Irwin, G. 1985. *The emergence of Mailu: as a central place in coastal Papuan prehistory*. Terra Australis 10, Department of Prehistory, Research School of Pacific and Asian Studies, Australian National University.

Lyman, R. Lee and O'Brian, M.J. 2000. Measuring and explaining change in artifact variation with clade-diversity diagrams. *Journal of Anthropological Archaeology* 19: 39–74.

Neiman, F.D. 1995. Stylistic variation in evolutionary perspective: inferences from decorative diversity and interassemblage distance in Illinois Woodland ceramic assemblages. *American Antiquity* 60(1): 7–36.

Palmer, B. 1974. Pottery in the South Pacific. In: Barnard, N. (ed), *Early Chinese art and its possible influence in the Pacific Basin*, pp. 693–721. Proceedings of a symposium arranged by the Department of Art History and Archaeology, Columbia University, New York City, Taiwan.

Rechtman, R.B. 1992. *The evolution of socio-political complexity in the Fiji Islands*. PhD thesis, Ann Arbor, Michigan.

Reepmeyer, C. and Clark, G. 2009. Post-colonisation interaction between Vanuatu and Fiji reconsidered: The reanalysis of obsidian from Lakeba Island, Fiji. *Archaeometry*.

Rice, P.M. 1987. *Pottery analysis. A source book*. University of Chicago Press, Chicago and London.

Sand, C. 1996. Recent developments in the study of New Caledonia's prehistory. *Archaeology in Oceania* 31: 45–71.

Sand, C. 1999. Lapita and non-Lapita ware during New Caledonia's first millennium of Austronesian settlement. In: Galipaud, J-C. and Lilley, I. (eds), *The Pacific from 5000 to 2000 BP. Colonisation and transformations,* pp. 139–159. Editions de IRD, Paris.

Schmidt, H. 2003. Loanword strata in Rotuman. In: H. Andersen (ed), *Language contacts in prehistory: Studies in stratigraphy*, pp. 201–240. John Benjamins, Amsterdam and Philadelphia.

Sheppard, P. and Walter, R. 2006. A revised model of Solomon Islands culture history. *Journal of the Polynesian Society* 115: 47–76.

Solheim, W.G. II. 1952a. Oceanian pottery manufacture. *Journal of East Asiatic Studies*. 1(2): 1–39.

Solheim, W.G. II. 1952b. Paddle decoration of pottery. *Journal of East Asiatic Studies*. 2(1): 35–45.

Spriggs, M. 1997. *The Island Melanesians*. Blackwell Publishers Ltd, Oxford and Massachusetts.

Spriggs, M. 2003. Post-Lapita evolutions in Island Melanesia. In: Sand, C. (ed), *Pacific archaeology: Assessments and prospects. Proceedings of the International Conference for the 50th anniversary of the first Lapita Excavation, Koné-Nouméa 2002*, pp. 213–220. Les Cahiers de L'Archéologie en Nouvelle-Calédonie, Museum of New Caledonia, Noumea.

Wahome, E.W. 1997. Continuity and change in Lapita and post-Lapita ceramics: A review of evidence from the Admiralty Islands and New Ireland, Papua New Guinea. *Archaeology in Oceania* 32(1): 118–123.

Wahome, E.W. 1998. Ceramic and prehistoric exchange in the Admiralty Islands, Papua New Guinea. Unpublished PhD thesis, Australian National University.

Webster, D. 1975. Warfare and the evolution of the state: A reconsideration. *American Antiquity* 40(4): 464–470.

Wilkes, C. 1985. *Narrative of the United States exploring expedition. Tongataboo, Feejee Group, Honolulu.* Vol. III. Fiji Museum, Suva.

Williams, T. 1985. *Fiji and the Fijians. Vol 1. The islands and their inhabitants*. Fiji Museum, Suva.

13

Compositional analysis of Fijian ceramics

Geoffrey Clark
Department of Archaeology and Natural History, The Australian National University

Douglas Kennett
Department of Anthropology, The University of Oregon

Introduction

The varied geological setting of the Fiji Islands gave rise to clays and temper sands that were combined by prehistoric potters to manufacture ceramics with distinctive constituents. Compositional analysis of pottery can be used to identify non-local sherds, and when comparative geochemical information is available, to delineate a potential ceramic source locale for local and exotic ceramics. The technique of examining mineral and non-mineral materials entrained in clays or added to clays by prehistoric potters was first used by Curtis (1951), who analysed 26 pot sherds excavated by Edward Gifford from the Navatu and Vuda sites in northern Viti Levu. Comprehensive petrographic study of Fijian sherds has been made by Dickinson (1971, 1973, 1980, 1998, 2001, 2006) and Best (1984), with additional work by Petchey (1995), Aronson (1999) and Bentley (2000). Fijian pot clays have been analysed by Best (1984:359–367, Appendix G) and Petchey (1995:142) using X-Ray Florescence and the Electron Microprobe. Kennett et al. (2004) and Bentley (2000) have investigated the chemical composition of Fijian ceramics with Neutron Activation Analysis (NAA) and Microwave Digestion Inductively Coupled Plasma Mass Spectrometry (MD-ICP-MS), and Cochrane (2004) employed Laser Ablation Inductively Coupled Plasma Mass Spectrometry (LA-ICP-MS) on ceramics from the Yasawa Islands.

Petrographic analysis is a potent technique able to reveal pottery transfer over short and long distances, with Fijian ceramics identified from as far afield as Rotuma, Tuvalu, Tokelau, Tonga and Samoa (Dickinson 2006:117–118). The petrographic study of thin sections is time consuming, however, and defining the origin of temper sands requires considerable skill and a detailed knowledge of island geology and geomorphology. Consequently, the number of sherds examined from a particular prehistoric site is often small in relation to the size of the excavated assemblage. It has also been difficult for archaeologists to establish just how common exotic sherds actually are in an assemblage, and whether temper sands were associated with particular vessel forms or decorative techniques (see Best 1984). It has also been argued that non-local ceramics were usually transported as already manufactured containers, rather than as raw materials, although the movement of temper sands has been recorded in several archaeological sites (Best 1984:352; Dickinson 1998:266).

The EPF ceramic collections were analysed using two methods aimed at examining prehistoric interaction in the Fiji Islands. First, our approach built on the proven technique of petrographic examination of sherds by William Dickinson, reinforced by optical examination of three sherd collections under low-power magnification to examine potential linkages between temper, surface decoration, vessel form and ceramic age.

Second, broader patterns of prehistoric interaction were examined through an MD-ICP-MS analysis of sherds from nine sites (Figure 138). In petrography, the mineral grains added or entrained in a clay are identified, but the approach cannot specify whether a sherd clay is exotic, or whether exclusively calcareous-tempered sherds are imports. Chemistry-based MD-ICP-MS measures the bulk element composition of the clay and the temper in a sherd sample. The chemical analysis of sherds using methods such as NAA, MD-ICP-MS and LA-ICD-MS is appealing to archaeologists because relatively large numbers of ceramic samples can be quickly analysed, compared with petrography, and because the recognition of non-local sherds using element data does not necessarily require a detailed knowledge of archipelago geology.

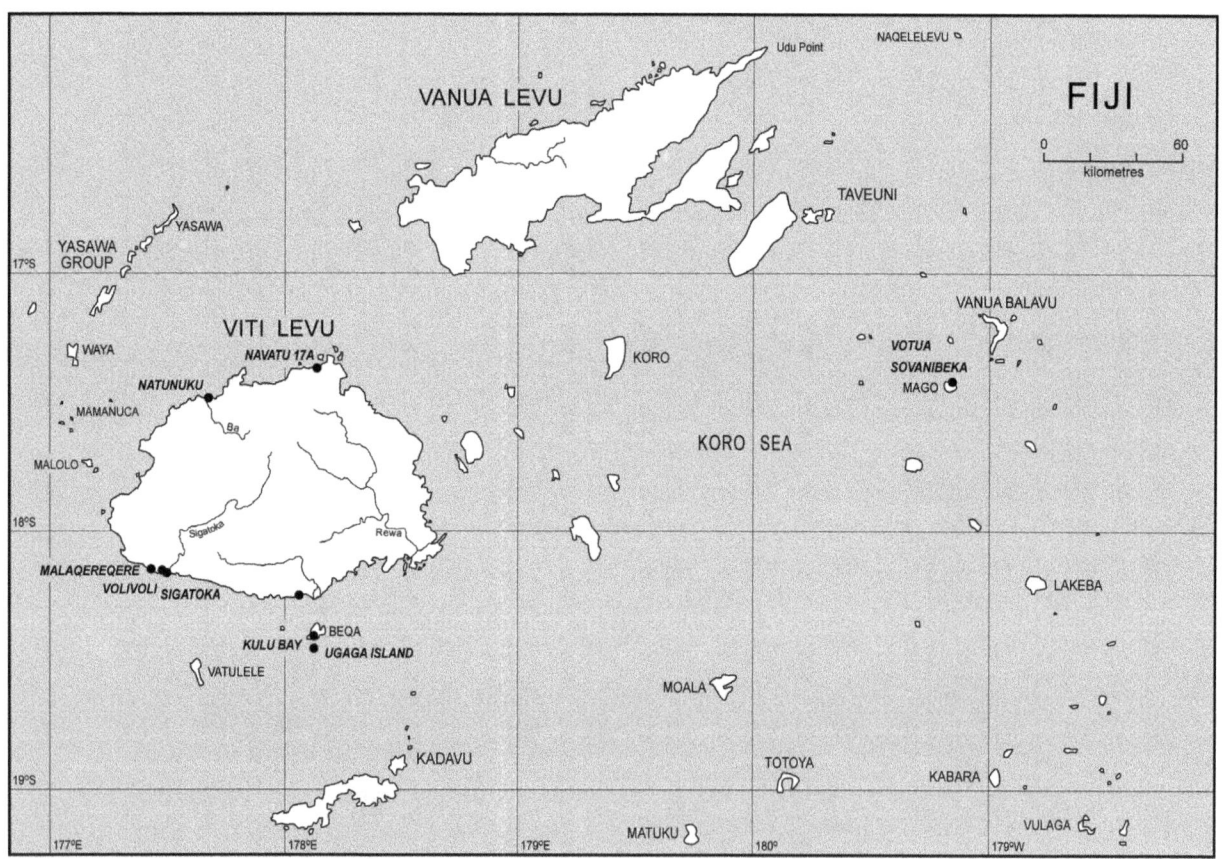

Figure 138. Location of EPF ceramic collections analysed with petrography and MD-ICP-MS.

To examine the correlation between petrographic and chemical results, ceramics from Navatu, Ugaga and Karobo examined with petrology, including identified non-local specimens, were also analysed with MD-ICP-MS.

The MD-ICP-MS results from Ugaga Island and Kulu Bay showed that sherds from the two sites were chemically distinct from one another, while Dickinson's petrology examination identified sherd tempers at both sites as compatible with an origin on Beqa Island, and consistent with the transport of pottery from Kulu Bay and other places on Beqa to the small islet of Ugaga, 2–3 km from the Beqa coast. The chemical signature of sherds may be affected by several factors, including the quantity and number of tempers added to a clay, the duration and intensity of firing, and the chemistry of the depositional environment. Analysis of MD-ICP-MS results from Ugaga Island and Kulu Bay suggest that burial conditions may have changed the element concentrations in pot sherds from one or both sites, and caution should attend multi-site analysis of ceramics based purely on chemical data.

Ceramic samples

A total of 98 sherds from eight archaeological sites was examined in thin section by William Dickinson (see Dickinson 2006 for details), who identified the mineralogy of temper sands and established megascopic guidelines for separating sherds into local temper groups. A total of 896 rim and body sherds from three sites – Navatu 17A, Ugaga and Karobo – was sectioned with a diamond saw, and the cleaned sections examined under low-power magnification and identified to one of Dickinson's megascopic temper groups (Table 60). A total of 219 sherds from nine sites was analysed with chemistry-based MD-ICP-MS, extending an earlier study of 43 Lapita-age sherds from the Ugaga and Kulu sites reported by Kennett et al. (2004).

Table 60. Ceramic samples from Fijian archaeological sites analysed with petrology, low-power microscopy and chemical methods.

Site Location	Petrography: Temper sand	Macroscopic: Temper sand	MD-ICP-MS: Clay + temper
Viti Levu: South Coast			
Sigatoka	1		10
Volivoli II + III			24
Malaqereqere			14
Karobo	10	238	15
Viti Levu: North Coast			
Natunuku	26		31
Navatu 17A	26	253	31
Offshore Islands			
Kulu Bay, Beqa	10		26
Ugaga Island, Beqa	17	405	38
Votua, Mago	5		27
Sovanibeka, Mago	3		3
Total	**98**	**896**	**219**

1. Petrographic and macroscopic examination of sherds from Navatu, Ugaga and Karobo

Generically distinctive temper provenances are empirically definable from an island's geotectonic environment. Indigenous pottery can be inferred from the similarity of temper sands to local island bedrock, while pottery transfer can be identified from the occurrence of exotic temper sands that could not be derived from local island bedrock. The texture of temper assessed from the degree of grain sorting and angularity indicates whether prehistoric potters collected sands from beach, stream or non-coastal terrestrial environments. Temper sands in sherds were examined in thin section, with frequency counts of individual mineral types made from a total of 300–400 identified grains per section (see Dickinson 1998, 2006). Calcareous grains are a common component of many sherd assemblages in Oceania that cannot be used to infer provenance because reef characteristics are similar throughout the region.

Megascopic examination of temper grains is inherently less accurate than petrography since the mineral assemblage is not identified, and the appearance of related tempers may be highly variable as proportions of associated grains of different colouration vary (Dickinson 1998:273). The approach has the advantage, however, that larger sherd samples can be examined to assess whether ceramic tempers vary systematically by excavation stratigraphy/unit, or by vessel form and type of surface decoration. Dickinson's petrographic study identified the temper groups present in three assemblages – Navatu, Ugaga and Karobo – and recorded the megascopic criteria associated with each. Sherds examined megascopically were sectioned with a diamond lapidary saw, and identified to one of Dickinson's temper groups using the megascopic guidelines. Calcareous inclusions were tested with 10% HCl and the strength of the reaction recorded on a scale of 1 (low) to 3 (high).

Navatu 17A temper groups

Temper sands from Navatu 17A sherds consist of a spectrum of related basaltic sands that were subdivided by Dickinson into four subgroups depending on the proportions of plagioclase feldspar and ferromagnesian grains, and the quantity and mineralogy of the extrusive and intrusive igneous rock fragments. Most temper sands were subangular to subrounded, fine to coarse in size, and moderately to well sorted. Calcareous grains occurred in sherds from all temper subgroups at a frequency of 1% to 5%. Temper variants are likely to represent local sands, collected from streams and beaches close to the Navatu 17A site, that eroded from the Ba Volcanic Group (Seeley and Searle 1970).

Standard (non-placer and non-lithic)

The standard tempers contain relatively even proportions of plagioclase feldspars and ferromagnesian grains (mean 22% and 23% respectively), followed by hornblende (10%). Hypabyssal and volcanic rock fragments have a combined frequency mean of 34%. Olivine, epidote and opaque iron oxide are under 10%, while quartz and biotite are rare or absent (≤1%).

Pyroxenic placer (PP)

In the PP temper, pyroxene is dominant, varying from 40% to 82% (mean 75%) of counted grains. Variation is considered to be due to the degree of beach placering. Plagioclase feldspars are present in amounts generally less than 10%, as are other minerals such as hornblende, olivine and opaque iron oxide. Quartz, epidote and biotite constitute 1% or less of the grain types. Hypabyssal fragments are also under 10%, and volcanic rock fragments range from 6% to 21%.

Opaque/Lithic rich (OL)

In these temper variants, the plagioclase feldspars (F) are significantly more abundant than clinopyroxene (C) (mean F/F+C=0.68). The variants are distinguished in thin section by the frequency of opaque iron oxides (16% versus 3%) and rock fragments (59% versus 26%). Hornblende, olivine, epidote and biotite are present in trace or low frequencies (≤3%).

Megascopically, it is difficult to distinguish between the opaque and lithic-rich temper variants, and these are combined into a single subgroup (OL) using the proportion of plagioclase feldspar/lithic to ferromagnesian grains as the main selection criterion. Subgroup identification using low magnification on a highly variable and allied temper spectrum was difficult and the megascopic temper identifications should be tested by additional petrographic work.

Navatu: Vessel form/decoration versus temper

Rim sherds used to establish vessel form (n=33) and 220 body sherds were sectioned and identified under low-power magnification to one of Dickinson's temper subgroups. The majority of these sherds were from Layer 4 (n=140) with 80 sherds from the Layer 1 assemblage. Comparison of vessel form with temper subgroup reveals little association in Layer 1 (Table 61). The clearest trend is the apparent restriction of the opaque and lithic-rich variants to the Layer 4 assemblage, where they were used in making double-spouted vessels and decorated bowls, but not apparently in the manufacture of utilitarian cooking jars with everted rims. The double-spouted containers, some with a stirrup handle, are complex vessel forms likely to have been drinking vessels for high-status individuals (Clark and Sorovi-Vunidilo 1999).

Navatu non-local tempers

In the sample of 220 sectioned body sherds, only one sherd was identified in the Layer 1 assemblage (NAV-1015) as having an unusual spectrum of temper grains and it was sent to Dickinson. Petrographic examination shows it to contain a non-local temper. Reappraisal of the Gifford excavation sherds by Dickinson reveals another sherd with an anomalous temper from a context equivalent to Layer 4 (No. 11-8764).

The temper in NAV-1015 contains moderately sorted, subangular grains of fine sand size that might represent natural temper sands embedded in the clay paste. Quartz and plagioclase feldspars are abundant (30% and 34% respectively), with pyroxene, hornblende, epidote and opaque iron oxide present in amounts under 10%. A specific origin for this sherd could not be determined, but the mineral suite is consistent with derivation from the dissected orogen of interior or southern Viti Levu. The sherd almost certainly dates to the past 600 years, considering its location (Trench B: 40–50 cm depth) and incised surface decoration.

The second non-local Navatu sherd (No. 11-8764) has a temper composed of subrounded to subangular, fine to medium-grained sand. Quartz, which in local Navatu sherds occurs at a frequency of 1% or less, is present at 7%. Total plagioclase (16%) and clinopyroxene (11%) values is lower than local Navatu sherds, while olivine is present in trace amounts. Biotite levels are slightly higher at 2%. Microlitic to felsitic volcanic rock fragments were abundant (41%). Gifford (1951:Plate 22, z) illustrates this rim sherd which was decorated with three rows of oval end-tool impressions on the rim, and cross-hatch relief on the body.

The temper belongs to the dissected orogen type derived from the Wainimala orogen exposed in the interior of Viti Levu, and the Rewa River watershed of eastern Viti Levu is a likely location. Sherd No. 11-8764 was recovered by Gifford from Rectangle EF3–4: 250–265 cm depth, which suggests it dates to ca.1000–1500 cal. BP.

Table 61. Navatu temper groups by vessel form and surface modification.

Navatu Layer 1			
Vessel form	**Standard Non-Placer**	**Pyroxenic Placer**	
Jar – everted rim	8	2	
Bowl – everted rim	2	–	
Single orifice ≤ 10cm	1	1	
Total	**11**	**3**	
Decoration	**Standard Non-Placer**	**Pyroxenic Placer**	**Other**
Shell impressed	59	6	–
Incised symmetric	4	–	1
Appliqué	4	1	–
Side tool (shell)	5	–	–
Total	**72**	**7**	**1**
Navatu Layer 4			
Vessel form	**Standard Non-Placer**	**Placer Pyroxenic**	**Opaque/ Lithic**
Jar – everted rim	5	2	–
Bowl – everted rim	–	1	–
Bowl – inverted rim	1	1	1
Bowl – inverted 'flange' rim	–	1	2
Single orifice ≤ 10cm	1	–	–
Double spout and stirrup handle	1	–	3
Total	**8**	**5**	**6**
Decoration	**Standard Non-Placer**	**Placer Pyroxenic**	**Opaque/ Lithic**
Cross-hatch relief	37	8	5
Parallel-rib relief	21	7	4
Curvilinear relief	34	4	–
Side tool (rounded)	4	2	4
End tool	9	1	–
Total	**105**	**22**	**13**

Ugaga Island temper groups

Three temper groups were identified in the Ugaga Island assemblage by Dickinson, with the same temper groups found in the ceramic assemblage excavated from the nearby heavily-disturbed Lapita site at Kulu Bay on Beqa Islands. The temper sands are mineralogically and texturally varied, indicating pottery transfer to Ugaga Island from multiple locations.

Quartzose-Feldspathic (QF)

The QF temper grains are fine to coarse in size and subrounded to subangular. Plagioclase feldspar grains are abundant (mean 31%), with clinopyroxene (13%) and hornblende (8%) in roughly equal proportions. Subordinate amounts of quartz, epidote and micro-angular rock fragments from extrusive sources are also present in amounts generally less than 10%.

Calcareous grains were not identified in the sherds examined by Dickinson, but small fragments of reef detritus are identified in the sectioned sample. A likely origin for the QF temper sands is Kulu Bay, which is surrounded by atypical exposures of feldspar-rich shoshonitic rock, but in the absence of an examination of beach sands from Kulu Bay, a south Viti Levu origin for these sherds remains a possibility. Shoshonite also outcrops in the north and south of Yanuca Island in the Beqa lagoon (Band 1968:27) and some sherds with the QF temper could derive from Viti Levu and Yanuca Island, as well as Kulu Bay.

Pyribole rich (PY)

Temper sands in the PY temper group are fine-to-medium, moderately sorted, with subangular to subrounded form. Pyroxene (35–50%) and hornblende (20–31%) are prevalent, followed by opaque iron oxide and small amounts of plagioclase feldspar (<10%) and volcanic rock fragments. Quartz, epidote and calcareous grains are absent or rare. Outcrops of hornblende-augite andesite occur at Vaga Bay on Beqa Island (about 2 km from Kulu Bay), where there are also dykes of hornblende dolerite, and at the southern end of Malumu Bay. However, Band (1968:37) notes that hornblende was virtually absent at Malumu Bay, but common at Vaga Bay. The green-to-brown pleochroism of the hornblende grains in the temper sands is similar to that recorded for Vaga Bay, indicating the likelihood of a Beqan origin.

Mixed placer (MP)

Calcareous grains of reef detritus vary from 9% to 60% of the counted grains. The 9% value is probably low and due to weathering of embedded shell fragments. The mineral temper is well sorted, subrounded-to-rounded, and fine-to-medium grained. The main mineral is clinopyroxene (19–65%), followed by opaque iron oxide (2–35%), volcanic rock fragments, and plagioclase feldspars. Hornblende and biotite are present in small amounts (≤3%). A Beqan source, excluding Kulu and Vaga Bays, is considered likely for this temper in view of the significant pyroxene and low hornblende content.

Ugaga: Vessel form/decoration versus temper

A total of 405 rim and body sherds were sectioned and identified to one of Dickinson's temper groups (Table 62). The QF temper is common in jars with abruptly thickened rims, also known as 'collar rims' or 'expanded rims', while PY and MP tempers are frequently associated with utilitarian jars with everted rims. A dentate-stamped dish with a flat base has the QF temper, suggesting the restriction of this temper type to the Lapita period. In post-Lapita times, the MP temper became increasingly popular and was mixed with clay to make jars with everted rims.

Temporal change in the use of QF temper is clearly illustrated in the sample of 290 sectioned body sherds with distinctive surface modification. About 82% of all dentate-stamped sherds have the quartzose temper, supporting the inference that it is restricted to the first ceramics brought to Ugaga Island. Carinated sherds and those of unspecified form described as lugs or stands also yield a high proportion of QF sherds (12/19 or 63%), suggesting most date to the Lapita period ca. 3000–2600 cal. BP. There is a slight indication in the temper data for a decline in PY and an increase in MP tempers in post-Lapita sherds. Dented and parallel-rib relief sherds have PY values of 30–34%, whereas the sherds with diamond and square relief have lower PY values, at 16–17%.

Table 62. Ugaga temper groups by vessel form and surface modification.

Vessel form	QF	PY	MP	Non-local
Jar – everted rim	4	17	48	1
Jar – abruptly thickened rim	9	3	6	–
Bowl – everted rim	2	3	8	–
Bowl – inverted rim	–	1	5	–
Bowl – inverted 'flange' rim	–	1	2	–
Dish – flat base	1	–	–	–
Double spout	–	1	–	–
Double spout and stirrup handle	–	–	2	–
?Vessel form	–	–	–	1
Total	**16**	**26**	**71**	**2**
Surface modification				
Body sherds	QF	PY	MP	Non-local
Dentate stamped	41	2	6	1
Dents	–	9	21	–
Parallel-rib relief	–	31	59	–
Square relief	–	5	25	–
Diamond relief	–	14	75	1
Total	**41**	**61**	**186**	**2**

Ugaga Island non-local tempers

Six sherds in the megascopic sample did not appear to match any of the temper groups, and were sent to Dickinson for examination. Four of the sherds proved to be from two provenance areas beyond Beqa Island. The sherd description and provenance, and the inferred source of the tempers is given in Table 63.

Two sherds had an unusual temper that required staining of the thin sections to determine their mineralogy. Sherds UGA-1158 and UGA-2064 are quartz rich (56%), with significant plagioclase feldspars (38%) and small quantities of felsitic volcanic rock fragments, opaque iron oxide and clinopyroxene. The temper sand is moderately sorted (fine to coarse sand size), and grains are subangular to subrounded. UGA-1158 also contains calcareous reef fragments. On the available geological evidence, and in the absence of a comprehensive Vanua Levu temper suite, Dickinson suggests a source from the Udu Volcanic Group on the northern Vanua Levu peninsula. The quartz-rich Ugaga sherd (UGA-1158) with dentate stamping is undoubtedly of an early age and was brought to the island with the first pottery assemblages. Two more sherds with the same decoration and temper are identified, but the vessel form(s) could not be determined.

The temper grains in two sherds (UGA-1106 and UGA-2079) indicate an origin from the southern coast of Viti Levu (or from an interior drainage leading to the south coast). These sherds contain moderately sorted, subangular to subrounded quartzose temper sands that are likely to be of stream origin and of dissected orogen type. The ratio of quartz (Q) to plagioclase feldspar (F) is similar for both sherds (Q/Q+F=0.64 and 0.66), but they differ from each other in the amount of ferro-magnesian and intrusive igneous rock fragments. The presence of overlapping, deep and irregular cross-hatch paddle impressions on UGA-1106 suggests a likely time of transport in the mid-sequence (ca. 1700–1200 BP), but the age of the plain rim sherd, UGA-2079, cannot be determined.

Table 63. Ugaga sherds identified by petrology as having a non-local temper.

Description	Sherd No.	Square and Depth (cm)	Inferred origin
Body sherd with deep irregular cross-hatch relief, 5.9mm thick. Blackened interior surface.	UGA-1106	M6: 20–30	South coast or inland Viti Levu, ?Rewa Delta
Plain rim with flat-rounded lip.	UGA-2079	F8: 30–40	South coast or inland Viti Levu, ?Rewa Delta
Body/rim sherd with dense dentate stamping, 11.7mm thick.	UGA-1158	L5: 20–30	Udu Point, northeast Vanua Levu
Plain rim with pointed lip, 8.7mm thick. Joins to dentate-stamped sherd UGA-906.	UGA-2064	F8: 10–20	Udu Point, northeast Vanua Levu

Karobo temper groups

The local Karobo temper in five thin-sectioned sherds (KAR-1A, 3A, 4A, 5A, 7A) is a moderately sorted, subangular to subrounded quartz-bearing sand of varied mineralogy and fine to coarse grain size. Quartz (average 29%) and plagioclase (average 24%) are abundant, while hornblende (average 8%) is generally greater than clinopyroxene (average 1%). Opaque iron oxide and epidote are present at 10% or less, and rock fragments, including those from sedimentary/metasedimentary deposits, are common (average 28%). Fragments of volcanic rock and red lateritic soil, some of which are more than 1 cm in length, are common in the megascopic examination of Karobo sherds, as are fragments of a pale white chert/metachert. No calcareous grains are recorded reacting with HCl, although recessive pits in sherds could indicate their former presence. On textural and mineralogical grounds, Dickinson considers that the indigenous Karobo tempers do not derive from beaches, and were probably collected from a variety of local drainages tapping the Wainimala bedrock near Karobo. One sherd (KAR-8A) contains small amounts of weathered volcanic rock as temper, which may represent fluvial debris transported from Wainimala exposures near Karobo.

Karobo: Vessel-decoration versus temper

Sectioning and examination of temper grains in 220 body sherds and 18 vessel rims does not reveal a strong association between temper type and vessel form, or type of surface modification (Table 64). There is no evidence for the spatial restriction of temper types to different excavation areas. The available site information does not allow temper types, however, to be correlated with stratigraphy. Around 81% of body sherds have the QF temper of dissected orogen type expected from drainages near the site, such as the Taunovo, Waisese and Wainiyabia. Sherds with sparse temper sands make up 3% of the sample, and have a similar appearance to the sherd containing weathered volcanic rock fragments (VRF temper).

Karobo non-local tempers

Megascopic examination of Karobo sherds revealed the presence of another reasonably common non-quartzose temper group, and four sherds from this group were sent to Dickinson. Petrographic identification of the mineral suite suggests importation of temper sands from one or two locations.

The non-local temper in three sherds (KAR-155, 204, 811) consists of a well-sorted, subangular to subrounded placer sand of beach origin. Quartz is rare or absent and clinopyroxene is

Table 64. Karobo temper groups by vessel form and surface modification.

Vessel form	Quartzose Feldspathic	Pyroxenic Placer	Opaque Oxide
Jar – everted rim	7	3	–
Bowl – everted rim	1	1	–
Bowl – inverted 'flange' rim	1	–	–
Platter	3	–	1
Double spout and stirrup handle	1	–	–
Total	**13**	**4**	**1**
Surface modification			
Body sherds	Quartzose Feldspathic	Pyroxenic Placer	Volcanic Fragments
Parallel-rib relief	61	8	1
Square relief	56	12	2
Diamond relief	61	15	4
Total	**178**	**35**	**7**

the most common grain type (average 73%). Opaque iron oxide is higher (average 17%) than in local Karobo sherds (average 5%), while other distinguishing characters include the presence of minor and deeply weathered biotite (1%) and the absence of hornblende. The most likely source for the pyroxene sand of beach origin (PY temper), after comparison with Navua Delta sherds, is the nearby Navua Delta about 6.5 km from Karobo. The three sherds carry cross-hatch relief, and, like the majority of the Karobo assemblage, probably date to ca. 1500 BP.

A base sherd from a flat-based platter bearing leaf impressions (KAR-V2) contains a fine-grained temper unlike the quartz-rich or pyroxene-rich variants. Opaque iron oxide is the most common mineral in the sherd (46%), followed by plagioclase (22%) and pyroxene (11%). It contains biotite at 5% and oxyhornblende at 1%, minerals not found in other Karobo sherds. Volcanic rock fragments are also present (13%). This temper could have derived from the Navua Delta, although Dickinson considers that the plagioclase level is too low and the opaque iron oxide and pyroxene levels too high in comparison with the few sherds from Navua he has examined. In addition, hornblende (2%) does not occur in any of the inferred Navua sherds so far examined.

An origin from Kadavu 65 km to the south is a possibility, considering the presence of oxyhornblende and biotite. However, other Kadavu sherds examined by Dickinson have a much greater proportion of plagioclase (62–72%), and hornblende is the dominant pyribole (average 16%). Further, the Karobo sherd has a higher frequency of opaque iron oxide and volcanic rock fragments (in Kadavu sherds opaque iron oxide=11–12% and VRF=4%), so the attribution of the Korobo sherd to Kadavu remains provisional. Nonetheless, once fired, the large platters, like those recorded from Karobo and Sigatoka Level 2 (Birks 1973), would have been difficult to transport, suggesting that the raw materials were taken to Karobo and the platters were manufactured at the site.

Discussion of petrographic and optical results

The megascopic examination of sectioned sherds has in each assemblage been able to identify sherds with non-local tempers. In this case, 'non local' means the temper sand is likely to have come from a location 6–10 km or more from where the sherd was found. The proportion of each excavated assemblage examined megascopically comprises between 2% and 13% of the total assemblage, with non-local tempers making up only 0.4%–1.5% of that amount. It is clear that potters at the three sites made use of locally available temper sands to manufacture ceramics, and there is no reason to suspect the large-scale importation of pottery. Temporal change in temper sources is identified at Ugaga, where the use of QF temper is limited to the Lapita phase, and at Navatu 17A, where the OL temper is associated with the oldest ceramics. The reason for a change in temper sand is unclear, and might result from site/location abandonment, a decline in the availability of a temper sand as a result of natural or anthropogenic environmental change, the imposition of social boundaries, and/or ceramic specialisation.

The majority of the non-local ceramics are decorated, and as with the dentate-stamped sherds found on Ugaga Island, likely to have been made with temper sands collected from Udu Point on Vanua Levu some 300 km away (a sherd from the Mulifanua Lapita site in Samoa [Dickinson 2006:118] is also thought to have Udu Point temper). At Navatu 17A and Ugaga, non-local sherds indicate transfer of ceramics from southern and eastern Viti Levu, with the possibility that temper sands from Kandavu were brought to Karobo to make large platters used to produce salt by evaporation of sea water (Burley 2005).

2. Chemistry-based MD-ICP-MS

The common practice of analysing clay and temper components in a sherd to examine prehistoric interaction can be problematic because of the heterogeneous composition of ceramics (Neff et al. 1988, 1989; Elam et al. 1992), and the possibility that the depositional environment has altered sherd composition (Ambrose 1993). To test whether chemistry-based MD-ICP-MS could be used to identify Lapita ceramics from individual islands and sites, Kennett et al. (2004) analysed sherds from Kulu Bay and Ugaga Island in Fiji, and compared results with those from analysed samples from Tonga (Vuki Mound) and New Ireland (Kamgot). Bivariate plots of Ho versus Mn separate Fijian sherds from Tonga and New Ireland, while Ga and Be differentiate Kulu Bay sherds from Ugaga Island ceramics.

The study also identified four sherds from Ugaga Island and two from Kulu Bay with anomalous compositions that were likely to represent imports to Beqa Island. Clear element distinctions between sites and islands led to the analysis of another 176 sherds of Lapita and post-Lapita age from nine assemblages excavated in the EPF. Samples were analysed with a Hewlett-Packard 4500 quadropole ICP-MS at California State University. Before analysis, sherd surfaces were abraded with a dremal tool and ground in a synthetic agate mortar, with sample digestion and ICP-MS processing as reported in Kennett et al. (2004:38). The abundance of 37 matrix and rare earth elements was measured (Be, Mg, Al, K, Sc, V, Cr, Mn, Fe, Co, Ni, Cu, Zn, Ga, Rb, Sr, Y, In, Cs, Ba, La, Ce, Pr, Nd, Sm, Eu, Gd, Tb, Dy, Ho, Er, Yb, Lu, Pb, Bi, Th and U). Instrumental precision was 2–3% and detection limits for most elements were in the parts per billion (ppb) range.

The MD-ICP-MS analysis of pot sherds was designed to build on the petrology and optical temper results, as it was unclear whether the bulk composition of a sherd might produce erroneous results by identifying chemical outliers that are actually composed of different proportions of local clays and tempers. Another possibility is that sherds made with a non-local component could have been mixed with a local clay or temper, potentially obscuring the partially exotic origin of a ceramic from bulk composition. Sherds examined with petrology were used in the MD-ICP-MS study to determine whether it was a effective tool to investigate prehistoric interaction in Fiji. The first step was to determine whether MD-ICP-MS could correctly identify non-local sherds in a particular prehistoric pottery assemblage. Second, the utility of recent chemical characterisation techniques is that relatively large numbers of sherds can be analysed,

332 Geoffrey Clark and Douglas Kennett

making multi-assemblage comparisons viable. As reported by Kennett et al. (2004), sherds from Ugaga Island are chemically distinct from Kulu, but petrology results indicate transfer of pottery from Kulu Bay to Ugaga Island. The discrepancy suggests the depositional environment may be influencing element concentrations in pottery at either Kulu or Ugaga.

MD-ICP-MS identification of non-local sherds

The ability of MD-ICP-MS to discriminate non-local pottery in an assemblage was tested by analysing local and non-local sherds from Navatu, Karobo and Ugaga used in the petrographic study (Table 65). Descriptive statistics were calculated for the log-transformed MD-ICP-MS

Table 65. Sherd samples examined with petrography and MD-ICP-MS. The inferred origin of sherds is based on the identification of temper grains by Dickinson.

Sherd code	Sherd	Decoration	Age group	Local	Inferred origin
Navatu					
NAV-1A	Body	Cross-hatch impressed	Post Lapita	Yes	Ba volcanics
NAV-2A	Body	Plain	Post Lapita	Yes	Ba volcanics
NAV-3A	Body	Plain	Post Lapita	Yes	Ba volcanics
NAV-4A	Body	Cross-hatch impressed	Post Lapita	Yes	Ba volcanics
NAV-7A	Body	Plain	Post Lapita	Yes	Ba volcanics
NAV-9A	Body	Wavy impressed	Post Lapita	Yes	Ba volcanics
NAV-109	Rim	Punctate and finger impressed	Post Lapita	Yes	Ba volcanics
NAV-1015	Rim	Incised cross-hatching	Late prehistoric	No	South Viti Levu
Ugaga					
UGA-1A	Body	Irregular 'dents'	?Post Lapita	Yes	Vaga Bay, Beqa
UGA-2A	Body	Incised	Lapita	Yes	Beqa unlocalised
UGA-3A	Rim	Notched applied band	Lapita	Yes	Kulu Bay, Beqa
UGA-4A	Rim	Plain	?	Yes	Kulu Bay, Beqa
UGA-8A	Body	Cross-hatch impressed	Post Lapita	Yes	Vaga Bay, Beqa
UGA-10A	Body	Parallel impressed	Post Lapita	Yes	Beqa unlocalised
UGA-11A	Body	Cross-hatch impressed	Post Lapita	Yes	Beqa unlocalised
UGA-1106	Body	Cross-hatch impressed	Post Lapita	No	South Viti Levu, ?Rewa Delta
UGA-2671	Rim	Tool notched collar	Lapita	Yes	Kulu Bay, Beqa
UGA-2064 petro/ UGA-906 ICP-MS	Rim	Dentate stamped	Lapita	No	Udu Point, Vanua Levu
Karobo					
KAR-1A	Double spout	Plain	Post Lapita	Yes	Wainimala drainage
KAR-3A	Body	Cross-hatch impressed	Post Lapita	Yes	Wainimala drainage
KAR-5A	Body	Plain	Post Lapita	Yes	Wainimala drainage
KAR-8A	Body	Parallel impressed	Post Lapita	Yes	Wainimala drainage
KAR-V2	Rim	Leaf impressed	Post Lapita	No	?Kadavu
KAR-204	Body	Cross-hatch impressed	Post Lapita	No	Navua Delta
KAR-811	Rim	Plain	Post Lapita	No	Navua Delta

element data (37 elements) from each site to identify outlier samples that might be exotic, followed by hierarchical cluster analysis (HCA), and multidimensional scaling (MDS) to test the robusticity of individual sample classifications. Discriminant function analysis (DFA) was used on the total sample of sherds from nine sites to locate potentially non-local sherds to a possible source area and to test group association. To examine the DFA placement of a sherd in an exotic assemblage, an additional HCA (Average Linkage) was run using the assemblage from which the non-local sherd was recovered against the possible source assemblage identified in the DFA. All statistical analyses were made with SPSS (Version 13). The hierarchical cluster analysis results for Navatu, Ugaga and Karobo are shown in Figures 139–141.

Navatu MD-ICP-MS

There were 31 sherds in the MD-ICP-MS sample from Navatu, and eight of these had been examined in thin-section by Dickinson, who had identified NAV-1015 as a late-prehistoric import from southern Viti Levu. The HCA of element data placed the Navatu sherds in two clusters, with two sherds (NAV-1015, NAV-2) separate from the main cluster and distinct from two sherds (NAV-19, NAV-25) on a separate branch of the dendrogram (Figure 139). The NAV-2 sherd associated with NAV-1015 is marked with wavy-impressions and comes from the

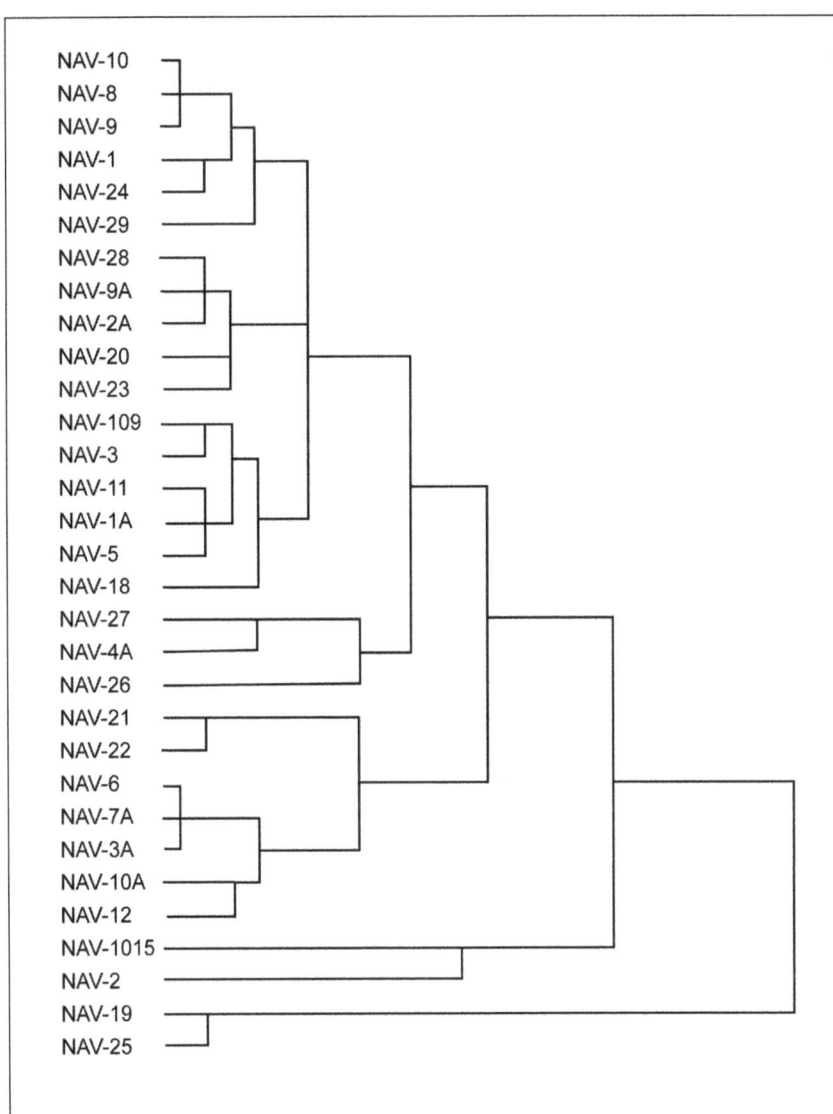

Figure 139. Cluster analysis of Navatu sherd composition determined with MD-ICP-MS. Outlier NAV-1015 was examined with petrology and MD-ICP-MS and identified as likely to originate from south Viti Levu.

early Layer 4 occupation (Table 65). Similarly, NAV-19 and NAV-25, also possibly exotic to the site, were recovered from Layer 2 and Layer 4 respectively.

When entered as 'ungrouped cases' in a discriminant function analysis (DFA) containing all samples, NAV-1015 grouped closest to sherds from Volivoli in southwest Viti Levu, NAV-19 and NAV-25 clustered with sherds from Malaqereqere (southwest Viti Levu), and NAV-2 grouped with Natunuku ceramics (north coast Viti Levu). An HCA study of these sherds with those from Malaqereqere and Natunuku did not reveal a close connection between the non-local Navatu sherds and sherds from other sites. However, NAV-1015 was placed in the main group of Volivoli sherds in the HCA, indicating a possible origin for the sherd in the Volivoli area.

Both petrography and MD-ICP-MS were able to identify sherd NAV-1015 as of probably south-coast Viti Levu origin, with MD-ICP-MS indicating that pottery from the south and the west of Navatu was being brought to the site from ca.1500 cal. BP.

Ugaga Island MD-ICP-MS

The MD-ICP-MS sample from Ugaga consisted of 38 sherds, including 10 that had been examined in thin section by Dickinson (Table 65). Of these, eight were identified as deriving from Beqa Island, with two sherds containing the pyribole-rich temper (PY), three with the mixed-placer (MP) temper, and three with quartzose-feldspathic (QF) temper.

Sherd UGA-1106 has a quartzose temper likely to derive from the south coast of Viti Levu (or from an interior drainage leading to the south coast), and UGA-2064 is quartz-rich with significant plagioclase feldspars, suggesting derivation from the Udu Volcanic Group on the northern Vanua Levu Peninsula. Sherd UGA-906 was conjoined to UGA-2064, and was analysed with MD-ICP-MS. The HCA dendrogram clearly identified the exotic sherd UGA-906/UGA-2064, which was sourced with petrography to the Udu Peninsula, along with a further 'anomalous' sherd UGA-1352 (Figure 140). However, UGA-1106, had a temper suggesting importation from the south coast of Viti Levu but was grouped with two sherds of probable Lapita age that may have been made on Beqa.

Sherds containing the PY, QF and MP tempers were spread across several of the main cluster groups, and did not group together on the basis of temper. This suggests the temper groups might in fact derive from more than one location. An alternative is that if most of the tempers derive from the same location, such as the QF temper, then either the quantity of temper has a significant impact on sherd composition, or a variety of clays were being used with the temper types.

The antiquity of samples was estimated in the HCA by decoration/vessel form attributes, as either 'Lapita' or 'post Lapita', with dentate-stamped and other distinctive-decoration/form sherds attributed to the 'Lapita' group, and impressed types of decoration to the 'post Lapita' group. Sherds that could not be placed in either group were assessed as '?Lapita' and '?post Lapita' based on vessel/rim form criteria that are less diagnostic than decoration. By age-class, both 'Lapita' and 'post Lapita' sherds formed discrete clusters, suggesting similar clay-temper mixes. For example, post-Lapita sherds UGA-68, 83, 96 and 114 grouped together, as did UGA-1A, 11A 14, while sherds UGA-661 to UGA-5A were all of Lapita age (excluding the post-Lapita non-local sherd UGA-1106). These sherds were made with components that were not apparently used by potters in post-Lapita times, and considering their frequency, were probably made with materials obtained on Beqa Island.

The Ugaga sherds are chemically varied. Two non-local sherds from Vanua Levu were able to be differentiated with MD-ICP-MS, but the technique was not able to clearly distinguish UGA-1106 as an import from southern Viti Levu.

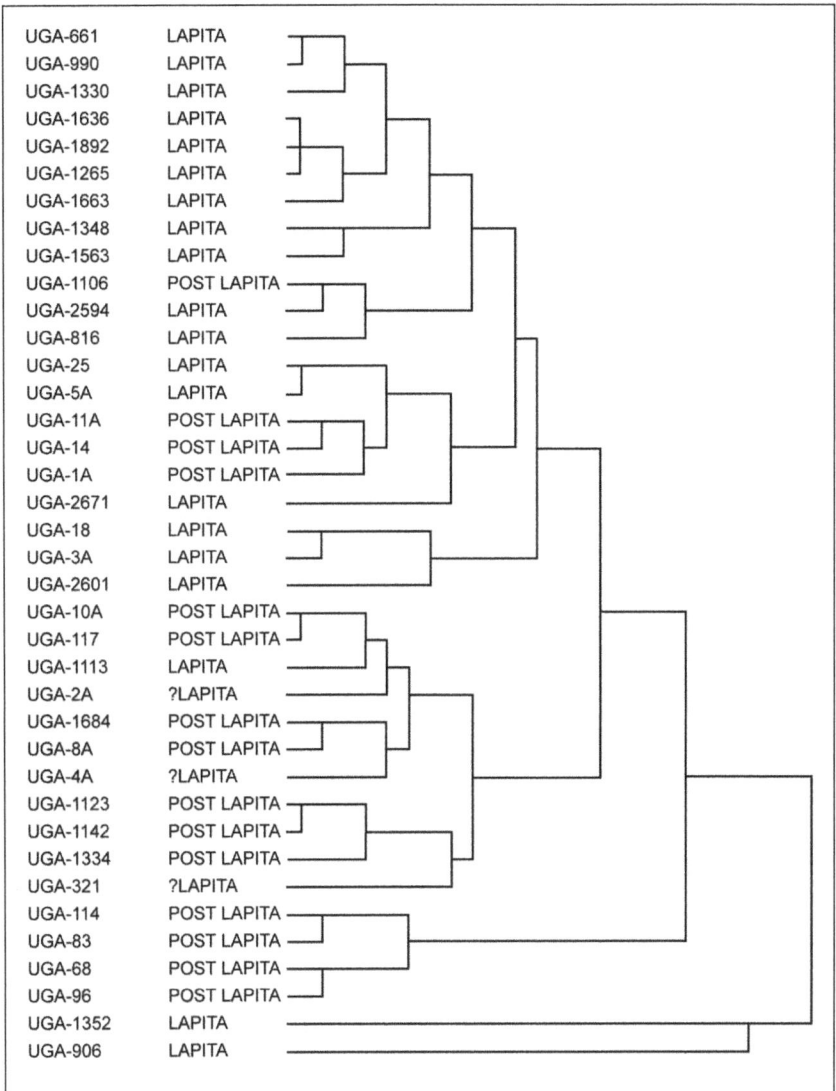

Figure 140. Cluster analysis of Ugaga sherd composition determined with MD-ICP-MS. UGA-1106 was identified as of likely south Viti Levu origin by petrography. UGA-2064 was identified as of likely north Vanua Levu origin by petrography. Two sherds from the same vessel (UGA-906 and UGA-2064) analysed with MD-ICP-MS are outliers.

Karobo MD-ICP-MS

The Karobo sample was the smallest of the three collections analysed, and consisted of 15 sherds. Seven of these had been examined in thin section by Dickinson (Table 65), who identified two sherds (KAR-204, 811) with temper sands that probably derived from the nearby Navua Delta, and one sherd (KAR-V2) as a potential import from Kandavu Island 65 km to the south. Univariate and multivariate statistics showed there was substantial variation within the Karobo sherd collection, displayed in the HCA dendrogram (Figure 141). The plot groups the three non-local sherds together (KAR-204, 811, V2), while sherds containing local temper (KAR-1A, 3A, 4A, 5A, 7A, 8A) are distributed through the two main clusters. Without petrographic analysis, it is unlikely that KAR-204, 811, V2 would be identified as non-local on element results, although a larger sample might produce a better discrimination.

Sample KAR-9 is an outlier in the HCA (Figure 141), which nonetheless groups with the Karobo sample in a DFA using all analysed sherds. KAR-9 is a fragment of a platter marked on the base with leaf-impressions. The presence of platter sherds from two or three distinct locations at Karobo (Navua Delta, ?Kadavu, unknown) suggests possible importation of clay/temper sands from several areas to manufacture the distinctive and fragile vessels that may have been used to produce salt.

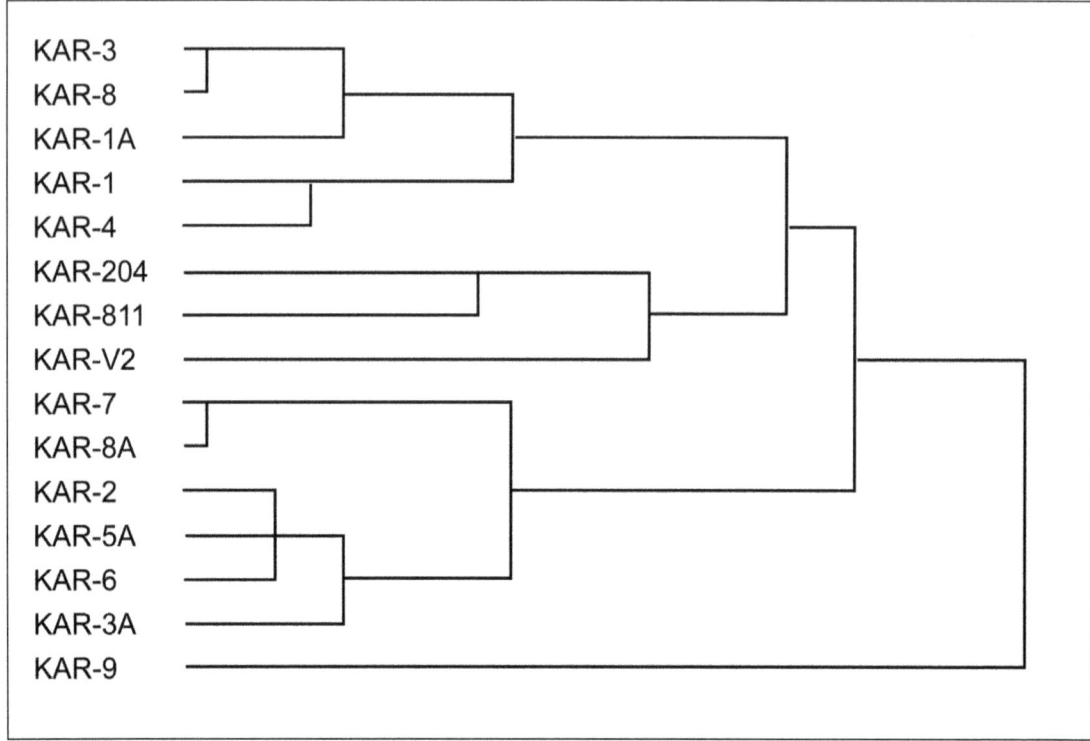

Figure 141. Cluster analysis of Karobo sherd composition determined with MD-ICP-MS. KAR-V2 and KAR-204 were identified as non-local by petrography (?Kadavu and Navua Delta).

MD-ICP-MS of sherds from other sites

The ability of MD-ICP-MS to identify non-local sherds in three assemblages was evaluated by investigating temper composition independently of chemistry-based MD-ICP-MS. Results demonstrate that significant outliers in the HCA plots of element data were non-local sherds in the case of Ugaga and Navatu, and although some ceramics identified with petrography as exotic were not easily identified in all MD-ICP-MS results, those from Ugaga and Navatu indicate that extreme outliers, like KAR-9 from Karobo, might well represent ceramic imports. The analysis was extended to six other sherd collections to identify potentially non-local sherds using the univariate and multivariate techniques used above.

Viti Levu southwest coast and Beqa Island

The three ceramic collections from Sigatoka, Malaqereqere and Volivoli were collected from coastal or near-coast sites in southwest Viti Levu, and the Kulu Bay sherds were from Beqa Island, about 10 km off the south Viti Levu coast (Figure 138).

The smallest assemblage analysed with MD-ICP-MS is made up of 10 surface sherds collected during EPF investigations at the Sigatoka Sand Dunes (Anderson et al. 2006). Based on decorative style, eight sherds bear impressed markings of post-Lapita age, one plain sherd is of indeterminate age, and a lug sherd similar to those identified by Birks (1973) probably dates to the late-Lapita era ca. 2600 cal. BP. HCA shows one cross-hatch impressed sherd (SIG-6) is an outlier. Discriminant function analysis places this sherd with the Navatu sample, but an HCA limited to only the Navatu and Sigatoka samples shows SIG-6 is an outlier from both sites, and Navatu is unlikely to be the sherd source.

The Malaqereqere sherd collection consists of 14 plain body sherds, all of which appear to date to ca. 750 cal. BP or later. In the HCA, there is a main cluster containing 13 sherds with one outlier, MAL-2, from 50–60 cm depth. Additional HCA and DFA of this sherd with other south-coast ceramics included the sample within the range, suggesting that MAL-2 might not be a long-distance import from beyond the south coast.

Volivoli II and Volivoli III are two adjacent rock shelters, and a combined sample of 23 plain sherds from the two excavations was used in the HCA. Two sherds from Volivoli III were identified as outliers (VOLI-1, VOLI-4). A DFA of all sherds was then run, which placed the two Volivoli sherds, along with another sample (VOLI-3), with ceramics from nearby Sigatoka. An additional HCA of Volivoli versus Sigatoka demonstrated the expected compositional similarity of sherds from Sigatoka and Volivoli to one another, and confirmed the outlier status of the probable non-local sherd, SIG-6.

From Kulu Bay on Beqa Island, 26 sherds were analysed with MD-ICP-MS. Most are stylistically of Lapita age, with only three impressed post-Lapita sherds. The HCA identified two main clusters in the chemical data, and DFA of two cluster outliers (KULU-3, KULU-27) placed the ungrouped cases with ceramics from the Votua site in the Lau Group. The linkage was tested with an HCA of Kulu Bay and Votua sherds which did not place either of the two Kulu sherds with the Votua ceramics. The two sherds might be non-local, or might represent local variation in the Beqa Island ceramic suite.

Viti Levu north coast and Lau

In the HCA, 30 Natunuku sherds were placed on a main branch of the dendrogram, separate from two sherds. One of the latter is a dentate-stamped and notched Lapita rim sherd (NAT-16), and the other (NAT-28) is a plain rim of indeterminate age. Further analysis with DCF and HCA suggested these samples may have been imports, or their composition reflects local variation in clays and tempers in the vicinity of Natunuku. When labelled by indicative sherd age, the dendrogram spread of Lapita pottery at Natunuku suggests significant compositional variation, suggesting clays and tempers were collected from several local sources.

Ceramics from the Lapita site at Votua site on Mago Island dating to 2750 cal. BP were examined, along with three post-Lapita sherds bearing impressed markings from the nearby limestone shelter site of Sovanibeka. The dendrogram located a 'wavy' impressed sherd from Sovanibeka on a separate branch to other samples, with VOT-32 also located away from the main cluster group. An all-sample DFA placed VOT-32 with other Votua-Sovanibeka sherds, and located the SOV-4 sherd with those from Karobo in southern Viti Levu. An HCA of Votua and Karobo sherds identified the compositional similarity of SOV-4 to three Karobo sherds (KAR-2, 3A, 5A, 6), indicating a possible south Viti Levu origin for the SOV-4 sherd.

Inter-site comparison: Ugaga Island and Kulu Bay

MD-ICP-MS results from 219 sherds from nine sites identified a relatively small number of sherds as probable imports. These include the unambiguous non-local sherds (NAV-1015, NAV-2, NAV-19, NAV-25, UGA-906, UGA-1352, SIG-6, SOV-4), as well as sample outliers like KAR-9, NAT-16 and NAT-28 that might well be imports. Moreover, the chemical data displayed coherent patterns when sherd age was considered, particularly at Ugaga, where clusters of Lapita and post-Lapita sherds were recognised. However, non-local sherds identified with petrology, such as UGA-1106, KAR-204, KAR-811 and KAR-V2, were not seen to be distinct from presumed locally made sherds in some analyses.

At the assemblage level, chemistry-based MD-ICP-MS was able to discriminate non-local sherds from the majority, which are inferred to have been made with locally available materials. It is reasonable to expect that an inter-site analysis, then, should differentiate sherds from distinct localities because the chemical signature of locally produced sherds from each site was able to identify statistical 'non-local' outliers.

Indeed, DFA can separate ceramic samples from nine sites (combining samples from Votua and Sovanibeka, and Volivoli II and Volivoli III), suggesting the feasibility of employing larger samples from many more archaeological sites to comprehensively investigate the movement of prehistoric pottery in Fiji over 3000 years (Figure 142).

However, while the MD-ICP-MS results from Ugaga Island and Kulu Bay show significant chemical differences between the two sherd collections, petrographic work by Dickinson on pottery from Kulu Bay and Ugaga Island and sherds collected from Beqa Island by Crosby (1988) indicated that the main temper groups present in the Ugaga assemblage were probably collected from places on Beqa Island, including Kulu Bay.

Sherds from Ugaga Island and Kulu Bay with the QF temper had mineralogical characteristics that were: 'not shared jointly to [a] similar degree by any other tempers known to date from either Fiji or elsewhere, and provisionally stand as a potentially unique fingerprint of tempers derived from the vicinity of Kulu Bay' (Dickinson 1997). A comparison of the QF-tempered sherd UGA-2671 with the mineralogy of three QF sherds from Kulu Bay is shown in Table 66, and the close similarity is evidence that both were made with temper sands collected from Kulu Bay.

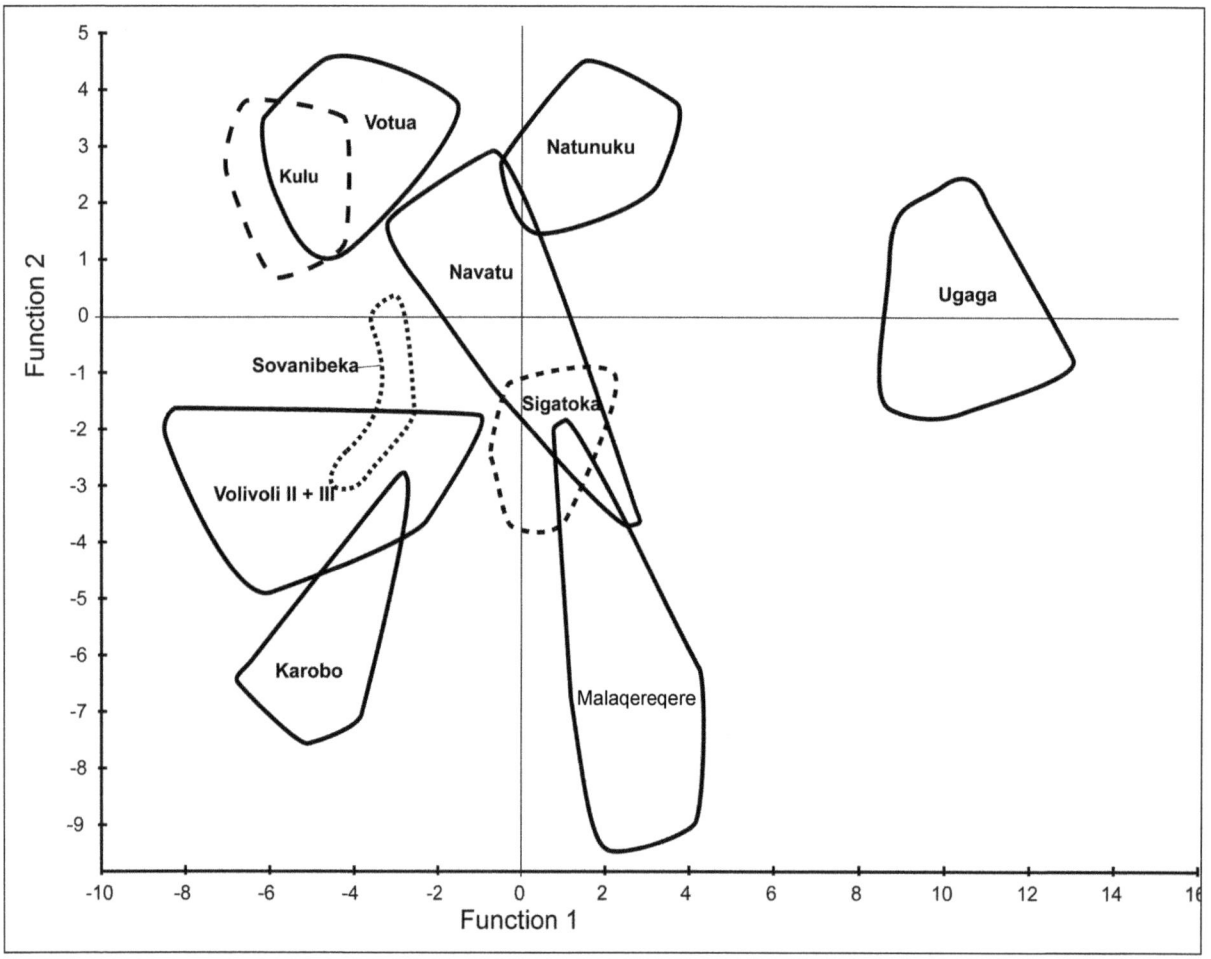

Figure 142. Discriminant function analysis of pot sherds from nine sites (Natunuku, Volivoli II+III, Malaqereqere, Sigatoka, Votua-Sovanibeka, Ugaga, Kulu Bay, Karobo, Navatu). The two functions account for 72.2% of variance. Note that compositional boundaries include local and non-local sherds. Note the separation between Kulu Bay and Ugaga Island ceramics and also between Votua and Sovanibeka sherds, suggestive of post-depositional change in sherd composition.

Table 66. Comparison of a Lapita shed from Ugaga Island with the QF temper compared to average grain counts from three Lapita-age QF-tempered sherds from Kulu Bay.

Grain type	UGA-2671	Kulu Bay (N=3)
Quartz	7	8
Plagioclase	41	41
K-feldspar	2	2
Pyroxene	12	4
Hornblende	2	6
Opaque	4	6
Epidote	2	2
Biotite	1	1
Microphanerite	4	10
Microlitic VRF	18	14
Glassy VRF	7	8

VRF = Volcanic rock fragment

The two other temper groups found in Ugaga ceramics, PY and MP, are also likely to derive from Beqa Island, and a common origin for a proportion of ceramics from Ugaga and Kulu is strongly implied, considering the similar mineralogy of the tempers, the proximity of the two locations to one another in the Lapita period, and the absence of suitable pottery-making clays on the small islet of Ugaga.

The discrepancy between MD-ICP-MS and petrology results is shown in an MDS diagram of Ugaga and Kulu assemblages (Figure 143), and was repeated in HCA (centroid, Ward's, nearest neighbour), regardless of whether non-local sherds were removed from the analysis, or whether the most influential elements responsible for group separation were omitted. Restriction of the Ugaga sample to seven sherds identified with the QF temper thought to originate from Kulu Bay also failed to reveal any similarity to sherds from Kulu Bay.

The elements most influencing group separation include Be, Co, Ni, Cu, Zn, Ga, In, Cs, Ba, Lu and Bi. The elements are significantly correlated with each other (Pearson Correlation Significance (two-tailed) at the 0.05 level), except for Co versus Lu. Compared with assemblages with a reasonable number of sherd analyses (Volivoli II+III, Votua + Sovanibeka, Navatu, Natunuku, Ugaga), Kulu sherds have mean element levels that were elevated in Cu, Zn, Ga, Cs, Ba, La, Ce, Pr, Nd, Sm, Eu and Gd. Of these, Cu, Zn and Ga are related transition metals subject to oxidisation, while most of the remainder belong to the Lanthanide rare earth elements (LREE).

The elevation of clusters of elements, particularly the LREE, suggests either the enrichment/stabilisation of the elements in ceramics recovered in the wet and sticky clay at Kulu Bay, or the depletion of these elements in sherds deposited at other locations. The Kulu Bay sherds were washed in saltwater after excavation, which might affect element concentration from the subsequent precipitation of mineral salts. The loss of Ca in sherds has been recorded when $CaCO_3$, as shell-temper, is eroded from ceramics (Descantes et al. 1998). However, only a portion of the Ugaga Island and Kulu Bay sherds contained shell temper and it appears that burial conditions at one or both of the sites altered the chemical composition of the pottery in ways that are as yet unclear. In a study of Mycenaean pottery, alkali elements and some

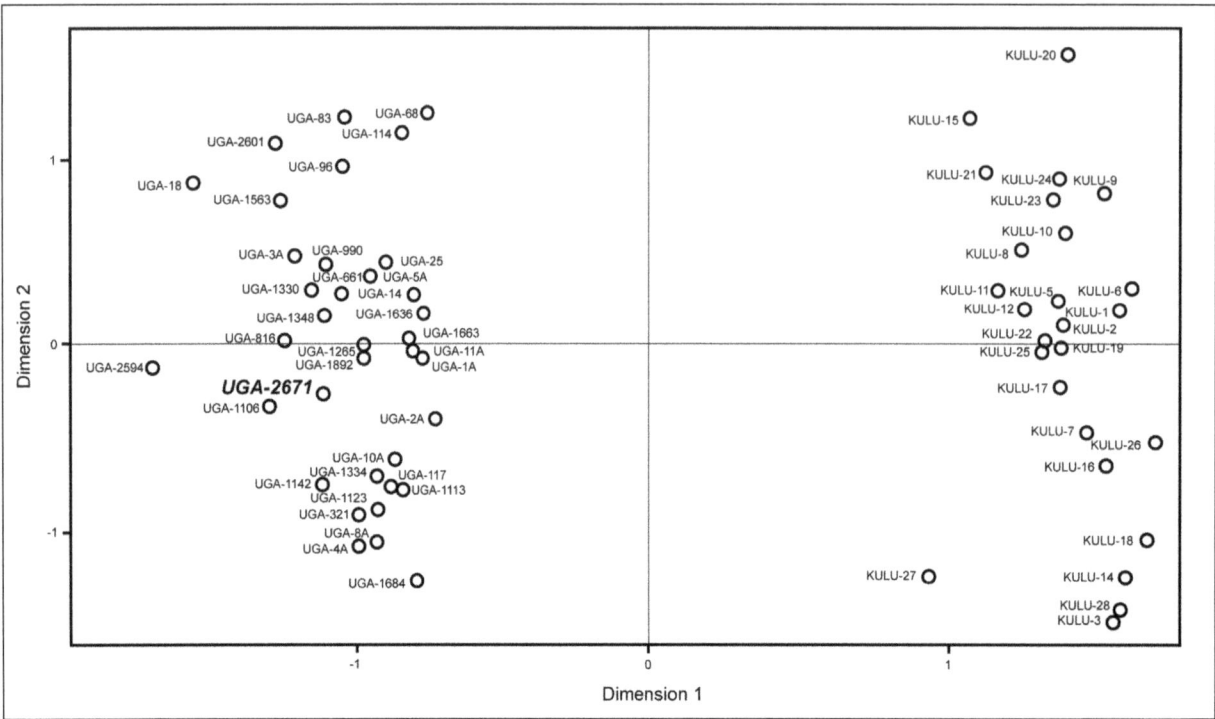

Figure 143. MDS diagram of sherd composition from Ugaga Island and Kulu Bay determined with MD-ICP-MS (37 elements). Petrographic analysis indicates that sherds from Kulu Bay were brought to Ugaga Island and this was also indicated by the similarity in vessel form and decoration and site proximity. Geochemical analysis, however, shows no overlap between the two assemblages, suggesting that sherd composition has been altered by the burial environment. Sherd UGA-2671 from Ugaga Island has a mineral suite almost identical to QF tempered sherds from Kulu Bay, but does not group with any Kulu Bay sherds.

REE were found to have been leached by burial conditions, but instances of post-burial change in prehistoric sherds is overall comparatively rare (Schwedt et al. 2004). Alteration of alkali metals post-burial, especially Cs, Na, K, Rb and P, has also been recognised in other studies, but generally most REEs in ceramics have not been recorded as being significantly altered by the depositional environment (Freestone et al. 1985; Garrigos et al. 2001; Garrigos et al. 2002).

There is no parallel in the literature for the deviation in ceramic composition recorded between the Ugaga and Kulu Bay sherds. If the petrology results are accurate, then the MD-ICP-MS results may be differentiating ceramic assemblages that were made with similar materials, and at the end of their use-life interred in unique burial environments that have altered the chemical composition of sherds. Element variation in pottery can occur because of chemical and mineralogical variation in the clay deposit (Elam et al. 1992; Druc and Gwyn 1998), the addition and subtraction of elements during the manufacturing phase (Carpenter and Feinman 1999), and post-depositional alteration and contamination of the sherds (Garrigos 1999). Pottery use can also enhance element concentrations (Hally 1986).

Post-depositional alteration of ceramics is suggested in the current data, but the conclusion needs to be tested by studies combining petrology and MD-ICP-MS of prehistoric ceramics known to have been made in one place and interred elsewhere. In Fiji, such a comparison might usefully focus on pottery produced in the Rewa Delta of Viti Levu, and found in many parts of the archipelago, to examine how the depositional environment affects sherd composition. Another line of investigation would be to analyse sediments from Kulu Bay and Ugaga Island to determine whether chemical differences in the soil mirror ceramic element concentrations observed in pot sherds, and the use of LA-ICP-MS on sherd clays to investigate whether diagenesis is primarily affecting the concentration of elements in sherd clay. The latter possibility may be significant, as Cochrane (2004) used LA-ICP-MS to target sherd clay in an analysis of ceramic interaction from the Yasawa Islands.

The results of the MD-ICP-MS study demonstrate that it is a useful technique to investigate intra-site ceramic variation, as several outliers examined with petrology were confirmed to be non-local. However, uncertainties remain about the reliability of a multi-site study because the Ugaga ceramics were shown to have a distinct composition from the pottery from Kulu Bay sample, even though some pottery analysed was almost certainly made with similar clay and temper.

Ceramic interaction patterns

The different methods used to examine sherd constituents (petrology, megascopic and chemical) confirm the long-distance movement of pottery in the Fiji Islands in the Lapita period, with ceramics on Ugaga Island that probably derive from Vanua Levu, and in the post-Lapita era, with an impressed sherd on Mago Island that grouped with ceramics from southern Viti Levu. It is difficult to draw conclusions about the frequency of interaction over time considering the relatively small size of the sherd samples analysed from each site. During the Lapita period, it is evident a variety of clays and tempers were used to manufacture ceramics, given the chemical diversity observed in sherds from Ugaga and Natunuku. This is consistent with high rates of population mobility in the islands of Fiji during Lapita colonisation that is likely to have resulted in potters having to use locally available, and at times sub-optimal, clay and temper. Significant differences in the quantity of temper grains added by potters to clay suggest a high rate of experimentation, consistent with this.

A byproduct of high mobility is a higher rate of material-culture production and discard than at permanently occupied settlements (Schiffer 1972). This might be significant for Lapita ceramics as pottery made with new combinations and types of raw materials should experience greater amounts of manufacture and use failure, in addition to significant ceramic discard and breakage from canoe travel and community relocation. A further consequence of local ceramic production coupled with frequent site relocation and site abandonment is the caching of valued material culture items. The transport of artefacts with particular functional attributes, as well as artefacts whose value was connected to the belief system, is also anticipated, and several non-local Lapita sherds were from decorated vessels.

In post-Lapita times the movement of pottery continued, but there was reduced chemical variability as the overall rate of community mobility declined and populations were aggregated in permanent/semi-permanent settlements. One exception to this appears to be the coastal site of Karobo where groups from different areas appear to have been making flat-based platters, possibly to extract salt from seawater.

The presence of non-local pottery in post-Lapita sites might be the result of formal inter-group events (trade and exchange, marriage, death, title bestowal) rather than community mobility, as was suggested to have been common during the colonisation phase. Reduced community mobility and relatively stable access to quality clay and temper sources could lead to full, or partial, craft specialisation, as in the case of Rewa ceramics that were transported widely in late prehistory as well as the production of large pots on Kadavu Island (Hunt 1979).

In the Yasawa Islands, sherd clays analysed with LA-ICP-MS indicated that the spatial extent of interaction in the western Fiji Islands (Mamanuca-Yasawa Islands) contracted after 1000 BP (Cochrane 2004). The increasing frequency of pottery from the northern Yasawas in upper levels of the Y2-39 rock shelter in the south of the Yasawas suggests, if the element data is reliable, increased importation of pottery in late prehistory, although exotic sherds interpreted as being from outside the Yasawas-Mamanucas were also present. The possible demise, or reduced emphasis, on pottery production in islands to the south of the Yasawas, such as the Mamanucas and Malolo (no sherds were examined by Cochrane (2004) from these islands), and the possibility of a greater emphasis on pottery manufacture in the northern islands of the Yasawsas suggests informal or part-time craft/product specialisation. Highly valued pottery from Rewa was moved through the Fiji Islands in late prehistory, and was used by chiefs (Best 1984:606-611), while other small islands in the proto-historic era were associated with particular products and crafts (see also Hooper 1982; Young 1982). There are hints that the geographic association of some islands with particular products used in trade and exchange relationships also occurred in the Yasawas, which were known for the quality of their sail mats that were sought after by Tongans in the 19th century (Derrick 1974:121). Rather than reduced interaction in west Fiji, as surmised by Cochrane (2004), the compositional data he obtained may be tracking change in pottery production as a result of craft specialisation, that in turn is related to the development of complex Fijian chiefdoms in late prehistory whose influence spanned the archipelago.

Chemical analysis of prehistoric pottery can reveal the spatial extent of interaction and variation in rates of community mobility, when ceramics accompany people to a new destination or are used extensively in trade and exchange networks. Compositional data from ceramics will not specify interaction patterns accurately when ceramics manufactured at a particular location were produced primarily for domestic requirements and pottery was not used in exchange networks.

The term 'interaction', which can be defined as 'contact between individuals in a population' (Cochrane and Neff 2006:379), does not take into account the likelihood of increased community mobility during the colonisation era, which correlates, in terms of ceramic production, with increased compositional variability within a site assemblage. This variability is generally interpreted as the result of 'interaction' rather than the effects of community mobility and relocation. For instance, a Lapita group travelling from Viti Levu to islands in the Lau Group could leave ceramic debris at several temporarily occupied locations from pots made at several islands, even though there was no 'interaction' or contact with individuals from outside the voyaging community.

When a community is tethered to a location, as is argued to occur more frequently in the post-colonisation era, interaction at the inter-group level is suggested to have increased in importance, but exactly how pottery was incorporated into community events and activities in prehistory is difficult to determine. A large volume of non-local pottery suggests regular contact and exchange between post-Lapita groups, while small amounts of non-local pottery indicate that ceramics were not an important exchange item. Vessels may have been transported to a location as food and water containers, or were kin-related gifts representing visits between extended families rather than formal inter-group exchanges. In addition, while trade and exchange networks involving pottery or stone tools should be archaeologically identifiable, not all communities necessarily engaged in the production of these items, and their interaction histories may not be deduced confidently from the compositional study of ceramics. In such instances, details of ceramic form and decoration can supplement compositional data to refine our views about prehistoric population connectivity within and between Fijian islands.

References

Ambrose, W.R. 1993. Pottery raw materials: Source recognition in the Manus Islands. In: Spriggs, M., Yen, D.E., Ambrose, W., Jones, R., Thorne, A. and Andrews, A. (eds), *A community of culture. The people and prehistory of the Pacific,* pp. 206–217. Department of Prehistory, Research School of Pacific Studies, Australian National University.

Anderson, A., Roberts, R., Dickinson, W., Clark, G., Burley, D., De Biran, A., Hope, G. and Nunn, P. 2006. Times of sand: Sedimentary history and archaeology at the Sigatoka Dunes, Fiji. *Geoarchaeology* 21: 131–154.

Aronson, K.F. 1999. A compositional analysis of ceramics from the Qaranicagi rockshelter: Implications for exchange. Unpublished MA thesis, University of Hawaii.

Band, R.B. 1968. *The geology of southern Viti Levu and Mbengga.* Geological survey of Fiji, Bulletin No. 15.

Bentley, R.A. 2000. Provenience analysis of pottery from Fijian hillforts: Preliminary implications for exchange within the archipelago. *Archaeology in Oceania* 35: 82–91.

Best, S. 1984. Lakeba: the prehistory of a Fijian Island. Unpublished PhD thesis, Department of Anthropology, University of Auckland.

Birks, L. 1973. Archaeological excavations at Sigatoka dune site, Fiji. *Bulletin of the Fiji Museum* No.1.

Burley, D. 2005. Mid-sequence archaeology at the Sigatoka Sand Dunes with interpretive implications for Fijian and Oceanic culture history. *Asian Perspectives* 44(2): 320–348.

Clark, G. and Sorovi-Vunidilo, T. 1999. Fijian double-spouted vessels. *Domodomo* 11: 6–14.

Carpenter, A.J. and Feinman, G.M. 1999. The effects of behaviour on ceramic composition: Implications for the definition of production localities. *Journal of Archaeological Science* 26: 783–796.

Cochrane, E.E. 2004. Explaining cultural diversity in Ancient Fiji: The transmission of ceramic variability. Unpublished PhD thesis, University of Hawaii.

Cochrane, E.E. and Neff, H. 2006. Investigating compositional diversity among Fijian ceramics with laser ablation-inductively coupled plasma-mass spectrometry (LA-ICP-MS): Implications for interaction studies on geologically similar islands. *Journal of Archaeological Science* 33: 378–390.

Crosby, A. 1988. Beqa: archaeology, structure and history in Fiji. Unpublished MA thesis, Department of Anthropology, University of Auckland.

Curtis, G.H. 1951. Appendix I. Petrography of pottery. In: Gifford, E.W. Archaeological excavations in Fiji, pp. 239–241. *University of California Anthropological Records* 13: 189–288.

Derrick, R.A. 1974. *A history of Fiji*, Government Press, Suva.

Descantes, C., Neff, H., Glascock, M.D. and Dickinson, W.R. 1998. Chemical characterization of Micronesian ceramics through neutron activation analysis. *Journal of Archaeological Science* 28: 1185–1190.

Dickinson, W.R. 1971. Petrography of some sand tempers in prehistoric pottery from Viti Levu, Fiji. Final report No. 2. *Records of the Fiji Museum* 1: 108–121.

Dickinson, W.R. 1973. Appendix 1. Sand temper in prehistoric potsherds from the Sigatoka Dunes, Viti Levu, Fiji. In: Birks, L. Archaeological excavations at Sigatoka dune site, Fiji, pp. 69–73. *Bulletin of the Fiji Museum* No.1.

Dickinson, W.R. 1980. Appendix B. Foreign temper at Yanuca on Viti Levu. In: Hunt, T.L. Toward Fiji's past: archaeological research on southwestern Viti Levu, pp. 216–217. Unpublished PhD thesis, University of Auckland.

Dickinson, W.R. 1997. Sand tempers in prehistoric sherds from Kulu Bay, Beqa Island, Fiji. Unpublished Petrographic Report WRD-161 (15 November 1997).

Dickinson, W.R. 1998. Petrographic temper provinces of prehistoric pottery in Oceania. *Records of the Australian Museum* 50: 263–276.

Dickinson, W.R. 2001. Petrography and geological provenance of sand tempers in prehistoric potsherds from Fiji and Vanuatu: South Pacific. *Geoarchaeology* 16: 275–322.

Dickinson, W.R. 2006. *Temper sands in prehistoric Oceanian pottery: Geotectonics, sedimentology, petrography, provenance.* The Geological Society of America Special Paper 406.

Druc, I.C. and Gwyen, Q.H.J. 1998. From clay to pots: a petrographical analysis of ceramic production in the Callejon de Huaylas, North-Central Andes, Peru. *Journal of Archaeological Science* 25: 707–718.

Elam, M.J., Carr, C., Glascock, M.D. and Neff, H. 1992. Ultrasonic disaggregation and instrumental neutron activation analysis of textural fractions of Tucson Basin and Ohio Valley pottery. In: Neff, H. (ed), *Ceramic characterization of ceramic pastes in archaeology.* Monographs in World Archaeology No. 7, Prehistory Press, Madison, Wisconsin.

Freestone, I.C., Meeks, N.D. and Middleton, A.P. 1985. Retention of phosphate in buried ceramics: An electron microbeam approach. *Archaeometry* 27: 161–177.

Garrigos, J.B. 1999. Alteration and contamination of archaeological ceramics: The perturbation problem. *Journal of Archaeological Science* 26: 295–313.

Garrigos, J.B., Kilikoglou, V. and Day, P.M. 2001. Chemical and mineralogical alteration of ceramics from a late Bronze Age kiln at Commos, Crete: The effect on the formation of a reference group. *Archaeometry* 43: 349–372.

Garrigos, J.B, Mommsen, H. and Tsolakidou, A. 2002. Alteration of Na, K and Rb concentrations in Mycenean pottery and a proposed explanation using X-ray diffraction. *Archaeometry* 44: 187–198.

Gifford, E.W. 1951. Archaeological excavations in Fiji. *University of California Anthropological Records* 13: 189–288.

Hally, D.J. 1986. The identification of vessel function: A case study from northwest Georgia. *American Antiquity* 51: 267–295.

Hunt, C. 1979. Fijian pottery and the manufacture of cooking pots on Kadavu Island. *The Artefact* 4: 27–35.

Hooper, S.P. 1982. A study of valuables in the Chiedfdom of Lau, Fiji. Unpublished PhD thesis, University of Cambridge.

Kennett, D.J., Anderson, A., Cruz, M.J., Clark, G. and Summerhayes, G. 2004. Geochemical characterization of Lapita pots via Inductively Coupled Plasma Mass Spectrometry (ICP-MS). *Archaeometry* 46: 35–46.

Neff, H., Bishop, R.L. and Sayre, E.V. 1988. A simulation approach to the problem of tempering in compositional studies of archaeological ceramics. *Journal of Archaeological Science* 15: 159–172.

Neff, H., Bishop, R.L. and Sayre, E.V. 1989. More observations on the problem of tempering in compositional studies of archaeological ceramics. *Journal of Archaeological Science* 16: 57–69.

Petchey, F. 1995. Archaeology of Kudon: archaeological analysis of Lapita ceramics from Mulifanua, Samoa and Sigatoka, Fiji. Unpublished MA thesis, Department of Anthropology, University of Auckland.

Schiffer, M.B. 1972. Archaeological context and systematic context. *American Antiquity* 37: 157–165.

Schwedt, A., Mommsen, H. and Zacharias, N. 2004. Post-depositional element alterations in pottery: Neutron activation analyses of surface and core samples. *Archaeometry* 46: 85–101.

Seeley, J.B. and Searle, E.J. 1970. Geology of the Rakiraki district, Viti Levu, Fiji. *New Zealand Journal of Geology and Geophysics* 13: 52–71.

Young, J. 1982. The response of Lau to foreign contact: An interdisciplinary reconstruction. *The Journal of Pacific History* XVII: 29–50.

14

Stone artefact manufacture at Natunuku, Votua, Kulu and Ugaga, Fiji

Chris Clarkson
Archaeology Program, The University of Queensland

Lyn Schmidt
Department of Archaeology and Natural History, The Australian National University

Introduction

Pacific flaked-stone assemblages after ca. 3000 years ago are often portrayed as simple, expedient, homogeneous and typologically depauperate. Recent technological analyses, however, are beginning to reveal significant variation in the types of reduction strategies employed in different regions and sites, as well as in the degree to which raw materials of various origins were reduced, conserved and curated (Halsey 1995; Sheppard 1992, 1993; Swete Kelly 2001). These studies have largely been concerned with identifying the mechanisms and quantities in which raw materials (but typically obsidian) were distributed across the Pacific at different times. Yet there is a growing concern that flaked-stone assemblages of all kinds, and not simply those derived from long-distance exchange, should be better described and integrated into current research questions in Pacific prehistory. Such questions include the tempo and economic basis of Lapita expansion, changing mobility, settlement and subsistence patterns, Lapita and post-Lapita innovation, and the continuity and nature of local and regional interaction. Although Allen and Bell (1988) called for greater reporting of basic information on aspects of Pacific assemblage variability nearly 20 years ago, there is still an alarming lack of data on such basic issues as the types, origins and proportions of raw materials found in assemblages, the form in which they were procured and imported, the various reduction techniques employed, the types and abundance of technological categories represented, their size and form, the function of stone tools, and the impact of various taphonomic processes on assemblage size and composition.

At present, only a few, small stone artefact assemblages have been recovered from a handful of well-dated sites in Fiji. In addition, little is known of the origins, form or abundance of many of the raw materials that make up these assemblages. There are also very few past studies of stone artefacts to draw on, and most of these are typological in nature, concentrating on the minority of morphologically regular artefacts in an assemblage (e.g. adzes and retouched flakes) rather than whole assemblages. Early studies have identified the presence of various reduction techniques as well as some commonly used raw materials, but overall, our understanding of the nature and organisation of lithic technology in Fiji is still rudimentary.

We therefore aim to address four basic questions in this paper:

1. What was the nature of stone procurement on different islands?

2. What was the range of reduction strategies and manufacturing activities undertaken at each site?

3. Are there differences in reduction intensity between sites?

4. Might assemblage variability reflect levels of mobility or economic and social differentiation between sites?

Our analysis is essentially a base-line technological study on which future studies of Fijian stone artefacts may build. It is primarily descriptive, rather than analytical, and the few hypotheses we propose are based on simple data rather than extensive inter-site comparisons.

Previous work

Previous stone-artefact studies in Fiji reflect past approaches to stone-artefact analysis world-wide, with attention given primarily to the construction of typologies and the range of possible tool functions, rather than the range of reduction strategies and material remains produced. Before 1979, no systematic descriptions of Fijian flaked-stone-artefact assemblages were undertaken. Gifford (1949, 1951) was the first to mention stone artefacts in Fijian sites, but only formal types such as adzes, hammerstones and whetstones were mentioned. Sixteen years later, Birks and Birks (1967) reported the presence of stone artefacts in their excavations at the Sigatoka Dune site and the Yanuca site on southwest Viti Levu. Their description focused on raw-material types and imputed tool functions, but no assemblage data was provided (Birks and Birks 1967:18). In a later study, Birks (1973) reported flakes of chalcedony found at the Sigatoka site, but again, no detail about the artefacts was provided. In 1975 and 1976, Best (1977, 1984) began excavating open sites and rock shelters on Lakeba and recovered hundreds of flakes.

Charles Hunt's (1979) study provided the first basic description of stone artefacts from Fiji. He recovered numerous chert flakes and cores from a ring-ditch site near the Samabula River. He described the flakes as amorphous with few signs of use, but described truncated triangular cross-sectioned blades and thick, narrow flakes resembling drill points. Cores were described as 'pyramidal', with large square platforms and more than four flake scars. Terry Hunt (1980) later analysed an assemblage from the site of Yanuca on southwest Viti Levu. The assemblage consisted of 41 flaked pieces, some of which exhibited use-wear and retouch. Raw materials used in the manufacture of the assemblage varied and reflected the local geology of the area. A selection of adzes was also analysed, building on Birks and Birks (1968) earlier description of these artefacts.

Best's (1984) dissertation on sites on Lakeba provides the first detailed description of a Fijian flaked-stone industry, as well as some details on the range of raw materials and manufacturing strategies employed. Best noted the presence of rotated and unrotated cores, as well as bipolar cores and flakes made from a range of raw materials. He developed a typology that divided utilised, retouched and unretouched flakes of various shapes and sizes into the categories of 'drills', 'shallow pointed flakes', 'heavy duty flakes', 'oval ended flakes', and 'blades and concave scrapers'. Artefacts were made from chert and a chalcedony-like silicified coral found outcropping on Vanuabalavu, with the latter material dominating the assemblages of Lapita age. Exotic obsidian was rarely found, and was most abundant after the Lapita period. Best (1984) also classified adzes on the basis of cross section and performed chemical sourcing analysis, although no source workshops were identified in his study.

Finally, Hunt et al. (1999) have recently mentioned flake assemblages recovered from excavations in the Yasawa Islands, including small cores and other artefacts made from basalt, chert, and quartzite. These showed no signs of retouch or use-wear.

In summary, there is little data available with which to formulate general statements about the organisation of flaked-stone technology in Fiji. Our own analysis therefore attempts to provide a more thorough technological description for the four assemblages recovered from the recent excavations at Natunuku, Kulu, Ugaga and Votua.

Technological analysis

The following analysis presents information on a variety of aspects of lithic technology for each site. The analysis is based on macroscopic inspection of artefacts and the recording of up to 39 morphological and technological variables for flakes, 18 for cores and 13 for adzes, as well as microscopic inspection of artefacts for traces of use-wear. The excavation strategy and chronology for each of the sites analysed in this chapter are reported in earlier chapters and are not repeated here. Because sites were argued in earlier chapters to either exhibit marked disturbance or represent single-phase occupations, we present assemblage data as single units rather than spatial or temporal components.

Assemblage size and density

Table 67 presents data on the size and contents of each of the excavated assemblages. From this table, we see that Votua is the largest assemblage in both size and density, and is more than twice the size of any other site reported here. Natunuku is the next largest assemblage, followed by Kulu and Ugaga. With only five artefacts, Ugaga is too small to provide a reliable basis for statements about reduction technology and is therefore omitted from much of the following discussion and analysis.

Assemblage richness

In keeping with the notion that rare artefacts tend only to appear as sample size increases (Hiscock 2001), a clear relationship exists between sample size and the number of technological categories present for Natunuku, Kulu and Ugaga (Figure 144). Votua, on the other hand, represents a clear outlier in that it is the largest of the excavated assemblages and yet has very low assemblage diversity. This situation could reflect real differences in the diversity of economic and manufacturing activities undertaken at Votua compared with the other sites.

Raw material procurement

Table 68 provides information on the proportions of different raw materials found at each site. Chalcedony dominates the Kulu and Natunuku assemblages, whereas chert is most abundant at Votua. Volcanic stone makes up the majority of the five artefacts found at Ugaga. It is worth considering first whether the proportions of raw materials found in each assemblage might reflect the relative availability of different raw materials in the vicinity of each site.

Table 67. Assemblage breakdown for each of the excavated assemblages.

Site	Kulu	Ugaga	Natunuku	Votua
Flaked and ground adze	1	3	3	
Flaked adze blank		1		
Adze rejuvination flake	4		1	4
Biface				1
Unidirect. bipolar core	1		5	
Multi-direct. bipolar core	5		3	
Bipolar flake	3		11	3
Bipolar drill	1		1	
Bipolar retouched flake			1	
Multi-platform core				1
Core fragment				
Drill	4		5	
Flake	26		45	100
Flaked piece	9	1	25	153
'Pot lid' flake	1			
Flaked quartz crystal			1	
Hammerstone				2
Retouched flake			5	9
Retouched flake piece			2	
Total	**55**	**5**	**106**	**274**
Number of categories	10	3	13	8
% Bipolar	18.2	0	19.8	1.1
Total weight (g)	162	1946.4	586.3	2053.7
Artefacts/m^3 deposit	19	3	31	88

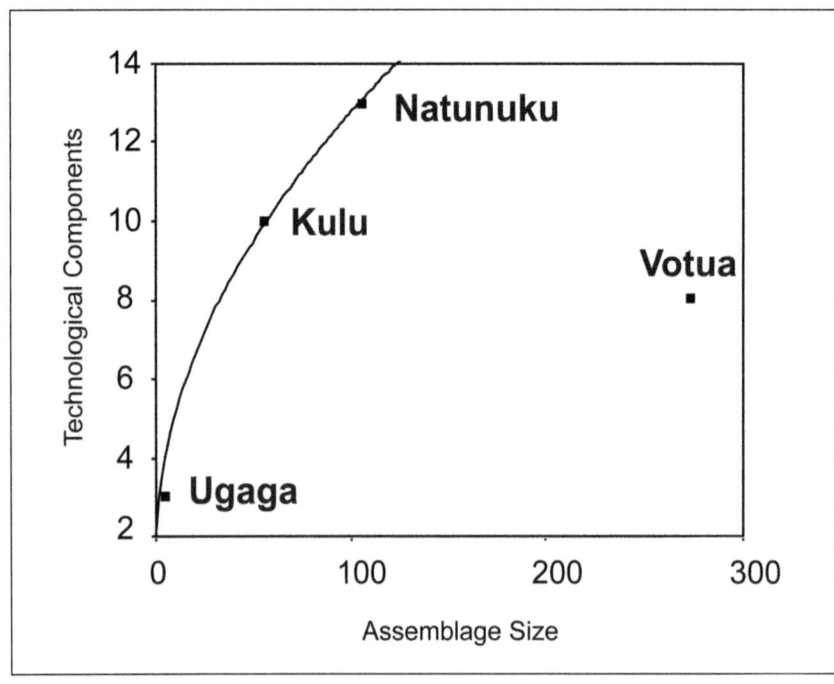

Figure 144. Relationship between assemblage size and richness for Fijian assemblages.

At present, little is known about the availability of stone suited to artefact manufacture in the Fiji Islands. However, examination of the geological and archaeological literature helps identify a number of potential sources of chert, chalcedony and other materials, such as novaculite, flinty tuff and mudstone, on some of the larger islands.

From this literature, it appears that chalcedony is abundant at various locations across Viti Levu (Figure 145), and is probably available less than 50 km inland from Natunuku in at least two locations (Bartholomew 1960:14; Band 1968:12; Harvey 1958 cited in Hunt 1979:37). From the available descriptions, this material occurs in a variety of sizes, up to large boulders and blocks, the larger sizes probably better suited to the manufacture of stone artefacts. Jasper and a variety of other chert types, and fine-grained siliceous rocks such as mudstones and tuff also appear to be obtainable within ca. 80 km of Natunuku (Bartholomew 1960:14; Houtz 1963:4), although it is possible that undiscovered sources of these and other materials exist closer to the site.

Votua is apparently the closest of any site to a stone source (Best 1984). Jasper outcrops in large blocks, up to 1 m in diameter, on Vanuabalavu, only 23 km northeast of Mago Island, and no doubt accounts for much of the chert in the Votua assemblage (see Chapter 6). Chalcedony

Table 68. Percentages of raw material types used at each site.

Site	Chalcedony	Chert	Quartz crystal	?Quartz	Volcanic
Kulu	65	18	–	–	16.8
Ugaga		20			80
Natunuku	75	10	1.9	0.9	11
Votua	10	84	–	–	5.8

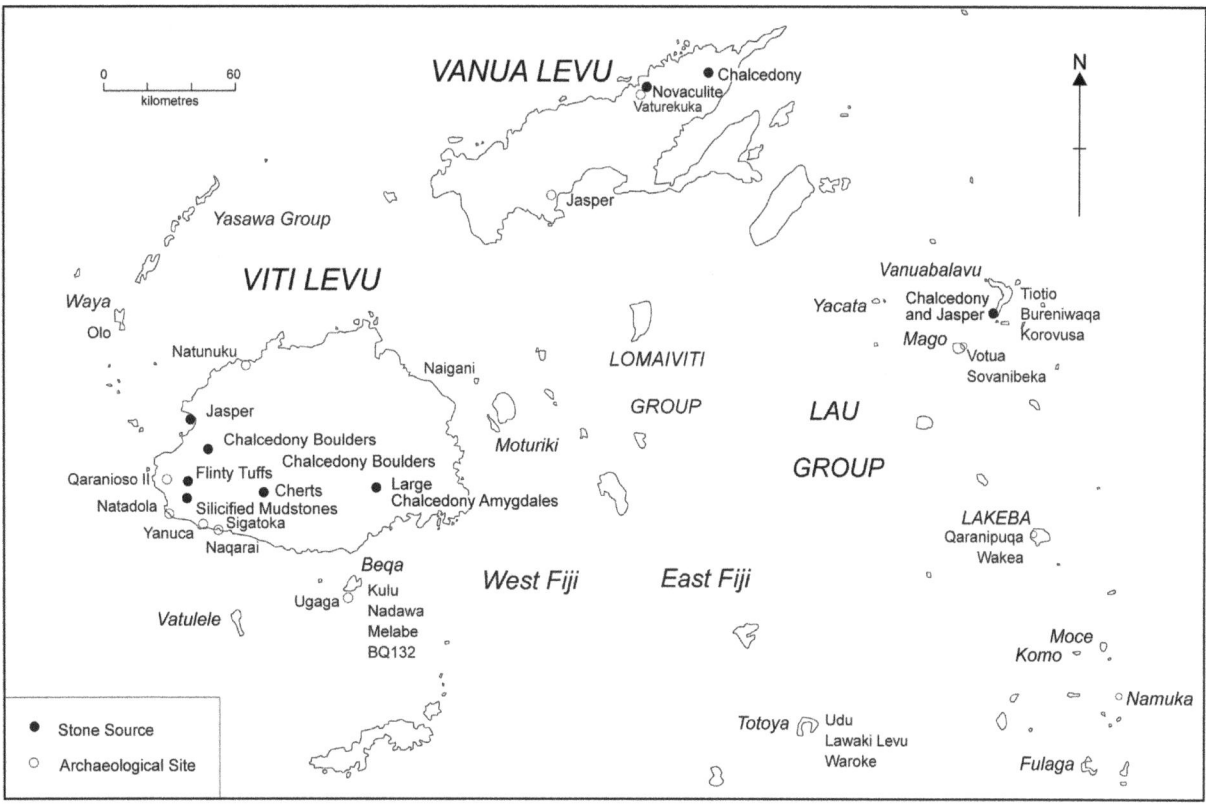

Figure 145. Location of archaeological sites and reported stone sources in Fiji.

and silicified coral heads were also found adjacent to the jasper source on Vanuabalavu by Best (1984).

As no sources of non-volcanic flakeable stone are mentioned in the geological reports for Beqa Island, it is possible that chalcedony and chert had to be imported to Kulu and Ugaga from sources on Viti Levu, as far away as 40–80 km.

A wide variety of flakeable non-volcanic rocks are also available on Vanua Levu (including chalcedony, jasper and novaculite) and probably on other islands in the Fijian Group (Ibbotson 1969:6). In addition to siliceous materials, there is an abundance of different types of volcanic rocks on most islands in Fiji. Some are likely suited to flaking and/or adze manufacture. Best (1984) identified several sources of basalt, tuff and andesite in the Lau Group, some of which were certainly used in adze manufacture. It remains for future surveys and sourcing studies to determine the exact location and nature of other volcanic and siliceous stone sources, and to discover rare and recognisable raw-material types that might allow investigation of inter-island transport.

From this review of the literature, the only known sources of flakeable stone close to the coast and easily accessed by people reliant on ocean transport are the jasper sources in the Nadi riverbed and around Savusavu Bay, as well as the silicified coral and jasper sources on Vanuabalavu. Overland travel would have been necessary to access the larger chalcedony blocks in the interior of the islands. At the minimum, people would have had to travel 13 km inland to access these sources of chalcedony, chert, tuff and mudstone; however, some of the larger sources of chalcedony are as far as 36 km inland. Future physical and elemental characterisation of these sources should help determine the relative quality and importance of each source in the past. As a side note, inspection of a small collection in the Fiji Museum of chert and chalcedony flakes from the Natunuku site revealed large pieces of chalcedony, one of which still had an oyster shell adhering to its surface. Whether this results from post-depositional exposure within the littoral zone, or indicates the existence of a local source of chalcedony right on the coast requires investigation.

Returning to the data presented in Table 68, it appears that the proportions of raw materials present in the Natunuku and Votua assemblages probably reflect the relative availability and quality of raw materials in the local area. The inhabitants of Natunuku made greatest use of chalcedony sources that perhaps outcrop no further than 50 km away (in a straight line) from the site, while at Votua, greatest use was made of jasper which was probably obtained as large nodules from nearby Vanuabalavu. Kulu mainly contains chalcedony, but as sources on the island are unrecorded, we assume this material had to be imported from sources 40–80 km away on Viti Levu or other islands.

Further clues about the form in which stone was procured and its likely origins can be obtained from examining the size ranges and type of cortex on stone artefacts of each raw-material type. This information is presented in Table 69 and indicates that artefacts made from volcanic materials at Natunuku are the largest, followed by chert and then chalcedony. At Kulu and Votua, the maximum size of chert and volcanic artefacts is the same. However, a sample of large cores collected from the surface of the Votua site, which has probably eroded from the same single occupation layer as the excavated material, enlarges the maximum size of chert and chalcedony artefacts considerably. These consist of a jasper core measuring 200 mm in diameter and a chalcedony core measuring 83 mm in diameter (as indicated in brackets in Table 69).

Given the size of the assemblages, it is possible that the mean and maximum lengths of artefacts are partially attributable to the small sample size. Regression analyses confirm that the max-

Table 69. Mean and maximum length (mm) and dominant cortex type for each raw material type.

Material	Kulu	Natunuku	Votua
Chalcedony			
Mean	13 ± 6	17 ± 7	16 ± 5
Max.	26	36	27 (83)
Cortex	Irregular	Irregular	Irregular
Chert			
Mean	20 ± 11	29 ± 17	21 ± 10
Max.	44	66	82 (200)
Cortex	Irregular	Irregular	Irregular
Volcanic			
Mean	17 ± 12	30 ± 16	36 ± 24
Max.	44	71	82
Cortex	None	Angular	Irregular
Dominant cortex			
Angular	0%	31%	21%
Irregular	100%	62%	71%
Rounded	0%	8%	8%

imum lengths of artefacts increase with sample size for chert and chalcedony (chert: R^2=0.99, p=0.06; chalcedony: R^2=0.99, p=0.04), but not for volcanic artefacts (R^2=0.74, p=0.34). However, the results do not rule out the possibility that size also reflects real differences in the form in which materials were procured or the degree to which they were subsequently reduced. Cortex type may provide further clues as to the form and geological setting in which materials were obtained, whereas the effects of reduction intensity on artefact size are explored below.

Examining the dominant type of cortex found on artefacts as indicated in Table 69, it appears that most raw materials preserve irregular cortex, except for the volcanic stone found at Natunuku. In fact, 79% of all chalcedony and 71% of all chert artefacts preserve irregular cortex. This type of cortex is more suggestive of procurement from primary outcrops, rather than beaches or watercourses, where cortex would tend to be rounded from water-transport (although conglomerates might also contain rounded cobbles). Some chalcedony artefacts from Natunuku also have a thick crystalline cortex suggestive of volcanic origins, although silicified coral is also present in all sites.

In summary, the scarcity of intact and relatively unreduced nodules at sites renders the determination of exact patterns of raw-material procurement very difficult. The type of cortex found on artefacts from all sites, however, suggests the use of primary outcrops rather than secondary sources of water-transported cobbles. The size of these cobbles is very difficult to determine. The mean and maximum size of artefacts does appear to be related to sample size, with the largest artefacts only appearing in the biggest assemblage. However, it is conceivable that these differences in mean and maximum size also relate to distance from a stone source and hence the degree to which raw material was reduced. In the next section, we examine evidence for the types and intensity of reduction found at each site.

Core reduction

An indication of the reduction strategies employed at the Fijian sites can be ascertained from the technological characteristics of cores and flakes. As shown in Table 67, bipolar reduction dominates both the Natunuku and Kulu assemblages, as indicated by cores and flakes exhibiting opposed crushed platforms, wedging initiations and flat or sinuous compression fracture planes (Cotterell and Kamminga 1987:689) (Figure 146). Cores from these sites are also extremely small, with numerous flake scars. In contrast, both the excavated and collected cores from Votua are predominantly worked by freehand percussion, and are much larger than those found at Kulu and Natunuku.

The common assertion that bipolar working represents a later stage in the reduction of cores than freehand percussion can be tested by plotting the weight of cores against maximum face length (Figure 147). Although the sample size is small, a good separation exists between core types, suggesting that real stages in the core-reduction process existed. From this graph, then, it appears that cores were initially worked on a single platform. They were subsequently rotated once platform angles became too great or step and hinge terminations began to appear on each face. Finally, reduction switched to a bipolar technique once cores hit inertia thresholds and flakes could no longer be struck while cores were held in the hand (Hiscock 1982). The bipolar cores shown in the bottom left-hand corner of Figure 147 are nearing the absolute limits of reduction, and could barely have been held between thumb and finger. It is possible that some other method of stabilisation was at this point used to hold these tiny cores in place while blows were delivered from above. Overall, the greater abundance of bipolar cores at Kulu and Natunuku suggests that later stages of core reduction were carried out at both these sites than at Votua.

Changes to core size, geometry and the nature of force input that result from the use of different reduction strategies also have implications for the size and morphology of flakes. Table 70 presents data on the mean characteristics of flake scars found on cores at each stage

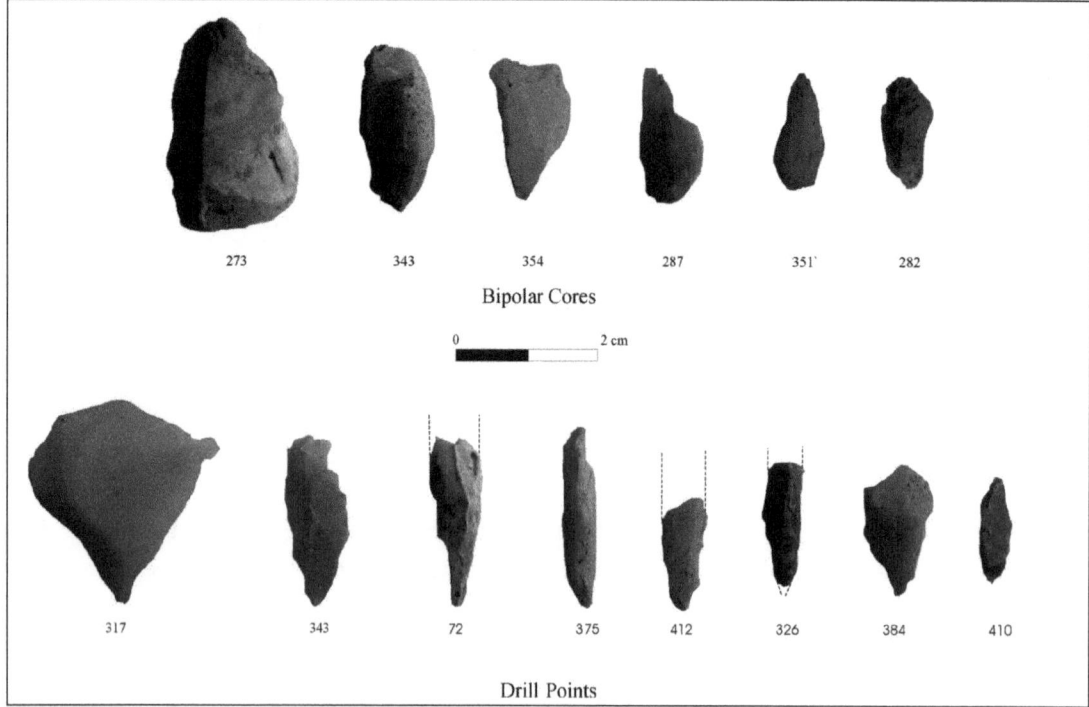

Figure 146. Bipolar cores and drill points from Kulu and Natunuku.

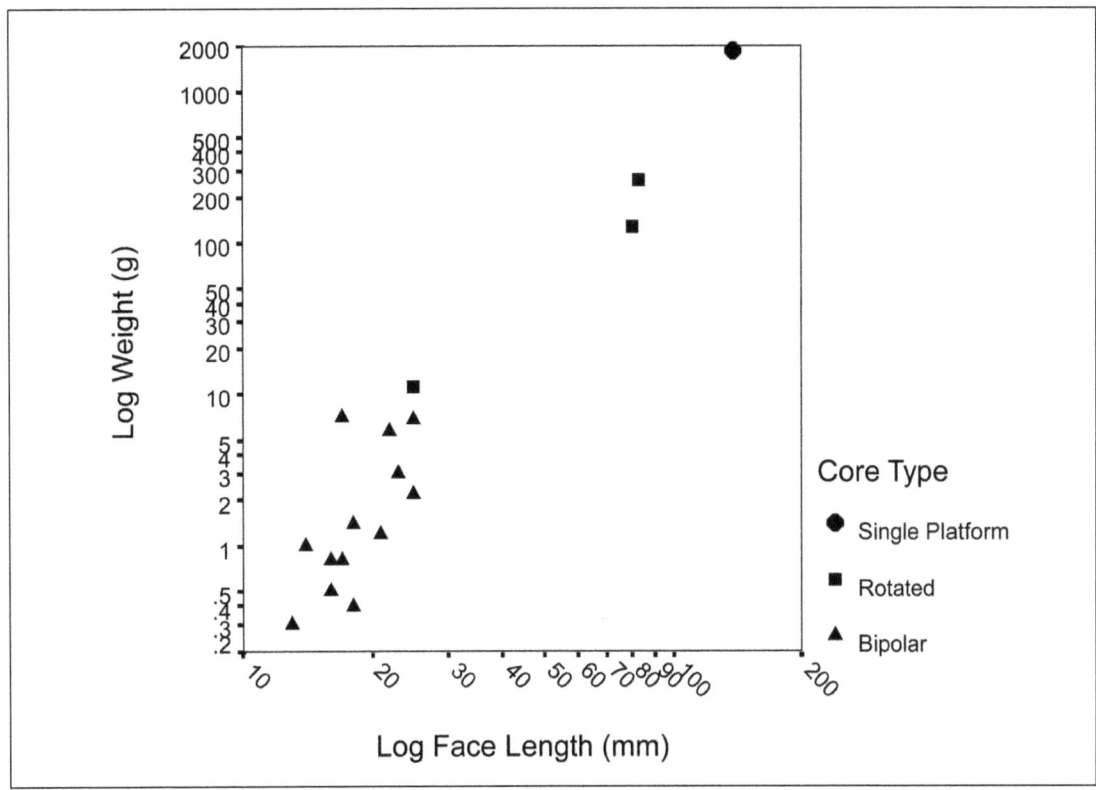

Figure 147. Relationship between core face length and weight at each stage of reduction.

Table 70. Mean dimensions and characteristics by core type.

Core type	Single platform	Rotated	Bipolar
Dominant material	Chert/jasper	Chalcedony	Chalcedony
Number	1	3	13
Platform area	6650	796	0
%Cortex	80	17	5
Number of rotations	0	5	1
Longest face	140	58	19
Feather/Non-feather	2	5	6
Number of parallel scars	0	0	2
Elongation of final scar	0.8	1.9	3.2

of reduction, and helps describe the changing nature of flakes throughout this process. For instance, the gradual decortication of cores should result in flakes with little or no cortex at later stages of reduction. The shrinking size of core platforms should similarly be reflected in a decrease in the size of flake platforms as knappers try to conserve what is left of the core. As more mass is struck from a core, the maximum face length also decreases, and so too should the length of flakes. As feather terminations are produced more regularly at later stages of core reduction, flakes should also possess fewer non-feather terminations. Finally, as parallel ridges (or arises) are set up, and flaking is increasingly aligned along a single plane (as, for example, in bipolar reduction), flakes should become more elongated and parallel sided.

Flake characteristics and reduction

Examining the nature of flakes found at each site, those from Kulu and Natunuku are indeed more characteristic of later stages of reduction than those found at Votua. Table 71 presents this data and shows that flakes from Kulu and Natunuku are shorter, have smaller platforms and less cortex, are more elongate and parallel sided, and have fewer aberrant terminations than those found at Votua.

The data for platform attributes also supports the trend for later stages of core reduction at Kulu and Natunuku. Table 72 gives the percentages of platform types found on flakes at each site. Crushed and focalised platforms are most common at Kulu and Natunuku. Crushing typically results from bipolar percussion or the delivery of excessive force to a small platform. Focalisation results from placing blows close to the edge of the platform, and may be indicative of greater precision in the placement of blows, the conservation of raw material, or the working of small cores. Platforms formed by cortex and single and multiple scars that are indicative of the reduction of single platform and rotated cores are most abundant at Votua.

Table 71. Mean characteristics of flakes.

Site	Kulu	Natunuku	Votua
Length	16	18	21
Mean platform area	6	16	27
%Cortex	3	7	16
%Bipolar crushing	18.2	19.8	1
%Parallel and elongate	4	8	1
Number of arises	1.3	1.1	0
Feather/Non-feather	2.5	1.9	1.7

Table 72. Percentages of flake platform types by site.

Site	Crushed	Focalised	Multiple	Single	Cortical
Kulu	56.7	6.3	16.0	26.7	
Natunuku	50.9	5.7	9.4	32.1	1.9
Votua	17.0	1.1	17.0	53.2	11.7

Retouching

If we turn to flake retouching, we find that Kulu and Natunuku artefacts again show signs of greater reduction than those from Votua. Table 73 presents data on the mean extent of retouch found on flakes using three measures of retouch intensity. These indices provide a measure of the coverage, lateral extent and steepness of retouch on flakes. The Index of Invasiveness (Clarkson 2002), for example, measures retouch coverage over both the dorsal and ventral surfaces of an artefact. A result of 0 indicates no retouch and a result of 1 indicates the artefacts are completely covered in retouch over both faces. The perimeter of retouch, on the other hand, simply calculates the percentage of the flake margin that has been retouched. The last measure, or Kuhn's (1990) geometric index of reduction, calculates edge attrition as the ratio of the height of retouch to the maximum thickness of the flake. Again, a score of 0 indicates no retouch, while a score of

1 indicates that retouch height has equalled (or exceeded) flake thickness. All three measures indicate that retouch is greatest at Kulu, followed by Natunuku and Votua. These measures also indicate that retouching in Fijian sites tends to be flatter and more invasive than steep-edged and marginal.

Table 73. Degree of retouch exhibited at each site.

Site	Index of invasiveness	%Perimeter of retouch	Kuhn Index
Kulu	0.4	65	.11
Natunuku	0.2	57	.02
Votua	0.1	43	.01

Manufacturing products and tool use

Drill points

Drill points are a poorly defined implement class technologically and functionally, yet the term is widely employed in Pacific archaeology (but see Smith et al. 1996; Allen et al. 1997). For this analysis, we define drill points as flakes exhibiting steep bi-directional flaking and/or crushing on their margins, tapering to a point (Figure 146). The tip itself must show signs of damage or working. Ten drill points were identified in the analysis, at various stages of reduction. From this sample, there are indications of the nature of drill-point manufacture and discard thresholds. At present, there is no demonstrated link between these particular implements and the function their name implies. It is relevant, though, that their morphology closely resembles drill points of known function from other parts of the Pacific (Kamminga 1982; Smith et al. 1996:197; Allen et al. 1997) and the world (Grace 1989), that there are numerous examples of drilled shell artefacts in the Fijian Islands, and that use-wear studies conducted on other Fijian drill points have revealed torsion fractures and striations consistent with use as drills, as well as calcium-carbonate residues likely derived from working shell (D. Davenport, pers. comm., ANU).

All of the drill points examined were made from a high-quality chalcedony free of cortex or internal flaws. It seems that a diverse range of flake blanks were employed in the manufacture of these artefacts. A large proportion of drill points was probably made on bipolar flakes, however, as most were broken or had distal ends badly damaged by use, it was often difficult to be sure. One drill point clearly at an early stage of reduction was also clearly made from a non-bipolar flake, and showed two distinct pointed tips initiated at opposite ends of the margin (Figure 146, No. 317). Another drill point was made from a burin spall, as indicated by the presence of truncated retouch scars running along the dorsal ridge of the flake (Figure 146, No. 375).

Most identified drill points were actually broken tip fragments that probably snapped off during use. Only one intact drill point appears to have been worked down to a very small slug. This artefact is only 12 mm long, suggesting that hafting enabled a very long use-life for some of these tools. Only one drill point appeared to have a distinct haft element, as indicated by an abrupt change in the width of the flake and the invasiveness of retouch (Figure 146, No. 72).

Thus, while drill points were clearly made from high-quality raw materials, and probably served a specialised purpose, they were selected from a wide range of flake types and varied considerably (at least initially) in size and shape. This last observation is supported by very high coefficients of variation (CV) for the width (CV=104) and thickness (CV=29) of drill points. Unfortunately, there are too few complete drill points to examine variation in length.

Adzes

Nine adzes and adze-blanks were found at the four Fiji sites, and these were highly variable in size and shape, as shown in Figure 148. In order to understand the sequence of adze manufacture and rejuvenation and the effects that reduction intensity might have had on adze variability, it is possible to explore the relationship between the extent of flaking and grinding found on adzes and changes to their shape.

If adzes were gradually flaked, ground and resharpened over their use-life, we should expect a strong positive correlation between the amount of flaking an adze has received and the proportion of its surface covered by grinding (see also Ulm et al. 2005). To explore this proposition, we conducted a regression analysis on the relationship between the Index of Invasiveness and the percentage of surface grinding found on each adze. This test returns a strong and significant *negative* relationship between the amount of visible retouch and the percentage of surface grinding on an adze (R^2=-0.865, p=0.002). This suggests adzes were entirely covered with flake scars before grinding, and grinding gradually removed these scars as it extended to cover the entire surface. When flake scar and grinding coverage are calculated for Best's (1984) 15 illustrated Lakeba adzes, and the data added to our own sample, the results become even more significant (R^2=-0.705, p=<0.0005), as shown in Figure 149. We have excluded Best's adzes with high-backed, triangular cross sections (the so-called Samoan-type adzes) as these appear to have been manufactured from a very different type of blank to the other adzes in the collection. As Best only illustrated one side and one edge of each adze, we have assumed symmetry in the amount of flaking and grinding on the opposite surface. This has no doubt introduced error into our analysis, but we feel this is unlikely to be excessive, given the excellent results.

In Figure 150, we again pool Best's adze data with the present study to plot the percentage

Figure 148. Adzes and adze flakes from Fijian assemblages.

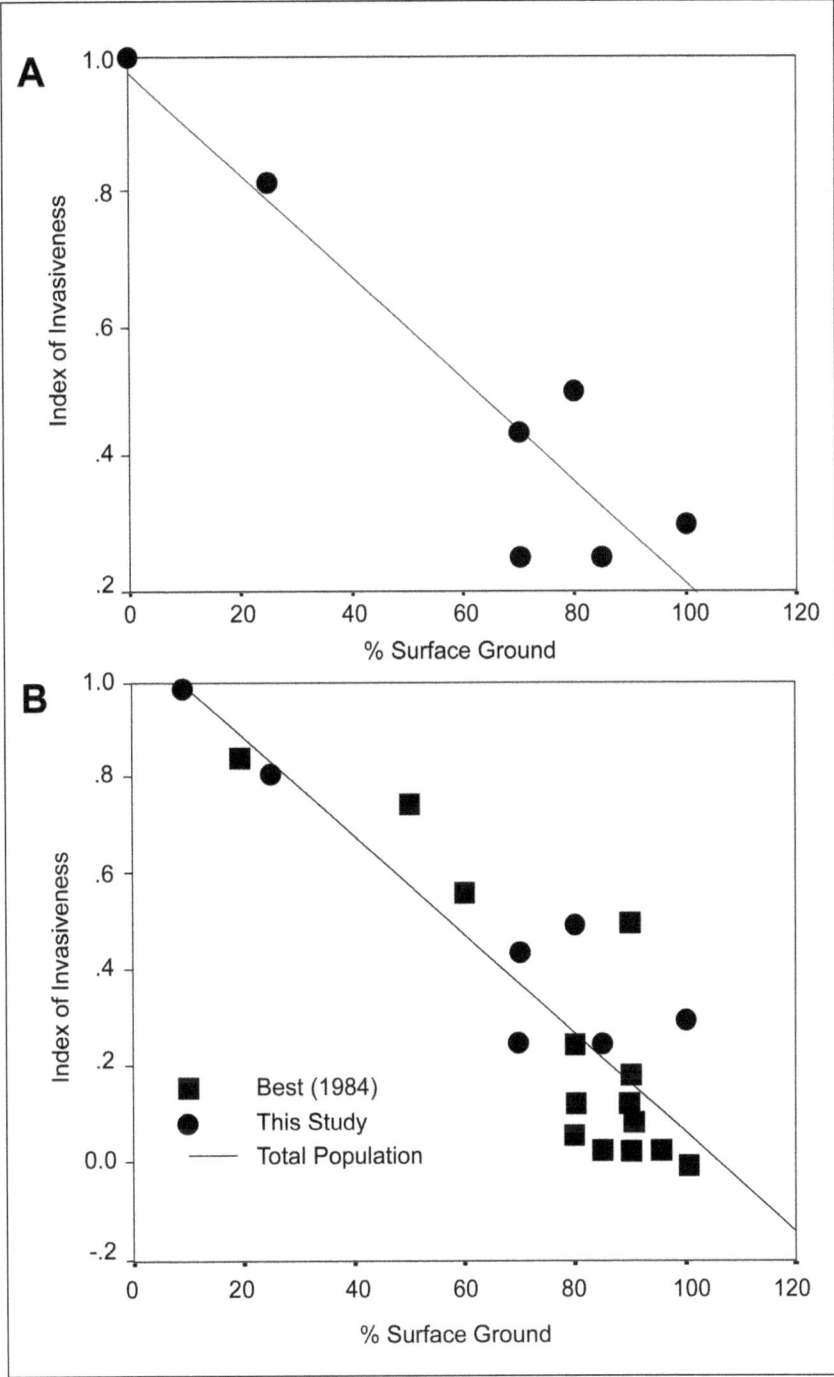

Figure 149. Relationship between the amount of retouch visible on adzes and the percentage of surface grinding for A) adzes from the excavated collection, and B) Best's (1984) illustrated adzes combined with those from the present study.

of surface grinding against the number of grinding facets found on each adze. It is clear that as more of the surface area is covered in grinding the number of grinding facets also increases ($R^2=0.582$, $p=0.001$).

Finally, Figure 151 shows that mean elongation decreases as the percentage of surface grinding increases, indicating that the blade tends to be successively worked back towards the butt end of the adze as it is resharpened (note that these results mirror the description by Smith et al. 1999 of Shag River Mouth adze rejuvenation). We do not explore size as a factor of reduction intensity as it is highly likely that different-sized adzes were manufactured for different purposes. Nevertheless, we are confident that the same changes to shape and surface morphology should hold for adzes of all sizes.

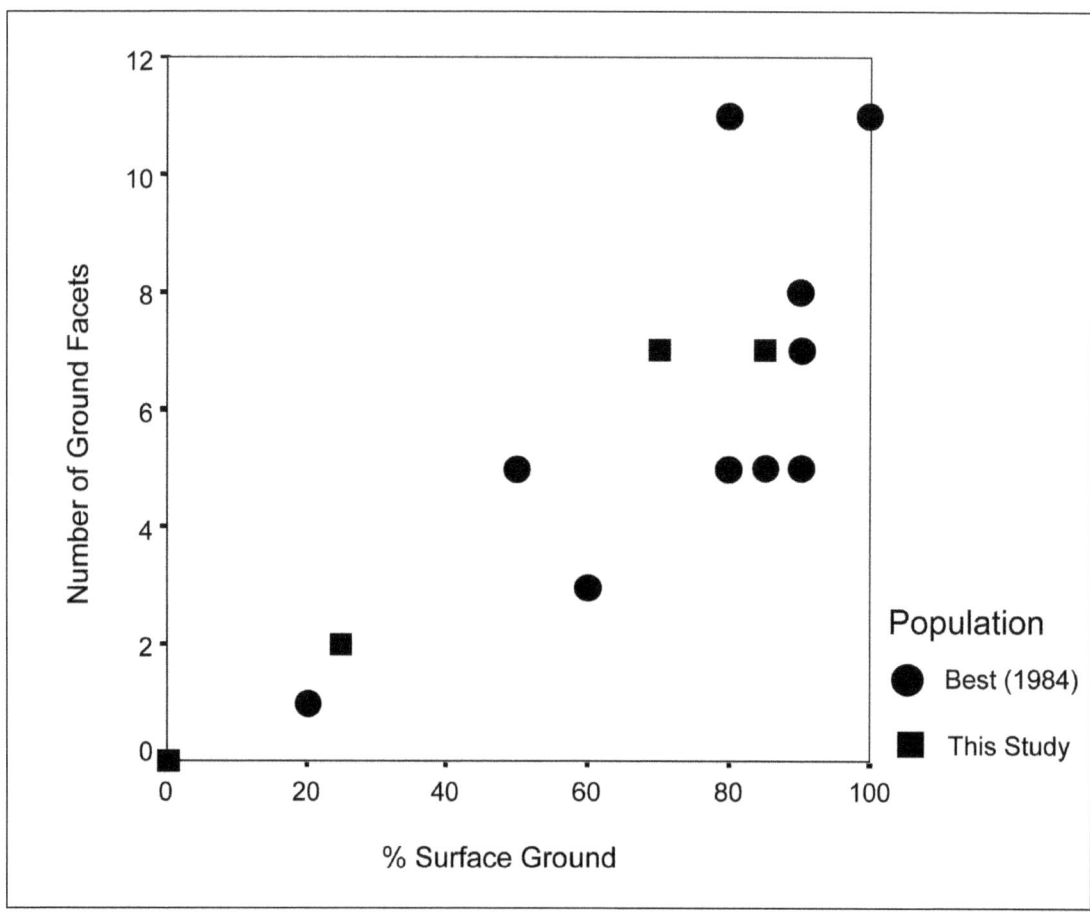

Figure 150. Relationship between the number of grinding facets on adzes and the percentage of ground surface area.

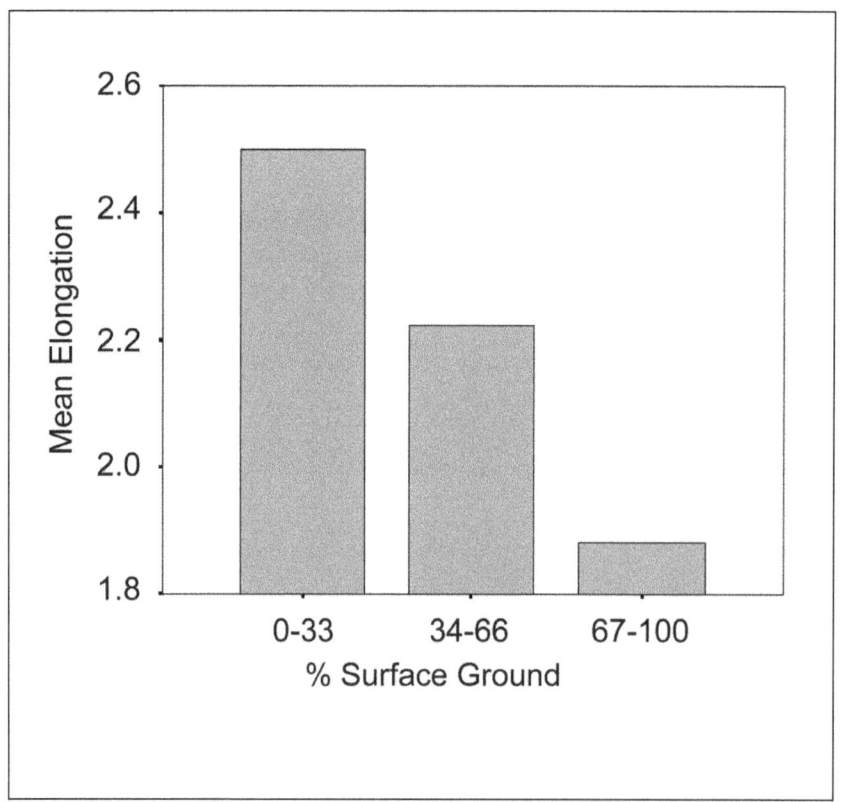

Figure 151. Relationship between adze elongation and the percentage of the ground surface area.

The preceding three tests allow us to form a basic model of Fijian adze manufacture and rejuvenation. Adzes were initially roughed out as ovate bifaces (Figure 152, No. 1). These were then steeply flaked around the perimeter to give a thick rectangular block tapering to a sharp edge at one end. Flake scars would tend to cover the entire blank at this stage. Grinding then initially adds an even edge to the adze, but also gradually increases in area and results in a growing number of facets as the adze continues to be shaped and resharpened. This process gradually removes old flake scars from the surface. With successive resharpening, whether involving regrinding or more drastic edge renewal (involving the removal of flakes that preserve grinding on their dorsal surfaces, e.g. top row of Figure 152), the edge is steadily worked back towards the butt, reducing length and elongation over its use-life.

If this model of adze reduction is correct, and the mean area of grinding and the mean number of facets are examined for each site, it appears that adzes from the Beqa sites are more heavily worked (mean surface grinding=75%, mean facets=6) than those found at Natunuku (mean surface grinding=53%, mean facets=3).

Use-wear analysis

Use-wear studies observe the degree of modification on an artefact's edge due to use. These can include edge rounding, striations, polish, abrasion and edge fractures (Kamminga 1982:4–17). Use-wear analysis is undertaken to determine the function to which the tool has been put. Ethnographic and ethnoarchaeological studies (White 1967:406; Gould et al. 1971:149; White et al. 1977; Shackley and Kerr 1985:95) have discovered that debitage and unmodified primary flakes are used for a wide range of purposes. In addition to these ethnoarchaeological studies, analyses of lithic assemblages from the Pacific have revealed that as well as complete flakes, broken flakes and flaked pieces were also used as tools (Sheppard 1993:133). These factors

Figure 152. Adze blank and rejuvenation flakes.

should be taken into consideration when analysis is undertaken and the lithic assemblages studied in their entirety. In keeping with these findings, the entire assemblages from all three sites were examined for traces of use-wear.

From microscopic analysis of the lithics recovered from the excavations, it is evident that only a small percentage of each assemblage carried any signs of use-wear. This consisted of edge fracturing (step fractures caused by friction) and edge rounding. Both forms of wear typically occurred together on these specimens, and are best attributed to the action of scraping. No attempt was made to identify the types of contact materials worked. Most flakes were large enough to have been hand held, and no signs of hafting were discovered, even on the proximal ends of drill points which were closely examined for this type of wear. The occurrence of use-wear at the three main sites is listed below.

Kulu

Use-wear occurs on six items, one flake made from chalcedony (C9:40–50 cm) and one bipolar flake (C11:130–140 cm) constructed from quartz, and four drill points. This represents 11% of the total assemblage. Use-wear consists of rounding and fractures on distal and lateral margins on the flakes, and damage to the distal points of the drill points.

Natunuku

Use-wear occurs on eight flakes (two bipolar) and six drill points, totalling 13% of the assemblage. Use-wear consists of tiny fractures and smoothing on the margins and distal ends of the drills. For unretouched flakes, the lateral margins most commonly exhibited wear, although two flakes did possess wear on the distal margin. One flake had wear on both the lateral and distal margins, while another showed wear on the dorsal ridge.

Votua

From Votua, 12 artefacts had use-wear (all flakes), making up 4% of the assemblage. This damage consisted of step fractures, striations and rounding, most commonly on the lateral margins, with only one flake displaying damage on the distal margin.

Manufacturing activities

Table 74 summarises evidence for the total range of technological activities conducted at each site. Kulu and Natunuku display the widest range of technological activities, despite smaller assemblage sizes. They also possess the highest frequencies of retouching, adze manufacture/use, and drill-point manufacture/use. The relative scarcity of retouching, adzes and drill points, in addition to the presence of large volcanic hammerstones and the absence of use-wear on artefacts, suggests a different set of manufacturing/use activities at Votua (Tables 74 and 75). These activities appear to be focused more on procurement and early-stage reduction than at Kulu or Natunuku. Overall, assemblage differences are attributable to the degree to which raw materials were reduced, as well as the range of manufacturing activities at each site. While

Table 74. Percentages for various manufacturing activities conducted at each site.

Site	%Retouched	%Adze products	% Drill points	% Hammerstones	% Use-wear
Kulu	14	9	9		11
Natunuku	12	4	6		13
Votua	4	1		1	4

Table 75. Summary of the abundance of technological activities and artefact types found at Fijian sites.

Nature/Activity	Kulu	Ugaga	Natunuku	Votua
Assemblage size	Small	Very small	Medium	Large
Richness	Normal	Normal	Normal	Low
Siliceous stone availability	Poor	Poor	Fair	Good
Reduction intensity	High	None	Medium	Low
Drill points	High	None	Medium	None
Flakes with use-wear	Low	None	High	None
Adzes	Low	High	Medium	None
Adze rejuvenation	High	None	Low	Low
Adze manufacture	None	None	Low	Very low
Adze reduction	High	None	None	Low

the range of manufacturing activities (and hence the range of technological classes) at three sites (Natunuku, Kulu and Ugaga) appears largely related to sample size, Votua stands out as technologically impoverished, consistent with primary core reduction as the single dominant technological activity at the site.

Discussion and conclusion

At the outset of this analysis, four basic questions were formulated:

1. What was the nature of stone procurement on different islands?
2. What was the range of reduction strategies and manufacturing activities undertaken at each site?
3. Are there differences in reduction intensity between sites?
4. Might assemblage variability reflect levels of mobility or economic and social differentiation between sites?

Technological analysis of the Fijian assemblages has provided partial answers to some of these questions, and these may be summarised as follows.

The nature of the stone-procurement strategies at each of the Fijian sites appears to reflect the availability of raw materials in the surrounding landscape, with the closest raw materials tending to dominate assemblages. In all cases, however, raw materials had to be imported over considerable distances, sometimes involving water-crossings of more than 40 km. A range of reduction strategies was employed at each site, with all sites exhibiting evidence for the use of both freehand percussion and bipolar reduction techniques. Bipolar reduction dominates the Natunuku and Kulu assemblages, with cores tending to be worked to a very small size and flakes tending to be more characteristic of later stages of reduction. In contrast, the Votua assemblage displays far greater use of freehand percussion, with cores and flakes exhibiting characteristics of earlier stages of reduction. Kulu and Natunuku also display the widest range of technological activities, despite their smaller assemblage sizes, and possess the highest frequencies of retouch, adze and drill-point manufacture/use. Votua, on the other hand, suggests a more limited set of manufacturing/use activities, focused more on procurement and early-stage reduction.

Our last question moved the focus from questions of a direct technological nature to one of cultural significance – might assemblage variability reflect levels of mobility or economic and social differentiation between sites? At present, this question cannot be answered satisfactorily, although a number tentative suggestions are made below.

As outlined, assemblage variability is greatest at the sites of Natunuku and Kulu, where both assemblages exhibit dominant bipolar reduction and a reliance on chalcedony. Occupants of Natunuku accessed the raw materials at the range of up to 50 km inland, while at Kulu the nearest source is perhaps no closer than 40–80 km away on Viti Levu. The extreme degree of bipolar working at Kulu would appear to reflect the scarcity of lithic resources on the island, with a water-crossing necessary to access them. The fact that the same strategies were undertaken at Natunuku suggests that the distance of 50 km inland was also enough to require that raw materials were conserved and curated. Considering the maritime nature of Fijian society, the 40 km sea-crossing would be no more arduous or less frequently travelled than a distance of 50 km over land. Both sites seem to demonstrate, however, that travel to and from these sources was not frequent.

The assemblage at Votua is markedly different from the others, with freehand percussion dominating the assemblage, resulting in larger cores and flakes, with more cortex and fewer retouched artefacts. The distance between Mago and Vanuabalavu Island, where the source of the jasper that makes up the bulk of the Votua assemblage is located, is only 23 km, and the casual use of this resource suggests frequent contact between these two islands. Further work on the Fijian islands would serve to provide further baseline data to tackle these interesting questions of social relations, inter-island visitation and resource use.

The greater range of activities, technique variations and the degree of reduction exhibited at each of the sites analysed in this paper indicates a level of technological differentiation not previously documented for Fijian sites of Lapita age. Whether such differences are related to varying levels of residential mobility, the range or intensity of economic activities, the location of sites on islands of vastly different size, or differential access to raw materials, remains an open question at this stage. Addressing these questions in more detail requires attention to multiple lines of evidence, such as site sizes, the diversity and quantity of non-stone artefacts, evidence of inter-island contacts, and the range of subsistence opportunities offered in each location, as well as the taphonomic processes at work at each individual site. At this stage, only tentative conclusions can be reached regarding the wider implications of assemblage variation in Fiji, and as such, the questions raised in this paper remain an imperative for future research in the area.

Appendix: Inventory of artefacts made in shell, coral, bone and stone

Geoffrey Clark and Katherine Szabó

Archaeology and Natural History, The Australian National University

Table 76. Artefacts made in shell and other materials found in EPF and Karobo excavations (with permission of the Fiji Museum).

Number	Type of Artefact	Material	Location	Quantity	Comments
	Natunuku				
1	Bead	Shell-?species	Trench 3, Square B6, 50–60 cm	1	Diameter 8.8 mm, 4.2 mm thickness, hole diameter 4.0 mm. Drilled biconically.
2	Bead	Shell-?species	Trench 3, Square B6, 40–50 cm	1	Bivalve shell. Diameter 8.6 mm, 1.7 mm thickness, inner diameter 2.5 mm.
3	Bead	Bone-fish	Trench 3, Square B6, Layer 1 30–40 cm	2+7 frags	Fish vertebrae – probably shark or other cartilaginous fish. Diameter 16.0 mm, 3.5 mm perforation.
4	Bead	Bone-fish	Trench 3, Square A3, Layer 2 (light brown)	1	Fish vertebrae – probably shark or other cartilaginous fish. Diameter 12.0 mm, internal perforation 1.7 mm.
5	Bead	Shell-*Conus* sp.	Trench 3, Square B5, 0–10 cm	1	Two perforations, one on spire, one on side. Diameter of largest hole 10.95 mm, 19.3 mm length.
6	Bead-long unit	Shell-*Tridacna* sp.	Test Pit 2, 10–20 cm	1	*Tridacna*. Biconical perforations. Flat polished back. Length 28.8 mm, width 11.9 mm, height 6 mm.
7	Bead-long unit	Shell-*Tridacna* sp.	Trench 3, Square B6, Layer 1, 50–60 cm	1	Burnt *Tridacna*. Biconical perforations with one end broken. Length 18.8 mm, width 15.3 mm, height 7.4 mm.
8	Bead-long unit	Shell-*Tridacna* sp.	Test Pit 1, 0–10 cm	1	Unfinished (beginning of a perforation). Length 24.0 mm, width 13.9 mm, height 9.8 mm.
9	Ring-armband	Shell-*Conus* sp.	Test pit 1–2, 0–10 cm	1	Thickness (height) uneven, ranging from 5.9 mm to 4.1 mm, width 16.4 mm. Finished and broken. Rectangular cross section.
10	Ring-armband	Shell-*Conus* sp.	From brown-black surface soil on west side of ditch between depression and shore	1	Width 6.4 mm, height 5.7 mm, internal diameter 55 mm. Finished and broken. Semi-circular cross section.
11	Ring-armband	Shell-*Conus* sp.	Trench 3, Square A4, 0–10 cm	1	Width 8.4 mm, height 5.2 mm, internal diameter 65 mm. Finished and broken. Semi-circular cross section.
12	Ring-armband	Shell-*Conus* sp.	Trench 3, Square A6, 40–50 cm	1	Width 9.7 mm, height 6.3 mm, internal diameter 55 mm. Finished and broken. Semi-circular cross section.
13	Ring	Shell-*Conus* sp.	Trench 3, Square A6, 40–50 cm	1	Finished and broken. Constructed from outer perimeter of a ground *Conus* spire. Width 4.0 mm, height 2.0 mm.
14	Ring	Shell-*Conus* sp.	Test Pit 1–2, 20–30 cm	1	Complete ring. Constructed from ground *Conus* spire. Diameter 17.5 mm, height 2.8 mm, hole diameter 8.6 mm.
15	Ring	Shell-*Trochus* sp.	Test Pit 1, 0–10 cm	1	Preform fragment.
16	Armband unit	Shell-*Conus* sp.	Test Pit 2, 10–20 cm	1	Rectangular unit. Four perforations – one at each corner. Polished. Perforations not biconical. One edge snapped off. Two others ground down and one flat. Finished and broken.
17	Armband unit	Shell-?species	Trench 3, Square A3, 0–10 cm	1	Rectangular unit. Two perforations. One at each end.

Continued on next page

Table 76 continued

Number	Type of Artefact	Material	Location	Quantity	Comments
18	Miscellaneous-Spire	Shell-*Conus* sp.	Trench 3, Square A4, 0–10 cm	1	Natural shape of spire has been smoothed. Ground flat on underside. Diameter 26.4 mm, diameter of perforation 4.9 mm.
19	Miscellaneous	Shell-*Spondylus* sp.	Test Pit 2, 10–20 cm	1	Fragment shaped to a rough drill shape, not finished. Length 25.2 mm, width 19.1 mm.
Navatu					
20	Ring-armband	Shell-*Trochus* sp.	Square 17A, Trench B, 20–40 cm	1	Circular fragment from base of *Trochus* shell flaked into shape. Unfinished ring blank. Diameter of shell 65 mm.
Malaqereqere					
21	Ring-armband	Shell-*Trochus* sp.	Square A2, 0–10 cm	1	Finished and broken. Constructed from outer perimeter of a ground spire. Diameter of original shell 5 mm, height 3.2 mm.
22	Ring-armband	Shell-*Trochus* sp.	Square A2, 10–20 cm	1	Incomplete. Base of shell starting to be shaped into ring.
Ugaga					
23	Ring-armband	Shell-?species.	Square A14, 10–20 cm	1	Finished and broken. Height 17.9 mm, width 18.9 mm. Triangular cross section.
24	Ring-armband	Shell-*Conus* sp.	Square D13, 40–60 cm	1	Finished and broken. Width 9.7 mm, height 5.6 mm. Rectangular cross section.
25	Miscellaneous	Shell-?species.	Square D13, 10–20 cm	1	Rectangular fragment. Width 23.1 mm, length 19.8 mm, height 4 mm. Smoothed and shaped on edge, engraved on inner side with triangular geometric pattern.
26	Miscellaneous	Shell-pearl shell	Square C12, 20–30 cm	1	Cut and smoothed on all edges. Rectangular in shape with drilled hole commenced on inside surface. Diameter of hole 7.2 mm, length 35.5 mm, width 25.3 mm, height 6.7 mm.
27	Miscellaneous	Shell-*Conus* sp.	Square P10, 10–20 cm	1	Rectangular cut section of shell. At start of working process. Length 40.6 mm, width 18.6 mm.
28	Miscellaneous	Shell-*Tridacna* sp.	Square J5, 40 cm	1	Large bivalve shell worked by removal of edge. Length 120.5 mm, width 154.0 mm.
Votua					
29	Ring-armband	Shell-*Conus* sp.	Area 1, surface	1	Finished and broken. Width 6.6 mm, height 3.5 mm. Semi-circular cross section.
30	Ring-armband	Shell-*Conus* sp.	Area 1, 20–30 cm	1	Finished and broken. Width 9.2 mm, height 3.6 mm. Rectangular cross section.
31	Ring-armband	Shell-*Conus* sp.	Area 2, Square 1, 50–60 cm	1	Finished and broken. Width 6.8 mm, height 5.1 mm. Semi-circular cross section.
32	Ring-armband	Shell-*Conus* sp.	Area 2, Square 1, 10–20 cm	1	Finished and broken. Width 12.7 mm, height 8.1 mm. Rectangular cross section.
33	Ring-armband	Shell-*Conus* sp.	Area 2, Square 2, 40–50 cm	1	Finished and broken. Width 2.7 mm, height 3.2 mm. Rectangular cross section.
34	Ring-armband	Shell-*Conus* sp.	Area 2, Square 1, 40–50 cm	1	Finished and broken. Width 6.7 mm, height 5.3 mm. Semi-circular cross section.
35	Armband unit	Shell-Shell-*Conus* sp. sp.	Area 2, Square 3, 50–60 cm	1	Curved rectangular segment. Four holes drilled at corners. Length 40.5 mm, width 16.5 mm, height 2.9 mm. Rectangular cross section. Complete.

Continued on next page

Table 76 *continued*

Number	Type of Artefact	Material	Location	Quantity	Comments
36	Armband unit	Shell-*Conus* sp.	Area 2, Square 2, 50–60 cm	1	Curved rectangular segment. Two drilled holes, one at each end. Length 30.8 mm, width 11.4 mm, height 2.7 mm. Rectangular cross section. Complete.
37	Armband unit	Shell-*Conus* sp.	Area 2, Square 2, 0–10 cm	1	Broken curved rectangular segment. Two corner holes along intact edge. Length 27.4 mm, width 20.4 mm, height 3.3 mm. Rectangular cross section.
38	Beads	Shell-?species	Area 2, Square 1, 40–50 cm	1	Circular shaped fragment of shell with central perforation, smoothed on all edges. Diameter 6.3 mm, central hole diameter 3.1 mm. Complete.
39	Beads	Shell-?species	Area 2, Square 4, 40–50 cm	1	Circular shaped fragment of shell with central perforation, smoothed on all edges. Diameter 13.6 mm, central hole diameter 3.5mm. Complete.
40	Miscellaneous	Shell-*Tridacna* sp.	Area 2, Square 1, 0–10 cm	1	Adze preform. Length 119.0 mm, width 26.0 mm, height 32.6 mm. Flaked along length.
41	Miscellaneous	Sea urchin spine	Area 2, Square 1, 50–60 cm	1	Broken sea urchin spine shaped at end to form point. Length 37 mm.
42	Miscellaneous	Shell-pearl shell	Area 2, Square 1, 40–50 cm	1	Fish-hook blank, roughed out section in L shape. Length 15.2 mm, width 14.7 mm.
43	Miscellaneous	Shell-pearl shell	Area 2, Square 2, 50–60 cm	2	Flaked shell, possibly blanks at first stage of working.
Karobo					
44	Miscellaneous	Shell-*Trochus* sp.	Square Q3, Layer 1/2	1+6	Spire with hole drilled in one side, Diameter of hole 13.9 mm and lowest ring segment removed, opposite to hole. First stage reduction to make ring. Six other fragments.
Votua					
45	Abrader	Coral	Area 2, Square 2, 20–30 cm	1	Grooved coral cobble. Length 122.8 mm, width 83.3 mm, depth 52.0 mm. Three grooves on ground surface (6.7–8.2 mm wide, depth 3.5–5.5 mm). Two shallow grooves running across main grooves. One groove on side of cobble.
46	Abrader	Coral	Area 2, Square 3, 40–50 cm	1	Grooved coral. Length 63.6 mm, width 57.8 mm, depth 50.2 mm. Four grooves on surface and two sides. Width of grooves 8.3–9.7 mm, depth 6.2–7.3 mm.
47	Abrader	Coral	Area 2, Square 4, 10–50 cm	1	Grooved coral. Length 49.5 mm, width 42.4 mm, depth 39.2 mm. Two grooves, one on top and one on side. Width of grooves 11.6–11.8 mm, depth 7.9–8.2 mm.
48	Abrader	Coral	Area 2, Square 3, 50–60 cm	1	Grooved coral. Length 60 mm, width 48.2 mm, depth 30.3 mm. Two grooves on surface. Width is 10.5–10.9 mm, depth 9.1 mm.
49	Ornament/gaming piece?	Quartz/calcite?	Area 2, Square 1, 10–20 cm.	1	Stone disk. Ground on surfaces and circumference. Diameter 33.9 mm, depth 9.5 mm.
Ugaga					
50	File/abrader	Sandstone	P10, 40–50 cm	1	Stone file made in laminated material. Top and bottom surface ground flat, sides rounded. Length 146.5 mm, width 42.0 mm, depth 33.8 mm.

Continued on next page

Table 76 *continued*

Number	Type of Artefact	Material	Location	Quantity	Comments
51	Abrader	Coral	M8, 30–40 cm		Grooved coral. Length 109.8 mm, width 80.2 mm, depth 39.9 mm. Two grooves on surface, one on opposite face and one on side. Width is 13.1–13.4 mm, depth 7.4–9.2 mm.
	Karobo				
52	Stone pot anvil	Volcanic conglomerate	Square A2, 1.5 m depth	1	Material with pyroxene/amphiboles. Length 62 mm, width 46 mm, depth 32.5 mm. Surface is incised by lines creating a checker-board pattern of squares ca. 5–6 mm in size.
53	Stone pot anvil	Volcanic conglomerate	Square A2, 1.5 m depth	1	Material with pyroxene/amphiboles. Length 62 mm, width 43 mm, depth 17.5 mm. Surface is incised by lines creating a checker-board pattern of squares ca. 5–6 mm in size.

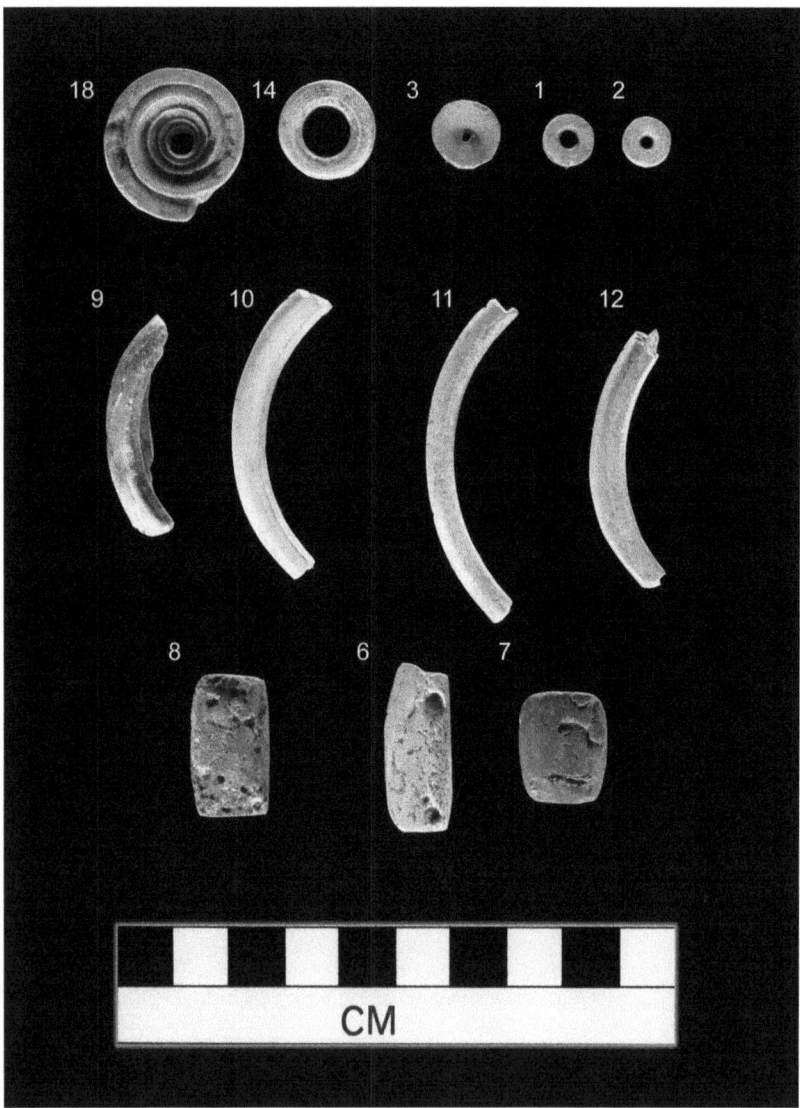

Figure 153. Natunuku shell and bone artefacts.

Figure 154. Ugaga shell artefacts.

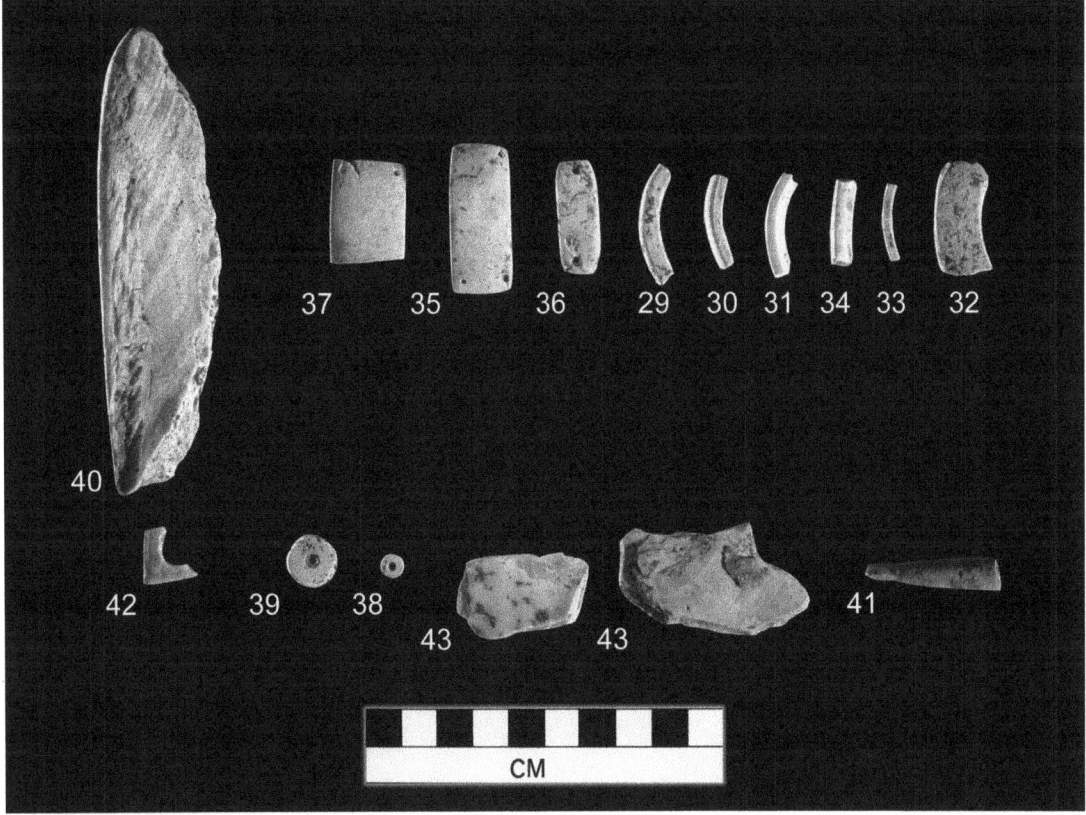

Figure 155. Votua shell artefacts and a worked sea urchin spine (41).

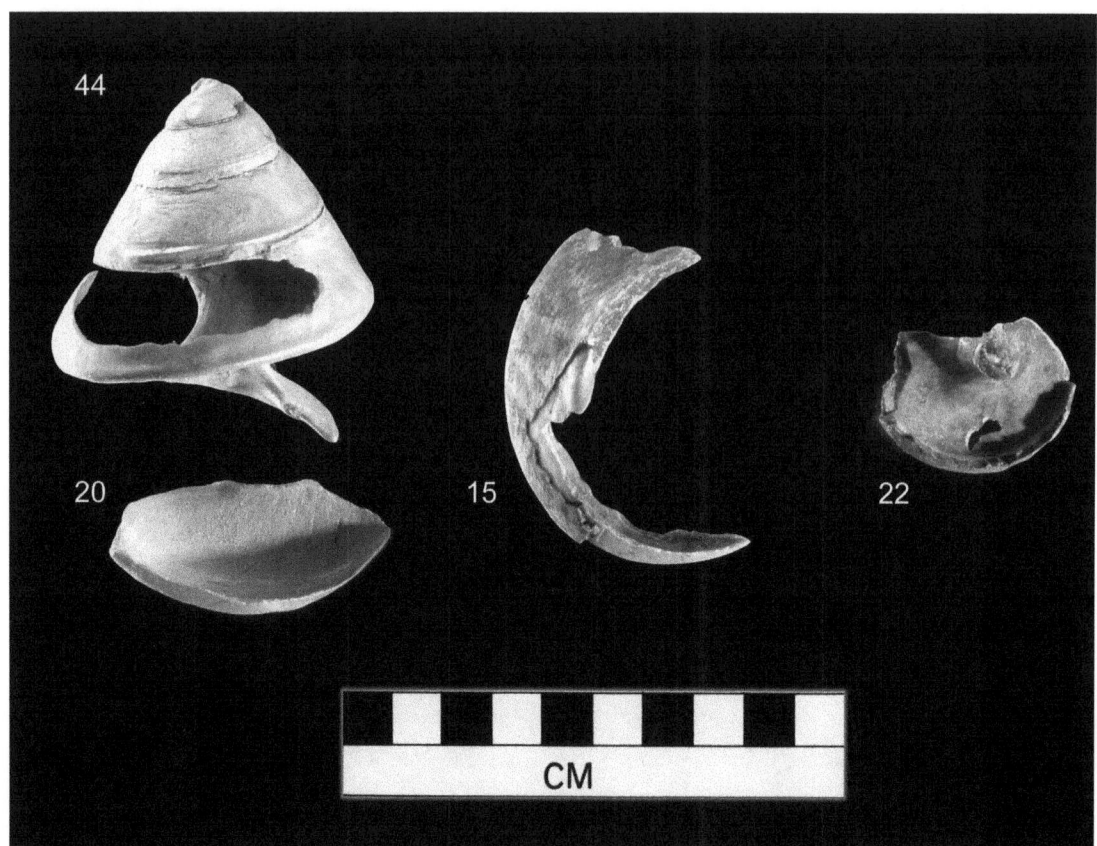

Figure 156. Worked *Trochus* shell from Karobo, Navatu, Malaqereqere and Natunuku.

Figure 157. A quartz/calcite stone disk from the Votua Lapita site.

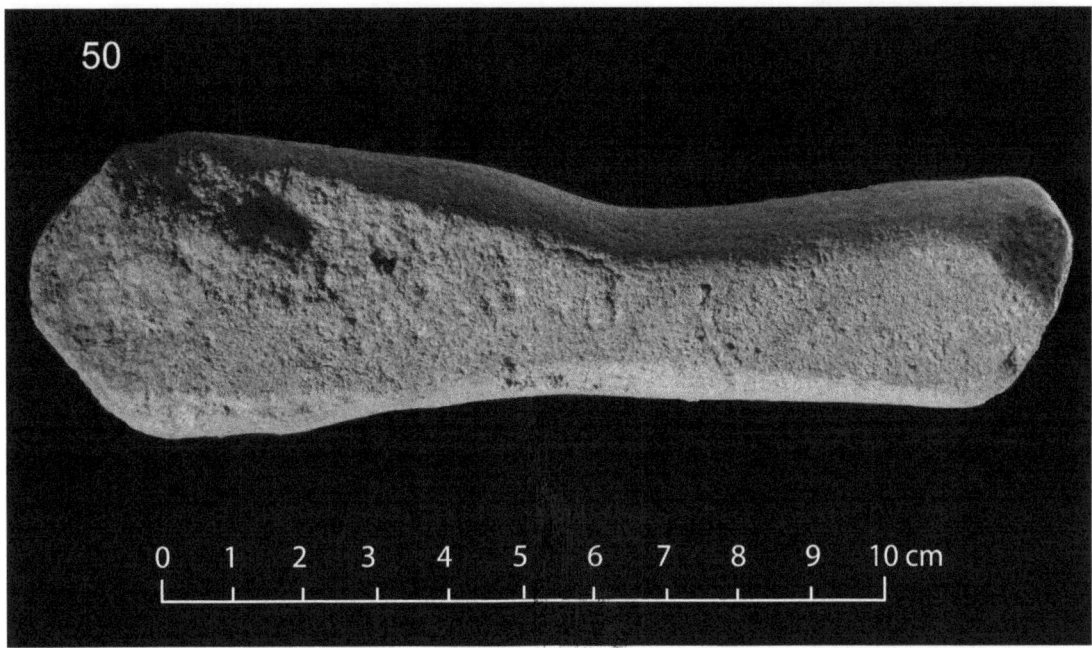

Figure 158. Sandstone file from Ugaga Island.

Figure 159. Grooved coral artefacts from Ugaga (51) and Votua (46 and 45).

Figure 160. Top, grooved stone artefacts from Karobo made in a pyroclastic rock/tuff (Sq. A2, Layer 5, 1.5 m depth) used to mark pots with cross-hatch relief. Bottom, sherd with cross-hatch relief on right and impression in modelling compound taken from grooved stone (52) on left.

References

Allen, M.S. and Bell, G. 1988. Lapita flaked stone assemblages: Sourcing, technological, and functional studies. In: Kirch, P.V. and Hunt, T.L. (eds), *Archaeology of the Lapita cultural complex: A critical review*, pp. 83–98. Thomas Burke Memorial Washington State Museum Research Report No. 5. The Burke Museum, Seattle.

Allen, J., Holdaway, R. and Fullagar, R. 1997. Identifying specialisation, production and exchange in the archaeological record. the case of shell bead manufacture on Motupore Island, Papua. *Archaeology in Oceania* 32: 13–38.

Band, R.B. 1968. *The geology of southern Viti Levu and Mbengga*. Bulletin 15, Ministry of Lands and Mineral Resources, Fiji.

Bartholomew, R.W. 1959. *Geology of the Lautoka area, north-west Viti Levu*. Bulletin 2, Ministry of Lands and Mineral Resources, Fiji.

Best, S. 1977. Archaeological investigations on Lakeba, Lau Group, Fiji. *New Zealand Archaeological Association Newsletter* 20: 28–34.

Best, S. 1984. Lakeba. Prehistory of a Fijian Island. Unpublished PhD thesis, Department of Anthropology, University of Auckland.

Birks, L. 1973. *Archaeological excavations at the Sigatoka Dune Site, Fiji*. Fiji Museum Bulletin 1. Fiji Museum, Suva.

Birks, L. and Birks, H. 1967. A brief report on excavations at Sigatoka Dune Site, Fiji. *New Zealand Archaeological Association Newsletter* 10: 16–25.

Birks, L. and Birks, H. 1968. Adzes from excavations at Sigatoka, Fiji. *Archaeology and Physical Anthropology in Oceania* 3(1): 105–115.

Clarkson, C. 2002. An index of invasiveness for the measurement of unifacial and bifacial retouch. A theoretical, experimental and archaeological verification. *Journal of Archaeological Science* 29: 65–75.

Cotterell, B. and Kamminga, J. 1987. The formation of flakes. *American Antiquity* 52: 675–708.

Elm, S., Cotter, S., Cotter, M., Lilley, I., Clarkson, C. and Reid, J. 2005. Edge-ground hatchets on the southern Curtis Coast, Central Queensland. A preliminary assessment of technology, chronology and prevenance. In: McFarland, I., Paton, R. and Mountain, M-J. (eds), *Many exchanges: Archaeology, history, community and the work of Isabel McBride*, pp. 323–342. Aboriginal History Monograph 11, Canberra.

Gifford, E.W. 1949. Excavations in Viti Levu. *Journal of the Polynesian Society* 58: 83–90.

Gifford, E.W. 1951. Archaeological excavations in Fiji. *University of California Anthropological Records* 13: 189–288.

Gould, R.A., Koster, D.A. and Sontz, A.H. 1971. The lithic assemblage of the Western Desert Aborigines of Australia. *American Antiquity* 36: 149–169.

Grace, R. 1989. *Interpreting the function of stone tools*. British Archaeological Reports International Series 47. Archaeopress, Oxford.

Halsey, A. 1995. Obsidian resource maximisation. A comparison of two Lapita assemblages. Unpublished BA Honours thesis, Department of Prehistory, La Trobe University, Melbourne.

Hiscock, P. 1982. A technological analysis of quartz assemblages from the south coast. In: Bowdler, S. (ed), *Coastal Archaeology in Eastern Australia*, pp. 32–45. Department of Prehistory, RSPAS, Australian National University.

Hiscock, P. 2001. Sizing up prehistory. Sample size and the composition of Australian artefact assemblages. *Australian Aboriginal Studies* 1:48–62.

Hunt, C. 1979. A flaked stone industry from Fiji. *The Artefact* 4: 37–30.

Hunt, T. 1980. Towards Fiji's past. Archaeological research on Southwestern Viti Levu. Unpublished MA thesis, Department of Anthropology, University of Auckland.

Hunt, T.L., Aronson, K.A., Cochrane, E.E., Field, J.S., Humphrey, L. and Reith, T.M. 1999. A preliminary report on archaeological research in the Yasawa Islands, Fiji. *Domodomo* 12: 5–43.

Ibbotson, P. 1960. *Geology of the Suva Area, Viti Levu.* Bulletin 4, Ministry of Lands and Mineral Resources, Fiji.

Ibbotson, P. 1969. *The geology of east-central Vanua Levu.* Bulletin 16, Ministry of Lands and Mineral Resources, Fiji.

Kamminga, J. 1982. *Over the edge. Functional analysis of Australian stone tools.* University of Queensland Occasional Papers in Anthropology 12, University of Queensland.

Kuhn, S. 1990. A geometric index of reduction for unifacial stone tools. *Journal of Archaeological Science* 17: 585–593.

Shackley, M. and Kerr, H. 1985. Ethnography and experiment in the interpretation of quartz artifact assemblages from Namibia. An optimistic attempt. *Lithic Technology* 14: 95–97.

Sheppard, P.J. 1992. A report on the flaked assemblages from three southeast Solomons Lapita sites (SE-SZ-8, SE-RF-2 and SE-RF-6). In: Galipaud, J.C. (ed), *Poterie Lapita et Peuplement*, pp. 145–154. Orstom, Noumea.

Sheppard, P.J. 1993. Lapita lithics. Trade/exchange and technology. A view from the Reefs/Santa Cruz. *Archaeology in Oceania* 28: 121–137.

Smith, I., Campbell, M. and Bristow, P. 1996. Flaked stone tools. In: Anderson, A., Allingham, B. and Smith, I. (eds), *Shag River Mouth. The Archaeology of an Early Southern Maori Village*, pp. 77–102. ANH Publications, RSPAS, Australian National University.

Swete Kelly, M.C. 2001. Lapita lithics. An analysis of obsidian acquisition, utilisation and discard on the Anir Islands. BA Honours, School of Archaeology and Anthropology, Australian National University.

Ulm, S., Cotter, S., Cotter, M., Lilley, I., Clarkson, C. and Reid, J. 2005. Edge-ground hatchets on the southern Curtis Coast, central Queensland: A preliminary assessment of technology, chronology and provenance. In: Macfarlane, I., Mountain, M-J. and Paton, R. (eds), *Many exchanges: Archaeology, history, community and the work of Isabel McBryde*, pp. 323–342. Aboriginal History Monograph 11, Canberra.

White, J.P. 1967. Ethno-archaeology in New Guinea. Two examples. *Mankind* 6: 409–414.

White, J.P., Modjeska, N. and Irari, H. 1977. Group identification and mental templates. An ethnographic experiment. In: Wright, R.V.S. (ed), *Stone tools as cultural markers*, pp. 380–390. Australian Institute of Aboriginal Studies, Canberra.

15

Characterisation and sourcing of archaeological adzes and flakes from Fiji

Barry Fankhauser
Department of Archaeology and Natural History, The Australian National University

Geoffrey Clark
Department of Archaeology and Natural History, The Australian National University

Atholl Anderson
Department of Archaeology and Natural History, The Australian National University

Introduction

This chapter focuses on the characterisation and sourcing of lithic artefacts (adzes and flakes) found in excavations conducted in 1996 and 1997 on Beqa Island, Mago Island and Viti Levu. Although the primary focus is on basalt because of accumulated knowledge, other rock types are represented due to the diversity of lithic materials found in Fiji in contrast to oceanic basalts in the island groups of Polynesia. Lithic material found in the Fijian Islands could be from the island on which it was found, from within the archipelago, or imported from another island group, especially from Samoa (Best 1984; Best et al. 1992; Weisler 1993a). Determination of the provenance of raw materials found during excavation of a site can be valuable in providing information on contacts between that location and others. Provenance is defined here as the material's place of origin, i.e. the geological source (see Weisler 1993c:62).

Most studies have focused on basalt, which was the most widely distributed commodity in prehistoric Polynesia to the east of Fiji, and therefore has the potential to contribute most to the understanding of prehistoric trade and social interaction. In addition to Samoa, basalt sourcing studies have been undertaken in several island groups of Polynesia, including the Cook Islands

(Walter 1990; Weisler 1994; Walter and Sheppard 1996; Sheppard et al. 1997), Pitcairn and Mangareva (Weisler 1993b, 1994, 1995, 1996a, 1996b) and Hawaii (Cleghorn et al. 1985; Weisler 1990a, 1990b, 1990c). Determining the source of an object depends on regional geological knowledge, i.e. the macroscopic, petrographic and geochemical attributes of source material. Basalt sources in much of Polynesia have been extensively studied and chemically analysed. This is not the case for Fiji. Fijian lithic sources have not been geochemically characterised except for some analyses conducted by Best (1984). Fiji is more petrologically diverse given its location to the west of the Andesite Line, which separates Samoa and the rest of Polynesia (alkali and tholeitic oceanic basalts) from the andesite-plutonic rocks of Tonga and Fiji (Dickinson and Shutler 1979; Sinton et al. 1985). The results of a second project investigating the chemical composition of siliceous artefacts are presented in the Appendix.

Geochemical characterisation of adze rocks

Weisler (1993c) has given a summary of references which deal with different types of analysis for basalt sourcing in Polynesia. These include macroscopic descriptions of adzes and polished flakes (R. Green 1974:141; Kirch 1988:192), thin-section analysis (Buist 1969; Emory 1975; Kirch 1975; Best 1984; T. Green 1984; Cleghorn et al. 1985; White 1987; Weisler 1990b; Withrow 1990, 1991), and geochemical analysis of adze material (Best 1984; Walter 1990; Best et al. 1992; Weisler 1989, 1990b, 1993a). Additional references for geochemical analysis include: Walter and Sheppard 1996; Weisler and Kirch 1996; Weisler and Woodhead 1995; Weisler et al. 1994; and several articles in a monograph edited by Weisler (1997a).

Macroscopic observations can at times be useful, but given similar colour, mineralogy and weathering effects of lithic materials, conclusions based on these observations should be approached with caution. Thin-section descriptions have some of the limitations above, but can provide useful data to discriminate sources in certain circumstances (Best 1984; Cleghorn et al. 1985; White 1987). Either of the above techniques should be combined with geochemical techniques to be most effective in discriminating provenance. Weisler (1993c:68) gives the following reasons for the power of geochemical analysis as an analytical tool: (1) its results are reproducible; (2) instrument specifications and operating conditions can be reported in full; (3) identification of chemical components is not subject to human error; (4) elemental abundances can be determined with accuracy and precision parameters noted; (5) use of standards facilitates inter-laboratory comparisons of databases; and (6) the analytical sample taken to analyse bulk chemical constituents more closely represents the whole specimen, in contrast to a two-dimensional thin-section.

Major and minor element compositions of basalts in the Pacific have been found by researchers doing sourcing studies to be similar over wide areas (Weisler and Woodhead 1995; Sinton and Sinoto 1997), making assignment to a specific source difficult. Assignments to sources from petrographic examination can also be problematic because of similarities in mineralogy (Weisler and Kirch 1996). Also, quarried stone weathers over time and at different rates depending on ambient conditions (Best et al. 1992). Weathering not only affects the petrography but also the chemical make-up (the elemental signature) of the stone. However, the combination of elemental analysis and petrological analysis is more likely to identify identical source material.

Ideally, for sourcing of individual artefacts using geochemical data, it is necessary for all potential sources to have been described and analysed (Wilson 1978; Rapp 1985; Weisler and Sinton 1997:177). This ideal probably is never realised and certainly in the case of basalt in the Pacific, many prehistoric quarries have not been characterised (Weisler and Sinton 1997).

However, several sourcing studies have been successful and have demonstrated intra-archipelago as well as inter-archipelago transfer of basalt. Island quarries which have been most studied are those of Hawaii and Samoa.

In this research, 10 major and minor elements were analysed using energy dispersive X-Ray analysis (EDXA). The advantages of this method over, for example, X-Ray Fluorescence (XRF) are the ease of sample preparation and presentation to the instrument and a much smaller sample size. However, EDXA is not as accurate as XRF. Analytical accuracy is about 6% for a 10 wt% concentration of an element, and improves at higher concentrations. The limit of detection is about 0.1 wt% (Williams 1987; Goodhew and Humphreys 1988). Sheppard et al. (1997:Table 6.2) present accuracy and precision information for XRF data. It is possible using XRF to analyse whole specimens, but with less accuracy than prepared samples (Weisler 1993a).

Nineteen trace elements were analysed using inductively coupled plasma-mass spectrometry (ICP-MS). ICP-MS has detection limits of parts per billion for most of the elements in the periodic table and requires only small sample sizes of ca. 100 mg (Jarvis et al. 1992). This is a much smaller detection limit and sample size than required for XRF. Historically, most analytical work for sourcing in the Pacific has been done using XRF with its limitations, but ICP-MS will probably become more popular in the future. XRF performs best analysing certain elements and this characteristic has often defined the element suite used to characterise lithic sources.

Weisler and Sinton (1997:179) indicate the elements least affected by the combination of real, local source variability and analytical uncertainty are Si, Ti, Al, Fe, Mg, Ca, K, V, Sr, Y, Zr and Ba. Best (1984) and Best et al. (1992) indicate the best discriminators of the major/minor elements are SiO_2, TiO_2 and P_2O_5 and they plotted these values to show relationships between sources. For Weisler and Sinton (1997), the most efficient discriminators are SiO_2, TiO_2 and K_2O.

Best's (1984) analyses of adzes and rocks from southern Lau were chosen for comparison with Fiji lithics. These samples were chosen because they would be most likely to furnish information on the possible origins of the adzes and flakes analysed in the present project. Best divided the rock types into five main groups: basalts, andesites, tuffs, all other igneous rocks, and sedimentary rocks. He further divided the basalts into six subgroups:

1. Those with a distinctive glassy texture;
2. Those containing celadonite/biotite;
3. Those containing olivine;
4. Limburgite – oceanic basalt;
5. Leucite – feldspathoidal basalt; and
6. All others.

Best found that the preference for, or presence of, various rock types changed considerably through time. Eight of the Lauan adzes and a Taveuni specimen grouped with two Samoan sources. For Best (1984:406), the most interesting aspect of the island's adze material was that so much of it came from so far away.

In addition to Best's samples, a database of basalt analyses from several researchers was compiled. Sample analyses were chosen from this database for comparison with the chemical analyses of excavated flakes and adzes. Sinton and Sinoto (1997) have constructed a database of basalt analyses from Polynesia containing chemical analyses of 280 individual samples from 36 quarries.

Cluster analysis was used to find out which analyses in a data set were similar. Cluster analysis is a method for describing the similarities among objects in a sample (Romesburg 1984). Cluster analysis results in a diagram called a dendrogram that shows the hierarchy of similarities among all pairs of objects. Other methods of analysing the data were tried, such as plotting ratios of elements or oxides (see, for example, Best et al. 1992) and principal components analysis. Results were similar to results from other methods of data analysis, but dendrograms are more clearly visualised, especially when there are many data points. The cophenetic correlation coefficient is an index that tells us how much the clustering method distorts the information in its input in order to produce its output or the dendrogram. Values for the cophenetic correlation of around 0.8 indicate the distortion is not great. Cophenetic correlations were calculated in this study and varied from 0.85 to 0.92.

Some samples from the Fiji excavations were closely linked with Best's (1984) samples. In addition, some of the 25 samples were closely linked with each other through both major oxide and minor element clustering, as well as being similar petrologically. No samples were similar to those from Samoa, but this could be expected given the morphology of the analysed artefacts.

Adze samples: Materials and methods

Various lithic flakes and adze fragments were provided from excavations conducted in 1996 and 1997 in Fiji, on Beqa Island, Viti Levu and Mago Island. Most of the samples were basalt, but other rock types were represented. Although the sample size was limited, 25 artefacts which were obviously flakes and adze fragments were sampled.

After visually inspecting, weighing and measuring the artefacts, small pieces were cut from each piece using a diamond saw. Samples for energy dispersive X-Ray analysis (EDXA) weighed approximately 50 mg and those for inductively coupled plasma spectroscopy-mass spectrometry (ICP-MS) ranged from 250 mg to 400 mg.

The samples for ICP-MS were polished on 240 grit wet emery paper to remove possible contamination from the diamond saw blade. The samples were then washed and put into an ultrasonic bath to remove any adhering particles. Samples were weighed and put into separate micro-centrifuge tubes for posting to the Advanced Analytical Centre at James Cook University for trace-element analysis. Samples were whole pieces and were not pulverised in order to avoid contamination from any grinding apparatus.

The pieces for EDXA were washed and dried. They were then mounted in a jig holding 26 samples, especially made for the mount available for the electron microscope. The samples were epoxied into holes in the jig. This allowed them to be polished flat for analysis. Polishing was done using 240, 400 and 600 grit wet emery cloth, followed by polishing compound (cerium oxide) on glass. The mounted samples were washed in detergent in an ultrasonic bath. The polished samples were viewed with a microscope at 20x magnification.

Samples were dried at 120°C for 17 hours and were weighed before and after heating to give a loss on drying (LOD) expressed as a percentage. Dried samples were then fired in a muffle furnace at 500°C for four hours. The percentage mass loss on ignition (LOI) was determined.

Energy dispersive X-Ray analysis

The SEM-EDXA instrument is located in the Electron Microscopy Laboratory at the Research School of Biological Sciences, ANU. The instrument used was a JEOL JSM-6400 scanning electron microscope (SEM), fitted with an Oxford 138 eV SATW 10 mm^2 detector. The analysis system was an Oxford ISIS using SEMQUANT. Samples were coated with carbon before analysis. Analyses were done using 15 keV at 1 nA for 200 seconds live time. Most analyses were done at 150–180x magnification, although this ranged from 150x to 400x depending on the homogeneity of the sample. Lower magnifications were used on non-homogeneous samples to 'average' the surface. Results were in element percent and the oxides were calculated stoichiometrically.

Inductively coupled plasma spectroscopy with mass spectrometry

The sample preparation at James Cook University was done using a method from Jarvis et al. (1992:Chapter 7). The solid samples along with a reference standard (Hawaiian basalt: BHVO-1) were prepared by digesting with a mixture (4:1) of concentrated hydrofluoric acid and concentrated nitric acid, and finally taken up in 2% nitric acid. The ICPMS (Model 'Ultramass') was manufactured by Varian Australia. The instrument parameters are given in Table 77. Phosphorus was analysed separately using ICP-atomic emission spectroscopy (ICP-AES).

Table 77. Varian ICP-MS instrument settings for trace-element analysis.

Instrument Parameters	Segmented Scan Mode
Plasma Flow 15.0 L/min	
Auxillary Flow 1.50 L/min	
Nebuliser Flow 1.07 L/min	
Sampling Depth 5.0 mm	
Forward Power 1.2 kW	
Sample Pump Rate 25 rpm	
Extraction Lens -600 V	Reading Space 0.025 AMU
First Lens -360 V	Points per Peak 3
Second Lens -13.60 V	Scans Replicate 5
Third Lens 0.60 V	No. of Replicates 5
Fourth Lens -10 V	Dwell Time 1000 mS
Photon Stop -15.60 V	Sample Delay 40
Entrance Plate 0 V	Stabilisation Time 15
Exit Plate 0 V	Rinse Time 70

Cluster analysis

The agglomerative hierarchical clustering algorithms available in the statistical system NCSS 6.0.1 were used to build a cluster hierarchy displayed as a tree diagram or dendrogram. The group average (unweighted pair-group) method was used.

Comparison samples

A database of basalt chemical analyses was constructed which incorporated results from several researchers. Analyses were either typed or scanned from journal articles and especially from a monograph edited by Weisler (1997a) which contains values from most basalt sourcing studies. Samples were selected from the database for cluster analysis to provide a comparison with the excavated flakes and adzes.

Adze samples: Results and discussion

Description of samples

The samples analysed in this project and site details are given in Table 78 (see also Table 79). The adzes and flakes listed turned out to be not all basalts. This would be expected for lithics in

Table 78. Description of analysed archaeological samples from Fiji.

Lab No.	Sample Context	Sample Description	Dimensions Length x Width (cm)	Mass (g)	LOD %	LOI %
F1	Beqa Is, Kulu Bay, C10, 90–100 cm	Dark grey, fine-grained adze	5.5 x 2.8	36.72	0.06	0.17
F2	Beqa Is, Kulu Bay, C10, 90–100 cm	Black, fine-grained adze flake	2.4 x 1.5	1.44	0.00	0.10
F3	Beqa Is, Kulu Bay, C10, 90–100 cm	Dark grey, fine-grained adze flake	2.9 x 1.8	2.19	0.59	0.30
F4	Beqa Is, Kulu Bay, C11, 10–20 cm	Grey, fine-grained adze flake	2.3 x 1.0	0.81	0.58	0.88
F5	Beqa Is, Kulu Bay, C10, 30–50 cm	Grey, fine-grained adze flake	5.6 x 4.5	32.37	0.42	0.60
F6	Beqa Is, Kulu Bay, C10, 30–50 cm	Greenish, fine-grained adze flake	4.3 x 4.2	13.99	0.06	0.22
F7	Beqa Is, Kulu Bay, C10, 30–50 cm	Greenish, fine-grained adze flake	2.2 x 1.9	1.70	0.08	0.31
F8	Beqa Is, Ugaga Is, L9: 40 cm	Grey, very fine-grained adze	6.5 x 2.3	31.29	0.38	0.51
F9	Beqa Is, Ugaga Is, D8: 30–40 cm	Grey, fine-grained adze flake	2.7 x 1.3	1.69	0.28	0.09
F10	Natunuku, Trench 3, Level 1: 20–30 cm	Dark grey, fine-grained, adze flake	8.5 x 7.4	232.34	0.04	0.00
F11	Mago Is, Votua TP1: 20–30 cm	Thin, fine-grained, dark grey adze flake	2.8 x 1.2	0.83	0.04	0.24
F12	Natunuku, Trench 3, Level 1: 10–20 cm	Dark grey and brown, fine-grained adze tip. Appears similar to F10	5.0 x 6.1	90.91	0.54	0.28
F13	Natunuku, TP 2-4, Level 1: 10–20 cm	Greenish, fine-grained adze flake	6.4 x 3.8	27.50	0.17	0.27
F14	Natunuku, TP 2, Level 1: 10–20 cm	Grey, fine-grained adze flake	3.4 x 2.1	6.90	0.09	0.24
F15	Natunuku, TP 2, Level 1: 10–20 cm	Grey, fine-grained adze flake	3.3 x 1.7	3.29	0.17	0.21
F16	Natunuku, Trench 3, B5, Layer 2	Greenish-grey, fine-grained adze (?) flake	6.7 x 3.4	49.32	0.14	0.29
F17	Beqa Is, Kulu Bay, C10: 50–70 cm	Black, fine-grained adze flake	4.5 x 2.0	4.89	0.11	0.14
F18	Beqa Is, Kulu Bay, C11: 20–30 cm	Grey, very fine-grained adze flake	3.7 x 1.2	2.11	0.49	0.61
F19	Beqa Is, Kulu Bay, C11: 30–40 cm	Grey, fine-grained core with flake scars	2.0 x 1.9	4.81	0.13	0.10
F20	Beqa Is, Kulu Bay, C11: 30–40 cm	Grey, fine-grained adze flake	2.5 x 1.7	3.45	0.04	0.00
F21	Beqa Is, Kulu Bay, C11: 90–100 cm	Grey, fine-grained adze flake	2.3 x 1.6	1.85	0.08	0.08
F22	Beqa Is, Kulu Bay, C11: 110–120 cm	Grey, fine-grained thin adze flake	2.6 x 1.7	1.46	0.68	0.59
F23	Beqa Is, Kulu Bay, C11: 110–120 cm	Grey, very fine-grained thin adze flake	2.0 x 0.7	0.30	nd	nd
F24	Beqa Is, Ugaga Is, N10: 40 cm	Grey, fine-grained adze flake	5.2 x 2.8	75.74	0.07	0.11
F25	Beqa Is, Kulu Bay, C11: 30–40 cm	Grey, ?adze flake with black and white crystals	2.8 x 1.3	3.07	0.74	0.39

LOD = loss on drying at 120°C; LOI = loss on ignition at 500°C; nd = not determined

Fiji (Best 1984), where several rock types are represented. The samples which visually appeared to be basalt are numbers: F5–F8, F15, and F17–F22. The green and black crystals would likely be olivine and biotite (or iron oxide), respectively. Brown crystals could be weathered biotite or celadonite (Best 1984). Other rock types could not be identified because this is an area for a specialist and no thin-sections were made. Samples which by eye appeared similar and could be from the same sources are groups: F5, F6, F7; F13, F16; F17, F20; F24, F25; and possibly F9, F11.

Some samples appeared quite weathered, especially samples F10, F12, F15, F20 and F25. The greenish appearance of some flakes (Table 78) might be due to weathering. The descriptions presented in Table 79 are more reliable because the samples had a fresh polished surface. Texture and crystals could easily be seen and compared.

The loss on ignition (LOI) values are all less than one (Table 78). Best et al. (1992:53) indicate that if a sample is badly weathered and has an LOI>1%, it plots away from the main group. They therefore omitted such samples from plots of chemical analyses.

Database samples

The publications which provided major/minor element oxide data are given in Table 80. The number of samples incorporated into the database is also given. Most authors have included all of the relevant oxides and this is a consideration in the selection of samples for comparison. The number of samples actually available for comparison is much less than the total number indicated. This is because of the repetition involved when researchers incorporate sample values presented in the literature for their own sourcing comparisons.

Table 79. Description of lithic samples as viewed in mounting plate at 20x magnification.

Lab. No.	Description	Homogeneous?
F1	Black, fine grained	Yes
F2	Black, very fine grained	Yes
F3	Dark grey, some white phenocrysts	Fairly
F4	Brown, fine grained	Yes
F5	Grey, some white and brown inclusions	Yes
F6	Light grey, small black inclusions	Yes
F7	Light grey, light green (olivine?) and black crystals	Fairly
F8	Grey, fine grained	Yes
F9	Dark grey, small black and brown crystals	Fairly
F10	Grey to black, large white and black phenocrysts	No
F11	Black, very fine grained	Yes
F12	Grey, large white crystals	No
F13	Grey, very small black crystals	Yes
F14	Dark grey, small black crystals	Yes
F15	Black, large white crystals	No
F16	Brown, fine grained, appearance of silt stone	Yes
F17	Brown to black, coarse grained, white and brown crystals	Fairly
F18	Grey, fine grained, some small black crystals	Yes
F19	Black, very fine grained	Yes
F20	Black, course grained, white crystals, similar to F15	No
F21	Dark grey, fine grained with few very small white crystals	Fairly
F22	Dark grey, fine grained, very small black flecks	Yes
F23	Grey, very fine grained	Yes
F24	Black, very fine grained	Yes
F25	Very weathered, large crystals, similar to F12	No

Table 80. Publications containing lithic source and artefact major/minor element oxide data.

Oxide	This report	Best 1984	Best et al. 1992	Anderson et al. 1997	Weisler 1993a	Ayres et al. 1997	Clark et al. 1997	Sheppard et al. 1997	Allen and Johnson 1997	Rolett et al. 1997	Weisler and Sinton 1997	Sinton and Sinoto 1997
N	25	44	163	10	3	7	37	97	20	20	9	33
SiO_2	■	■	■				■	■	■	■	■	■
TiO_2	■	■	■	■	■		■	■	■	■	■	■
Al_2O_3	■	■	■		■	■	■	■	■	■	■	■
Fe_2O_3	■	■	■	■	■	■	■	■	■	■	■	■
MnO	■	■	■	■	■		■	■	■	■	■	■
MgO	■	■	■	■	■	■	■	■	■	■	■	■
CaO	■	■	■	■	■	■	■	■	■	■	■	■
Na_2O	■	■	■	■	■		■	■	■	■	■	■
K_2O	■	■	■	■	■	■	■	■	■	■	■	■
P_2O_5	■	■	■	■	■		■	■	■	■	■	■

N = number of samples. Grey (■) = oxide included in study.

A large number of samples with trace-element analyses was available for incorporation into a database (Table 81). However, there was a problem of incompatibility between analyses performed in different and, at times the same, laboratories. Even though a large suite of elements was analysed in some studies (e.g. the present project; Best et al. 1992; Allen and Johnson 1997), results on several elements could not be used because only those elements common to all samples being considered could be used. For example, the element suite in this study contains 19 elements, but only 11 of these could be used for the clustering analysis.

Major/minor element oxides

The EDXA results are given in Table 82. The results for F1, F2, F3, F5, F14 and F16 are averages of duplicate analyses. The EDXA spectrum for sample F19 is presented in Figure 161. The phosphorus peak in this spectrum is not discernible by eye. Although P_2O_5 was analysed by EDXA, results from ICP-AES are included in this table because they are more accurate. EDXA values below ca. 1% are not reliable. The P_2O_5 values have been corrected to BHVO-1 standard values. Total iron is presented as Fe_2O_3 although it would be better presented as ferrous iron (FeO) because most of the iron in basalts is in this form (Wright 1971). However, most people doing sourcing research in the Pacific present Fe as Fe_2O_3. SiO_2 values are generally higher and TiO_2 values lower than those for oceanic island basalts (see Weisler and Sinton 1997:Table 10.5). There is a wide range of oxide concentrations and this may represent the diversity of rock types available locally. The sum of analyses varies from 94.78% to 104.70%, with an average of 98.85%. There appear to be no systematic errors in the values except for F19, which has an unusually high TiO_2 value of 7.08% and an MnO value of 1.62%. It appears that the EDXA beam sampled a Ti-rich mineral inclusion. The analysis of solid polished samples gives the most reliable results for EDXA, although non-homogeneous solid samples can present problems because of the small area analysed.

Some samples were powdered and analysed as a comparison to solid samples (Table 83).

Table 81. Publications containing lithic source and artefact trace element data.

Element	This report	Best et al. 1992	Anderson et al. 1997	Weisler 1993a	Ayres et al. 1997	Clark et al. 1997	Sheppard et al. 1997	Allen and Johnson 1997	Weisler and Sinton 1997	Sinton and Sinoto 1997
Number	25	36	10	3	7	31	77	17	8	32
Sc	■				■			■	■	■
V	■	■					■	■	■	■
Cr	■	■	■		■		■	■	■	■
Ni	■	■	■	■			■	■	■	■
Cu	■	■	■	■				■	■	■
Zn	■	■	■	■			■	■	■	■
Rb	■	■	■	■		■	■	■	■	■
Sr	■	■	■	■	■	■	■	■	■	■
Y	■	■	■	■		■	■	■	■	■
Zr	■	■	■	■	■	■	■	■	■	■
Nb	■	■				■	■	■	■	■
La	■	■		■	■	■	■			
Ce	■			■	■			■		
Nd	■				■			■		
Sm					■			■		
Eu					■			■		
Dy					■			■		
Er								■		
Yb					■			■		
Pb		■						■		
Th	■	■			■		■	■		
U								■		
Ba	■	■			■				■	■
Ga	■		■							
Fr				■						
Co					■					
As	■	■		■						
Tb					■		■			
Ra							■			
Lu					■					
Ta					■					
Hf					■					

Grey areas = measured elements.

Table 82. EDXA percentage concentrations for adzes and flakes from Fiji. Note P_2O_5 values determined by ICP-AES.

Location	Lab. No.	SiO_2	TiO_2	Al_2O_3	Fe_2O_3	MnO	MgO	CaO	Na_2O	K_2O	P_2O_5
Kulu Bay	F1	55.07	1.07	17.01	9.38	0.12	3.36	4.61	6.81	1.15	0.077
Kulu Bay	F2	71.37	0.40	15.09	2.90	0.07	0.19	1.69	4.83	4.32	0.087
Kulu Bay	F3	52.47	1.78	15.88	9.69	0.15	4.13	7.35	2.86	0.73	0.111
Kulu Bay	F4	62.98	1.19	12.12	9.87	0.06	2.43	1.30	4.05	1.03	0.185
Kulu Bay	F5	71.69	0.97	13.38	3.05	0.27	0.54	1.22	5.77	2.08	0.143
Kulu Bay	F6	59.15	1.83	12.32	8.15	0.20	1.93	9.42	1.58	0.66	0.121
Kulu Bay	F7	60.87	1.19	15.05	7.44	0.23	2.10	7.61	2.58	0.79	0.154
Ugaga Is	F8	57.32	0.83	14.75	8.34	0.21	2.83	6.36	4.34	0.19	0.090
Ugaga Is	F9	56.60	0.98	15.31	10.24	0.32	4.06	9.39	3.35	0.37	0.197
Natunku	F10	52.78	0.71	17.20	7.98	0.32	8.20	10.48	2.78	0.16	0.154
Votua	F11	65.14	0.67	16.80	4.80	0.13	0.77	4.40	4.95	2.37	0.351
Natunuku	F12	53.93	0.57	19.77	5.82	0.08	4.98	9.12	2.63	1.79	0.372
Natunuku	F13	61.35	1.20	13.69	8.05	0.20	2.86	7.08	2.00	0.69	0.130
Natunuku	F14	55.33	1.50	15.04	9.86	0.19	2.54	8.03	4.37	0.10	0.123
Natunuku	F15	53.76	1.04	15.58	10.14	0.23	4.71	12.29	2.37	0.38	0.134
Natunuku	F16	57.07	0.86	14.77	10.09	0.11	3.08	4.79	2.90	0.98	0.133
Kulu Bay	F17	55.26	1.48	15.78	15.26	0.15	5.17	4.38	6.86	0.24	0.122
Kulu Bay	F18	54.78	0.90	16.56	8.47	0.19	3.28	10.04	5.36	0.52	0.089
Kulu Bay	F19	52.41	7.08	13.44	13.89	1.62	3.95	5.97	3.33	0.96	0.086
Kulu Bay	F20	59.80	0.86	17.08	6.19	0.18	4.07	6.58	6.98	0.03	0.098
Kulu Bay	F21	56.73	0.89	13.83	9.83	0.16	4.73	7.86	4.87	0.40	0.102
Kulu Bay	F22	52.17	0.85	17.99	8.56	0.16	3.19	10.43	4.31	0.37	0.063
Kulu Bay	F23	65.58	0.91	14.05	6.95	0.14	2.51	7.60	2.80	0.46	0.128
Ugaga Is	F24	47.22	0.77	18.08	9.20	0.22	8.57	12.72	1.63	0.32	0.114
Kulu Bay	F25	55.02	0.51	19.56	5.15	0.09	2.32	5.98	4.25	2.70	0.320

Note that these analyses are normalised to 100%; powdered samples have analyses adding up to less than 100% and this can be much less than 100% in the case of porous samples with an uneven surface and charging effects. There is fairly good agreement between results for the two methods of preparation. Both homogeneous (F16 and F24) and non-homogeneous (F10 and F20) samples were picked for comparison (see Table 79). The analytical results for solids and powders have similar differences for homogeneous and non-homogeneous samples. This is most likely due to the care taken during analysis to avoid non-homogeneous areas of polished solids. The results indicate that samples for EDXA can be either solid or powdered. Powdered samples are generally easier to prepare and there would be an advantage to obtaining samples by drilling artefacts where minimum damage is usually desirable. Sample sizes for EDXA would require a depth of only ca. 2 mm for a 2 mm diameter drill. Note that there can be problems with contamination from drills, corers and grinding equipment. This is generally not a problem for major/minor element determinations but must be considered for trace elements.

The dendrogram of analysed Fijian lithics (Figure 162) shows close similarities between

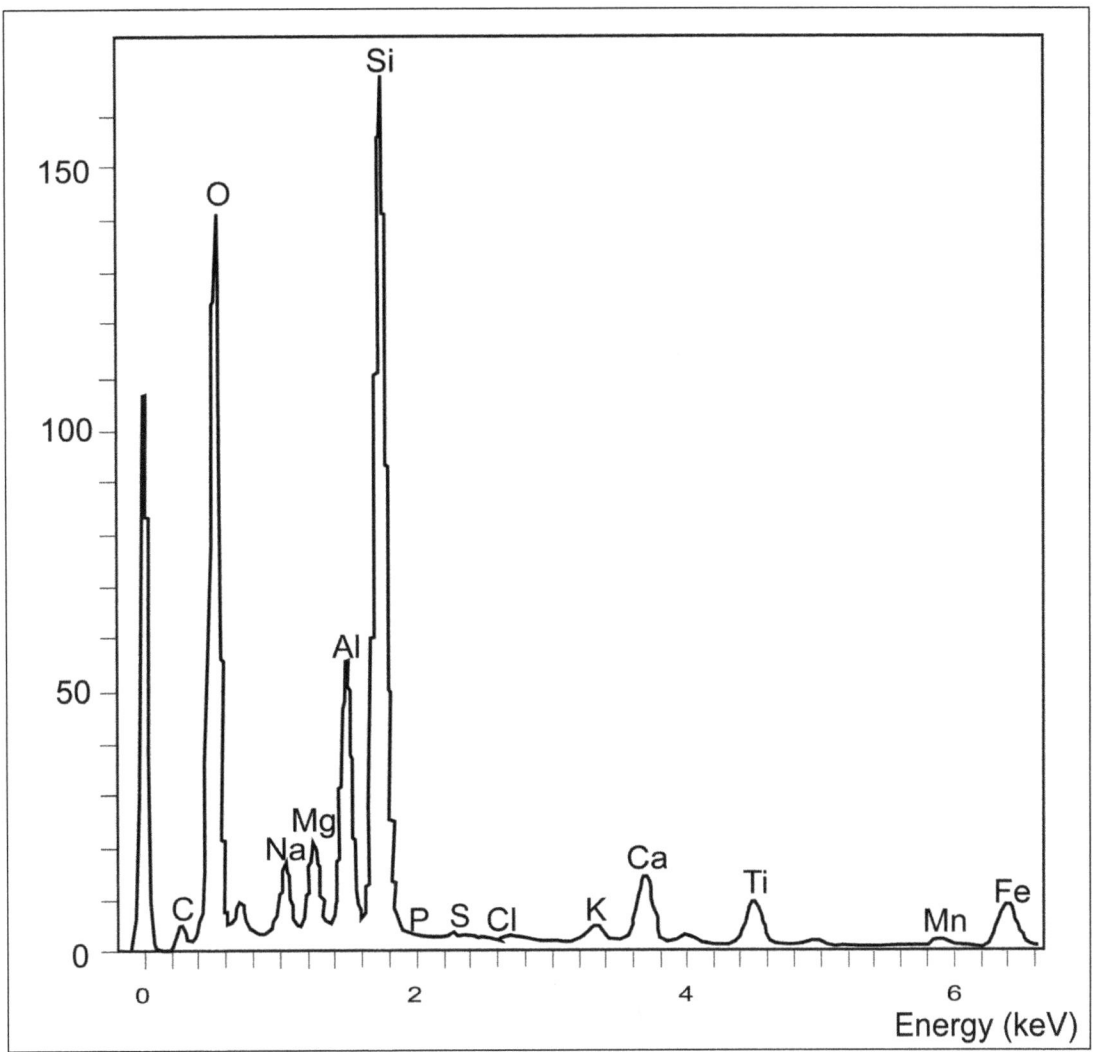

Figure 161. EDXA spectrum of sample F19.

Table 83. Comparison of EDXA results for powdered and solid samples. Results are normalised to 100%.

	Natunuku		Natunuku		Kulu Bay		Ugaga	
	F10-S	F10-P	F16-S	F16-P	F20-S	F20-P	F24-S	F24-P
Oxide	Solid	Powder	Solid	Powder	Solid	Powder	Solid	Powder
SiO_2	52.40	49.82	60.24	57.36	58.72	57.56	47.81	48.88
TiO_2	0.70	0.56	0.91	0.81	0.84	0.68	0.78	0.90
Al_2O_3	17.08	17.66	15.59	15.18	16.77	14.20	18.30	17.11
Fe_2O_3	7.92	10.16	10.65	11.32	6.08	7.14	9.32	10.03
MnO	0.32	0.16	0.12	0.30	0.18	0.19	0.22	0.18
MgO	8.14	8.42	3.25	3.87	4.00	7.04	8.68	8.07
CaO	10.40	10.35	5.06	7.41	6.46	7.63	12.88	12.04
Na_2O	2.76	2.59	3.06	2.70	6.85	5.45	1.65	2.43
K_2O	0.16	0.18	1.03	0.89	0.03	0.05	0.32	0.32
P_2O_5	0.12	0.09	0.09	0.17	0.07	0.05	0.04	0.06

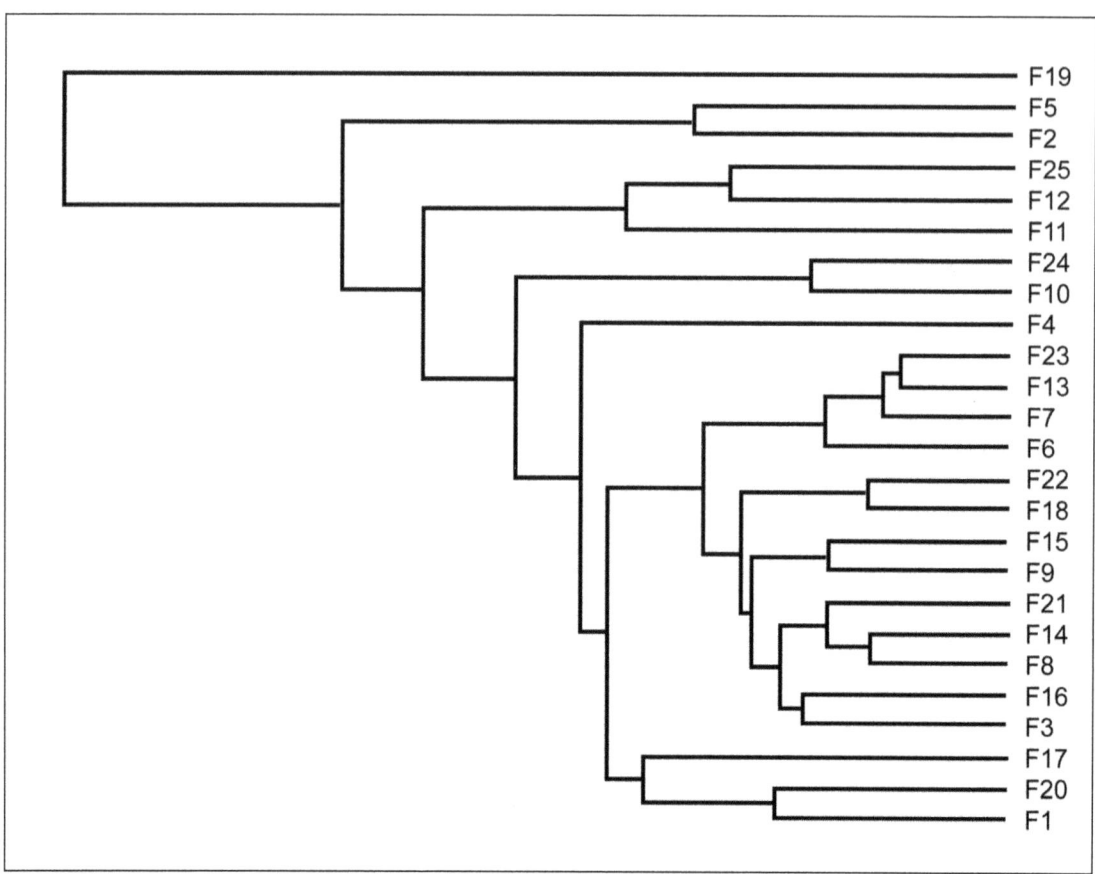

Figure 162. Hierarchical clustering report for oxide analysis of excavated flakes and adzes.

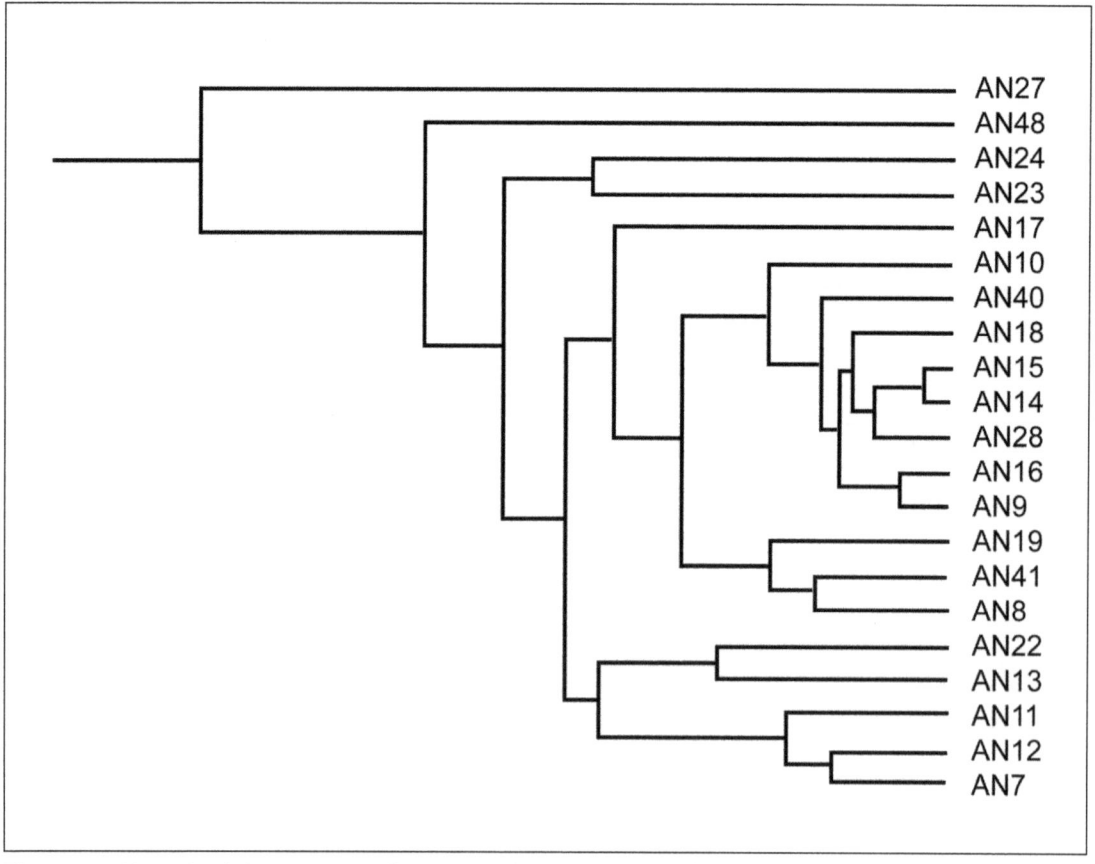

Figure 163. Hierarchical clustering report for samples from Best (1984:A74-A75).

sample numbers: F1, F20; F2, F5; F3, F16; F6, F7, F13, F23; F8, F14, F21; F9, F15; F10, F24; F12, F25; and F18, F22. Results of visual examination of the artefacts (Tables 78 and 79) combined with cluster analysis indicate only groups F6, F7, F13; F12, F25; and F18, F22 are probably from three different sources. Samples F6 and F7 are from the same bag labelled Beqa Is, Kulu Bay, and F13 is from Natunuku VL 1/1. Sample F12 is also from Natunuku, from a depth of 10–20 cm and closely resembles F25 from Beqa Is, Kulu Bay, Sq. 11 at a depth of 30–40 cm. In both cases, this represents inter-island use of stone from the same source. Samples F18 and F22 are from the same square at Beqa Is, Kulu Bay, but at depths of 20–30 cm and 110–120 cm respectively. This could indicate that the same stone source was being used over a long time period, but given the archaeological evidence for deposit mixing at Kulu Bay this cannot be confirmed.

All of Best's analyses (1984) for the Lau Islands and Samoan adzes and rocks are included in Table 84. The four adzes from Samoa are from Roger Green's excavations in Samoa (Green and Davidson 1969). Petrographic descriptions of most of these samples are given in Table 85. The data matrix in Table 84 was cluster analysed.

Results for the clustering analysis of Best's data are shown in Figure 163. As expected, the results are similar to those found by Best (1984) and Best et al. (1992). Best found several Lauan adzes were closely associated with adzes and quarry material from Samoa. Lauan adzes AN16

Table 84. XRF analyses (%) of selected adzes and rocks (from Best 1984). Note that 'AN' numbers are Best's (1984) analysis numbers.

Sample	Label	SiO_2	TiO_2	Al_2O_3	Fe_2O_3	MnO	MgO	CaO	Na_2O	K_2O	P_2O_5
Samoa Adze	AN7	47.287	4.228	13.536	13.695	0.171	8.034	8.939	3.181	1.134	0.624
Samoa Adze	AN8	45.306	4.576	15.331	14.464	0.188	5.672	8.093	3.674	1.218	0.686
Samoa Adze	AN9	48.901	3.103	15.697	13.321	0.179	4.556	7.208	4.382	1.599	0.966
Samoa Adze	AN28	49.635	3.215	15.469	13.334	0.178	4.508	7.51	4.013	1.719	0.896
Lakeba Adze	AN27	63.957	0.802	15.117	7.345	0.173	1.410	4.269	4.396	2.425	0.378
Lakeba Adze	AN10	46.066	3.162	14.527	13.014	0.191	4.539	7.177	3.833	1.399	0.984
Lakeba Adze	AN11	47.200	4.675	13.700	13.794	0.197	6.815	8.723	3.147	0.985	0.578
Lakeba Adze	AN12	46.897	4.600	13.938	13.406	0.164	6.413	8.505	3.285	1.015	0.606
Lakeba Adze	AN13	44.514	2.120	14.914	11.821	0.181	9.514	9.959	2.547	1.360	0.668
Namuka Adze	AN14	47.852	3.374	15.390	13.833	0.175	4.633	7.517	4.067	1.446	0.889
Kabara Adze	AN15	47.731	3.318	15.436	13.558	0.173	4.758	7.436	3.990	1.496	0.878
Vanuabalavu Adze	AN16	48.751	3.051	16.011	13.059	0.182	4.666	7.082	4.270	1.625	0.939
Taveuni Adze	AN17	46.414	4.794	15.724	14.632	0.127	5.944	8.380	3.530	1.214	0.661
Moce Adze	AN18	48.613	3.363	15.519	13.895	0.157	4.789	7.488	4.045	1.485	0.872
Fulaqa Adze	AN19	46.421	4.824	15.654	14.939	0.213	5.700	8.511	3.523	1.259	0.673
Kabara Rock	AN22	45.421	2.190	15.302	12.217	0.153	8.598	10.537	3.238	0.810	0.600
Lakeba Rock	AN23	44.106	1.363	13.767	11.840	0.168	3.775	7.805	2.834	0.764	0.292
Lakeba Rock	AN24	52.808	1.393	15.585	12.251	0.141	3.174	7.084	3.627	1.019	0.311
Samoa Leone Q.	AN40	48.580	3.340	15.490	14.080	0.190	4.790	7.550	3.680	1.600	0.880
Samoa Leone Q.	AN41	45.860	4.780	15.530	14.770	0.170	5.640	8.480	3.140	1.240	0.670
Henderson Rock	AN48	50.930	2.350	16.310	11.250	0.200	2.870	6.740	4.970	2.420	1.170

Table 85. Petrographic descriptions of samples in Table 84 (from Best 1984:A70-A72).

Petrology No.	Sample	Label	Petrographic Description
1	Lakeba Adze	AN27	Glassy basalt, with small pyroxene needles and iron-oxide in volcanic glass
7	Vanuabalavu Adze	AN16	Basalt, celadonite, some small plagioclase phenocrysts, microphenocrysts of olivine
9	Lakeba Adze	AN10	Olivine basalt, celadonite replacing olivine phenocrysts, plagioclase phenocrysts
10	Lakeba Adze	AN11	Olivine basalt, similar to AN10
12	Lakeba Adze	AN12	Olivine basalt, similar to AN10
17	Namuka Adze	AN14	Basalt, similar to AN16
20	Kabara Adze	AN15	Olivine basalt, felspathic, with celadonite
22	Moce Adze	AN18	Olivine basalt, similar to AN15
23	Fulaqa Adze	AN19	Olivine basalt, similar to AN15
26	Lakeba Adze	AN13	Alkaline olivine basalt, with titaniferous augite
94	Lakeba Rock	AN23	Fine-grained felspathic basalt
96	Lakeba Rock	AN24	Fine-grained felspathic basalt with celadonite-filled cavities
101	Kabara Rock	AN22	Olivine basalt, olivine phenocrysts, microphenocrysts of plagioclase, iron oxide
105	Samoa Adze	AN7	Olivine basalt (olivine phenocrysts); groundmass with augite and ores
106	Samoa Adze	AN8	Olivine feldspar basalt; contains green and brown celadonite in cavities
107	Samoa Adze	AN9	Felspathic basalt; contains brown biotite (celadonite)

and AN10 were thought to be from Tutuila and are grouped as such, with AN10 being an outlier. The Samoan adze (AN28, AN9, AN8) and quarry (AN40, AN41) samples form a large cluster with several Lauan adzes (Lakeba AN10, Moce AN18, Kabara AN15, Namuka AN14, Vanuabalavu AN16 and Fulaga AN19). The larger cluster can be divided into two smaller clusters, which was also noted by Best (1984:403). One Samoan adze sample forms a cluster with Lakeba adzes AN11 and AN12. It can be seen in Figure 163 that some Lauan adzes are closely linked with Samoan adzes and quarry samples. Best concluded the adzes were sourced to Samoa and specifically to Tutuila. According to Best (1984:403), AN23 and AN24 are rock samples from the two mineralogically nearest sources. They are linked, but not closely. Lakeba adze AN13 and an andesitic-basalt from Delaioloi (Kabara, AN22) are similar.

The dendrogram in Figure 164 has the results of a cluster analysis for the analyses from Best (Table 84) and excavated Fiji flakes and adze fragments (Table 82; also compare Figures 162 and 163). Interestingly, there are few closely associated artefacts among Best's samples and those of the current project. None of the excavated samples is closely associated with the Samoan material. This could be expected given that no adzes resembling those of a Samoan origin were available for analysis. In addition, flakes would be unlikely to have a Samoan origin given that Samoan adzes would have been imported in finished form and the only possibility of finding flakes sourced to Samoa would be flakes from retouching adzes.

However, there are a few linked samples. These include AN27, F11; AN24, F3, F16; and less so with AN23, connected to a group of samples from the present project. Best found that Lakeba rock (AN23 and AN24) clustered by itself in a ternary diagram. This most likely indicates a local source of rock for associated samples in this project. Although the analysis of a

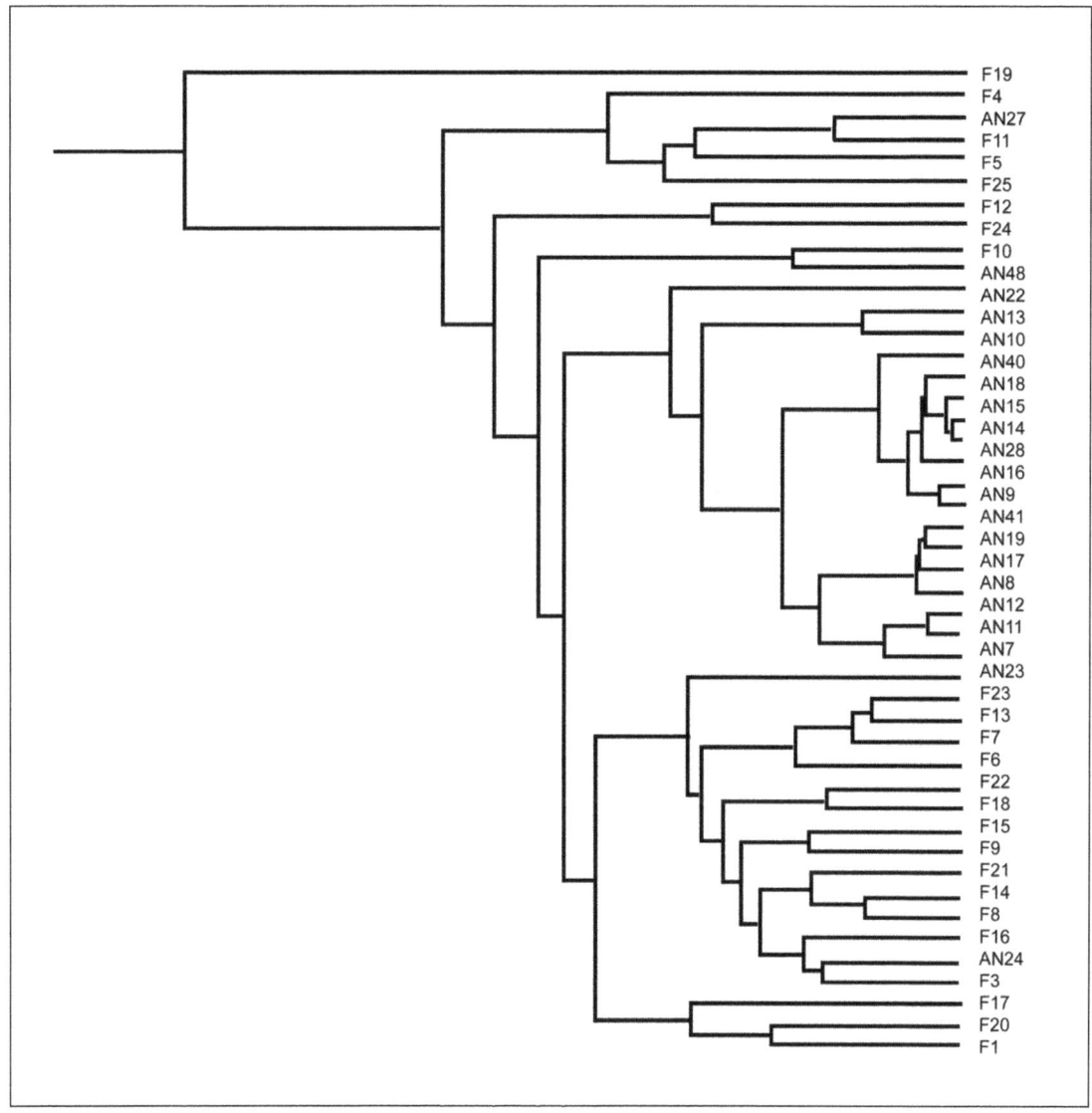

Figure 164. Hierarchical clustering report for excavated samples and Best (1984:A74-A75).

Lakeba adze (AN27) appears in Best (1984:A70, A74) it 'disappears' from further consideration there and in Best et al. (1992). Note that it is an outlier in Figure 163 but is clustered here with F11 and F5 (Figure 164). However, its petrographic description (Tables 78 and 79) does not resemble those of the latter samples, and it most likely is not from the same source.

Additional selected samples from the database will now be considered (see Table 86). Several samples were obtained from sites on American Samoa and some were sourced to Samoa (e.g. RW-M and RW-F labelled Ma'uke in Best et al. 1992), with other Cook Island samples likely to be from Samoa (Sheppard et al. 1997:101–103).

Results of cluster analysis for all samples with major/minor elemental analyses considered in this report are presented in Figure 165. Note that the dendrogram is split into two sections. A large cluster is formed, with AN23 and AN24 linked closely with Alega 1 and F3 and less so for several other excavated (F) samples. Another large cluster contains mostly Samoan samples, with closely associated Lauan adzes and samples from other island groups having artefacts possibly sourced to Samoa. Some Hawaiian samples form a group which includes AN23 and AN13 (previously found to be off by themselves in Best's ternary diagram), but there is unlikely to be

Table 86. Additional basalt reference samples (oxides in %).

Reference	Archipelago	Information	Label	SiO_2	TiO_2	Al_2O_3	Fe_2O_3	MnO	MgO	CaO	Na_2O	K_2O	P_2O_5
Clark et al. 1997:75	A. Samoa	Weisler	Taputapu	49.56	3.38	15.35	13.72	0.17	4.55	7.56	3.96	1.54	0.79
Clark et al. 1997:75	A. Samoa	TUT-II.2	Asiapa	50.24	2.94	16.01	12.87	0.18	4.11	7.26	3.99	1.77	1.25
Clark et al. 1997:75	A. Samoa	TUT-II.3	Le'aeno	47.80	3.71	16.09	12.74	0.18	4.84	7.71	3.65	1.61	0.76
Clark et al. 1997:76	A. Samoa	H1	Fagasa	48.90	3.19	15.90	13.24	0.19	4.45	7.21	3.71	1.70	0.84
Clark et al. 1997:76	A. Samoa	TUT-II.7	Alega 1	49.80	3.16	15.50	12.09	0.18	4.07	7.39	3.56	1.61	0.08
Clark et al. 1997:76	A. Samoa	TUT-II.4	Lau'agae	47.95	3.82	15.96	13.91	0.16	4.89	7.71	3.63	1.51	0.73
Clark et al. 1997:76	A. Samoa	TUT-11.10	Nu'u'uli	52.80	2.03	16.30	9.25	0.17	3.23	6.10	4.20	2.20	1.25
Weisler and Sinton 1997:179	A. Samoa		Tataga-matau	48.52	3.42	15.51	13.66	0.18	4.79	7.54	3.76	1.55	0.78
Allen and Johnson 1997:121	Cook Islands	5	Aitutaki	49.58	3.13	15.90	13.39	0.17	4.53	7.54	3.54	1.64	0.90
Sheppard et al. 1997:96	Cook Islands	R63-19	Rarotonga	48.17	2.65	16.24	11.96	0.24	4.13	6.86	4.42	1.82	1.00
Sheppard et al. 1997:96	Cook Islands	RAR-6	Rarotonga	47.83	3.04	16.13	13.08	0.21	4.50	7.24	3.95	1.68	0.83
Sheppard et al. 1997:96	Cook Islands	R92-1	Rarotonga	47.21	3.16	15.75	13.07	0.22	4.73	7.19	3.70	1.63	0.78
Sheppard et al. 1997:96	Cook Islands	RW-M	Ma'uke	47.92	3.43	15.53	13.57	0.21	4.77	7.74	3.91	1.54	0.81
Sheppard et al. 1997:96	Cook Islands	RW-F	Ma'uke	49.45	2.73	16.61	11.91	0.20	4.19	7.13	4.55	1.88	1.00
Weisler and Sinton 1997:179	Pitcairn		Tautama	49.93	2.68	15.57	13.45	0.22	3.49	7.09	4.55	1.99	1.25
Weisler and Sinton 1997:179	Marquesas		Eiao	46.95	3.90	15.23	13.53	0.16	6.47	9.32	3.18	1.00	0.54
Weisler and Sinton 1997:181	Hawaii	Kaho'olawe	Pu'umaiwi	52.37	2.98	14.02	13.18	0.17	4.60	8.37	3.00	0.85	0.88
Sinton and Sinoto 1997:200	Hawaii	Hawai'i	Mauna Kea	47.99	3.95	13.44	15.32	0.21	5.07	9.58	3.08	1.13	0.56
Sinton and Sinoto 1997:200	Hawaii	Maui	Haleakala	51.00	2.02	17.49	10.57	0.25	2.49	6.27	6.25	2.25	0.88
Sinton and Sinoto 1997:200	Hawaii	Lana'i	Kapohaku	51.48	2.11	13.96	12.11	0.16	7.10	10.06	2.29	0.52	0.25
Sinton and Sinoto 1997:200	Hawaii	Ovahu	Waiahole	52.81	2.19	13.77	11.37	0.15	6.54	9.14	2.69	0.71	0.34
Sinton and Sinoto 1997:202	Easter Island		Ova he	51.28	2.46	14.69	13.96	0.22	3.29	7.16	3.91	1.32	0.82
Sinton and Sinoto 1997:203	Society Islands	Ra'iatea	Ra'iatea II	42.37	4.54	15.07	13.83	0.18	5.16	10.69	3.72	1.82	0.64
Sinton and Sinoto 1997:203	Society Islands	Tahiti	Tahinu II	42.73	3.93	15.15	13.83	0.19	5.01	10.45	3.65	1.98	0.67

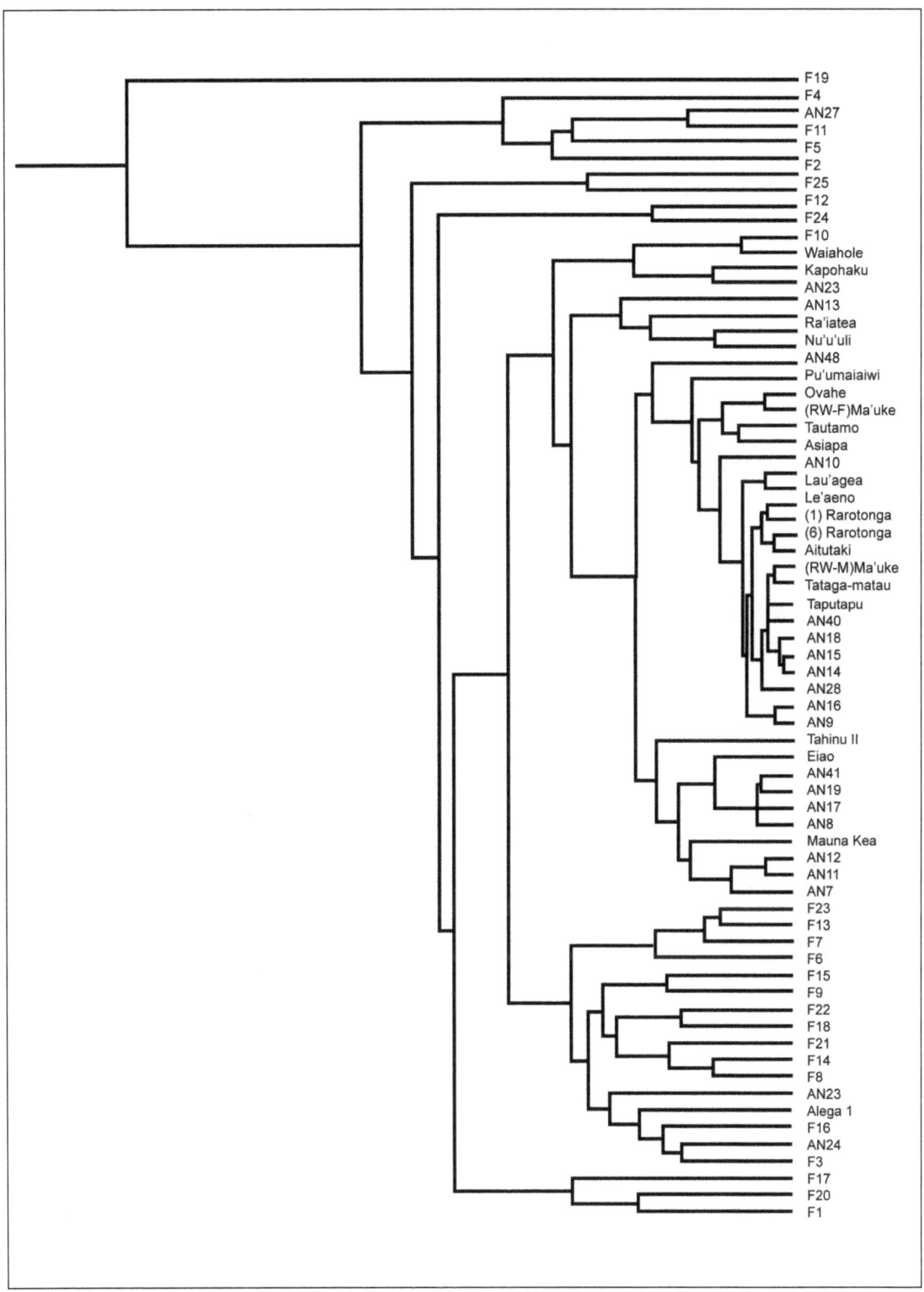

Figure 165. Hierarchical clustering report for excavated and all reference samples.

any relationship between samples from Hawaii and Fiji. What is clear here is that several Lauan adzes have their origin in Samoa and are most likely from Leone (Tutuila). The sample from Alega is out of place here. According to Clark et al. (1997:76), Alega samples cluster tightly with the bulk of the Fagasa samples. Alega 1 cannot be associated with source rock from Lakeba.

Trace elements

Table 87 gives the ICP-MS results for trace-element analysis of the excavated flakes and adzes. Nineteen elements were included in the analyses. The limit of detection was 1 part per million (1µg/g) for Nb, Ni, Pb and Th, and 5 ppm for As. Values below this limit are indicated by a < sign. Note that these limits of detection are to some extent laboratory dependent and the actual limit of detection with ICP-MS for these elements is <1 part per billion (Rubinson 1987:227–228). Literature and determined values for BHVO-1 are presented. In addition to some being

Table 87. ICP-MS analysis results (ppm) for excavated adzes and adze flakes from Fiji.

Sample	Analysis Ref.	As	Ba	Ce	Cr	Cu	Ga	La	Mb	Nd	Ni	Pb	Rb	Sc	Sr	Th	V	Y	Zn	Zr
F1	AAC Ref:2430-01	<5	135.1	7.5	16.3	85.3	16.3	2.6	3.2	6.5	9.3	3.5	16.9	35.8	171.6	2.2	314.4	17.6	67.0	33.7
F2	AAC Ref:2430-02	<5	1114.3	37.9	3.7	27.7	15.8	16.5	10.6	21.5	<1	4.5	79.6	11.6	126.2	4.3	5.8	36.7	88.5	240.5
F3	AAC Ref:2430-03	<5	1194.4	8.3	13.4	126.2	18.0	2.8	2.8	7.9	9.2	2.4	9.6	36.6	216.8	1.5	339.3	26.1	121.5	63.1
F4	AAC Ref:2430-04	54.5	479.8	11.4	7.7	52.7	15.5	5.2	6.4	11.2	6.0	2.8	10.2	30.1	203.8	1.9	138.5	34.6	168.3	87.5
F5	AAC Ref:2430-05	<5	411.3	16.8	3.4	10.3	16.9	6.3	3.7	15.8	3.7	1.8	16.9	19.7	127.8	1.2	31.3	56.7	133.9	126.1
F6	AAC Ref:2430-06	39.5	176.6	9.1	7.5	60.2	16.1	3.1	3.8	8.5	6.2	1.4	8.0	33.0	467.3	1.0	184.2	29.7	106.5	74.3
F7	AAC Ref:2430-07	17.4	267.4	9.5	8.4	35.5	16.6	3.6	4.7	9.7	8.2	1.3	20.1	31.5	451.1	1.1	155.4	33.5	400.0	66.1
F8	AAC Ref 2430-08	<5	101.7	5.7	10.4	6.5	12.3	2.9	1.8	7.1	12.0	1.0	38	34.0	227.8	1.0	194.2	24.9	70.2	73.4
F9	AAC Ref:2430-09	142.5	323.1	9.3	17.8	9.3	17.2	3.8	6.4	9.4	11.3	6.4	17.9	29.4	300.0	1.9	249.8	25.9	94.4	50.1
F10	AACRef:2430-10	<5	72.2	11.7	271.4	44.4	152	4.5	<1	86	106.8	2.0	1.6	29.1	186.5	<1	268.4	16.6	81.2	51.1
F11	AAC Ref:2430-11	<5	784.0	32.6	28	29.5	16.9	13.6	6.6	22.1	<1	2.9	42.0	18.6	251.1	2.5	32.0	37.6	111.0	161.7
F12	AAC Ref:2430-12	166.1	558.7	18.3	8.2	95.0	17.4	9.1	5.5	13.1	10.5	2.6	58.6	28.2	743.8	1.8	265.3	20.7	91.7	58.0
F13	AAC Ref:2430-13	<5	512.7	11.7	12.9	64.2	16.4	3.8	35.5	11.3	8.8	1.1	11.4	28.8	373.8	<1	200.0	39.5	129.4	68.8
F14	AAC Ref:2430-14	<5	279.4	10.1	10.0	89.3	17.5	3.1	4.6	8.9	7.2	1.0	1.4	33.5	420.9	<1	276.6	29.0	112.5	75.4
F15	AAC Ref:2430-15,	<5	43.3	2.8	15.6	9.9	15.9	1.1	30.2	2.8	17.8	1.1	7.0	39.0	167.6	<1	257.3	15.6	73.4	45.0
F16	AAC Ref:2430-16	<5	502.4	10.7	10.8	67.7	17.6	7.0	30.2	15.3	11.8	1.1	19.9	32.4	309.5	<1	201.4	55.9	125.2	54.9
F17	AAC Ref:2430-17	<5	3052	6.6	13.8	643.6	20.9	2.5	4.6	6.7	13.1	1.0	3.5	39.9	140.1	<1	561.2	26.1	74.0	50.7
F18	AAC Ref:2430-18	<5	1187	4.0	9.8	148.2	16.6	1.9	2.7	4.9	17.4	<1	22.8	42.2	298.7	<1	234.5	25.3	99.0	87.8
F19	AAC Ref:2430-19	130.4	175.1	6.0	11.4	213.3	17.3	2.4	1.2	5.8	14.0	4.7	22.2	40.3	106.2	<1	348.0	19.8	93.2	34.5
F20	AAC Ref:2430-20	<5	29.0	1.6	16.5	17.0	15.3	<1	23.1	1.9	14.6	<1	1.6	28.5	93.1	<1	305.1	17.6	106.3	30.1
F21	AAC Ref:2430-21	<5	53.4	3.8	15.1	28.3	14.9	2.0	<1	3.7	13.0	<1	9.3	40.5	102.2	<1	340.8	20.8	50.1	47.5
F22	AAC Ref 2430-22	<5	147.9	2.2	26.8	48.3	12.0	<1	2.0	1.5	18.7	<1	5.6	28.4	230.6	<1	201.1	10.3	93.6	60.0
F23	AAC Ref:2430-23	<5	333.1	7.2	6.5	46.3	14.0	2.4	1.5	6.6	7.5	<1	7.2	27.7	223.4	<1	153.7	26.5	89.1	51.8
F24	AAC Ref: 2430-24	<5	86.7	5.3	389.3	46.0	16.1	1.8	<1	4.9	123.2	<1	2.7	33.7	111.4	<1	268.0	13.1	76.4	34.3
F25	AAC Ref: 2430-25	<5	337.4	23.0	58.7	145.9	18.7	11.1	3.1	17.0	24.9	2.6	33.5	32.6	535.1	<1	272.7	24.9	93.0	89.5
BHVO-1	Determined	<5	129.8	36.4	257.4	136.0	22.0	16.2	19.3	21.6	115.1	2.0	13.7	32.1	318.9	1.0	310.3	25.5	116.4	182.5
BHVO-1	Lit. Value	0.4	139.0	39.0	289.0	136.0	21.0	15.8	19.0	25.2	121.0	2.6	11.0	31.8	4030	1.1	317.0	27.6	105.0	179.0

below the level of detection, values for Th and Pb were low and too similar to be of use and were removed from the data set. Because arsenic (As) results appear useful for discrimination, values <5 were set to 1. Other elements with values <1 were set to 0.1. The element values were further corrected to reflect the standard BHVO-1.

Cluster analysis for the trace-element analysis of Fijian excavated material is given in Figure 166. NCSS has divided the results into four clusters with six outliers. Cluster 1 contains F10, F24; Cluster 2: F13, F16; Cluster 3: F2, F11; and Cluster 4: F1, F21, F18, F8, F23, F22, F4, F6, F14, F15, F20, F9, F19. Closely linked (similar) samples include F1, F21, (F18); F8, F23, (F22); F6, F14, (F4); F15, F20; F13, F16; and F10, F24. Note that samples not as closely linked are indicated within parentheses. Other samples which are linked include F2, F11; F12, F25; F9, F19. Note that the clustering analysis of trace elements for Fiji where all elements are used is similar to clustering with a reduced number of elements. The exception is that F9 and F19 are linked with the full data set.

Linkages common to dendrograms for major/minor and trace elements (Figures 162 and 166) are: F12, F25 (and similar petrology); F10, F24 (petrology different); F8, F22, F23 (similar petrology); and F6, F14 (similar petrology). These commonly linked samples should be considered as coming from the same sources. Samples F10 and F24 do not appear the same petrologically but differential weathering may be involved and they may be from the same source.

Ideally, the same samples which were used to form Table 86 for the oxides should have been considered for trace elements. The trace-element database unfortunately does not contain any samples of possible Fijian origin for comparison with the excavated material. Best (1984) and Best et al. (1992) have results only for oxides (Table 84) of Fijian lithics. The table of reference

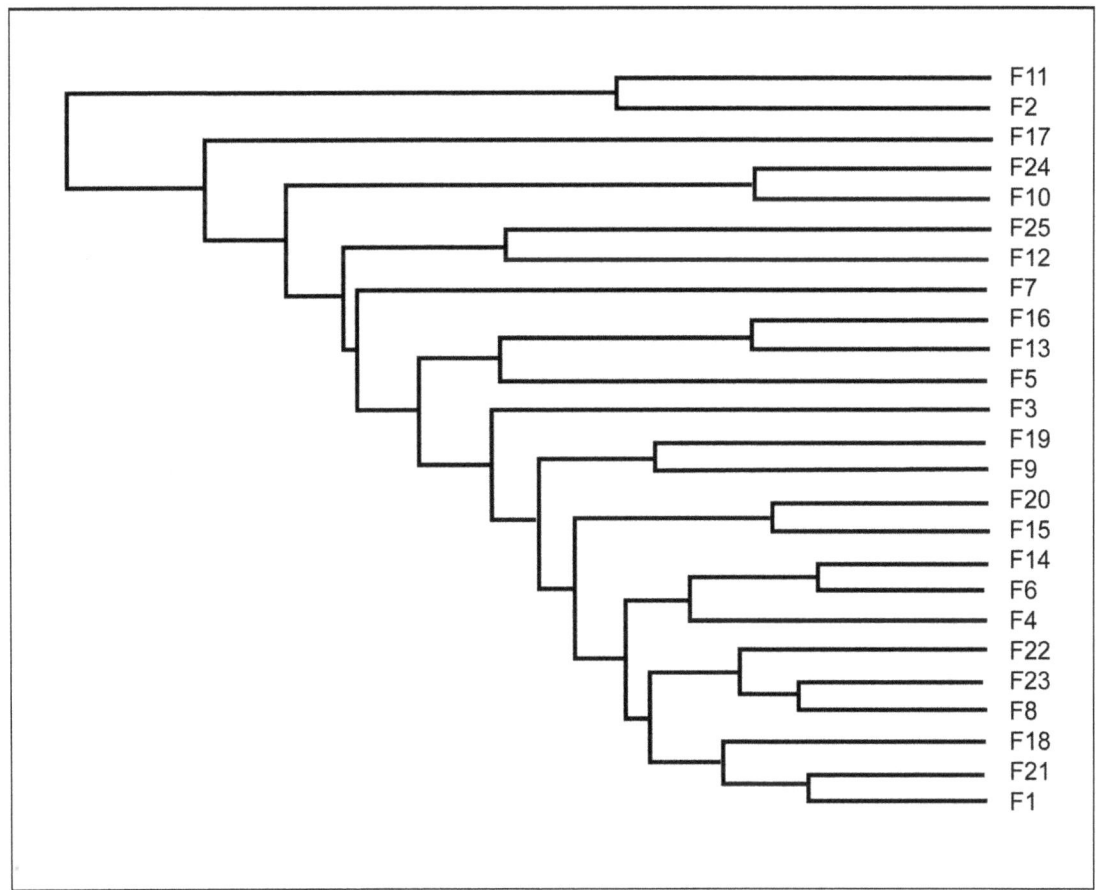

Figure 166. Hierarchical clustering report for trace-element analysis of Fiji excavated flakes and adze fragments.

samples contains analyses of flakes either directly or indirectly sourced to American Samoa and other lithic material from Polynesia (see Table 88). Several of these references are unlikely to have a connection with the excavated artefacts, but they were included to see how they would cluster.

Trace-element analyses for excavated adzes and flakes, along with selected reference samples, are shown in Table 89. The samples in this table have only 11 analysed elements in common, although the original analyses contained more. The data matrix was cluster analysed.

Results of the cluster analysis are given in Figure 167. Most of the excavated samples cluster together and away from the reference samples. This would be expected because there are no likely source rocks in the reference database to link with the Fijian artefacts. It can be seen that samples from Samoa are closely linked and form a cluster, although Tautama and Ovahe are in the cluster but not closely linked. Sample AN41 is linked with F7, but it should be in the Samoan cluster and this appears to be a faulty chemical analysis. Some of the linkages indicate the similarities in trace-element make-up of certain basalts from widely separated sources. At this time, it appears that major-element analyses were of more use than trace elements because of the availability of reference samples.

Table 88. Trace-element analyses (ppm) for basalt references.

Reference	Archipelago	Information	Label	V	Cr	Ni	Cu	Zn	Rb	Sr	Y	Zr	Mb	Ba
Best et al. 1992:85	Cook Islands	Ma'uke	Cooks1	279	0	54	42	159	27	598	42	347	39	264
Best et al. 1992:85	Cook Islands	Ma'uke	Cooks2	248	0	19	34	110	20	717	33	241	63	370
Best et al. 1992:85	A. Samoa	Flake, Area 1	15 (TTM-A1)	221	0	0	7	195	44	710	50	406	44	297
Best et al. 1992:85	A. Samoa	Flake, Area 1	17 (TTM-A1)	214	0	0	8	191	38	720	50	406	42	330
Best et al. 1992:85	A. Samoa	Flake, Area 3	23 (TTM-A3)	209	0	6	15	190	41	721	50	407	44	314
Best et al. 1992:85	A. Samoa	Flake, Leone	AN40	197	0	0	0	197	50	742	51	424	44	326
Best et al. 1992:85	A. Samoa	Flake, Leone	AN41	305	0	41	26	549	28	622	43	350	40	271
Best et al. 1992:85	A. Samoa	II.2	Asia pa	153	0	17	23	193	41	755	55	451	48	426
Sinton and Sinoto 1997:201	A. Samoa	Tutuila	Maupua	198	1	36	30	150	342	107	50	473	60	317
Sinton and Sinoto 1997:201	A. Samoa	TUT-II.3	Le'aeno	247	0	23	25	181	39	764	43	391	47	303
Sinton and Sinoto 1997:201	A. Samoa	Tutuila	Tataga-matau	210	1	0	5	182	42	708	49	383	49	305
Sinton and Sinoto 1997:201	Pitcairn		Tautama	109	8	1	15	171	39	589	48	417	89	458
Sinton and Sinoto 1997:201	Marquesas		Eiao	297	87	100	47	130	18	591	37	306	28	187
Sinton and Sinoto 1997:200	Hawaii	Kaho'olawe	Pu'umoiwi	345	59	60	75	145	16	396	65	228	17	299
Sinton and Sinoto 1997:200	Hawaii	Hawai'i	Mauna Kea	427	0	30	35	137	30	538	39	314	44	405
Sinton and Sinoto 1997:200	Hawaii	Maui	Haleakala	38	6	0	8	133	55	1105	41	412	77	886
Sinton and Sinoto 1997:200	Hawaii	Lana'i	Kapohaku	304	291	118	103	106	7	357	64	136	10	97
Sinton and Sinoto 1997:200	Hawaii	O'ahu	Waiahole	272	225	123	106	104	10	445	25	167	10	119
Sinton and Sinoto 1997:202	Easter Island		Ovahe	162	1	7	5	154	28	299	74	459	53	260
Sinton and Sinoto 1997:203	Society Islands	Ra'iatea	Ra'iatea II	158	8	3	12	118	63	1882	42	433	74	864
Sinton and Sinoto 1997:203	Society Islands	Tahiti	Tahinu II	381	1	53	110	114	53	740	34	311	60	587

Table 89. Trace-element analyses (ppm) for excavated and selected reference samples.

Sample	Label	V	Cr	Ni	Cu	Zn	Rb	Sr	Y	Zr	Nb	Ba
Kulu Bay	F1	321.1	18.3	9.8	85.3	60.4	13.6	216.8	19.1	33.1	3.1	144.7
Kulu Bay	F2	5.9	4.1	0.1	27.7	79.8	64.2	159.5	39.7	235.9	10.4	1193.5
Kulu Bay	F3	346.5	15.0	9.7	126.2	109.6	7.8	274.0	28.3	61.9	2.8	1279.3
Kulu Bay	F4	141.5	8.6	6.3	52.7	151.8	8.2	257.6	37.5	85.8	6.3	513.9
Kulu Bay	F5	32.0	3.8	3.9	10.3	120.8	13.6	161.5	61.4	123.7	3.6	440.5
Kulu Bay	F6	188.2	8.4	6.5	60.2	96.1	6.4	590.6	32.2	72.9	3.7	189.2
Kulu Bay	F7	158.8	9.4	8.6	35.5	360.8	16.2	570.1	36.3	64.8	4.7	286.4
Ugaga Is.	F8	198.4	11.7	12.6	6.5	63.3	3.0	287.9	27.0	72.0	1.8	108.9
Ugaga Is.	F9	255.2	19.9	11.8	9.3	85.2	14.4	379.1	28.1	49.1	6.3	346.0
Natunuku	F10	274.2	304.7	112.2	44.4	73.3	1.3	235.6	18.0	50.1	0.1	77.3
Votua	F11	32.7	3.1	0.1	29.5	100.1	33.9	317.3	40.7	158.6	6.5	839.8
Natunuku	F12	271.0	9.2	11.0	95.0	82.8	47.3	940.0	22.5	56.9	5.4	598.4
Natunuku	F13	204.3	14.5	9.3	64.2	116.7	9.2	472.4	42.8	67.5	34.9	549.1
Natunuku	F14	282.5	11.3	7.5	89.3	101.5	1.1	532.0	31.4	73.9	4.5	299.2
Natunuku	F15	262.8	17.6	18.7	9.9	66.2	5.7	211.8	16.9	44.2	29.7	46.3
Natunuku	F16	205.8	12.2	12.4	67.7	112.9	16.0	391.1	60.6	53.9	29.7	538.1
Kulu Bay	F17	573.2	15.5	13.8	643.6	66.8	2.8	177.1	28.2	49.7	4.5	326.9
Kulu Bay	F18	239.5	11.0	18.3	148.2	89.3	18.4	377.4	27.5	86.1	2.7	127.1
Kulu Bay	F19	355.5	12.8	14.7	213.3	84.1	17.9	134.2	21.4	33.8	1.2	187.6
Kulu Bay	F20	311.6	18.6	15.3	17.0	95.9	1.3	117.6	19.1	29.5	22.7	31.1
Kulu Bay	F21	348.1	16.9	13.7	28.3	45.2	7.5	129.2	22.5	46.6	0.1	57.2
Kulu Bay	F22	205.4	30.1	19.7	48.3	84.4	4.5	291.4	11.1	58.8	1.9	158.4
Kulu Bay	F23	157.0	7.3	7.8	46.3	80.4	5.8	282.3	28.7	50.8	1.5	356.7
Ugaga Is.	F24	273.8	437.0	129.5	46.0	68.9	2.2	140.8	14.2	33.6	0.1	92.9
Kulu Bay	F25	278.6	65.9	26.2	145.9	83.9	27.0	676.3	26.9	87.7	3.1	361.4
Ma'uke	Cooks1	279	0	54	42	159	27	598	42	347	39	264
Ma'uke	Cooks2	248	0	19	34	110	20	717	33	241	63	370
Flake, Area 1	15 (TTM-A1)	221	0	0	7	195	44	710	50	406	44	297
Flake, Area 1	17 (TTM-A1)	214	0	0	8	191	38	720	50	406	42	330
Flake, Area 3	23 (TTM-A3)	209	0	6	15	190	41	721	50	407	44	314
Flake, Leone	AN40	197	0	0	0	197	50	742	51	424	44	326
Flake, Leone	AN41	305	0	41	26	549	28	622	43	350	40	271
II.2	Asiapa	153	0	17	23	193	41	755	55	451	48	426
Tutuila	Maupua	198	1	36	30	150	342	107	50	473	60	317
TUT-II.3	Le'aeno	247	0	23	25	181	39	764	43	391	47	303
Tutuila	Tataga-matau	210	1	0	5	182	42	708	49	383	49	305
Pitcairn	Tautama	109	8	1	15	171	39	589	48	417	89	458
Marquesas	Eiao	297	87	100	47	130	18	591	37	306	28	187
Kaho'olawe	Pu'umoiwi	345	59	60	75	145	16	396	65	228	17	299
Hawai'i	Mauna Kea	427	0	30	35	137	30	538	39	314	44	405
Maui	Haleakala	38	6	0	8	133	55	1105	41	412	77	886
Lana'i	Kapohaku	304	291	118	103	106	7	357	64	136	10	97
O'ahu	Waiahole	272	225	123	106	104	10	445	25	167	10	119
Easter Island	Ovahe	162	1	7	5	154	28	299	74	459	53	260
Ra'iatea	Ra'iatea II	158	8	3	12	118	63	1882	42	433	74	864
Tahiti	Tahinu II	381	1	53	110	114	53	740	34	311	60	587

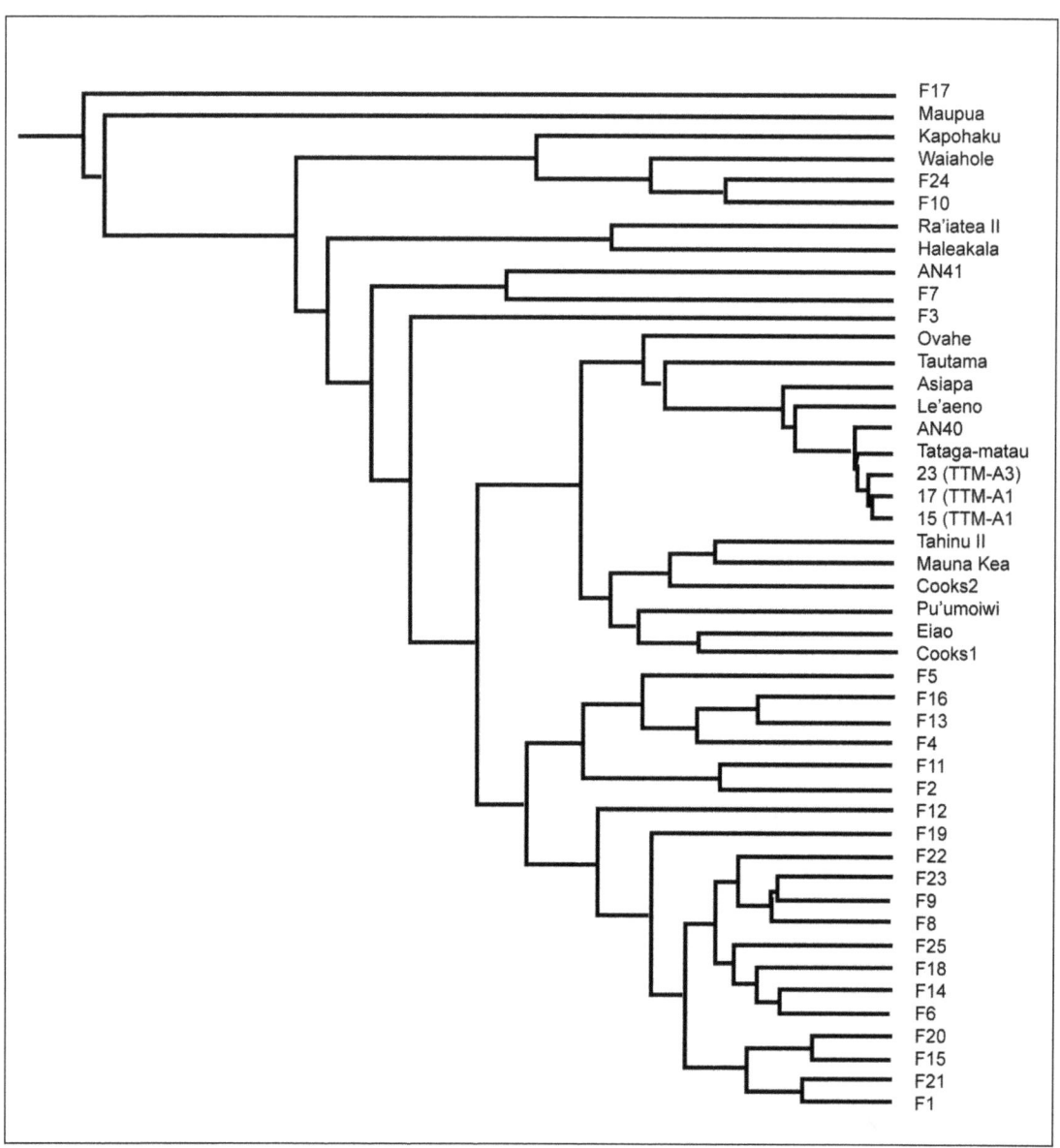

Figure 167. Hierarchical clustering report for trace element analysis of Fiji excavated samples and reference samples.

Adze samples: Conclusion

Among the small sub samples cut from 25 excavated flakes and adzes, some showed a high degree of weathering which would influence the petrography and chemical make-up. The pieces were successfully analysed for major/minor element oxides using EDXA and for 17 trace elements by ICP-MS. In addition, phosphorus was determined by ICP-AES.

EDXA works best on polished flat specimens, which was the reason for preparing such samples in this project. A comparison of solid versus powdered samples indicates that powdered samples may be successfully analysed and the results normalised to 100%. This method of sample preparation is preferred when minimal damage to an artefact is necessary – for example, in museum specimens, where a sample can be obtained by drilling. Contamination of samples during the sampling and pulverising process is not a great concern for major/minor element oxide determinations. However, trace-element concentrations can be affected by sampling and pulverising processes.

ICP-MS is an excellent method for the determination of trace-element concentrations because of its sensitivity and small sample size requirements. Most analytical determinations for sourcing studies in the Pacific have been done using XRF. This has limited the number of chemical elements which have been determined and various researchers have selected different element suites, further restricting comparisons. A non-destructive EDXRF method used by Weisler is probably the ideal for museum specimens, but the lack of instrumentation and reduced sample output restricts this technique.

The analyses reveal that some of the samples from the Fiji excavations are closely linked with Best's (1984) samples. A Lakeba adze (AN27) is closely linked with sample F11, but they do not resemble one another petrologically. Lakeba rock (AN24) is closely linked with F3 and F16 and they could be from the same source. Lakeba rock (AN23) is linked to a cluster of excavated samples and some of these may be from the same source, samples that also include AN24.

None of the excavated samples are closely associated with Samoan reference samples. However, no adzes resembling those of known Samoan morphology were found. All of the flakes which were analysed are most likely from local sources.

Closely linked samples which should be considered as coming from three separate sources are F12, F25; F8, F22, F23; and F6, F14. Another pair, F10, F24, with differing petrology, may be from the same source. These closely linked samples indicate inter- and intra-island usage of rock from the same sources. Also, there may be a considerable time depth to this usage.

Trace-element analyses characterised the excavated samples but there were no relevant reference samples from local quarries to carry out sourcing. It is clear from the clustering analyses that none of the artefacts was from Samoa.

Best (1984) and Best et al. (1992) analysed archaeological lithic samples from Fiji and Samoa as well as the wider Pacific. Their interest, after the discovery that basalt adzes could be sourced to the island of Tutuila, has centred on basalt and Samoa to the detriment of Fijian lithics. Other rock types are to be found to the west of the Andesite Line, making sourcing of rocks found in archaeological sites in Fiji more complex. There is little data available except for some initial work by the above authors.

Appendix: Chemical characterisation of chert artefacts from Fiji

Geoffrey Clark

Department of Archaeology and Natural History, The Australian National University

Introduction

Flake tools made in siliceous rock have been found in numerous archaeological sites in Fiji and such materials might represent prehistoric movement and interaction in the Central Pacific (Green 1996). Crypto-crystalline rocks fracture conchoidally and were commonly used to make expedient sharp-edged artefacts. Primarily composed of silica (SiO_2), with minor oxides of Al, Fe, Ca, Mn, Na, K and Mg, chert develops in different environments often over long periods and varies in its colour, texture and composition. In geology, 'chert' is a term that includes flint, chalcedony, jasper, silicified coral and other crypto-crystalline material. The different colours of chert often reflect the amount and form of minor elements, particularly Fe, which in red 'jasper' is in the form of hematite (Fe_2O_3), while in yellow chert Fe is in the form of lepidocrocite (FeO(OH)). White chert, whether partially or completely translucent, often indicates a low concentration of minor elements. Accidental and purposeful heating as well as weathering can affect the colour, hardness and flaking characteristics of chert (Hatch and Miller 1996).

Ward and Smith (1974) used X-Ray Fluorescence (XRF) to compare the chemical signatures of cherts from the Solomon Islands with those from Australia, New Zealand and New Guinea, and, from a comparison of trace elements, demonstrated the likely transfer of chert from Ulawa to the Reef Santa Cruz Islands. In an important paper, Sheppard (1996:101) summarised the distribution of chert, obsidian and basalt in Near and Remote Oceania and noted that chert had a wide areal extent but a low regional frequency, and was usually not abundant at an individual source. Chert could be divided using petrology into different types based on quartz mineralogy and micro-fossil content and structure, with the possibility that chert from Futuna was taken to Tikopia around ca. 1500 AD. Geochemical analyses appeared to reflect the major depositional environment, suggesting that cherts that were formed in comparable geological settings and conditions might have similar chemical signatures.

The diverse geology of the Fiji Islands indicates the existence of numerous chert sources (see Chapter 14), with two sources of jasper and two sources of silicified coral reported from Vaunuabalavu in the Lau Group. Best (1984:415–416) identified a silicified coral source on Vanuabalavu as the likely source of flakes from an early site on Lakeba, which demonstrated the transfer of silicious stone within the Lau Group. A pilot project to examine the chemical composition of chert tools recovered in the EPF excavations was instigated as no geochemical analyses of Fijian chert had been made, and the presence of silicious tools in sites could represent the widespread transfer of crypto-crystalline material in prehistory.

Materials and methods

Twenty chert tools recovered from EPF excavations were selected for analysis: Votua (n=12), Kulu Bay (n=4), Natunuku (n=3), Ugaga Island (n=1) and Yacata Island (n=2, see Clark and Hope 2001). A jasper outcrop was sampled at Tiotio on Vanuabalavu (n=1). Additional chert tools were obtained from existing archaeological collections in Fiji (Sigatoka n=5, Natunuku n=3, Cikobia n=2, Lakeba n=6, Totoya n=4), making a total of 43 samples (Table 90). Chert artefacts from Votua and Sigatoka date to the late-Lapita era, but the dating of chert samples from other sites is uncertain, as at Kulu Bay and Ugaga, where Lapita and post-Lapita artefacts were mixed together, and at Totoya and Yacata, where chert flakes were surface collected.

Table 90. Chert samples submitted for chemical analysis. FJ09 was not analysed.

Lab. No.	Location	Type	Description
FJ01	Mago, Votua, Area 1: 0–10 cm	core	Red banded fine-grained material, pitted with thin veins of grey-blue and brown.
FJ02	Mago, Votua, Area 1: surface	core	White fine-grained with pale yellow areas and grey veined.
FJ03	Mago, Votua, Area 1: surface	core	Red banded fine-grained and pitted with grey-blue and brown vacuoles.
FJ04	Mago, Votua, Area 1: 0–10 cm	flake	Yellow-brown banded and fine-grained.
FJ05	Mago, Votua, Area 1: 20–30 cm	flake	Dark red fine-grained homogeneous material.
FJ06	Mago, Votua, Area 2: 0–10 cm	flake	Red with micro-layering, fine-grained with a thin lens of brick red material in section.
FJ07	Mago, Votua, Area 2: 30–40 cm	flake	Dark red fine-grained surrounding a light orange-red area 4 mm^2. Cortex in cross section has a thin white covering.
FJ08	Mago, Votua, Area 2: 0–30 cm	flake	Yellow-brown fine-grained with diffuse patches of grey-black, possible cortex on one face.
FJ09	Mago, Votua, Area 2: 30–40 cm	flake	Brown fine-grained material with small vacuoles.
FJ10	Mago, Votua, Area 2: 30–40 cm	flake	Dark red fine-grained with patches of mottled pink and a few small vacuoles.
FJ11	Mago, Votua, Area 2: 0–10 cm	flake	Brown with thin branches of red-brown and diffuse patches of quartz.
FJ12	Mago, Votua, Area 2: 10–20 cm	flake	Mottled yellow brown and a vein of red penetrating 3 mm from cortex.
FJ13	Viti Levu, Sigatoka, 45A, Y/2/2	flake	Pale white with diffuse inclusions of dark red. White cortex on one face.
FJ14	Viti Levu, Sigatoka, 45A, Y/2/4	flake	Yellow with red patches near cortex. Small crystals on thin cortex layer.
FJ15	Viti Levu, Sigatoka, 45A, S	flake	White fine-grained material with an area of yellow and red on one edge. Numerous small grey vacuoles.
FJ16	Viti Levu, Sigatoka, 45A, Y/2/4	flake	Yellow-white coarse-grained and veins of grey-green.
FJ17	Viti Levu, Sigatoka, 45A, Z/2/1	flake	White fine-banded material with stained patches of yellow.
FJ18	Cikobia, CIK-06B: 130–140 cm	flake/core	Brown fine-grained and banded material with veins of quartz and small grey vacuoles.
FJ19	Cikobia, CIK-06D: 80–90 cm	flake	Dense dark red material with small pinkish pits near cortex and a few interior grey-blue vacuoles.
FJ20	Viti Levu, Natunuku, Tr. 3: Layer 2A	flake	White mottled with grey-to-yellow quartz. No visible banding or vacuoles.
FJ21	Viti Levu, Natunuku, Tr. 3: 30–40 cm	flake	Red glassy material with a coarse-grained inclusion of ?red-black glass. Near the edge the material is coarse-grained with particles of white, red and ?black.
FJ22	Viti Levu, Natunuku, surface. FJM	flake	White fine-grained and banded material stained with pale yellow-brown. Sample had a small oyster growing on surface.
FJ23	Viti Levu, Natunuku, surface. FJM	flake	Pink-red quartz coarse material with a plate-like structure.
FJ24	Viti Levu, Natunuku, Tr. 3: 50–60 cm	flake	Dark red dense material with veins of purple-red and numerous grey-blue vacuoles.
FJ25	Viti Levu, Natunuku, surface. FJM	flake	Orange-brown cortex. Interior has blocky grey-white inclusions with coarse and irregular banding.
FJ26	Beqa, Kulu, C10: 30–50 cm	flake	White coarse-grained material with very small patches of black and yellow-brown. No banding present.
FJ27	Beqa, Kulu, C10: 30–50 cm	flake	White-grey material with diffuse white patches and inclusions. Pale yellow towards edge.
FJ28	Beqa, Kulu, C11: 30–40 cm	flake	Pink-white material with round inclusions of red-orange and angular white particles. Vacuoles and possible micro-fossils.
FJ29	Beqa, Kulu, C10: 0–30 cm	flake	White homogeneous material lacking vacuoles or coloured inclusions.
FJ30	Beqa, Ugaga, P9: 30–40 cm	flake	Interior has angular fragments of quartz surrounded by irregular areas of yellow and red.
FJ31	Lakeba, 196-12-B-1(1)	flake/drill bit	White homogeneous fine-grained material.
FJ32	Lakeba, 101/7/47(16A)	flake	Irregular coarse areas of pinkish-red and brown.
FJ33	Lakeba, 196-B-B-3(2)	flake	White course-grained quartz.
FJ34	Lakeba, 196-16-B-1(1)	flake	Mottled coarse white and grey-brown with possible micro-fossils.
FJ35	Lakeba, 196-16-B-3(8)	flake	Dark red fine-grained and homogeneous material.
FJ36	Lakeba, 196-23-B14	flake	Dark red fine-grained with micro-vacuoles and mottled with brick red.
FJ37	Yacata, Natuiwaqa, TP1: 0–30 cm	flake	Dark brown fine-grained material.
FJ38	Yacata, 200m southeast of village	flake	Brick-red interior intruded by crystal-filled vacuoles and dark brown patches.
FJ39	Vanuabalavu, Tiotio	cobble	Dark red, fine-grained homogeneous material with very small vacuoles .
FJ42	Totoya, Jigojigo, TO31/43/32	flake	Dark red, fine-grained homogeneous material with very small vacuoles. Thin veins of blue ?quartz.
FJ43	Totoya, Keteira 1, TO31/46	flake	Interior crystal-filled vacuoles surrounded by irregular and coarse patches of pink and red material.
FJ44	Totoya, Waroka 3	flake	Dark red fine-grained material with irregular pink and white streaks.
FJ45	Totoya, Udu, TO31/1/2	flake	Mottled grey-yellow coarse material with small black grains and partially absorbed lathe structures.

Chert samples were cut with a hydraulic diamond wire saw with the wire-cut surface analysed with proton and gamma induced X-Ray emissions (PIXIE/PIGME) at the ANSTO 3 MV van de Graff accelerator at Lucas Heights. Elements measured in ppm were F, Na, Al, Si, K, Ca, Ti, Cr, Mn, Fe, Zn, Rb, Sr, Y, Zr, Nb and Pb (Table 91). Sample FJ09 from Votua was too small to examine, leaving 42 analysed samples. Following the geochemical study, chert sections were scanned at 4800 dpi to facilitate the description of colour and texture (Table 90), and to check whether the area sampled by the proton beam – visible in most sample scans as a grey or brown circle – included any voids or anomalies that might affect element concentrations. Element values were log10 transformed, with individual element values checked against sample colour to identify elements that were highly correlated with Fe. Associated with 'red' iron-rich chert samples were Pb, Zn, Ti, Rb, F, Ca, Cr and Mn, while Al, Na, K, Sr, Y, Nb and Zr were not strongly correlated with Fe. SPSS Version 13 software was used to perform two hierarchical cluster analyses (between-groups linkage, squared Euclidean distance).

The first HCA used nine iron-correlated elements in the red chert samples (Fe, Pb, Zn, Ti, Rb, F, Ca, Cr, Mn), as colour is a common criterion that is used to group archaeological chert artefacts, and similar-coloured chert tools at different sites could result from the exploitation of a particular source. For red 'jasper' artefacts found in the Lau Group this was especially plausible as there were two known sources of jasper on Vanuabalavu, and artefacts made in red chert were found at the Votua Lapita site on nearby Mago Island. A second HCA was run with remaining elements that were not correlated with Fe. This was to investigate the geochemical variability in samples once the elements largely responsible for sample colour had been removed.

Analysis results

All samples were composed of a high proportion of Si (75.7%–99.9%), with variable amounts of Fe, ranging from 0.01% to 23.4%, reflecting colour variation between red, white and variegated cherts. Trace elements were extremely low for Sr, Y, Zr and Nb and slightly higher for F, Ca, K and Cr (Table 91).

The HCA dendrogram of the Fe-correlated elements contains two main clusters (Figure 168). The top cluster contains the majority of chert from archaeological sites in west Fiji, such as Sigatoka, Natunuku and Kulu, with a few samples from east Fiji (Totoya, Votua, Lakeba). These samples are low in Fe, as indicated by their white-to-yellow colour, although two artefacts of reddish chert from Natunuku (FJ21, FJ24) were also placed in the cluster. Most of the white-yellow samples in the upper cluster were fine-grained and relatively homogeneous, in contrast to six samples forming a separate sub-branch of the lower cluster (FJ16, FJ25, FJ28, FJ30, FJ26, FJ43). These cherts were coarse-grained and heterogeneous with diffuse coloured areas, often with veining and vacuoles. The lower branch of the base cluster was dominated by red chert from the Lau Group and Cikobia Island, north of Udu Point on Vanua Levu, including a sample from the Tiotio outcrop on Vanuabalavu. Individual Votua artefacts were found to be similar to those from Totoya (FJ01 with FJ42), Lakeba (FJ06 with FJ36), and Yacata (FJ11 with FJ37). The Tiotio chert (FJ39) grouped with two artefacts from Lakeba and Votua (FJ10 and FJ35). These samples were similar to one another and were dark red and fine-grained and had only a few small vacuoles.

The second HCA examined elements Al, Na, K, Sr, Y, Nb and Zr that were not strongly correlated with sample colour (Figure 169). Such elements might represent the origin of a chert with greater reliability than elements responsible for sample colour, particularly if the same source of crypto-crystalline material contained chert of different colours. There is greater variation in

Table 91. Fijian chert element analysis (ppm).

Sample	Location	F	Na	Al	Si	K	Ca	Ti	Cr	Mn	Fe	Zn	Rb	Sr	Y	Zr	Nb	Pb
FJ01	Votua	5.6	272.4	155.3	585084	131	102	151	549	0	43956	2	2	2	0	2	1	40
FJ02	Votua	4	79.1	–	573976	185	102	0	41	0	123	4	0	1	1	1	2	0
FJ03	Votua	6.6	90.2	–	580546	149	183	230	104	139	68942	16	2	0	0	2	2	86
FJ04	Votua	7.3	217	–	556984	461	302	216	894	467	69134	22	4	0	0	0	2	97
FJ05	Votua	292.6	219.9	–	515240	167	12265	423	1778	268	133434	28	26	8	0	0	4	130
FJ06	Votua	8.2	241	–	569991	179	365	309	1165	0	97621	18	0	0	0	2	0	60
FJ07	Votua	60.5	276.1	136.9	511404	79	2586	480	1760	255	158406	107	7	3	0	5	3	150
FJ08	Votua	6.2	503.9	532	547908	690	394	89	465	1068	37072	8	0	5	0	1	1	12
FJ10	Votua	29.2	268.9	–	523852	81	2006	292	17	99	105730	11	6	5	0	4	1	77
FJ11	Votua	3.1	300.5	–	564198	495	123	25	67	209	11213	4	0	1	1	1	1	2
FJ12	Votua	3.3	183.9	–	553315	308	109	0	82	30	4530	3	1	1	1	1	1	2
FJ13	Sigatoka	3.5	146.4	135.6	561059	152	249	0	120	32	112	1	0	1	0	0	1	0
FJ14	Sigatoka	2.6	182	172.2	568646	116	157	0	92	0	268	0	0	2	0	0	1	0
FJ15	Sigatoka	2.6	955.8	577.1	560531	346	63	0	9	6	337	0	0	1	0	1	0	1
FJ16	Sigatoka	10.5	725.4	3277.1	569699	735	957	171	65	22	2454	5	0	7	2	2	1	0
FJ17	Sigatoka	2.6	376.5	518.4	582253	376	143	0	76	5	81	0	1	1	1	1	1	2
FJ18	Cikobia	5.7	125.5	248	541222	216	18265	182	458	504	53409	7	5	4	0	1	0	43
FJ19	Cikobia	4.5	101	–	574904	142	235	90	433	249	30400	6	2	2	0	2	0	20
FJ20	Natunuku	3.2	106.8	204.5	581342	102	141	0	0	3	224	1	1	2	0	1	1	1
FJ21	Natunuku	4.8	24.8	–	599117	126	20684	0	127	4	663	2	0	12	0	1	1	1
FJ22	Natunuku	2.6	1203.7	320.8	574729	314	0	0	34	0	61	2	1	0	0	2	3	0
FJ23	Natunuku	2.8	332.7	343.8	562690	335	97	0	107	8	330	2	1	1	1	2	2	0
FJ24	Natunuku	4.3	230.6	–	565118	240	0	0	354	50	25036		1	0	0	0	3	17
FJ25	Natunuku	43.2	1558.3	3677.3	556349	1152	1334	188	122	11	682	1	0	13	2	6	0	1
FJ26	Kulu	11.4	15.9	204.2	571314	16	106	1574	9	1	148	2	1	2	1	97	1	5
FJ27	Kulu	4.4	112.5	–	566835	49	67	0	80	0	188	0	0	5	3	4	4	0
FJ28	Kulu	3.6	186.5	188	564416	139	226	3351	161	6	296	1	2	3	1	4	3	4
FJ29	Kulu	1.5	167.5	357.5	575126	214	261	9	44	12	156	4	1	3	0	2	2	1
FJ30	Ugaga	4.1	40.6	132.7	566088	224	107	6322	120	0	4003	2	0	2	2	10	3	6
FJ31	Lakeba	3.3	192.7	322.3	599963	210	464	20	158	8	356	7	1	2	1	2	2	7
FJ32	Lakeba	5.3	150.5	246.6	564536	528	212	149	247	572	30726	10	2	3	0	0	1	18
FJ33	Lakeba	1.8	79.3	–	568402	141	128	0	216	4	186	2	2	2	1	1	2	1
FJ34	Lakeba	12.3	104.4	–	570234	90	133	13	86	12	230	0	1	2	2	0	1	2
FJ35	Lakeba	6.2	237.1	221.1	547460	187	1027	402	100	43	50980	8	0	5	4	2	3	13
FJ36	Lakeba	7.3	125.3	223.3	573053	128	110	321	1181	0	109461	7	1	0	0	6	5	188
FJ37	Yacata	2.3	38	–	561106	505	345	28	208	731	15833	4	2	3	2	1	0	4
FJ38	Yacata	50.4	571.2	3790.1	541650	3142	261	1051	1433	119	106580	11	18	3	0	11	3	130
FJ39	Tiotio	8.8	261.5	3772.6	545718	1392	583	298	58	5	22287	1	3	8	3	8	3	17
FJ42	Totoya	6.1	60.6	43.5	557957	10	157	129	588	0	45740	2	2	0	0	12	1	15
FJ43	Totoya	5.9	32.6	58.8	547170	91	233	4769	0	28	3831	3	0	2	2	16	2	5
FJ44	Totoya	5	216.9	–	563570	265	138	0	149	28	5258	2	0	2	2	0	2	0
FJ45	Totoya	9.7	141.4	177.2	586752	174	154	9712	553	0	66733	6	0	26	0	44	1	44

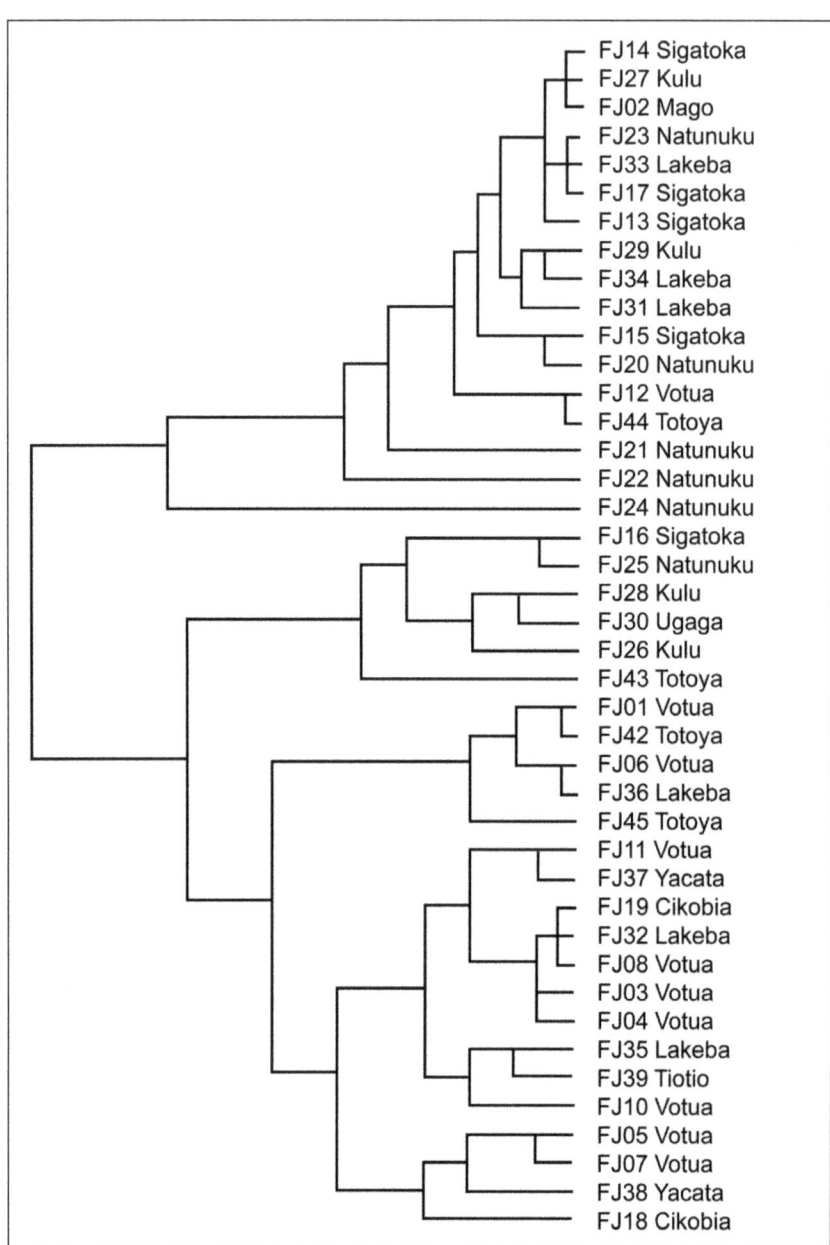

Figure 168. Hierarchical clustering report for chert samples using Fe-correlated elements.

the distribution of samples in the HCA, with Votua artefacts in the major clusters. The ability to discriminate chert with the seven minor and trace elements does not appear great, as the Tiotio source (FJ39) did not group with any of the Votua artefacts, despite Vanuabalavu being the closest known source of red chert to Mago Island. However, the majority of cherts from Sigatoka were in the top cluster, while three artefacts from Totoya were grouped together in a subcluster (FJ42, FJ43, FJ45), indicating that the artefact groupings are not entirely arbitrary.

Conclusions

Chert is a heterogenous material compared with some basalts, and particularly obsidians, which form by the rapid cooling of a relatively homogeneous magma fluid (Lyons et al. 2003). Attribution of an artefact to a particular source is further complicated by the number of potential sources in the Central Pacific, as chert can be formed by diagenesis in limestone environments as nodules, or be deposited in thin or thick beds, especially in geosynclinal deposits that have been uplifted. Potential sources of chert have been recorded on Viti Levu (Hunt 1979), Vanua

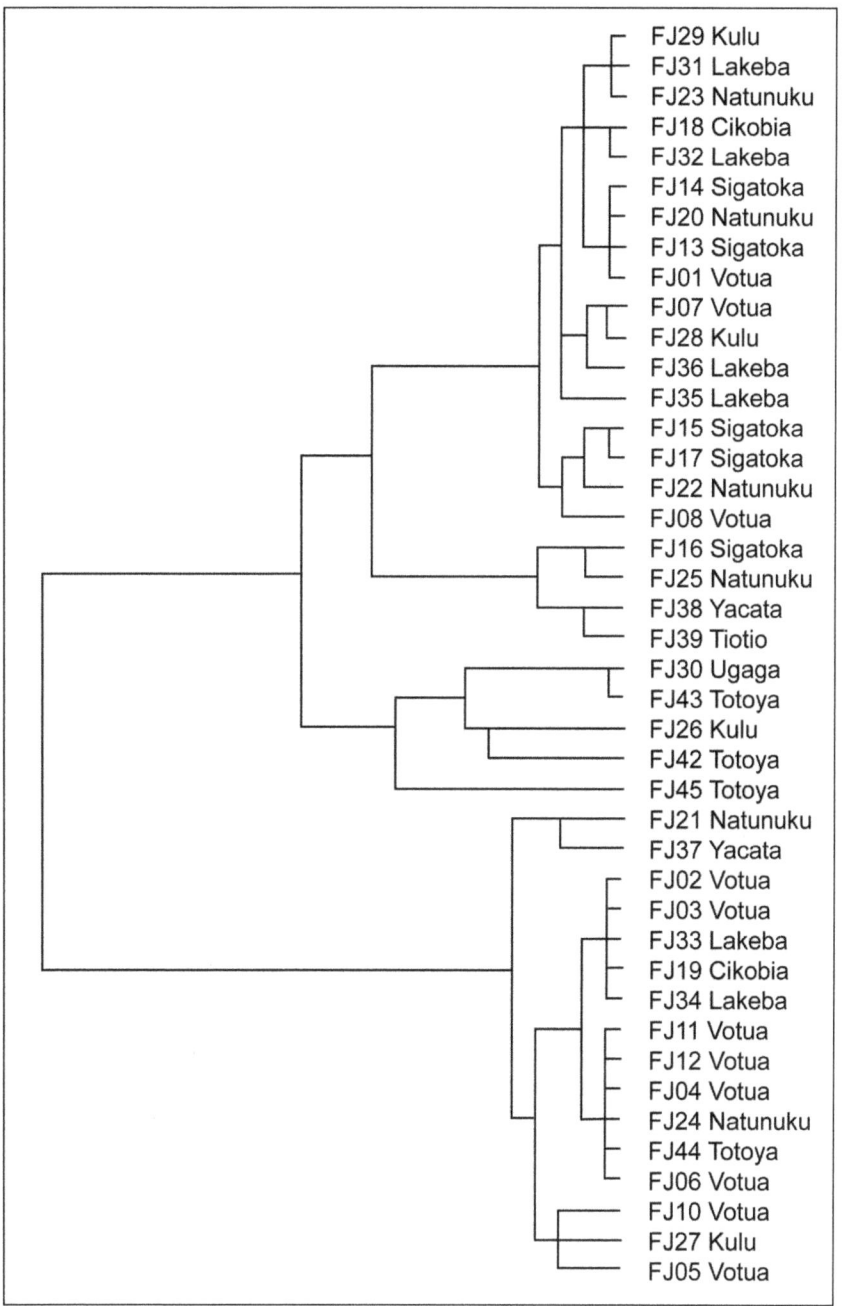

Figure 169. Hierarchical clustering report for chert samples using elements not strongly correlated with sample colour (Al, Na, K, Sr, Y, Nb, Zr).

Levu and Vanuabalavu, but many more must be present considering the complicated geology and number of islands in the Fiji archipelago.

Chemical analysis of chert artefacts revealed a group of elements strongly correlated with Fe, which in different forms is the main contributor to chert colour. As expected, these elements in a HCA grouped samples by colour, but the analysis also correctly sorted the majority of samples by texture. The similar visual and textural properties of chert were reinforced by the chemical results that placed chert from an outcrop on Vanuabalavu with artefacts from the Votua Lapita site. Results also indicated that a white-yellow chert found at Natunuku and Sigatoka may be from the same source (probably Viti Levu), and chert from this source might also have been taken to Beqa Island and Lakeba. Red and yellow chert artefacts from Votua, Lakeba, Yacata and Totoya are likely to originate from a source in the Lau Group and may have been taken as far afield as Cikobia, while the red chert appears to be from a different source. It is interesting that a red chert (presumed to be local) circulates mainly in the Lau Group and outer islands, while on Viti Levu, a white chert-chalcedony may have been distributed as far as the Suva area in late prehistory, as Hunt (1979:38) reports that flakes from a ring-ditch overlooking the Samabula River were of the same material as flakes found at Sigatoka. A number of early sites contain chert artefacts, but the temporal association of crypto-crystalline tools with Lapita pottery is unclear due to site disturbance, except at Votua where chert artefacts are numerous. On Lakeba, silicified materials were certainly present in Lapita-age deposits and are common at the Ulunikoro (Site 47) fortification, dating to about AD 1100 (Best 1984:492–493).

Minor and trace elements for chert artefacts did not produce coherent geographic clusters, and several trace elements were present at low concentrations, meaning that they have a limited capacity to confidently differentiate prehistoric artefacts. Chert was almost certainly transported through the Fiji Islands in prehistory and future work should concentrate on establishing the chemical and petrological variation in the known chert sources so that archaeological artefacts can be identified to a source with greater confidence.

References

Allen, M.S. and Johnson, K.T.M. 1997. Tracking ancient patterns of interaction: Recent geochemical studies in the southern Cook Islands. In: Weisler, M.I. (ed), *Prehistoric long-distance interaction in Oceania: An interdisciplinary approach*, pp. 111–113. New Zealand Archaeological Association Monograph 21, NZAA, Auckland.

Anderson, A., Ambrose, W., Leach, F. and Weisler, M. 1997. Material sources of basalt and obsidian artefacts from a prehistoric settlement site on Norfolk Island, South Pacific. *Archaeology in Oceania* 32: 39–46.

Ayres, W.S., Goles, G.B. and Beardsley, F.R. 1997. Provenance study of lithic materials in Micronesia. In: Weisler, M.I. (ed), *Prehistoric long-distance interaction in Oceania*, pp. 53–67. New Zealand Archaeological Association Monograph 21.

Best, S. 1984. Lakeba: The prehistory of a Fijian island. Unpublished PhD thesis, University of Auckland.

Best, S. 1989. *Lakeba: The prehistory of a Fijian island*. University Microfilms, Ann Arbor, Michigan.

Best, S., Sheppard, P. Green, R. and Parker, R. 1992. Necromancing the stone: archaeologists and adzes in Samoa. *Journal of the Polynesian Society* 101(1): 45–85.

Buist, A. 1969. Field archaeology on Savai'i. In: Green, R. and Davidson, J. (eds), *Archaeology in Western Samoa* 1: 34–68. *Bulletin of the Auckland Institute and Museum 6*, Auckland.

Clark, G and Hope, G. 2001. Archaeological and palaeoenvironmental investigations on Yacata Island, northern Lau, Fiji. *Domodomo* 13: 29–47.

Clark, J.T., Wright, E. and Herdrich, D.J. 1997. Interactions within and beyond the Samoan archipelago: Evidence from basaltic rock geochemistry. In: Weisler, M.I. (ed), *Prehistoric long-distance interaction in Oceania: An interdisciplinary approach*. New Zealand Archaeological Association Monograph 21, NZAA, Auckland.

Cleghorn, P.L., Dye, T., Weisler, M. and Sinton, J. 1985. A preliminary petrographic study of Hawaiian stone adze quarries. *Journal of the Polynesian Society* 94: 235–251.

Dickinson, W.R. and Shutler, R. 1979. Petrography of sand tempers in Pacific Islands potsherds: Summary. *Geological Society of America Bulletin* 90: 993–995.

Dye, T.S., Weisler, M.I. and Riford, M. 1985. Adz quarries on Moloka'i and Oahu, Hawaiian Islands.

Report 093085 on file, Department of Anthropology. Bernice P. Bishop Museum, Honolulu.

Emory, K.P. 1975. Material culture of the Tuamotu Archipelago. *Pacific Anthropological Records 22.* Bernice P. Bishop Museum, Honolulu.

Goodhew, P.J. and Humphreys, F.J. 1988. *Electron microscopy and analysis.* Taylor and Francis, London.

Green, R.C. 1974. Review of portable artifacts from Western Samoa. In: Green, R.C. and Davidson, J. (eds), *Archaeology. in Western Samoa* 2: 245 275. Bulletin of the Auckland Institute and Museum 7, Auckland:

Green, R.C. 1996. Prehistoric transfers of portable items during the Lapita horizon in Remote Oceania: A review. *Bulletin of the Indo-Pacific Prehistory Association* 15: 119–130.

Green, T. 1984. Appendix I: Petrologic evaluation of artifact material from Norfolk Island, In Specht, J. (ed), *The Prehistoric Archaeology of Norfolk Island:* 53–56. Pacific Anthropological Records 34. Bishop Museum, Honolulu.

Green, R.C. and Davidson, J. (eds). 1969. Archaeology in Western Samoa, Volume 1. *Bulletin of the Auckland Institute and Museum* 7.

Hatch, J.W. and Miller, P.E. 1996. Procurement, tool production, and sourcing research at the Vera Cruz jasper quarry in Pennsylvania. *Journal of Field Archaeology* 12: 219–230.

Hunt, C. 1979. A flaked stone industry from Fiji. *The Artefact* 4: 37–39.

Jarvis, K.E., Gray, A.L. and Houk, R.S. 1992. Sample preparation for ICP-MS, Chapter 7. *Handbook of inductively coupled plasma mass spectrometry.* Chapman and Hall, London.

Kirch, P.V. 1975. Excavation at sites *A1-3* and *A1-4:* Early settlement and ecology in Halawa Valley. In: Kirch, P.V. and Kelly, M. (eds), *Prehistory and Ecology in a Windward Hawaiian Valley: Halawa Valley, Moloka'i:* 17–70. Pacific Anthropological Records 24. Bishop Museum, Honolulu.

Kirch, P.V. 1988. Niuatoputapu: The Prehistory of a Polynesian Chiefdom. *Thomas Burke Memonal Washington Stale Museum Monograph 5.* Seattle.

Leach, H. and Witter, D. 1987. Tataga-matau "rediscovered". *New Zealand Journal of Archaeology* 9: 33–54.

Leach, H. and Witter, D. 1990. Further investigations at the Tataga-matau site, American Samoa. *New Zealand Journal of Archaeology* 12: 51–83.

Lyons, W.H., Glascock, M.D. and Mehringer, Jr. 2003. Silica from sources to site: Ultraviolet fluorescence and trace elements identify cherts from Lost Dune, southeastern Oregon, USA. *Journal of Archaeological Science* 30: 1139–1159.

Rapp, G., Jr. 1985. The provenance of artifactual raw materials. In: Rapp, G. Jr. and Gifford, J.A. (eds), *Archaeological geology.* Yale University Press, New Haven.

Romesburg H.C. 1984. *Cluster analysis for researchers.* Lifetime Learning Publications, Belmont, California.

Rolett, B.V., Conte, E., Pearthree, E. and Sinton, J.M. 1997. Marquesan voyaging: archaeometric evidence for inter-island contact. In: Weisler, M.I. (ed), *Prehistoric long-distance interaction in Oceania: An interdisciplinary approach.* New Zealand Archaeological Association Monograph 21, NZAA, Auckland.

Rubinson, K.A. 1987. *Chemical analysis.* Little, Brown and Company, Boston.

Sheppard, P.J. 1996. Hard rock: Archaeological implications of chert sourcing in Near and Remote Oceania. In: Davidson, J.M., Irwin, G., Leach, B.F., Pawley, A. and Brown, D. (eds), *Oceanic Culture History: Essays in honour of Roger Green*, pp. 99–115. New Zealand Journal of Archaeology Special Publication, New Zealand.

Sheppard, P.J., Walter, R. and Parker, R.J. 1997. Basalt sourcing and the development of Cook Island exchange systems. In: Weisler, M.I. (ed), *Prehistoric long-distance interaction in Oceania: An interdisciplinary approach*, pp. 85–110. New Zealand Archaeological Association Monograph 21, NZAA, Auckland.

Sinton, J. M. 1990. Geologic and archaeologic reference collections for south Polynesian adze studies. Hawaii Bishop Research Institute, Honolulu.

Sinton, J.M. and Sinoto, Y.H. 1997. A geochemical database for Polynesian adze studies. In: Weisler, M.I. (ed), *Prehistoric long-distance interaction in Oceania: An interdisciplinary approach*, pp. 194–204. New Zealand Archaeological Association Monograph 21, NZAA, Auckland.

Sinton, J.M., Johnson, K. and Price, R. 1985. Petrology and geochemistry of volcanic rocks from the northern Melanesian borderland. In: Brocher, T. (ed), Investigations of the Northern Melanesian Borderland, pp. 35-65. *Earth Science Series* Vol. 3. Circum-Pacific Council for Energy and Mineral Resources, Houston.

Walter, R. 1990. The Southern Cook Islands in Eastern Polynesian Prehistory. Unpublished PhD thesis, University of Auckland.

Walter, R. and Sheppard, P.J. 1996. The Ngati Tiare adze cache: Further evidence of prehistoric contact between West Polynesia and the Southern Cook Islands. *Archaeology in Oceania* 31: 33–39.

Ward, G.K. and Smith, I.E. 1974. Characterization of chert sources as an aid to the identification of patterns of trade, Southeast Solomon Islands: A preliminary investigation. *Mankind* 9: 181–186.

Weisler, M.I. 1989. Towards documenting exchange in a complex chiefdom: An essay in method. Paper presented at the 54th Annual Meeting of the Society for American Archaeology, Atlanta, Georgia.

Weisler, M.I. 1990a. Sources and sourcing of volcanic glass in Hawai'i: Implications for exchange studies. *Archaeology in Oceania* 25: 16–23.

Weisler, M.I. 1990b. A technological, petrographic, and geochemical analysis of the Kapohaku adze quarry, Lana'i, Hawai'ian Islands. *New Zealand Journal of Archaeology* 12: 29–50.

Weisler, M.I. 1990c. Chemical characterization and sourcing of volcanic glass artifacts from Poka'i Bay, O'ahu. Environmental and Energy Services Co, Honolulu.

Weisler, M.I. 1993a. Chemical characterisation and provenance of Manu'a adz material using a non-destructive X-Ray Fluorescence technique. In: Kirch, P.V. and Hunt, T.L. (eds), The To'aga Site: Three millennia of Polynesian occupation in the Manu'a Islands, American Samoa. *Contribution to the University of California Archaeological Research Facility Berkeley, Number 51*, pp. 167–188. Berkeley.

Weisler, M.I. 1993b. Long-distance interaction in prehistoric Polynesia: Three case studies. Unpublished PhD thesis, Department of Anthropology, University of California, Berkeley.

Weisler, M.I. 1993c. Provenance studies of Polynesian basalt adze material: A review and suggestions for improving regional data bases. *Asian Perspectives* 32(1): 61–83.

Weisler, M.I. 1994. The settlement of marginal Polynesia: New evidence from Henderson Island. *Journal of Field Archaeology* 21: 83–102.

Weisler, M.I. 1995. Henderson Island prehistory: Colonization and extinction on a remote Polynesian island. *Biological Journal of the Linnean Society* 56: 377–404.

Weisler, M.I. 1996a. An archaeological survey of Mangareva: Implications for regional settlement models and interaction studies. *Man and Culture in Oceania* 12: 61–85.

Weisler, M.I. 1996b. Taking the mystery out of the Polynesian 'mystery' islands: A case study from Mangareva and the Pitcairn Group. In: Davidson, J., Irwin, G., Leach, F., Pawley, A. and Brown, D. (eds), *Pacific culture history. Essays in Honour of Roger Green*, pp. 615–629. New Zealand Journal of Archaeology Special Publication, Dunedin.

Weisler, M.I. (ed) 1997a. *Prehistoric long-distance interaction in Oceania: An interdisciplinary approach*. New Zealand Archaeological Association Monograph 21, NZAA, Auckland.

Weisler, M.I. 1997b. Prehistoric long-distance interaction at the margins of Oceania. In: Weisler, M.I. (ed), *Prehistoric long-distance interaction in Oceania: An interdisciplinary approach*, pp. 149–172. New Zealand Archaeological Association Monograph 21, NZAA, Auckland.

Weisler, M.I. and Kirch, P.V. 1996. Interisland and interarchipelago transfer of stone tools in prehistoric Polynesia. *Proceedings of the National Academy of Sciences, USA* 93: 1381–1385.

Weisler, M.I., Kirch, P.V. and Endicott, J.M. 1994. The Mata'are basalt source: Implications for prehistoric interaction studies in the Cook Islands. *Journal of the Polynesian Society* 103: 203–216.

Weisler, M.I. and Sinton, J.M. 1997. Towards identifying prehistoric interaction systems in Polynesia.

In: Weisler, M.I. (ed), *Prehistoric long-distance interaction in Oceania: An interdisciplinary approach*, pp. 173–193. New Zealand Archaeological Association Monograph 21, NZAA, Auckland.

Weisler, M.I. and Woodhead, J. 1995. Basalt Pb isotope analysis and the prehistoric settlement of Polynesia. *Proceedings of the National Academy of Sciences, USA* 92: 1881–1885.

White, A.J.R. 1987. Appendix 7. Petrography of some stone adzes from Tongatapu, Tonga group. In: Poulsen, J. (ed), Early Tongan prehistory, pp. 279–281. *Terra Australis 12*. Department of Prehistory, Research School of Pacific Studies. The Australian National University, Canberra.

Williams, K.L. 1987. *An introduction to X-Ray Spectrometry: X-Ray Fluorescence and electron microprobe analysis*. Allen and Unwin, London.

Wilson, A.L. 1978. Elemental analysis of pottery in the study of its provenance: A review. *Journal of Archaeological Science* 5: 219–236.

Withrow, B. 1990. Prehistoric distribution of stone adzes on Hawaii Island: Implications for the development of Hawaiian chiefdoms. *Asian Perspectives* 29: 235–250.

Withrow, B. 1991. Prehistoric production, distribution, and use of stone adzes: Implications for the development of Hawaiian chiefdoms. Unpublished PhD thesis, University of Minnesota, Minneapolis.

Wright, T.L. 1971. Chemistry of Kilauea and Mauna Loa lava in space and time. *Geological Survey Professional Paper 735*. United States Government Printing Office, Washington, D.C.

terra australis 31

16

Colonisation and culture change in the early prehistory of Fiji

Geoffrey Clark
Department of Archaeology and Natural History, The Australian National University

Atholl Anderson
Department of Archaeology and Natural History, The Australian National University

Introduction

The arrival of humans in the Fiji Islands at ca. 2950–3050 cal. BP was, in historical and ecological terms, a momentous event in Pacific prehistory that nonetheless comprised only a relatively small part of the Lapita expansion in Near and Remote Oceania. In turn, Lapita colonisation was only one of several prehistoric migratory movements in Oceania that began during the late Pleistocene movement to Near Oceania (Allen and O'Connell 2008), with the frequency and scale of maritime movements increasing during the late Holocene (Anderson 2001; Green 2003). In this chapter, we situate the colonisation of Fiji and the Early Prehistory of Fiji Project results in the Lapita expansion, contrasting it with human arrival in western Micronesia and the colonisation of East Polynesia. These prehistoric migratory movements suggest a preference for colonisation of uninhabited landmasses. In the case of Lapita migration, suspected avoidance of the main Solomon Islands and Samoa raises, among other critical issues, questions about seafaring capacity and colonisation pattern during the Lapita era. These are particularly important when considering human arrival in Fiji–West Polynesia because the 800+ km water gap separating Vanuatu–New Caledonia from Fiji was the largest inter-archipelagic voyage in the Lapita world, and it is generally held to be a significant barrier to Lapita movement (Green 1991; Irwin 1992; Clark and Murray 2006).

A seafaring ability that was able to bypass extensive island groups like the Solomons and Fiji (Burley and Dickinson 2001; Sheppard and Walter 2006) alludes to a maritime capacity with the potential to transport large migrant numbers to Fiji from several western archipelagos settled by Lapita groups. However, the evidence for systematic long-range voyaging in Remote Oceania is equivocal (Anderson 2003, 2008a; Irwin 2008), and a predominantly incremental pattern of movement is suggested by the distribution of Kutau/Bao obsidian and the localisation of ceramic designs, notwithstanding the likelihood that some long-range passages occurred in Lapita times. At the intra-archipelagic level, the Lapita dispersal in Fiji is examined using stylistic variation among early ceramic assemblages, site characteristics and the subsistence economy. The post-Lapita period, starting at ca. 2500 BP, is argued to represent a significant shift in settlement approach, landscape use, and mobility patterns, which, by the first millennium AD, contributed to the increased diversity of human systems in Fiji.

Lapita colonisation and oceanic migration

The late-Holocene migration of people in the Pacific Ocean took in three distinct geographic areas that in orthodox scholarship represent independent dispersal events during the period ca. 3500 BP to 700 BP (Figure 170).

The smallest and possibly oldest dispersal was to western Micronesia. It probably originated from eastern Indonesia–southern Philippines (Callaghan and Fitzpatrick 2009) and encompassed Palau and the Mariana Islands, with indirect evidence that it also included Yap (Donaldson and Intoh 1999). The dating of this expansion is uncertain, with archaeological sites in Palau and Saipan dating no older than 3500–3100 cal. BP (Clark 2005; Liston 2005; Clark et al. 2006; Carson 2008), but palaeoecological data that might indicate human activity as early as 4500 cal. BP (Athens et. al 2004; Dickinson and Athens 2007). Archaeological dates on marine bivalves extend to 3100–3000 cal. BP on Palau and to 3500 cal. BP on Saipan (Carson 2008), but the latter determinations are probably affected by burning and are too old. If so, western Micronesia was probably settled at 3400–3200 cal. BP, although a robust colonisation chronology for the region has yet to be established (Clark 2004).

The second dispersal was the Lapita migration, which extends from Manus in the west (146° 57') to Samoa in the east (172° 03'). It has been considered a separate event from the colonisation of western Micronesia, although both have a similar antiquity of ca. 3400–3000 cal. BP based on radiocarbon dates from archaeological sites (Clark 2005; Specht 2007; Green et al. 2008), and both involved groups that derived ultimately from Island Southeast Asia and produced various types of red-slipped pottery. A direct connection between the two migrations has been proposed (Craib 1999), and Bellwood (2005) suggests a direct origin for Lapita culture in the Mariana Islands of western Micronesia. Accepting the generic similarities in material culture, there are, however, also significant differences in the two cultural assemblages, including an absence of pig, dog and *Rattus exulans* remains in western Micronesia before about 2000 BP (Anderson 2008b). Analysis of modern pig DNA suggests that the western Micronesian source is East Asian, while pigs in Melanesia and Polynesia belonged to a Pacific clade (Larson et al. 2007). There are also dissimilarities in pottery and shell ornaments (Szabo and Summerhayes 2002; Carson 2008; DeFant 2008).

The third migration was of Polynesians from the Tonga–Samoa region eastward to the Cook Islands, Society Islands and Marquesas. The chronology of this expansion is debated, with current radiocarbon dates for migration at 1200–800 BP (Anderson and Sinoto 2002; Green and Weisler 2002; Conte and Anderson 2003). This movement, possibly divided into earlier tropical and later sub-tropical to temperate-zone migrations, eventually encompassed New Zealand, Easter Island and Hawaii (Hunt and Lipo 2008; Wilmshurst et al. 2008), along with numerous islands and atolls within triangle Polynesia, including some that were abandoned in

Colonisation and culture change in the early prehistory of Fiji 409

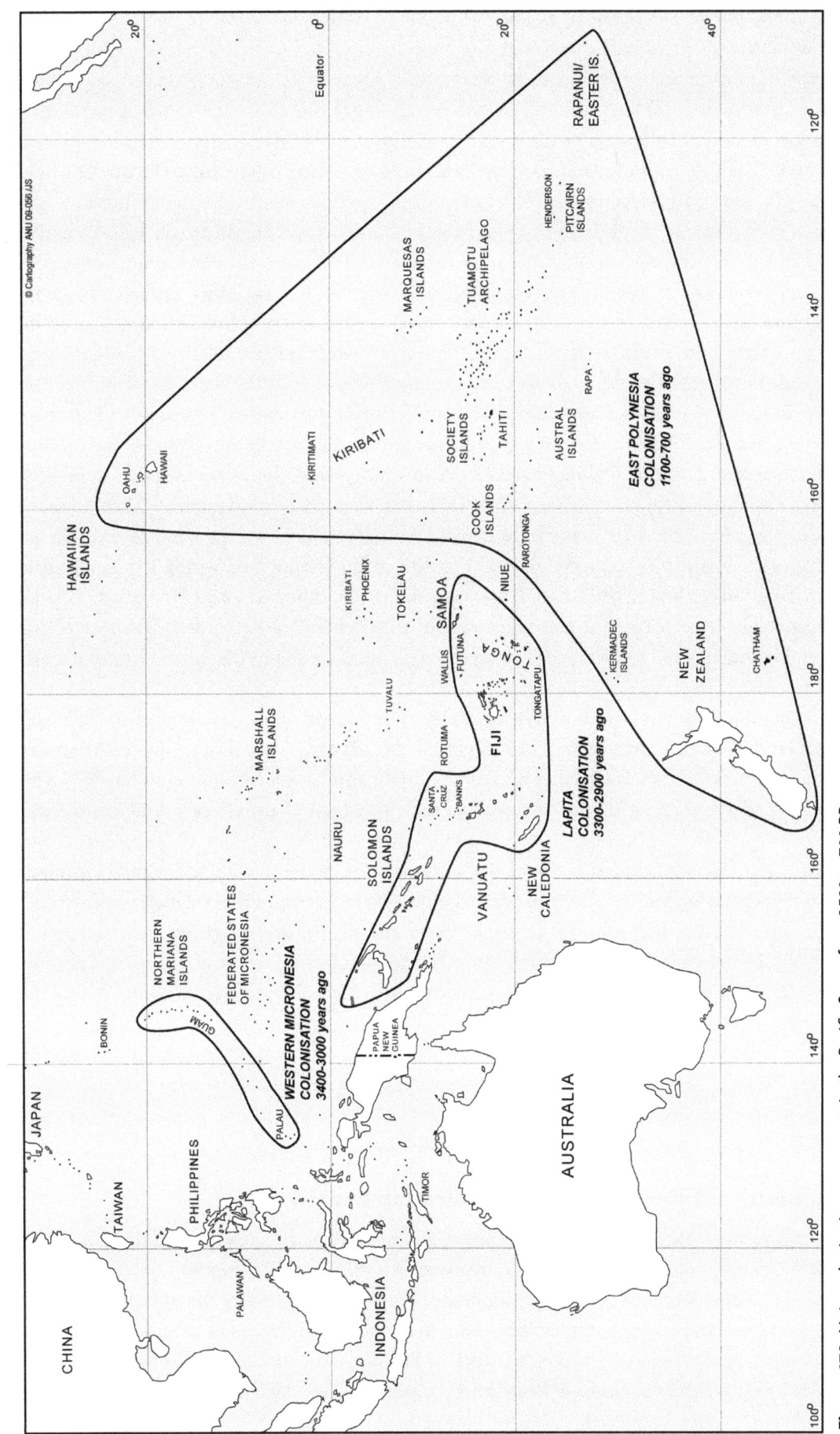

Figure 170. Major colonisation movements in the Pacific Ocean from 3500 to 700 BP.

prehistory (Weisler 1994; Anderson and White 2001; Anderson 2002).

Whatever the proximate cause(s) of migration in Remote Oceania (Anderson et al. 2006a), it is useful to compare dispersal among the regions. Dispersal to western Micronesia occurred over a distance of 2300 km and took in between 9° and 13° of latitude (north), depending on an origin in eastern Indonesia or the southern Philippines. Lapita dispersal extended 4680 km and took in 21° of latitude (south). The East Polynesian language-culture distribution spans some 7400 km and a staggering 68° of latitude. As the periods involved are a few hundred years in each case, the rate of dispersal was increasing (cf. Irwin 1992). Anderson (2001) suggests this was also happening within the Lapita expansion. Whether the rates reflect changes in dispersal capability, for example in seafaring technology, or in some other variables, is open to conjecture. The wind conditions for eastward travel are less favourable in Micronesia and East Polynesia than in the Lapita region, where monsoonal westerlies are relatively predictable and seasonally persistent. The ability to move a large colonising propagule, which is partly a function of proximity between source and destination, would affect the demography of colonisation and it may be, for example, that many fewer people reached western Micronesia than Santa Cruz in the Lapita era and that their ability to sustain continuing migration was attenuated accordingly. Again, it might be a function of incentive. There is not much beyond western Micronesia, but beyond Santa Cruz there are many large islands. It may have been for the latter reason that west Micronesian expansion captured only 1600 sq. km of land, compared with a Lapita expansion across 146,000 sq. km of land. East Polynesian migration captured 288,520 sq. km, although this cannot have been by land-area incentive, which declined eastward, the discovery of New Zealand being entirely unpredictable and representing more than 90% of the East Polynesian land area.

If migration success is measured by the proportion of land area to dispersal area, the capture rate of land, then this gives an index of migration success (MI), which has western Micronesia with an MI of 0.08, East Polynesia with an MI of 0.48 and Lapita colonisation with the highest MI of 1.5 (Figure 171). Using ocean area (sq. km) for the three expansions produces the same pattern (Figure 171), indicating that Lapita migration might be considered the most successful of the three movements in terms of locating and colonising island territory. The migration index values could also suggest that because Lapita colonisation was supported by high territory yields relative to the costs and risks of dispersal, the migration stream may have been continuous, especially in the region from the Bismarck Archipelago area to the Vanuatu–New Caledonia area, where the size of islands/archipelagos is relatively large, island inter-visibility is high and intervening water gaps are 350 km or less.

The early movements in Remote Oceania thus show a contrast in dispersal versus land capture. West Micronesia was low on both counts, East Polynesia had high dispersal but relatively low capture – and it would be exceedingly low if New Zealand had not been found (see Figure 171), while Lapita has moderate dispersal and high land capture.

Colonisation movements and inhabited landscapes

How population movements were constrained or absorbed by the presence of already-inhabited islands is an important consideration in migration studies, and has implications for Lapita expansion and the colonisation of Fiji. In the case of Polynesian expansion, the prevailing approach was to discover and occupy uninhabited and remote islands in the eastern Pacific, even though large but already populated archipelagos such as Fiji, Vanuatu and New Caledonia lying to the west of Samoa–Tonga could have been reached, particularly from Tonga, using the prevailing southeast trade winds. Indeed, there are Polynesian settlements to the west of Tonga–Samoa

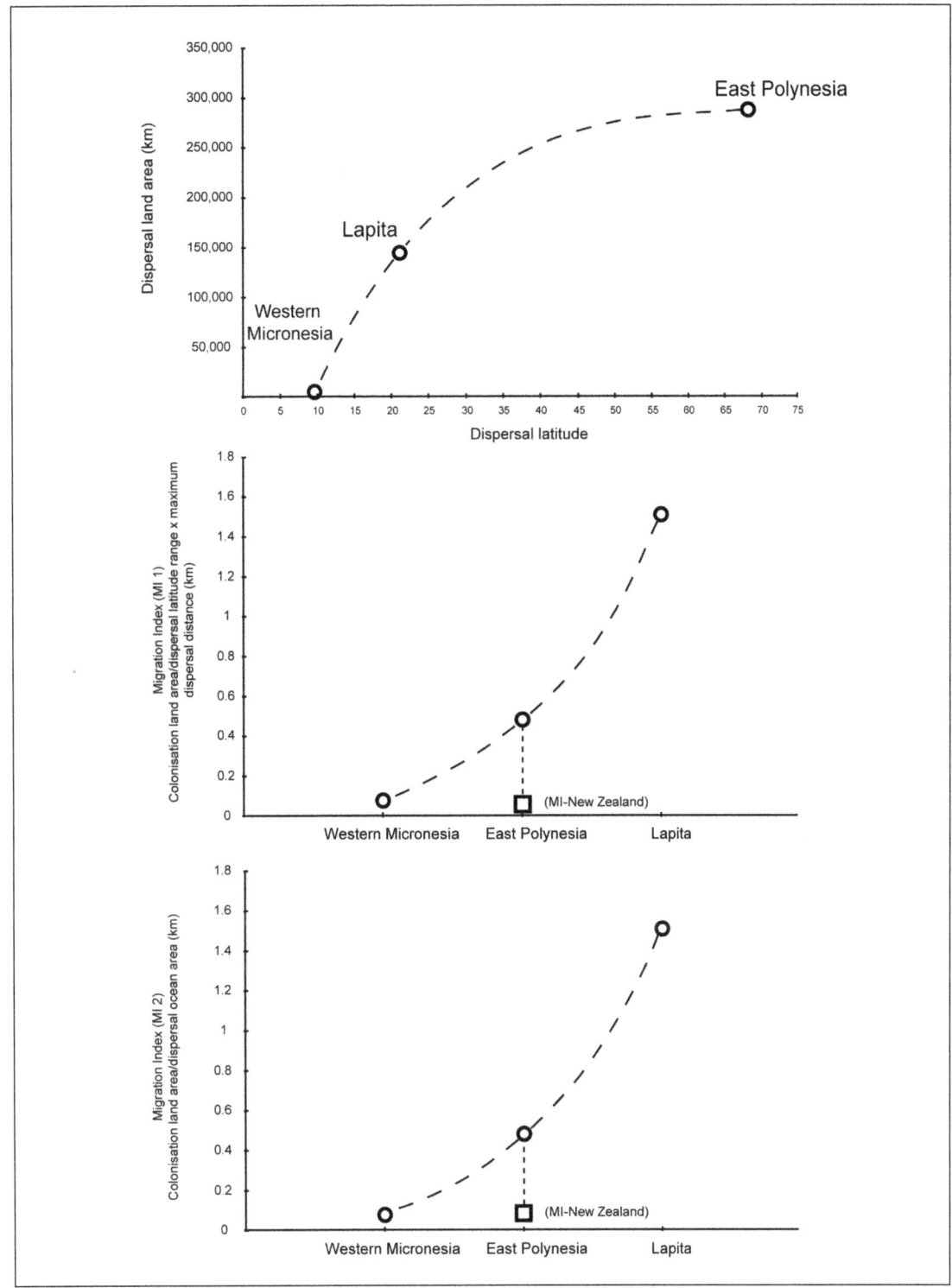

Figure 171. Comparative views of three prehistoric migration events. Top, island land area colonised versus dispersal latitude range. Middle and bottom, migration index values for three colonisation events calculated by dividing the land area colonised in each event by dispersal area (MI 1=latitude range x maximum dispersal distance, MI 2=dispersal ocean area). Western Micronesia may have been colonised by separate colonisation movements, but it is included as an entity because the expansion(s) appears to have originated from Island Southeast Asia at approximately the same time (3300-3000 cal. BP). For East Polynesia, two MI values were calculated. The first (circle symbol) is based on the prehistoric culture distribution, while the second (square symbol) is the index value after removal of New Zealand's land area, which comprises more than 90% of the colonised land in East Polynesia. Note that Lapita colonisation was the most successful of the three movements in terms of land capture.

known as the Polynesian Outliers (Kirch 1984b), yet almost all are isolated or in peripheral positions adjacent to larger islands, and most are atolls or raised coral (*makatea*) environments that are relatively poor in terrestrial resources. The marginal tendency of Outlier geography might result from resistance to colony emplacement on large volcanic/island arc islands that were already supporting large established populations.

Linguistic subgrouping based on shared innovations places the Polynesian Outliers in Nuclear Polynesian (Northern Pre-Polynesian) and separating before the formation of Eastern Polynesian (Marck 2000; Kirch and Green 2001). Eastern Polynesian can be archaeologically dated to about 1200–1000 BP (Anderson and Sinoto 2002; Anderson 2003; Conte and Anderson 2003; Hunt and Lipo 2008). If occupation of the Outliers was not the result of involuntary voyages, and the linguistic sequence is accurate and not skewed by variation in the rate of lexicon replacement and borrowing, then there may have been an earlier phase of Polynesian voyaging westward, presumably at a time before the Society Islands and other uninhabited islands were discovered to the east. Although Polynesians may have reached Australia and South America (Storey et al. 2007; cf. Gongora et al. 2008), no definitive evidence for a prehistoric settlement has yet been reported on either continent. The western limit of Polynesian colonisation (excluding sites in southern New Zealand) is currently the Emily Bay site on Norfolk Island (Anderson and White 2001), some 1400 km from Australia, and the eastern limit of Polynesian settlement remains Easter Island/Rapa Nui.

The dominant pattern of avoidance of already inhabited landmasses needs to be considered in relation to Lapita colonisation, which clearly failed to reach or avoided Australia and New Guinea, and which, judging by the location of many Lapita sites on offshore islands, may have been relatively unsuccessful initially on large islands such as New Britain and New Ireland (Spriggs 1995; Specht 2007:56). Torrence and Swadling (2008) propose that mid-Holocene social networks in New Guinea and surrounding islands, marked by the distribution of stemmed obsidian stone tools and stone mortars and pestles, could have encouraged the uptake and spread of Lapita material culture among indigenous groups – an idea that can be examined from the discovery of non-Austronesian sites that are contemporary with Lapita settlements in Island New Guinea. The existence of complex interaction networks involving what are likely to be prestige items in New Guinea–Island New Guinea implies the presence of stable social groups, which, alternatively, might have resisted migrant entry, or at least resisted the material culture of migrants. One possible indication of this is the inland distribution of 'bird and wing' mortars in New Guinea where Lapita pottery has yet to be recorded (Torrence and Swadling 2008).

The almost complete absence of knowledge about the nature of Lapita and non-Lapita interaction anywhere in the Bismarck Archipelago means that we cannot yet evaluate the effects of migrant-indigenous interaction in relation to Lapita colonisation (but see Lilley 2002; Pawley 2007, n.d.), which might also have been influenced by the Witori W-K2 eruption on New Britain at 3500 BP (Torrence and Doelman 2007) and the prevalence of malaria in the region (Groube 1996). Nonetheless, an apparent preference for uninhabited islands seen in Polynesian colonisation and the admittedly slender evidence for limited engagement in the Bismarck Archipelago could suggest that the location of early Lapita colonies was influenced by the presence of indigenous populations in Near Oceania.

Archipelago avoidance by Lapita migrants?

A view that Lapita migrants avoided occupied island groups has recently been put forward in relation to the main Solomon Islands. The northern islands in the Solomons were first occupied in the Pleistocene by non-Austronesians, judging by dates of 20–28 ka at Kilu Cave on Buka, although prehistoric sites older than 6000 BP have yet to be found further south even though the Buka-Guadalcanal landmasses were of much greater size during periods of low sea level (Spriggs 1997; Chappell 2005). Sheppard and Walter (2006:48) suggest that the absence of early Lapita sites in the main Solomons suggests these islands were entirely leap-frogged, with migrants travelling directly from Island New Guinea to the Reef/Santa Cruz Islands.

Such a leap-frogging pattern of movement of early Lapita colonists is thought to be the result of negative and positive factors. On the one hand, an already established population in the main Solomon Islands inhibited early Lapita occupation, and on the other, the discovery that uninhabited islands east of the main Solomons held dense and easily accessible marine and terrestrial resources encouraged long-distance movement and avoidance of the main Solomons. While there are linguistic and archaeological critiques of the idea (Felgate 2007; Clark and Bedford 2008; Pawley n.d.), including the fact that substantial quantities of chert found in early Lapita sites in the Reef/Santa Cruz Islands originate from Ulawa/south Malaita 400 km away in the central Solomons (Sheppard 2003), it remains a valid hypothesis (e.g. Lilley 2008).

The possible avoidance of the main Solomon Islands is also significant for ideas about Lapita seafaring and colonisation patterns once the previously uninhabited island groups east of the Reef/Santa Cruz Islands had been discovered. To reach Vanuatu and New Caledonia from the Reef/Santa Cruz Islands requires voyaging south over a total of 10 degrees of latitude, although no inter-island distance is greater than 250 km. However, if the main Solomon Islands were avoided by Lapita colonists, and extensive contact between the Bismarck Archipelago and the Reef/Santa Cruz Islands was maintained, as the volume of Talasea obsidian in the RF-2 site suggests (Sheppard 2003), then canoe voyages of more than 800 km might have been routinely undertaken during Lapita expansion to Remote Oceania.

There are significant implications of this for the colonisation of the Fiji Group and West Polynesia because the ocean gap of 800 km separating Fiji from southern Vanuatu has long been seen as a barrier that reduced the volume and frequency of Lapita migration (Green 1991; Irwin 1992). Further, once in the Fiji Group, voyages of 370 km were needed to reach Tongatapu, and voyages of 500–700 km to reach Samoa. One indication that Lapita voyaging thresholds were being approached in Fiji–West Polynesia might be the fact that small and relatively remote islands like Rotuma, 470 km from Fiji, and Niue, 410 km from Tonga (Vava'u), do not appear to have been settled in Lapita times (Walter and Anderson 2002), or indeed 'Ata, fewer than 100 km south of Tongatapu. If uninhabited island groups were perceived as being of high value to oceanic migrants and were the main target of dispersal, then the discovery of Fiji–West Polynesia, with a combined land area of some 22,100 sq. km, could well have stimulated a major phase of migration, especially if accurate voyages of 800 km were within the capacity of Neolithic seafarers.

However, measured by numbers of sites with dentate ceramics, the Lapita occupation of Fiji–West Polynesia exhibits significant patchiness indicative of a migration movement that was slowing. In northern Tonga and Samoa, the number of recorded Lapita sites is much fewer than in southern Tonga. For northern Tonga, across the 71 islands of Vava'u only five Lapita sites have been identified, all small and covering no more than 1500 sq. m each (Burley 2007). The number is in striking contrast to central and particularly southern Tonga, where the density of ceramic sites suggests rapid population expansion during Lapita and post-Lapita phases (Burley et al. 2001; Burley 2007). The western end of 'Upolu has a single Lapita site, Mulifanua, which is submerged from flexural subsidence of the lithosphere under volcanic loading (Dickinson and Green 1998). Radiocarbon dates from archaeological sites in Samoa and American Samoa when filtered through 'chronometric hygiene' protocols suggest that permanent settlement of Samoa did not take place until 2500–2400 BP (Reith et al. 2008).

Natural and anthropogenic factors have transformed the landscape of the Samoan Islands (J. Clark 1996; Green 2002; Reith et al. 2008) to a greater extent than Fiji–Tonga, but despite this, Addison and Morrison (In press) and (Reith et al. 2008) believe that the radiocarbon record demonstrates the failure of Lapita colonisation in Samoa. Unlike the main Solomon Islands 'gap', the Lapita avoidance of Samoa cannot result from the restrictive effects of an already resident population, or from the size of inter-archipelagic distances if voyages of 800 km were commonly undertaken. Demographic exhaustion is a potential explanation if Lapita populations were concentrated in the Fiji Islands, either because of a preference for large continental islands or because migrant numbers were low and contained by the extensive coastlines of Viti Levu and Vanua Levu.

Different patterns of archipelago colonisation are suggested for Tonga, where the Nukuleka site on Tongatapu Island has tan-paste ceramics, some of which have a quartz-pyroxene temper indistinguishable from temper in a non-local sherd from a Lapita site on Nendo in the Reef/Santa Cruz Islands. The source of this distinctive temper must lie west of Tonga, and while a source in Fiji cannot be excluded, the presence of subordinate hornblende in the exotic sherds suggests an origin in Vanuatu (Dickinson 2006). Of the numerous alternatives suggested by the presence of the tan-paste sherds in Tonga, Burley and Dickinson (2001) propose direct settlement of southern Tonga by a Lapita group that bypassed the Fiji Islands, signalling a canoe voyage of 1750 km (central Vanuatu–Tongatapu) or 2300 km (Nendo/Santa Cruz–Tongatapu).

This idea is initially attractive when considered together with an apparent Lapita avoidance of northern Tonga and Samoa, as it suggests that the founding population of Tonga was small and perhaps unable or unwilling to expand initially northward beyond the Ha'apai Group. Second, disparate colonisation movements from different parts of the migration stream are a plausible explanation for the physical differences observed today between the populations of Fiji and Tonga–Samoa, glossed as the 'Melanesia–Polynesia' divide (Clark 2003). These differences are elsewhere held to have developed in the post-Lapita period (e.g. Burley 2005; Cochrane 2008), but Donohue and Denham (2008) suggest that Lapita migration included 'Asiatic' Austronesian and 'Papuan' non-Austronesian components, either as separate population strata or in a migration stream that combined the two.

Yet, while it is an intriguing proposition, a Lapita canoe voyaging range of 1700–2300 km is not otherwise well attested, except for a potential late-Lapita/post-Lapita presence in Australia that might derive from the Solomon Islands and/or New Guinea (Felgate and Dickinson 2001; Felgate 2007), and colonisation movements to western Micronesia. Open ocean voyages of such magnitude are uncommon until Polynesian expansion some 1800 years later, and if such distances were a feature of Lapita seafaring, you would expect that at least some parts of East Polynesia would have been colonised earlier. The prospect of a Lapita migration stream containing groups with different physical characteristics that resulted ultimately in the Polynesia–Melanesia divide is feasible, although it raises the uncomfortable prospect that inter-group biological variability among Lapita groups has been concealed in the archaeological record by the material-culture similarities of Lapita ceramics, ornaments and adzes.

The proposed Lapita avoidance of Samoa, either through demographic exhaustion or a west Fiji colonisation pattern that was different from the Lapita colonisation of east Fiji–Tonga–Samoa, has two logical deficiencies. The first is that several islands near to Samoa have prehistoric records that begin in Lapita times and indicate occupation thereafter. The second is that the post-Lapita ceramic record of Samoa does not currently have a close relationship with any other assemblage in the region, even though Samoa is argued to have been permanently occupied by pottery-making people who settled there at 2500–2400 BP.

The small island of Futuna, some 560 km from Samoa, has four Lapita sites (Sand 1990:125) and Uvea, 360 km from Samoa, has at least three sites with dentate-stamped ceramics (Frimagacci and Siorat 1983; Sand 1996). Niuatoputapu is only 280 km from Samoa and has one Lapita site (Kirch 1988), but Futuna, Uvea and Niuatoputapu have post-Lapita deposits with plainware ceramics and radiocarbon dates indicating continuous occupation since the Lapita era. Further, design motifs and elements from the NT-90 site on Niuatoputapu analysed by Kirch (1988) showed close relationships between Lapita sites in Fiji–West Polynesia (Sigatoka-Uvea 0.90, Mulifanua-Niuatoputapu 0.91, Niuatoputapu-Uvea 0.93), suggesting a degree of inter-island mobility and contact towards the end of the Lapita period when Samoa is suggested to have been abandoned (Reith et al. 2008).

The mobility indicated by the ceramic data is reinforced by archaeological evidence for Lapita movement in Fiji–West Polynesia. Obsidian from Lapita deposits in Lakeba has been sourced to northern Tonga (Best 1984:434; Reepmeyer and Clark 2009), and the same material has been recorded from a late-Lapita site in southern Tonga, while a quartz-bearing sherd from the Mulifanua site in Samoa most likely derives from Vanua Levu in Fiji (Dickinson 2006:118). It does not seem probable that highly mobile colonising groups would settle small islands close to Samoa, but fail to occupy the large islands of the Samoa Group for 400 years (Clark and Bedford 2008).

Another objection concerns the nature of Samoan ceramic assemblages. Post-Lapita pottery from west Fiji and the Lau Group, as well as from southern Tonga, Futuna, Uvea and Niuatoputapu, is different from the exclusively plainware-bowl assemblage in Samoa dating to at least 2400–1700 BP. Since the Samoan plainwares cannot be derived convincingly from known prehistoric assemblages in the region (or from Vanuatu and New Caledonia), they are likely to represent a local development, signalling that older ceramic sites are likely to be present in Samoa. Notwithstanding the results of radiocarbon-date reviews and GIS modelling (Reith et al. 2008; Addison and Morrison In press), we suggest that ceramic assemblages from Fiji–West Polynesia do not support a hypothesis that Samoa was re-settled at 2500–2400 BP.

An underlying problem in this discussion is whether patterns of voyaging are discerned adequately from ceramic data. Migration voyaging, whether in exploratory or colonising mode, probably carried little pottery and conserved what it had, in the expectation that cooking could be carried out by alternative means during short stops along the way and that new pots would be made immediately on arrival; which, in the latter case, is what sourcing studies generally suggest to have been the case. Therefore, while the distribution of pottery in any quantity indicates places where people settled, its absence elsewhere does not necessarily show that those places were avoided as temporary landfalls, brief encampments and so on, the evidence for which is very much harder to find or recognise, yet might well exist along the coasts of the Solomons and Fiji. In short, to read absence of pottery as evidence of very long-distance passages accomplished without stopping is quite probably inaccurate both in terms of sailing capability and migration behaviour.

Incremental colonisation and Kutau/Bao obsidian

If archipelago 'avoidance' models and long-distance 'point-and-arrow' migration movements (Burley and Dickinson 2001; Sheppard and Walter 2006; Lilley 2008) are not convincingly supported, as we argue in relation to Samoa, then it is necessary to ask whether there is archaeological data consistent with incremental movement, recognising that oceanic expansions may have involved elements of both gradual and punctuated movement.

Comparison of ceramic motifs in Lapita sites is a valuable method for tracking Lapita movement at the archipelagic scale, but there is uncertainty about the processes of decorative change, with researchers interpreting the stylistic data as evidence for ongoing interaction across the Lapita range, or, alternatively, rapid localisation of ceramic assemblages (Sand 2001; Summerhayes 2001; Clark and Murray 2006).

Instead, we examine the distribution of obsidian from the Kutau/Bao source in west New Britain, which was the most widely distributed material in Lapita times, although it was not always the most abundant obsidian in a number of West Pacific Lapita sites (Spriggs 1991; Wickler 2001; Specht 2002; Summerhayes 2004). Models of obsidian use suggest it was employed and discarded in a utilitarian manner, with the procurement of Kutau/Bao obsidian representing the importance of ongoing social connections among Lapita groups, particularly those in the Reef/Santa Cruz Islands (Sheppard 2003; Specht 2002).

If obsidian transfer from west New Britain was essentially a byproduct of Lapita social connectivity, then variation in the quantity of obsidian across the Lapita range should reflect elements of the broader dispersal pattern. For instance, a Lapita movement that was predominantly incremental should be manifested by a typical down-the-line distribution characterised by high obsidian frequencies around the source, low-to-absent frequencies at the migration terminus, and intermediate amounts of obsidian in between. Alternatively, long-distance voyaging and archipelago avoidance would leave a different obsidian footprint, as movements originating from locations with abundant Kutau/Bao obsidian, like the Reef/Santa Cruz Islands, should have significantly more obsidian than Lapita movements originating from locations where there was little. In brief, incremental archipelago movement should be characterised by obsidian amounts that decrease monotonically with distance from source, while an expected feature of 'point-and-arrow' movement is an obsidian distribution where there is no linear relationship between obsidian abundance and distance from source.

The high proportion and volume of Kutau/Bao obsidian in several Reef/Santa Cruz sites supports the maintenance of social relations among Lapita groups separated from each other by the main Solomon Islands (Sheppard 2003; Sheppard and Walter 2006). In Remote Oceania, the amount of Kutau/Bao obsidian declines rapidly with distance from the Reef/Santa Cruz Islands (Figure 172), consistent with a predominantly incremental pattern of colonisation, as several other researchers have also argued (Sand and Sheppard 2000; Reepmeyer et al. In press). Since the Reef/Santa Cruz sites have significant amounts of Kutau/Bao obsidian, but are around 2000 km from the source, it appears that Lapita migration in Near Oceania was very different than in most of Remote Oceania. Lapita settlements might have involved higher rates of community interaction throughout the Bismarcks-Reef/Santa Cruz region, compared with rapid dispersal and post-colonisation fragmentation of social networks beyond the Reef/Santa Cruz Islands (Green and Kirch 1997; Anderson 2001). Thus, the Reef/Santa Cruz Islands appear to have been an important colonisation node or 'gateway' to Remote Oceania, through which the migration stream funnelled when the existence of the large and uninhabited island groups of Vanuatu and New Caledonia became known to Lapita communities.

Lapita colonisation of the Fiji Islands

Lapita groups occupied the varied landscapes of Fiji probably as a result of numerous factors, including migrant numbers, maritime capacity, subsistence economy, physical geography and the nature of migrant social systems, few of which can be estimated accurately with existing archaeological information. In its stead and acknowledging the deficiencies in our data sets, we review the Lapita settlement of Fiji using radiocarbon dates and inter-site ceramic variation to examine the colonisation pattern, before outlining the site characteristics and evidence for

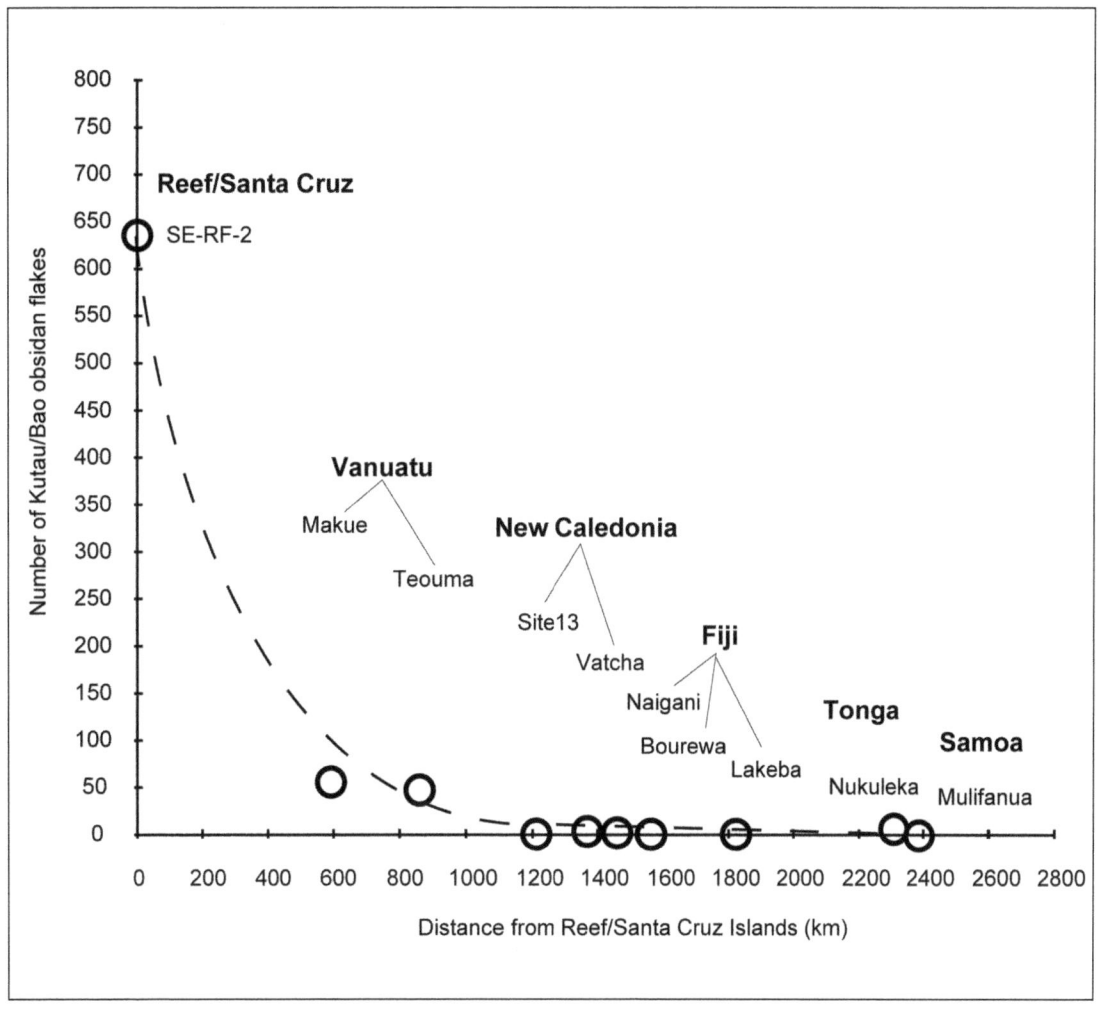

Figure 172. Number of flakes of Kutau/Bao obsidian found in archaeological sites in Remote Oceania increasingly distant from the Reef/Santa Cruz Islands. The quantity has not been standardised by excavation area/volume as this information is not available for all sites. Most sites yielding Kutau/Bao obsidian have been investigated in medium to large-scale investigations (e.g. SE-RF-2, Makue, Teouma, Naigani, Bourewa, Lakeba-Wakea, Nukuleka). Recent excavations at Nukuleka by David Burley (pers. comm.) found an obsidian flake that may be from the Kutau/Bao source.

a Lapita subsistence economy. Historical linguistics has developed a detailed model of intra-archipelagic colonisation that can be compared with archaeological data, but skeletal and genetic studies, although supporting a complex settlement history, are currently unable to determine the dispersal pattern (Pietrusewsky 1990; Visser 1994; Serjeantson and Gao 1995; Kelly 1996; van Dijk 1998).

Dialect variation

Linguistic studies suggest that the Central Pacific subgroup (CP) of Oceanic was a dialect chain that initially spanned the Fiji–Tonga region (Marck 2000; Kirch and Green 2001:56–61). During the first centuries of Lapita settlement, morphological and lexical innovations developed between central and western Fiji (Viti Levu and southwest Vanua Levu) and northeast Vanua Levu, the Lau Group and Tonga. The latter branch of CP was termed 'Tokalau Fijian-Polynesian' by Geraghty (1983), as 'tokalau' means 'northeast' in Fijian, and Pawley (n.d.) suggests that the 'Tokalau' innovations developed before permanent occupation of islands north of Tonga. When permanent settlement of Samoa and adjacent islands did take place at about 2700–2800 BP there was a further set of diagnostic innovations that defined Nuclear Polynesian. In Fiji, the affiliation of the Tokalau Fijian–Polynesian dialect subsequently changed, with the dialects of northeast Vanua Levu and the Lau Group resynthesising with the dialects of central and western Fiji, creating a 'Proto-Fijian' dialect chain over most of the Fiji Group.

Dating dialect-chain developments is notoriously difficult, but the archaeological record shows Lapita movement to the Lau Group–southern Tonga and then southern Tonga–Samoa within a short period between 2950 cal. BP and 2750 cal. BP. Each expansion (central and western Fiji to northeast Fiji–southern Tonga, and southern Tonga to Samoa and nearby islands) appears to have led to the development of significant language innovations in newly established settlement frontiers. The resynthesis of central and western Fijian with Tokalau Fijian–Polynesian must have occurred after Rotuman and Pre-Polynesian diverged from the CP dialect chain, and prior to the development of substantial inland populations on Viti Levu (Pawley and Sayaba 1971; Pawley 1999) in the period 2000–1000 BP. An age estimate of 2500–2000 BP for the 'Proto-Fijian' period appears reasonable, as it provides several centuries for the language innovations marking Tokalau Fijian–Polynesian and Nuclear Polynesian to develop.

The complicated sequence of language development in the Central Pacific and particularly in Fiji suggests that there may be evidence for an early material-culture divide between central and western Fiji and northeast Fiji–southern Tonga, which closed with language resynthesis across Fiji in the period 2500–2000 BP, before the dialect diversification documented by Geraghty (1983), shown in Figure 173.

Archaeological data

We now examine the archaeological evidence for Lapita colonisation of Fiji, particularly the ceramic record, as it is the most abundant and best described category of prehistoric material culture. Other types of information relevant to this issue are omitted due to space restrictions (see Chapters 4–10).

Lapita sites with stylistically early ceramics are found only on Viti Levu and nearby islands (Bourewa, Naigani, Yanuca, Natunuku and Naitabale). Intricate dentate stamping also occurs on a small number of sherds at Lakeba (site 101/7/196) (Best 2002:41), but no Lapita sites in the Yasawa Islands or in the Lau Group appear to be as early as those found on, or near to, Viti Levu. The apparent consolidation of early Lapita settlements on the large island of Viti Levu, followed by later movement to smaller landmasses, is consistent with incremental movement from the largest island in the archipelago, but it is a view that could, in part, stem from the small number and size of early Lapita sites relative to late-Lapita sites, which means that early sites will be harder to locate in archaeological survey, even on small islands. A similar pattern of expansion from a large island to small islands is proposed for Tonga, where the oldest Lapita site is found on Tongatapu (Burley and Dickinson 2001; Burley 2007), and in New Caledonia Lapita sites on the Grand Terre are older than those found on smaller offshore limestone islands like the Loyalty Group that appear to have been colonised one or two centuries later (Sand 1998).

The concentration of early Lapita groups on Viti Levu and a subsequent clinal pattern of movement through the Fiji Group suggested by decorated ceramics is not well attested in the radiocarbon dates. The oldest adequately dated sites in the early group are Bourewa on the southwest coast of Viti Levu, with an estimated range of 2950–3050 cal. BP, Naigani at 2800–2900 cal. BP, and Lakeba (site 196), at 2750–2950 cal. BP (NZ 4590). The remaining sites are not well dated. Yanuca has a potential age range of 2750–2950 cal. BP from a result on the shell of *Batissa violcea* (ANU-11414, Clark and Anderson 2001b), and Naitabale might be dated by Wk-11481 to 2850–3050 cal. BP, but other determinations from the site indicate an

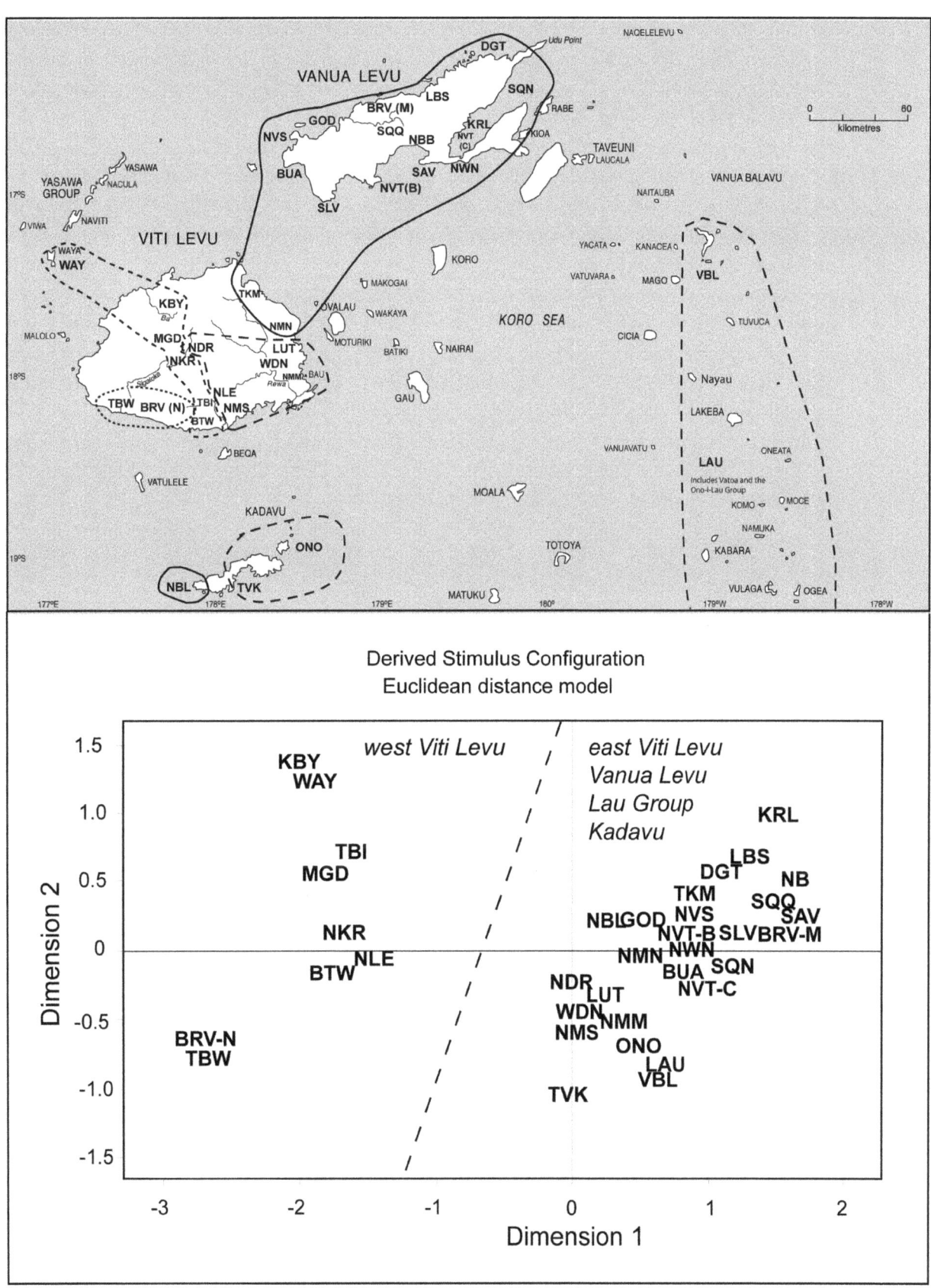

Figure 173. Map of Fiji (top) showing results of an MDS analysis of communalect association based on phonological innovations in 32 communalects recorded by Geraghty (1983:Table 16). MDS analysis of phonological innovations (bottom) divides the communalects of west Viti Levu from the communalects of east Viti Levu, Vanua Levu, Kadavu and the Lau Group, suggesting that the east Viti Levu division from west Viti Levu is of considerable antiquity and possibly dates to the post-Lapita period (see Pawley and Sayaba 1971).

age of 2700–2850 cal. BP (Nunn et al. 2007). In contrast, several late-Lapita sites, including Sigatoka Level 1 (2450–2650 cal. BP) and Votua on Mago Island (2700–2800 cal. BP), are well dated (see Chapter 7).

The radiocarbon dates on their own are too few and have an age span that prohibits the detection of any clear pattern of archipelago movement, other than the observation that Viti Levu appears to have the earliest sites, bearing in mind the absence of archaeological work on Vanua Levu. Lapita pottery was made in Fiji for at least 400–500 years (cf. Anderson and Clark 1999), providing ample time for significant stylistic change in the ceramic corpus and the proliferation of Lapita settlements in the archipelago. With the discovery of Lapita and post-Lapita sites containing complete or nearly complete vessels, ceramicists will increasingly use information from the whole container to assess inter-site and intra-site relationships (see vessel data and analyses in Birk 1973; Sand et al. 1998; Burley 2005; Bedford 2006; Clark 2007; Clark and Wright 2007). But at the present time, it is necessary to investigate site relationships using a variety of ceramic data, including the percentage of vessels decorated, types of vessel form, and motif presence/absence. The frequency of dentate-stamped and incised motifs in an assemblage is an important source of information (Best 1984; Clark and Murray 2006), which is not yet available for the early sites of Bourewa and Naitabale.

Ceramics: Percentage decorated

The frequency of dentate-stamped and incised decoration in Fijian assemblages is highest at Natunuku, Yanuca and Naigani (ceramics from Bourewa are under analysis). Best (2002:Table 4) calculated a relative site age from the percentage of three early traits in ceramic assemblages: rouletting, flat-based dishes and carinations (calculated against the percentage of all dentate-stamped and incised sherds in an assemblage). Taking the average of the three percentage values, the sites in order from oldest to youngest are Natunuku, Yanuca, Lakeba, Naigani and the TO-2 Nukuleka site in Tonga. Pottery from the Naitabale site was not able to be analysed in Best's 2002 study, but is considered earlier than that of Naigani (Best in Nunn et al. 2004b:218). A percentage comparison of ceramic decoration by Nunn et al. (2007:Table 3), from oldest to youngest, ordered the sites: Naigani, Natunuku, Yanuca, Nukuleka (Tonga), Haateiho (Tonga) and Naitabale. However, the 0.6% decorated percentage in the Naitabale assemblage is consistent with radiocarbon dates from the site that indicate the presence of a later and larger Lapita occupation (Best 2002:84; Nunn 2007; Nunn et al. 2007:Table 3). The Naigani values for dentate-stamping (33.0%) and incised decoration (27.9%) in the Nunn et al. (2007) study are incorrect according to Best (2002:84).

Rather than a spilt between Lapita groups in west Fiji and those of east Fiji (see Clark and Anderson 2001a), Best's percentage data suggest a relatively early dispersal through Fiji to the Lau Islands and Tonga, along with the possibility that Lapita groups were continuing to arrive on Viti Levu, as suggested from Kutau/Bao obsidian at Naigani, which also has an unusually high frequency of decorated sherds (dentate-stamped 24%, incised 9.5%, see Best 2002:84), similar to the Vatcha site in New Caledonia, which also contains Kutau/Bao obsidian (Sand and Sheppard 2003; Nunn et al. 2007:Table 3).

Ceramics: Vessel form

The amount of decoration in Fijian Lapita assemblages declines over time, as does the number of complex vessel forms. Fragmentation of pottery containers varies within and between sites, making an intersite comparison difficult, and for sites such as Naitabale and Bourewa the form of ceramic containers has yet to be published. Restricting ourselves to those assemblages where there is sufficient information to determine vessel form (Clark and Anderson 2001a:Table 2) reveals seven vessel categories (bowls, constricted orifice, jars, jars with large applied bands, jars with carinations/convex shoulders, wide-mouthed carinated jars/dishes, dishes with flaring rims and flat bases) in six sites (Yanuca, Natunuku, Lakeba (sites 196 and 197), Naigani, Sigatoka and Votua).

The relationship of assemblages based on vessel form is shown in Figure 174, and suggests that Yanuca and Natunuku are the oldest, followed by Naigani and Lakeba, and then the late-Lapita assemblages of Sigatoka Level 1 and Votua. The site order is somewhat similar to that suggested by Best (2002), and the results also support the view that Lapita migration to Fiji from the west was still occurring at 2800–2900 cal. BP, some 50–150 years after initial colonisation if Bourewa is dated to 2950–3050 cal. BP.

Ceramics: Motif presence/absence

There have been several attempts to code Lapita designs to enable inter-site and archipelago comparisons to track Lapita movement. In the case of Fijian ceramic assemblages, pioneering work by Mead and others attempted to investigate the design process and pattern-making 'rules' (Mead et al. 1973), while other researchers restrict themselves to creating design inventories (Anson 1983; Best 1984; Poulsen 1987; Chiu 2003). There are several problems with an inventory approach for Lapita decoration that varies markedly in the number, complexity and density of designs in early sites – especially those in the west of the distribution – compared with Lapita designs in Fiji–West Polynesia, which are fewer in number, simplified in pattern and executed in an open and sparse style. One of the most basic issues is that decoration in a few 'type assemblages' forms the majority of a design reference catalogue that may omit many of the designs present in other assemblages, even though some of these may be comparable to

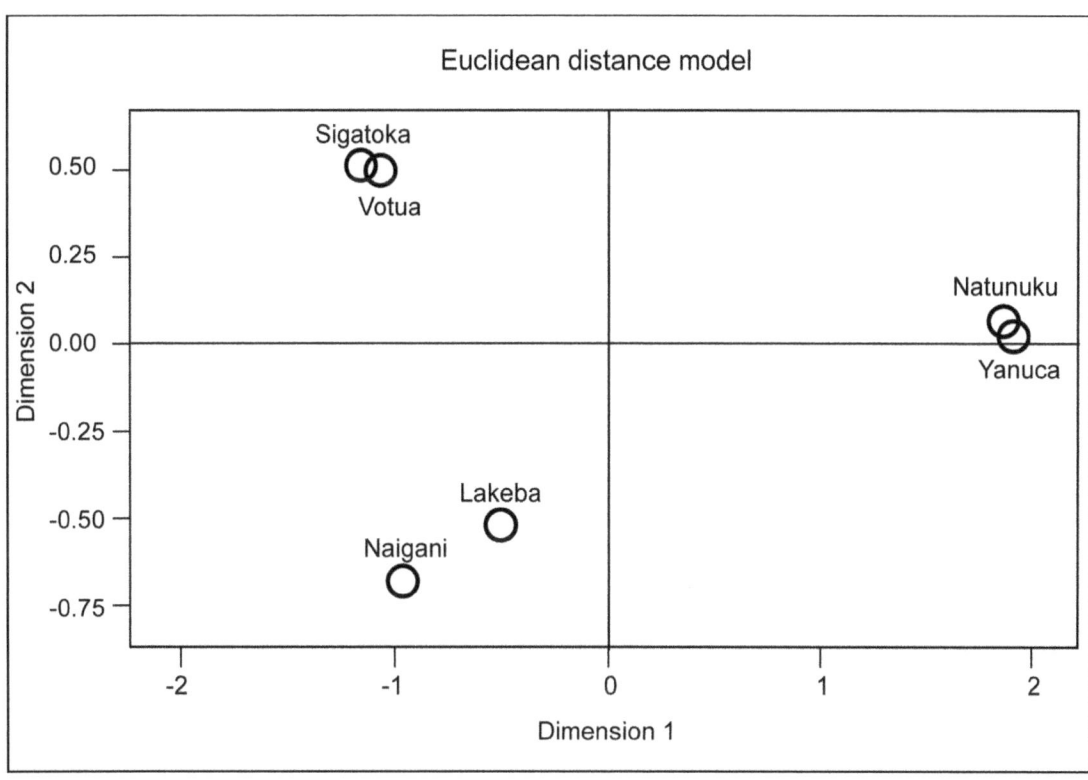

Figure 174. Lapita assemblage relationships from an MDS analysis of seven vessel form categories from six Lapita sites in Fiji (Yanuca, Natunuku, Sigatoka, Votua, Lakeba, Naigani).

designs in an inventory. Several researchers have used Anson's (1983) motif catalogue to examine Lapita movements and inter-site relationships (Summerhayes 2001), and to describe Lapita assemblages (Bedford 2006), including those recently excavated in Fiji (Nunn et al. 2007), and the approach is followed here.

The presence/absence of motifs in five early Lapita sites in Fiji (Natunuku, Yanuca, Naigani, Naitabale and Lakeba (site 196 and 197)) was tabulated from published sources (Anson 1983; Kay 1984; Nunn et al. 2007). The simplified Lakeba motifs were recorded using a different system (Best 1984), but the majority could be assigned to motifs or motif variants listed by Anson (1983). To examine site relationships within Fiji, two motif outgroups were included in the analysis. The first was the SC-RF-2 motifs from the Reef/Santa Cruz Islands and the second was the Site 13 motifs from New Caledonia recorded by Anson (1983). The purpose of the outgroups was to illustrate the relative similarity/difference among Fijian assemblages by comparing them with assemblages from other island groups that should be dissimilar, particularly if Lapita expansion in Remote Oceania was predominantly incremental or clinal, which would have provided time for local ceramic development in each island group before movement to new island groups. Late-Lapita ceramics from Sigatoka and Votua were not included due to the small number of motifs/part motifs. These late assemblages are important, however, as they demonstrate that by 2700–2800 cal. BP, the Lapita design system of Fiji had decomposed to a point where dentate-stamping of pottery vessels was rare, and in design terms, stylistically minimal.

Motifs from the seven Lapita assemblages were binary coded for presence/absence and analysed with MDS (squared Euclidean distance), and compared with HCL results using the squared Euclidean distance and simple matching coefficient, which produced the same results. Previous motif studies of Lapita site relationships have used the Jaccard coefficient index in which joint absences are excluded from consideration and equal weight is given to matches and nonmatches (Best 1984, 2002). However, as the Lapita design system declines, the number of joint absences will rapidly increase and this aspect of stylistic change should be included in an inter-site measurement. As a result, the simple matching coefficient, which measures the ratio of matches to the total number of values and gives equal weight to matches and nonmatches, was preferred.

The results of the MDS motif analysis are shown in Figure 175. As expected, the motifs in the Fijian assemblages group together, away from the motifs in the RF-2 site in the Reef/Santa Cruz Islands and the Site 13 motifs in New Caledonia. Revised dating of the RF-2 site (Green et al. 2008) suggests it is similar in age or slightly younger than the oldest sites in Fiji (RF-2 age: 68% CI 2825–2983, 2949–3145 and 95% CI 2724–3062, 2878–3271). Sand (1997) has dated surviving components of Site 13 to about 3100–3000 cal. BP (WKO013A/B). Among the Fijian assemblages, those of Lakeba and Naitabale group together, with Naigani more distant. The HCL analysis suggests that the sites in order from oldest to youngest are: Yanuca, Natunuku, Naigani, Naitabale and Lakeba, which is similar to the site-age order in the vessel-form analysis. Natunuku and Yanuca are closest to the other Fijian assemblages, but are the most distant from the Reef/Santa Cruz and New Caledonia motif sets, even though they may well have a similar age. If Fiji was settled from Vanuatu, then Vanuatu motifs dating from 3000–2900 cal. BP should be similar to motifs from Yanuca and Natunuku, a hypothesis that can be examined from a comparison of the Bourewa motifs and new assemblages excavated from Vanuatu (e.g. Bedford 2006).

The similarity of the east Fiji Lakeba motifs to those from the Naitabale site close to Viti Levu could result from devolution of the Lapita design system or interaction between east Fiji and west Fiji. First, design decay may have removed the majority of complex dentate-stamped

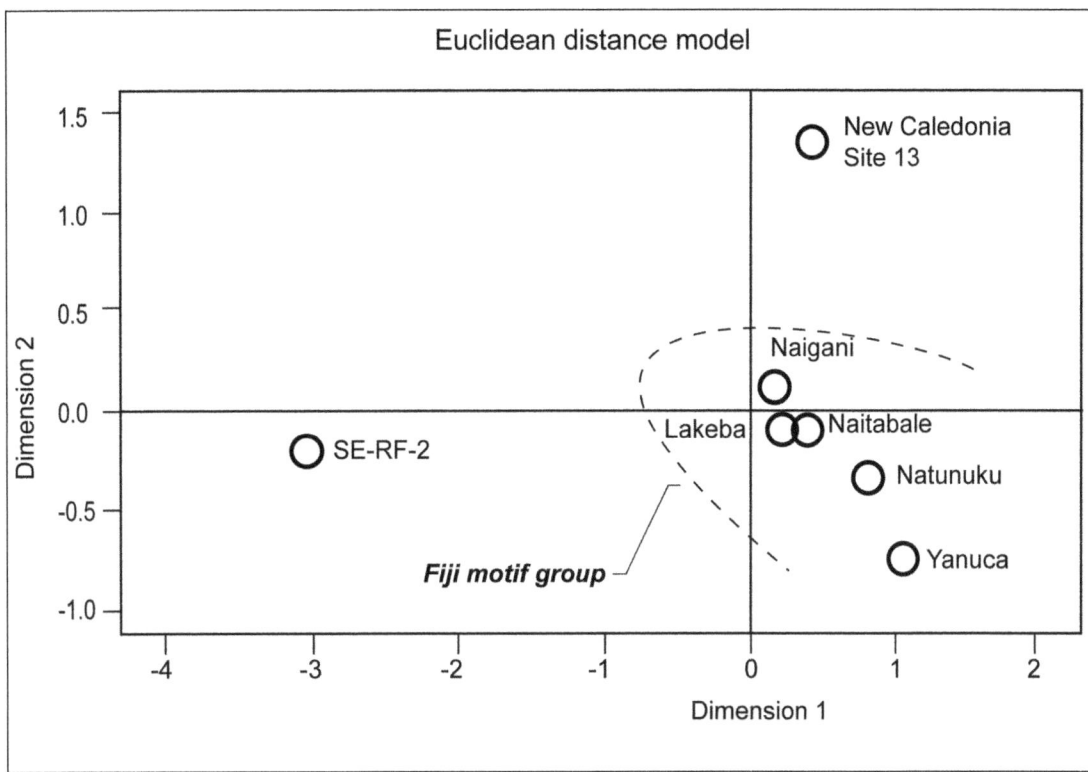

Figure 175. Lapita assemblage relationships from an MDS (squared Euclidean distance) analysis of motif presence/absence (simple matching coefficient) from five Fijian sites (Yanuca, Natunuku, Naitabale, Lakeba, Naigani), SE-RF-2 (Reef/Santa Cruz) and Site 13 (New Caledonia).

and incised designs by about 2800 cal. BP, with the remainder consisting of the most frequently used designs in the decorative corpus. The stylistic association among decorated Lapita ceramics would increase through time, therefore, due to the similarity of the decay pathway, with assemblages from Naitabale and Lakeba towards the end of the sequence grouping together because of their late age. Given the number of motifs recorded from Naitabale (40), this idea is not well supported. An alternative is that Lapita groups in the west and east of Fiji were in frequent contact with one another and the motif presence/absence reflects ongoing interaction across the archipelago at the same time as language innovations were accumulating in west–central Fiji and east Fiji–Tonga. The latter would mean that language innovations were largely decoupled from changes to ceramic material culture. Lapita and post-Lapita ceramics and material culture from intermediate locations such as southern Lau, located between Tonga and west Fiji, would clarify the alternatives (see Clark 2009).

Lapita sites: Size and characteristics

Turning to the size of sites as a proxy for Lapita group/community size, the earliest components at Naitabale, Naigani, Bourewa and Lakeba are small and appear to have been around only 1000 and 2500 sq. m (Best 1984; Nunn 2007). The Yanuca rock shelter and Natunuku sites were also likely to have occupied a small area, although erosion and development means their size cannot be determined. The late-Lapita Level 1 component at the Sigatoka Sand Dunes is also in this range (although Burley (2003) suggests the Level 1 deposit is not an occupation), as is the Votua site on Mago, and the sites on Qoqo Island and Beqa Island, among others (Clark 2000; Clark et al. 2001; Jones et al. 2004; Nunn et al. 2006; Cochrane et al. 2007). The anomaly is Lakeba, where Wakea (site 196) is estimated to cover 15,000 sq. m of the coastal flat (Best 2002), and the site could well be considerably larger, based on the surface distribution of dentate-stamped sherds and the inclusion of the nearby Qaranipuqa (site 197) rock shelter. Elsewhere on Lakeba, sites larger than the Wakea Lapita site are rare and only occur in the late prehistoric period when large fortifications and community settlements were developed (Best 1984:Table 2.1).

The large size of the Wakea site could result from the concentration of migrants in 'gateway' communities (Hirth 1978), which acted as fixed points for exploration, dispersal and population consolidation in frontier environments. Several studies emphasise the significance of known points in new landscapes in migration (Lee 1996; Moore 2001), and whatever the actual number of Lapita people arriving in Fiji, the population density during colonisation must have been low relative to archipelago size and land area. A dendritic coastal settlement pattern of a few relatively large sites in strategic locations across the archipelago would allow for efficient exploration of the hinterland and would provide a staging post for further expansion by a numerically small and mobile population.

Lapita sites in Fiji are located in diverse environments and situations different from the restricted criteria suggested by Lepofsky's (1988) innovative catchment analysis. In southern Lau, Lapita and post-Lapita ceramic sites are located in leeward settings on palaeoshorelines around shallow embayments that would have provided canoe shelter, but more importantly, access to concentrations of *Anadara* and *Gafrarium* bivalves (Clark 2009). On Mago Island, the Votua site is behind a headland in a small cove containing mangroves and dense concentrations of bivalves close to an intermittent stream. Proximity to broad fringing reefs and estuary environments appears to have been the most important consideration for locating the prehistoric communities at Sigatoka and Natunuku, as well as Bourewa, Naitabale, Qoqo and Rove, reported by Nunn and colleagues (Nunn et al. 2004a, 2005, 2006; Kumar et al. 2004), and may have been critical to the establishment of the Wakea site on Lakeba, and the Kulu Bay and Ugaga sites in the Beqa lagoon. Neither a reef-break 'canoe passage' nor a permanent fresh water source appear to have been necessary factors in Lapita site placement compared with the presence of a significant fringing reef and sheltered embayments with abundant gregarious bivalves. Fresh water may have been obtained at some sites, such as Wakea and several others in the Lau Group, from intertidal springs debouching from the limestone substrate, while on Ugaga Island in the Beqa lagoon, fresh water must have been carried to the island.

No inland sites with complex dentate-stamped decoration have yet been found in Fiji. There is a late-Lapita shell-impressed arc on a rim from the Qaranioso II shelter several kilometres inland (Anderson et al. 2001), and simple dentate markings were found on a sherd at another inland location on Viti Levu (Kumar and Nunn 2003). Best (2002:22) found inland settlement on Lakeba only occurred in Period II at ca. 2500 cal. BP, consistent with a late-Lapita inland presence on Viti Levu. Excavations at Tatuba Cave some 45 km from the mouth of the Sigatoka River indicate use of the interior by 1700–2000 cal. BP (Field 2004), similar to the age of several EPF cave/rock shelters (see Chapter 7). The archaeology of island interiors is an important and under-researched topic in Pacific prehistory, although human activity and occupation in areas distant from coastal resources in Fiji has been examined in several studies (Parry 1987; Kuhlken and Crosby 1999), particularly the development of fortified sites (Field 2004, 2005) in relation to climate change in the past 750 years (Kumar et al. 2006; Nunn 2007; Nunn et al. 2007).

The potential effects of climate change on the development of human societies in Fiji requires fine-grained archaeological and palaeoecological studies of human activity in a variety of inland landscapes (i.e. valley floors, ridge lines, rock shelters, riparian zones, agricultural systems, fortifications) before as well as after 1000 BP. Furthermore, it is vitally important, in making those connections, to be able to rule out the obvious alternative that movement into new habitats and changes in subsistence and settlement patterns, plus increasing evidence of defensive structures or warfare, are more clearly associated with population growth, as the late activation of the Sigatoka Sand Dunes, probably through increased rates of erosion and sedimentation, might represent (Anderson et al. 2006b).

Current site locations point to a Lapita presence in Fiji that was tethered in the main to coastal settlements, but which involved forays to the interior to collect resources such as fine-grained rocks for adze manufacture, for the hunting of endemic fauna and for the collection of economic food and craft plants. The dispersal of Lapita groups through terrestrial landscapes was clearly substantially slower than dispersal across water gaps to islands, suggesting that coastal resources and environments were basic to migration subsistence, an issue we examine further below.

Subsistence economies

The issue of subsistence strategies involved in Lapita migration is contentious in large part because the subsistence mode is connected to theories of Neolithic migration, especially the hypothesis of a cohesive spread of farming, language and people (and their genes) over large parts of the world (Diamond and Bellwood 2003; Bellwood 2005). For Lapita migration, the central issue is whether initial dispersal carried a suite of domesticated fauna and flora with it, or whether transported biotas arrived in a piecemeal fashion perhaps over several centuries (Groube 1971; Clark and Anderson 2001a; Davidson and Leach 2001; Burley 2007). What is not in dispute is that, as on other oceanic islands, human arrival in Fiji had a significant impact on native fauna, particularly the avifauna, but also on endemic reptiles like the extinct giant iguana (*Lapitiguana impensa*), terrestrial crocodilian (*Volia athollandersoni*) and giant ground frog (*Platymantis megabotoniviti*) (Chapter 3).

Skeletal remains from introduced animals (pig, dog, chicken) found in Fijian Lapita sites were critically evaluated in Chapter 10, with only the chicken and the non-food commensal Pacific rat (*Rattus exulans*) and spiny rat (*Rattus praetor*) able to be confirmed as Lapita-era introductions in the Lau Islands. Pig remains are present in early Lapita sites in the Bismarck Archipelago, as well as in northern and central Vanuatu, but they have not been found in Lapita sites in New Caledonia, southern Vanuatu or Tonga (see Chapter 10), and reports of dog remains at Naigani and Yanuca in Fiji similarly need to be confirmed. On Lakeba, remains of the pig and dog do not appear in the sequence until about 1000 BP (Best 1984:197, 555).

Adventive land snails from early levels of Yanuca have also been used to infer early horticulture, with *Lamellaxis gracilis* and *Gatsrocopta pediculus* potentially transported on plants, although not necessarily cultigens (Hunt 1981; Clark and Anderson 2001a:83), and the basal sediments of Yanuca have been redeposited (Hunt 1980:39; Clark and Anderson 2001b). Direct evidence for transported crops has been identified at Bourewa where Horrocks and Nunn (2007) report microfossil remains of *Colocasia esculenta* (taro) and *Dioscoria esculenta* (lesser yam).

The first point to note about the presence of taro and yam at Bourewa is that the sediment sample from Pit X20 at 55–63 cm depth post-dates two radiocarbon determinations on marine shell, with a range of 2440–2710 cal. BP, indicating a late-Lapita age for the sediment sample. Ploughing of the upper 40 cm and the presence of four post-Lapita burials in Pit X20, mostly below the plough zone, suggests that the sediment sample need not be associated with the Lapita component of the site. The other sediment sample yielding identified microfossils of taro and lesser yam was collected from Pit X25 at 134 cm depth. A ^{14}C determination on *Conus* sp. shell from 140 cm depth at the base of a marine-shell midden deposit (Wk-17544) has an age of

3250–3450 cal. BP, which is older than all other determinations from the site, and it may date naturally deposited beach shell (Nunn 2007:172). It is uncertain whether the sediment dates to the early Lapita occupation or later.

Horrocks and Nunn (2007:746) place use of taro and yam at Bourewa in 'mid-Lapita' rather than late-Lapita times, as is suggested by the radiocarbon results for Pit X20, and they propose that the impetus for horticulture was sea-level fall that exposed dry land suitable for root-crop planting around the former tidal inlet. However, if the X25 sample from the base of the cultural deposit dates to ca. 3000 cal. BP it would demonstrate the early arrival of horticulture in Fiji before sea-level fall when Bourewa was a low elongate sand spit/barrier island that would have been unfavourable for growing root crops. In a recent paper, Nunn (2009) says that cultivars were not introduced to Bourewa until 2800 cal. BP, but the reason for rejecting the association between the early radiocarbon age (Wk-17544) and sediment sample yielding remains of taro and lesser yam in Pit X25 is not discussed.

At other Lapita sites in Fiji, the environmental location appears to have been orientated towards marine and wild terrestrial resources rather than optimal horticultural zones. For instance, sandy beach flats backed by steep limestone/volcanic slopes backed by cliffs is inimical to horticulture (e.g. Kulu Bay, Wakea, Votua), and narrow coastal sand flats/spits fronting fringing reefs also have limited horticultural potential (e.g. Bourewa, Votua, Ugaga, Qoqo Island, Naitabale).

There is another issue in Horrocks and Nunn (2007) – the identification of starch. Hardy et al. (2009) point to basic problems in starch identification, noting that the current 'best fit' morphological method is unreliable for species identification. As Horrocks and Nunn used a reference collection composed exclusively of material from plants cultivated in Pacific prehistory, there is a possibility that their identifications of cultivated plants are merely by default and that a much wider range of potential source material would provide different results.

Recognising the difficulty of identifying evidence of agriculture, especially of plant remains in early Lapita sites, the available subsistence data still supports Best's (1984:650–653, 2002:23–25) argument for a primary focus on wild resources from the oldest layers of the Lakeba (site 197) rock shelter that show an emphasis on turtle and birds, including the hunting of now-extinct species (Chapter 10; and see Field et al. 2009). In Tonga, Burley (1998:35) found the location of Lapita sites on Tongatapu and Ha'apai suggested that access to wild resources was more important than proximity to horticultural land. However, in Vava'u, Lapita sites were positioned close to inland swales suitable for wet taro production (Burley 2007), and similar small-scale topographical variation could be hidden beneath sediments at Natunuku, Bourewa, Sigatoka and Kulu Bay. Alternatively, Lapita-era gardens may have been located some distance from coastal settlements and reconstruction of Lapita site palaeogeography, particularly the location of soils of high horticulture potential in addition to back-beach swales, could be used to identify locations where traces of Lapita horticulture could be sought.

The initial subsistence mode in Fiji and the change in the inventory of domesticated plants and animals during the Lapita era needs to be established by directly dating and recovering remains from secure Lapita contexts, and employing robust analytical methods to securely identify economic plant remains. We believe that some cultigens were probably introduced during the Lapita era, but nonetheless suggest the default position should be 'absent until demonstrated', as archaeological proof of prehistoric subsistence is essential for evaluating variability in prehistoric migrations (e.g. Kirch 1997:203–212; Bellwood 2005).

Post-Lapita transformations

A Lapita period in Fiji lasting 400–500 years that involved relatively small mobile populations which settled the coastal margins of islands and utilised inland resources cannot be envisaged as a homogeneous culture/society, as the early linguistic dialect divisions and the results of motif analysis attest (Figure 175). However, by 2500–2000 cal. BP community mobility had declined relative to the Lapita period when inter-archipelagic movement through the Central Pacific was relatively common, and when the settlement hierarchy appears to have involved strategically positioned sites like Wakea on Lakeba. Such sites were located along voyaging routes and on occupation frontiers that were connected to a range of smaller sites in the hinterland. Some contact between island groups persisted post-Lapita, but the locus of group/community interaction shifted once population growth and population distribution led to backfilling of empty/sparsely inhabited territory so that inter-group encounters for economic materials and social activity such as spouse exchange no longer required long-distance voyaging and the concentration of migrants in gateway communities.

A focus by post-Lapita groups on specific island environments is suggested by the reduction in long-distance intra-archipelagic imports, the reduced scale of intra-archipelago movement, the predominance of local production modes seen in the manufacture of post-Lapita ceramics (Chapter 13) and the local geochemistry of stone adzes/flakes (Chapter 15). The re-analysis of obsidian from post-Lapita levels on Lakeba shows that it is not from northern Vanuatu as originally thought, which means there is currently a total absence of geochemical evidence for any inter-archipelago contact with Fiji during the period 2500–1000 BP. This result can be attributed in part to a focus on colonisation sites of the Lapita era, on the one hand, and the highly visible late-period fortifications/structures, on the other.

Even so, the similarity in the evidence for early Lapita mobility (3000–2500 BP) and that of late prehistoric social interaction (1000–200 BP) indicates that two very different events – early colonisation/migration and the late prehistoric development of complex societies – created archaeological signatures of extensive social interaction that are somewhat similar. The signatures of long-distance interaction are only superficially related, however, because the movement of non-local material products during migration/colonisation relates to the volume and direction of the migration stream, and the social value of items, like obsidian, in it, whereas in stratified chiefly societies non-local goods are frequently prestige items involving craft specialisation and the return of items to socio-political centres, as is likely to be the case with adzes manufactured on Tutuila in Samoa that were transported widely in the Pacific (Best et al. 1992; Kirch and Green 2001; Clark 2002).

The resynthesis of central and western Fijian with Tokalau Fijian dialects, and its spilt with Tongic is estimated to have taken place during the early part of the post-Lapita period (Pawley 1999, n.d.). If dialect resynthesis was influenced by the infilling of archipelago environments, then human impact on island landscapes should be evident through the expansion of settlements in a larger number of locations and increased anthropogenic activity on islands. On smaller islands, these events may well have occurred earlier than on large islands due to the increase in population size in relation to finite resources, particularly productive arable land (see Kirch 1984a). However, palaeoecological records from the Lau Group, the Yasayasa Moala Group and Viti Levu document increasing environmental impact on large and on small islands after 2500 cal. BP (see Chapter 4).

On Lakeba (59 sq. km), the Waitabu Swamp core indicates that burning and erosion were underway on the southeast coast before 2000 BP, but increased massively during the period from 1900 to 1750 cal. BP (Latham et al. 1983). The main phase of vegetation clearance and erosion on Yacata Island (8.5 sq. km) dates to 2530–1100 BP (Clark and Hope 2001), similar to Totoya (28 sq. km), where palaeoecological cores suggest the 'onset of substantial burning and sedimentation by the end of Period I.2 [2500–2000 BP]', with a second round of substantial vegetation disturbance around 1700 BP (J. Clark and Cole 1997:152). On Viti Levu (10,531 sq. km), forest clearance and erosion in the highlands near the source of the Sigatoka River created a levee in which 6 m of sedge peat developed within the past 2100 years (Hope et al. 1999; Anderson et al. 2006b:151), while the poorly dated Bonatoa Bog in the Rewa Delta also suggests the decline of lowland forests after about 2500 BP (Chapter 4; Hope et al. 1999: Figure 3).

An increased focus on island landscapes in the early post-Lapita period relative to the multi-island and predominantly near-coast focus of Lapita times must have involved new settlement strategies and an increasing concern with ownership and access to land and economic resources that involved negotiation and competition among groups. Archaeological data for this is currently inadequate, although it might be represented in central and southern Lau by the presence of Period 2 sites (ca. 2500–2100 BP) in every part of the landscape, including the highest hilltops (Best 2002:21). Best (1984:562) considered the coincidence in the archaeological record of cannibalism and use of interior hilltops after 2500 BP as being 'diagnostic of stress, and presumably internal strife'.

On Viti Levu during the middle of the first millennium AD settlements appear in new locations that also suggest an increasing concern with control of land and its defence. Navatu 17A was positioned on the flanks of a steep volcanic plug and in the Sigatoka Valley easily defended hilltops termed 'territorial fortifications' came into existence (Field 2004). At the same time, open coastal sites existed at Sigatoka on the stable Level 2 palaeosol formed during a period of low ENSO activity from 2400 to 1600 cal. BP (Moy et al. 2002; Burley 2005; Anderson et al. 2006b). Human remains from the Sigatoka Sand Dune and Lakeba post-Lapita sites, however, do not have injuries consistent with conflict (Visser 1994), although cannibalism may be an early post-Lapita trait (Best 1984:Appendix O). Status differentiation in the post-Lapita period is shown by the burial treatment at Sigatoka (Best 1989; Visser 1994:170–186), and by the concentration of ornate and complex double-spouted vessels from the lower levels of Navatu 17A associated with potentially high-status food items such as cannibalised human remains and turtle bone (Chapter 10). Economic specialisation is also likely at this time from the large flat-based ceramic pans recorded from Viti Levu and the Yasawas (Lambert 1971; Clark and Sorovi-Vunidilo 1999:10), which may have been used to produce salt from evaporation of seawater (Burley 2005). Salt was an important late-prehistoric exchange commodity between coastal and inland groups (Williams 1985 [1858]:94) that may have been traded inland during the post-Lapita period.

Dialect variation on Viti Levu increased with settlement of the interior and separation of east and west populations, by the topographical barrier of the Nadrau Plateau, which can be archaeologically dated to about 1500–2000 BP (Chapters 4–6). The Eastern dialect group covered the largest area, encompassing most of the Fiji Group (eastern Viti Levu, Vanua Levu, Lau Group), while the Western dialect was restricted to western Viti Levu, the Yasawas and Vatulele (see Pawley (1981) and Pawley and Ross (1995) for general models of *in situ* language diversification in Melanesia). Geraghty's (1983) study of dialect variation examined phonological innovations in 32 communalects, which preserves the main east Viti Levu–west Viti Levu division (Figure 173) and shows the emergence of additional dialect variability in Fiji. Phonological innovations provide a relatively coarse measure of language relationships, as is the case with northeast Viti Levu grouping with Vanua Levu, but northeast Viti Levu differs in its lexicon and grammar from Vanua Levu (Geraghty 1983). The main point to keep in mind is that the process of dialect variation in the post-Lapita period does not disclose any evidence that language variability was influenced by migration/contact with Vanuatu/New Caledonia, and that local processes of communalect development were also dominant in the late-prehistoric era, notwithstanding a significant Tongan influence in parts of Fiji.

In the first and second millennium AD dialect divergence can be attributed to geographic proximity, topographic barriers and influence of social groups/chiefdoms. For instance, Geraghty (1983) suggests the existence of a southeast Viti Levu (Koro Sea) prestige dialect area, implying that the Verata-Bau-Rewa seat of political power in the 19th century had been influential long before. Thus, while language change and social transformation in the Lapita era of Fiji–West Polynesia can be viewed as the outcome of migrant arrival and interaction in frontier environments, in post-Lapita times a new and complicated set of local relationships developed within Fiji that controlled community and social development. One outcome of this with high archaeological visibility was change in post-Lapita ceramics, but inter-group competition, settlement of the interior and other previously under-used landscapes, accompanied by subsistence adaptations and economic specialisation, are hallmarks of the post-Lapita period that require much more archaeological investigation (see Hunt 1986).

In the West Pacific, studies have shown that genetic differences between inland and coastal populations are amplified by island size and the ruggedness of island topography, which combine to increase rates of genetic drift (Friedlander et al. 2007). While Fiji was settled much more recently, it is likely that similar factors contributed to the cultural and physical differences noted between inland and coastal groups in Fiji in the 19th century that fuelled a theory that Fiji had an early 'Melanesian' population stratum and a more recent 'Polynesian' population stratum (Clark 2003). Linguistic studies demonstrate that landscape topography on Viti Levu led to dialect variation (Pawley and Sabah 1971; Geraghty 1983) and it is reasonable to suggest that variation in genetic composition and cultural traits also increased in the post-Lapita period. Long-distance interaction/contact with Vanuatu/New Caledonia has been proposed as an important factor influencing the course of post-Lapita Fiji, but there is currently little archaeological and linguistic support for it, and the effects of local processes on the development of human diversity in Fiji need to be taken up in future research.

References

Addison, D.J. and A.E. Morrison In press. The Lapita settlement of Samoa: Is a continuous occupation model appropriate? In: Proceedings of the VII International Conference on Easter Island and the Pacific Islands: Migration, identity, and cultural heritage, Gotland, Sweden.

Allen, J. and O'Connell, J.F. 2008. Getting from Sunda to Sahul. In: Clark, G.R., Leach, F. and O'Connor, S. (eds), *Islands of inquiry: Colonisation, seafaring and the archaeology of maritime landscapes*, pp. 31–46. Terra Australis 29. Canberra, ANU E Press.

Anderson, A.J. 2001. Mobility models of Lapita migration. In: Clark, G.R., Anderson, A.J. and Vunidilo, T. (eds), *The archaeology of Lapita dispersal in Oceania*, pp.15–23. Terra Australis 17, Pandanus Press, Canberra.

Anderson, A.J. 2002. Faunal collapse, landscape change and settlement history in Remote Oceania. *World Archaeology* 33: 375–390.

Anderson, A.J. 2003. Initial dispersal in Remote Oceania: Pattern and explanation. In: Sand, C. (ed), *Pacific archaeology: Assessments and prospects*. Les cahiers de l'archéologie en Nouvelle-Calédonie 15, pp. 71–84. Départment Archéologie, Service des Musées et du Patrimoine de Nouvelle-Calédonie, Noumea.

Anderson, A.J. 2008a. Traditionalism, interaction and long-distance seafaring in Polynesia. *Journal of Island and Coastal Archaeology* 3: 240–250, 268–270.

Anderson, A.J. 2008b. The rat and the octopus: Initial human colonization and the prehistoric introduction of domestic animals to Remote Oceania. *Biological Invasions* DOI 10.1007/s10530-008-9403-2.

Anderson, A. and Clark, G. 1999. The age of Lapita settlement in Fiji. *Archaeology in Oceania* 34: 31–39.

Anderson, A., Clark, G. and Worthy, T. 2000. An inland Lapita site in Fiji. *Journal of the Polynesian Society* 109(3): 311–316.

Anderson, A., Bedford, S., Clark, G., Lilley, I., Sand, C., Summerhayes, G. and Torrence, R. 2001. A list of Lapita sites containing dentate-stamped pottery. In: Clark, G.R., Anderson, A.J. and Vunidilo, T. (eds), *The archaeology of Lapita dispersal in Oceania*, pp. 1–13. Terra Australis 17, Pandanus Press, Canberra.

Anderson, A.J. and White, J.P. (eds) 2001. *The Prehistoric Archaeology of Norfolk Island, Southwest Pacific*. Supplement 27, Records of the Australian Museum.

Anderson, A.J. and Sinoto, Y.H. 2002. New radiocarbon ages of colonization sites in East Polynesia. *Asian Perspectives* 41: 242–257.

Anderson, A.J., Chappell, J., Gagan, M., and Grove, R. 2006a. Prehistoric maritime migration in the Pacific Islands: An hypothesis of ENSO forcing. *The Holocene* 16: 1–6.

Anderson, A., Roberts, R., Dickinson, W., Clark, G., Burley, D., De Biran, A., Hope, G. and Nunn, P. 2006b. Times of sand: sedimentary history and archaeology at the Sigatoka Dunes, Fiji. *Geoarchaeology* 21: 131–154.

Anson, D. 1983. Lapita pottery of the Bismarck Archipelago and its affinities. Unpublished PhD thesis, University of Sydney.

Athens, J.S., Dega, M.F. and Ward, J. 2004. Austronesian colonisation of the Mariana Islands: The palaeoenvironmental evidence. *Bulletin of the Indo-Pacific Prehistory Association* 24: 21–30.

Bedford, S. 2006. *Pieces of the Vanuatu Puzzle: Archaeology of the North, South and Centre*. Terra Australis 23. Canberra: Pandanus Books, The Australian National University.

Bellwood, P. 2005. Coastal south China, Taiwan, and the prehistory of the Austronesians. In: Chey, C-Y and Pan, J-G (eds), *The Archaeology of Southeast Coastal Islands of China Conference*, pp. 1–22, Executive Yuan, Council for Cultural Affairs, Taiwan.

Best, S. 1984. Lakeba: The prehistory of a Fijian island. Unpublished PhD thesis, Department of Anthropology, University of Auckland.

Best, S. 1989. The Sigatoka dune burials (Site VL 16/1). Unpublished report to the Fiji Museum, Suva.

Best, S. 2002. *Lapita: A view from the east*. New Zealand Archaeological Association Monographs 24, Auckland.

Best, S.B., Sheppard, P., Green, R.C. and Parker, R. 1992. Necromancing the stone: Archaeologists and adzes in American Samoa. *Journal of the Polynesian Society* 101: 45–85.

Birks, L. 1973. Archaeological excavations at Sigatoka dune site, Fiji. *Bulletin of the Fiji Museum* No.1.

Burley, D. 1998. Tongan archaeology and the Tongan past, 2850–150 B.P. *Journal of World Prehistory* 12(3): 337–392.

Burley, D.V. 2003. Dynamic landscapes and episodic occupations: Archaeological interpretation and implications in the prehistory of the Sigatoka Sand Dunes. In: Sand, C. (ed), *Pacific archaeology: Assessments and prospects*, pp. 307–315. Les Cahiers de l' Archéologie en Nouvelle-Calédonie Number 15, New Caledonia.

Burley, D. 2005. Mid-sequence archaeology at the Sigatoka Sand Dunes with interpretive implications for Fijian and Oceanic culture history. *Asian Perspectives* 44(2): 320–348.

Burley, D.V. 2007. In search of Lapita and Polynesian Plainware settlements in Vava'u, Kingdom of Tonga. In Bedford, S., Sand, C. and Connaughton, S.P. (eds), *Oceanic Explorations: Lapita and Western Pacific settlement*, pp. 187–198. Terra Australis 26. ANU E Press, Australian National University.

Burley, D.V. and Dickinson, W.R. 2001. Origin and significance of a founding settlement in Polynesia. *Proceedings of the National Academy of Sciences* 98: 11829–11831.

Burley, D.V., Dickinson, W.R., Barton, A. and Shutler, R. Jr. 2001. Lapita on the periphery: New data on old problems in the Kingdom of Tonga. *Archaeology in Oceania* 36: 89–104.

Callaghan, R. and Fitzpatrick, S.M. 2009. Examining prehistoric migration patterns in the Palauan Archipelago: A computer simulated analysis of drift voyaging. *Asian Perspectives* 47: 28–44.

Carson, M.T. 2008. Refining earliest settlement in Remote Oceania: Renewed archaeological investigation at Unai Bapot, Saipan. *Journal of Island and Coastal Archaeology* 3: 115–139.

Chappell, J. 2005. Geographic changes of coastal lowlands in the Papuan past. In: Pawley, A., Attenborough, R., Golson, J. and Hide, R. (eds), *Papuan pasts: Cultural, linguistic and biological histories of Papuan-speaking peoples,* pp. 289–328. Pacific Linguistics, Canberra.

Chiu, S. 2003. Social and economic meanings of Lapita pottery: A New Caledonia case. In: Sand, C. (ed), *Pacific archaeology: Assessments and prospects*. Les cahiers de l'archéologie en Nouvelle-Calédonie 15, pp. 159–182. Départment Archéologie, Service des Musées et du Patrimoine de Nouvelle-Calédonie, Noumea.

Clark, G. 2000. Post-Lapita Fiji: Cultural transformation in the mid-sequence. Unpublished PhD thesis, Australian National University.

Clark, G. 2002. Adzes of interaction: Samoan basalt artefacts in Fiji. In: Bedford, S., Sand, C. and Burley, D. (eds.), *Fifty years in the field*, pp. 227–238. New Zealand Archaeological Association Monograph.

Clark, G. 2003. Shards of meaning: Archaeology and the Melanesia–Polynesia distinction. *Journal of Pacific History* 38(2): 197–213.

Clark, G. 2004. Radiocarbon dates for the Ulong site in Palau and implications for western Micronesian prehistory. *Archaeology in Oceania* 39: 26–33.

Clark, G. 2005. A 3000-year culture sequence from Palau, western Micronesia. *Asian Perspectives* 44: 349–380.

Clark. G. 2007. Standardization, specialization and Lapita ceramics. In: Bedford, S., Sand, C. and Connaughton, S.P. (eds.), *Oceanic explorations: Lapita and Western Pacific settlement*, pp. 289–299. Terra Australis 26. ANU E Press, Australian National University.

Clark, G. 2009. Early ceramic sites in southern Lau, Fiji. *Archaeology in New Zealand* 62: 81–89.

Clark, G. and Sorovi-Vunidilo, T. 1999. Double-spouted vessels from Fiji. *Domodomo* 11(2): 6–11.

Clark, G. and Hope, G. 2001. Archaeological and palaeoenvironmental investigations on Yacata Island, northern Lau, Fiji. *Domodomo* 13(2): 29–47.

Clark, G. and Anderson, A. 2001a. The pattern of Lapita settlement in Fiji. *Archaeology in Oceania* 36: 77–88.

Clark, G. and Anderson, A. 2001b. The age of the Yanuca Lapita site, Viti Levu, Fiji. *New Zealand Journal of Archaeology* 22: 15–30.

Clark, G., Anderson, A. and Matararaba, S. 2001. The Lapita site at Votua, northern Lau Islands, Fiji. *Archaeology in Oceania* 36: 134–145.

Clark, G. and Murray T. 2006. Decay characteristics of the eastern Lapita design system. *Archaeology in Oceania* 41: 107–117.

Clark, G., Anderson, A. and Wright, D. 2006. Human colonization of the Palau Islands, western Micronesia. *Journal of Island and Coastal Archaeology* 1: 215–232.

Clark, G. and Wright, D. 2007. Reading Pacific pots. In: Anderson, A., Green, K. and Leach, F. (eds), *Vastly Ingenious: The archaeology of Pacific material culture in honour of Janet M. Davidson*, pp. 173–190. University of Otago Press, Dunedin.

Clark, G. and Bedford, S. 2008. Friction zones in Lapita colonisation. In: Clark, G.R., Leach, F. and O'Connor, S. (eds), *Islands of inquiry: Colonisation, seafaring and the archaeology of maritime landscapes*, pp. 59–73. Terra Australis 29. Canberra, ANU E Press.

Clark, J.T. 1996. Samoan prehistory in review. In: Davidson, J.M., Irwin, G., Leach, B.F., Pawley, A. and Brown, D. (eds), *Oceanic culture history: essays in honour of Roger Green*, pp. 445–460. New Zealand Journal of Archaeology Special Publication.

Clark, J.T. and Cole, T. 1997. Environmental change and human prehistory in the Central Pacific: Archaeological and palynological investigations on Totoya Island, Fiji. Unpublished report to the Fiji Museum, Suva.

Cochrane, E.E., Matararaba, S. and Nakoro, E. 2007. Lapita and later archaeology of the Malolo and Mamanuca Islands, Fiji. *Journal of Island and Coastal Archaeology* 2: 245–250.

Cochrane, E.E. 2008. Migration and cultural transmission: Investigating human movement as an explanation for Fijian ceramic change. In: O'Brian, M.J. (ed), *Cultural transmission and archaeology: Issues and case studies*, pp. 132–145. Society for American Archaeology, The SAA Press, Washington, DC.

Conte, E. and Anderson, A.J. 2003. Radiocarbon ages for two sites on Ua Huka, Marquesas. *Asian Perspectives* 42: 155–160.

Craib, J. 1999. Colonisation of the Mariana Islands: New evidence and implications for human movements in the western Pacific. In: Galipaud, J-C. and Lilley, I. (eds), *The Pacific from 5000 to 2000 BP. Colonisation and transformations*, pp. 477–486. IRD Editions, Paris.

Davidson, J.M. and Leach. B.F. 2001. The strandlooper concept and economic naivete. In: Clark, G.R., Anderson, A.J. and Vunidilo, T. (eds), *The archaeology of Lapita dispersal in Oceania*, pp. 115–123. Terra Australis 17, Pandanus Press, Canberra.

DeFant, D.G. 2008. Early human burials from the Naton beach site, Tumon Bay, Island of Guam, Mariana Islands. *Journal of Island and Coastal Archaeology* 3: 149–153.

Diamond, J. and Bellwood, P. 2003. Farmers and their languages: The first expansions. *Science* 300: 597–603.

Dickinson, W.R. 2006. *Temper sands in prehistoric Oceanian pottery: Geotectonics, sedimentology, petrography, provenance*. Geological Society of America Special Papers 406. The Geological Society of America, Boulder, Colorado.

Dickinson, W.R. and Green, R.C. 1998. Geoarchaeological context of Holocene subsidence at the Ferry Berth site. Mulifanua, Upolu, Western Samoa, *Geoarchaeology* 13: 239–263.

Dickinson, W.R. and Athens, J.S. 2007. Holocene paleoshoreline and paleoenvironmental history of Palau: Implications for human settlement. *Journal of Island and Coastal Archaeology* 2: 175–196.

Dodson, J.R. and Intoh. M. 1999. Prehistory and palaeoecology of Yap, Federated States of Micronesia. *Quaternary International* 59: 17–26.

Donohue, M. and Denham, T. 2008. The language of Lapita: Vanuatu and an early Papuan presence in the Pacific. *Oceanic Linguistics* 47: 433–444.

Felgate, M.W. and Dickinson, W.R. 2001. Late-Lapita and Post-Lapita pottery transfers: Evidence from intertidal-zone sites of Roviana Lagoon, Western Province, Solomon Islands. In: Jones, M. and Sheppard, P.J. (eds), *Proceedings of the 2001 Australasian Archaeometry Conference*, pp. 105–122. Research Papers in Anthropology and Linguistics, Number 5, Auckland.

Felgate, M. 2007. Leap-frogging or Limping? Recent evidence from the Lapita littoral fringe, New Georgia, Solomon Islands. In: Bedford, S., Sand, C. and Connaughton, S.P. (eds), *Oceanic Explorations: Lapita and Western Pacific settlement*, pp. 123–140. Terra Australis 26. ANU E Press, Australian National University.

Field, J.S. 2004. Environmental and climatic considerations: A hypothesis for conflict and the emergence of social complexity in Fijian prehistory. *Journal of Anthropological Archaeology* 23: 79–99.

Field, J.S. 2005. Land tenure, competition and ecology in Fijian prehistory. *Antiquity* 79: 586–600.

Field, J.S., Cochrane, E.E. and Greenlee, D.M. 2009. Dietary change in Fijian prehistory: Isotopic analyses of human and animal skeletal material. *Journal of Archaeological Science* 36: 1547–1556.

Friedlaender, J.S., Friedlaender, F.R., Hodgson, J.A., Stoltz, M., Koki, G., Horvat, G., Zhadanov, S., Schurr, T.G. and Merriwether, D.A. 2007. Melanesian mtDNA complexity. *PLoS One* 2: 1–13.

Frimagacci, J.P. and Siorat, B.Vienne. 1983. *Inventaire et fouille des sites archeologiques et ethnohistoriques de l'ile d'Uvea*. Centre de Noumea Sciences Humaines, ORSTOM, Nouvelle-Caledonie.

Geraghty, P.A. 1983. The history of the Fijian languages. *Oceanic Linguistics Special Publication* No. 19. University of Hawaii Press, Honolulu.

Gongora, J., Rawlence, N.J., Mobeg V.A., Jianlin, H., Alcalde, J.A., Matus, J.T., Hanotte, O., Moran, C., Austin, J.J., Ulm, S., Anderson, A.J., Larson, G., and Cooper, A. 2008. Reply to Storey et al.: More DNA and dating studies needed for ancient Arenal-1 chickens. *Proceedings of the National Academy of Sciences of the USA* 105: E100.

Green, R.C. 1991. Near and Remote Oceania – disestablishing 'Melanesia' in culture history. In: Pawley, A.K. (ed), *Man and a half: essays in honour of Ralph Bulmer*. pp. 491–502. Polynesian Society, Auckland.

Green, R.C. 2002. A retrospective view of settlement pattern studies in Samoa. In: Ladefoged, T. and Graves, M. (eds), *Pacific Landscapes Archaeological Approaches*, pp. 125–152. California: The Easter Island Foundation, Bearsville Press.

Green, R.C. 2003. The Lapita horizon and traditions – signature for one set of Oceanic migrations. In: Sand, C. (ed.), *Pacific archaeology: Assessments and prospects*. Les cahiers de l'archéologie en Nouvelle-Calédonie 15, pp. 95–120. Départment Archéologie, Service des Musées et du Patrimoine de Nouvelle-Calédonie, Noumea.

Green, R.C. and Kirch, P.V. 1997. Lapita exchange systems and their Polynesian transformations: seeking explanatory models. In: Weisler, M.I. (ed), *Prehistoric long-distance interaction in Oceania: an interdisciplinary approach*. pp. 19–37. New Zealand Archaeological Association Monograph 21.

Green, R.C. and Weisler, M.I. 2002. The Mangarevan sequence and dating of the geographic expansion into southeast Polynesia. *Asian Perspectives* 41: 213–241.

Green, R.C., Jones, M. and Sheppard, P. 2008. The reconstructed environment and absolute dating of SE-SZ-8 Lapita site on Nendo, Santa Cruz, Solomon Islands. *Archaeology in Oceania* 43: 49–61.

Groube, L.M. 1971. Tonga, Lapita pottery, and Polynesian origins. *Journal of the Polynesian Society* 80: 278–316.

Groube, L.M. 1996. The geometry of the dead. In: Davidson, J.M., Irwin, G., Leach, B.F., Pawley, A. and Brown, D. (eds), *Oceanic culture history: essays in honour of Roger Green*. pp. 133–165. New Zealand Journal of Archaeology Special Publication.

Hardy, K., Blakeney, T., Copeland, L., Kirkham, J., Wrangham, R., and Collins, M. 2009. Starch granules, dental calculus and new perspectives on ancient diet. *Journal of Archaeological Science*, 36: 248–255.

Hirth, K.G. 1978. Interregional trade and the formation of gateway communities. *American Antiquity* 43(1): 35–45.

Hope, G., O'Dea, D. and Southern, W. 1999. Holocene vegetation histories in the Western Pacific – alternative records of human impact. In: Lilley, I. and Galipaud, J-C. (eds), *The Pacific from 5000 to 2000 BP. Colonisation and transformations*, pp. 387–404. IRD Editions, Paris.

Horrocks, M. and Nunn, P.D. 2007. Evidence for introduced taro (*Colocasia esculenta*) and lesser yam (*Dioscorea esculenta*) in Lapita-era (3050–2500 cal. yr BP) deposits from Bourewa, southwest Viti Levu Island, Fiji. *Journal of Archaeological Science* 34: 739–748.

Hunt, T.L. 1980. Toward Fiji's past; archaeological research on southwestern Viti Levu. Unpublished MA thesis, University of Auckland.

Hunt, T.L. 1981. New evidence for horticulture in Fiji. *Journal of the Polynesian Society* 90: 259–269.

Hunt, T.L. 1986. Conceptual and substantive issues in Fijian prehistory. In: Kirch, P.V. (ed), *Archaeological approaches to evolution and transformation*, pp. 20–32. Cambridge University Press, Cambridge.

Hunt, T.L. and Lipo, C.P. 2008. Evidence for a shorter chronology on Rapa Nui (Easter Island). *Journal of Island and Coastal Archaeology* 3: 140–148.

Irwin, G. 1992. *The Prehistoric exploration and colonisation of the Pacific*.: Cambridge University Press, Cambridge.

Irwin, G. 2008. Pacific seascapes, canoe performance, and a review of Lapita voyaging with regard to theories of migration. *Asian Perspectives* 47: 12–27.

Jones O'Day, S., O'Day, P. and Steadman, D.W. 2004. Defining the Lau context: Recent findings on Nayau, Lau Islands, Fiji. *New Zealand Journal of Archaeology* 25: 31–56.

Kay, R. 1984. Analysis of archaeological material from Naigani. Unpublished MA thesis, University of Auckland.

Kelly, K.M. 1996. The end of the trail: The genetic basis for deriving the Polynesian peoples from Austronesian speaking palaeopopulations of Melanesian Near Oceania. In: Davidson, J.M., Irwin, G., Leach, B.F., Pawley, A. and Brown, D. (eds), *Oceanic culture history: essays in honour of Roger Green*, pp. 355–364. New Zealand Journal of Archaeology Special Publication.

Kirch, P.V. 1984a. *The evolution of the Polynesian chiefdoms.* Cambridge University Press, Cambridge, New York, Port Chester, Melbourne, Sydney.

Kirch, P.V. 1984b. The Polynesian outliers: Continuity, change, and replacement. *Journal of Pacific History* 19: 224–238.

Kirch, P.V. 1988. Niuatoputapu: The prehistory of a Polynesian chiefdom. *Thomas Burke Memorial Washington State Museum Monograph* No. 5. The Burke Museum, Seattle.

Kirch, P.V. 1997. *The Lapita Peoples. Ancestors of the Oceanic world.* Blackwell Publishers, Cambridge and Oxford.

Kirch, P.V. and Green, R.C. 2001. *Hawaiki, Ancestral Polynesia. An essay in historical anthropology.* Cambridge University Press, United Kingdom.

Kuhlken, R. and Crosby, A. 1999. Agricultural terracing at Nakauvadra, Viti Levu: A late prehistoric irrigated agrosystem in Fiji. *Asian Perspectives* 38: 62–89.

Kumar, R. and Nunn, P.D. 2003. Inland and coastal Lapita settlement on Viti Levu Island, Fiji: New Data. *Domodomo* 16: 15–20.

Kumar, R., Nunn, P.D., Katayama, K., Oda, H., Matararaba, S. and Osborne, T. 2004. The earliest-known humans in Fiji and their pottery: The first dates from the 2002 excavations at Naitabale (Nartururuku), Moturiki Island. *South Pacific Journal of Natural Science* 22: 15–21.

Kumar, R., Nunn, P.D., Field, J. and De Biran, A. 2006. Human response to climate change around AD 1300: A case study of the Sigatoka Valley, Viti Levu Island, Fiji. *Quaternary International* 151: 133–143.

Lambert, R. 1971. Botanical identification of impressions on archaeological potsherds from Sigatoka. Final Report No. 3. *Records of the Fiji Museum* 1: 124–148.

Larson, G., and 31 additional authors. 2007. Phylogeny and ancient DNA of *Sus* provides insights into Neolithic expansion in Island Southeast Asia and Oceania. *Proceedings of the National Academy of Sciences, USA*, 104: 4834–4839.

Latham, M., Hughes, P.J., Hope, G. and Brookfield, M. 1983. Sedimentation in the swamps of Lakeba and its implications for erosion and human occupation of the island. In: Latham, M. and Brookfield, H.C. (eds), *The eastern Fiji Islands. A study of the natural environment, its use and man's influence on its evolution*, pp. 103–119. General Report No. 3 of the UNESCO/UNFPA Project, ORSTOM, Paris.

Lee, E.S. 1996 [1965]. A theory of migration. In: Cohen, R. (ed), *Theories of migration*, pp. 14–57. Edward Elgar, United Kingdom.

Lepofsky, D. 1988. The environmental context of Lapita settlement location. In: Kirch, P.V. and Hunt, T.L. (eds), *Archaeology of the Lapita culture complex: A critical review*. pp. 33–47. Thomas Burke Memorial Washington State Museum Research Report No. 5. Burke Museum, Seattle.

Lilley, I. 2002. Lapita and Type Y pottery in the KLK site, Siassi, Papua New Guinea. In: Bedford, S., Burley, D. and Sand, C. (eds), *Fifty years in the field. Papers in honour of Richard Shutler*, pp. 79–90. New Zealand Archaeological Association, Auckland.

Lilley, I. 2008. Flights of fancy: Fractal geometry, the Lapita dispersal and punctuated colonisation in the Pacific. In: Clark, G.R., Leach, F. and O'Connor, S. (eds), *Islands of inquiry: Colonisation, seafaring and the archaeology of maritime landscapes*, pp. 75–86. Terra Australis 29. ANU E Press, Canberra

Liston, J. 2005. An assessment of radiocarbon dates from Palau, western Micronesia. *Radiocarbon* 47: 295–354.

Marck, J. 2000. *Topics in Polynesian language and culture history*. Pacific Linguistics, Canberra.

Mead, S., Birks, L., Birks, H. and Shaw, E. 1973. The Lapita pottery style of Fiji and its associations. *Journal of the Polynesian Society Memoir* 38: 1–98.

Moore, J.H. 2001. Evaluating five models of colonization. *American Anthropologist* 103: 395–408.

Moy, C.M., Seltzer, G.O., Rodbell, D.T. and Anderson, D.M. 2002. Variability of El Nino/Southern Oscillation activity at millennial time scales during the Holocene epoch. *Nature* 420: 162–165.

Nunn, P.D. 2007. Echoes from a distance: Research into the Lapita occupation of the Rove Peninsula, southwest Viti Levu, Fiji. In: Bedford, S., Sand, C. and Connaughton, S.P. (eds), *Oceanic Explorations: Lapita and Western Pacific settlement*, pp. 163–176. Terra Australis 26. ANU E Press, Australian National University.

Nunn, P.D. 2009. Geographical influences on settlment-location choices by initial colonizers: A case study of the Fiji Islands. *Journal of the Institute of Australian Geographers* 47(3): 306–319.

Nunn, P.D., Matararaba, S., Ishimura, T., Kumar, R. and Nakoro, E. 2004a. Reconstructing the Lapita-era geography of Northern Fiji: A newly discovered Lapita site on Yadua Island and its implications. *New Zealand Journal of Archaeology* 26: 41–55.

Nunn, P.D., Kumar, R., Matararaba, S., Ishimura, T., Seeto, J., Rayawa, S., Kuruyawa, S., Nasila, A., Oloni, B., Ram, A.R., Saunivalu, P., Sing, P and Tegu, E. 2004b. Early Lapita settlement site at Bourewa, southwest Viti Levu Island, Fiji. *Archaeology in Oceania* 39: 139–143.

Nunn, P.D., Pepe, C., Matararaba, S., Kumar, R., Sing, P., Nakoro, E., Gwilliam, M., Heorake, T., Kuilanisautabu, L., Nakoro, E., Narayan, L., Pastorizo, M.A., Robinson, S., Saunivalu, P. and Tamani, F. 2005. Human occupations of caves of the Rove Peninsula, southwest Viti Levu Island, Fiji. *South Pacific Journal of Natural Science* 23: 16–23.

Nunn, P.D., Matararaba, S., Kumar, R., Pene, C., Yuen, L., Pastorizo, M.A. 2006. Lapita on an island in the mangroves? The earliest human occupation at Qoqo Island, Southwest Viti Levu, Fiji. *Archaeology in New Zealand* 49: 205–212.

Nunn, P.D., Hunter-Anderson, R., Carson, M.T., Thomas, F., Ulm, S. and Rowland, M.J. 2007. Times of plenty, times of less: Last-millennium societal disruption in the Pacific Basin. *Human Ecology* 35(4): 385–401.

Parry, J. 1987. *The Sigatoka valley – pathways into prehistory*. Fiji Museum Bulletin No. 9. The Fiji Museum, Suva.

Pawley, A. 1981. Melanesian diversity and Polynesian homogeneity: A unified explanation for language. In: Hollyman, J. and A. Pawley (eds), *Studies in Pacific languages and cultures: Essays in honour of Bruce Biggs*, pp. 269–309. Linguistic Society of New Zealand, Auckland.

Pawley, A. 1999. Chasing rainbows: implications for the rapid dispersal of Austronesian languages for subgrouping and reconstruction. In: Zeitoun, E. and Jenkuei Li, P. (eds), *Selected papers from the eighth international conference on Austronesian linguistics*. Symposium Series of the Institute of Linguistics (Preparatory Office), Academia Sinica, Number 1, Taiwan.

Pawley, A. 2007. The origins of early Lapita culture: The testimony of historical linguistics. In:

Bedford, S., Sand, C. and Connaughton, S.P. (eds), *Oceanic explorations: Lapita and Western Pacific settlement*, pp. 17–49. Terra Australis 26. ANU E Press, Australian National University.

Pawley, A. n.d. Polynesian paradoxes: Subgroups, wave models and the dialect geography of Proto Polynesian. Draft paper for the Eleventh International Conference on Austronesian Linguistics (11·ical), 22–26 June 2009, Aussois, France.

Pawley, A. and Sayaba, T. 1971. Fijian dialect divisions: eastern and western Fijian. *Journal of the Polynesian Society* 80: 405–436.

Pawley, A. and Ross, M. 1995. The prehistory of the Oceanic languages; a current view. In: Bellwood, P., Fox, J.J. and Tryon, D. (eds), *The Austronesians*. pp. 39–74. Department of Anthropology, Research School of Pacific and Asian Studies, Australian National University.

Pietrusewsky, M. 1990. Lapita-associated skeletons from Watom Island, Papua New Guinea, and the origins of the Polynesians. *Asian Perspectives* 28(1): 83–89.

Poulsen, J. 1987. Early Tongan Prehistory. (2 volumes). *Terra Australis* 12. Department of Prehistory, Research School of Pacific Studies, Australian National University.

Reepmeyer, C and Clark, G. 2009. Post-colonisation interaction between Vanuatu and Fiji reconsidered: The reanalysis of obsidian from Lakeba Island, Fiji. *Archaeometry*.

Reepmeyer, C., Spriggs, M., Bedford, S. and Ambrose, A. In press. Provenance and technology of lithic artefacts from the Teouma Lapita site, Vanuatu. *Asian Perspectives*.

Reith, T.M., Morrison, A.E. and Addison, D.J. 2008. The temporal and spatial patterning of the initial settlement of Samoa. *Journal of Island and Coastal Archaeology* 3: 214–239.

Sand, C. 1990. the ceramic chronology of Futuna and Alofi: An overview. In: Spriggs, M. (ed), *Lapita design, form and composition*. pp. 123–133. Occasional Papers in Prehistory, No. 20, Department of Prehistory, Australian National University.

Sand, C. 1996. Archaeological research on Uvea Island, Western Polynesia. *New Zealand Journal of Archaeology* 18: 91–123.

Sand, C. 1997. The chronology of Lapita ware in New Caledonia. *Antiquity* 71: 539–547.

Sand, C. 1998. Recent archaeological research in the Loyalty Islands of New Caledonia. *Asian Perspectives* 37(2): 194–223.

Sand, C. 2001. Evolutions in the Lapita Cultural Complex: A view from the Southern Lapita Province. *Archaeology in Oceania* 36: 65–76.

Sand, C., Coote, K., Bole, J. and Outecho, A. 1998. A pottery pit at locality WKO013A, Lapita (New Caledonia). *Archaeology in Oceania* 33: 37–43.

Sand, C. and Sheppard, P. 2003. Long distance prehistoric obsidian imports in New Caledonia: Characteristics and meaning. *Earth and Planetary Sciences* 331: 235–243.

Serjeantson, S.W. and Gao, X. 1995. *Homo sapiens* is an evolving species: origins of the Austronesians. In: Bellwood, P., Fox, J.J. and Tryon, D. (eds), *The Austronesians*. pp. 165–176. Department of Anthropology, Research School of Pacific and Asian Studies, Australian National University.

Sheppard, P. 2003. Lapita lithics: Trade/exchange and technology. A view from the Reefs/Santa Cruz. *Archaeology in Oceania* 28: 121–137.

Sheppard, P. and Walter, R. 2006. A revised model of Solomon Islands culture history. *Journal of the Polynesian Society* 115: 47–76.

Specht, J. 2002. Obsidian, colonising and exchange. In: Bedford, S., Sand, C. and Burley, D. (eds), *Fifty years in the field*, pp. 37–49. New Zealand Archaeological Association Monograph.

Specht, J. 2007. Small islands in the big picture: The formative period of Lapita in the Bismarck Archipelago. In: Bedford, S., Sand, C. and Connaughton, S.P. (eds), *Oceanic explorations: Lapita and Western Pacific settlement*, pp. 51–70. Terra Australis 26. ANU E Press, Australian National University.

Spriggs, M. 1991. Nissan: The island in the middle. In: Allen, J. and Gosden, C. (eds), *Report of the Lapita homeland project*, pp. 222–243. Department of Prehistory, Research School of Pacific and Asian Studies, The Australian National University.

Spriggs, M. 1995. The Lapita culture and Austronesian prehistory in Oceania. In: Bellwood, P., Fox, J.J. and Tryon, D. (eds), *The Austronesians*, pp. 112–133. Department of Anthropology, Research School of Pacific and Asian Studies, Australian National University.

Spriggs, M. 1997. *The Island Melanesians*. Blackwell Publishers Ltd, Oxford and Massachusetts.

Storey, A.A., Ramirez, J.M., Quiroz, D., Burley, D.V., Addison, D.J., Walter, R., Anderson, A.J., Hunt, T.L., Athens, J.S., Huynen, L. and Matisoo-Smith, E.A. 2007. Radiocarbon and DNA evidence for a pre-Columbian introduction of Polynesian chickens to Chile. *Proceedings of the National Academy of Sciences of the USA* 104: 10335–10339.

Summerhayes, G. 2001. Far Western, Western, and Eastern Lapita: A re-evaluation. *Asian Perspectives* 39(1–2): 109–118.

Summerhayes, G. 2004. The nature of prehistoric obsidian importation to Anir and the development of a 3,000 year old regional picture of obsidian exchange within the Bismarck Archipelago, Papua New Guinea. *Records of the Australian Museum, Supplement* 29: 145–156.

Szabo, K. and Summerhayes, G. 2002. Worked shell artefacts – new data from early Lapita. In: Bedford, S., Sand, C. and Burley, D. (eds), *Fifty years in the field*, pp. 91–100. New Zealand Archaeological Association Monograph.

Torrence, R. and Swadling, P. 2008. Social networks and the spread of Lapita. *Antiquity* 82: 600–616.

Torrence, R. and Doelman, T. 2007. Problems of scale: Evaluating the effects of volcanic disasters on cultural change in the Willaumez Peninsula, Papua New Guinea. In: Gratten, J. and Torrence, R. (eds), *Living under the shadow: Cultural impacts of volcanic eruptions*, pp. 42–66. Walnut Creek (CA), Left Coast Press.

Van Dijk, N. 1998. The Melanesians: An osteological study of their biological relationships within the Pacific. Unpublished PhD thesis, Australian National University.

Visser, E.P. 1994. The prehistoric people from Sigatoka: An analysis of skeletal and dental traits as evidence of adaptation. Unpublished PhD thesis, University of Otago, New Zealand.

Walter, R. and Anderson, A. 2002. The archaeology of Niue Island West Polynesia. *Bishop Museum Bulletin in Anthropology* 10. Bishop Museum Press, Honolulu.

Weisler, M.I. 1994. The settlement of remote Polynesia: New evidence from Henderson Island. *Journal of Field Archaeology* 21: 83–102.

Wickler, S. 2001. *The prehistory of Buka: A stepping stone island in the northern Solomons*. Terra Australis 16. Department of Archaeology and Natural History and Centre for Archaeological Research, The Australian National University.

Williams, T. 1985 [1858]. *Fiji and the Fijians. The islands and their inhabitants*. Fiji Museum, Suva.

Wilmshurst, J.M., Anderson, A., Higham, T.F.G. and Worthy, T. 2008. Dating the late prehistoric dispersal of Polynesians to New Zealand using the commensal Pacific rat. *Proceedings of the National Academy of Sciences of the USA* 105: 7676–7680.

terra australis 31

www.ingramcontent.com/pod-product-compliance
Lightning Source LLC
Chambersburg PA
CBHW061546010526
44114CB00027B/2945